# THE CAMBRIDGE COMPANION TO PLUTARCH

Plutarch is one of the most prolific and important writers from antiquity. His *Parallel Lives* continue to be an invaluable historical source, and the numerous essays in his *Moralia* are crucial evidence for ancient philosophy and cultural history. This volume provides an engaging introduction to all aspects of his work, including his method and purpose in writing the *Lives*, his attitudes toward daily life and intimate relations, his thoughts on citizenship and government, his relationship to Plato and the second Sophistic, and his conception of foreign or "other." Attention is also paid to his style and rhetoric. Plutarch's works have also been important in subsequent periods, and an introduction to their reception history in Byzantium, Italy, England, Spain, and France is provided. A distinguished team of contributors together helps the reader begin to navigate this most varied and fascinating of ancient writers.

FRANCES B. TITCHENER is Distinguished Professor of History and Classics at Utah State University. Involved with the International Plutarch Society (IPS) since 1987, she is a coeditor of *Ploutarchos*, the journal of the IPS. She is also a coeditor of *Fame and Infamy* (Oxford 2015) and of *Plutarch's Cities* (Oxford 2022).

ALEXEI V. ZADOROJNYI is Senior Lecturer in Greek Language and Culture at the University of Liverpool. He has published numerous articles and chapters on Plutarch as well as other Greek and Roman authors of the imperial period.

D1610384

# THE CAMBRIDGE
# COMPANION TO PLUTARCH

EDITED BY

FRANCES B. TITCHENER

*Utah State University*

ALEXEI V. ZADOROJNYI

*University of Liverpool*

CAMBRIDGE
UNIVERSITY PRESS

Shaftesbury Road, Cambridge CB2 8EA, United Kingdom

One Liberty Plaza, 20th Floor, New York, NY 10006, USA

477 Williamstown Road, Port Melbourne, VIC 3207, Australia

314–321, 3rd Floor, Plot 3, Splendor Forum, Jasola District Centre, New Delhi – 110025, India

103 Penang Road, #05–06/07, Visioncrest Commercial, Singapore 238467

Cambridge University Press is part of Cambridge University Press & Assessment,
a department of the University of Cambridge.

We share the University's mission to contribute to society through the pursuit of
education, learning and research at the highest international levels of excellence.

www.cambridge.org
Information on this title: www.cambridge.org/9780521766227

DOI: 10.1017/9780511986451

First published 2023

*A catalogue record for this publication is available from the British Library.*

*A Cataloging-in-Publication data record for this book is available from the Library of Congress*

ISBN 978-0-521-76622-7 Hardback
ISBN 978-0-521-17656-9 Paperback

# Contents

# *Figures*

# Contributors

ERAN ALMAGOR is an independent scholar based in Israel.

MARK ALEXANDER BECK is Associate Professor of Classics at the University of South Carolina.

JOHN DILLON is Emeritus Regius Professor of Greek at Trinity College Dublin.

TIMOTHY DUFF is Professor of Greek at the University of Reading.

FRANÇOISE FRAZIER was Professor of Greek Language and Literature at Paris Nanterre University.

JULIA GRIFFIN is Professor of Renaissance Literature at Georgia Southern University.

NOREEN HUMBLE is Professor of Classics and Associate Director of the Calgary Institute for the Humanities at the University of Calgary.

ROBERT LAMBERTON is Emeritus Professor of Classics at Washington University–St. Louis.

KATHERINE MACDONALD is a barrister and solicitor. She was formerly Senior Lecturer in the Department of French at University College London.

JUDITH MOSSMAN is Professor of Classics and Pro-Vice-Chancellor for Arts and Humanities at Coventry University.

KATERINA OIKONOMOPOULOU is Assistant Professor of Classics at the University of Patras.

JAN OPSOMER is Professor of Philosophy at KU Leuven.

MARIANNE PADE is Professor of Classical Philology at Aarhus University and Editor at the Royal Danish Academy of Sciences and Letters.

CHRISTOPHER PELLING is Emeritus Regius Professor of Greek at the University of Oxford.

AURELIO PÉREZ JIMÉNEZ is Emeritus Professor of Greek Philology at the University of Málaga.

DONALD RUSSELL was Professor of Classical Literature and Fellow of St John's College, University of Oxford.

PHILIP STADTER was Eugene H. Falk Professor in the Humanities and Professor of Classics and of Comparative Literature at the University of North Carolina–Chapel Hill.

FRANCES B. TITCHENER is Distinguished Professor of History and Classics at Utah State University.

MANUEL TRÖSTER is Scientific Officer at the Max Planck Society.

ALEXEI V. ZADOROJNYI is Senior Lecturer in Greek Language and Culture at the University of Liverpool.

# Acknowledgments

The editors both thank their families for their love, support, and tolerance during the long hours and frustrating delays this book encountered. We are also in debt to a number of professional colleagues. In particular, we thank Katherine Low for her fine translation of Françoise Frazier's chapter. We also thank the various individuals who helped with our manuscript's preparation, including Sabine Barcatta, Marie Skinner, Daniel Porter, and Rebecca Van Der Horst. The staff at Cambridge University Press have been outstanding and we particularly thank Michael Sharp for his help over the years. We are saddened that three of our authors (Françoise Frazier, Philip Stadter, and Donald Russell) are no longer with us as the volume goes to press but it is comforting to think that they had finished their revisions and were pleased with their work.

The co-editors are also grateful to the Musée des Augustins in Tolouse (especially Anna de Torrès) for authorizing use of the painting by Jean-Charles Nicaise Perrin as cover image. The painting (1782; inv. 2004.I.259) presents the Theban noblewoman Timocleia brought before Alexander the Great – the story which is narrated at length in Plutarch's *Alexander* 12 and *Virtues of Women* 259D–260D.

Finally, we could not have completed this project without the consistent correction, help, and encouragement of Christopher Pelling. His contributions go far beyond the two chapters in this book. We thank him profusely for his assistance while remaining solely responsible for any infelicities or errors.

# Introduction

*Frances B. Titchener and Alexei V. Zadorojnyi*

> For centuries Plutarch retained a direct appeal which seemed to make
> any introduction superfluous.[1]

The writings of Plutarch of Chaeronea offer a rich, often vividly nuanced
retrospective assessment of Greek and Roman history, as well as revealing
a good deal about the intellectual culture of Roman Greece in Plutarch's
own lifetime. From the sheer scope and size of the manifold works Plutarch
left behind we can deduce that he spent a lifetime of effort and energy not
just writing but also reading and thinking.

We hope that you will enjoy meeting this major literary figure of his time
and in later periods of Western culture. Our aim is to provide general
information on Plutarch and his intellectual position in the discursive and
sociocultural context(s) of the Greco-Roman world in the first and second
centuries CE, as well as on the Plutarchan corpus: its range and significance,
the axial themes, and possible approaches to the ordering of knowledge and
argument within it. Ideally, this all leads to the importance of appreciating
Plutarch as a unified intra/intertextual phenomenon. But Plutarch (like any
noteworthy author, for that matter) is also a product of readerly reception –
a text that cannot help being reinvented by its readership, based on their long-
term yet evolving (of course) sensitivities, imagination, and sociopolitical
attitudes. Source criticism lay at the center of scholarship on Plutarch until
the middle part of the twentieth century, which downplayed Plutarch's own
cultural program and literary artistry. Current scholarship, like that in this
volume, tends to focus on Plutarch himself, as a human, scholar, and narrator
who shared his own attitudes, intentions, and methods through his texts.[2]

---

[1] Jones (1974: 280).

[2] Titchener (2011: 37–38): "In the latter third of the twentieth century, commentaries on Plutarch's *Lives*
became historical, rather than grammatical or school-oriented, and large-scale works began to compare
Plutarch to his tradition in history and literature rather than argue over his use of sources. After Pelling's
groundbreaking article on simultaneous preparation in the Roman lives, other studies continued to
address methodology. Recent work has centered on the use of *hypomnēmata*, or commonplace books,

## Plutarch's Writings and Impact

For many today, the name "Plutarch" ought to ring a bell in connection with biographical accounts of famous Greek and Roman statesmen. A certain familiarity with Plutarch's *Parallel Lives* is common among students of ancient history and the general public alike, and with good reason. Plutarch's *Parallel Lives* are paired biographies of Greek and Roman figures, as a rule with a comparative coda (*synkrisis*) at the end.[3] Engaging and deeply complex, the *Parallel Lives* aim to improve their readers as historians, philosophers, and citizens.

Plutarch did not invent the genre of biography,[4] but his biographies gained truly unrivalled recognition over the centuries. There are other ancient biographers, to be sure, and situating Plutarch in the development of the ancient biographical tradition was an important part of the earlier scholarship on his oeuvre. Cornelius Nepos, a contemporary of Cicero's, wrote a series of *Vitae*, or *Lives*, but they are not on the same scale or as unified a project as Plutarch's *Parallel Lives*.[5] Suetonius, Plutarch's close contemporary, wrote *The Lives of the Twelve Caesars*, biographies of Roman rulers starting with Julius Caesar, but his format and tone are markedly different from Plutarch's flowing narrative and the comparative, gently moralistic approach. So while there may be other ancient biographers important to the tradition, all the same there is no one who presents a package quite like the Chaeronean. He is unparalleled.

Indeed, there would be no exaggeration in arguing that it was Plutarch the biographer who consolidated the canon of "great men" of Greece and Rome for posterity[6] – the individuals Plutarch wrote about became *ipso facto* central within that canon. While Plutarch's ultimate goal was, as he declares himself, to uncover and reflect upon the psychological and ethical

---

particularly in the *Moralia*, but in the *Lives* also. As in the essays, there is new focus on structure, particularly the use of various literary devices like dramatic structure that facilitate instruction."

[3] On Plutarch's biographical comparisons, see Duff (1999a: 243–286); Boulogne (2000); Pelling (2005a); Tatum (2010); Larmour (2014). A relatively recent attempt to revive the Plutarchan method of paired biographies is Lloyd George (2016).

[4] The best, richly illustrated histories of biographical writing in antiquity are Hägg (2012) and De Temmerman (2020). See Pelling's Chapter 1 in this volume for Plutarch's place in the history of ancient biography.

[5] Nepos' biographies are "sketches of their subjects, very selective in content and focus. The brevity of Nepos' biographies simply cannot convey the thematic complexity and historical detail of a biography by Plutarch, and comparison of Nepos to his major successors is inherently disadvantageous to him" (Stem 2012: 16).

[6] So Ziegler (1951: 898). Compare the claim by the eighteenth-century French art critic Étienne La Font de Saint-Yenne (1754: 52) that as a source of material for historical paintings, "Plutarch alone [*seul*] can provide storylines fit to keep busy the brushes of all the artists in Europe."

issues behind historical agency,[7] he ended up as a kind of gatekeeper of ancient heroism broadly understood. He wrote about heroic and otherwise remarkable women, too, although his approach to gender as biographer-cum-moralist is clearly not even-handed.[8]

While Plutarch is most renowned as the author of the *Parallel Lives*, he also bequeathed to us the *Moralia* – this blanket term refers to the collection of over seventy-five essays that cover a wide spectrum of issues. Those works are no less seminal in our conversation with Plutarch and underlie many of the essays in this *Companion*. The range of the *Moralia* is astonishingly diverse in terms of intellectual content, literary formats, and settings. Here we find essays containing hands-on advice on ethical and societal demeanor, philosophical dialogues, scrutiny of all sorts of cultural and antiquarian subjects (notably in *Quaestiones convivales*), collections of memorable sayings, rhetorical showpieces, some "hard-core" philosophical exegesis, and so on and so forth. There is advice on how to behave in almost any circumstance: funerals, dinner parties, political gatherings, religious ceremonies, wars. The reader of Plutarch's *Moralia* learns how to tell a flatterer from a genuine friend and whether it is good to have many friends, why Menander is better than Aristophanes, whether chickens or eggs came first, why meat-eating is immoral, what Egyptian mythology is really about, what in the world is wrong with Herodotus' *Histories*, how the souls are judged in the afterlife, and other lively topics.

The so-called Lamprias Catalog, which lists many titles of Plutarch's lost works,[9] builds up the picture of Plutarchan erudition and versatility even further. It is positively regrettable that we do not have, for example, his biography of Caligula or the treatise(?) *On Euripides* (Lamprias Catalogue no. 31 and no. 224, respectively).

## The Life of Plutarch

The best place to look for Plutarch is in Plutarch. Consider his words in his essay *An seni respublica gerenda sit*:

---

[7] Pelling (2002a); Duff (1999a); Chrysanthos (2018). In this volume, see Duff's Chapter 3, "Plutarch As Moral Educator," for Plutarch's agenda and strategies; also Stadter's Chapter 9, "Plutarch and Classical Greece," for Plutarch's attitude toward the past of that country.

[8] See e.g. Stadter (1999a); McInerney (2003); Buszard (2010). In this volume the late Françoise Frazier brings out the philosophically enlightened conventionality of Plutarch's outlook on sex, women, and family (Chapter 11).

[9] Irigoin (1986).

> Now surely you know that I have been serving the Pythian Apollo for many
> Pythiads, but you would not say: "Plutarch, you have done enough sacri-
> ficing, marching in processions, and dancing in choruses, and now that you
> are older it is time to put off the garland and to desert the oracle on account
> of your age." (792F)[10]

This vivid portrait of a senior religious official in action exemplifies why
people have been reading and writing about Plutarch for almost 2,000
years: he is extraordinarily approachable. He "talks" about things that
people can relate to.[11] Moreover, his generous nature, as well as broad
curiosity and learning, shines through in his writings. Because of their
significance, there is almost no aspect of Western civilization where the
influence of his works is not felt, from Shakespeare's plays and Montaigne's
essays to important political developments (inter alia, the creation of the
United States constitution) and even whole literary genres such as miscellany. In fact, it is difficult to find a new way to introduce him and his work,
or even to contextualize his writings, without treading some awfully well-
worn territory, not that we have not tried in this volume.

In that spirit, we suggest that the reader encounter the essays in this
*Companion* as interlocutors – onlookers of a leisurely dialogue with Plutarch
himself. Envision our authors as Plutarch's companions; yourselves his fellow
travelers. As we set out on this journey together, what do we want to know
about each other? We'd presumably ask one another where we are from, what
our families are like, and what are our professions. We might discuss literature
and entertainment. Later, as we grow to know one another better, we might
explore personal beliefs having to do with philosophy, politics, and religion.
And finally, late at night or perhaps in symposium when the servants are not
listening, we might quietly talk about what it is like to live under Roman rule.

In Plutarch's case, we know he was born in Chaeronea ca. 49–50 CE and
lived there all his life until his death near the end of the emperor Hadrian's
rule, ca. 120 CE.[12] He tells us that he remained in his small hometown "lest
it become even smaller" (*Demosthenes* 2.2). But despite its size, Chaeronea
was hardly isolated, with easy access via the Corinthian gulf to Italy,
Macedonia, and the Black Sea, as well as Egypt and the eastern
Mediterranean, all well pacified and safe to travel through in those days.
Friends and travelers from all over the Roman world would have found it

---

[10] This and other translations are from the Loeb Classical Library, unless otherwise indicated.
[11] For instance, in this volume see Mossman and Zadorojnyi's Chapter 14, "Plutarch and Animals," for
Plutarch's thoughts on vegetarianism and the "usefulness of animals to think with"; also Pelling's
Chapter 12 in this volume on wealth as a factor of moral and historical causation according to Plutarch.
[12] See Jones (1971: 1–64) for details on Plutarch's dates.

easy to visit him. Plutarch was interested in the past of his native town; notably, he records that several generations before his birth, Chaeronea had experienced a fair measure of both benign and brutal Roman interventions (*Cimon* 1.2–2.1; *Antony* 68.7–8).

We know many of his relatives' names, including his great-grandfather Nicarchus, his grandfather Lamprias, his father Autobulus, his wife Timoxena, his brothers Lamprias and Timon, his sons Chairon and Soclarus and daughter Timoxena who died young, and his surviving sons Plutarchus and Autobulus. Many appear as characters in the essays, either as interlocutors or subjects of anecdotes. We must tread carefully here, however, since the majority of this information comes from Plutarch's *Quaestiones convivales* (*Table talk*), charming reported dialogues purporting to be transcriptions of dinner parties hosted or attended by Plutarch but not necessarily "realistic" in the modern sense.[13] On the other hand, essays such as his *Consolatio* to his wife upon the death of their daughter or *Coniugalia praecepta* (*Advice to bride and groom*) surely capture genuine emotions and contribute to the sense that we see Plutarch as a man, not just a writer, in his writings.

Plutarch also led an active public life, particularly in religion. We know from an inscription and his own essays that he served as a priest at Delphi for many years.[14] In three dialogues entitled collectively the *Pythikoi Logoi*, which Plutarch sent as a gift to his friend Serapion,[15] Plutarch's strong religious convictions come into focus, especially his feeling that sacred ceremonies were an important part of any politically active individual's life. He also drew a sharp distinction between authentic belief and superstition. To him, ignorance of the gods leads in the long run to irrationality and

---

[13] Great-grandfather: *Antony* 68.7. Grandfather: *Quaestiones convivales* 622E, 669C, 738B. Father: *Quaestiones convivales* 615E, 641F, 656C, 657E. Wife: *Coniugalia praecepta* 145A, *Consolatio ad uxorem* 608A–612B. Brothers: *Quaestiones convivales* 615C-E, 617E, 639B, 643E, 726D, 740A, *De fraterno amore* 487E. Daughter: *Consolatio ad uxorem* 611D. Sons: *Quomodo adolescens poetas audire debeat* 15A, *Consolatio ad uxorem* 609D; *De animae procreatione in Timaeo* 1012B. Consider, for instance, the opening of *Amatorius* 749B, where Plutarch describes a quarrel between his parents and parents-in-law just after his marriage; see Titchener (2009: 395–401). In this volume, see Oikonomopoulou's Chapter 7, "Plutarch at the Symposium," for the special significance of the symposiastic genre on Plutarch's intellectual and social horizon.

[14] *An seni respublica gerenda sit* 792F; see *CIG* 1713 = *SIG* 1.379, 588 for an inscription on the base of a statue dedicated to Hadrian upon the emperor's visit, which records Plutarch as the officiating priest.

[15] *De E apud Delphos* (384D–394C) discusses various explanations for the three possible meanings of the Greek letter E on Apollo's temple at Delphi. *De Pythiae oraculis* (394D–409D) discusses the fact that oracles used to be delivered in hexameter verse, but were no longer, and concludes that the present time called for directness and simplicity rather than vagueness and riddling speech. It contains a guided tour of the Delphic statues and monuments, accompanied by anecdotes and former oracles as seen by young visitors. *De defectu oraculorum* (409E–438F) discusses but does not resolve the question of why the oracle was becoming obsolete.

atheism.[16] In fact, as he sees it, superstition is worse than atheism because atheists remain unmoved in respect to the divine, but through their fear that same impulse misleads the superstitious into making wrong-headed decisions (*De superstitione* 165C). Timidity of this sort lies at the heart of Plutarch's intense disgust with superstition, since to him it results from a fear so intense that it completely debilitates and flattens the affected individual (*De superstitione* 165B). Without involving deities directly in his works the way Herodotus or a tragedian does, Plutarch suffuses his world with the deeply felt convictions of a man who is willing to question the moral order but not the gods.[17]

Plutarch was active in politics as well. From a famous anecdote, we know that as a young man he undertook diplomatic missions of some sort on behalf of Greece:

> I recollect that when I was still a young man I was sent with another as envoy to the proconsul; the other man was somehow left behind; I alone met the proconsul and accomplished the business. Now when I came back and was to make the report of our mission, my father left his seat and told me in private not to say "I went" but "we went," not "I said" but "we said" and in all other ways to associate my colleague in a joint report. (*Praecepta gerendae reipublicae* 816D–E)

From this we learn not only that Plutarch had undertaken this mission but also that his father was clearly experienced and savvy, and engaged with his son's career – a role model that the young Plutarch clearly admired and emulated.

### The Plutarchan Macrotext

In short, Plutarch offers plenty of first-rate material both for studying Greek and Roman history and religion and for gauging the sociocultural and intellectual atmosphere of imperial Greece during the first decades of the period that was later designated as the Second Sophistic.[18] Until relatively (by the classicists' yardstick) recently, however, Plutarch was regarded as an author whom one would read primarily for self-perfection and inspiration; that is to say, for the sake of paradigmatic values that can

---

[16] *De superstitione* 164E; see Titchener (2008).
[17] In this volume, see Lamberton's Chapter 6, "Religion and Myth in Plutarch," describing Plutarch's religious views as a synthesis of traditionalism and philosophical inquiry.
[18] For Plutarch in the context of the Second Sophistic, the ideal starting point is Schmitz (2014). In this volume, see Russell's Chapter 8, "Language, Style, and Rhetoric," appraising Plutarch's relationship with rhetoric and laying out the principal features of Plutarch's language and writing style.

improve one's personality and energize one's career. The Plutarchan *Lives* in particular used to be the formative matrix for generations of Western Europe's royalty and intelligentsia since the Renaissance. Plutarch's texts were not just popular among the educated class – they were essential; their impact was enormous and long-lasting.[19] The downturn happened around the middle of the nineteenth century, when scholars of antiquity stopped seeing Plutarch as a reliable informant, while for the wider reading public his moralism and the whole discursive mentality felt increasingly alien and outdated. The Plutarchan heroes were losing their appeal and relevance.[20] In many ways, the decline and marginalization of Plutarch mirrors the overall trajectory of Europe's reception of classical antiquity, from the Renaissance into the modern age.[21]

Valuable comments about Plutarch were being made, nonetheless, at the time when his ideological and cultural supremacy started to ebb. A leading French literary critic of the mid-nineteenth century compared the *Memoirs* of Marquis de Lafayette (who had covered himself in glory during the US War of Independence, then played a prominent part in events of the French Revolution, and kept going as the embodiment of dignified republicanism until his death in 1834) with Plutarch's *Lives*: Lafayette's multivolume autobiography, claims the critic, reveals immanent integrity and cohesion, "just as the set of Plutarch's *Lives* is never incomplete, even if there is only one volume" ("Ce sont là de ces volumes, qui comme ceux des vies de Plutarque, ne sont jamais dépareillés, même quand on n'en a qu'un").[22] This seemingly casual insight prefigures the suggestion put forward by Gennaro D'Ippolito in the 1990s that Plutarch's works ought to be read as a polyphonous and yet fundamentally unified macrotext.[23] The concept of the macrotext is important because it encourages us to think through the various (leit)motifs, cross-references, and echoes, which are found aplenty across the Plutarchan corpus, in a more disciplined and searching manner. For instance, Plutarch's habit of recycling the same quotations and apophthegms

---

[19] See, more recently, Gallo (1998a); Ribeiro Ferreira (2002: esp. 293–368); Ribeiro Ferreira and Leão (2003: 179–261); Aguilar and Alfageme (2006); Candau Morón et al. (2011: 533–673); Guerrier (2012); Beck (2014a: 531–610); North and Mack (2018); Xenophontos and Oikonomopoulou (2019); Kingston (2022). In this volume, see Humble's Chapter 15, "Plutarch in Byzantium," Pade's Chapter 16, "Plutarch in the Italian Renaissance," Pérez Jiménez's Chapter 17, "Plutarch and the Spanish Renaissance," Griffin's Chapter 18, "Plutarch and Shakespeare: Reviving the Dead," and MacDonald's Chapter 19, "Plutarch in France: Sixteenth to Eighteenth Centuries" for later reception.

[20] See Gefen (2012); David-de Palacio (2012); Zadorojnyi (2018a; 2019); Cazals (2001).

[21] Goldhill (2002: 246–251, 282–293); Hartog (2005: 99–103, 115–147).

[22] Sainte-Beuve (1839: 245) = (1844: 196). [23] D'Ippolito (1991; 1996).

(and whole citational clusters) in different contexts[24] looks entirely rational from the macrotextual perspective. Moreover, it is clear that manifold synergies exist between the *Lives* and the *Moralia*;[25] a number of recurrent, macrotextually cogent propositions emerge, such as the insistence on philosophically oriented *paideia*, the desirability of equitable balance between the rational and nonrational forces in the soul and likewise in the polity, and the caveats against competitive ambition and anger as disruptive ethico-political drives. (Plutarch appears to endorse wholeheartedly the status quo of the Empire: *De Pythiae oraculis* 408B–C, *Praecepta gerendae reipublicae* 824C.)

On the other hand, the macrotextual reading of Plutarch throws into relief some formidable fault-lines and high-stakes interpretive challenges. Is Plutarch a serious philosopher of the Middle-Platonic persuasion,[26] or is he mainly interested in providing the Greco-Roman elite with commonsensical and only loosely philosophical moral guidance[27] – or maybe both? (After all, he believes, in his own crisp phrase, that "it is most clever to philosophize without appearing to talk philosophy": *Quaestiones convivales* 614A.) Is his moral judgment open-ended or, deep down, prescriptive? Is he driving a biographically centered (anecdotal, episodic) idea of history, or does he at the same time contemplate more global and long-term historical patterns?[28] The constructive approach to the Plutarchan microtext must neither demand absolute consistency nor foreground the discrepancies,[29] but rather recognize and embrace the layered, contrapuntal complexity of Plutarch's writing, and accept the often seeming contradictions in the recycled clusters of topics and quotations (see pp. 7–8 above).

A saliently macrotextual fault-line of Plutarch's thought is the awareness of the compelling allure but also the dangers entailed in the spectacle of suffering. The notions of drama and tragedy are regularly invoked by

---

[24]  See e.g. Bowie (2008); Van der Stockt (1999b; 1999c; 2004); Beck (2010); Xenophontos (2012).

[25]  E.g. Valgiglio (1992); Nikolaidis (2008); Xenophontos (2016). In this volume, see Tröster's Chapter 2, "Romanness and Greekness in Plutarch"; Almagor's Chapter 13, "Plutarch and the Barbarian 'Other'," which takes stock of Plutarch's opinion of "barbarians" as the indispensable foil to Greco-Roman identity; and also Beck's Chapter 10, "Great Men: Leadership in Plutarch's *Lives*."

[26]  On Middle Platonism, see Dillon (1996) and Boys-Stones (2018). In this volume, see Opsomer's Chapter 4, "In the Spirit of Plato," in which Plutarch's position as a Middle Platonist is fleshed out; also Dillon and Zadorojnyi's Chapter 5, "Plutarch as a Polemicist," which samples the polemical strand in Plutarch's construal of history and philosophy.

[27]  Van Hoof (2010; 2014); Roskam and Van der Stockt (2011).

[28]  See, respectively, Zadorojnyi (2018b) and Pelling (2010).

[29]  These obviously are there: see Nikolaidis (1991; 1994).

Plutarch.[30] This is how he likes to label human behavior or language that in his eyes is overly ostentatious and bombastic and that, at the end of the day, belongs with folly and falsehood. Yet alongside such Platonizing censure of toxic theatricality, Plutarch may turn tragedy into a poignant diegetic caption when the magnificent volatility or sheer horror of a real-life scenario are entitled to bona fide dramatism (e.g. *Demetrius* 53.10; *Crassus* 33.7; *Brutus* 31.4–6). Plutarch thus appears to make room for the existential dimension of tragedy, even though in his more didactic passages he would normally deflate and neutralize the tragic experience[31] by reducing it to interpretable value-statements, which are frequently problematic but sometimes valid (e.g. *Quomodo adulator ab amico internoscatur* 63A, "the tragic Merope advises . . ."). Yet he is not complacent about such didactic filtering of tragedy either, given that he dwells on several striking instances of aberrant, even criminal spectatorship. At the banquet of the Parthian king, the violence of Euripides' *Bacchae* is reenacted literally – and applauded (*Crassus* 33).[32] A cruel Greek tyrant weeps in the theater, but emphatically shows no remorse over the atrocities he has committed or is going to commit (*Pelopidas* 29.9–10; *De Alexandri fortuna aut virtute* 334A). With a will, the last anecdote could be taken as Plutarch's wry riposte to Aristotle's *Poetics*: tragedy stirs pity and fear, but the tragic broadcast of these emotions does not necessarily change the human self for the better.

## Conclusion

In the proem to the *Lives* of Theseus and Romulus, Plutarch draws an analogy between the past and a map of the earth (*Theseus* 1.1).[33] Transposing the metaphor, it can be said that the aim of this volume is to give the reader a tour of Plutarch's own expansive and varied macrotext. The essays of the *Companion* trace out and explore the must-visit discursive zones and axial avenues, as it were, that run through the Plutarchan oeuvre. His treatment of "public" and "private" themes (which are so often fused rather than held asunder by Plutarch) will be addressed from different angles, yet working toward a joined-up vision of the ancient author whose

---

[30] The rest of this paragraph is a very basic summary of several full-scale and subtle discussions of Plutarch's engagement with tragedy: key studies are De Lacy (1952), Tagliasacchi (1960), Mossman (2014), and especially Pelling (2016b).
[31] On Plutarch's exploitation of literature as educational resource, see Konstan (2004); Saïd (2005a); Bréchet (2007); Lather (2017).
[32] Zadorojnyi (1997a: 179–182); Chrysanthou (2018: 116–120).
[33] On the role of topography and the spatial dimension generally in Plutarch's writing, see further Beck (2012); Georgiadou and Oikonomopoulou (2017).

cultural baggage and intellectual range are impressive and, what is more, so eminently convertible into narrative, commentary, and debate – again, in Plutarch's writing these three modes of textuality tend to merge together.[34] It is for this reason that the contributors were not assigned a rigid agenda, with the editors preferring to reach out to readers, whether general or expert, in different areas looking for a *tour d'horizon* as a background, or perhaps a launching pad, for some more specific interest, and a reassurance that they are not missing something important.

We hope that when your journey with your companion Plutarch is over, you will know and appreciate him a little better, and even more importantly, as Apollo charges us all, you will know yourself and your own world in greater depth and detail after an unparalleled journey!

We are especially proud to include his essay and to dedicate this volume to Donald Russell. Many elegant tributes have been published since his passing on February 9, 2020, all praising his tremendous learning, deep humanity, and skilled teaching. Coeditor Fran Titchener in particular was the beneficiary of all three of those things. From their earliest acquaintance, Donald was extremely kind, inviting Fran to meals at St. John's, where he discreetly advised on whether to use a knife and fork on a banana. He also hosted her frequently in his own home, leading serious discussions not just on classical literature and scholarship but on everything from place names ("Titchener" seems to mean something like "people who lived where two paths meet") to antiques roadshow to train schedules. As a wide-eyed visiting student in Oxford back in 1995, Alexei Zadorojnyi (whose surname, in turn, means "over the road") received similar hospitality and precious advice from Donald Russell on several occasions. Donald Russell was one of the most genuine, candid, and forthright people imaginable. He is greatly missed. In one of Plutarch's myths about the afterlife (*De genio Socratis* 593E), the souls of exceptional individuals carry on overseeing and giving friendly encouragement to the living who are, to quote from Russell's fine translation of this work, "still practising for the same goal." We hope that Donald Russell himself, having moved on to become the patron daemon of Plutarchan studies, would look kindly upon this *Companion*.

---

[34] Easily the most striking example is the narrated dialogue *De genio Socratis*: see Nesselrath (2010).

CHAPTER I

# Plutarch and Biography

## Christopher Pelling

Plutarch has a lot to answer for. It is not just that he did so much to fix the canon of great Greeks and Romans in the popular imagination, though that too is true. We have also grown so used to the distinctive aspects of a Plutarchan biography that we almost take them for granted in our own generic expectations: the linear narrative from birth to death; the concentration on public actions but with an eye to family life; the delight in anecdotes; the respect for historical truth; and a commitment to getting the character right. These are still the features that characterize many books in the "biography" section of a bookshop, at least those that deal with the sort of public, political figures that Plutarch took as his own subjects. We are unsurprised too that Plutarch chose to write his *Lives*, or most of them, in a series – the *Lives of the Caesars* and then the *Parallel Lives* (though we should not forget the freestanding *Lives* as well, the extant *Aratus* and *Artaxerxes* and the lost *Heracles, Hesiod, Pindar, Crates, Daiphantus,* and *Aristomenes*); we have become used to *Lives of the Saints* or *Composers* or *Admirals* or *Pirates* or even *Great Rugger Players*. Plutarch himself has so dominated Western biography that his influence has surely played a part in shaping these traditions; at times, the modeling is direct (e.g. Bullock 1991). Yet none of these features could be taken for granted when Plutarch settled down to write. He faced many choices, ones that might well have been made differently.

Was there a "genre" of biography at all? Genre in ancient biography is difficult; in fact, genre in ancient literature is difficult, and there have been suggestions that we should talk instead about individual models, father-figures whom their literary descendants always have in mind and from whom they Oedipally try, with varying success, to break away.[1] That is an extreme view, and genre is a sensible way of looking at literature that has a performance context: we know what a tragedy is; it is what was performed

---

[1] Rosenmeyer (1985).

at the tragic festival. Prose-genres take longer to be identified and tend to have more fluid boundaries.[2] Even "history" is not spoken of as a genre until Aristotle (*Poetics* 1450a36–51b11, 1459a21–24);[3] the word *biographia* is not found until late antiquity[4] but it looks as if life-writing is thought of as something identifiable by the first century BC. Thus Cornelius Nepos speaks of "this type of writing" (*hoc genus scripturae*) in his proem and mentions his fear "that, if I begin to set out what happened, I might seem to be writing history rather than telling his life" (*non uitam eius enarrare, sed historiam ... scribere*, *Pelopidas* 1.1): the phrasing is snappy and casual enough to suggest that the distinction is familiar. But it is best to think of any genre as very loosely defined, with various works that have something in common but no firm generic boundaries to police. There were works, for instance, on Alexander the Great in which he was inevitably the central figure, but they did not start at birth or include his early life; Arrian's *Anabasis* is the best-known extant example. Are these biographies? If so, should not the *Odyssey* count as a biographical poem? What of Xenophon's *Memorabilia*, centering on the figure of Socrates but doing so in a mass of little narratives rather than one big one? The conventional story of the genre takes it back to two fourth-century BCE origins, Xenophon's work on the Spartan king Agesilaus and Isocrates' on the Cyprian Evagoras, with a nod to fifth-century BCE antecedents in Stesimbrotus and Ion of Chios.[5] Both the *Agesilaus* (10.3) and the *Evagoras* (8, 11, 65) more precisely describe themselves as "encomia," rhetorical works of praise – but, again, is there anything to mark off encomium as a separate genre from biography rather than a subclass of it? There would not even have been the theoretical vocabulary to phrase such a question. And if we think in formal terms, we might equally concentrate on a different work of Xenophon as a progenitor of biography, his account of the sixth-century BCE Persian king Cyrus in *Cyropaedia*. That work does start at the beginning and develop a linear narrative in the way we have come to expect of biography.

Still, here looms a further complication, for we should not be so ready to regard that cradle-to-grave form as a basic indicator of biography. Even

---

[2] Geiger (1985: 11–18) and McGing and Mossman (2006b: ix–xiii) here have good remarks.

[3] For a sketch of the theoretical questions raised by historiography as a genre, see the papers in Kraus (1999), especially Marincola (1999); I had my own say in the same volume (Pelling 1999b) and, turning to biography rather than history, in Pelling (2006). For the broader issues raised by genre, see e.g. Depew and Obbink (2000), Barchiesi (2000), and Swift (2010: 6–34).

[4] Momigliano (1993: 12).

[5] On Ion, see now Jennings and Katsaros (2007); on Stesimbrotus, Pelling (2016a; 2020).

today, celebrity biographers often do not do it in that way; books on actors and football stars may start from a brilliant moment of success and then jump all over the place, more in the style of a talk-show interview than of the staid linear narratives of political biography.[6] Before Plutarch, too, cradle-to-grave was just one way among many. At least one work, Satyrus' *Life of Euripides*, was even written in dialogue form. Life-writing could be so broad a concept that it did not even need a personal subject at all: Dicaearchus wrote a *Life of Greece*, collecting together snippets about the way different Greeks lived, their feasting and their dress and their political institutions, and glancing back to the origins of these customs.

So we should think of genre as a repertory of possibilities, not a straitjacket. There might be "on-the-whole" expectations,[7] ones that no reader would be surprised to find were not met; but, for Plutarch, expectations may not even have got as far as that.

To bring out how different Plutarch's biography might have been, while also keeping half an eye on the modern genre as well as its ancient forerunners, let us turn to Hermione Lee's short but magisterial *Biography* (2009). Lee begins by mapping "ten rules for biography," all of which except the last can be broken but all corresponding to modern expectations. Her interest is admittedly more in literary biography, where she is herself a distinguished practitioner, than in political biography. Plutarch wrote literary biographies too – the lost *Hesiod*, *Pindar*, and *Crates* – but we cannot know what form they took. Lee's rules are still illuminating. So: How does Plutarch match up to these modern expectations and how does he compare under each heading with other ancient productions?

### Rule 1: The Story Should Be True

Yes, Plutarch would have agreed – on the whole. His frequent discussions of his sources (Rule 4, pp. 18–19 below) are usually targeted on truth: "if this story is true, I cannot understand why Cicero did not mention it in his account of his consulship" (*Caesar* 8.3–4). The impressive discussion of Aristides' wealth at *Aristides* 1 weighs different indications and uses an argument from letter-forms to show that a certain inscription is not as relevant as had been claimed. When Plutarch explains that in *Theseus* he is

---

[6] Lee (2009: 123) notes the greater freedom she, as a literary biographer, has found in organizing her material than a political counterpart would have done.

[7] Pelling (1999b: 329). This is also the position taken by Burridge (2004: esp. 33–36), drawing illuminating conclusions about the relationship of the Gospels to Greco-Roman biography.

entering a new, more distant period when he can only "make myth look like history" (*Theseus* 1), that tells a story about his other *Lives* too, the ones where he has not had to plead for such readerly indulgence. Still, Plutarch's idea of truth, or way of getting at the truth, may not be the same as ours. We find many cases where Plutarch tells the same stories in incompatible fashion in different *Lives*;[8] he cannot have thought them all equally true. It takes a modern reader aback when he defends his inclusion of the meeting of Solon and Croesus despite its chronological difficulties: "when a story is so famous and well-attested, when (most important) it fits Solon's character so well and is so worthy of his wisdom and largeness of spirit, I am not prepared to reject it because of the so-called rules of chronology" (*Solon* 27.1).

Yet there is more to that than meets the eye.[9] The chronologists' calculations *were* often insecure. Just as important is his reason for retaining the story: it fits Solon's character so well. A modern reader might say that this was a good reason why it should have been made up, but it does point to Plutarch's overriding desire to be true to life, his character's life. In cases where he does bend the truth in detail, for instance in making the young Antony more susceptible to the pernicious Curio (*Antony* 2) or tailoring the ostracism of (?) 415 BCE to make Nicias more directly responsible for his own undoing (contrast *Nicias* 11 with *Alcibiades* 13),[10] we might see him as "helping the truth along," bending details to accentuate traits and themes that he believes important to grasping what the man was really like and building a picture of his identity (Rule 8, pp. 23–25 below). We would be shocked at this in a modern biography (though much less so in a bio*pic*, as we allow more latitude in films) but we should still accept the element of truth in that mix as well as of falsity. The material is true *enough*, and that is what matters, rather (in a way) as with Thucydides' treatment of speeches (1.22); and 95 percent of any *Life* Plutarch would surely have thought simply true, without further qualification.

However much truth we find in Plutarch, it is more than might have been expected and certainly more than could be taken for granted. Momigliano argued that "the borderline between fiction and reality was thinner in biography than in ordinary historiography";[11] that overgeneralizes, but there were certainly works like Xenophon's *Cyropaedia* where the level of truthfulness was anything but complete. Readers of such a work,

[8] Cf. Pelling (2002a: 91–102, 152–156); Nikolaidis (1991: 154–155). Licona (2017) productively compares the differences in the four Gospels with Plutarch's technique.
[9] Cf. Duff (1999a: 312–314).
[10] On the first, see Pelling (1988a: 118); on the second, Pelling (2000a: 49–52).
[11] Momigliano (1993: 56; cf. 46).

like those of Philostratus' *Apollonius of Tyana* or perhaps even of the Christian Gospels,[12] would have to work out as they went how much truth and what *sort* of truth the work conveyed; readers of Satyrus' dialogues could equally not assume that everything everyone said was literally true, even if the work conveyed the broader truth that Euripides was a figure about whom people always argued and always would. That, too, is a sort of truth, but not the sort that was to be found in Plutarch.[13]

### Rule 2:  The Story Should Cover the Whole Life

Yes, in the sense of covering all its span. We can often see Plutarch working hard to reconstruct childhood from a few scattered hints:[14] *Coriolanus* is a good instance of that, where the young Marcius' relationship with his mother is elaborated from a few sentences in his source Dionysius of Halicarnassus (see below, p. 25). It is therefore striking (and relevant to Rule 1) to note what he does *not* do: several of his *Lives* have blank patches, for instance the hole in *Themistocles* from 493 to 483 BCE, and there are great gaps in *Lives* such as *Publicola* and *Aristides*. But he does not fabricate anything to fill them, nor does he pretend to have much to say about how Solon or Flamininus died.

Once again, this was not the only way Plutarch could have chosen to write. He could have fabricated; *Cyropaedia* did. Alternatively, many one-person narratives had concentrated only on significant parts of a person's story; that was true of the Alexander narratives, Xenophon's *Anabasis*, and Cicero's *On His Consulship*, works that Plutarch certainly knew. It was already true of the *Odyssey*. Even works that covered a whole life did not necessarily do so evenly. In Rome a culture had developed of writing of "the deaths of famous men" (*exitus uirorum illustrium*), particularly men like Thrasea Paetus and Helvidius Priscus who had stood up self-destructively to hated emperors. Such works may have covered the life but clearly dwelt especially on the death. They left their mark on Tacitus' *Agricola*, written probably just as Plutarch was beginning his *Parallel Lives*: the mention in Tacitus' proem of the *Lives* of Thrasea and Helvidius written by Arulenus Rusticus and Herennius Senecio (*Agr.* 2.1) is not casual.[15] Plutarch may well have known some members of that

---

[12] On the Gospels' relation to Greco-Roman biography, see Burridge (2004) and Averintsev (2002), reaching different conclusions, and now Licona (2017).
[13] On all this, see further Pelling (2002a: 143–170), where I compare Plutarch's standards of veracity with those of historiography.
[14] Pelling (2002a: 301–338).    [15] Whitmarsh (2006b: 307–310).

philosophical circle personally.[16] He anyway almost certainly knew literature of that kind, as he apparently used Thrasea's *Life* of Cato Minor as a source for his own *Life*.[17] But, rich though Plutarch's description of Cato's death is, he stays close to his usual balance in the distribution of narrative.

There is another aspect of "the whole life," one that features more in Lee's discussions of modern biography: the expectation that all *aspects* of a life should be covered, in particular the sexual. Here Plutarch is discriminating. He does bring in sexual items at times. That is particularly so when they impinge on public life, for instance Antony's affair with Cleopatra, or Pompey's delight in spending time with his wives away from the political hurly-burly (*Pompey* 53.1–6; cf. 74–75); but there are other cases too, as with the young Pompey as an ardent lover (*Pompey* 2.5–9), or the scandal that surrounded the young Cimon (*Cimon* 4.6–9), or – much more gently – Pericles' kissing Aspasia every time he left home or returned at night (*Pericles* 24.9). Sulla's, Cicero's, and both Catos' treatment of their wives becomes important to their evaluation (*Sulla* 35–36.2; *Cicero* 41; *Cato Maior* 24; *Cato Minor* 7, 25, 52.5–9); so does Agesilaus' behavior in homosexual affairs (*Agesilaus* 11.6–10, 20.9; cf. 25.1–26.1).[18] Here he is not wholly isolated as sex played an important part in the traditions concerning some of the figures he treated (Theseus, Alcibiades, Caesar, Demetrius, Antony), but not in all, and Plutarch could find nothing to say about the family life or sexuality of men like Nicias or Fabius or Marcellus. He cannot even tell us whether Philopoemen was married, presumably because Polybius did not say so in his encomium.

Here one often senses the personality of Plutarch himself:

> And so Cato married Atilia, daughter of Serranus, and this was the first woman with whom he had intercourse: the first, but not the last, so here he differed from Scipio's friend Laelius. Laelius was the more fortunate of the two, to have just the single partner, the woman he originally married, in the many different stages of his life. (*Cato Minor* 7.3)

None of this has the prurience of much modern biography or indeed of Suetonius; but Plutarch knew that such aspects of personal life mattered if one was to come to know one's figures as one wished.

---

[16] Jones (1971: 23–24, 51–54): notice especially *De curiositate* 522D–E, with Arulenus in the audience when Plutarch lectured at Rome.

[17] Cf. especially *Cato Minor* 25.2, 37.1; Geiger (1979b).

[18] On Plutarch's interest in his heroes' sexuality, see Stadter (1995) and especially Beneker (2012); cf. Schmitt Pantel (2009: 31–33, 117–154).

## Rule 3:   Nothing Should Be Omitted or Concealed

But no *Life* can ever be full; molding a narrative always excludes as well as shapes what remains. It is also one of Plutarch's historiographic principles that there *should* be omissions: there should be no irrelevant material to a figure's discredit (*De Herodoti malignitate* 855C–E). He gives a fuller treatment of his attitude toward flaws in the proem to *Cimon*:

> It is just like our expectations of portrait-painters, when their subjects are beautiful and very attractive. If there is a small flaw, we do not want them either to omit it completely or to make too much of it, for the one makes the representation defective and the other makes it ugly. In the same way, just as it is hard or rather impossible to show any person's life as totally irreproachable and pure, we must dwell on the good things to round out the truth as a likeness; as for the mistakes and destructive elements in one's actions that come from some emotional experience or some political necessity, one should regard them more as fallings-short in virtue rather than cases of evil or vice. We should not be wholly eager or excessive in pointing to them in our writing, but rather behave as if we were embarrassed on behalf of human nature, if it cannot find a character to depict of unqualified goodness and indisputable virtue. (*Cimon* 2.4–5)

And Plutarch duly does not mince his words when he finds defects even in those he admired. Timoleon's most repellent act was his failure to stop the execution of his enemies' wives and daughters (*Timoleon* 33.2); Brutus' handing over of Thessalonica and Sparta for plunder is "the one charge in his *Life* to which no defense can be found" (*Brutus* 46.2). Room is also found in the series for some deterrent examples. Just as the musician Ismenias used to teach the flute by pointing out "you should not play like that" as well as "you should," so Plutarch will include some cases of "bad men and those who are blamed" (*Demetrius* 1.6)[19] – Demetrius and Antony, at least, and perhaps more (Coriolanus and Alcibiades are the ones most usually touted). Not that even those are uniformly bad, any more than the exemplary figures are uniformly good. The really bad, a Cleon or a Clodius or a whole range of tyrant-figures, require a fuller omission – total omission from the series, as such men are not morally interesting.

So Plutarch's view of moral omissions is a nuanced one. It is clear that not all his predecessors were so nuanced. Aristoxenus' fourth-century BCE lives of philosophers had dwelt on Socrates' irascibility and Plato's plagiarism (frs. 54b, 56, 67 Wehrli): they do not sound particularly balanced. Encomium in contrast dwelt only on the good. Polybius contrasted the

---

[19] Cf. Duff (2004).

needs of his history, with its blend of praise and blame, with the "summary and inflated" way he had treated Philopoemen in the separate encomium (10.21.8), and Plutarch's criticisms of Philopoemen's irascibility and contentiousness (3.1) will be his own rather than drawn from Polybius. With Agesilaus we can see something similar: first, that Xenophon omits in his encomium some unfavorable materials that he includes in his *Hellenica*; second, that Plutarch is more critical of Agesilaus than Xenophon had been in either work.[20] This readiness of Plutarch to portray characters as mixed, even if largely admirable, goes with that "embarrassment on behalf of human nature" that we saw in *Cimon*. He knows that human nature is mixed too; his readers can see and ponder how this has been true even with the great.

### Rule 4:   All Sources Used Should Be Identified

Ancient and modern expectations are again different. Historians tended to quote their predecessors mainly in disagreement or sometimes (as in Livy) to note divergences in, say, casualty numbers; occasionally quotation is more extensive, as in Thucydides' treaty documents (4.118–19, 5.18–19) or Herodotus' grave-epigrams (7.228). Plutarch quotes sources of a wider range and in much greater profusion. Thus *Alcibiades* quotes Plato, Euripides, comic poets (especially Aristophanes), Thucydides, Duris of Samos, Antiphon, Demosthenes, Isocrates, and Critias. The Roman *Lives* are less rich in literary quotations, presumably because Plutarch had not read Latin literature so extensively, but he can still quote Horace (*Lucullus* 39.5),[21] and *Caesar*, for instance, quotes Caesar himself, Asinius Pollio, Livy, Cicero, C. Oppius, Tanusius Geminus, and Strabo. It has long been disputed how many of these writers Plutarch knew at first hand but scholars today are much readier to believe in Plutarch's wide reading than they were sixty years ago.

Just as relevant is the range of genres he cites and the reasons for which he does so. For instance, historians do not usually quote Cicero's works as a source for events,[22] but Plutarch does; thus, for instance, *Antony* quotes and makes extensive use of the *Second Philippic* (esp. at 6.1, 9.5–9, 10, and 21), while *Cicero*, *Caesar*, and *Crassus* similarly exploit *On His Own Consulship* (quoted at *Caesar* 8.3–4 and *Crassus* 13.3–4; not quoted in *Cicero*, but clearly used a great deal[23]). Nor are writers simply quoted to

[20] Shipley (1997: 49–50).   [21] Stadter (2015c).
[22] Millar (1964: 54–55); cf. Pelling (2002a: 148).
[23] *Second Philippic*: Pelling (1988a: 26–27). *On His Own Consulship*: Moles (1988: 26); Pelling (2002a: 45–53).

score points against them; we have already noticed the judicious weighing of different types of evidence to establish Aristides' personal wealth (*Aristides* 1; see above, p. 13), and often a source is quoted to add credibility to an item that might otherwise be doubted, very much in the modern manner.

It does not look as if Plutarch's predecessors cited material so extensively, but he is not alone among biographers. Suetonius too quotes extensively, perhaps influenced by an antiquarian tradition that concentrated on more literary figures (this was argued by Friedrich Leo and has been much discussed since[24]). Thus his *Diuus Iulius* quotes contemporary pamphlets and lampoons, Cicero, Pollio, C. Oppius, Balbus, Brutus, Hirtius, and Caesar himself, as well as literary works – Calvus, Catullus, Curio – more in the manner of Plutarch's Greek *Lives* than his Roman. So some biography, at least, is prepared to parade a scholarly apparatus to a degree that historiography found stylistically inappropriate.

## Rule 5: The Biographer Should Know the Subject

Many ancient encomiasts and biographers did. Polybius carried the urn at Philopoemen's funeral (Plutarch, *Philopoemen* 21.5), Tacitus was Agricola's son-in-law, and the Roman "deaths of famous men" (see above, pp. 15–16) were typically written by younger disciples of the martyred dead. In works of more distant literary forms, Xenophon and Plato both knew Socrates, Ion talked of his own meetings with the great, and the first versions of Alexander's campaigns were written by participants Callisthenes, Aristobulus, and Ptolemy. Plutarch's subjects were more removed; the nearest he came to his own day was in the *Lives of the Caesars* and the only one of those Caesars he had a chance even to see was Nero.[25] He was, however, acquainted with some who had participated in the events, notably the consular Mestrius Florus with whom he toured the battlefield of Bedriacum (*Otho* 14.2).

The *idea* of personal knowledge is still important to Plutarch's self-presentation. In the prologue to *Aemilius Paulus* he describes the biographical experience:

> It was thanks to others that I took up the writing of *Lives*, but I have come to stay with it, and delight in staying, for my own sake. It is just like using history as a mirror to find a way of ordering and molding my own life in the

---

[24] Leo (1901); Momigliano (1993: 18–21, 86–88, 112–121) reviews the debate.
[25] Especially *De E apud Delphos* 391E; Jones (1971: 16–17).

image of the virtues of others. The experience resembles nothing so much as living with them as house-guests; it is as if I am entertaining each of them in turn, receiving them through the medium of history and exploring "the greatness and quality of the man,"[26] selecting from their actions the most important and most illuminating. "Oh, what greater joy could you ever have than this?"[27] – and what could be a more effective way of self-improvement? (*Aemilius Paulus* 1.1–2)

It is hard to think that Plutarch found all his mental house-guests equally congenial, or that he recognized much of himself when he looked in the mirror offered by, say, Coriolanus or Demetrius, but his moralism is subtler here than it may at first appear, as we shall see under Rule 9 (below, pp. 26–27).

Such imagery retains its appropriateness, and Lee herself goes further than "house-guest": writing biography can be "a kind of marriage."[28]

## Rule 6:   The Biographer Should Be Objective

By this Lee makes it clear that she means "impersonal and authoritative," though she also emphasizes that this aspect has always been in question.[29] Plutarch's ways of building authority are complex; source-citation (Rule 4) is one, projecting not merely the research he has done but also his readiness to weigh it critically. Another is the distance he keeps from his subjects. For all his attempts to see his figures' point of view, we have also seen (Rule 3) that when they deserve criticism, he states it strongly.

Impersonality is a different matter. The *Lives* project a strong impression of Plutarch's personality. Sometimes, though rarely, this is through a reference to his own experience: the battlefield tour (*Otho* 14.2; above, p. 19); the family reminiscences in *Antony* (28.3–12, 68.6–8); the student-friend Themistocles who was the great man's descendant (*Themistocles* 32.6). Much more often it is the implicit self-portrait that emerges through his writing as we receive an impression of (as Philip Stadter has put it) "being in contact with an understanding and intellectually curious person, someone who is serious yet not stuffy, aware of life in all its manifestations, yet deliberately avoiding the unseemly and trying to present the best side of his subjects."[30] Those moral judgments on his heroes, sympathetic but not pulling any punches, are an important part of that self-characterization. They appeal to moral categories and values that he can assume his readers will share or will at least feel guilty if they do not. So in this case it is the

---

[26] Homer, *Iliad* 24.630.     [27] Sophocles, fr. 636 Radt, from the *Tympanistai*.
[28] Lee (2009: 134).     [29] Lee (2009: 12).     [30] Stadter (1988: 292).

personality, not the impersonality, that builds his moral authority, as the "I" of the writer deftly becomes a shared "we" of writer and reader together.[31] This is not so much objectivity as an adroitly molded shared subjectivity.

Encomium generally leaves a less strong impression of the speaker's personality; it also operates with a predictable range of moral categories. Tacitus' *Agricola*, however, conveys much more personal engagement, especially in the concluding chapters when he reflects on the final, murderous phase of Domitian's reign (*Agr.* 45.1): that bonds author and reader together as they reconstruct what it was like to live in those years, and links them with Agricola's experience too. One of the most interesting cases is, again, Xenophon's *Cyropaedia*. The narrative voice is superficially impersonal but it would be a lazy reader who did not find it arresting that an Athenian intellectual and military man could find so much to admire, and so much material for imaginative play, in a Persian king of a century and a half before. That too draws readers in to wonder how far such a hero might really provide an example for their own world.

Still, none of these writers manages to project quite so likable an image as Plutarch; and when Ion of Chios gossiped about his encounters with the great, a frisson of disapproval or envy probably jostled in most readers' minds with admiration and awe. For a parallel to Plutarch's skillful use of likability we need to go to other genres – to Herodotus, perhaps, or to Horace.[32]

### Rule 7:   Biography Is a Form of History

On the contrary, one might feel, biography defines itself *against* history. Andrew Wallace-Hadrill has teased out the implications for Suetonius of his defining his own biography as "non-history,"[33] and Plutarch phrases his project similarly:

> In this pair I shall treat the lives of Alexander the king and of Caesar, the conqueror of Pompey. There is a mass of material to cover, and by way of introduction I shall say only one thing. I ask my readers not to quibble if I do not report all the most famous achievements or cover them in detail, but generally abbreviate: for it is not histories that we are writing but *Lives*, and it is not always the most brilliant exploits that reveal a person's virtues or vices. On the contrary, it is often a small thing, a remark or a joke, that creates a stronger impression of character than engagements where

---

[31] Pelling (2002a: 237–254, 267–282).    [32] Russell (1993).    [33] Wallace-Hadrill (1983: 8–10).

thousands die or the greatest of pitched battles or the sieges of cities. (*Alexander* 1.1–2)

Those who want full details can go to "the histories that go through everything" (*Fabius Maximus* 16.6). He had already said something similar in the *Lives of the Caesars*, though without the emphasis on character: "a detailed narrative is appropriate for a pragmatic history, but I too should not omit anything of note in the doings and sufferings of the Caesars" (*Galba* 2.5). Nepos had used a similar history–biography contrast (see above, p. 12).

Yet one does not define one's writing against something else unless the borders are close: there is only point in comedy's presenting itself as "not-tragedy"[34] because they share so many features of dramatic form. We should also note how guarded the *Alexander* passage is: "not *always* the most brilliant exploits . . . it is *often* a small matter." The opposite is also sometimes true; *Nicias* appears (though there is a textual issue) to justify the inclusion of so much on the Sicilian disaster precisely because it reveals so much of Nicias' character (*Nicias* 1.5). Tim Duff has pointed out that the words *historia* and *historein* are more often used by Plutarch to refer to what he does, not to what he avoids.[35] We should notice too where the programmatic passage is placed – before the *Lives* of two particularly big-thing people. In fact, the contrast is not wholly carried through: *Alexander* and particularly *Caesar* have a fair amount to say about those big things as well as the small, even if (with the exception of Gaugamela and Pharsalus) they do not go through every battle in detail. The *Lives* vary; *Crassus* or *Sertorius* are much less interested in setting their central figures against their society than *Tiberius Gracchus* or *Caesar* itself. And history is certainly *relevant* to biography, especially biographical evaluation. Dionysius of Syracuse was the sort of tyrant that needed to be removed, but Caesar was not: that is a crucial point in comparing Dion and Brutus (*Comparatio Dion-Brutus* 2).

The way in which the *Lives* complement one another is also relevant. With other ancient biographers we see how a series of *Lives* can become a way of *doing* history, especially intellectual history: thus the story of ancient philosophy is tracked through Diogenes Laertius' *Lives of the Philosophers* and that of the "Second Sophistic" through Philostratus' *Lives of the Sophists*. In Plutarch's case, it is increasingly suggested that not merely the synkritic couplings but also further groupings are relevant, that *Demetrius, Pyrrhus*, and *Eumenes* should be seen against the template

---

[34] Cf. especially Taplin (1986).    [35] Duff (1999a: 17–18); cf. Valgiglio (1987).

of *Alexander*, that *Caesar*, *Crassus*, and *Pompey* work as a triad and *Lysander* and *Alcibiades* as a syzygy, that *Lycurgus* and *Solon* encourage comparison of the two lawgivers and *Fabius* and *Marcellus* of the two generals, that *Alexander–Caesar* and *Pyrrhus–Marius* should be read against one another, and that the two *Cato*s each benefit if the reader also has the other in mind.[36] It is possible too to see the Spartan *Lives* as forming a group, all under the shadow of what *Lycurgus* has told us of the city and its institutions,[37] and to see the late Republican *Lives* tracing the way in which forces unleashed under the Gracchi finally destroy the state through Julius Caesar.[38] The more such links are seen, the more tempting it becomes to see the whole series not so much as "not-history" as an alternative mode of history, exploring a culture through the actions and experiences of its great men; rather as, after Suetonius, biography became a natural mode of tracking the Roman principate. Any such view has to have qualifications. Plutarch certainly leaves some periods and aspects uncovered; straightforward tyrants, in particular, have no appeal for him, though unstraightforward ones like Caesar do.[39] But there is a strong case for seeing history and at least political biography as less divorced than a simple reading of *Alexander* 1 might suggest, just as their standards of truthfulness may not be very different (Rule 1).

### Rule 8:   Biography Is an Investigation of Identity

"Identity," like "objectivity," is a problematic word, riddled with modern suggestions, and this is not the place to attempt to unravel them. But it is legitimate to ask how far Plutarch was concerned to isolate what was special about each of his figures, and how far he sought to "get under their skin," to try to understand them.

   Exemplary life-writing can easily go with idealizing and stereotyping, and the figures' individuality (to use a favorite modern concept) can suffer; nor is that necessarily a defect, as a familiar character-pattern may make it easier for an audience to grasp, even to identify with, a person, as Stephen Halliwell has argued with reference to Isocrates' *Evagoras*.[40] At least in American English, it is no bad thing to be "a regular guy." Even in Britain, defense barristers usually present their clients, and parliamentary

---

[36] For these suggestions, see, respectively, Mossman (1992: 103–104); Beneker (2005); Rodrigues (in press); H. Beck (2002); Alexiou (2010); Buszard (2008); Beck (2014b).
[37] Compare the papers in Davies and Mossman (forthcoming in 2023).
[38] Pelling (2011a: 34–35); Stadter (2010) traces other thematic links within those *Lives* and their pairs.
[39] Pelling (2010).     [40] Halliwell (1990: 42–56).

candidates present themselves, as model members of society; if they wish
jurors or electors to relate to them, they are ill advised to dwell on whatever
habits mark them out as unusual or strange. And in ancient rhetorical
culture too, stereotypes provided an indispensable kit for speakers' *etho-
poiia* – that is, the characterization of their subjects in easily recognizable
terms.

Many of Plutarch's characters do have *something* of a stereotype about
them – the man of overriding ambition, the soldier lost in politics, the
high-principled philosopher who cannot compromise – and we can recognize something of Theophrastus' "superstitious man" in his Nicias. They
certainly show fewer unexpected combinations of qualities than Suetonius'
emperors, and Suetonius' presentation by categories allows an emphasis on
each heading at a time, without the same need to integrate the characteristics into a unified whole. But even in Plutarch there is always more to it: the
military Pompey's uxoriousness, the philosophical Cato's irascibility, the
religious Nicias' nervousness before the Athenian *demos*. Plutarch's skillful
use of anecdotes is relevant here too, with that eye for "a small thing,
a remark or a joke" that he pinpoints in *Alexander* 1 as a way to create an
"impression of character" (see above, pp. 21–22).[41] To take examples just
from that pair, we have, for instance, the young Alexander's skillful
calming of the agitated horse Bucephalus (*Alexander* 6); the trust
Alexander shows in a suspected doctor, downing a draught with
a radiant smile (*Alexander* 19.5–10); the young Caesar's arrogant treatment
of his pirate captors (*Caesar* 2); the dinner on the night before the Ides of
March, when conversation turns to the ideal death and Caesar says "the
unexpected" (*Caesar* 63.7). That suits modern tastes: Lee notes the advice
that Elizabeth Gaskell gave herself for her life of Charlotte Brontë – "if you
love your reader and want to be read, get anecdotes!"[42] It suited ancient
tastes too,[43] though here again encomium tended to be more generalized
than other biographic literature. Xenophon's *Cyropaedia* is full of stories,
for instance those of the precocious young Cyrus' clever remarks when first
brought to Astyages' court; his *Memorabilia* collected good stories of
Socrates, and Ion's *Epidemiai* good ones of himself; Suetonius too knows
a good story when he sees one, for instance the tale of Gaius executing forty
prisoners during his wife's siesta and returning to tell her "what a lot of
work I have done while you were taking your nap" (*Caligula* 38.3). But
Plutarch does it more, and more illuminatingly, than most.

[41]  On anecdotes, see Schmitt Pantel (2009: 180–196) and works cited there.    [42]  Lee (2009: 59).
[43]  Momigliano (1993: 68–73, 76).

Sometimes – not always – he also tries hard to get under the skin and to understand what made a man what he was.

> Others are brave in search of fame and glory; Marcius' aim was his mother's approval. Nothing could make him feel more honored or happier than for her to hear him being praised, or see him being crowned, or to embrace him in tears of delight. . . . He felt he owed his mother the joy and gratitude that would normally fall to a father as well and could never be satisfied with giving Volumnia pleasure or paying her honor. He even chose his wife according to his mother's wishes and request, and he continued to live in the same house with her even after his wife had borne her children. (*Coriolanus* 4.5–7)

Plutarch knew from his source Dionysius of Halicarnassus only that the father was dead, that mother and wife seemed to be living in the same house, and that at the decisive moment of his narrative the intransigent Coriolanus would crumble before his mother's pressure.[44] The rest is his own psychological reconstruction.

There was a vast way to go along the path of psycho-biography before Erikson could reconstruct Martin Luther's infant relationship with his parents on the basis of his later life, or Strachey could give a Freudian interpretation of the childhood of the future Elizabeth I and her relationship with her stepfather.[45] But a first step is taken here.

## Rule 9:   The Story Should Have Some Value for the Reader

For Plutarch, that value is a moral one. Narrative biography can inspire "an emulative desire to imitate" those who have achieved such things, and "stimulate enthusiasm and a drive to make oneself like" the great men of the past (*Pericles* 1–2) – or unlike Demetrius and Antony (see above, p. 17). He has tried to become a better man himself for his biographical studies, examining his own behavior in that mirror of other people's lives (above, pp. 19–20).

The comparative method is basic here, using one life as a foil to bring out what is distinctively good or bad, or at least less good, about the other (cf. *Mulierum virtutes* 227C–D). That technique is not new: it was a well-known technique in literary criticism (familiar enough to be played off in the Aristophanic *Frogs*), and we can see something of it in Isocrates' *Evagoras*, with comparisons to Persian kings (so also Xenophon, *Agesilaus* 9) and to the heroes of the Trojan War. Nepos' *On Famous Men* seems to

---

[44] For the details, see Russell (1963); Pelling (2002a: 155–156, 309–310, 394–398).
[45] Erikson (1958); Strachey (1928). Cf. Lee (2009: 136–138) on the psycho-biography of Shakespeare.

have compared Romans and foreigners in groups, for example generals and historians.[46] But Plutarch took this much further, and the complexities of his comparative technique have been a central interest of recent scholarship. It is now clear that the emphases of one *Life* can affect the selection of material for its pair, as for instance in the focus on both men's dealings with unscrupulous opponents in *Pericles–Fabius*;[47] that structural strategies can shape the pair as much as the individual *Life*, as in the chiastic hour-glass structure of *Aemilius Paulus–Timoleon* or *Cimon–Lucullus*;[48] and that imagery can run through a whole pair, as in the recurrent theatrical figures of *Demetrius–Antony*.[49] It is arguable too that second *Lives* often revisit the themes of first but in a more complex and subtle register.[50] There are also questions about the comparative epilogues: can they be seen as providing new, alternative perspectives on themes developed in the narrative?[51] And should we assume that epilogues have been lost in the four cases where they are absent (*Phocion–Cato Minor*, *Pyrrhus–Marius*, *Themistocles–Camillus*, *Alexander–Caesar*), or can we identify reasons why Plutarch might have chosen not to round off those pairs in his usual manner?[52]

All this makes the *Lives* morally thought-provoking, even if the reader is never challenged to reassess moral values too radically: Plutarch does not generate the sort of defamiliarization a fifth-century Athenian audience might feel in exploring what is wrong with democracy or what defeat must have felt like for the Persians – or, for that matter, the strangeness that a first-time reader of Xenophon's *Cyropaedia* might feel in pondering the merits of a barbarian king (see above, p. 21). Still, the moralism is not straightforward either. Mirrors can distort as well as reflect;[53] wise readers would be cautious about assuming an exact correspondence with their own situations, just as the wise politician has to be discriminating in drawing morals from history (*Praecepta gerendae reipublicae* 814A–C). Duff in particular has stressed that the *Lives* often avoid simple moral lessons.[54] A final judgment on, say, Lysander or Phocion may be complex and elusive – far more elusive than the straightforward praise of Xenophon's *Agesilaus* or Isocrates' *Evagoras*, and less explicit than Suetonius' verdict

---

[46] Duff (1999a: 243–245); Gossage (1967: 60 and n. 48); Geiger (1985: 87–95, 97–98); Larmour (2014: 407–408).
[47] Stadter (1975).
[48] Geiger (1981: 99–104); Swain (1989a); Pelling (2002a: 373–374); Larmour (2014); and especially Duff (2011c).
[49] De Lacy (1952); Pelling (1988a: 21–22).
[50] Pelling (2002a: 349–364); Roskam (2011a); De Pourcq and Roskam (2016).
[51] Duff (1999a: 243–286).      [52] Erbse (1956); Duff (1999a: 254–255); Pelling (2002a: 365–386).
[53] Zadorojnyi (2010).      [54] Duff (1999a).

after weighing the case for and against Julius Caesar, "The balance is tilted by his other actions and words, so that he is thought to have abused his power and to have been justly killed" (*Diuus Iulius* 76.1; cf. *Diuus Vespasianus* 1.1 on Domitian).

Less explicit, though, not less powerful. It is still possible, as Duff emphasizes, to take the *Lives* as moral thought-experiments. Stadter puts it well, again using Plutarch's image of the mirror (*Aemilius Paulus* 1; see above, pp. 19–20):[55]

> He invites the reader, using the life he is reading as a mirror, to consider his own qualities: "am I acting in the same ambitious way that Marius did?" The introspection may go further: recognizing the modes of self-justification employed by Marius, as present in oneself – "after all, I deserve it." Again, the reader of *Antony* might ask, "am I allowing myself to be swayed by smooth talking but pernicious flatterers?"

And why should we expect such questions to have easy answers?

Explicit preaching is not to our taste, but modern biographers too, especially political biographers, can hardly avoid all evaluation. After all, politicians trade in the public's evaluation all their lives, and few careers end in farewell rich in acclaim from a grateful nation. Biographers have to revisit the issues; even as figures recede into history, a writer about Churchill, say, will naturally discuss the strengths and weaknesses of his war-leadership.[56] Many modern biographies are not too far, in fact, from the balance struck by Plutarch, with an attempt to see a life from the central figure's viewpoint balanced by a readiness to criticize when appropriate, though inevitably some prefer to reach for the hatchet or the halo.

Few modern readers would put such moral assessment in terms of value for themselves. Still, Plutarch is again something of a forerunner here, at least in the insistence that biography and a moral dimension go hand in hand – even if it is now immorality, not morality, that sells books, and authors typically maintain a mask of non-judgmentalism.[57]

## Rule 10:   There Are No Rules for Biography

There were no rules in Plutarch's day either, only (as we saw) some on-the-whole expectations. But any series – biographies, novels, TV soaps – creates its own rules as it goes, and the readers of Plutarch's series will soon have grasped what to expect. Even there they will have noticed variations, most

---

[55] Stadter (2000: 505).    [56] As is done, for instance, by Hastings (2009).
[57] Cf. Lee (2009: 17 [immorality and popularity], 91, 133 [reluctance to moralize]).

explicitly in the different texture of *Theseus–Romulus* (see above, pp. 13–14); but the more remarkable feature is the way he shapes each *Life* to the same pattern, despite their very different source-material. In some cases – Agesilaus, Philopoemen, the younger Cato – there would have been classic biographical material already; sometimes he will have been wrestling with a detailed historical narrative – Thucydides or Dionysius or Pollio; in other cases – Publicola, Cimon – he will not have had much material at all. His controlling hand is so light that, once again, we easily take for granted what was in fact quite remarkable.

So there were many choices that Plutarch made, and many other forms his biographies might have taken. No less remarkable is the way that, time and again, those distinctive choices can be seen to prefigure modern biographical tastes. Of course, this should not be overstressed; modern biography is a capacious genre too, and Plutarch has less in common with the latest stocking-filler on a Hollywood or footballing celebrity than with a measured discussion of Churchill or JFK. But it is worth noting our feeling of familiarity, not least as a warning. When we find so much that feels so modern, we can read him too easily, and fail to sense what is alien as we too are drawn into the community of "us" that Plutarch so assiduously builds. One purpose of this *Companion* is to remind us that there is more to Plutarch's *Lives* than an easy read.

## Further Reading

Momigliano (1993) has become the standard treatment of ancient biography, but Hägg (2012) is fuller and less idiosyncratic. For compact synoptic discussion of ancient biography, see Pelling (2009). Duff (forthcoming) collects important articles. A helpful bibliographic survey is Zadorojnyi (2020). For case studies in ancient biography, interesting and useful collections are McGing and Mossman (2006a), de Temmerman and Demoen (2016), and de Temmerman (2020), while French and St Clair (2002) offers thought-provoking perspectives from other periods and cultures. Schmitt Pantel (2009) provides a novel interpretation of the history–biography relation, showing how the fifth-century Athenian *Lives* illuminate Athenian culture and "identité politique," and comparing Plutarch with his fifth-century antecedents. On ancient literary biography, see Lefkowitz (1981) and with less drastic claims (2012), Fletcher and Hanink (2016), and, specifically on Homer, Graziosi (2002); on political (rather narrowly defined) biography, Geiger (1985), with the review by Moles (1989).

# CHAPTER 2

# Romanness and Greekness in Plutarch

## Manuel Tröster

Plutarch's oeuvre covers a remarkably broad range of topics related to both Greek and Roman culture, society, and history. Considering the extraordinary scope and versatility of his work, he is often viewed as epitomizing a shared Greco-Roman culture among the political and intellectual elite of the Empire.[1] From such a perspective, it has been argued that his writings ultimately serve to promote a more ambitious program of reconciliation or even of fusion between Greek philosophy and Roman power.[2] The former view would imply interethnic cooperation, while the latter would go beyond this by creating a kind of universalist synthesis.

There are several good reasons for assuming that Plutarch pursued an agenda of rapprochement and integration. First of all, he was not only a Greek scholar but also a Roman citizen (*SIG*³ 829A). While it is true that Plutarch was strongly attached to his native town of Chaeronea (*Demosthenes* 1–2), as well as to the sanctuary of Apollo at nearby Delphi, his connections extended far beyond the confines of Boeotia and central Greece.[3] This is reflected in a large number of Romans and highly Romanized Greeks among his friends and acquaintances, many of whom belonged to the upper echelons of the imperial administration.[4] Quite a few of Plutarch's works, including the *Parallel Lives*, are dedicated to people from this circle, thus indicating that the intended audience consisted of Greeks and Romans alike.[5] Given the mixed nature of Plutarch's

I am grateful to Geert Roskam and Alexei Zadorojnyi for their helpful comments and suggestions. Research for this chapter was supported by the Deutscher Akademischer Austauschdienst (DAAD).

[1] Cf., for example, Jones (1971); Sirinelli (2000).
[2] Cf. Barigazzi (1984); Boulogne (1994); also, with a greater appreciation of remaining differences, Pinheiro (2013: 347–398).
[3] See Stadter (2004) on Plutarch's use of his contacts to the benefit of the Delphic oracle.
[4] Cf. Jones (1971: 39–64); Sirinelli (2000: 167–188), as well as the prosopographical data in Ziegler (1951: 665–696); Puech (1992).
[5] As convincingly argued by Stadter (2002). Also note Stadter (2015a) on Plutarch's relationship to powerful Romans in terms of patronage.

social and intellectual milieu, it would have been difficult for him not to embrace a vision of dialogue and understanding. In this context, it should also be noted that the imperial elite as a whole was undergoing a major transformation during Plutarch's lifetime and increasingly incorporated provincials from the Greek-speaking part of the Empire.[6] Consequently, intersecting and overlapping identities were very common in the aristocratic society to which Plutarch belonged: he and his peers were accustomed to thinking and acting as Romans no less than as Greeks, and frequent code-switching was a matter of course. In this setting, the line between Greek and Roman became ever more blurred.

Secondly, Plutarch appears to have been quite satisfied at least with some of the staple features of the political environment under the Empire. In the treatise *Praecepta gerendae reipublicae*, he remarks that

> of the greatest blessings that cities can enjoy – peace, liberty, prosperity, abundance of men, and concord – so far as peace is concerned, the peoples have no need of statesmen at present; for all war, both Greek and barbarian, has fled from us and has disappeared; and of liberty the peoples have as great a share as our rulers grant them, and perhaps more would not be better. (*Praecepta gerendae reipublicae* 824C)[7]

As will be seen toward the end of this chapter, Plutarch's attitude to Roman rule is actually more ambivalent and cannot be separated from his views on political relations within the *polis* of his day. Nevertheless, the fact remains that he appreciated the benefits of a relatively peaceful environment in which well-educated and affluent provincials like him could play a limited but powerful role at the local level and, increasingly, beyond.[8] Judging from the works of other writers from the High Empire, most notably Dio Chrysostom and the more enthusiastic Aelius Aristides, this attitude was fairly widespread among the contemporary Greek elite. However, it also needs to be borne in mind that these authors and the literary movement known as the Second Sophistic are first and foremost concerned with Greek culture and its classical heritage, which they reinterpret in light of a present shaped by Roman domination.[9] In this vision, Rome is a significant and in many ways acceptable factor, but continues to be approached from an essentially Greek perspective.

[6] Cf. Halfmann (1979: esp. 71–81).
[7] Cf. also *De Pythiae oraculis* 408B–C; *De tranquilitate animi* 469E; *An seni respublica gerenda sit* 784F. Translations are adapted from the Loeb Classical Library.
[8] Dillon (1997) goes a step further by suggesting that Plutarch viewed the Roman Empire as the end of history. Against this interpretation, see Stadter (2005a).
[9] Cf., for example, Bowie (1970); Swain (1996: 65–100), but also note the reservations voiced by Veyne (2005: 204–207).

Finally, the focus and structure of a number of Plutarch's works suggest that he sought to strike some sort of balance between Greek and Roman culture. Above all, this applies to the *Parallel Lives*, in which he compares the careers and qualities of some of the greatest statesmen of Greek and Roman history. Significantly, Plutarch does not strive to demonstrate the general superiority of the Greek over the Roman protagonists, or vice versa, but chooses to treat them on equal terms. Thus, he appreciates political acumen, strategic brilliance, and personal integrity in all of his heroes, applying more or less the same standards throughout the series.[10] While this compositional strategy may be read as a statement about the continuing relevance of Greek civilization,[11] it cannot be stressed enough that the pairs are not framed in terms of hostile confrontation. Rather than staging a contest of cultures, the biographer employs the dual structure of the *Lives* to explore moral questions from various angles, frequently inviting his readers to ponder the issues involved and to make their own judgments. This agenda is perhaps most apparent in the formal comparisons, which conclude most of the pairs by highlighting similarities and differences; for, despite having a fundamentally competitive element, they eschew expressing a clear preference for one or the other of the respective heroes.[12] In fact, Plutarch often makes a point of balancing his account, first establishing the greatness of Theseus and then arguing in favor of Romulus (*Comparatio Theseus-Romulus* 1–3 and 4–6), or outlining the strengths and weaknesses of Cimon and Lucullus before insisting that they both had "good and god-like natures" (*Comparatio Cimon-Lucullus* 3.6). In this sense, then, Plutarch may be said to transcend the dichotomy between Greek and Roman culture, yet it remains to be asked what kind of concepts, values, and beliefs actually underlie and inform his universal ethico-political perspective.

Given his educational background, Plutarch is of course more familiar with Greek literature and history than with their equivalents on the Roman side. This is reflected throughout the collection in the tremendous wealth of scholarly references and literary embellishments derived from Greek

---

[10] Cf. Späth (2007: 146–152).

[11] Cf. Valgiglio (1992: 4027–4050); also Desideri (1992: 4481–4486) = (2012: 240–245). See also text at n. 19 in this chapter.

[12] Cf. Duff (1999a: 257–286). The competitive nature of the *synkriseis* is stressed by Tatum (2010: 10–18). By contrast, Boulogne (1994: 57–71; 2000) views the balanced comparisons as serving to construct an ideal third person who combines the virtues of the Greek and Roman heroes. Also note the systematic analysis in Mora (2007a: 165–186), who concludes that there is a tendency to present the Greek protagonists as moderately superior.

authors whose writings formed part of Plutarch's intellectual repertoire. However, the omnipresence of Greek learning should not obscure the fact that he made a major effort to conduct research specifically for the Roman *Lives*, which included the consultation of Latin sources (*Demosthenes* 2.2–4).[13] Taken as a whole, the series provides a remarkably comprehensive panorama of Greek and Roman history, tracing the long trajectory from the mythical founders and lawgivers of the archaic period to the Roman conquest of Greece and the end of the Roman Civil Wars, respectively.[14] While it is true that Plutarch himself insists on being a biographer rather than a historian,[15] it would be misguided to deny his debt to the genre of historiography and the broader significance of the collection as a framework for interpreting the Greco-Roman past. Beyond the balance established between the protagonists of the individual pairs, the ambitious project of the *Lives* thus encourages the reader to think of Greece and Rome as historical spaces of equal importance.

Nevertheless, Plutarch's work is also marked by significant tensions between the Greek and Roman spheres. This is chiefly because his outlook, his patterns of interpretation, and his criteria of judgment are to a large extent determined by the classical tradition of Greek thought, the cultural imperatives of the incipient Second Sophistic, and the perspective of a local aristocrat caught up in the vicissitudes of *polis* life. Accordingly, Hellenic culture and civilization are central to Plutarch's analysis even when he is dealing with Roman affairs and personalities. This will emerge very clearly from the following case studies, which focus in turn on a biographical pair involved in the Roman conquest of Greece (*Philopoemen–Flamininus*), on a successful general who rejects Greek education to his own detriment (*Marius*), and on a philhellenic benefactor who eventually falls victim to the allure of barbarian luxury (*Lucullus*). Subsequently, a brief analysis will look at the Greekness of Plutarch's representation of Roman politics and culture in general and in a number of mid-Republican *Lives* in particular. Beyond this, selected pieces from the *Moralia* will be considered in order to establish the nature and limitations of Plutarch's engagement with Roman tradition (*Quaestiones Graecae* and *Quaestiones Romanae*), as well as the

---

[13] On Plutarch's use of Latin material, see Theander (1951: 68–78); Jones (1971: 81–87); Strobach (1997: 32–46); also Zadorojnyi (1997b) on poetry and Stadter (2015c) on nonhistorical works in general.

[14] Cf. Pelling (2010) on the extent to which Plutarch attempts to provide a "global" history. Of course, this did not occur in an ideological void. See Mora (2007a: 154–160) on the significance of the biographer's choice of heroes and parallels in terms of "correcting" previous views of Greco-Roman history and, arguably, of improving the record of the Greeks.

[15] Cf. most notably *Alexander* 1, with the analysis in Duff (1999a: 14–22).

ambivalence of his attitude to Roman rule (*Praecepta gerendae reipublicae*). Thus, it will become apparent that Plutarch's writings are in no small measure shaped by broader phenomena of hybridity and modes of cultural dominance, assertion, and resistance, making them highly relevant to current debates on such topics and inviting fresh readings from interdisciplinary and intercultural perspectives.

One of the most conspicuous features of the *Lives* is the extent to which Greek education and benefactions to Greece serve as a yardstick for judging the Roman protagonists.[16] In Plutarch's view, *paideia* is crucial in accounting for a politician's ability to develop statesmanlike qualities and, more specifically, to control his passions and curb his ambition (*philotimia*).[17] This line of analysis is especially appropriate for the Roman *Lives*, in which the absorption of Greek culture by the central figures cannot necessarily be taken for granted, thus allowing Plutarch to demonstrate its impact with greater facility. Furthermore, the biographer's character portrayals regularly highlight values and concepts associated with Greek civilization, such as *praotēs* ("mildness") and *philanthrōpia* ("humanity").[18] While this requires little explanation in the case of the Greek heroes, it implies that the Roman protagonists have to prove themselves on a playing field defined by the parameters of Greek tradition and culture. Consequently, Plutarch's evaluative categories reflect a pronounced cultural bias – or, to put it differently, his conceptual spectacles prevent him from seriously exploring the distinctive nature of Roman or any other non-Greek identity.[19]

At the same time, Plutarch's approach is inclusionary in the sense that his criteria are used to judge Greeks and non-Greeks alike on the basis of their actual behavior and, in particular, with a view to their attitude toward Greece and Greek culture. Roman statesmen can therefore earn the biographer's acclaim by conforming to roughly the same standards that are applied to their Greek counterparts. In other words, the boundary they are expected to cross is not defined along ethnic lines but according to moral and cultural values. To the degree that Romans display philhellenism and *philanthrōpia*, they have the potential to equal or even to surpass Greeks in

[16] Cf. Swain (1990a); also (1996: 139–144); further García Moreno (1995: 136–147; 2002).
[17] Cf. Pelling (1989: *passim*); Swain (1990a: 131–134) = (1995: 239–243); more generally, Duff (1999a: 72–89).
[18] Cf. Martin (1960; 1961); Panagopoulos (1977: 216–222); de Romilly (1979: 275–307); Frazier (1996: 231–239); Becchi (2009a).
[19] Cf. Duff (1999a: 287–309); Preston (2001: 97–109); Goldhill (2002b: 254–271); Roskam (2004: 255–264). Also note Leeck (2010: esp. 57–63 and 167–175), who describes this in more negative terms as a failure to promote cultural understanding. For a judicious and balanced assessment, see Van der Stockt (2013: esp. 33–39).

terms of Greekness. Thus, in the case of Numa, who is idealized as a just king and institution builder, Plutarch draws the remarkable conclusion that he was "far more Hellenic" a lawgiver than his equally idealized pair Lycurgus (*Comparatio Lycurgus-Numa* 1.10). Conversely, Greeks as well as Roman philhellenes can be likened to barbarians when they fail to live up to certain standards of behavior.[20] Evidently, Plutarch considers cultural boundaries to be permeable and penetrable, yet this does not mean that they are irrelevant. It is therefore misleading to claim that his biographical project is strictly confined to the realm of political philosophy and, as such, has little or nothing to do with Greek and Roman identity.[21]

In several respects, the pair of Philopoemen and Flamininus is key to understanding Plutarch's views on Greek and Roman history and culture. Firstly, these *Lives* are concerned with the Roman conquest of Greece and hence with the end of Greek political independence. While Plutarch's choice of Greek heroes gives center-stage to the glorious achievements of the fifth and fourth centuries, relatively little attention is devoted to the erosion of power in the Hellenistic age (*Eumenes, Demetrius, Pyrrhus, Agis/Cleomenes, Philopoemen*).[22] This is undoubtedly related to the zeitgeist of the High Empire and the overriding significance of the classical era for the redefinition of Greek identity.[23] In the *Philopoemen*, however, the biographer explicitly deals with "the last of the Greeks" (*Philopoemen* 1.7), who in many ways acts like his celebrated predecessors yet operates in an environment that leaves little room for military exploits and political maneuvering. Flamininus, on the other hand, is the first of Plutarch's heroes to show how a Roman politician should ideally treat the Greeks, conferring benefactions on them and paying homage to Hellenic culture. The overall positive assessment of Flamininus' policies is by no means unparalleled in other ancient authors, but nevertheless remains remarkable, given that he was not only a benefactor but also a conqueror of Greece.[24]

Secondly, this is the only pair in which Plutarch compares and contrasts the biographies of two contemporaries. One of the implications is that the

[20] Consider the case of Lucullus, which will be discussed later, and see Pelegrín Campo (1997: 374–375) on the notion of "barbarization" in Plutarch; also Schmidt (1999: 296–299) (on the *Alexander*).
[21] As is argued by Späth (2007: esp. 152–166).
[22] *Aratus* is relevant too, but does not belong to the *Parallel Lives*. For Plutarch's view of this period, see Muccioli (2012: 209–253).
[23] See Geiger (1981: 89–94); Colonnese (2007: 109–114).
[24] The same applies to Aemilius Paulus. On Plutarch's historical judgment in both these *Lives*, see Bremer (2005); also Tröster (2009).

historical context itself comes into sharper focus than in pairs that establish links between the protagonists across time. The fall of Greece is thus contemplated from two different angles that offer complementary perspectives on one and the same process. Considering this historical overlap, it is striking that neither the Greek nor the Roman hero plays a major role in the *Life* dedicated to his respective counterpart. While there is a sense of personal rivalry between them,[25] Plutarch seems to steer the narrative away from any major confrontation – a tactic that arguably helps him to present the two readings on equal terms.

Thirdly, the ambitions and frustrations of the two protagonists serve to epitomize the whole of Greek and Roman history.[26] In spite of his individual excellence and bravery, Philopoemen fails to attain his objectives because of his own contentiousness (*philonikia*) and because of the continual bickering and divisions among the Greeks. Notwithstanding the final outcome, however, Plutarch does not reject Philopoemen's political agenda, but rather looks with respect at the affirmation of Greek liberty and independence in the face of Roman ascendancy (*Philopoemen* 17.2–3; *Comparatio Philopoemen-Flamininus* 3.4). In the end, the honors bestowed on the Achaean leader are even validated by the Roman conquerors themselves (*Philopoemen* 21.10–12). As for Flamininus, his policies in Greece are not only more successful but also earn him admiration as a just statesman and benefactor. The following reflections are put into the mouths of the Greeks in the aftermath of the celebrated declaration of liberty at the Isthmian Games in 196 BCE:

> Undoubtedly, valor and wisdom are rare things among men, but the rarest of all blessings is the just man. For men like Agesilaus, or Lysander, or Nicias, or Alcibiades understood how to conduct wars well and how to be victorious commanders in battles by land and sea, but they did not know how to use their successes so as to accomplish noble and honorable ends. Indeed, if one excepts the action at Marathon, the sea-fight at Salamis, Plataea, Thermopylae, and the achievements of Cimon at the Eurymedon and about Cyprus, Greece has fought all her battles to bring servitude upon herself, and every one of her trophies stands as a memorial of her own misfortune and disgrace, since she owed her overthrow chiefly to the baseness and contentiousness (*philonikia*) of her leaders. Whereas foreigners who were thought to have only slight sparks and insignificant traces of a common remote ancestry, from whom it was astonishing that any helpful

---

[25] Cf. *Philopoemen* 15.1–2; *Flamininus* 13.2–3; 17.2; also Polybius 23.5.2; Livy 35.30.13; 35.47.4; Justin 31.3.4. For the historical background, see Raeymaekers (1996).

[26] Cf. Pelling (1997b: 148–153, 254–258); also Walsh (1992: 212–218).

word or purpose should be devoted to Greece – these men underwent the greatest perils and hardships in order to rescue Greece and set her free from cruel despots and tyrants. (*Flamininus* 11.4–7)

Thus, it is through the eyes of the Greeks and the lens of Greek history that Plutarch chooses to evaluate Flamininus' character and policies at this momentous juncture. Interestingly, the passage explicitly refers to the *philonikia* of the Greek leaders, thereby taking up the central characteristic of Philopoemen as established in the first *Life* of the pair.[27] However, Flamininus is favorably contrasted not only with contemporary politicians but also with some of the most eminent statesmen of the Greek past. This suggests a remarkably negative view of the whole of Greek history, yet Plutarch may well have expected his readers to remember at this point that Rome would not always remain as benign and peaceful as she promised to be in the days of the Isthmian Declaration. After his departure from Greece, moreover, Flamininus himself falls victim to excessive ambition in the competitive struggles among the Roman nobility, standing by his brother in spite of the latter's murderous *luxuria* and hunting down the defenseless Hannibal, who had been spared by the noble Scipio Africanus (*Flamininus* 18.3–21.14). At the end of the day, Flamininus' *philotimia* is therefore not too different from the *philonikia* associated with Philopoemen.[28]

Evidently, these points are also relevant to Plutarch's own present. In the *Flamininus*, he actually mentions the parallel of the declaration of Greek liberty by the emperor Nero in 67 CE (*Flamininus* 12.13), which plainly made a strong impression on the biographer's generation. However, he is somewhat reluctant to spell out any political lessons, and much is left to the reader's interpretation.[29] What are the implications of Plutarch's respect for Philopoemen's courage and leadership? To what extent does his depiction of Flamininus involve criticism of the harsher Roman policies at a later stage? And how is the reader supposed to resolve the inherent tension between self-destruction and foreign liberation? Despite these uncertainties, it is not too difficult to form an idea of Plutarch's general recommendations regarding

---

[27] Cf. *Philopoemen* 3.1; 17.7, as well as *Comparatio Philopoemen-Flamininus* 1.4; 1.7, with the analysis in Pelling (1997b: 129–135); also Walsh (1992: 209–212); Duff (2008b: 11–13); Stadter (2011: 251–253) = (2015a: 282–283). Nevertheless, Swain (1988: 345) considers it "unlikely that Plutarch is here [*sc.* at *Flamininus* 11.6] stigmatizing Philopoemen."

[28] Cf. Swain (1988: 343–347); also Pelling (1989: 208–214; 1997b: 249–254); Pinheiro (2013: 210–227). Owing to her political culture, however, Rome was in a much better position to survive the excesses of *philotimia* than Greece, as is pointed out by Pelling (2012: 66–67).

[29] Compare n. 26 in this chapter and, more broadly, Pelling (1995); also Duff (2011b). Furthermore, note that the emperors are mentioned very rarely in Plutarch's extant works. See Ash (2008), with references.

Greek *philonikia* and the exercise of Roman power. As will be seen in the discussion of *Praecepta gerendae reipublicae* at the end of this chapter, concord among the Greeks and justice in the administration of Empire are among Plutarch's chief concerns as a political practitioner and adviser. Similar points are frequently made in the *Lives*. Just as Roman politicians are regularly commended for conferring benefactions on Greeks, one of the yardsticks applied to Greek statesmen is the ability to benefit their country as a whole rather than tearing it apart by aggressively pursuing particularist interests.[30]

While Flamininus is praised for his philhellenism and *philanthrōpia*, the *Life of Marius* paints a much more critical portrait of a protagonist who flaunts his disregard for Greek learning and culture (*Marius* 2.2).[31] Accordingly, this biography is often considered one of the "negative" *Lives*, in which Plutarch depicts personalities whose behavior is meant *not* to be imitated (*Demetrius* 1.5–6), yet this assessment should not obscure the fact that both good and bad traits can be found in all Plutarchan heroes.[32] In the case of Marius, the biographer duly recognizes the protagonist's good natural disposition (*Marius* 3.5), as well as his outstanding qualities as a soldier and general. By contrast, his civilian career is marked by failure and excess, which is to a large extent attributable to his rejection of Hellenism and *paideia*. Marius' increasingly immoderate behavior thus illustrates the negative potential of (Roman) power when it lacks the guidance of Greek philosophy. What is more, his disrespectful attitude toward the heritage of Greece stands in stark contrast to the appreciation of archetypal Roman virtue and probity in the parallel *Life of Pyrrhus*.[33]

At the beginning of the *Marius*, Plutarch cites the protagonist's willful ignorance of Greek culture as the principal reason for his violent outbursts and untimely ambition in old age. Significantly, this attitude is rejected as being contrary to the wisdom of Plato:

> Accordingly, just as Plato used to say to Xenocrates the philosopher, who had the reputation of being rather morose in his disposition, "My good

---

[30] Consider, for example, the pan-Hellenic exploits of Cimon, who unites the Greek allies (*Cimon* 6.2–3), vanquishes the barbarians (12.1–13.4 and *passim*), and seeks good relations between Athens and Sparta (16 and, picking up on all of these points, *Comparatio Cimon-Lucullus* 2.1–4). See Tröster (2014) for further discussion.

[31] Cf. also Sallust, *Bellum Iugurthinum* 63.3; 85.12; 85.32; Cicero, *Pro Archia* 19; Valerius Maximus 2.2.3.

[32] Cf. Duff (1999a: 45–49, 53–65); also Stadter (2000: 500–506) = (2015a: 237–243). This is further confirmed by Mora (2007a: 177–180) on the basis of quantitative analysis of positive and negative elements in the *synkriseis*.

[33] Cf. Schepens (2000); Mossman (2005b). On the idea of Roman decline in the *Pyrrhus–Marius*, see Buszard (2005a; 2005b).

Xenocrates, sacrifice to the Graces," so if Marius could have been persuaded
to sacrifice to the Greek Muses and Graces, he would not have put the
ugliest possible end to a most distinguished career in field and forum, nor
have been driven by the blasts of passion, ill-timed ambition, and insatiable
greed upon the shore of a most cruel and savage old age. (*Marius* 2.3–4)

The implication is clear: as he chooses to ignore Plato's advice, Marius is
destined to go astray.[34] The remarks just quoted are taken up later in the
narrative when the protagonist's unbridled aspirations in old age are
condemned as juvenile behavior and meet with the disapproval of the
"better people" (*Marius* 34.5–7).[35] At the end of the *Life*, moreover, the
biographer unfavorably contrasts Marius' lamentations and unyielding
ambition with Plato's good humor in the face of death, and goes on to
reflect on the importance of *logos* and *paideia* for leading a virtuous and
happy life (*Marius* 45.10–46.5). This critical assessment carries all the more
weight as Plutarch not only rejects excessive ambition as a bad thing in
itself but also considers it particularly reprehensible in old men, whom he
expects to wield their influence in a more restrained and less ostentatious
fashion.[36] In other words, the elderly Marius is wrong both from a political
and a philosophical point of view since his actions are contrary to the
requirements of his age (*par' hēlikian*).[37]

In a rather different way, this latter charge also applies to Lucullus, who
supposedly retired from public activity after a long campaign in the East,
only to embark on a life of luxury and self-indulgence.[38] Notwithstanding
Plutarch's negative verdict on the protagonist's final years, the *Life of
Lucullus* is often considered to be more positive than it should have
been.[39] As the biographer states in the proem, he decided to set up
a literary monument out of gratitude for the benefactions conferred by
Lucullus on his native Chaeronea at the time of the Mithridatic Wars
(*Cimon* 1–2). In fact, the greater part of the *Life* portrays the protagonist as
an exemplary philhellene both in terms of his cultural interests and with
regard to his political course of action. Following the account of the

---

[34] Cf. Swain (1990a: 138–140); Cacciari (1995: 368–377); Duff (1999a: 107–111, 118–121); also Duff
(2008b: 17–18).

[35] Cf. also *Sulla* 7.2; *Lucullus* 38.3.

[36] Compare the treatise *An seni respublica gerenda sit*, especially 793A–796C, which will be briefly
discussed later.

[37] For further examples, see Byl (1977: 110–113); Cacciari (1995: 377–380 and *passim*); Frazier (1996:
72–76).

[38] On Lucullus' "retirement," see Hillman (1993); Tröster (2008: 70–72).

[39] Cf. most notably Swain (1990a: 143–145) and (1992b), and the discussion in Tröster (2008: 149–151).

Roman victory at Tigranocerta and the resettlement of the city's inhabitants, Plutarch notes that

> Lucullus was loved as a benefactor and founder. And whatever else he did also prospered, in a way worthy of the man, who was yearning for the praise that is consequent upon justice and humanity (*philanthrōpia*), rather than for that which follows military successes. For the latter, the army also was in no slight degree, and fortune in the highest degree, responsible; but the former qualities were the manifestation of a gentle and educated spirit, and in the exercise of these virtues Lucullus now, without recourse to arms, subdued the barbarians. (*Lucullus* 29.5–6)

Evidently, this is a rather generous reading of Lucullus' policies, with a characteristic focus on philhellenism and *philanthrōpia* as the driving forces behind his decisions. And yet it would be erroneous to regard Plutarch's idealizing interpretation as mere fiction, for other sources confirm that the general went out of his way to rally the support of the Greeks, mainly to strengthen his own position and to further the war effort against Mithridates.[40] As so often, the biographer is not fabricating evidence but rather adapting and reinterpreting the material at his disposal.[41]

Following his return to Rome, Lucullus is initially commended for checking his ambition, thus avoiding the sad fate met by Marius and others (*Lucullus* 38.3–4). However, Plutarch then shifts his attention to the excesses of the protagonist's private life, which he not only condemns as unsuitable for a statesman but also connects with the notion of barbarian luxury (*Lucullus* 41.7; *Comparatio Cimon-Lucullus* 1.5).[42] There is a sharp separation between Lucullus' extravagant lifestyle on the one hand and the more decent sentiments of his Greek friends, whom he continued to support, on the other (*Lucullus* 41.2). In the concluding *synkrisis*, Plutarch further reinforces his criticism of the retired politician's debauchery by pointing out that he acted contrary to the teachings of Plato and the Academy, adopting instead the attitude of an Epicurean sensualist (1.2–3). This appears all the more blameworthy as Lucullus has shortly before been depicted pursuing and promoting philosophical studies, being himself an adherent of the Academic tradition (*Lucullus* 42.1–4).

Considering the omnipresence of *paideia*, Platonic philosophy, and philhellenic benefactions, it is fair to conclude that Plutarch's Roman

---

[40] Cf. Tröster (2008: 44–47, 127–148), with references.

[41] Cf. generally Pelling (1979; 1980; 1990).

[42] Note that Lucullus was dubbed *Xerxes togatus* (*Lucullus* 39.3; Velleius Paterculus 2.33.4; Pliny the Elder, *Naturalis Historia* 9.170). On the polarity between Greek and barbarian characteristics in Plutarch, see Nikolaidis (1986); Schmidt (1999: 49–65, 89–100, 120–137); also Almagor's Chapter 13 in this volume.

*Lives* have a distinctly Greek flavor. On the one hand, this Hellenicity can be observed in terms of cultural concepts and a consistent concern for the well-being of Greece. On the other, as Christopher Pelling has shown, it features in Plutarch's analysis of Roman politics, which is to a large degree determined by the notion of a fundamental divide between Senate (*boulē*) and people (*dēmos*).[43] This interpretive framework undoubtedly owes a lot to Greek ideas about the balance of constitutions and to the stereotype of an aristocracy facing stiff opposition from a fickle multitude. At the same time, it makes it difficult for Plutarch to understand the dynamics of competition and consensus in Roman political culture with its emphasis on *dignitas*, *auctoritas*, and *mos maiorum*. Furthermore, the biographer generally pays little attention to the specific role of groups like the *equites*, the veterans, or the rural *plebs*, who left a profound mark on the violent conflicts of the late Republic.

As a result, the protagonists of the *Lives* are usually depicted as either siding with the "conservative" majority of the Senate or championing the cause of the people, often in association with "demagogues." Thus, Pompey is criticized during his first consulship for "devoting himself more to the people than to the Senate" (*Pompey* 21.7), and later obtains the command against Mithridates "due to the favor of the people and the flattery of the demagogues" (*Lucullus* 35.9). As for the Gracchi, they are actually viewed as demagogues in their own right, alongside their Spartan counterparts Agis and Cleomenes, despite having good intentions in the first place (*Agis/Cleomenes* 2.7–10). Only very rarely do Plutarch's heroes manage to gain equal respect among the nobility and the people at large (*Cicero* 10–11; *Aemilius Paulus* 38.2–6 and *passim*). To be sure, this antithetical reconstruction does capture an important aspect of Roman political life. After all, a similar contrast between aristocracy and people can be found in many a historian's account, perhaps most explicitly in Sallust,[44] who had first-hand experience of Republican politics. However, Plutarch tends to use this framework more systematically and more exclusively than other ancient authors.

To some extent, the Greekness of the biographer's perspective is of course due to the fact that his thought is closer to the life of the Greek *polis* both of his own day and of the classical past than to the world of the *res publica*. This is not merely a matter of historical knowledge and cultural

---

[43]  Cf. Pelling (1986a: 165–187) = (2002a: 211–225); also de Blois (1992: *passim*); Mazza (1995: *passim*); Sion-Jenkis (2000: 66–69). On the *dēmos* theme in the Greek *Lives*, see Prandi (2005).
[44]  Cf. especially *Bellum Iugurthinum* 41–42; *Bellum Catilinae* 38.

understanding but also reflects Plutarch's political concerns as a Greek aristocrat harboring deep suspicions about the aspirations of the *dēmos*.[45] Beyond this, the dual structure of his biographical project arguably helped to produce a common and mutually reinforcing emphasis on the confrontation between statesman and multitude. In fact, it has been suggested that, despite the obvious prominence of Greek elements in the series, the Greek *Lives* are in turn colored by Roman practices and stereotypes.[46] Thus, the experience of patronage and public munificence in the Roman context may lie behind the idea that Nicias put on expensive shows to win the goodwill of the people (*Nicias* 3). More broadly, it might be argued that Plutarch was induced by the weight attached to military skills and political authority at Rome to simplify the complexities of democratic life in fifth- and fourth-century Athens. On one level, these considerations put into perspective the previous points about the core conceptual Greekness of the *Lives*. On another, the existence of common features may not be all that surprising in a cycle of biographies that focuses on character and statesmanship rather than trying to explore the specifics of disparate historical circumstances. If Plutarch conceived the arrangement in pairs as a distinctive structural principle of the series, some blurring of the boundaries between Greek and Roman settings must have been unavoidable and indeed desirable.

A further qualification needs to be added. However important Greek concepts may be for understanding the character of Plutarch's Roman heroes, it would be simplistic to conclude that Greek-style *paideia* is all that counts. Thus, a man like Aemilius Paulus is held in high regard not only on account of his philhellenism and *philanthrōpia* but also because of his steadfast attachment to ancestral values and religious ceremonial in accordance with Roman tradition (*Aemilius Paulus* 3.2–7).[47] Does this mean that the biographer actually understands this tradition and is prepared to recognize it as equally valid? In this context, it should not be overlooked that the concerns of the Roman nobility were in many ways quite similar to Plutarch's own preoccupations as a member of the Greek elite under the Empire. Some of the ideas they have in common are their preference for a powerful aristocracy, reverence for experienced statesmen, and the great value attached to religious customs. In other words, quite a few elements of Roman tradition appealed to Plutarch rather naturally, without requiring him to engage with the particulars of their cultural setting and historical

[45] Cf. Mazza (1995: 264–268) and, on the largely negative depiction of the people in the *Lives*, Saïd (2005b).

[46] Cf. Pelling (1986a: 175) = (2002a: 217–218), citing Gomme (1945: 72–74).

[47] See Tröster (2012).

background. Still, as far as Aemilius Paulus is concerned, it is telling that
the biographer is at pains to highlight his eagerness to broaden the training
of his sons by adding Greek *paideia* to the traditional Roman curriculum
(*Aemilius Paulus* 6.8–10).[48]

In contrast to Aemilius Paulus, Cato Maior (another champion of *mos
maiorum*) refuses to draw on the expertise of Greek tutors for the education
of his son (*Cato Maior* 20.5–7). As for his broader reservations about
Hellenization, it is hardly surprising that Plutarch uses strong words to
reject them as unfounded (*Cato Maior* 23). Beyond this, the biographer
exposes the weakness of Cato's stance by pointing out that his thinking was
in fact influenced by Greek philosophy and learning to a certain extent
(*Cato Maior* 2.3–6). While this is true, Plutarch fails to explore more fully
the rationale behind his subject's attitude, which can only be understood
with reference to Roman values, traditions, and debates.[49] A similar neglect
of the historical parameters of Roman society can be seen, for instance, in
the *Marcellus*, where the protagonist is presented from the start as self-
controlled (*sōphrōn*), humane (*philanthrōpos*), and full of respect for
Hellenic *paideia* and *logoi* (*Marcellus* 1.3). Later on, he is responsible for
war atrocities in Sicily and the sack of Syracuse, yet this is reinterpreted as
an attempt to bring Greek civilization to Rome (*Marcellus* 21).[50]

The Greekness of Plutarch's outlook and the limitations of his interest
in Roman history and culture also emerge from some of his writings
beyond the *Lives*. Particularly relevant are two collections of questions
and answers centering on a variety of customs and practices from, respectively, the Greek and Roman worlds. These anthologies are embedded in
the tradition of etiological writing, which is concerned with causation and
explanation as a way of relating the past to the present and hence of
defining identity. While the two works belong to the same genre and
resemble each other in terms of structure and content, it is chiefly the
differences between them that help to shed further light on Plutarch's
attitude to otherness.[51]

---

[48] Also note *Aemilius Paulus* 28.11 on the acquisition of Perseus' library.
[49] On the meaning and limitations of Cato's anti-Hellenism, see Gruen (1992: 52–83); Jehne (1999),
with further references.
[50] Compare also *Fabius Maximus* 22.7–8 and note the contrast with Polybius 9.10 and Livy 25.40.1–3;
also 27.16.7–8. On Plutarch's adaptation of his source-material, see Pelling (1989: 199–208); Swain
(1990a: 140–142); also H. Beck (2002: 481–486; 2003: 255–259).
[51] For the following argument, compare Preston (2001); also Goldhill (2002: 265–271). A different
reading is proposed by Boulogne (1992; 1994: 75–146), who suggests that the Greekness of
*Quaestiones Romanae* primarily serves to promote a universalist ideal.

Not surprisingly, *Quaestiones Graecae* shows the author's extensive knowledge of obscure traditions and local peculiarities, by and large without questioning their functional value. In this rich panorama of myth and history, Greece emerges as a vibrant community of cultural diversity. By contrast, Plutarch's answers in *Quaestiones Romanae* often address the very raison d'être of the practices concerned, which is thus considered not to be self-evident. What is more, the Greek issues are appropriately discussed with reference to Greek concepts and institutions, whereas many of the problems drawn from the Roman world can only be filled with meaning by transcending their cultural setting. This goes well beyond the common tendency to highlight the Greek origins of Roman customs and traditions. In many cases, Plutarch seems to use Roman practices to launch a broader discussion of Greek paradigms and parallels that do little to illuminate the phenomena themselves but rather deflect the reader's attention away from them. Occasionally, Roman explanations are explicitly rejected in favor of more abstract or specifically Greek alternatives, which Plutarch finds more appropriate and pertinent.[52] Addressing the question of why the Romans worship Fortuna Primigenia (*Quaestiones Romanae* 289B–C), for instance, he first presents the view of the majority of the Romans, linking the practice with Servius and the ancient kings. After that, however, it becomes clear that Plutarch prefers what he calls "an explanation more natural and philosophic," suggesting that, irrespective of the Roman context, Fortune is the origin of everything.

Undoubtedly, these differences are partly due to the fact that the intended audience for both works is Greek. Still, it is significant that the perspective adopted toward Rome is that of an outside observer, though one with a fair amount of inside knowledge. While Plutarch claims authority on the problems involved to the point of declaring his Roman sources wrong, his answers are often inconclusive and tend to multiply hypothetical explanations, even if these are frequently arranged in a more or less recognizable hierarchy.[53] This tentativeness is admittedly characteristic of many of his writings, yet it helps to account for the fact that, amidst the numerous Greek models and parallels, the essence of Roman culture remains somehow elusive.

While *Quaestiones Graecae* and *Quaestiones Romanae* focus on the remote past, Plutarch's attitude to the Romans of his own day is expressed most openly in *Praecepta gerendae reipublicae*. As noted earlier, this treatise

---

[52] On Plutarch's use of Latin and Greek sources in this work, see Van der Stockt (1987).
[53] Cf. the data compiled and discussed by Mora (2007b: 359–370).

includes a statement indicating that Plutarch warmly appreciated some of
the benefits brought about by Roman rule. Peace, prosperity, and stability
were obviously crucial factors in preventing major upheavals, thus helping
to entrench the position of Plutarch and his peers in the government of the
Greek *poleis*. Granted, there were moments of unrest, violence, and inse-
curity even under the High Empire,[54] but this does not alter the overall
picture of a relatively calm and stable environment.

However, *Praecepta gerendae reipublicae* is not a piece of imperial panegyric but a practical guide addressed to a Greek aristocrat who is aspiring to
a political career. Far from heaping uncritical praise on Rome, it shows
unmistakable signs of nostalgia for the glorious days of Greek independence and supremacy. For all its positive effects, the Roman presence is also
viewed as burdensome and restrictive:

> When entering upon any office whatsoever, you must not only call to mind
> those considerations of which Pericles reminded himself when he assumed
> the general's cloak: "Take care, Pericles; you are ruling free men, you are
> ruling Greeks, Athenian citizens," but you must also say to yourself: "You
> who rule are yourself ruled, ruling a city subject to proconsuls, the agents of
> Caesar . . . . You should arrange your cloak more orderly and from the
> general's office keep your eyes upon the orator's platform, and not have
> great pride or confidence in your crown, since you see the proconsul's boots
> just above your head." (*Praecepta gerendae reipublicae* 813D–E)

An explicit contrast is drawn in this passage between the cherished
freedom of Periclean Athens on the one hand and the woeful dependence
of the Greeks under Roman domination on the other. In fact, Plutarch's
dislike of external intervention is so strong that its avoidance becomes one
of the foremost objects of political action both among and within the *poleis*.
Only if the Greeks maintain order, live in concord, and settle internal
conflicts among themselves does Plutarch see any prospect of preserving
what is left of their local autonomy (814E–816A). He thus rejects the more
aggressive course advocated by those who strive to revive the spirit of the
distant past by emphatically evoking the battles of Marathon, the
Eurymedon, and Plataea (814A–C).[55] Having accepted the Roman presence as a fact of life, he rather seeks to defend the privileges of the Greek
aristocracy within the parameters set by imperial rule. Accordingly, Roman

---

[54] Cf. Woolf (1993: 185–189); Brélaz (2008: 184–190).
[55] On this statement and the changing relevance of past Greek exploits, cf. Oudot (2010); also Gascó
(1990); more broadly, Connolly (2001: 359–362). See further Marincola (2010) on the presentation of
those battles in the *Lives*.

politics remains largely outside Plutarch's focus, though he does stress the advantages of being well connected with Roman men of power (814C–D). Conversely, he is highly critical of those among his fellow Greeks who lose sight of the interests of their native cities because of their eagerness to pursue a career in the imperial administration (814D–E).[56]

At the same time, Plutarch's argument about the threat of Roman intervention serves to add punch to his related points about local government and the role of his own class as a guarantor of stability and autonomy. In his view, the aristocracy is required to thwart the designs of ambitious demagogues and to check the often-irrational impulses of the multitude, even by circuitous means (813A–C; 818A–819B). As this can only be achieved by avoiding divisions and rivalry among the ruling establishment, the conclusion of *Praecepta gerendae reipublicae* again stresses the importance of concord and consensus in local politics (823F–825F). In a nutshell, Plutarch suggests that aristocratic solidarity would keep the Romans out and the masses down. Evidently, this is in many ways a distinctly conservative program, and it is therefore logical for Plutarch to entrust its implementation to the older generation of experienced politicians. Thus, in the essay *An seni respublica gerenda sit*, he calls on the most seasoned members of the political elite to offer guidance, make the toughest decisions, and transmit their wisdom and expertise to their younger colleagues (790C–791C; 793A–796C). This idea of a regime based on the experience and authority of old men is developed into a veritable system of informal gerontocracy.[57]

As far as the imperial presence is concerned, modern scholars have variously described the views advanced in *Praecepta gerendae reipublicae* as either pro- or anti-Roman, stressing Plutarch's acceptance of, or at least acquiescence in, Roman rule or, conversely, his bitterness and sense of humiliation.[58] Undoubtedly, his attitude is pro-Roman in the sense that he defends the status quo as basically unalterable and as providing some major benefits. Nevertheless, Plutarch also represents Rome as an alien and potentially oppressive element that serves to restrict the autonomy of the Greek *poleis*. It should not be overlooked, however, that his objectives in

---

[56] The potential pitfalls of such a career are also addressed in *De tranquilitate animi* 470C as part of a larger warning against the insatiable desire for ever greater achievements, but without implying general disapproval of Greeks assuming high office at the imperial level. Cf. Stadter (2002: 124–125) = (2015a: 46–47); also Swain (1996: 169–171).

[57] Cf. Desideri (1986: 379–381) = (2012: 120–123); also Byl (1977: 113–123).

[58] The former opinion is expressed e.g. by Jones (1971: 110–121); the latter by Halfmann (2002). For a balanced assessment, cf. Swain (1996: 161–186). Also note Duff (1999a: 291–298).

the political treatises are more limited than in the *Lives*, where his target audience extends to the very top of the imperial administration. Consequently, the crude alternative of a pro- or anti-Roman reading may be a red herring. Instead of arguing the case for either of these interpretations, it may be more appropriate to reiterate the emphasis on Plutarch's class interests and practical concerns within the world of local politics and, to some extent, beyond.

Similar conclusions may be drawn for his work as a whole. Time and again, it has been seen that Plutarch's oeuvre needs to be interpreted against his personal background as a Greek aristocrat, a Platonic philosopher, and a priest at Delphi. Moreover, his literary production clearly bears the marks of the revival of classical Greek culture at his time of writing. Thus, Roman statesmen and their sociocultural setting tend to be measured against Greek concepts and standards. While this does not mean that Plutarch's perspective is anti-Roman, it is certainly fair to call it Hellenocentric. If he pursues a broader program for his society, it is that of a present that ought to be shaped by the heritage of Greek culture and civilization.

## Further Reading

Jones (1971) remains the fullest treatment of Plutarch's relationship with Rome and the Romans, complemented by Stadter (2015a) on Plutarch's Greco-Roman audience. The fundamental importance of Greek culture for understanding the Roman *Lives* and Plutarch's writings in general emerges from Pelling (1989), Swain (1990a; 1996: 135–186), and Duff (1999a), as well as from García Moreno (1995; 2002). Their views are challenged implicitly by Boulogne (1994), who suggests that Plutarch promotes a program of cultural fusion, and explicitly by Späth (2007), who argues that the *Lives* are basically a timeless philosophical project. Questions of Greek and Roman identity are also explored by Van der Stockt (2013) and, with more particular foci, by Schmidt (1999) on Plutarch's perception of barbarians, Preston (2001) on *Quaestiones Graecae* and *Quaestiones Romanae*, and Roskam (2004) on otherness. Plutarch's general view of Greek, Roman, and "global" history is discussed by Pelling (2010) and, more systematically, by Mora (2007a), who detects a moderate pro-Greek bias in the texture of the *Lives*. Plutarch's reading of Roman politics and society is analyzed by Pelling (1986a), de Blois (1992), and Mazza (1995). Geiger (2017) suggests that there is a tendency in Plutarch to eschew the more recent Roman material.

CHAPTER 3

# Plutarch As Moral and Political Educator

## Timothy Duff

Plutarch's extant corpus, at over a million words, is one of the largest to survive from classical antiquity.[1] His works span a staggering number of literary genres and forms (biographies, speeches, dialogues, letters, essays, collections of anecdotes, miscellanies,[2] and more) and cover a wide variety of themes (history, philosophy, practical advice for living, advice for the statesman, education, etc.).[3] But a common thread running through almost all Plutarch's works is their interest in morality – that is, in what defines, and how one should live, a good and honorable life – and their concern to "improve" their readers.

It is not surprising that morality should be such a central concern, as moralism – a tendency to think in terms of right and wrong, virtue and vice – was such a strong reflex in Plutarch's world. Ancient society was steeped in the language of virtue and vice. When the Greeks thought about human character, they thought in moral terms: a person's character was less about the traits that individuated them, that made them different or unique, and much more about the person's virtues or vices, their conformity to a set of norms of correct behavior, how they measured up against a set of accepted standards.[4] Most ancient literature was in some sense moral: historians looked for lessons from the past; philosophers discussed the nature of virtue and claimed to be able to teach their students to live well. Inscriptions in cities throughout the Roman Empire, including

---

[1] At 1.037 million words, it is almost twice the size of Plato (591,000); of authors up to the fourth century CE, it is smaller only than Galen (2.499 million) and, marginally, Aristotle (1.076 million). Compare the much smaller corpora of e.g. Xenophon at 315,000, Demosthenes at 297,000, and Thucydides at 150,000. Figures from the *Thesaurus Linguae Graecae*.

[2] Miscellanies: e.g. *Table talk*, *Greek questions*, and *Roman questions*. See Klotz and Oikonomopoulou (2011a).

[3] On the variety of literary forms in the *Moralia*, see especially Ziegler (1949: 60–257) = (1951: 696–895); Gallo (1998b). Cf. Russell (1993: xii–xiii); Van Hoof (2010: 68–70).

[4] On this aspect of ancient concepts of character, see Gill (1983; 1986; 1990; 1996); Duff (1999a: 13–14).

47

Plutarch's own Chaeronea, honored benefactors for their virtues. And Roman emperors paraded their supposed virtues and were assessed for their virtues and their vices by later biographers or historians.[5]

Plutarch presents himself explicitly as a teacher of correct behavior in some texts. His *On tranquillity of mind*, for example, takes the form of a letter addressed to a plainly important man, Paccius.[6] This Paccius, Plutarch claims in the opening lines, has written to him from Rome to ask Plutarch to write something on "contentment" or "tranquillity of mind" (*euthumia*), as well as on Plato's *Timaeus*. Not wishing to let Paccius down, Plutarch continues:

> I gathered together some observations on tranquillity of mind from the notes which I happened to have made for myself, believing that you were requesting this discourse not for the sake of hearing a work aimed at elegance of style, but for the practical help (*khreias boēthētikēs*) that it might offer. (1, 464E–F)

Plutarch presents himself here as a guide for correct living, and in what follows he mixes practical advice with philosophical analysis.[7] In other texts, Plutarch is less explicit about their morally educative value. But all have matters of morality, of right and wrong, of correct and incorrect behavior, at their heart.

In what follows, I will attempt to give an overview of Plutarch's moralizing approach across his corpus, paying particular attention to works of literary criticism, works of practical morality, political texts, and biographies. A number of themes will emerge. One is the importance in Plutarch's works of examples (*paradeigmata*), whether drawn from history, literature, or everyday life, as models for imitation or the reverse. Another is the profound influence of Plato, and especially Platonic conceptions of the soul, in all Plutarch's moral thinking. A third theme is that many texts are marked by a great interest in the *practical* application of philosophical principles to the problems faced by Plutarch's wealthy and powerful readers, and in keeping with this practical bent, Plutarch presents himself not as a preacher but as a congenial guide, sensitive to the weaknesses of human nature. Finally, and perhaps most importantly, Plutarch teaches the importance of readers' learning to think for themselves about moral

---

[5] Most notably by Suetonius. For this aspect of Suetonius' work, see e.g. Wallace-Hadrill (1983: 66–72, 142–117); Lewis (1991: 3626–3640).

[6] Not necessarily a senator, as Jones (1971: 59) claims, but nonetheless, as is clear from numerous references in *On tranquillity of mind*, a powerful and wealthy man. See Stadter (2002: 125) = (repr. 2015a: 47); Puech (1992: 4865); Van Hoof (2010: 87–89).

[7] On this passage, see Van der Stockt (1999b); Van Hoof (2010: 110–115).

issues, rather than waiting to be told how to react or what to do, and assumes such an alert and independent reader of his own works.

## Morality and Literary Criticism

The way in which a concern with right and wrong behavior runs through Plutarch's work like a seam can be glimpsed in two texts that deal with what might to modern eyes seem a topic far removed from morality: literary criticism.[8] In one work, *On the malice of Herodotus* (*Peri tēs Hērodotou kakoētheias*), Plutarch attacks the historian Herodotus for giving a distorted picture of the Greek resistance to Persia in the Persian Wars. But Plutarch's rationale for his critique of Herodotus does not have to do with Herodotus' use of evidence or with his capabilities as a historian. It is rather that the over-critical attitude Herodotus adopts towards the Greeks is indicative, Plutarch claims, of Herodotus' own malicious disposition (*kakoētheia*). Of course, we need not assume that the way Plutarch presents Herodotus in this work is the sum total of what he had to say about him; Plutarch speaks highly elsewhere of Herodotus and uses him copiously in the *Lives*.[9] What is significant, however, is that the criticism of Herodotus here is couched in moral terms: Herodotus' biases spring from and reveal his own ethical disposition.[10]

The second text that we shall consider is a treatise on how the young should be taught to read poetry. But far from dealing with aesthetics, plot, meter, or the host of other themes a modern reader might expect,[11] Plutarch's preoccupation in *How the young man should listen to poetry* is with the potentially harmful moral effect that reading Homer or the tragedians might have on the young.[12] Behind this approach lies the

---

[8]  Cf. Russell (1989: 302–306).
[9]  On Plutarch's use of Herodotus in the *Lives*, see e.g. Hershbell (1993: 147–148, 151–152); Dognini (2007: 494–502); Pelling (2007a); Duff (2010b); and the papers in Duff and Fletcher (forthcoming). For *On the malice of Herodotus* as a rhetorical invective or display speech, and therefore not a simple statement of Plutarch's views of Herodotus, see e.g. Seavey (1991); Hershbell (1993: 158–159); Teodorsson (1997); Ramón Palerm (2000; forthcoming).
[10]  See Hershbell (1993: 152–163); Marincola (1994; 2015a: 89–94); Roskam (forthcoming). In the same way, Dionysius of Halicarnassus commended Herodotus and criticized Thucydides for their choice of subjects and of where to begin and end their narratives, both of which, he argued, revealed their moral disposition (*diathesis*) (*Letter to Pompey* 3–6). For this criterion for judging a historian, see Luce (1989: 21–23); Fox (1993: 37–38); Duff (1999a: 56–59).
[11]  Cf. Hunter and Russell (2011: 2, 8–9); Hägg (2012: 277); Bowie (2014: 178, 187–188).
[12]  On *How the young man should listen to poetry*, see especially Hunter and Russell (2011); also Russell (1973a: 51–53); Schenkeveld (1982); Carrara (1988); Valgiglio (1991); Van der Stockt (1992: 39–49, 122–131); Díaz Lavado (1996); Jouan (2001: 191–193); Zadorojnyi (2002); Konstan (2004; 2005: 2–4, 6, 14–15); Bowie (2014: 183–185); Xenophontos (2016: 79–91).

assumption that heroes or gods in poetry might in some sense be considered models of behavior, exemplars to be imitated. From as early as Xenophanes in the sixth or early fifth century BCE, some Greeks had been concerned about the many instances of immoral or unedifying actions or words, by both men and gods, to be found in Homer.[13] Plato in the *Republic* had responded to this problem by wishing to ban poetry from his ideal city;[14] Plutarch's answer in this text is less radical and more realistic: the young must be taught to evaluate critically what they are reading.[15]

The young man should not, Plutarch advises, simply assume that the great figures he reads about "were wise and just men, outstanding kings and models of all virtue and correctness." For "he will be greatly harmed if, in amazement, he approves of everything and resents nothing" (8, 25E). Instead the young reader should learn that "poetry is an imitation of characters and lives (*mimēsin . . . ēthōn kai biōn*), and of people who are not perfect or pure or completely irreproachable." In other words, not everyone or everything one meets in poetry is admirable or worthy of imitation. The reader's attitude should, therefore, include not only "elation and enthusiasm for noble deeds and words" but also "repugnance and resentment at the base" (*ta . . . phaula*). Furthermore, the young reader must learn to distinguish between good and bad behavior themselves: they should "boldly shout out, as a matter of habit, 'Wrong!' and 'Improper!' (*ouk orthōs kai ou prosēkontōs*), no less than 'Right!' and 'Proper!' (*orthōs kai prepontōs*)" (8, 26A–B). Young readers should, in other words, read with their moral faculties alert and be prepared to make their own judgments on the behavior and opinions of the characters in poetry.

Plutarch now performs a reading of Books 1 and 9 of the *Iliad* to demonstrate the way this approach might work, and the kind of independent judgment that the young reader must learn. Some of Achilles', Agamemnon's, or Phoenix's actions are commended (e.g. "This was right and moderate and proper", *orthōs tauta kai metriōs kai prepontōs*) and some condemned ("No longer right and moderate", *ouket' orthōs oude metriōs*, 26D) (8, 26B–27A). In these cases, Plutarch says, "the distinction is clear" (*hē diaphora prodēlos*). "But," he continues, "in most cases where the poet's opinion is unclear, distinctions should be made (*dioristeon*) along the

---

[13] Xenophanes frs. 11–12 D–K.    [14] Especially *Republic* Books 2–3 and 10.
[15] See Halliwell (2002: 296–302) and Zadorojnyi (2002) on the relationship of Plutarch's position here with Plato's in the *Republic*. Cf. Hunter and Russell (2011: 8–9) on the way in which Plutarch's attitude to poetry parallels his attitude to the emotions: neither are to be done away with, but they should be controlled and directed by reason; both positions involve explicit rejection of Stoic views (e.g. *How the young man should listen to poetry* 7, 25C; *On moral virtue* 10, 450B–D).

following lines" (27A). Analysis of some passages from the *Odyssey* follows: if Nausicaa falls in love with Odysseus simply because she is overcome by desire on seeing him, then "her boldness and lack of restraint are to be condemned" (*psekteon*); but if she is attracted by his character and his conversation, "it is right to admire her" (27B). Similarly, if Odysseus' pleasure that the suitors are giving his wife gifts is motivated simply by venality (*dōrodokia*) and greed, he is in effect prostituting his wife; but if it is because he would have the over-confident suitors more easily in his power, then "his pleasure and confidence are reasonable" (27C).

By encouraging young readers to adopt this critical attitude, Plutarch continues, "we shall not allow them a leaning towards bad characters (*pros ta phaula . . . tōn ēthōn*) but encourage an emulation and preference towards the better (*tōn beltionōn zēlon kai proairesin*), if we unhesitatingly award censure to one and praise to the other" (8, 27E–F). Significantly, we have here not just an allotting of praise and blame, in which the young readers are expected to see the moral import of particular actions or words and to label them with abstract words defining virtues or vices. Young readers are also encouraged to look beyond the actions or words of characters themselves to consider motivation, an exercise that necessarily involves thinking hypothetically and debating alternative moral readings of the same action.

Finally, Plutarch advises that the young must be taught to question the opinions expressed in poetry, especially in those tragedies "in which persuasive and unscrupulous words accompany disreputable and base acts." The right response to ignoble opinions expressed is to answer back and ask why this or that opinion should be considered right; what was the motivation of the person saying it (8–9, 27F–28D)? "For he who in this way confronts and resists (*apantōn kai antereidōn*), and refuses to hand himself over, broadside on, to every argument, as to a wind . . . will thrust aside much of what is not truly or profitably said" (28D). Readers, then, must "resist" attractive but immoral notions, and not give way to them. Once again, their own active engagement and discrimination is crucial.[16]

A few points stand out in this text. First, as we noted, poetry is conceived in moral terms: whatever the beauty of the words or the dramatic power of the plot – or rather, *because of* the beguiling power of its language and plot, and the potential attractiveness of its characters (1, 15D–F; 2, 16B–D) – the young must be taught to read morally; that is, to always to have in mind the

---

[16] On this passage as arguing for "critical" readers, see Goldhill (1999: 105–106); Whitmarsh (2001: 49–54); Konstan (2004); Duff (2011b: 80–82). For such "active" reading as encouraged or assumed in ancient texts more broadly, see Yunis (2003: 201–212); Konstan (2006).

moral import of what they read. But rather than keeping from the young reader all but the most unambiguously moral or edifying stories, this text advocates a reading stance that looks for moral lessons in, and applies a moral sensibility to, even texts whose characters or plot do not make for simple models for imitation.

Secondly, as part of this moralizing reading, the characters that appear in poetry are to be evaluated in terms of their function as role models: are they good examples whom one should imitate, or the reverse? Finally, the young are to be taught to be active moral readers: that is, they should learn to evaluate *for themselves* the character and behavior of those they read about, and to select those worthy of imitation or those to be condemned. They should be taught to exercise their own judgment or discrimination (*krisis*: 1, 15D; 4, 20D; 8, 26B) in deciding what is good or bad behavior, to look behind actions and assess possible motivations, and not to accept uncritically the words of a character as right or true, but rather to "resist" some opinions expressed.

As we shall see, the approach to literature advocated here, which pre-supposes not only a moralizing reading, in which the protagonists might serve as examples for imitation or the reverse, but also an active, discriminating reader, is central to Plutarch's moral programme elsewhere and finds its culmination in the *Parallel Lives*.[17]

## Philosophy

We see Plutarch's interest in questions of morality, and some of the psychological assumptions that lie behind it, at its most abstract in one of his more theoretical philosophical treatises, *On moral virtue*.[18] This is a highly technical work, heavily influenced by Plato and Aristotle.[19] Its purpose is to investigate the nature of what Plutarch calls "moral virtue" or "virtue of character" (*ēthikē aretē*).[20] Central to Plutarch's understanding of the nature of virtue here and throughout his works is the conception of the

[17] Cf. the similar insistence on active reading in *On listening* (e.g. 3, 39C; 7-9, 40F–42E; 17, 47B–D; 18, 48C–D): see Kidd (1992: 24–25); Goldhill (1999: 106–107); König (2007: 48–49).
[18] On this text, see the commentaries of Babut (1969a) and Becchi (1990b) and the discussion of Gill (2006: 219–238). I discuss it, in relation to the *Lives*, in Duff (1999a: 72–77).
[19] But also contributing and responding to contemporary philosophical debates. On Plutarch's conceptions of the human soul in *On moral virtue*, see e.g. Opsomer (2012). For the relationship between the influence of Plato and Aristotle on Plutarch's conception of the soul in this treatise (whose positions Plutarch attempts to harmonize), and of the contemporary Platonic and Aristotelian schools, see also Babut (1969a: 61–76); Donini (1974: 63–125); Becchi (1975; 1978; 1981; 1990b: 27–49); Opsomer (1994); Gill (2006: 229–238); cf. Duff (1999a: 72–73).
[20] As opposed to "contemplative" or "theoretical" virtue (*theōrētikē aretē*: 1, 440D).

soul as divided into a rational part and an irrational part, from the latter of which spring our emotions or "passions" (*pathē*). When correctly functioning, the rational should lead and guide the irrational (3, 441D–442C). Not, says Plutarch, that one should aim to suppress the irrational part of the soul entirely or, as the Stoics did, deny its existence;[21] the emotions (ambition, shame, anger, sexual desire, etc.) are necessary for the exercise of virtue. But they must be strictly controlled and subordinated to reason, and must act in "harmony" with it; otherwise they can be harmful.[22] And crucial for the exercise of such reasoned self-control is, says Plutarch, the laying down of correct habits, an idea that Plutarch underlines by punning on the Greek words for character (*ēthos*) and habit (*ethos*) (4, 443C).[23] It follows from this that virtue can be learnt and taught[24] and can be exercised by everyone.[25]

The Platonic (or Platonic-Aristotelian) conception of the human soul and of the nature of virtue and vice espoused in *On moral virtue* underlies all Plutarch's works and provides the psychological and ethical framework for them. The notion of the soul as a site of conflict between reason and passion is central. The passions, though necessary and natural, need to be strictly controlled; the question of whether, in the face of disturbing circumstances, one is able to assert one's reason (*logos*) or reasonings (*logismoi*), or is overwhelmed by passion (*pathos*), is an important moral indicator for Plutarch throughout his works. Two emotions that receive particular attention are ambition and anger: both are in themselves necessary spurs to action; without them a person would be entirely passive. But they can so easily get out of control; ambition, for instance, which can inspire men to great achievement, can easily give rise to a destructive self-regard and rivalry, in which peers are seen as competitors and enemies.[26]

---

[21] On Stoic theories of emotion, see e.g. Brennan (1998; 2003).

[22] For Plutarch's criticism of Stoic doctrines of the soul, see Gill (2006: 229–238); Opsomer (2012: 315–316, 319–320; 2014: 94–98).

[23] Both Plato and Aristotle had argued that character (*ēthos*) is formed by habituation (*ethos*): e.g. Plato, *Laws* 792e "the whole character is implanted through habit" (*to pan ēthos dia ethos*); Aristotle, *NE* 1103a11–b25 (esp. 1103a17–18 "[virtue] of character results from habit" (*hē ēthikē [aretē] ex ethous periginetai*), hence its name"); *EE* 1220a38–1220b7; *MM* 1185b38–1186a8. Cf. ps.-Plutarch, *On education* 4, 2F–3B; Plutarch, *On talkativeness* 18, 511E.

[24] A case Plutarch argues in the (probably) fragmentary or unfinished *Can virtue be taught?* (439A–440C). Cf. Barigazzi's (1993) suggestion that the fragments of that text (Lamprias Catalogue no. 180) and four others – *On chance* (97C–100A), *On virtue and vice* (100B–101E), *Is vice sufficient to cause unhappiness?* (498A–500A), and *Are the passions of the soul worse than those of the body?* (500B–502A), only the last of which is listed in the Lamprias Catalogue (no. 208) – should be regarded as fragments of a single work on whether virtue can be taught.

[25] And therefore that, since virtue can be taught and learnt, a good education and upbringing in childhood are vital for the formation of character. See e.g. Gill (1985); Duff (1999a: 76–77; 2008b).

[26] See Duff (1999a: 75–97); Nikolaidis (2014: 352–353). See also pp. 71–72 in this chapter.

*On moral virtue* is just one amongst a number of technical philosophical treatises; Plutarch also wrote a commentary on Plato's *Timaeus* (*On the creation of the soul in the 'Timaeus'*) and further attacks on both the Stoics (*On Stoic contradictions*; *Against the Stoics on common conceptions*) and the Epicureans (*It is not possible to live pleasantly according to Epicurus*; *Against Colotes*; *Whether 'Live unknown' is good advice*). The Stoics believed that only the philosopher was virtuous, and what is more, that there were no gradations of virtue;[27] Plutarch, on the contrary, believed in the efficacy of philosophy to help also those who did not devote their lives to studying it. Through gaining a correct understanding of themselves and their weaknesses, and through taking a series of small steps, it was possible for all men to effect real moral improvement.[28] In fact, it is this very point that Plutarch argues explicitly in *How to understand that one is making progress in virtue*,[29] a work dedicated to a very important man of affairs indeed: the Roman statesman and administrator Sosius Senecio.[30]

## Practical Morality: The "Popular-Philosophical" Works

This sense of philosophy as a practical tool for better living[31] finds its clearest expression in the so-called popular-philosophical texts.[32] These texts are "popular" in the sense that they apply philosophical principle to the real world, but the audience they presuppose is as much an elite one as in all Plutarch's works: the addressees of these texts, where there is a specific addressee, and the world imagined is that of wealthy men, deeply involved

---

[27]  On Plutarch and Stoicism, see Babut (1969b); Hershbell (1992b); Opsomer (2014), and nn. 21–22 in this chapter.

[28]  See Van Hoof (2010), especially Chapter 1.

[29]  On *Progress in virtue*, see e.g. Russell (1973a: 87–90); Valgiglio (1989); Roskam (2005b: 220–363, 405–412). The text is explicitly aimed at opposing the Stoic belief that gradations of virtue were impossible (on which see Roskam 2005b: *passim*).

[30]  Senecio was twice *consul ordinarius* and a legionary commander in Trajan's Dacian Wars and also the dedicatee of both the *Parallel Lives* (*Theseus* 1.1; *Demosthenes* 1.1; 31.7; *Dion* 1.1) and the *Table talk* (references in Duff (2011c: 219, n. 29); discussion in Klotz (2007: 651–652) [= 2011a: 162–164]; (2014: 209–210)). On Senecio, see Syme (1958: ii, 599); Jones (1970: 101–104; 1971: 54–57); Halfmann (1979: 211); Caballos Rufino (1990: 295–298); Puech (1992: 4883); Swain (1996: 144–145, 426–427); Stadter (2015a: 36–42, 122).

[31]  Van Hoof (2010: 34).

[32]  The term ("Popularphilosophisch-ethische Schriften") is Ziegler's (1949: 1, 66–67) = (1951: 637, 702–704). He analyzes the texts he groups under this heading at (1949: 131–168) = (1951: 768–825); cf. Tsekourakis (1983). Van Hoof (2010) offers a complete reassessment of these texts in which she places them in their social context and examines Plutarch's self-presentation in them; she critiques Ziegler's term, preferring to call them works of "practical ethics," and modifies the group of texts included (6–7, 257–261), as does Nikolaidis (2011: 205); cf. Xenophontos (2014a). See also the surveys in Van Hoof (2014); Nikolaidis (2011).

in the public affairs of their own *polis*, and sometimes in the Roman imperial administration. There is a remarkable variety of literary form amongst these texts. Some are essays dedicated to friends or powerful figures; others are epistolary or dialogues.[33] But all offer practical advice on how such men might improve themselves in relation to a particular trait of character or behavior. The advice is moral in that it advocates correct, morally upstanding behavior. But it is also highly practical, and always links morally correct behavior with social and political success: living a virtuous life is not about withdrawing from the world and from politics, as the Epicureans taught (a point Plutarch makes explicitly in *Live Unknown*),[34] nor does it involve trying to live up to the impossible standards advocated by the Stoics, but is about living an honorable and happy life.[35]

A good example is *Control of anger* (*Peri aorgēsias*).[36] The form of this text is a dialogue between two speakers as they travel together (1, 453C) – a setting that would immediately bring Plato to mind[37] and that places the text, for all its practicality, in a serious philosophical tradition. It opens with a man called Sulla, who has been away in Rome for a year, saying that he has noticed that his friend, Fundanus, has become much less prone to fits of anger than he used to be; he asks Fundanus to explain "what cure, as it were, did you use, to make your *thumos* so obedient to the rein and so gentle, so mild and submissive to reason" (1, 453C). The thought and the language here, especially the notion of the *thumos* (the "spirited" part of the soul, a subdivision of the irrational, and here especially its tendency to anger) as a horse that needs to be controlled by reason, is thoroughly Platonic.[38] And in the next few chapters, this philosophical flavor is continued, as Sulla talks of the difficulty of reason's getting control of anger once it has taken hold, and of the necessity of preparing oneself beforehand, as for a siege, "with the help that philosophy brings" (2, 454A).[39]

---

[33] Noted by e.g. Ziegler (1949: 82) = (1951: 719); Van Hoof (2010: 1). See also n. 3 in this chapter.
[34] See Trapp (2004: 198); Kechagia-Ovseiko (2014: 116–118). On *Live unknown*, see Roskam (2007b). On Plutarch and Epicureanism, see Hershbell (1992a); Boulogne (2003); Kechagia-Ovseiko (2014).
[35] Van Hoof (2010: 28–40, 255–256, and *passim*; 2014: 144).
[36] On *Control of anger*, see Russell (1968: 140–146); Ingenkamp (1971: 14–26, 74–145 *passim*); Laurenti and Indelli (1988); Becchi (1990a); Duff (1999a: 87–89); Stadter (2000: 503–504) = (repr. 2015a, 240–241); Van der Stockt (2003–4; 2008); Van Hoof (2007).
[37] Especially *Phaedrus* 227a–b; *Laws* 625a–c. Cf. Van Hoof (2007: 62).
[38] See especially Plato, *Phaedrus* 253c–254e (cf. 255e–256a; *Republic* 588e–591d). Plutarch refers to the *Phaedrus* passage, and uses the metaphor of the passions as a horse, frequently in his works: Duff (1999a: 78–79).
[39] Cf. Russell (1968: 141) on the siege metaphor as probably Stoic in origin.

But despite the Platonic setting and vocabulary, and the Platonic way in which the soul is envisaged throughout the text (e.g. 11, 459B), this is above all a practical text, and theoretical analysis or definition of anger plays very little role.[40] Fundanus realized, he says, once he had on one or two occasions successfully stood up against his own fits of rage, that it was possible for reason to conquer anger – just as the Thebans, after once standing up to the Spartans in the fourth century, realized that the Spartans were not invincible (3, 454C).[41] The rest of the text is given over to Fundanus' description of what, in practice, helped him. First, a series of observations and reflections that Fundanus made.[42] Fundanus observed the ill effects of anger on others; it makes them look ugly and harsh, and he hated the idea of appearing that way to his friends, or to his wife and daughters (6, 455F). In such moments it would be useful, he thought, if a friend could hold up a mirror to him so he could see how unpleasant he had become (6, 456A–B). Observing others also taught him that angry words can cause long-lasting enmities; the better alternative is dignified silence (7, 456D–E). He also saw that anger is not a sign of strength but of weakness. Along with these "negative examples" (*phaula paradeigmata*), he also collected, he says, "fine" ones too (9, 457C), and proceeds to give a list of historical kings, tyrants, and orators who acted in a dignified way by restraining their anger and who achieved their goals thereby, followed by a few examples of men who, conversely, because they acted in anger, did not achieve what they desired (9–10, 457E–459B).

Fundanus now turns to describe a series of practical exercises that helped him to become habituated to restraining his anger. Control of anger, he says, can be learnt by practicing on one's slaves; that is, by practicing not to rush to anger at their misdeeds (11, 459B–460C). Part of the solution is not to have excessive desires: if one is accustomed to dining modestly, one will not be enraged when a dinner is not done to perfection (13, 461A–462F). Similarly, one should limit one's expectations of other people, so as not to become enraged when they do not live up to them (16, 463B–E). We should also "turn our reasoning inward" and consider whether we are not prone to the same faults that anger us in others (16, 463E–F). Fundanus also

---

[40] Van Hoof (2007: 63–65; 2010: 62–63).
[41] The reference is probably to the Battle of Tegyra in 375 BCE, or the series of battles beginning with the return of the Theban exiles in 378 and including Tegyra (*pace* Helmbold (1939) and Kidd (1992, ad loc.), who assume it refers to the Battle of Leuctra). See *Pelopidas* 13.4–7; 15.1–8; 17.11–13.
[42] Observations and reflections (*epilogismoi*), chs. 6–10; practical exercises (*ethismoi*), chs. 11–16, but the lines are blurred. Other works of practical ethics begin with a section of "conviction" (*krisis*), where the reader grasps the harm that the passion in question brings (see *On talkativeness* 16, 510C–D). See Ingenkamp (1971: esp. 112); Van Hoof (2007: 71; 2010: 47–49).

claims that he tried to limit his meddlesomeness and not worry about minor matters ("a slave's task, a friend's action, a son's pastime, a wife's whisper", 16, 464A), as doing so brings constant outbursts of rage over small matters, which can become "a habit that affects more important matters" (16, 463F–464B). Fundanus concludes by comparing himself with those who take a vow to refrain from sex or wine, or from telling lies. In the same way, he refrained from anger first just for a couple of days; then, as he made progress, he was able gradually to go without for longer. In so doing, he claims, he proved right the argument that a calm and humane disposition benefits its possessor even more than it does those who come into contact with him (16, 464C–D).

Several features are worth noting here. First, although this is a text about right and wrong behavior, it does not actually *tell* the reader to do anything;[43] still less is there a heavy-handed narratorial voice, preaching at the audience.[44] The dialogue form is important: readers listen along with Sulla to Fundanus' narration of the observations he made about his own condition and the steps that he found helpful; the reader is encouraged to share his judgments, a step made easier to take by the frequent first-person plural verbs and pronouns ("we," "us") that Fundanus uses.[45] Just as he compared himself to others, so the reader is encouraged to compare him or herself both to them and to him. Interestingly, Fundanus himself is not instructed by any teacher; it was his own observation of himself and of the effect his behavior had on others that was his chief guide.[46]

Secondly, although *Control of anger* is deeply informed by Plutarch's Platonist philosophy, and although the first few chapters, in which Fundanus talks of anger as a passion and the difficulty of it being controlled by reason, are heavily Platonic, and its assumption that small steps in virtue are worth making is anti-Stoic, this is not a work of philosophical theory.[47] Plutarch was certainly, as we have seen, competent to write such a work. Rather, this is a work that shows philosophy *in action*. Not "philosophy light," but the practical application of philosophical principles to real life,

---

[43]  Van Hoof (2007: 71; 2010: 42–47).

[44]  There were certainly sermonizing texts of this nature in existence in the ancient world – the name "diatribe" was sometimes applied to them: e.g. the surviving texts of Bion (fourth to third centuries BCE) or Teles (mid-third century BCE). The exact meaning of the term and how far the diatribe was considered a separate literary form is debated. See Tsekourakis (1983); Moles (1996); Uthemann and Görgemanns (2006). For possible influences of the diatribe on Plutarch, see Burns (2015).

[45]  Van Hoof (2007: 78; 2010: 53–54, 95; cf. 143 on the *On exile*; 2014: 144).

[46]  Stadter (2000: 503–504) = (repr. 2015a: 240–241); Van Hoof (2007: 71–72).

[47]  And indeed, as in others of Plutarch's "popular-philosophical" works, there is material from other philosophical traditions: Van Hoof (2014: 142–143; cf. 2010: 71–73).

in which the reader sees with Fundanus and Sulla not only how one might go about changing one's behavior for the better but also how an ordinary member of the ruling classes might perform philosophy in the real world.[48] There are also some striking psychological insights here: that anger, for example, often comes from a belief that one is being despised or slighted by others (12, 460C–F) or from setting too high one's expectations.[49]

Thirdly, Fundanus frequently refers to his observation of others both as a motivating force in making him want to change and as a means of learning about his own weaknesses and how to overcome them (e.g. 6, 455E). Such examples (*paradeigmata*) may be good or bad, as he says explicitly at 9, 457C; that is, they may be models to imitate or avoid. Implicit here is a comparison of self with exemplary others, and the power that such comparison, and the introspection that goes along with it, have to bring about reform. While many of the exemplars in this text are drawn from Fundanus' everyday world (friends, family, the relationship of masters and slaves), some are drawn from history. Indeed, the very notion that one might learn from examples is itself introduced with a historical example: Fundanus learnt about anger from observing others, just as the ancient Spartans used to learn about drunkenness from observing their helots (6, 455E). And Fundanus claims that stories about "kings and tyrants" and their handling of their own anger are more useful to collect than stories about philosophers (9, 457D) – citing, amongst other examples from history, how the Macedonian king Antigonus once exercised restraint when he overheard some of his men standing outside his tent abusing him (9, 457E).[50] Similarly, he mentions the story of the Athenian leader Phocion urging his fellow-citizens, when news first reached them of Alexander the Great's death in Babylon in 323 BCE, to pause before revolting from Macedon in case it should prove false – a model, he says, for not acting precipitately when in a rage (11, 459E–F).

Finally, although the *Control of anger* seems to be set mainly in the "private" sphere of home and family, two points should not escape us. First, this is an elite world. Both Fundanus and Sulla are wealthy and

---

[48] This interest in the practical application of philosophy is also apparent in some pairs of Lives, especially *Dion–Brutus* and *Phocion–Cato Minor*. On this aspect of those Lives, see e.g. Pelling (1989: 222–226); Swain (1990b); Duff (1999a: 131–160); Dillon (2008). See also n. 69 and p. 75 in this chapter.

[49] Cf. Aristotle, *Rhetoric* 1380a; Seneca, *On anger* 2.22.2.

[50] In *Sayings of kings and commanders* 182C–D, the Antigonus to whom this anecdote is attached is Monophthalmus (died 301 BCE); in the parallel passage in Seneca, *On anger* 3.22, some details would better fit Antigonus Gonatas (died 239 BCE) or Doson (died 221 BCE): see Laurenti and Indelli (1988: 101).

powerful men; Sextius Sulla had just returned after a year in Rome – perhaps, the reader might surmise, on official business; he appears in the *Table talk* as the host of a banquet in Plutarch's honor upon his own arrival in Rome (8.7, 727B).[51] Fundanus, an Italian, would go on to be consul in 107 CE and governor of Achaea in 122/3.[52] The world Fundanus evokes is one in which banquets are given (13, 461D), and in which one might have favorite sets of tableware, or costly drinking cups, gems, and seal-stones (13, 461E).[53] Furthermore, though the context is largely a domestic one, the kind of behavior assumed to be desirable here does not concern the private world alone, or the mere cultivation of an inner serenity: there is a close fit between the behavior recommended or pilloried here and the behavior that would also lead to social and political success on the public stage.[54]

In fact, many of Plutarch's popular-philosophical texts address the kind of issues facing wealthy, politically engaged men, and have political life at their heart. One, dedicated to Antiochus Philopappus, grandson of the exiled king Antiochus IV of Commagene,[55] addresses a problem that plagued wealthy or politically active men: *How to tell a flatterer from a friend.*[56] The theme of managing social relations, especially the reciprocal ties of friendship that played such an important role in social and political life at all levels, is also central to *Having many friends* and *How to profit from one's enemies.*[57] Both are addressed to Cornelius Pulcher, a wealthy man from the Greek city of Epidaurus and later *iuridicus* of Egypt,[58] a very powerful position in the Roman administration, and take as their starting point the fact that a man of affairs will have false friends and enemies.

---

[51] On Sextius Sulla, see Jones (1971: 60); Puech (1992: 4878–4879). Although he is designated as "Sulla the Carthaginian" in *Table talk* 727B and *Romulus* 15.3, he was almost certainly a Roman citizen of some standing.

[52] On C. Minicius Fundanus, see Syme (1958: i, 114; ii, 468–469, 650, 801); Jones (1971: 58); Puech (1992: 4861).

[53] A point made by Van Hoof (2010: 20, 87–88) with reference to all the popular-philosophical works.

[54] Van Hoof (2010: 54–57; cf. 33–37, 40, 190–193).

[55] Philopappus rose to be a member of the Roman Senate and consul suffect in 109 CE; he also reached the archonship in Athens. A grandiose monument to him survives on the top of the Hill of Muses in Athens, in which he styles himself "king" (*basileus*). For bibliography, see Salmeri (2000: 58, n. 21).

[56] See Engberg-Pedersen (1996); Van Meirvenne (2002); Whitmarsh (2006c), all on how this text is about the political as much as the personal. Also on this text, Papadi (2005). For the flatterer as a pervasive type in the literature of this period, see Russell (1973a: 95–96, 108, 123–124); Whitmarsh (2000: 307–314).

[57] On these two texts, see O'Neill (1997); Van der Stockt (2011).

[58] Puech (1983: 17–21; 1992: 4843).

Other texts deal with the issue of when and how it is right to speak or remain silent: *On talkativeness* and *On being a busybody* lay out the social dangers of talking too much, especially of gossiping about others' private misfortunes; such behavior, Plutarch argues, is not only morally wrong but in fact damages the perpetrator's own social standing.[59] On the other hand, *On bashfulness* discusses ways of avoiding the social disgrace brought on by excessive timidity: not that such timidity is a vice itself, Plutarch reassures his reader (1, 528D), but it can lead to shameful and cowardly compliance with the wishes of others. Another text, *On praising oneself inoffensively*, is not an abstract discussion of what might have been presented as the vice of self-praise, but a practical discussion for the man of affairs, for whom standing up for himself and his achievements was a necessity, but for whom success might create envy amongst his peers;[60] the sense here of a world of high politics is all the stronger if the dedicatee, Herculanus, is to be identified with C. Julius Eurycles Herculanus, one of the richest men in the Peloponnese and one of the earliest Greeks to become a senator in Rome.[61] The audience constructed in these works, then, is wealthy and politically active: whether in their own small *polis*, as Plutarch presents himself, or in the wider Greek world, in the Roman administration or indeed in Rome itself.[62] The advice Plutarch gives may be moral, but it is social and political too.

## The Power of the *Exemplum*: *Political Advice*

It is traditional to classify Plutarch's political works such as *Political advice* and *Should an old man engage in politics?* under a separate category from his works on practical morality.[63] However, the audience envisaged is the same (elite men engaged in political life in their own *polis* or beyond), and while these works do not focus on a single problem faced by such men, they aim in the same way to give practical advice, based on philosophical principles,

---

[59] Van Hoof (2010: 157–161, 190–199).
[60] On *Inoffensive self-praise* see e.g. Radermacher (1897: 419–424); Vallozza (1991); Fields (2009); Miletti (2014).
[61] Jones (1971: 41); Puech (1992: 4850–4855).
[62] On the social position of Plutarch's imagined readers, see Jones (1971: 40–47); Van Hoof (2010: 19–27; 2014: 141–142). On whether Plutarch might have had Roman readers (in addition to Greek) in mind: Stadter (2000; 2002); Duff (2005; 2007–8: 7–11).
[63] See n. 32 in this chapter. Van Hoof (2010: 258–259) does align these two texts with the works of practical ethics. Similar can be said of *Inoffensive self-praise*, a work of both moral, practical, and political advice: cf. Radermacher (1897: 419).

about how to live a successful and moral life as a member of the governing class.[64]

The *Political advice* addresses a certain Menemachus, apparently a well-born young man from Sardis.[65] Menemachus, Plutarch explains, does not have time in his busy political life in his own city to study philosophy but has asked for some advice about public affairs, and Plutarch has obliged with this treatise, which contains, as he puts it, "a wide variety of examples" (1, 798B–C). In the opening lines, Plutarch refers to other philosophers who give general exhortations but no advice; they are, he says, like men "who trim their lamps but fail to pour in oil." Plutarch's stance here, then, is as a philosopher, but a philosopher who gives practical advice to wealthy elite men in the real situations they face – in this case, how to live a life of statesmanship;[66] he distinguishes himself from those philosophers, probably Stoics especially, who do not actually offer any advice about how to live in the real world. In writing this, Plutarch is putting into practice his own advice in *Should an old man engage in politics?*,[67] which was probably written about the same time,[68] and putting into practice Plato's conviction that the good man should enter public life and the philosopher should teach him.[69]

In the work that follows, the advice is certainly grounded in philosophy. One must, Plutarch says, enter politics not on impulse or stirred by the prospect of public acclaim – that is, under the influence of passion ("excitement caused by vain glory or contentiousness [*philoneikia*]") – but as the result of a "deliberate choice on the basis of judgement and reason" (*hē proairesis arkhēn ekhousa krisin kai logon*, 2, 798C).[70] The advice is also moral in the sense that it advocates virtue. Since the statesman will live the rest of his life "as

---

[64] On Plutarch as attempting to apply philosophical principles to the world of statesmanship, see e.g. Trapp (2004); Stadter (2012); Pelling (2014).

[65] The Sardian context is implied at 17, 813E–F; 32, 825D. On Menemachus, see Renoirte (1951: 69–79); Carrière (1984: 29–33); Puech (1992: 4859). On *Political advice*, see Renoirte (1951); Jones (1971: 110–121); Valgiglio (1976); Carrière (1977; 1984); Pavis d'Escurac (1981); Desideri (1986; 1991a; 2011); Caiazza (1993); Mueller-Goldingen (1993: 206–210); Masarrachia (1995); Massaro (1995); Swain (1996: 162–183); Duff (1999a: 293–298); Prandi (2000); Halfmann (2002); Trapp (2004); Pelling (2014: 153–160); Xenophontos (2016: 128–139, 146–149); Kemezis (2016).

[66] Van Hoof (2010: 74–75).

[67] On *Should an old man engage in politics?*, see e.g. Desideri (1986); Masarrachia (1995); Trapp (2004); Xenophontos (2012; 2016: 139–149); Pelling (2014: 153–159).

[68] *Political advice* was probably written between 96 and 114 CE; that is, when Plutarch was between about fifty and seventy. See Jones (1966: 72); Carrière (1984: 9–25); Caiazza (1993: 8–11). On the date of *Should an old man engage in politics?*, see also Follet (1972).

[69] Plato famously set an example of such political engagement when he attempted to influence Dionysius I and II, tyrants of Syracuse. Plutarch tells the story of his interactions with the latter in his *Dion*, which draws on Plato's own *Seventh Letter*.

[70] And "from conviction and by reasoning" (*apo gnōmēs kai logismōi*), 2, 798E. See Roskam (2004–5; 2005a).

though on an open stage" (*hōsper en theatrōi . . . anapeptamenōi*), he must put
his own character in order (4, 800B), since the people trust men of good
character and see through those without (4, 800F–801A). Later in the text, love
of money and making financial gain out of holding office are roundly
condemned (26, 819E). But the advice is also highly practical: this is philosophy
and moralism applied to the real world of public life. Complete virtue,
Plutarch claims, again with Stoic doctrine in his sights, is difficult to achieve,
so the statesman should start by tackling his most "flourishing and conspicuous" vices (4, 800B). Furthermore, virtue alone is not enough: practical
oratorical skills are necessary too (5, 801C); a section on the kind of oratory
that the statesman should adopt follows (5–9, 801C–804C).[71]

Plutarch then proceeds to discuss the best ways to enter public life, the
importance of choosing one's friends carefully, and ways of dealing with
enemies (10–14, 804C–811A): topics to which, as we have noted, Plutarch
devoted whole treatises (*On having many friends, How to profit from one's
enemies*). He illustrates his advice to treat with respect one's colleagues in office
with a personal reminiscence: "I remember how once, when I was still young,
I was sent with another man as envoy to the proconsul"; that is, to the Roman
governor. The colleague, Plutarch continues, was "somehow left behind"[72]
and Plutarch proceeded on his own. But on his return, Plutarch's father
advised him, in making his report of the mission, to include his colleague
and associate him with its success and to say not "'I' went but 'we' went, not 'I'
said, but 'we' said" (20, 816D) – just the kind of careful modesty recommended
in *On praising oneself inoffensively* (esp. 19, 546D–E). Similarly, the advice, if
one is not among the super-rich, not to compete with them in lavish benefactions to the city ("foot races, theatrical shows and banquets"), and certainly not
to borrow money in order to do it, but to "try to lead the state through virtue
and wisdom combined with reason" (31, 822F), is both practical and moral,
and overlaps with the concerns of the treatise *That one ought not to borrow*.[73]

Two other things are worth noting. First, Plutarch's success in projecting for
himself a persona of philosophical moderation and sense should not blind us to
the strong ideological content of this text. The kind of statesmanship envisaged
here is statesmanship at the *polis* level. Although some Greeks had at this time
started to rise high in the Roman administration, the wider Roman imperial
context is here for the most part ignored; powerful friends "up there" (*anō*) are

---

[71] Cf. Pelling (2014: 155–156).
[72] *apoleiphthentos de pōs ekeinou*. In leaving the reasons for the colleague's absence vague, and not
naming him, Plutarch gives the impression here of practicing what he preaches: that is, not drawing
attention to a colleague's weaknesses or lessening his dignity.
[73] Cf. Pavis d'Escurac (1981: 289–290); Desideri (1985: 398–399).

useful to have, but should not be used to try to seek a career in the Roman administration for oneself (18, 814C–E).[74] Where Rome is mentioned, it stands as an external threat; and the statesman's most important duty is to avoid the conditions that might lead to Roman intervention (17–19, 813D–816A; 32, 823F–825D). Furthermore, the people are dangerous; like a "suspicious and capricious beast," they need be led and controlled, albeit (says Plutarch) benevolently (4, 800C). Whatever their private differences, the elite must maintain a united front in dealing with the people, giving the impression of like-mindedness (*homonoia*),[75] else disorder and revolution, which would inevitably bring a strong Roman reaction, result.[76] In most Greek cities the popular citizen assembly theoretically had some power,[77] but Plutarch suggests various subterfuges to make sure that that power was not actually exercised:[78] one member of the governing class should speak against a measure to avoid giving the impression that they have stitched things up beforehand (as indeed they have) (16, 816F); games, shows, and public distribution of money, while not good in themselves, can be used to keep the people quiet (24, 817F–818E); in other cases, "roundabout and circuitous means" must be used to prevent the people's making misguided decisions (25, 818E–819B).[79] In all this Plutarch reveals the biases and assumptions of his class.[80]

[74] On the attitude to Rome in the *Political advice*, see Jones (1971: 111–118); Pavis d'Escurac (1981: 291–300); Desideri (1986: 373–375) = (repr. 2012: 113–116); (2011: 94–97) = (repr. 2012: 136–138); Swain (1996: 162–183); Duff (1999a: 293–298); Pelling (2014: 158–159).

[75] The importance of maintaining like-mindedness or concord (*homonoia*) amongst the elite is a key theme in the *Political advice* (e.g. 20, 816A; 32, 823F–825A; cf. Cook (2004)), and prominent in contemporary inscriptions and in the speeches of Dion of Prusa: see Kienast (1964); Jones (1978: 83–94); Sheppard (1984–6: 241–252). Cf. also Thériault (1996) on the widespread cult of a deified *Homonoia* (Concord).

[76] On the danger that unrest might lead to Roman intervention, see Salmeri (2000: esp. 74–76); cf. Jones (1978: 20). Cf. John's Gospel 11.48 where the Jewish Council (*sunedrion*), concerned at the possibility of unrest inspired by Jesus, declares, 'If we let him go on like this, everyone will believe in him and the Romans will come and take away both our place [i.e. the temple] and our nation.'

[77] On the continuing role of popular assemblies in the *poleis* in the early imperial period, see Salmeri (2000: 71–73; 2011: 202–206); Zuiderhoek (2008: 418–425); Fernoux (2011); van Nijf (2011: 232–236). For more on the Greek city in this period, see e.g. Dmitriev (2005); Gleason (2006); van Nijf and Alston (2011).

[78] It is true that Plutarch uses the term "democracy" to describe the constitution of the kind of *polis* he has in mind (*Political advice* 21, 816F): but in this period this meant simply autonomy and constitutional rule, with the different organs of power (i.e. assembly, council, courts, magistracies) functioning (cf. Swain (1996: 173); Chaniotis (2010); Van Nijf (2011: 232–236); cf. 19, 815A, where the state that would be overthrown in the event of external intervention is summed up as "council, people, courts, every office" (*kai boulē kai dēmos kai dikastēria kai arkhē pasa*). At 10, 805D Plutarch uses "oppressive and oligarchic" (*epakhthē kai oligarkhikēn*) to refer disparagingly to the untrammeled power of the Areopagus council in pre-Ephialtic Athens.

[79] On Plutarch's attitude to the people as shown here, see Desideri (1986: 375–379) = (repr. 2012: 116–121); (2011: 97–98) = (repr. 2012: 138–139). His advice here probably influenced Machiavelli: Desideri (1995b).

[80] On Plutarch's assumptions about political leadership, see Carrière (1977: 238–241); Aalders (1982: 28–36); de Blois (1992: 4600–4611); Duff (1999a: 89–90); Pelling (2014: 156–158).

Secondly, although its concerns are with the present, this text – as often in Plutarch – uses a host of examples drawn from history, both Greek and Roman, in order to illustrate, amplify, and concretize its moral and political advice throughout (cf. 1, 798C). Thus, when Plutarch discusses the two ways in which one might inaugurate one's political career, and mentions the possibility of a quick and glorious rise to prominence, he gives a series of historical parallels: one might burst onto the scene suddenly by overthrowing a tyrant, as Aratus of Sicyon did in 251 BCE, or through making a brilliant wartime alliance, like Alcibiades in 418, or through glorious military service, like Pompey or Scipio Aemilianus (10, 804E–805A). True, he acknowledges, times have changed and such exploits are not normally available to the young Greek statesman[81] – though one might still enter politics by attacking a bad politician, such as Cleon, or an oligarchic Council, as Ephialtes did (both examples drawn from the fifth century BCE); or, a better and less risky model, by acting as a reconciler between opposing factions, like Solon several hundred years earlier (10, 805B–E). As an example of the second, "safer and more leisurely way" of entering public life, Plutarch cites Aristides, Phocion, Lucullus, Cato the Elder, Epaminondas, and Agesilaus, who all attached themselves to a worthy patron (11, 805E–F).

But not all the great men of history are to be imitated; Plutarch also mentions some negative examples: whereas other men honored their patrons, the Spartan king Agesilaus, "out of untimely ambition and jealousy of his reputation," later insulted and rejected his own promoter, Lysander (11, 805F). And some modern-day patrons, out of envy, try to deprive their protégés of glory, as Marius did when, after promoting Sulla, he tried to marginalize him, thus precipitating civil war (12, 806C–D). Similarly, in discussing how to deal with friends, Plutarch begins by introducing two contrasting negative examples: Cleon, who renounced all his friends in order not to be influenced by bias in their favor, and Themistocles, who prided himself on enriching his friends at every opportunity (13, 806F–807A). In almost all cases, Plutarch does not explain either who these historical figures mentioned were or what they did: he assumes that his readers know

---

[81] "Now, when the affairs of the cities do not include leadership in wars, putting down tyrannies or acts of alliance, what beginning of a conspicuous and brilliant public career could one find? There remain public law-suits, embassies to the emperor. . ." (10, 805A): a point of view that ignores the possibility, for those with Roman citizenship, of service in the Roman army such as Arrian had (see Grassl (1982); Bosworth (1988: 18–19)), though that might have less impact on one's reputation in one's own *polis*.

them already and employs brief incidents from their lives to back up and amplify his argument at any given point.[82]

## The *Parallel Lives*: Learning from Examples

The use of historical figures as exemplars to guide conduct finds its greatest expression in Plutarch's largest and most well-known work, the *Parallel Lives*. Written at about the same time as the *Political advice*, and after most of the other texts in the *Moralia*,[83] the *Parallel Lives* constitute a vast series of biographies of statesmen, both Greek and Roman, which stretch chronologically from Theseus and Romulus, the mythical founders of Athens and Rome, to the Hellenistic kings and the dynasts of the late Roman Republic.[84] The *Parallel Lives* owe their name to their unique structure. They were designed to be read not as individual biographies but in "parallel": that is, in pairs, each pair consisting of a Greek Life and a Roman one, usually in that order. Thus, for example, Alexander the Great is paired with another conquering general, Julius Caesar; the Athenian orator Demosthenes is paired with the Roman orator Cicero; and Themistocles, Athenian victor in the Persian invasion of Greece, is paired with Camillus, Roman victor in the Gallic invasion of Italy.[85] Most pairs of *Lives* are followed by a comparison (*synkrisis*) of the two men, and about half open with a prologue, which introduces them both.[86]

Plutarch declares an explicitly moral purpose for the *Parallel Lives* in several of these prologues.[87] At the start of *Alexander–Caesar*, he warns his readers not to expect large-scale historical narrative, since his most pressing concern is to reveal the moral character of the statesmen whose Lives he is writing about: "For," he declares, "it is not so much histories that we are writing but lives, and there is not always in the most outstanding deeds

---

[82] On the historical examples in *Political advice*, cf. Carrière (1984: 56–60); Desideri (1991a); Prandi (2000).

[83] Between ca. 96 and perhaps 120 CE: Jones (1966: 68–70). See n. 68 in this chapter.

[84] The latest Greek Life is that of Philopoemen (253–182 BCE), general of the Achaean League, and the latest Roman is Mark Antony (82–30 BCE). Plutarch also wrote a separate series of *Lives of the Caesars* (on which see e.g. Georgiadou (1988; 2014); Ash (1997); Giannattasio Andria (2000; 2006); Stadter (2005b)), of which only the *Galba* and *Otho* survive; and several free-standing Lives, of which the *Aratus* and *Artaxerxes* survive.

[85] One book, uniquely, contains a double pair of Lives: *Agis* and *Cleomenes* (third-century kings of Sparta) paired with the *Gracchi*; there is a common prologue and *synkrisis*. On the structure of this book, see Duff (2011c: 237, 253, 256, and esp. 266–268).

[86] On the structure of Plutarchan paired Lives, see Duff (2011c).

[87] On the moralism of the *Lives*, see Martin (1995); Pelling (1995); Stadter (1997; 2000; 2003–4); Duff (1999a; 2007–8; 2011b); Nikolaidis (2014).

a revelation of virtue or vice – but often a little matter like a saying or a joke hints at character more than battles where thousands die, huge troop deployments or the sieges of cities" (*Alexander* 1.2). A key aim, then, of the *Lives* is to reveal the character of their subjects, which, Plutarch claims, can often be best understood through well-chosen anecdotes about them or revealing pronouncements that they made. And character, glossed here in terms of "virtue and vice," is conceived in moral, or judgmental, terms; it is about right and wrong, good and bad behavior.[88]

Uncovering the moral character of the subject in this way is meant to have a practical benefit for the reader, a point Plutarch makes in the prologue to another pair of Lives, the *Aemilius Paulus–Timoleon*.[89] He claims that he himself tries, through looking in the "mirror of history," to "adorn my life and make it like the virtues of these men." He imagines himself, and by extension his readers, communing with the great men of the past "when they visit us through history." "We examine" (*anatheōrōmen*), he says, each of these men, "taking from his deeds the most important and most beautiful to know." The purpose of studying these men and their noble deeds is a practical one, to improve oneself: what, he concludes, could be more pleasurable "and more effective for the correction of character?" (*pros epanorthōsin ēthōn*) (*Aemilius Paulus* 1.1–3). Plutarch here imagines himself and his readers not only observing the actions of the statesmen of the past, assessing their behavior and judging it on a moral scale, but also comparing themselves with those great men: by looking into history, as in a mirror, he says, he sees himself reflected, good points and bad, and considers his own behavior in the light of that of the great men of the past. The process is analogous to that described in *Control of anger* by Fundanus, who studied the behavior of others to try to improve his own, and who also appealed to the image of the mirror for the kind of comparative introspection that he imagined, which should lead to self-improvement.[90]

That such an act of moral comparison is meant to have a practical application in the life of the reader is made clear in another prologue, that to the *Pericles and Fabius*, where Plutarch clarifies the mechanism by which this improvement might take place: imitation (*mimēsis*). While our

[88] On the *Alexander–Caesar* prologue, see Wardman (1971); Desideri (1995a); Duff (1999a: 14–22; 2014: 339–340); Hägg (2012: 268–272); Chrysanthou (2017: 133–138).
[89] The *Aemilius Paulus–Timoleon* is one of the few pairs of Lives in which the Roman Life precedes the Greek: see Duff (2011c: 213–214, n. 2, 221, 239). On this prologue, see Desideri (1989: 199–200, 212–213) = (repr. 2012, 201–202, 215–216); Duff (1999a: 30–34; 2011c: 220–221, 223; 2014: 341); Whitmarsh (2001: 54–57); Hägg (2012: 272–273); Nikolaidis (2014: 355–356, 358).
[90] See Stadter (2000: 500–505) = (repr. 2015a: 237–241); (2003–4: 89–91).

senses, Plutarch says in this prologue, have to pick up all external stimuli that reach them, we have the ability to turn our intellect away from stimuli that might be harmful and direct it at what is useful: "Such things" (that is, objects that are beneficial to study), he continues, "are found in works done out of virtue, which implant in those that investigate them a sort of emulation and desire which leads to imitation" (*Pericles* 1.4). One may admire, Plutarch continues, a painting or a sculpture, but not wish to become a painter or sculptor oneself; in contrast, virtuous deeds "implant an active impulse" (*hormē*), which leads to imitation. His *Parallel Lives*, he implies, which present the virtuous deeds of the great men of the past, should not only give pleasure but also benefit readers, because they encourage them not just to admire the men of the past but to actively imitate them.[91]

A deeper insight into the kind of process envisaged here can be found in a passage in *Progress in virtue*. There Plutarch warns that history, along with philosophy and poetry, should not be studied merely for pleasure but for the benefit they can bring in terms of "correction of character" (*epanorthōsis ēthous*) and "alleviation of passion" (*pathous kouphismos*) (8, 79C–E). We should, Plutarch argues a little later, desire "to do what we admire" and not even tolerate what we condemn (14, 84B). The proper response to virtuous men, he continues, is emulation (*zēlos*) and imitation (*mimēsis*). That Plutarch is thinking here of the great figures from the past soon becomes clear from the examples he cites (15, 84E–85B): we should love good men, even when they suffer misfortune, admiring Aristides even when he is exiled, Socrates even though he is poor, and Phocion even when condemned to death.[92] Before undertaking any action, Plutarch tells his readers that they should "set before their eyes good men of the present or the past and ask, 'What would Plato have done in this circumstance, what would Epaminondas have said, what sort of a man would Lycurgus have showed himself, or Agesilaus?,' adorning and refashioning themselves as though before a mirror" (15, 85A–B).[93]

It is just this process, by which one compares oneself with the great men of the past, as in a mirror, and tries to imitate them, that Plutarch imagines for the *Parallel Lives*. But this process does not involve blind imitation, and it is not just deeds that matter; readers are expected to deduce from their actions the moral character of the historical figures described and their motivations; in this way, as this passage from *Progress in virtue* makes clear,

---

[91] On the *Pericles–Fabius* prologue, see Duff (1999a: 34–45; 2001; 2011c: 220; 2014: 335, 336, 342).
[92] "For that inspiration (*enthousiasmon*) which holds true even to the point where one is not appalled at apparent disaster but still admires and emulates (*thaumazein kai zēloun*), this no-one can ever turn away from what is good" (15, 85A).
[93] On this passage in relation to the *Lives*, see Duff (1999a: 32–33); Stadter (2000: 502–503).

even in defeat and misfortune the virtuous men of the past can, through their virtues, form role models.

Not that all examples are ones to imitate. We have seen how in *Control of anger* and *Political advice* Plutarch made frequent use of negative examples. In the same way, he makes clear at the start of the *Demetrius–Antony* that the correct response to some of the subjects of his biographies – or at least, to some of their deeds and character-traits – is the opposite of imitation. The Spartans, he argues, used to make their helots drunk in order to teach their young men the dangers of drunkenness. Fundanus had cited the same example in *Control of anger* to show how one might improve oneself by reflecting on other people's bad behavior. Here Plutarch's argument is rather more subtle: we should *not* be like the Spartans, whose action he character-izes as "hardly humane or the act of a statesman."[94] The fact that Plutarch cites the same historical exemplum in two places but uses it for entirely different purposes demonstrates how malleable such anecdotes can be, as they are redeployed in different contexts to serve different ends.[95] But still, he continues, "perhaps it is not such a bad idea for me to insert into the examples of the Lives (*ta paradeigmata tōn biōn*) one or two pairs of men who conducted themselves in a rather unreflecting way and who became in their positions of power and amid great affairs notorious for their vice." The reason for introducing such negative examples is, he claims, not entertain-ment but so that "we will be more enthusiastic both as spectators and as imitators of the better Lives, if we do not leave unexamined the base and the castigated" (*tōn phaulōn kai psegomenōn*).[96] That is, the Lives of less morally admirable figures will provide readers with a set of negative paradigms – conduct or character-traits to be deplored – and in so doing will throw into sharper contrast the more positive examples.

## The Themes of the *Parallel Lives*

The *Parallel Lives*, then, provide a cast of historical exemplars to whom readers are meant to compare themselves, looking for virtues or virtuous actions to imitate, and vices, weaknesses, or despicable actions to avoid. The two Lives in a pair often bring out the same or related character-traits in their protagonists, as well as similarities in their actions or the circum-stances of the careers. Indeed, the prologues sometimes declare explicitly

---

[94] See Duff (2004: 276–277); Van der Stockt (2008: 297–298); Nikolaidis (2014: 328).
[95] Cf. e.g. Van der Stockt (1999a; 1999b; 2002; 2003–4); Stadter (2008). Cf. n. 82 above.
[96] On the *Demetrius–Antony* prologue, see Duff (1999a: 45–49; 2004; 2014: 335–336); and pp. 72 and 75–76 in this chapter.

what the chief moral focal points will be: for example, the prologue to Book 10, after naming the two figures who form its subject (Pericles and Fabius Maximus), characterizes them as "men who were alike in their virtues, especially in their calmness and justice and their ability to endure the follies of their peoples and of their colleagues in office, and who so proved most beneficial to their countries" (*Pericles* 2.5). Demetrius and Antony are introduced in their prologue as men who confirmed "Plato's assertion that 'great natures' produce great vices as well as great virtues."[97] They were, Plutarch explains, "similarly given to love and drink, were soldierly, munificent, extravagant and domineering, and they had resultant similarities in fortune" (*Demetrius* 1.7–8). In the same way, the *Demosthenes–Cicero* prologue finishes by noting the two men's similarities in moral character ("their love of honor and freedom in their political activities and their lack of courage in wars and dangers," 3.3), before picking out some similarities in their careers (3.4–5).[98] In all these cases, the reader is alerted in the prologue to some of the moral and political foci of the two Lives.

In many other cases, even without such explicit initial guidance, individual Lives or pairs of Lives highlight particular virtues or vices, which they bring out both through direct character analysis and by showing them in action, through either narrative or carefully chosen characterizing anecdotes.[99] The character-traits in which Plutarch is interested, as befits a work on the lives of the great military and political figures of the past, are generally those related to public life and statesmanship, and there is a good deal of overlap with the themes in the popular-philosophical and political works that we examined earlier.[100] Indeed, the *Parallel Lives* are dedicated to the same powerful Roman, Sosius Senecio, as *Progress in virtue* was, and we may assume a wider readership amongst the Greek, and possibly Greek-speaking Roman, elite: men of affairs, for whom political models had

---

[97] On Plutarch's use of this Platonic concept, drawn from *Republic* 6, 491d–492a, see Duff (1999a: 47–49, 60–65, 205–208, 224–228, and s.v. Index of themes; 1999b).

[98] Cf. the *Pelopidas–Marcellus* prologue, which ends by noting that both men were "most formidable in hand-to-hand fighting" and brought successes to their country, but recklessly threw away their lives in battle "without any reasoning" (a vice) (*Pelopidas* 2.10–11). Cf. Beneker (2012: 68–72).

[99] On characterizing anecdotes in the *Lives*, see Stadter (1996; 2008: 57–64); Duff (2003; 2008b; 2008c; 2011b: 47–52, 54–55; 2011c: 224–228).

[100] These are Lives of statesmen, intended as models for men of affairs, not Lives of philosophers, teachers, or literary figures (cf. *Demosthenes* 3.2, where Plutarch explicitly denies that he will compare Demosthenes and Cicero as orators). There were biographies of that latter kind in existence: e.g. the Gospels, the numerous Lives of poets, and the ps.-Plutarchan *Lives of the ten orators*; later Philostratus' *Lives of the Sophists* and *Life of Apollonius of Tyana*, and Diogenes Laertius' *Lives of the Philosophers*.

a direct applicability. The *Coriolanus*, for example, can be read as a case-study in the dangers for the statesman of pride, unsociability, and anger; some passages overlap directly with *Control of anger*.[101] *Nicias* shows the dangers of caution and hesitancy in public life, and of excessive religious fear, and overlaps with both *On compliancy*[102] and *On superstition*.[103] *Pyrrhus* and *Marius* explore the dangers of discontent, and overlap with *On tranquillity of mind*[104] – though in all cases, the circumstances in which readers might be expected to apply these insights are very different to those that confronted the great men of the past who form the subjects of the *Lives*.[105]

Just as in the popular-philosophical texts, the tone is one of understanding for weakness rather than simple condemnation of vice. This tone – moral but sympathetic – stems partly from the fact that in telling each man's Life Plutarch adopts something of his perspective and sees events from his point of view.[106] But it also stems, as Plutarch himself explains at the start of the *Cimon–Lucullus*, from a belief, born out of "respect for human nature," that no man's life is "pure or blameless," and from a consequent determination to regard "mistakes" or "sins" (*hamartiai*) as "shortcomings in a particular virtue rather than the wickedness of vice" (*Cimon* 2).[107]

The *Parallel Lives* also share the same political assumptions as the texts we have examined, especially *Political advice* – though the distinction

---

[101] Duff (1999a: 205–240, esp. 210–215) on the overlap with *Control of anger*; cf. Alexiou (1999).
[102] It is true that, as Van Hoof (2008: 297) points out, Plutarch does not use the term "compliancy" (*dusōpia*) in the *Nicias*, and rarely at all in the *Lives*; but the characteristics of Nicias overlap with those of the compliant man – though Nicias', unlike the latter's, are displayed in the context of a great war in which Nicias played a leading role, and accordingly have more serious consequences.
[103] On Plutarch's *Nicias*, see Nikolaidis (1988); Piccirilli (1990b; 1993: ix–xvi); Titchener (1991; 2008); Duff (1999a: 56); Fletcher (2017; forthcoming).
[104] Duff (1999a: 101–130, esp. 104–107 on the overlap with *On tranquillity of mind*).
[105] See p. 74. And the overlap of themes should not be pressed too far: as Van der Stockt (2008) notes, none of the *Lives* deal with the vice of meddlesomeness (*polupragmosunē*), even though it gets a whole treatise in the *Moralia*.
[106] Contrast the different viewpoints from which Athens' response to the threat of Macedon is seen in the *Phocion* and *Demosthenes*; or conflict between Sparta and Thebes in the 370s and 360s BCE in *Agesilaus* and *Pelopidas*; or resistance to Roman domination of Greece in *Philopoemen* and its paired Life, *Flamininus*; or the events in the last years of the Roman Republic in *Lucullus, Cicero, Pompey, Crassus, Cato the Younger, Caesar, Brutus*, and *Antony* (on which see Pelling (1979; 1980); Beneker (2005)). Similarly with e.g. *Themistocles* and *Aristides*, or *Nicias* and *Alcibiades*, which each cover some of the same ground. See Duff (1999a: 133–135, cf. 307–308; 2011b: 73–74, with further bibliography).
[107] On *Cimon* 2 and its implications, see Duff (1999a: 55–56, 59–60, 162, 271; 2014: 339); Nikolaidis (2014: 356–357, 361). For similar comments on human nature never being wholly good, cf. *Agis/Cleomenes* 37[16].8; *How the young man should listen to poetry* 7, 25B–D; 26A; *Can virtue be taught?* 1, 439B; *On praising oneself inoffensively* 17, 545E.

between the political and the moral is not one that Plutarch would have recognized. In many Lives, the *demos* is presented as a fickle and potentially dangerous force, which needs kind but firm management (e.g. *Phocion, Pericles, Fabius*). Many also bring out the danger of a lack of harmony amongst the ruling elites (e.g. *Themistocles, Camillus*),[108] or the inadvisability of bringing in external powers to solve intra-Greek problems (*Philopoemen*; the standalone Life, *Aratus*). In the Roman Lives, Roman political institutions are assimilated to those of a Greek *polis*; the Senate, for example, becomes the Council, while the complex set of Roman popular electoral or legislative bodies becomes simply the Assembly.[109]

Finally, the *Parallel Lives* make the same Platonic dualistic assumptions about the soul we noted in the *On moral virtue:* in particular, the soul as a site of conflict between reason and passion, and the importance of education.[110] Coriolanus' failings, for example, are put down to a failure to adequately control his passions, which is itself shown to be a result of deficient education (*Coriolanus* 1.4–5; 15.4–5);[111] Pericles controls his own passions through reasoning, just as he controls the passions of the mob.[112] A recurrent focus in many Lives is ambition: in Greek, "love of honor" (*philotimia*), or "love of victory" (*philonikia*). In the Platonic conception of the soul, ambition, as we have seen, is an ambiguous force: it is absolutely necessary for the performance of anything worthwhile; a man without any "love of honor" would be in a sorry state. However, arising as it does from the irrational part of the soul, ambition must be properly controlled, and can easily topple over into contentiousness, spite, and a destructive desire to win at all costs and in all circumstances.[113] Almost all Lives explore this idea; it is particularly central to, for example, *Alexander–Caesar*; in the case

---

[108] On the theme of harmony (or its lack) amongst the elite in the *Lives*, see Wardman (1974: 57–63); Duff (1999a: 89–90). For this theme in Plutarch's treatment of the Persian Wars in particular, see Marincola (2010: 134–139; 2012); in *Themistocles–Camillus*, Duff (2010b). On concord (*homonoia*) as a contemporary concern, see n. 75 in this chapter.

[109] See Pelling (1986a). This leads to a flattening of the complexities of Roman political life, as Plutarch's Greek model had no space for e.g. the *equites* or the differences in composition of the different Roman popular assemblies. Similarly, Caesar's constitutional position at the end of his life is assimilated to a Greek tyranny: it is "acknowledged tyranny" in *Caesar* 57.1, a quotation of Plato, *Republic* 569b (Pelling 1997d: 221).

[110] Duff (1999a: 72–98). The importance of education in the *Lives*: Swain (1989b: 62–66; 1990a; 1996: 140–144); Pelling (1989); Duff (1999a: 72–78; 2008b).

[111] With an explicit quotation of Plato at *Coriolanus* 15.4. Discussion in Duff (1999a: 206–215).

[112] A virtue shared with Fabius Maximus, with whom he is paired: see Stadter (1975: 81–85; 1989: xxx–xxxi). On the way Plutarch projects the soul as a microcosm of the city, see Duff (1999a: 90–94).

[113] On *philotimia* in Plutarch, see Wardman (1955: 105–107; 1974: 115–124); Bucher-Isler (1972: 12–13, 31, 41, 58–59); Frazier (1988; 2014a); Duff (1999a: 83–87); Stadter (2011); and the papers in Roskam, De Pourcq, and Van der Stockt (2012).

of both men, desire for glory drives them on to great achievement, but also destroys them.[114]

## The *Parallel Lives*: The Reader as Moral Participant

The prologues, especially those to the *Demetrius–Antony* and *Aemilius Paulus–Timoleon*, might have led us to expect that each Life would provide either a positive paradigm to imitate or a negative one to avoid; that is, that there would be good Lives, whose subjects one should imitate, and bad Lives, whose subjects might act as deterrents, examples of what not to be. But, in fact, most Lives are a good deal more morally complex and less black and white than that. Even Demetrius and Antony, who are introduced as examples of "base and castigated lives," are admirable figures in many ways.[115] Conversely, even the most virtuous of Plutarch's biographical subjects are shown to have some less admirable qualities and to have made some mistakes; Pericles, for example, who is otherwise presented in a very positive light, is shown to have probably started the Peloponnesian War for disreputable personal reasons (*Pericles* 30–32);[116] and Agesilaus, whom Plutarch presents in the passage of *Progress in virtue* quoted earlier as one of the "good men" of the past to whom one might compare oneself, is presented in his Life, for all his military skill, his courage, and his love for his country, as also showing a deplorable pride and an inability to control his anger, which led to Sparta's total defeat.[117]

This complexity relates to a crucial difference between Plutarch's use of historical examples in the *Moralia* and in the *Lives*. In the *Moralia*, when Plutarch cites an example it is usually a single deed or characteristic that is highlighted, often in the form of a brief anecdote, and there is usually a single, fairly straightforward point; in the *Lives*, by contrast, we find an examination of whole careers, in which individual episodes are incorporated into a wider, and more complex, whole.[118] Thus, even though there is

[114] Cf. Steidle (1951: 13–24); Pelling (1997d); Duff (1999a: 85–87).
[115] Pelling (1980: 138) = (repr. 2002a: 105–106); (1988a: 10–18); Duff (1999a: 55–65; 2004: 282–283). On Demetrius and Antony as portrayed in some ways like heroes from tragedy, see De Lacy (1952: 168–171); Russell (1973a: 135); Pelling (1988a: 21–22); Mossman (1992: 100, 103; forthcoming); Andrei (1989: 78–82); Guillén Selfa (1997: 247–253); Duff (2004: 280–287); cf. Pimouguet-Pédarros (2011: 312–316). On the subjects of other Lives as tragic: Mossman (2014).
[116] Stadter (1987: 261–262); Piccirilli (1989; 1990a: xxxi–xxxii); Martin (1995: 15–16); Duff (1999a: 64).
[117] Luppino Manes (1989); Hamilton (1992: esp. 4205–4207; 1994); Hillman (1994: 272–279); Stadter (1999b; 2011: 247–249) = (repr. 2015a: 279–280).
[118] Stadter (2000: 498–500) = (repr. 2015a: 235–237).

considerable overlap, as we have noted, in the moral and political themes, and indeed in the historical personages and incidents treated,[119] the *Lives* are much more three-dimensional and much less reducible to simple black-and-white lessons.[120]

The *Lives* thus leave a lot more of the work of moral interpretation to the reader. In fact, although a major concern of each Life is the character of its subject, there is very little explicit comment about what he should or should not have done or what readers should or should not imitate.[121] In the works of practical ethics, even in those texts, such as *Control of anger*, where the advice and reflections are put in the mouth of a character within the text, the moral lessons are never in doubt.[122] This holds true at the level not only of such texts as a whole but also of the individual historical examples contained within them, which are each brought in to illustrate and confirm a single moral truth, which is usually stated explicitly. Thus, in *Control of anger*, after mentioning the example of Phocion urging the Athenians not to revolt from Macedonia in haste, Fundanus declares, "In the same way, I think, that the man hurrying to punish [a slave] in anger should say to himself . . ." (11, 459E–F). That is, the moral to be drawn from the historical example is stated clearly, as is, in this case, its practical application in the life of the reader. Similarly, in *Political advice*, after mentioning Sulla's generous sponsorship of his political protégés, Plutarch states, "To these men [i.e. to men who behaved like Sulla in this respect] one should attach oneself and cling closely" (12, 806E). When he turns to the subject of friends immediately after this, although he does not state so clearly the action the reader should take, he does make explicit how the historical examples he chooses should be judged: neither the examples of Cleon or Themistocles are to be praised, he says; Cleon "would have done better (*ameinon d' an epoiēse*) if he had rid himself of love of wealth, love of strife, envy and malice," whereas Themistocles "was also wrong" (*oud' houtos orthōs*) (13, 806F–807B).

---

[119] On the overlap between the subjects of the *Lives* and personages that occur in *Political advice*, see Mittelhaus (1911: 29–22); Carrière (1984: 14–18); Geiger (1981: 92–94). Cf. Stadter (2008) and Pelling (2002b) on the relationship of the *Lives* with *Political advice* and *Sayings of kings and commanders*.

[120] Pelling (1995); Stadter (1997; 2000); Duff (1999a: ch. 2 and *passim*); Hägg (2012: 275–277); Nikolaidis (2014: 355–358). Contrast the (simplistic) position of Jacobs (2018), who sees the *Lives* as providing "pragmatic advice" for contemporary statesmen and generals.

[121] For an analysis and categorization of the rare cases of such direct authorial comment in the *Parallel Lives*, see Duff (2011b: 61–64).

[122] Cf. Van Hoof (2010: 64–65; 2014: 45). Though, as she notes (2007: 71–72), the fact that Plutarch does not speak in his own voice in *Control of anger* does still leave some room for the reader's autonomy. See p. 57 in this chapter.

In the *Lives*, on the other hand, the moral or political lesson is generally left implicit.[123] In many cases, of course, commenting on a subject's character or labeling character-traits contains a strong implicit message, since in antiquity character was seen as essentially moral and character analysis often consists of the enumeration of virtues and vices. So, when Plutarch talks of Agesilaus' self-control (*sōphrosunē*) in the face of sexual pleasure (*Agesilaus* 11),[124] of Caesar's courage and sharing of his men's hardships (*Caesar* 17), or of Phocion's incorruptibility (*Phocion* 18), he invokes well-known virtues. In such cases it would be clear to an ancient reader, steeped in the language of virtue and vice, praise and blame, that virtues are admirable and to be imitated and vices despicable and to be both deplored and avoided. Plutarch himself makes that point, as we have seen, in several prologues. But he never says so explicitly in the body of the Lives. That is a step the reader is left to make for him- or herself.[125]

Furthermore, some Lives seem not to have clear-cut lessons. Take the *Life of Alexander*. There are, it is true, plenty of examples of virtuous, admirable behavior, and also, especially as the Life progresses, examples of conduct that is regrettable: Alexander's violence against his friends, his superstition, his arrogance. Some of this could be read as providing material for imitation and avoidance, though there is a fair amount of work to be done here by the reader in abstracting generalizable lessons from the incidents of Alexander's life, and then in seeing how they might be applied. But there is only so far that such an exercise could go: how many contemporary readers – important men, no doubt, in their own cities – would ever be faced with the challenges, opportunities, or dilemmas of an Alexander? How many would have even the opportunity to command an army, still less conquer a continent?[126] Furthermore, though one could attempt to go through the Life labeling each incident or action as "right" and "wrong," or listing Alexander's virtues and vices,[127] this would hardly do justice to its sophisticated literary texture, more tragedy than manual for

---

[123] See Duff (2011b).     [124] See Stadter (1995); Van der Stockt (2005).

[125] Compare *Political advice* 22, 817C, where Plutarch says explicitly that "it is citizen-like to endure the insults and anger of a man in office (*dēmotikon de kai blasphēmian enegkein kai orgēn arkhontos*)" and that "one should put off (*anatheteon*) one's defense until later," with *Pericles* 5 and 33–34 and *Fabius Maximus* 5, where Pericles and Fabius are said to have done just this, but where there is no authorial comment of approval, still less direct advice to the reader to do the same (though the prologue does highlight their ability "to endure the follies of their peoples and their colleagues" as a shared virtue: *Pericles* 2.5).

[126] Contrast Jacobs (2018), who ignores the gap between contemporary readers and the subjects of the *Lives* (see n. 120).

[127] As Plutarch does in the two speeches *On the fortune or virtue of Alexander*: encomia of Alexander that, in defending him from the charge of owing his success only to fortune, list his virtues in a one-sided way.

living. As Alexander moves inexorably eastwards towards the end of the *Life*, omens multiply and an aura of the supernatural overtakes him.[128] In such cases, if we can talk about a moralism, it is a deeper, less prescriptive one, which provokes thought rather than teaches a lesson.[129]

The paired structure of the *Lives* also deepens and complicates their moral texture. Some paired *Lives*, for example, when read against each other, seem to highlight ways in which different sorts of morality might conflict. Take the *Phocion–Cato Minor*, which provides two contrasting examples of how a statesman might react when faced with the inevitability of the imposition of autocracy on his state: Cato Minor bravely resisted Julius Caesar and, when all hope was gone, killed himself rather than compromise; Phocion, on the other hand, resisted Philip of Macedon while there was still a chance of success, then collaborated with Macedonian domination of Athens and sought, for the good of his fellow-citizens, to maintain good relations with the Macedonian kings. Cato's philosophical commitment to principle at all costs seems to be presented as virtuous and admirable, though even from the start several less attractive features seem to undermine this very positive presentation, suggesting he was extreme and over-rigid, as indeed is suggested in the prologue (*Phocion* 3.2–3). Might not Phocion's willingness to compromise his private principles for the common good, the reader is invited to ponder, have been the better course? But Phocion has no monopoly on virtue or political good sense; he ends up murdered by the *demos* that he had spent his life trying to guide and curb. At any rate, by juxtaposing these two *Lives*, Plutarch avoids providing a simple model for imitation or avoidance; rather, he invites the alert reader to engage in the job of weighing up their contrasting political choices.[130]

Indeed, this sense of the reader's own active involvement in the work of judging the subjects is prominent in both prologues and *synkriseis*. At the start of the *Demetrius–Antony* Plutarch argues that discrimination, or, as he puts it, "the power to make distinctions" (*tēn peri tas kriseis . . . dunamin, Demetrius* 1.1), is what marks out our rational capacity;[131] the senses, Plutarch argues, must passively receive all stimuli, but we can direct our

---

[128] Pelling (1997c: 247–250) = (repr. 2002a: 379–382).

[129] For this type of moralism in the *Lives*, see Pelling (1995); Duff (1999a; 2007–8; 2011b).

[130] For this reading of the *Phocion–Cato Minor*, see Duff (1999a: 131–160; 2011b: 68–69, 72–73). There is no *synkrisis* to the *Phocion–Cato Minor* to provide any kind of final judgment. On this pair of *Lives*, see also Trapp (1999); Zadorojnyi (2007). Similar questions are raised by the *Lysander–Sulla*: see Duff (1997; 1999a: 161–204); also Stadter (1992a; 2003–4: 91–94).

[131] On the emphasis on "discrimination" (*krisis*) in the *Demetrius–Antony* prologue, see Duff (2004). (Also on his prologue, see earlier in this chapter, p. 68.) Other prologues also distinguish ideal from

mind where we will. It is this power of discrimination, he continues, that
enables us to benefit from examples of bad conduct as much as good, so
that we can judge the correct response to each (1.1–5).[132]

The prologue to the *Pericles–Fabius* makes a similar point about our
ability to focus attention on what we choose. Towards the end of that
prologue Plutarch talks of how the study of the virtuous deeds of the past
"forms the spectator's character not through imitation but through the
investigation of the deed" (*tēi historiai tou ergou*). What Plutarch calls
"investigation" (*historia*) here probably refers not only to the author's
research and the resulting narrative but also to the reader's own thoughtful
analysis and reflection.[133] In fact, this sense of the reader's active involvement in a mutual investigation, in which he or she participates in the work
of assessing and judging the moral character of the subjects and responds
actively to the text through which these subjects are presented, recurs in the
very final words of the same prologue. After running briefly through some
of the similarities in character between Pericles and Fabius, Plutarch
concludes by inviting the reader's own participation: "But whether we
aim correctly at what we should, it is possible [sc. for you] to judge
(*krinein*) from my account" (*Pericles* 2.5). Several other prologues end
with an explicit or implied invitation to the reader to play an active part
in assessing the Lives of the two men that follow.[134]

Even in the closing *synkriseis*, where Plutarch weighs up the two subjects
against each other, the reader is accorded a good deal of autonomy. First,
the presentation of events in the *synkrisis* and the judgments made about
then can sometimes be radically different from that implied in the two
Lives: for example, Nicias' final surrender after the retreat from Syracuse is
treated in a much more negative way in the *synkrisis* than it had been in his
Life (*Nicias* 27.5–7 ~ *Nicias-Crassus* 5.4). This mismatch, which I have

---

less-than-ideal readers: *Nicias* 1.1; *Alexander* 1.1–3; see Pelling (2002c: 275–276); Duff (2014:
340–341).

[132] This notion is implied in the *Aemilius Paulus–Timoleon* prologue, where Plutarch talks (*Aemilius
Paulus* 1.2) of his "taking" or "selecting" (*lambanontes*) the most important and finest deeds of the
historical subjects (cf. Whitmarsh (2001: 55); Nikolaidis (2014: 358)); but it is not clear whether the
selectivity implied there refers to his activity as reader or as writer.

[133] On the prologue to the *Pericles–Fabius Maximus*, and on the interpretation of this sentence, see
Duff (1999a: 34–45). Further bibliography in n. 91.

[134] E.g. "You yourself will judge (*epikrineis autos*) these things from the narrative" (*Agis/Cleomenes* 2.9);
"We pass over perhaps some additional similarities, but it will not be difficult to collect them from
the narrative itself" (*Cimon* 3.3); "it would be difficult to judge whether nature made them more
alike in their manners or fortune in the facts of their lives" (*Demosthenes* 3.5); "they will make it
a matter of dispute (*diamphisbētēsin*) whether the greatest of their successes were a result of their
good fortune or their good sense" (*Aemilius Paulus* 1.6).

termed "closural dissonance," is a notable feature of several *synkriseis*; it has the effect of presenting the reader with two distinct views of the past, and with two distinct ways of evaluating the subjects of the two Lives that have preceded, which the reader is left to evaluate.[135] Secondly, the reader is invited throughout to rank the two subjects across a series of headings (military success, corruptibility, etc.): who was superior in this aspect or that? But in almost all cases neither of the two men is favored or judged superior overall and most end with no final verdict; there is, in other words, a studied even-handedness in how they are treated. In addition, even in the five *synkriseis* that conclude with a closing judgment, four invite the reader to judge for themselves whether they agree or disagree. For example, the *synkrisis* to the *Philopoemen–Flamininus* ends: "Since, after this examination, the difference [between them] is hard to define, consider (*skopei*) whether we shall seem to umpire unfairly if we award the Greek the crown for military experience and generalship, and the Roman the one for goodness and justice" (*Philopoemen–Flamininus* 3.5). The *synkrisis* of the unique double-pair *Agis/Cleomenes–Gracchi* prefaces the closing judgment with "You can see for yourself (*sunorais . . . kai autos*) the difference [between them] from what has been said" (*Agis/Cleomenes–Gracchi* 5.7).[136] The reader, far from being a passive observer, is a participant in the act of moral and political judgment.

This brings us back to the need for an active, engaged, and mature reader. In *How the young man should listen to poetry*, Plutarch envisaged the young reader learning to read morally: not waiting to be told whether an action was right or wrong, or assuming that every action or sentiment of the heroes about whom they read was to be imitated, but making their own moral judgments on them. Plutarch envisaged that as a first step to philosophy (14, 37B; cf. 1, 15F). In the *Lives*, Plutarch assumes a more mature reader, who is not only able to read morally and allot praise and blame but also takes part in the kind of active enquiry that the *Lives* invite: a reader who asks questions, who sees the moral and political complexity of the *Lives* as an opportunity to flex their philosophical muscles and employ their discrimination.[137] Through engaging with whole Lives and facing the

---

[135] For the term "closural dissonance," and examples and discussion, see Duff (1999a: 200–204, 263–286; 2000: 148–161; 2011b: 74–75).

[136] Picking up *Agis/Cleomenes* 2.9 (see n. 134 in this chapter). The passage continues: "But if it is necessary to set forth a decision about each one, I vote (*tithēmi*) that Tiberius was first of all of them in virtue, that the young Agis committed fewer errors, and that in achievement and daring Gaius fell far short of Cleomenes." Other examples at the end of *synkriseis* where readers are invited to judge for themselves: *Cimon–Lucullus* 3.6; *Philopoemen–Flamininus* 3.5; *Lysander–Sulla* 5.6.

[137] For the notion of the "critical" reader of the *Lives*: Duff (1999a: *passim*; 2007–8; 2011b); Whitmarsh (2001: 56–57); König (2007: 49–50).

moral complexities to which they give rise, the moral sensibilities of such readers are expanded. And if, in reading the *Lives*, the reader is confronted with difficult moral and political problems to which there is no straight-forward right answer, this is all to the good, since for Plutarch, as for Plato and Aristotle, "being at a loss" and "asking questions" was the beginning of philosophy.[138]

## Further Reading

On Plutarch's moral-educative programme in the *Lives*, the essential starting point is Pelling (1995) = (2002: 237–251). Duff (1999a) is a comprehensive study, emphasizing the complexity of the moral register and the lack of clear-cut lessons; the implications of this are expanded in Duff (2011a). Other important studies of this aspect of the *Lives* include Frazier (1996); Stadter (1997; 2000; 2003–4); Duff (2007–8; 2008a); Nikolaidis (2014). On the prologues, where Plutarch declares his moral-educative purpose, see also Stadter (1988); Duff (1999a: 13–51; 2011b; 2014). Pelling's (2002a) and Stadter's (2015a) collections of papers have much of value, as do the papers by various authors in Roskam and Van der Stockt (2011) and Beck (2014a). Gill (1990) is excellent on the judgmental aspect of ancient conceptions of character.

For the *Moralia*, the best starting point is Van Hoof (2010) on the popular-philosophical works; also Ingenkamp (1971); Nikolaidis (2011). Xenophontos (2016) provides a useful overview and summary. On *How the young man should listen to poetry* Konstan (2004) is excellent, as is the commentary by Hunter and Russell (2011). Good introductions to *On moral virtue* are provided by Gill (2006: 219–238) and Opsomer (2012: 319–328), and to *Political advice* by Desideri (1986) and Swain (1996: 162–183). There are now commentaries on each text in the Italian series *Corpus Plutarchi Moralium*.

---

[138] *On the E at Delphi* 1, 384E–F and 385C (*'epei de tou philosophein' ephē 'to zētein <arkhē, tou de zētein>* to thaumazein kai aporein*': probably alluding to Plato, *Theaetetus*. 115d); *Table talk* 5.7, 680C–D; 8.10, 734C–D; *Platonic questions* 1.4, 1000D–E. See Kechagia (2011a: 93–95). On the *Table talk* (literally, *Sympotic questions*) as encouraging the reader's own active engagement with the problems discussed (scientific in this case, rather than moral, e.g. 690F and 694D, see König (2007: esp. 44–50, 56); Klotz and Oikonomopoulou (2011b: 25); Oikonomopoulou (2011: esp. 120–121, 127–128).

CHAPTER 4

# In the Spirit of Plato

## Jan Opsomer

Philosophy is all-important in the work of Plutarch. The Chaeronean is the author of technical-philosophical treatises, he writes manuals describing the philosophical techniques of the care of the soul, he exemplifies philosophy as a living praxis by writing (to some extent idealized) philosophical dialogues, and in his biographies he offers further material – case studies – for philosophical reflection. The variety of topics, methods, and strategies is truly perplexing. Until not so long ago, confusion reigned concerning Plutarch's philosophical allegiance. Older scholarly literature often portrays him as an eclectic,[1] sometimes as a crypto-Stoic,[2] sometimes as a skeptic,[3] more often as an unorthodox Platonist.[4] A half-specialist like M. Foucault[5] occasionally quotes Plutarch as someone who practiced *Stoic* technologies of the self. However, since R. Jones' monograph *The Platonism of Plutarch* (1916),[6] it should have been clear that Plutarch was an outspoken Platonist.

Plutarch repeatedly and unambiguously professes his loyalty to Plato and the Academic tradition. His teacher Ammonius[7] led an informal school he called the "Academy." Plutarch followed in his footsteps: his

This chapter is part of a project that has received funding from the European Research Council (ERC) under the European Union's Horizon 2020 research and innovation program (grant agreement no. 885273).

[1] For a critique of the notion of eclecticism, see Dillon (1988); Donini (1988). Especially in non-specialized literature, but not only there (cf. Ziegler 1951: 938–939), Plutarch used to be portrayed as an unoriginal and second-rate philosopher, but these negative judgments (revealing their authors' own preconceptions about "good" philosophy) become rarer now. This may reflect a shift in philosophical taste but is certainly also due to a better understanding of Plutarch's intellectual project.

[2] Cf. Oakesmith (1902: xvii); Gréard (1880: 59).   [3] Cf. Schroeter (1911).

[4] Already in the first edition of his influential history of Greek philosophy, Zeller (1868: 141) labels Plutarch as a Pythagoreanizing Platonist, but at the same time calls him an eclectic and considers him to be strongly influenced by Stoicism (144-145).

[5] Cf. Foucault (2001: 108). Elsewhere Foucault mentions Platonizing tendencies: Foucault (1984: 209–210).

[6] Reprinted as Jones (1980).   [7] For Ammonius, see Whittaker (1969); Opsomer (2009).

writings teem with Platonic allusions, metaphors, and ideas; always he cites
Plato approvingly,[8] even reverently. Every year he celebrates Plato's and
Socrates' birthdays.[9] As regards other philosophical schools, Plutarch often
attacks them vehemently, in particular the "impious" Epicureans. The
Stoics are treated with more respect, yet their views too provoke harsh
criticism. If we look at the extant works, one wonders how there could be
any doubt about Plutarch's philosophical home: there are expositions of
Platonic philosophy (see later), invectives against the Epicureans (*Non posse
suaviter vivi secundum Epicurum, Adversus Colotem, An recte dictum sit
latenter esse vivendum*), and anti-Stoic works (*De Stoicorum repugnantiis,
De communibus notitiis adversus Stoicos*, but texts such as *De virtute morali*
and *De sollertia animalium* are also arguably anti-Stoic polemical tracts). So
how could learned readers have been mistaken or uncertain about
Plutarch's philosophical allegiance? The answer will become clear in this
chapter.

There can be no doubt that we now have a better understanding of the
thought of Plutarch and of the philosophy of his day. Plutarch's works give
expression to many voices, but scholars now realize that this does not mean
that a unity of intention is lacking. I shall argue that this combination of
unitary intention with polyphonic variety is connected to a particular
epistemological stance adopted by Plutarch that demands a certain caution
in the expression of one's own views and requires the serious examination
of the views of others. This should not, however, be confused with eclectic
doctrine shopping or doctrinal confusion on Plutarch's part.

Plutarch's Platonism is obviously not identical with the philosophy of
Plato himself.[10] Important philosophical developments had taken place
that inevitably shaped the interpretation of Plato's texts. Yet the latter
remain the main source for Plutarch's philosophy: Plutarch goes back to
the texts themselves and tries to understand them as testimonies of
a coherent philosophical system – what is more, of *the* philosophical
truth. His interpretation is influenced by at least two traditions: neo-
Pythagoreanism, which is in fact a Pythagoreanizing Platonism, and the
tradition of Plato's own Academy, which for an important part of the

---

[8]  Plutarch is even willing to agree with Plato where subsequent scientific discoveries had proven him
wrong, as is shown by *Quaestiones convivales* 7.1.
[9]  Compare *Quaestiones convivales* 717B.
[10]  Holtorf (1913) aims at offering a systematic doctrinal comparison between Plato and Plutarch,
criticizing Plutarch whenever the latter deviates from what Holtorf perceives to be the correct
interpretation of Plato.

intervening period had had a skeptical outlook, of various types and in varying degrees.[11]

At least as important as the question of philosophical affiliation is that of the very concept of philosophy adopted by Plutarch. Philosophy was not just a matter of doctrines, but also a praxis. As a praxis, it presupposed a strong commitment to an open-minded search for truth. It was, moreover, not a solitary praxis but held to be accomplishable only through cooperation in dialogue. As a social praxis, it was informed by cultural values and at the same time it strongly conveys a system of references as well as a certain ideal about culture and education to the cultural elite – an ideal to which Plutarch himself wishes to conform and wishes to be seen to conform.[12] Thus Plutarch offers himself up as a model for the philosophically educated person, who is knowledgeable in history, literature, natural science, cosmology, medicine, and religion, and applies to these domains a coherent philosophical template. This framework is supported by rational arguments and authoritative texts, the most important of which are the Platonic dialogues.

There is thus a continuum from works that would not seem to be philosophical at all, but on closer inspection turn out to be imbued with philosophical ideas, over works of practical ethics – misleadingly categorized by K. Ziegler as popular-philosophical works[13] – to the technical expositions of doctrine and exegesis of Plato. If we want to grasp the coherence of Plutarch's thought, we should start from the technical expositions before we examine the applications in different contexts. I suggest, however, that we should take a look first at what the Platonists from later antiquity considered to be Plutarch's core philosophical doctrines and interpretations of Plato.

### Reports on Plutarch's Philosophy from Late Antiquity

Later Platonists – those that are usually called Neoplatonists – did not regard Plutarch as a major philosopher, as was the fate of most if not all Platonists of the Early Empire prior to Plotinus. Yet the occasional

---

[11] These three aspects – Plato, neo-Pythagoreanism, Academy – are listed in Donini (2002: 267) and Bonazzi (2003: 237–240).

[12] A study of Plutarch's practical ethics, seen rather against its cultural and historical background and with special attention paid to the role of rhetoric and to the notion of cultural capital, is Van Hoof (2010).

[13] Ziegler (1951: 637). The term tells us more about the concept of "serious" philosophy tacitly assumed by those who use it to categorize Plutarch's works than about Plutarch's own understanding of these works. The so-called popular-philosophical works in fact address the cultural elite but differ from the more technical works in that they do not require their readers to be trained in Platonic philosophy. Cf. Pelling (2011b).

discussions of Plutarch's views and the use that was made of his works show that his interpretations were still held to deserve a serious treatment. Certainly, the later Platonists looked at Plutarch through their peculiar lens and by doing so highlighted important aspects of Plutarch's thought that were arguably central to Plutarch as well. Yet they also left certain aspects of Plutarch's philosophy in the dark – most importantly, the same aspect they had themselves forgotten about in their readings of Plato: that is, the dialogical and to some extent aporetic nature of Platonic philosophy.

In late antiquity[14] Plutarch was known – in some learned circles – for the following views, all considered to some extent as idiosyncratic:

1. The idea that the world was created through an active intervention by a creator god. This view is recognizably based on Plutarch's interpretation of Plato's *Timaeus*, which can be said to be "literal" in at least these two interrelated aspects: in Plutarch's interpretation of the role of a personal, thinking (i.e. deliberating) creator god – the Demiurge – and in Plutarch's claim that his demiurgic intervention chronologically precedes the origin of the world.[15]

2. The actual existence of a disordered state prior to the creation of the world.[16]

3. The distinction between pre-cosmic and cosmic time.[17]

4. The doctrine of a disordered world-soul as the principle of evil.[18]

5. The generation of the world-soul out of two elements: (i) an irrational soul – the "divisible nature" – and (ii) "indivisible being," in some sources described as a divine *soul*, in others as an intellect.[19]

6. The view that the Platonic Forms have their existence in the divine soul.[20]

7. The ungeneratedness of matter, understood as ontological independence and coevality with god.[21]

---

[14] The source for these doxographical bits of information was probably Porphyry's commentary on the *Timaeus*. See Opsomer (2001: 188). Plutarch's views are usually grouped with those of Atticus (ca. 150–200 CE).

[15] Cf. Proclus, *In Timaeum* 1.276.30–277.3; Philoponus, *De aet. mund.* 211.10–14; 519.22–25.

[16] Proclus informs us that Iamblichus and Porphyry criticized Plutarch and Atticus for accepting the actual existence of pre-cosmic matter and soul, as that would mean that there was a time when the Demiurge did not take providential care of matter and soul (*In Timaeum* 1.382.12–20; 384.2–5; 391.6–17). As we shall see, this is indeed what Plutarch believes: the Demiurge only exercises providence over his own works.

[17] Proclus *In Timaeum* 1.276.30–277.7; 1.286.26–29.

[18] Cf. Proclus, *In Timaeum* 1.381.26–382.12 (at 1.391.10 he attributes it to Atticus alone). Proclus refers to the same view, without naming its proponents, in *De mal. subst.* 40.4–7; 45.

[19] Proclus, *In Timaeum* 2.153.25–154.1.      [20] Syrianus, *In Met.* 105.36–106.5.

[21] Proclus, *In Timaeum* 1.384.2–5 (Plutarch and Atticus); cf. 1.391.6–17 (Atticus alone).

It was obvious to ancient philosophers that all of these views were based on readings of Plato's dialogues, taken as authoritative texts in which certain theological and cosmological truths are revealed.

This list may not be exhaustive. Late ancient authors will probably have known a great deal more about Plutarch's philosophy – including doctrines and works that we do not – but may not have bothered to quote him in all the cases in which they agreed. The list indeed contains only items that were somehow controversial. Plutarch's belief in divine providence, his views on virtue and vice, his opposition to the Stoics and Epicureans will have met with favor, and hence we do not know very much about their ancient reception, with some notable exceptions. Thus his treatise on the tardiness of divine punishment was a source of inspiration for Proclus, who freely quoted from it in his *Ten Questions on Providence*. And the final speech of Plutarch's teacher Ammonius in *De E apud Delphos* made some impression on the Christian bishop Eusebius,[22] who delighted in finding Christian views confirmed in a pagan author. He compares Ammonius' explanation that the Delphic god is addressed as "thou art" (*ei*) with the god of the Septuagint who claims that he is the One that *is*. In general, Plutarch's view of a personal, caring Demiurge, for being closer to popular views,[23] was more congenial to early Christian theological conceptions than the abstract metaphysical principles we find especially in later Platonists.[24] After all, Plutarch was a Delphic priest.

## A Methodological Difficulty

If we compare the doctrinal elements listed earlier with ideas expressed in Plutarch's own works, significant divergences appear. The reason is to be sought partly in the kind of slight distortions typical of doxographic reports, partly in the changed philosophical context: a case in point, as we shall see, is the emergence of a new concept of intellect that was to dominate the later Platonic tradition.

The readers of Plutarch who want to find out what Plutarch's final thoughts on specific issues were see themselves confronted with considerable difficulties. Plutarch's works teem with different voices expressing

---

[22] Eusebius, *Praep. ev.*, XI, 10, 15–16.

[23] See MacMullen (1997: Chapter 3) for popular views on providential intervention by personal deities, spirits, demons, and the like. The author provides a wealth of material from different sources spanning early Roman, later Roman, and early medieval times.

[24] Another Christian praising Plutarch as a true philosopher is Origenes (*Contra Celsum* 5.57 = Plutarch fr. 173).

various views. In a fraction of the corpus only does the author seem to speak to his readers directly, in his own voice, but even there he does not always seem to be fully consistent with what he says elsewhere. On closer inspection, however, a coherent body of thought transpires. It is as if Plutarch in this respect, too, imitates his master Plato, who was believed to be a thinker whose vocabulary is multifarious, but whose doctrines are unitary (*polyphōnos, ou polydoxos*).[25]

It is a sound methodological principle to start with the works in which Plutarch speaks in his own voice. These are often also the works that are more technical than others. Having thus established a doctrinal core, it will become much easier to disentangle the positions discussed in the works that have a more dialogical character, or where the narrator tends to hide (which is typically the case in the *Lives* or e.g. *Mulierum virtutes*). Recognizing the dialogical or dialectical character of his works[26] – in the dialogues, of course, but also in *Quaestiones convivales* and even in works that are not immediately dialectical in nature, such as the various *Quaestiones* (*Zētēmata, Aitia, Problēmata*) – is often the key to understanding Plutarch's philosophical observations.

## Platonism in Plutarch's Day

The dialogical nature of Plutarch's work is in two important ways connected with the time in which he was active: at this period of history, (a) the culture of philosophical debate was still alive and not yet dominated by the monological way of doing philosophy that would rule in late antiquity;[27] and (b) Platonism found itself in a transitional phase in which Platonists had not yet settled a number of dogmatic issues, but were examining and comparing quite divergent philosophical positions, Platonist and others. Let us elaborate these two points somewhat more.

In Hellenistic times Platonism went through a phase in which epistemological issues were held to be of primary philosophical importance. More particularly, any attempt to make doctrinal assertions seemed to be compromised by a kind of skepticism on behalf of the Academics. Under Arcesilaus and Carneades the Academy countered the strong truth claims made by other schools, especially the Stoics. In the course of these polemics, the Academics developed clever arguments and strategies to promote

---

[25] Stobaeus 2.7.4a, 55.5–6 Wachsmuth-Hense.
[26] Cf. Van der Stockt (2000a) and Brouillette and Giavatto (2011).
[27] Cf. Opsomer (2005: 199–200; 2007b: 287–288); Goldhill (2008).

the suspension of judgment. As the Hellenistic epoch drew to a close, Philo of Larissa (159–84 BCE) devised a more conciliatory position in the form of fallibilism: it is fine to hold and defend certain positive views and even say that one has a firm grasp on them, as long as one remains prepared to abandon them if a more satisfactory explanation presents itself.[28] It is this philosophical approach that is congenial to Plutarch's, but is also very much in the spirit of Plato himself. Plutarch expressly refers to the *eikōs logos* of Plato's *Timaeus* or the distinction between material conditions and teleological causes in the same dialogue, or also in the *Phaedo*, when discussing epistemological issues related to the study of natural phenomena.[29] Plutarch's attitude toward Philo's contemporary, Antiochus, is more ambivalent.[30] The latter attempted a new doctrinal synthesis, yet his views were held to be too close to other schools and too un-Platonic by many later Platonists – though he was in fact more influential than one might think.[31]

Plutarch's time also saw the gradual emergence of a Platonic system. As a matter of fact, many Platonists made attempts at systematizing Plato's works and what information they garnered from an indirect tradition, for instance in reports on Plato's philosophy found in Aristotle and others, or various texts that claimed, rightly or not, to represent an ancient tradition. These attempts at systematization were rarely in agreement and various tendencies fought for prevalence.[32] The drive behind the phenomenon may have come from competition from other schools. Not only did Stoicism constitute a strong system; the much-improved availability of Aristotle's esoteric works, too, coinciding with the revival of Aristotelianism that had set in at the end of the Hellenistic period, drew attention to a corpus that could convey the sense of a systematic body of thought.

A crucial factor in the development of Platonism in the Early Empire was the flourishing of Pythagoreanism. This was also the time, roughly, when most pseudo-Pythagorean literature was written. Plutarch himself was certainly influenced by these tendencies, yet seems to have been more cautious than others in integrating Pythagorean or Aristotelian ideas into

---

[28] See Brittain (2001: esp. 166–168).
[29] *Timaeus* 68e–69a; *Phaedo* 97b–99d; Plutarch, *De defectu oraculorum* 435E–436F; *Nicias* 23.4–5.
[30] Bonazzi (2009).    [31] Cf. Glucker (1978: 13–120); Brittain (2001); Sedley (2012).
[32] The results can be seen in doxographic reports and handbooks: Albinus, *Prologus*; Alcinous, *Didaskalikos*; Apuleius, *De Platone*; the doxography in Stobaeus, 2.7. 37.18–56.12 Wachsmuth, attributed (on rather shaky grounds) to Arius Didymus (cf. various contributions in Reydams-Schils 2011). Aspects of this systematization movement are studied in Bonazzi and Opsomer (2009). The contrast with older scholarly literature is revealing: Dörrie (1969: 524) considers Plutarch to be a heterodox Platonist, but recent scholarship has shown that there was no Platonic orthodoxy.

his philosophy. As far as the Chaeronean is concerned, Plato remains the ultimate authority. Plutarch's philosophy therefore has an essentially exegetical character. Since Plato was believed to have revealed deep truths in his works without always teaching in a straightforward way,[33] Plutarch regarded it as his principal task as a philosopher to explain obscure texts, to solve the difficulties posed by certain passages, to smooth out apparent inconsistencies, and to select passages that would provide optimal access to the truth.[34] This way of doing philosophy was typical of his time, to the extent that Plutarch could consider himself already as part of an exegetical *tradition*. Plato is not the only thinker clad with authority; other schools[35] and traditions were also believed to contain valuable insights. Also religious rites and customs, if properly explained, were believed to be reliable sources of primitive wisdom.[36]

## The Doctrinal Core of Plutarch's Philosophical Thought

What it is most important to have for a Platonist are true beliefs and, insofar as possible, knowledge, about three domains: the soul, divinity, and the cosmos. The world has been created by a divine craftsman, the Demiurge and at the same time highest deity, out of preexisting material. Plutarch thus understands the *Timaeus* literally in the sense that he considers the creation as a temporal[37] event that was preceded by a precosmic state. The divine craftsman imparted order – that is, rationality – to a preexisting disorderly soul. Thus this soul became a cosmic, well-ordered soul. With its help, the Demiurge structured the preexisting matter, making it the body of the world. Human souls have a structure analogous to that of the world-soul. They too have a dual nature: they contain a primeval recalcitrant element but also have a share in rationality, present

---

[33] Plato was believed to express himself occasionally in riddles in order to avoid those who were not yet philosophically mature enough wrongly thinking that they had understood his ideas. See, for example, *De defectu oraculorum* 420F. Similarly on Egyptian myths: *De Iside et Osiride* 354C.

[34] For this Plutarch could probably already fall back on existing lists or collections of passages that were held to be of key importance. For the practice of epitomizing Plato's works, see Baltes (2005a). The labeling and categorizing of the dialogues was another important means to make the corpus more accessible, but also to guide decisions on important interpretive issues. See Mansfeld (1994: 89–97); Tarrant (1993: 31–107; 2000: 1–9).

[35] On Plutarch's attitude to the Stoics, which strikes a subtle balance between criticism of certain tenets and respect for their general philosophical outlook, the standard work remains Babut (1969b). See also Dillon and Zadorojnyi's Chapter 5 in this volume and Opsomer (2014; 2017).

[36] This approach to philosophy, though not entirely new, gained prominence in post-Hellenistic times. See Frede (1999); Boys-Stones (2001).

[37] Strictly speaking, Plutarch would not say it took place *in time*, as he held that time originated together with the world-soul and thus with the cosmos. See later in this chapter.

in them somehow as a part of the Demiurge. Both elements are interwoven in such a way that neither of them exists, during our life on earth, in a pure, unmixed state. The traces of the original, disorderly soul constitute an ineradicable source of disorder; that is, of vice. It is of the highest importance for us to be constantly aware of this dual nature in order that we control the disorderly element as much as is humanly possible. At the same time, we should be confident that god exercises providence over the world and over our souls. For, as there is a part of him in both our souls and the cosmic soul, he is to be considered a father of these souls. This is Plutarch's philosophy in a nutshell. Let us now look at some points in greater detail.

## Plutarch on Cosmogony, Psychogony, and Transcendent Entities

Plato's works contain a striking contradiction regarding the nature of the soul: according to the *Phaedrus* (245c5–246a2), soul is without beginning, but according to the *Timaeus* (esp. 34b10–36d9), it has been created by the Demiurge.[38] Since it was Plutarch's firm conviction that the dialogues comprise a systematic body of thought, without any inconsistencies, he had to find a solution to this problem. Other Platonists facing the same problem had adopted a reading of the *Timaeus* that was in this respect nonliteral. Already the earliest successors of Plato had argued, in order to counter criticisms leveled by Aristotle, that according to Plato the world and the world-soul were in fact everlasting, without beginning or end. Plato, so they claimed, had merely told the story of the generation of the world for didactic reasons, to explain its structure.[39] For reasons that will become clear later in this chapter, Plutarch rejected this way out of the problem,[40] adopting instead a different solution that also agreed with his interpretation of the crucial passage, *Timaeus* 35a:[41] Plato is talking about

---

[38] Cf. *Platonicae quaestiones* 4, 1002E–1003A; *De animae procreatione in Timaeo* 1016A.
[39] See *De animae procreatione in Timaeo* 1013A, 1017B, referring to the view of the Old Academics Crantor and Xenocrates. Cf. Cherniss (1976a: 168–169, note e).
[40] *De animae procreatione in Timaeo* 1014A–B. Plutarch calls this literal interpretation unusual, yet it appears to have been not so unusual in Hellenistic times. Cf. Cicero's interpretation: *Tusc.* 1.70; *Timaeus* 2.5 (28b6–c7); *De nat. deor.* 1.2; and for the Epicurean reading of the *Timaeus*, Cicero, *De nat. deor.* 1.21; Lucretius 5.168–173; ps.-Plutarch, *Placita philosophorum* 881B–D (= *Doxographi Graeci* 300a18–301a19). The Lamprias Catalogue lists a work, *On the Fact That According to Plato the World Has Been Generated* (no. 66).
[41] For Plutarch's interpretation of this obscure passage, see Opsomer (2004). Plutarch finds further support in *Timaeus* 30a3–5, where a disorderly pre-cosmic motion is mentioned (assuming the principle that where there is motion, it is caused by a soul: cf. *De animae procreatione in Timaeo* 1014B–D; 1016D; 1017D). He also refers (*De animae procreatione in Timaeo* 1014B, 1015B, *De Iside et Osiride* 370F) to the "two souls" mentioned in *Laws* X, 897b–899b (see later in this chapter).

two different souls, or about two different stages of soul. When he calls the soul ungenerated, he refers to soul as such, a kinetic and cognitive force without temporal beginning or end. But when he describes the fabrication of the soul by the Demiurge, he refers to the origin of the cosmic – that is, the well-ordered – soul. The generation of the cosmic soul is inherent in the fact that the Demiurge bestows order, as somehow a part of himself, upon the preexisting soul. As soon as this soul becomes orderly, it starts to impose order on the world-body, thus assisting the god in his Demiurgic activity (e.g. *Platonicae quaestiones* 4, 1003A–B; *De animae procreatione in Timaeo* 1030C). The basic ingredients that make up the world are "soul itself," also called "the being that becomes divisible in the realm of bodies" and "indivisible, unchanging being"; that is, intellect that stems from the Demiurge himself. To this first mixture are added the principles of Identity and Difference (*Timaeus* 35a).[42]

Prior to the intervention of the Demiurge, soul was in a disorderly state and the cause of chaotic movement. Once it has been integrated into the cosmic soul, however, the motions of the whole are predominantly orderly, yet the influence of the original soul cannot be completely undone by the Demiurge. In our present world the original soul, though firmly encapsulated in the cosmic soul, makes its presence felt in what is irrational, excessive, disorderly – in other words, evil. Because of this theory of the disorderly soul, so Plutarch argues, Plato managed to avoid the problems that would later on vex the Stoics: the latter adopted Plato's idea of a providential god who steers the world (turning him into an immanent principle at the level of Plato's world-soul), but for lack of a counter-principle they cannot explain evil. They would see themselves forced either to deny its existence or to introduce it without its having a cause. Yet the acceptance of uncaused events constitutes a threat to the unity and consistency of the universe.[43]

Plato, on the contrary, accepts a counter-principle that is independent from god, at least in Plutarch's understanding. Plutarch thus endorses, and ascribes to Plato, a mitigated dualism – mitigated because the counter-principle is not equally strong and is dominated by the divine.[44] Here, as in many other cases, Platonism allegedly steers a sound middle course between the Epicureans, who reject divine providence, and the Stoics, who exaggerate its extension: "it is impossible for anything bad whatsoever

[42] *De animae procreatione in Timaeo* 1014D–E (1014E for the expression "soul itself"); 1024C; *Platonicae quaestiones* 2, 1001B–C.
[43] *De animae procreatione in Timaeo* 1015B–C; *De Iside et Osiride* 369D; 371A.
[44] *De Iside et Osiride* 371A.

to come about where god is the author of everything, or anything good where god is the author of nothing."[45]

Plutarch connects this cosmic dualism with a dualism of principles. Returning to the ingredients of the world-soul, Plutarch explains that indivisible being derives from what is in fact a higher principle, Identity, which in turn derives from an even higher principle, the One. Similarly, divisible being derives from Difference, which derives from the Dyad.[46] Thus Plutarch incorporates into his interpretation of the *Timaeus* a Pythagorean dualism of principles of the type that was popular among Platonists of his time. He supports this view by giving a brief doxography of dualism that supposedly shows Plato to be part of an ancient tradition.[47] It is remarkable, however, that Plutarch carefully avoids making the Dyad itself a principle of evil, and hence also introducing evil at the level of principles.[48] Actual division – loss of unity – is only introduced in the realm of bodies, as is indicated by the description of soul itself as "the kind of being that *becomes* divisible around bodies" (*Timaeus* 35a2–3).[49] Moreover, Plutarch points out that there is no interaction – and hence no evil action either – at the level of principles; the principles only become "fertile" (*gonimoi*) – that is, involved in becoming (*genesis*) – when mixed together in the soul.[50] Later Platonists were therefore right when they cited Plutarch for the view that an evil soul – and not the Dyad – is the principle of evil. Yet Plutarch did not hold the view, as is sometimes believed, that there are two separate, warring souls in the world. Where he expresses himself with precision, he makes it clear that the evil soul has been integrated into the world-soul; it has ceased to exist as an independent free-standing power. In the pre-cosmic state there was one soul, the original soul, and in the cosmic state too there is just one (universal) soul, which consists of a mixture of the former and a divine element.[51]

---

[45] *De Iside et Osiride* 369A–B.    [46] *De animae procreatione in Timaeo* 1024D.

[47] *De animae procreatione in Timaeo* 1026B–C. A slightly different doxography features in *De Iside et Osiride* 369D–371A. On these doxographies, see Mansfeld (1992: 274–290) and Donini (1994b: 5075–5082).

[48] One may usefully compare the view of Speusippus: fr. 45a–b Tarán, with Dillon (1996) 12. Plutarch's view is different, though, in that he does not claim, as Speusippus does, that the One is not good either.

[49] Cf. Opsomer (2004: 149–150, n. 56).

[50] *De animae procreatione in Timaeo* 1025F–1026A; *De Iside et Osiride* 369C–D. I defend this interpretation more extensively in Opsomer (2007c: 383).

[51] Sometimes Plutarch expresses himself less accurately and creates the impression that there are two opposing souls: cf. *De animae procreatione in Timaeo* 1016C and *De Iside et Osiride* 370F (discussing Plato's equally ambiguous account in *Laws* X 896d–897d; see, however, 897b2–3). The view to which he is committed, however, is clear from the more technical descriptions in *De animae procreatione in Timaeo*.

It should also be noticed that Plutarch implicitly equates the One with the Demiurge,[52] which fits his view that the Demiurge is at the same time the supreme god.[53] The latter view was not unusual for Platonists of Plutarch's day,[54] but would become highly problematic for later Platonists, who stressed the absolute simplicity of the One, which they held to be incompatible with the demiurgic activity. Plutarch's Demiurge is, moreover, an intellect,[55] which again agrees with later Platonic ortho-doxy. But this also means that for Plutarch the first principle is an intellect. This is a view that many, but not all later, Platonists reject, again because it does not seem to agree with the supposed absolute simplicity of the first principle. Plutarch's Demiurgic intellect is assisted in its creative activity by the world-soul, but unlike other Platonists, Plutarch does not create a whole hierarchy of Demiurges.

Some issues that were of great interest to (especially) later Platonists appear to have been less so for Plutarch. We find in the extant works no treatment of the structure of the intelligible cosmos (yet we know from the so-called Lamprias Catalogue[56] that he probably wrote more technical-philosophical works than we possess). The precise relationship between Platonic Forms and intellect remains unclear, for instance. What is clear is that the Demiurge, who is equated with the first god or the One or the Good, exists among the intelligibles, and that the Forms are around god. This presumably means that they are situated on the same ontological level without being identical. Plutarch assigns a certain priority to the Demiurge, but apparently rejects the popular "Middle" Platonic view that the Forms primarily exist as thoughts of the divine intellect.[57] Nor does he distinguish strictly between the intelligible and intellect as different ontological realms. He calls the Demiurge both an intellect and intelligible.[58] It was probably Plutarch's view that we have no way of knowing the precise relations that obtain between divine entities.[59] Hence it is a sign of respect for the gods, or caution (*eulabeia*), not to make strong pronouncements on such matters. In general, Plutarch does not appear to feel a strong urge to strictly demarcate ontological realms from each other. Thus the intelligible principles Identity

---

[52]  *De animae procreatione in Timaeo* 1027A, with Opsomer (2007c: 382).
[53]  *Platonicae quaestiones* 2, 1000E; 8, 1007E; *De Iside et Osiride* 352F.
[54]  It goes back as far as Xenocrates (fr. 15 Heinze = fr. 133 Isnardi[2]).
[55]  *De animae procreatione in Timaeo* 1024D; 1026E; *De Iside et Osiride* 371A–B.
[56]  Cf., for example, nos. 44, 49, 66–68, 71, 80, 134, 145, 163, 185. We cannot be certain that Plutarch was the author of these works.
[57]  For Plutarch's ontological views, see Ferrari (1995; 2000; 2002).     [58]  *De Iside et Osiride* 352A.
[59]  He does say, at *De animae procreatione in Timaeo* 1023C, that god is related to the Forms as imitator to pattern, but to the soul as artificer to finished product.

and Difference are said to *enter* the soul.[60] Whereas other, especially later, Platonists would hurry to point out that only copies of the intelligibles enter into lower realities while the former remain pure in their own realm, untainted by the latter, Plutarch does nothing of the sort. Fanatic transcendentalism is not his thing.

Similarly, Plutarch famously describes the divine part of the soul (of both the world-soul and human souls) as a part of the Demiurge present in the soul and compares it to the way a father is present in his offspring.[61] Other Platonists might find such talk objectionable as constituting a threat to god's transcendence. Plutarch, however, has a special reason for stressing the intimacy between the father-Demiurge and the soul: he is convinced that providential care can only exist between a maker and his product.[62] That is also why it is essential we accept that creation is a real event. The Demiurge has actually intervened and even imparted a part of himself to the soul and thus to the world. Plutarch's god does not have the same kind of caring relationship to entities that are not his products – for the pre-cosmic soul, for instance, or for matter.[63] This kind of caring relationship also does not obtain between intelligible principles that are derived onto-logically and timelessly the one from the other. It is in part because of providence that Plutarch insists on the reality of creation as opposed to the timeless derivation of transcendent principles. In Plutarch's philosophical texts both models, the temporal-demiurgic and the derivational, coexist peacefully and are assigned to different stages in the unfolding of reality.

Proclus attributes not just the view that the world was created in time but also the concept of a pre-cosmic time to Plutarch and Atticus.[64] As a matter of fact, Plutarch does not claim that the universe is generated in time. His view is rather that time, understood as ordered time, is generated simultaneously with the well-ordered movement of the world-soul. He is also committed to the idea, though, that the generation of the universe is *preceded*[65] by the pre-cosmic state, and to the view that in the pre-cosmic state there was a disorderly motion constituting an "amorphous matter of

---

[60] *De animae procreatione in Timaeo* 1025B; E–F.
[61] *Platonicae quaestiones* 2, 1001A–C; *De sera numinis vindicta* 559D; *De animae procreatione in Timaeo* 1024C–D. Cf. Ferrari (1996).
[62] This idea is more explicit in Atticus (fr. 4.8–13; cf. Seneca, *Ep.* 58.28). It is based on *Timaeus* 30b-c.
[63] *Platonicae quaestiones* 2, 1001A–B; *De animae procreatione in Timaeo* 1027A. Plutarch probably identified Providence with the Demiurge. Cf. Plutarch fr. 195 (Proclus, *In Timaeum* 1.415.18–20); *De facie quae in orbe lunae apparet* 926F; *Platonicae quaestiones* 1007C (with Cherniss' conjecture).
[64] Proclus, *In Timaeum* 1.276.30–277.7; 1.286.26–29. Also *In Timaeum* 3.37.12–13 (only Atticus).
[65] *De animae procreatione in Timaeo* 1014B; 1015A; 1016C; D; 1024C. Cf. Plato, *Timaeus* 37e; 48b; 52d; 53a. Also Sorabji (1983: 270–273).

time" (*Platonicae quaestiones* 8, 1007C). It is clear, then, that Plutarch accepts a basic temporal structure preceding the well-ordered time of the cosmos, yet refuses to call it time precisely because it lacks order; that is, it is not ordered according to regular time units like years, months, and days. Hence Proclus' report would seem to be essentially correct, the only difference being a terminological one.[66] Yet Proclus infers that if cosmic time measures the motion of the world-soul, disordered pre-cosmic time would measure the motion of the irrational soul. Proclus appears to be oblivious or unaware of the fact that Plutarch expressly rejects the premise that time is the concomitant of motion. According to Plutarch, time is rather "the cause and principle of the symmetry and order that hold together all the things that come to be, or rather that symmetrical and ordered movement itself."[67]

## Soul and Intellect

Although Plutarch sometimes seems to obfuscate the borders between ontological realms, he does treat the realm of intellect and the intelligible, on the one hand, and soul, on the other, as ontologically separate. Even when he says that intellect *enters* the soul, that which enters remains an intellect. And when the Demiurge is said to give something of himself to the soul, he does not abandon his post, giving up his own nature. In many passages Plutarch clearly separates soul from intellect.[68] Some scholars have nonetheless suggested that the indivisible being that enters into the soul is not an intellect, but a rational soul.[69] The main arguments in favor of this interpretation are (i) some passages in Plato, quoted by Plutarch, according to which intellect cannot come to be without soul (which is taken as the denial of a separate existence of intellect), and (ii) the fact that some Neoplatonists seem to attribute this theory to Plutarch.

Neither of these arguments is cogent.

(i)   The "principle" referred to does not amount to the claim that intellect can have no separate existence, but rather to the idea that it cannot be present in the world of becoming without the intermediary of a soul.[70]

---

[66] I should add that Plutarch himself describes the position of his opponents as the *negation* of chronological generation (*De animae procreatione in Timaeo* 1013A).
[67] *Platonicae quaestiones* 8, 1007B.
[68] For example, *De animae procreatione in Timaeo* 1024C; *De genio Socratis* 591D–E; *De facie quae in orbe lunae apparet* 943A.
[69] Schoppe (1994: 159–163); Dörrie and Baltes (1998: 257); Baltes (2000: 261–270; 2005b: 91–99).
[70] Cf. Plato, *Timaeus* 30b3 (quoted in *Platonicae quaestiones* 4, 1002F–1003A); *Sophist* 249a4–8; *Philebus* 30c9–10. I argue my case more extensively in Opsomer (2001: 195–197; 2004: 154–155).

Plutarch clearly and repeatedly says that soul partook of intellect (e.g. *Platonicae quaestiones* 4, 1003A; *De animae procreatione in Timaeo* 1014E). This is only possible if intellect existed prior to this participation; that is, independently of soul.

(ii) The Neoplatonic testimony is contradictory, hence unreliable. Moreover, it amalgamates Plutarch's views with those of Atticus, who in many respects indeed follows the Chaeronean. Regarding the generation of the soul, Proclus at *In Timaeum* 2.153.25–154.1 reports that according to Plutarch and Atticus, indivisible and divisible being (the ingredients out of which the soul is mixed in *Timaeus* 35a), are actually two souls: one a divine soul, the other an irrational soul. Both are combined in a hylomorphic manner, with the irrational soul acting as substrate, the divine as form, the product receiving the name "rational soul."[71] Scholars have combined this testimony with Syrianus' claim (*In Met.* 105.36–106.5) that according to the Platonists Plutarch, Atticus, and Democritus (not to be confused with the atomist), Platonic Forms are merely universal reason-principles (*katholou logoi*) existing in psychic substance. Adopting some additional assumptions, one may read this report as confirmation of Proclus' account of Plutarch's views about the generation of the soul. From there, one could construct a theory according to which the Forms according to Plutarch have their primary existence in the divine soul; that is, in "indivisible being." When this soul is mixed with the irrational soul, the Forms or their copies come to be present in the resulting rational soul.[72] Unfortunately for the advocates of this view, we find no trace of any such theory in the extant works of Plutarch.[73] Wherever Plutarch mentions indivisible being, he does not describe it as psychic, but uses expressions that refer to intellect or the intelligible. Perhaps Syrianus included Plutarch in his doxographic list because he had found the theory in Atticus, with whom

---

[71] The passage *De animae procreatione in Timaeo* 1024D–E seems to confirm this. Plutarch is talking about the cognitive faculties (*krisis*) of the soul that has already received order. Perception (*aisthēsis*) stems from Difference, intellection (*nous*) from Identity, and reason (*logos*) is common to both and a result of their being mixed. Even if one takes *aisthēsis* and *nous* to stand for the original ingredients of the soul, the passage does not equate the divine element with a higher soul. Yet the passage is close to Proclus' report at *In Timaeum* 2.153.25–154.1 and may have been taken by him, or more likely by his source – Porphyry – as providing evidence for this interpretation.

[72] The supporters of the view I am discussing (cf. n. 69) think that these *logoi* are *in* the mind of the divine soul (which is equated with the Demiurge) without being identical with it. See also Ferrari (1998).

[73] It would have been interesting to know the contents of the work listed as no. 63 in the Lamprias Catalogue: *Where Are the Forms?*

Plutarch is very often associated. Proclus' testimony is suspect for similar reasons. It is not about Plutarch alone, and is, moreover, contradicted by other things Proclus says about the Chaeronean. For at *In Timaeum* 1.381.26–382.12 Proclus claims that according to Plutarch, the irrational soul partakes of intellect, thus giving what I take to be the correct interpretation, as I have explained.[74]

The Neoplatonic testimony is interesting for another reason: the manner in which the Neoplatonists portray and then dismiss the views of their predecessors tells us something about the change of philosophical perspective between Plutarch's time and the fifth century CE. Clearly, a shift in philosophical perspective has taken place: in late ancient Athens it has become a matter of prime importance to distinguish hypostases in an unambiguous way, and to determine the exact relationships between ontological levels. Up to a certain degree this is important for Plutarch too: repeatedly he insists on making a strict distinction between soul and intellect.[75] The crucial difference, however, appears to be that Plutarch nowhere commits himself on the structure of the world transcending the soul, with the exception of the claim that the Demiurge is the highest god – and that is not something he argues for but rather presents as obvious. As for transcendence, this suffices, as we have seen: the Demiurge can remain an intellect while also being the One; the Forms belong to the same realm; the relationship between the dualistic principles and the Forms remains unspecified.

## Human Soul and Moral Psychology

There are no Neoplatonic doxographic reports on Plutarch's views on the human soul, on its therapy and moral philosophy, or on the relationship between philosophy and politics.[76] Yet these were at least as central to Plutarch's thought as the ontological views discussed earlier – which were singled out because of their importance for the history of the Platonic tradition.

---

[74] Two passages from Iamblichus' *De anima* pose similar problems: Iamblichus, *De an.* ap. Stob. 1, 374.21–375.5 and 379.25–380.5 Wachsmuth = Atticus frs. 10 and 11. The report in the first passage, which may also have been the direct or indirect source for Proclus at *In Timaeum* 2.153.25–154.1, may very well be the result of an unjustified extrapolation of the doxographical information on Atticus in the second passage. Cf. Opsomer (2001).

[75] Cf. n. 68 in this chapter.

[76] Plutarch's political philosophy, also in relation to the *Lives*, is a highly interesting topic, but will not be dealt with here. For important perspectives, see Roskam (2009b); de Blois et al. (2005).

Plutarch emphasizes the direct connection between cosmogony and the human soul.[77] Just as the world-soul governs the body of the world, so our human souls have command over our bodies. World-soul and human soul are composed of the same elements, welded together in the same manner. Unfortunately, there is one difference: in us the irrational forces are in comparison stronger than they are in the world-soul, which is why we also feel the pull of the body more strongly and are likely to succumb to desires connected to the body.[78] Yet our souls also have kinship with the divine and, indeed, have a divine part. This, on the one hand, gives human beings the craving for and the possibility of obtaining knowledge of things divine,[79] and, on the other, it makes god exercise providential care over individual human lives.[80]

However, nothing in human life is pure and unmixed.[81] It is this insight that Plutarch uses as the starting point for his thought on ethics, his moral philosophy, and the practical advice he gives in his works on moral philosophy, in the dialogues, and in the *Lives*. The *Lives* are of course no treatises on ethics, but moral philosophy is clearly crucial for the project. Many themes familiar from the *Moralia* also pop up at various places in the *Lives*.[82] The idea that nothing in human life is unmixed does not primarily refer to the vicissitudes to which we are subject, bouts of luck and bad luck, or just varying circumstances – although those too are attributable to the same facts about the sense-perceptible realm, where there is a tension between the works of providence and contingence – but first and foremost to the composition of the human soul: the soul is created essentially from an irrational substrate on which a rational order has been superimposed, but neither of these two elements exists in its pure state. They are always inextricably mixed. The main lesson to be derived from this assumption is that we can never free ourselves completely from irrationality. No matter how good we are, there is always the risk of irrational behavior; that is, behavior that is inspired by the passions and hence tendentiously vicious. On this view, the Stoic ideal of becoming passionless is misguided: our passions, stemming from the original soul, will always be

---

[77] *De animae procreatione in Timaeo* 1025C; 1026D–E; *De virtute morali* 441E–442A.

[78] *De animae procreatione in Timaeo* 1025D; 1026E.

[79] *Platonicae quaestiones* 1, 1000D–E; 3, 1002E; 6, 1004C–D.    [80] *Platonicae quaestiones* 1, 1000B.

[81] *De animae procreatione in Timaeo* 1025C–E; 1026C; *De virtute morali* 443B–C; *Platonicae quaestiones* 9, 1008C.

[82] See Valgiglio (1992); Duff (1999a: 60–61, 67, 72–98), as well as various contributions in Nikolaidis (2008) and Roskam and Van der Stockt (2011).

with us, whereas reason comes from outside.[83] Passions are thus due to the dyadic principle. They are not god's responsibility and are our innate portion of evil.[84] Whereas the Stoics ignored the true nature of the passions (to them, passions are mere erroneous judgments), the Aristotelians, so Plutarch claims, had mistaken views on reason (*logos*) and virtue.[85] For them, moral virtue is said to be nothing but moderated passions. Aristotelian virtue allegedly is the rightly proportioned mean (*logos*) *of* and *in* the passions; in other words, the irrational forces brought in a certain well-proportioned shape. The Platonist, however, knows that *logos* is a superior, independent principle that comes from outside to govern the passions.[86] Moral virtue thus amounts to a stable disposition of the irrational soul part that lets itself be governed by a principle superior to it.

Plutarch develops this theory of moral virtue in a technical treatise, *De virtute morali*, that is strongly indebted to the Peripatetic tradition. More precisely, Plutarch is representative of the Platonic reception of the Peripatetic theory of moral virtue.[87] The fact that Aristotle's doctrine of moral virtue as a mean (*metriopatheia*) has Platonic roots[88] was exploited by the Platonists to show that *metriopatheia*, correctly understood, is in fact a Platonic doctrine. What is more, Plutarch considers the Platonic original superior to Aristotle's adaptation of the theory. According to the doctrine of *metriopatheia*, moral virtue, which is a virtue of character (a stable disposition of the passions)[89] and therefore to be distinguished from the virtues of intellect, is located in the middle between opposed passions. In order to attain it, we should therefore look for the right mean between passions that tend toward opposite extremes; that is, toward vices. Courage, to take one of the easiest examples, is situated between the

---

[83] Cf. *De animae procreatione in Timaeo* 1026F: "The soul brings forth of herself the affective part but partook of intellect that got into it from the superior principle." See also 1026D–E and 1027A: "The soul is not entirely the work of god but, with the innate portion of evil in her has been ordered throughout by him."

[84] *De animae procreatione in Timaeo* 1027A.

[85] See *De animae procreatione in Timaeo* 1025D on the Stoics and Aristotle, who err in opposite directions. Platonism once more provides the right mean.

[86] *Platonicae quaestiones* 9, 1009B. *Logos* here denotes the mode of existence of *nous* when the latter is joined to the soul: cf. *De animae procreatione in Timaeo* 1025E and *De facie quae in orbe lunae apparet* 943A (with Bernardakis' emendation).

[87] The Peripatetic *metriopatheia* doctrine is expounded in Aspasius' *Commentary on the Nicomachean Ethics*, to which Plutarch's treatise can be usefully compared. Further similarities are with neo-Pythagorean texts on moral virtue (Metopus and Theages: cf. Opsomer 2012: 324) and with the Middle Platonic account of moral virtue in Alcinous, *Didaskalikos* 184.2–36. For a discussion of the complex problem of Plutarch's sources, see Babut (1969a: 44–54); Becchi (1981); Donini (1974: 63–125; 1986: 214).

[88] Opsomer (2012: 328).      [89] *De virtute morali* 443C–D.

passion of cowardice, on one side, and that of rashness, on the other.[90] Like any other moral virtue, courage consists in the right mean between excess and deficiency. This is comparable to the musical harmony produced out of deep and high notes.[91] The right mean should not be conceived as the position that is equidistant from the two extremes but is to be determined relative to personal character and circumstances.

Against what he presents as the Aristotelian view, Plutarch insists that the right mean is not a mixture of the two opposed passions.[92] It is rather a rational structure imposed upon the irrational soul by a higher, rational, and even divine principle: reason. In this manner, Plutarch connects the theory of moral virtue with his interpretation of the *Timaeus* and more precisely the generation and composition of the soul.[93] The main target of criticism in *De virtute morali* is the Stoic ideal of passionlessness or *apatheia*. This ideal is misguided, Plutarch thinks: we cannot get rid of the passions, as they belong to our very being. What we should do, however, is make the irrational forces harmonious and obedient to reason.

Yet final victory over the passions is illusory. Despite the presence of the divine in us, the passions constitute a constant threat – in some people more than in others, depending on their education, on the extent to which they have cared for their soul, but also on circumstances (luck always remains something to reckon with in human affairs). This is where the therapy of the soul[94] and the role of the philosopher as *directeur de conscience* come in.[95] Plutarch has written a large number of texts in which he gives practical advice, targeted at different types of people and applicable – adaptable – to all kinds of circumstances. And in the *Lives* he shows (great) people, with different natures and characters, coping with various situations, either getting the better of them or being overwhelmed by them. Plutarch's portrayal of character is very rich and multilayered and shows the complexities of morality in real life.[96]

The human condition is inextricably bound up with fortune; that is, luck (*tykhē*). The interplay between virtue and fortune as determinants of happiness, in its endless variety, is a recurrent theme of the

---

[90] *De virtute morali* 445A.    [91] *De virtute morali* 444C–445A.
[92] *De animae procreatione in Timaeo* 1025D; *De virtute morali* 444E. See Bellanti (2003).
[93] Cf. *De virtute morali* 441E–442A; *De animae procreatione in Timaeo* 1026D–1027A.
[94] The classic work on the ancient *Seelenheilungslehre* is Rabbow (1914). For Plutarch, see Ingenkamp (1971). See also Foucault (1984); Hadot (1995).
[95] For example, *Quomodo adolescens poetas audire debeat* 37F; 38B; *Coniugalia praecepta* 138B–D; *Mulierum virtutes* 242F; *De cohibenda ira* 454A; *De vitioso pudore* 529B. There is also the work whose title says it all: *Maxime cum principibus philosopho esse disserendum*.
[96] Cf. Nikolaidis (2011).

*Lives*[97] and the *Moralia*. Human action is set in the domain of the
contingent, where unexpected things can and will happen. That the
cosmic perspective is often present in Plutarch's thinking about morality and luck is evident, for instance, in the opening paragraphs of *De
fortuna Romanorum*.[98] Despite the fact that, for metaphysical reasons,
we will always be confronted with unforeseeable adversities, we should
not despair. Even if we are not immune to the vicissitudes of fortune,
our moral character is still the more decisive factor, since it will
determine whether we are resilient in adverse circumstances, and also
whether we are worthy recipients of good luck.[99] Moreover, as
a religious person, Plutarch believes we are not left alone to cope
with blind chance: although the gods leave room for chance and
refrain from steering the course of events down to the smallest details
(it is not quite clear how pervasive their control *could* be), they still
keep a benevolent eye upon humans and intervene at their
discretion.[100]

The achievement of virtue, however, is primarily our own responsibility
and is a matter of hard work. Contrary to intellectual virtue, which is
amenable to teaching, moral virtue is a virtue of character and acquired
through habituation. Since the passions cannot be eradicated, moral
training requires lifelong attention and the help of friends and family,
but also specialists. The therapy of the passions indeed pertains to an art
(*tekhnē*) and is modeled on medicine.[101] One has to recognize the passions –
that is, diagnose them – and then moderate them and keep them in check.
Habituation is of primary importance for the taming of the passions. This
therapy demands our continual attention. We should seek the assistance of
true friends (including family), especially if they are philosophers.
Philosophers are important because of their knowledge of human nature,
of good and evil. And we should not let ourselves be lulled into confident
contentment, thinking we have overcome our passions once and for all.
The passions' cleverest trick is to make us believe we do not have them.
Friends, however, have the duty to remind us of our moral shortcomings.
The main lesson provided by the philosopher is this: we should never

---

[97] E.g. *Dion* 47.7; 52.1–4; *Sulla* 30.5; *Sertorius* 10; *Marius* 46.1–2; *Cimon* 2.3–5. In the *Lives* the word
*tykhē* often bears connotations of divine intervention, whereas in the more technical treatments it
stands for "luck" – that is, chance in the domain of human action – and is distinguished from
*pronoia*, which stands for benevolent divine intervention.

[98] *De fortuna Romanorum* 316C–317C. Also *De virtute morali* 444A–B.

[99] E.g. *Dion* 21; *Sertorius* 10.2.      [100] E.g. *Sertorius* 1.1–3.

[101] For the technicalities and the different stages and procedures, see Ingenkamp (1971).

forget our dual nature, consisting of an element that is divine and rational but also of "irrationality, love of falsehood, and the emotional element" (*Quomodo adulator ab amico internoscatur* 61E).

Plutarch makes frequent use of Platonic imagery in illustrating his dualistic anthropology, for instance the image from the *Phaedrus* (246a6–d5; 248a1–b5; 253c7–255a1) according to which the soul is like a charioteer driving a pair of horses, one of which is good, the other bad. In a technical discussion of the soul parts Plutarch equates the charioteer with reason, the good horse with spirit,[102] and the bad horse with the passions (*Platonicae quaestiones* 9, 1008C–D). Reason has to restrain the passions with the help of spirit. In the *Life of Galba* Plutarch suggests that the military is like a bad horse totally out of control, with detrimental consequences for the "head" of state,[103] and in the *Life of Antony* the disobeying horse reveals itself in Antony's passion for Cleopatra that makes him act against his better judgment.[104] These examples show that, even where one would least expect it, philosophical ideas are interwoven with the textual and rhetorical strategies of the author.

Philosophy for Plutarch is, however, not just the subject matter of books, but is very much an activity conducted in a social context, in conversations with friends and acquaintances. In his dialogues, Plutarch paints in vivid tones philosophical conversations where the participants discuss questions about nature, customs, religion, theology, and philosophy in general. He shows the importance of what one may call dialectical virtues for a successful philosophical discussion, which ideally is a collaborative search for truth by people who rarely agree on everything, but do share a common philosophical culture and in some cases obtain a common overall perspective on the issues discussed. These philosophical dialogues, in particular *De Pythiae oraculis*, *De E apud Delphos*, *De defectu oraculorum*, *De facie quae in orbe lunae apparet*, *De sera numinis vindicta*, and *Quaestiones convivales*, show Plutarch at his best, both as an author and a philosopher. They display the good-natured humor and the humanity for which he was once famous.

## Further Reading

The classic survey of the history of Middle Platonism is Dillon (1977) = (1996); for thematically structured and searching discussion, richly illustrated from the ancient sources, see now Boys-Stones (2018). Jones (1980)

---

[102] Spirit (*to thymoeides*) is not of central importance in Plutarch's view of the soul. Cf. Opsomer (2012: 319–325).
[103] *Galba* 1.4; 6.4. Cf. Ash (1997).
[104] *Antony* 36.2. For more examples, see Fuhrmann (1964: 141–143).

(originally published in 1916) is a classic study of Plutarch's Platonism. A much richer picture is now provided in Frazier (2020) and Roskam (2021). On Plutarch's place in the history of the Platonic tradition, see Dörrie (1971) (somewhat outdated); Donini (2002) (reprinted with other useful articles in Donini 2011); Opsomer (2007b); Bonazzi (2007). Brouillette and Giavatto (2011) is a collection of articles, by various authors, on the different aspects of engagement with Platonism across the Plutarchan corpus. Cherniss (1976a) and (1976b) is the standard edition and English translation of some of the core philosophical works by Plutarch, with very helpful introductions and notes; for *De animae procreatione in Timaeo*, see also Ferrari and Baldi (2002).

Plutarch's views on the creation of the world and the divine are examined perceptively by Ferrari (1995; 1996; 2003; 2005; 2007–8); Dillon (2002); and several authors in Hirsch-Luipold (2005). Opsomer (2004) focuses on Plutarch's exegetical method in *De animae procreatione in Timaeo*. On the relationship between religion and philosophy in Plutarch, see also Frazier (2008c). Opsomer (2007c) explores the presence of Pythagorean dualism in Plutarch.

Roskam (2009b) elucidates Plutarch's political philosophy through a close reading of *Maxime cum principibus philosopho esse disserendum*. Van Hoof (2010) looks at Plutarch's philosophical praxis in its social context, drawing upon his works of practical ethics. Babut (1992) is a lucid study of the dialogue form as key to Plutarch's philosophical activity; Nesselrath (2010) contains essays, by various authors, on *De genio Socratis*.

CHAPTER 5

# Plutarch As a Polemicist

## John Dillon and Alexei V. Zadorojnyi

## I

We may tend to think of Plutarch as a generally even-tempered expositor of the great tapestry of Greek history, literature, and philosophy, and a benign counselor on questions of ethical conduct and social mores, yet it must be recognized that there is another side to him: that of the accomplished polemicist, primarily in the area of philosophy, but also in respect of his predecessors in the craft of history, and on occasion of the poets as well. What we propose to do here is, first, survey a selection of his critiques of previous historians, then cast a brief glance at his censure of the poets, before turning to an examination of his polemics against rival philosophical schools and, lastly, rival views within the Platonist tradition.

Plutarch's most notable sustained attack on a previous historian is his essay *De Herodoti malignitate*.[1] Stung by Herodotus' treatment of the medizing of Thebes in the Persian Wars, Plutarch performs a comprehensive hatchet-job on his credentials to impartiality as an historian, emphasizing his unfair and begrudging treatment of all other Greeks as well, from the beginning to end of the *Histories*.[2] Herodotus ends up on the wrong side of the ideological fence because of his noncelebratory view of the Greek past: "some people think that Herodotus is the one who glorified Greece, but he makes out that the victory of Artemisium was the product of bribery and theft."[3] Since

---

[1] See Hershbell (1993); Marincola (1994; 2018); Roskam (2017). It is also important to compare the essay with the use of Herodotus elsewhere in Plutarch's works, as well as with Plutarch's own manner of handling more controversial historical material – the wider context reveals interesting parallels as well as tensions: Wardman (1974: 191–195); Teodorsson (1997); Inglese (2003); Dognini (2007: 494–502); Pelling (2007a: 155–162); Marincola (2015a: 92–94); Chrysanthou (2018: 159–170; 2020).

[2] See Stadter's Chapter 9 in this volume.

[3] *De Herodoti malignitate* 867C (trans. Bowen 1992), referring to Herodotus 8.4–5. Compare and contrast the version Plutarch himself gives in *Themistocles* 7.5–7.

we have the text of Herodotus, this essay constitutes a good test case for observing Plutarch's treatment of his sources – careful attention to details of the text, along with selective quotation (and misquotation), and a number of unjustified inferences, such as to suggest very forcefully how he is treating, for example, the large corpus of the works of Stoic Chrysippus, which are lost to us.

The central thesis of *De Herodoti malignitate* is that behind the Herodotean narrative, notwithstanding its literary merits (874B),[4] there lurks a mean and cynical attitude summed up by the term *kakoētheia* (854E, 855A, 856B–C, 858A, 867C, 869F). That is to say, Herodotus' construal of history is ethically unsound and must be confronted as such:[5] Plutarch stands up against "not mere falsehood, but libelous falsehood" (870A–B). Early on in the essay (855B–856D), he describes some of the textual techniques for venting one's *kakoētheia*. These range from deliberate choice of words with negative connotations (855A, "the harshest nouns and verbs," *tois duskherestatois onomasi kai rhēmasin*) to various forms of chicanery built into the reportage itself, which is ever trying to insinuate and belittle.[6] Such elaborate theorizing is quite unusual, really, in the preamble of a Plutarchan polemical work. In the course of the ensuing discussion of Herodotus' passages Plutarch relaxes the analytical grip considerably, yet now and again his commentary echoes the insights that had been presented earlier. Thus, he kicks up a fuss (867D–F) about the fact that Herodotus calls the retreat of the Greek navy *drēsmos* ("run," "flight") after the Battle of Artemisium, which to Plutarch's ears is grating and ungenerous. Likewise, when Herodotus is found guilty of sneaky insinuation (861D–E, 864A–B) or gratuitous smear-mongering (864C, 871B–C), when his U-turns and disclaimers seem calculatedly half-hearted (862E–863A, 863C–D, 870C), or when his silence about noble deeds or sayings is interpreted as intentional omission (858A, 861B, 866C–D, 869C), it is both easy and necessary to make cross-references to Plutarch's checklist of the different guises of writerly *kakoētheia*. The general criteria are not wasted, then.

Plutarch backs his assault on Herodotus with a certain amount of evidence drawn from historiography (859B, 861C–D, 862B, 867A, 869A), poetry (869C, 871B–C, 872D–E), and versified inscriptions (867F–868A, 870D–F, 873B–C). It is telling that he also invokes the (unreferenced) lore

[4] On this passage, see Priestley (2014: 217–219); further Kirkland (2019: 484–489, 504–506).
[5] Roskam (2017); Kirkland (2019: 490–504).
[6] See Marincola (2015a); Ingenkamp (2016: 231–232); Kirkland (2019: 481–484, 489–490).

about the heroes of the Great Persian War (866A on the last charge at Thermopylae; 869C–D on the acumen of Themistocles) as the kind of patriotic knowledge any sensible person should uphold. There is plenty of engagement with Herodotus' text, naturally. Throughout the essay Plutarch keeps arguing that Herodotus' picture of the events and their causes fails to make good sense (859C–E, 860A–B, 865B–D, 866D–867B, 868C–F) and, worse, slides into outright self-contradiction (865B, *autos heautōi ta enantia legōn*, "he is contradicting himself"; 856F, 857D, 858D, 863A–B, 871E, 872D).

> To such extent his malice (*to kakoēthes*), which creeps into his narrative on any excuse at all, fills his history with confusion and inconsistency. (861A; trans. Pearson, modified)

The modern reader ought to remain wide awake, though, because Plutarch's own readings of Herodotus in the essay are very often cavalier, willful, and just plainly incorrect.[7] While historical and philological accuracy may not be his first concern here (particularly embarrassing is the conflation of the Spartan and Athenian calendars at 861E–862A), he shows rhetorical flair and wit in the way he deploys Herodotean intertextuality (specifically, 3.22.1 and 6.129.3–4) as a platform for shooting down Herodotus' reputation:

> Why not adopt what Herodotus himself says that the Ethiopian said about Persian perfume and purple clothes, that the myrrh was a pretense and the garments a pretense, and so say to him that his words are a pretense and his history a pretense. (863D–E; trans. Bowen)

> It looks to me as though, like Hippocleides standing on his head on the table and waving his legs in the air, Herodotus would dance away the truth and say, "Herodotus doesn't care." (867B; trans. Pearson)

On the whole, the essay's declamatory verve[8] tends to predominate over substantive polemics. Starting from the assumption that Herodotus is an ethically flawed author, Plutarch undertakes a blow-by-blow character assassination of the historian. He alludes to Herodotus' fundamental failings in regard to religion (e.g. 858A),[9] ethnicity (857A, *philobarbaros*, "pro-barbarian"), and polis-based identity (868A); the quasi-biographical anecdotes that cast Herodotus as would-be literary mercenary are brought

---

[7] Although it can be argued that Plutarch's criticisms willy-nilly help to throw into relief the discretion and subtlety with which Herodotus approaches political history and human motivation alike: see Baragwanath (2008: 9–20, 29–30) cf. Chrysanthou (2020: 68, 70).
[8] See Ramón Palerm (2000).     [9] See further Marincola (2015b).

into play, too (862A, 864D).[10] It appears that to Plutarch the polemical end justifies the means.

Other historians attacked, mainly during the course of the *Lives*, are Philistus (e.g. *Dion* 36.3), Timaeus of Tauromenium (e.g. *Nicias* 1), Duris (e.g. *Pericles* 28.2–3), Ctesias (on Persian affairs, e.g. *Artaxerxes* 6.9), Theopompus (e.g. *Lysander* 30.2), and the literary critic Caecilius of Caleacte (e.g. *Demosthenes* 3.2). These are criticized not so much for specific historical inaccuracies as for their general attitudes to history-writing. Thus, Philistus is accused of holding poisonous, "right-wing" political views – his account of Sicilian history manipulates language and arguments in order to put a positive spin (a sort of Herodotus in reverse, we might think) on the tyrannical regimes (*Dion* 36.3):

> although he is most skillful in furnishing unjust deeds and base characters with specious motives and in discovering decorous names for them, still, even he, with all his artifice, cannot extricate himself from the charge of having been the greatest lover of tyrants, and more than anyone else always an emulous admirer of luxury, power, wealth and marriage alliances of tyrants. (trans. Perrin, modified)

A more far-reaching example is Plutarch's treatment of Timaeus in the introduction to the *Life of Nicias*.[11] Plutarch's point here is that he himself will not attempt to vie with Thucydides in the way that Timaeus dares to do (*Nicias* 1.1):

> I think that Nicias is a suitable parallel to Crassus, and the Sicilian to the Parthian disaster. I must therefore at once, and in all modesty, entreat my readers not to imagine for an instant that, in my narration of what Thucydides has inimitably set forth, surpassing even himself in pathos, vividness and variety, I am so disposed as was Timaeus. He, confidently hoping to excel Thucydides in skill, and to make Philistus seem altogether tedious and clumsy, pushes his history along through the conflicts and sea-fights and harangues which those writers had already handled with the greatest success, showing himself, in rivalry with them, not even so much as
> *"By Lydian car a footman slowly plodding"*
> – to use Pindar's comparison; nay rather, a perfect example of senile learning and youthful conceit (*opsimathēs kai meirakiōdēs*), and, in the words of Diphilus,
> *"obese, stuffed to the full with Sicilian grease".* (trans. Perrin)

[10]  See Priestley (2014: 47–50).
[11]  On this, see the more comprehensive discussion of Muccioli (2000).

This carries on for some considerable time, performing a thorough hatchet-job on the wretched Timaeus. We may note the well-aimed adducing of poetic tags, including one from Plutarch's favorite fellow-countrymen Pindar, and the employment of witty verbal paradoxes such as "senile learning" (*opsimathēs kai meirakiōdēs*, literally "late-to-learn and puerile"), which are thoroughly characteristic of his philosophical polemics as well.

Before turning to that topic, however, we may look briefly at a reproof directed by Plutarch at the comic poets in response to their ill-conditioned gibes at his hero Pericles (*Pericles* 13.11–12):

> And why should anyone be astonished that men of wanton life (*anthrōpoi satyrikoi tois biois*) lose no occasion for offering up sacrifices, as it were, of contumelious abuse of their superiors, to the evil deity of popular envy, when Stesimbrotus of Thasos[12] has ventured to make public charge against Pericles of a dreadful and fabulous impiety with his son's wife? To such a degree, it seems, is truth hedged about with difficulty and hard to capture by research, since those who come after the events in question find that lapse of time is an obstacle to their proper perception of them; while the research of their contemporaries into men's deeds and lives, partly through envious hatred and partly through fawning flattery, defiles and distorts the truth. (trans. Perrin)

Here Plutarch's purpose is not primarily to assail the comic poets, but rather the wider one of lamenting the obstacles placed in the way of serious historical research by biased contemporary sources,[13] but it is interesting to see him here using the curious Aristotelian argument (aired in the *Poetics*, ch. 4, 1448b24–27) that authors who write about low-life characters must themselves be more or less vulgar people.

## II

But let us turn now from polemic against historians and poets to that against the philosophers, the chief topic of this chapter. Interschool philosophical polemic in the ancient world was not in general, as we know, an edifying process, having about as many procedural restrictions as Siamese kickboxing. It was an activity in which Plutarch indulged with considerable enthusiasm and expertise,[14] and it was, after all, an important strategy

---

[12] Stesimbrotus is, of course, not a comic poet but a biographer and historian. He is being introduced here as part of an a fortiori argument.

[13] Lenfant (2003). Yet see Xenophontos (2012: 616–621).

[14] Indeed, he draws up something close to an etiquette of conducting polemical discussion in an intellectually responsible and well-mannered way – although he does not himself always follow his own rules: see Roskam (2010–11).

for maintaining one's intellectual identity in a world of competing schools and traditions. His main targets, as might be expected, were the rival schools of Stoics and Epicureans,[15] but he also found occasion to lock horns, on at least one important topic, with his predecessors in Platonism, as we shall see.

What we propose to do here is to examine in turn Plutarch's treatment, first, of the Stoics, then of the Epicureans, and finally of his rivals in the Platonist tradition, basing ourselves primarily on his explicitly polemical works against the respective traditions, but supplementing these with relevant passages from other works. We will preface this, however, with some thoughts on Plutarch's philosophical environment, to set his polemic activity in perspective.

As has often been remarked,[16] ancient interschool polemic was generally provoked by thoroughly practical concerns. The Hellenistic and later schools were in direct competition with one another, both for pupils and for patrons, and this could be relied upon to lend a special edge to their controversies. Plutarch himself was not head of any organized Platonic school, being an independently wealthy local grandee, who had no need of support deriving from pupils, but he was well enough acquainted with the situation of those who were, such as (probably) his own teacher Ammonius, to empathize with his fellow sectaries, and, despite the personal friendships with contemporary Stoics and Epicureans portrayed in various of the dialogues,[17] he takes pleasure in laying into either school with vigor.[18]

It will be as well to list here the polemical works with which we shall be dealing.[19] Criticism of the Stoics is to be found primarily in the works

---

[15] Plutarch does not in general attack Aristotle or the Peripatetic School, as did, for example, the later Middle Platonist Atticus, as his own position in ethics was broadly Peripatetic (esp. in the essay *De virtute morali*),nor does he attack the skeptical tradition of the New Academy, as would such a figure as Numenius, on the Pythagoreanizing wing of Middle Platonism, as he himself was an advocate of the "unity" of the Academy (in his lost work *On the Unity of the Academy since Plato*, no. 63 in the Lamprias Catalogue), and liked to employ its dialectical methods against the Stoics. On Plutarch's relationship with the Aristotelian and the Academic traditions see, respectively, Karamanolis (2006: 85–126); Roskam (2011b); and Opsomer (1998: 161–221).

[16] For a good survey of relations between the schools in the imperial period, see Donini (1982); a more integrated account is offered in Trapp (2007). Babut (1969b: esp. 22–69) provides a good discussion of Plutarch's polemical strategies against the Stoics; see also incisive observations on the Platonists' engagement with Stoicism in Bonazzi (2016). Various remarks on the general topic of interschool polemic are found in the course of Dillon (1977).

[17] For example, Minicius Fundanus (in *De cohibenda ira*), Themistocles (in *Quaestiones convivales* 1.9), Demetrius of Tarsus (in *De defectu oraculorum*), Pharnaces (in *De facie quae in orbe lunae apparet*), or Boethus (in *De defectu oraculorum*).

[18] Hershbell (1992a; 1992b); Boulogne (2003); Opsomer (2014); Kechagia-Ovseiko (2014).

[19] There are a number of lost works listed in the Lamprias Catalogue of an apparently polemical nature, such as *On What Lies in Our Power: Against the Stoics* (no. 154), *Selections and Refutations of*

*De Stoicorum repugnantiis, De communibus notitiis adversus Stoicos*, and in a work surviving only as an extract (described oddly in the manuscripts as a *synopsis*), *Stoicos absurdiora poetis dicere*.[20] As for the Epicureans, the surviving works comprise the following: *Adversus Colotem, Non posse suaviter vivi secundum Epicurum*, and *An recte dictum sit latenter esse vivendum*. Lastly, we find a work, *De animae procreatione in Timaeo*, which is directed against Plutarch's predecessors in the Academy, particularly Xenocrates and Crantor, who maintained what was the general position of the Old Academicians after Plato, taken up in response to the criticisms of Aristotle in the *De Caelo*, that Plato had not intended the account of the temporal creation of the world by the Demiurge to be taken literally. Here we find Plutarch engaged not in interschool but rather in *intra*school polemic, although he is not much less acerbic for that.

As regards the discursive tactics of these polemics, certain salient features may be noted,[21] dependent as they are on the well-established procedures of Greek rhetoric. We shall find instances of apostrophe, or the direct address to the opponent, in this case generally either Chrysippus, for the Stoics, or Colotes, for the Epicureans; the adducing of passages of the opponent's works out of context (though this is a vice of which, as shall see, Plutarch accuses Colotes); and the use of vivid imagery, particularly similes, for satirical purposes. All of these serve to enliven the text while lowering the tone of the disputation. A further pervasive feature, which philosophical polemic, starting from Aristotle, adopts from forensic rhetoric, is to take any utterance of one's opponent that admits of ambiguity in the least favorable sense, for the purposes of reducing it to absurdity.

---

the Stoics and Epicureans (no. 148) – much of the contents of which doubtless finds its way into the surviving works – and several overtly anti-Epicurean works, such as *On the Contradictions of the Epicureans* (no. 129), *That the Epicureans Speak More Paradoxically Than the Poets* (no. 143), and *On What Lies in Our Power: Against the Epicureans* (no. 133), in all cases balancing corresponding titles against the Stoics. There are also lost works maintaining the unity of the Academy, *On the Unity of the Academy since Plato* (no. 63), and differentiating the skeptical Academics from the Pyrrhonists (no. 64) but, on the other hand, we find a treatise defending the view that the universe had a beginning in time (no. 66), which will have maintained the same line as Plutarch adopts in *De animae procreatione in Timaeo*, against his predecessors in the Old Academy.

[20] The latter text comprises, as it stands, just six points of comparison, the focus being on the Stoic concept of the Sage; the poets in all cases appear perfectly reasonable, while the Stoics are absurd.

[21] See also Babut (1969b: 22–69); Roskam (2007b; 2010–11); Weisser (2016); further, Boys-Stones (2019: 259–271).

# III

Let us turn first to the Stoics. Plutarch's chief ploy in attacking this set of opponents in his explicitly polemical works[22] is to impugn the consistency both of their doctrines with their way of life and of their doctrines with each other – this being a trait on which, traditionally, the Stoics particularly prided themselves.[23] Indeed, he begins *De Stoicorum repugnantiis* with a broadside:

> In the first place, I require that the consistency (*homologia*) of men's doctrines be observed in their way of living, for it is even more necessary that the philosopher's life be in accord with his theory than that the orator's language, as Aeschines says [*In Ctesiphontem* 16], be identical with that of the law. The reason is that the philosopher's theory is a law freely chosen for his own – at least it is if they believe philosophy to be not a game of verbal ingenuity played for the sake of glory, but as it really is, an activity worthy of the utmost earnestness.[24]

While reminding us that philosophy for the ancients was, in contrast to the modern era, viewed as a way of life, this is a lead-in to convicting the founders of Stoicism, Zeno, Cleanthes, and Chrysippus, of inconsistency, in that they all wrote much on politics, and indeed on involvement in public life, while none of them ventured to involve themselves in the public life either of their native cities or of their adopted ones – since all of them abandoned their native places, Kition, Assos, and Soli, respectively, in each case in favor of Athens (1033B–E).

Worse still, Plutarch continues (1033E–F), those Stoics who do go into public life are caught in contradiction (*makhē*) to their school's claim[25] that all laws and constitutions other than his ideal one are bogus, not laws or constitutions at all:

> As many as do enter government, however, are contradicting their own doctrines still more sharply, for in holding administrative and judicial offices, in acting as councilors and legislators, and in meting out punishments and rewards, they imply that they are taking part in the government of genuine states and that those really are councilors and judges who are at any time designated by lot, those really generals who are at any time so elected, and those really laws which were instituted by Cleisthenes, Lycurgus

---

[22] He also takes an anti-Stoic line in such essays as *De sollertia animalium* and *De virtute morali*, where he is taking a broadly Peripateticizing line, but these texts can be left aside for the present purpose.

[23] See e.g. Diogenes Laertius 7.40; Sextus Empiricus, *Adv. Math.* 7.17–19; Cicero, *Fin.* 3.74.

[24] All translations hereafter will be those from Cherniss (1976a; 1976b), lightly emended on occasion.

[25] A well-known Stoic paradox: compare *SVF* III 324, 327, 599, and so on.

and Solon, men whom they declare to have been base and stupid. So when they take part in government they are also in contradiction to themselves (*makhontai*).

Plutarch has thus put the Stoics in a double bind: they are damned if they don't take part in politics, and they are damned if they do. In this connection he is able to adduce all three of the early scholarchs to his purpose, as well as such later luminaries as Diogenes of Babylon and Zeno and Antipater of Tarsus (1033D). For the most part, however, he is content to focus on Chrysippus, whose voluminous writings on a wide variety of subjects, and in a wide variety of modes, give Plutarch ample occasion for generating contradictions.

To take a number of examples more or less at random, we may turn first to ch. 12 (1038A–C), where Plutarch sets up a contradiction between Chrysippus wearing his absolutist, "paradoxical" hat and Chrysippus in a protreptic mode, where he is necessarily addressing the *prokoptontes*, or those in the process of improvement. The paradox from which Plutarch takes his start is to the effect that "to the base man (*phaulos*) nothing is useful, profitable, or 'proper' (*oikeion*)."[26] This would, strictly speaking, make it futile to encourage "the base" as a category comprising all those who are not yet Sages to improve themselves. It would also seem to cut across the basic Stoic theory of *oikeiōsis*[27] as being something common to all (or almost all) creatures. Here is how he proceeds:

> Chrysippus says that to the base nothing is useful (*khrēsimon*), and that there is nothing for which the base man has any use or need. After stating this in the first book of *On Right Actions* (*Peri katorthōmatōn*), he says later on that both utility and gratification extend to the intermediates (*ta mesa*), none of which according to the Stoics is useful. Moreover, that nothing is either congenial (*oikeion*) or appropriate (*harmotton*) to the base man he states in these words: "Even as nothing is alien (*allotrion*) to the decent man (*asteios*), in the same way nothing is congenial to the base, since the latter property is good and the former bad.
>
> Why, then, again in every book of physics, yes and of ethics also, does he keep writing *ad nauseam* that from the moment of birth we have a natural congeniality (*oikeioumetha*) to ourselves, to our members, and to our own offspring? In the first book of his work *On Justice* he says that even the beasts have been endowed with congeniality to their offspring in proportion to its need, except in the case of fishes, for their spawn is nourished of itself. But

---

[26] *SVF* III 674. This "paradox" is aired also at *De communibus notitiis adversus Stoicos* 1068D–E, in the form "No one who is base derives benefit from anything (*ōpheleisthai*)."

[27] See e.g. Striker (1991); Schofield (2003).

even as there is no sensation in subjects for which there is nothing that is
perceptible by sense, so nor is there any congeniality for those for whom
nothing is congenial; for congeniality seems to be sensation or perception
(*antilēpsis*) of what is congenial.

The final sentence is rather convoluted in the Greek, but this, conceivably,
must be the sense of it. According to Chrysippus' *strict* doctrine, Plutarch
argues, the *phauloi* – and a fortiori the beasts – could not experience
*oikeiōsis* as nothing is *oikeion* to them.

This is very much representative of Plutarch's argumentative strategy
against the Stoics. When attacking a system that prided itself above all on
its complete consistency, one trawls through the vast oeuvre of an author
like Chrysippus, who plainly composed works on various levels of philosophical rigor and pragmatism, and fixes on anything that, on a malevolent
interpretation, gives an impression of contradiction.[28]

Another nice example occurs in ch. 21 (1044B–F). Here some summar-
izing will be necessary, as Plutarch's exposition is rather extended. The
contradiction he is seeking to set up on this occasion is between
Chrysippus' commendation of the simple life in his work *On the State*
(*Peri politeias*), which involves, among many other things,
a condemnation of people who keep peacocks and nightingales, with
his own remarks in the treatise *On Nature* that beauty is the purpose for
which many animals have been produced by nature; in the latter text,
Chrysippus refers to the beauty of the peacock's tail as a reason why the
peacock was created.

This seems to Plutarch to be not only inconsistent but arrogant, in
setting oneself up against the Creator of the world:

> To put it generally: even as the man is absurd who rebukes his table-
> companions for taking desserts and wines and relishes, but praises his host
> who has had these things prepared and has invited guests to share them,
> just so does he [sc. Chrysippus] seem to have no scruple about contradict-
> ing himself who extols providence for having provided fishes and birds and
> honey and wine, but objects to those who do not forgo these things and
> content themselves with "Demeter's grain and draughts of water clear,"[29]
> things ready to hand and our natural sustenance. (1044E–F)

---

[28] For a robustly structured appraisal of *De Stoicorum repugnantiis*, see Weisser (2016: 206–218, 226).
Roskam (2017: 171) rightly draws an analogy with Plutarch's efforts in *De Herodoti malignitate* to
expose inconsistencies in the historian's work.
[29] This being a reference back to Chrysippus' employment of two lines of Euripides (fr. 892 Kannicht-
Snell), which Plutarch asserts that he loved to quote (1043E, 1044B).

We may note here the use of imagery for his satirical purpose – in this case, the image of the boorish and ungrateful guest at a dinner-party.[30] Imagery is used again to good effect somewhat later (ch. 32, 1049B–D), in the course of an attack on Chrysippus for maintaining, in contradiction to the Stoic (and indeed Platonist) principle that the gods are good and responsible for no evil, that Zeus arranged the Trojan war for the purpose of disposing of surplus population (*apantlēseōs heneka tou plēthous tōn anthrōpōn*):

> Never mind the other absurdities in these remarks – for the subject of our examination is not whether the Stoics say anything wrong, but only how much they say in disagreement with themselves – but observe that, while his epithets for God are always fair and humane, the deeds which he imputes to God are harsh, barbarous, and Galatian. For there is no resemblance to colonization[31] in the destruction and annihilation of human beings to the extent wrought by the Trojan War, and again by the Persian and Peloponnesian, unless the Stoics know of some cities colonized in Hades and beneath the earth. No, it is the Galatian Deiotarus that Chrysippus makes God resemble, Deiotarus who, since he had got many sons and wished to bequeath his realm and household to one, slaughtered all the rest just as if he had pruned and cut back the shoots of a vine in order that one, the one he had spared, might grow large and strong.

So now we know the point of the mysterious reference to "Galatian" behavior! This is a deeply recherché, though not inelegant, comparison which contains within it a further comparison, to a vinedresser pruning unwanted shoots. It is a fine example of Plutarch's polemical strategy, and is in addition typically tendentious, since, from the point of view of the good of the cosmos as a whole, and therefore from the divine perspective, the culling of excess population is not an evil at all.[32]

Structurally, *De Stoicorum repugnantiis* leaves much to be desired. It begins abruptly, ends abruptly, and exhibits within its course very little sign of orderly progression – though there are some indications, for instance towards the end, of a certain association of ideas on the topics of Providence and the Gods.[33] It comes across rather as a transcription,

---

[30] On cultured dining as a major theme and focal trope of Plutarch's discourse, see Oikonomopoulou's Chapter 7 in this volume.

[31] Chrysippus, in a passage from Book III of his work *On the Gods*, which Plutarch has just quoted, compared Zeus' action to the authorities in an overpopulated city-state sending out a colony.

[32] There is also a minor instance of satirical imagery in the Plutarchan use of the term *apantlēsis*, in the sense of "draining off" of surplus water or other fluid, to describe the culling of the population.

[33] Chs. 31–40, specifically. Cherniss (1976b: 372–400) gives a full and sympathetic analysis of the structure of the work, with comments on previous authorities. See also Boys-Stones (1997; 1998).

without much concern for order, of the contents of Plutarch's notebooks, or *hypomnēmata*, on the Stoics, the fruit of prolonged and detailed studies of the works of Chrysippus but also of Zeno and Cleanthes, and even such later figures as Antipater of Tarsus.[34] It does incidentally provide a considerable store of valuable information on the doctrine of Chrysippus in particular – over seventy verbatim quotations from his works are included – but that is not our concern in the present context, even as it was not Plutarch's primary concern to provide such information but rather to mock the subject-matter he presents to us.

This is also his purpose in his other major anti-Stoic polemic, the *De communibus notitiis adversus Stoicos*. Yet here there is some effort to create a dramatic structure, and some degree of consequentiality. It is couched in the form of a dialogue between a certain Diadumenus[35] and an unnamed companion. The latter admits having been recently driven to distraction by Stoic friends of his, who have been directing a series of spiteful gibes against the Academy – particularly the New Academy – to the effect that their skepticism and denial of the possibility of knowledge of the physical world (*katalēpsis*) subverts the "common conceptions" (*koinai ennoiai*), or common sense. Plutarch, of course, is a partisan of the unity of the Academy (cf. notes 15 and 19 in this chapter), and he is prepared to take up the cudgels in their defense, but Diadumenus' companion decides that he prefers an attack on the Stoics to a defense of the Academics, so Diadumenus turns instead to that. The work is a good deal more structured than *De Stoicorum repugnantiis*, being divided into two major parts, the first (chs. 4–28) dealing with Stoic ethical theory, and the remainder (chs. 29–50) focusing on physics, and in both cases following a coherent line of argument.

His strategy is to turn the charge of subversion of common sense against the Stoics, and to demonstrate that, on a whole range of topics, ethical and physical, their doctrine is repugnant to common sense. He takes his start (1060B) from what he sees as the basic Stoic contradiction between commending "life in concordance with Nature" as an ideal, and then maintaining that "the things according to Nature" (*ta kata physin*) are

---

[34] The assumption of von Arnim (1903: xiv), that Plutarch must be using some previous compilation, rather than the works of Chrysippus himself, seems quite unwarranted. Babut (1969b: 32–33, 68–69) demonstrates convincingly that Plutarch must have known the larger contexts of many of the quotations he provides.

[35] This figure is otherwise unattested in Plutarch's work, though the name is common enough in inscriptions of the period. We may assume him to be a stand-in for Plutarch himself, though he may not be fictitious.

not goods but "indifferents" (*adiaphora*), the only good being Virtue. This allows Plutarch to develop a series of incoherencies and absurdities in their position, culminating in a fine flourish in ch. 29, 1073 C–D:

> Yet while casting away the theory of ethics on problems like this, *"twisted, unsound and all circuitous,"*[36] they belittle and disparage the rest of us, as if they alone uphold nature and common experience (*synētheia*) in the proper way, and alone put Reason in a position to turn away everything else, and to bring each man by his desires and pursuits and impulses to that which is naturally congenial (*oikeion*). Common experience, however, in becoming a conduit for their dialectic, has made no sound or useful gain, but, like a sickly ear, has been filled by senseless noises with uncertainty and hardness of hearing.

He then turns to deal with physics, and in particular the concepts of God and of the elements. As it turns out, the same doctrinal points can equally well be shown to clash with other Stoic doctrines and to be in conflict with the *koinai ennoiai*, so a certain amount of overlap results. To take one example out of many, in *De Stoicorum repugnantiis* Plutarch nails what he sees as a contradiction in Chrysippus between asserting, on the one hand, that God chastises evil or vice (*kakia*), while elsewhere maintaining that the existence of evil is in accord with nature, and indeed necessary for the manifestation of good (1050E–1051A). But of course the same point can be made in convicting the Stoics of running counter to the *koinai ennoiai*, and Plutarch accordingly brings this up again at *De communibus notitiis adversus Stoicos* 1065A–D, again with the help of the same quotation from Book II of Chrysippus' work *On Nature*.

Overall, Plutarch's strategy against the Stoics relies heavily, as did Aristotle's against the Academics, on selecting the most tendentious interpretation of a given doctrine and pursuing that to the maximum degree of absurdity, with the additional adornment of satirical imagery and quotations from the poets.

## IV

Against the Epicureans Plutarch's line of attack is rather different, though his techniques remain similar. Here it is no longer just a question of consistency; whereas the Stoics set store by virtue and reason, the Epicurean philosophy is rotten through and through, particular in respect

---

[36] Employing here a phrase from Euripides' *Andromache*, 448.

of their elevation of pleasure to a supreme end (*telos*) of life, and their dismissal of divine providence, and is to be challenged on a much more basic level. In one way, however, there is an analogy with the attack on the Stoics, and that is that in either case Plutarch finds just one chief enemy on whom to focus: in the case of the Stoics, Chrysippus; in that of the Epicureans, a favored pupil of Epicurus called Colotes.

Colotes is by no means so distinguished a member of the Epicurean tradition as was Chrysippus in the Stoic, but he merits his position as the chief butt of Plutarch's satire by reason of the fact that he had launched a number of attacks on Platonism,[37] as well as a more general attack on all other philosophies. This polemic especially attracts Plutarch's attention. The first of the two surviving works attacking him, *Adversus Colotem* (with subtitle, *In Defense of the Other Philosophers*)[38] is in the form of a dialogue between Plutarch and a companion or pupil of his, Aristodemus of Aegium, prefaced by an introduction explaining the circumstances of the dialogue – a reading of the book of Colotes at a session (*diatribē, skholē*) of Plutarch's philosophy group, presumably in Chaeronea.[39]

In the case of Colotes, then, the situation is rather different from that of Chrysippus, since here Plutarch is replying to an explicitly polemical work of his opponent.[40] Colotes' target, though he spreads his attack widely, is really his contemporary Arcesilaus, founder of the New Academy, and proponent of a skeptical version of Platonism. All the previous philosophers whom Colotes attacks, Democritus, Parmenides, Empedocles, Socrates, and Plato himself, are accused of making life impossible by propounding doctrines that make them the spiritual ancestors of Arcesilaus; to wit, that things are "no more this than that" and that it is impossible to have certain knowledge of anything. In the face of this, Plutarch's strategy is (a) to deny the accuracy of Colotes' accounts of his opponents' positions, and (b) to turn the accusations back on the Epicureans. The theme from which he takes his start is an accusation that Colotes makes against

---

[37] There exist in the Herculaneum papyri fragments of two works of his critique of Plato's dialogues, *Against Plato's Lysis* and *Against Plato's Euthydemus* (*PHerc.* 208, *PHerc.* 1032), while he also criticized the myth of Er and the implied view of an immortal soul (Proclus, *In Rep.* 2.109.11–12, 111.6–17).

[38] Thoroughly discussed by Kechagia (2011b).

[39] This incidentally brings to our attention the fact that the critical reading of polemical tracts from the opposition could form part of instruction in Platonic schools.

[40] Moreover, Colotes repeatedly breaches (according to Plutarch) the rules of healthy and constructive philosophical polemics: Roskam (2010–11: 137–141).

Democritus, someone for whom, as Plutarch remarks, he as an Epicurean should have more respect (1108E–F):[41]

> Colotes first charges him with asserting that no object is any more of one description than of another (*ou mallon toion ē toion*), and thus throwing our life into confusion. But so far is Democritus from considering an object to be no more of one description than another that he has attacked the sophist Protagoras for making this assertion and set down many telling arguments against him. (trans. Einarson and De Lacy)

This gives Plutarch his excuse for directing the same charge against the Epicureans, and he proceeds to develop that over a number of chapters (3–9). There follow defenses of Empedocles (10–12), then of Parmenides (13–14), Plato (14–16), Socrates (17–21), and Stilpon of Megara (22–23), all taking the same line, namely refutation of Colotes' account of their philosophies, and the turning back of his allegations upon the Epicureans. The final segment of the work (24ff.) concerns Colotes' attacks on his contemporaries, the Cyrenaics and in particular Arcesilaus, and Plutarch's defense of the latter especially is noteworthy in showing his sympathy for the position of the New Academy, as representing a legitimate approach to the legacy of Socrates and Plato, namely the aporetic aspect.

In *Non posse suaviter vivi secundum Epicurum* (which may be regarded as the "sequel" to *Adversus Colotem*), the strategy is different, since Plutarch is now on the offensive. What we find is an attack divided into two parts, one ethical, a critique of the Epicurean concept of pleasure as the end of life (chs. 3–19), the other "physical," or theological, criticizing the Epicurean attitude to the gods and the afterlife (chs. 20–31). For polemical purposes, the worst construction is put on Epicurus' concept of pleasure, as permitting man to be no better than the beasts, and in that connection Plutarch's praise of, first, the intellectual life (chs. 9–14), and then the "practical" or political life (chs. 15–19), is of great interest, as coming straight from the heart, and giving us a good insight into what makes Plutarch tick.

Here is a representative extract, which presents a nice contrast between the ideals Plutarch holds dear and those of Epicurus (1099D–E):

> Now suppose that, as they say, the recollection of past blessings is the greatest factor in a pleasant life. For one thing, not one of us would credit Epicurus when he says that while he was dying in the greatest pain and bodily afflictions he found compensation in being escorted on his journey

---

[41] On the links between Democritus and Epicureanism, see Warren (2002).

by the recollection of the pleasures he had once enjoyed; for you could sooner imagine a face reflected in water when the depths are stirred and the seas ride high than a smiling memory of pleasure in so great aching and convulsion of the body. And for another, no one, even if he should wish, could drive out of himself his memory of great actions. When could Alexander have possibly forgotten Arbela, Pelopidas Leontiades, or Themistocles Salamis? To this day the Athenians celebrate with a festival the victory at Marathon, the Thebans that at Leuctra, and we ourselves, as you know, that of Daiphantus at Hyampolis, and Phocis is full of sacrifices and honors;[42] and none of us gets such pleasure in what he has eaten or drunk himself at the feast as in what those men accomplished. (trans. Einarson and De Lacy)

Here Epicurus is firmly put in his place by this recital of great deeds, representative of the sort of life of public service the Epicurean tradition rejected, and which Plutarch regards as most honorable.

The short essay *An recte dictum sit latenter esse vivendum* ("Is 'Live Unknown' a Wise Precept?"), which may antedate the other two, and comes across as an incomplete sketch, continues the theme of the defense of a life of public engagement against the Epicurean injunction to quietism.[43]

# V

Having observed Plutarch in action against his two chief rivals, it is time to turn to his position within his own school. Like virtually all other Platonists of antiquity, Plutarch presents himself as (and indeed doubtless felt himself to be) nothing other than a faithful exegete of the doctrines of his master Plato. But on one important issue he finds himself in conflict with the virtual consensus (so far as we can observe) of his predecessors. The question is that of the temporal creation of the world out of a precosmic chaos, and in that connection the interpretation of Plato's account of demiurgic creation in the *Timaeus*.[44]

At the outset of his treatise *De animae procreatione in Timaeo*,[45] where he addresses this question, he states his position forcefully, in opposition to

---

[42] The speaker here, Aristodemus, is a Phocian.     [43] See Roskam (2007a; 2007b).

[44] For an overview (with rich bibliography) of the ancient Platonists' views on Plato's cosmogony, see Boys-Stones (2018: 147–211).

[45] As with the anti-Stoic treatises, one is much indebted here to the excellent comments of Harold Cherniss (1954; 1976a; 1976b) – though it is harder to agree with his (rather censorious) conclusions. The translations of Plutarch are once again his, lightly adapted. On this text, see also Hershbell (1987); Opsomer (2004) and Chapter 4 in this volume; Dillon (2010).

such predecessors as Xenocrates and Crantor, from the Old Academy, whom he presents as being far too subtle for their own good, and corrupters of the true doctrines of Plato. The following passage (1013A) is fairly representative of his position, in this case on the question of the true significance of Plato's description of the formation of the soul:

> All these interpreters are consistent in holding that the soul did not come to be in time and is not subject to generation, but that it has a multiplicity of faculties (*dynameis*) and that Plato, in analysing its essence into these, merely for theoretical purposes (*theōrias heneka*) represents it in his account as coming to be and being blended together; and they consider that it is with the same thing in mind concerning the universe too that, while knowing it to be everlasting and ungenerated, yet seeing the way of its organisation and management not to be easy if one does not first postulate its generation and a conjunction of generative factors at the beginning, he [sc. Plato] turned to this mode of exposition.

Plutarch, however, assuming the posture of a plain, bluff fellow from Boeotia, does not have much patience with this type of exegesis:

> Such being the gist of what they say . . . to me they both seem to be utterly mistaken about Plato's opinion, if one is to employ plausibility as a standard, not in the promotion of one's own doctrines, but rather with the desire to say something concordant with the views of that man [sc. Plato].

However, the fact is that Plutarch is far from being the impartial, straightforward exegete of Plato that he would have us believe. He has an agenda, and it is quite a significant one. The reason why it is important for him to establish that Plato really postulated a period of pre-cosmic chaos is that such a state of affairs will be presided over by a wayward and disorderly soul, and this ties in satisfactorily with an interpretation of Plato's thought that Plutarch wants to establish, namely the doctrine that there is in the world a force antithetical to God and the good order stemming from him, which is responsible for all the imperfection and moral evil manifest in the world, and can be identified with the second principle attested by Aristotle as constituting the foundation of Plato's "unwritten doctrines," the Indefinite Dyad, or "the Great-and-Small."

An aspect of the Dyad is the disorderly and irrational world-soul (1014B), which Plutarch discerns as animating the pre-cosmic state of things in the *Timaeus*, and which he equates with the "maleficent" soul of *Laws* X. This disorderly element, which Plato in the *Timaeus* (48a, 56c, 68e) calls Necessity (*anankē*), cannot be taken as something simply negative and characterless, such as matter, but must be a positive force, the disorderly or "maleficent" soul. It cannot simply be "matter"[46] because matter is something inert and devoid of impulse. As Plutarch says at 1014E–F:

> those, however, who attribute to matter and not to the soul what in the *Timaeus* is called "necessity" and in the *Philebus* measurelessness and infinitude in the varying degrees of deficiency and excess,[47] what will they make of the fact that by Plato matter is said always to be amorphous and shapeless and devoid of all quality and potency of its own and is likened to odorless oils which the makers of perfume take for their infusions? For what is without quality and of itself inert and without propensity (*arrhepes*) Plato cannot suppose to be cause and principle of evil and call ugly and maleficent infinitude (*apeirian aiskhran kai kakopoion*)[48] and again necessity which is largely refractory and recalcitrant to God.

This is a shrewdly chosen reference to *Timaeus* 50b–51a, where Plato does indeed present the Receptacle in this way – though without intending to distinguish it from the source of disorderly motion, as Plutarch would have us believe. What Plutarch, from a later perspective, is able to do, as has been said, is to project back the Aristotelian (and Stoic) concept of an inert and featureless matter onto the rather fuzzier concept of the Timaean Receptacle, and thus drive a wedge between Plato's various characterizations of it in the interests of postulating an actively disorderly principle.

He is also able to profit (1015F–1016A) from a contradiction that he can discern between the description of the soul in the *Timaeus* (taken literally) as created (at 34b–35a) and the assertion in the *Phaedrus* (245c–246a) that it is eternal – as being self-moving (1015F–1016A):

> A first proof is that it resolves what is called and indeed appears to be an inconsistency and self-contradiction of his. For one would not attribute even to a hung-over sophist (*sophistēi kraipalōnti*),[49] never mind Plato, in regard to doctrines about which he has been most seriously concerned, such confusion and incoherence as to declare of the same entity both that it is

---

[46] We may note that Plutarch, like all other ancient commentators on the *Timaeus*, has no compunction about attributing the Aristotelian concept of matter to the Platonic Receptacle and Nurse of Becoming. See further Boys-Stones (2018: 103–124).

[47] See Plato, *Philebus* 24a–25a and 25c5–d1.

[48] This suggestively combines references also to the *Philebus* (24a–25d) and *Laws* X (896d–898c), which will be discussed further later.

[49] In this connection, we may note other instances of Plutarch's equating of sophists with false and meretricious modes of discourse, for example *De genio Socratis* 580B, *De Herodoti malignitate* 855E. Cf. Stanton (1973); Mestre (1999).

ungenerated and that it came to be – in the *Phaedrus* that the soul is ungenerated, and in the *Timaeus* that it came to be.

Here Plutarch surely scores a significant point – if one takes the account of the creation of the soul in the *Timaeus* literally (and this is no doubt one of the many reasons that the members of the Old Academy did not wish to do so). If the soul is described by Plato as being generated in one passage, and is presented as ungenerated in another, then, if he is not to be convicted of contradicting himself in a most basic way, he must be talking about two different types of soul. A simple solution would be that the created soul is the rational and ordered soul, and the original, uncreated soul is the disorderly, irrational soul – what Plutarch would regard as "soul in itself."[50] Once again here, though, Plutarch's own distinctive doctrines are being introduced under the guise of a desire to give an accurate and essentially favorable exegesis of Plato. What he wants to demonstrate is that Plato in the *Timaeus* postulates an irrational, disorderly soul as a secondary principle in the universe as antithetical to the orderly and structuring principle constituted by the divine Monad. To reinforce his contention as to the existence of such an entity, he adduces a series of other significant passages from the Platonic corpus. First, he invokes (1014D) the opposition of Limit and Unlimitedness in the *Philebus*: "As for the substance of soul, in the *Philebus* he has called it limitlessness (*apeiria*), as being privation of number and ratio (*logos*), and having in itself no limit or measure of deficiency and excess and difference and dissimilitude."

The interesting thing about this parallel is that there is no question in the relevant passage of the *Philebus* (from 24a to 26b) of *apeiria* being equated with Soul. This is something that Plutarch is reading into the text. He has already decided that the Indefinite Dyad (which he views in a strongly dualist light: *De defectu oraculorum* 428Fff.) manifests itself as a disorderly world-soul, and this justifies him in making this connection; and he projects this back on the "nature divisible about bodies" of *Timaeus* 35a.

With this, in turn, as has been mentioned earlier, he connects the "maleficent soul" of *Laws* X, 896e, referring to "that disorderly and indeterminate but self-moved and motive principle which in many places he has called 'necessity' (*anankē*), but in the *Laws* has openly called

<hr>

[50] The awkward fact that the soul introduced in the *Phaedrus* and in *Laws* X is an orderly and rational soul, which, in *Laws* X at least, bids fair to being the ruling principle in the universe, is something that Plutarch is resolved to draw a veil over. Plutarch's distinctive view of the soul in itself is as something essentially irrational, though desirous of ordering; see Deuse (1983). Baltes (2000) works toward a unified account of Plutarch's ideas about the soul. For the bigger picture, see Boys-Stones (2018: 212–249).

disorderly and maleficent soul," characterizing this in turn as "the soul in itself" (*psykhē kath' heautēn*). This makes the assumption – admittedly, not all that unreasonable – that the soul "of the opposite capacity" is to be equated with the *anankē* of various places in the *Timaeus* (47e–48a; 56c; 68e–69a), a connection that Plato does not make in *Laws* X.

Plutarch is thus able to bring to bear a series of parallel Platonic passages to buttress his case that what is being portrayed in the *Timaeus* as the workings of the Receptacle, or of Necessity, is not simply the force of inertia proper to a passive material principle, but rather the disruptive activities of a disorderly, "evil" world-soul, and that there is a pre-cosmic period where this entity holds sway independent of the action of the Demiurge. This view he presents as the straightforward and natural interpretation of Plato's macrotext, in contradistinction to the over-subtle gyrations of certain members of the Old Academy, who have been over-hasty in succumbing to the criticisms of Aristotle.

Let us remember that we are concerned here not with Plutarch's own doctrinal position (though an appreciation of this is essential to an understanding of his exegetical strategy: see Opsomer's chapter in this volume), but primarily with that exegetical strategy itself. This strategy, as has been suggested, is founded upon a robust assertion of his faithful and unbiased exposition of Plato's doctrine, stated without fear or favor. We have seen, hopefully, how near this is to the truth. By way of coda, we may end with a vigorous piece of Plutarchan polemic against his opponents, emphasizing their excessive sensitivity to outside criticism (1013E).

> In any case, what frightens and embarrasses these men, in common with most of those who study Plato, leading them to manipulate and force and twist everything in the belief that they must conceal and deny it as something dreadful and unspeakable, is the generation and composition (*genesis kai systasis*) of the universe and of its soul, which have not been compounded from everlasting or in their present state for infinite time. To this, a separate treatise has been devoted;[51] on the present occasion it will suffice to state that these people confuse or rather utterly ruin (*synkheousi mallon de holōs anairousin*) the reasoning of Plato's case for the gods, which he admits he made against the atheists with a zeal extreme and unsuited to his years.[52] For,

---

[51] Presumably the lost treatise *On the Fact That the Cosmos Is Generated According to Plato*, listed as no. 66 in the Lamprias Catalogue, reminding us of how much of Plutarch's more technical philosophical work has been lost.

[52] Note here how Plutarch, in order to buttress his claim about the *Timaeus*, brings in two passages of *Laws* X, first the one arguing for the superior antiquity of soul over body (891e–899d), and secondly the one where Plato admits to speaking rather polemically, out of his zeal to prevail over the atheists (907b–c).

if the universe is ungenerated, there is an end of Plato's contention that the soul, being senior to the body, initiates all change and motion, installed in its position as established chief and, as he has said himself, as primary agent (*prōtourgos*).[53]

His opponents within the Academy, then, are undermining Plato's campaign against atheism.[54] And all this because embarrassment in the face of Aristotle's gibes have led them to distort the plain meaning of Plato!

## VI

In all of Plutarch's polemical procedure, then, we can discern common threads. His overriding concern, in the immortal words of W. C. Fields, is to "never give a sucker an even break." Stoics, Epicureans, and even his predecessors in the Platonic tradition have the incoherences in their positions relentlessly nailed, and the most absurd consequences of their misguided arguments teased out. What does come through, however, in the works surveyed here, besides Plutarch's accomplished polemical techniques, is the wide range of reading he was required to undertake in order to accomplish his self-appointed task, something for which collectors of fragments such as von Arnim and Usener, and all those who make use of them, have much reason to be grateful.

## Further Reading

The standard commentary in English on *De Herodoti malignitate* is Bowen (1992). Useful essay-length studies of this work are Hershbell (1993); Marincola (1994; 2015a; 2018); Roskam (2017); Kirkland (2019).

Thoughtful general analysis of philosophical polemics as a discursive (mine)field is Laks (2016). The most accessible overviews of Plutarch's attitude toward the Stoics and the Epicureans are Opsomer (2014) and Kechagi-Ovseiko (2014), respectively. Babut (1969b) remains essential; Roskam (2007a) and Kechagia (2011b) provide superb detailed exegesis. For insights into Plutarch's polemical procedures as such, short essays by Roskam (2007b; 2010–11) are particularly valuable.

---

[53] Again, a reminiscence of *Laws* 897a, where reference is made to the *prōtourgoi kinēseis* of the soul.
[54] An accusation, interestingly, picked up in the next generation by Atticus in his polemic against Aristotle (fr. 4 Des Places).

# CHAPTER 6

# Religion and Myth in Plutarch

### Robert Lamberton

## I Plutarch's Priesthood at Delphi

We know, thanks to a Delphic inscription supported by some oblique references in the text of Plutarch,[1] that near the end of his life he held the office of priest at the oracular shrine. While he writes in his flowery style of having "sacrificed, paraded, and danced" in the service of the god "for many Pythiads" (*An seni respublica gerenda sit* 792F), the only specific duty we can associate with Plutarch's tenure of this office is the overseeing of the erection by the Amphictyonic Council of a statue of the emperor Hadrian.[2]

These scraps of information, from an author who certainly depicts himself as quite at home at Delphi, raise hopes of a precious insider's view of the shrine and its obscure procedures, and even of an account of a Delphic priest's beliefs. Although he tells us a great deal about the shrine, Plutarch will deliver neither such a view nor such an account. Virtually everything he writes about Delphi belongs to the elusive genre of the dialogue and any certainty regarding the oracle, its rituals, and the vast array of artifacts and traditions that surrounded it is blurred by the play of personae, opinions, and conflicting interpretations.[3] If anything, Plutarch's priesthood may have placed upon him special obligations of secrecy. This is suggested by the portrayal in the essay *De E apud Delphos* of

---

[1] *Inscriptions de Delphes* no. 472 (= *CIG* 1713, *SIG*³ 829A) is on the base of a statue of Hadrian erected by the Amphictyons under the supervision of "Mestrius Plutarchus the priest." At *Quaestiones convivales* 700E, Plutarch refers to his "co-priest Euthydemus" and in *An seni respublica gerenda sit* (792F; cf. 785C) he writes of his service to Apollo Pythias.

[2] The capacity in which Plutarch carried out this task is nevertheless somewhat unclear. He seems, based on the inscription, to have acted as "epimelete" of the Amphictyons: Flacelière (1934: 61–62). There may, however, be some truth in Dittenberger's explanation (*SIG* 829a n. 2): the Amphictyons may have assigned this office to the priest because he was present more continuously at the shrine than others.

[3] Especially frustrating is the fact that Plutarch, for all his fascination with *daimones* and divination, commits himself to no general theory of divination or of the *daimones*' role in it. See Schröder (2010: esp. 168); cf. Opsomer (1996).

another Delphic priest, one Nicander, reminding a young and ebullient Plutarch that certain things are not to be explained to outsiders (391E). It is certainly true that, as a Delphic insider, Plutarch's testimony is especially precious for anyone attempting to understand Delphic ritual,[4] but it is equally true that for all he has to say, he very rarely tells us what we would like to know.

## II Religion and Rhetoric

This frustrating state of affairs extends to many areas in which we would like to tie down Plutarch's real intellectual commitments (his real "beliefs," if you will). The situation is not so dire as in the case of his model, Plato, of whom it can reasonably be argued that, while we know a great deal about his concerns, we know nothing of his philosophy, because (with the possible exception of the *Letters*, whose authenticity is dubious) he never committed to writing a single statement in his own voice. In Plutarch's dialogues as in Plato's, intellectual activity is dramatized, and philosophical discourse is presented as an end in itself.[5] Even in the essays that are not in dialogue form, Plutarch's discourse is always rhetorical, the speaker's persona carefully invented and reinvented to produce the desired effect on the reader. All too often one has the sense that, in the time-honored tradition of the rhetorical school, he could just as well be defending the thesis opposite to the one he supports.

In spite of all this, Plutarch's readers have included many who have found in the corpus evidence of religious beliefs held by the author,[6] and there are a number of reasons for doing so. First of all, one of Plutarch's most powerful rhetorical strategies is his capacity to generate a discourse that creates the impression that it is both intimate and confessional. This is essential, for example, to the genre of the consolation, which must sound heartfelt to its addressee, no matter how conventional the patterns and

[4] See e.g. Burkert (1996: 12).
[5] Or, if we take the principal goal of the dialogue form to be protreptic, we might say that it presents philosophical discourse as an exciting intellectual endeavor in which the intended reader will aspire to participate.
[6] Oakesmith (1902) and King (1908) represent the modern peak of concern with Plutarch the pious polytheist and Plutarch the theosophist, respectively. The modern literature on Plutarch and religion is large, and only sampled in the Further Reading at the end of the chapter. The scholar who has explored "religious themes" in Plutarch most thoroughly is Brenk (1977; 1986; 1987; 1998; 2007). The relatively brief remarks of Burkert (1996) are also particularly useful. For another perspective, see Hirsch-Luipold (2014).

even the *exempla* that constitute it.[7] The two consolations in the corpus (both on the deaths of children), one addressed to "Apollonius"[8] and the other to Plutarch's wife, illustrate the range of possibilities. The former is overloaded with illustrative texts and lacking intimate detail, while the latter has convinced most readers of its authenticity as a communication between spouses in a time of crisis, thanks largely to its (relatively) familiar tone and the inclusion of a few details that are unlikely to be known to outsiders. Yet the conventional pattern and the conventional succession of points essential to reducing the grief of the addressee remain. The line between authentic voice and conventional artifice is impossible to draw. The voices of Plutarch often aspire to sound confessional, and often succeed.

Another reason why the corpus of Plutarch has been ransacked so hopefully by searchers for evidence of genuine beliefs is the remarkable paucity of literary evidence for the nature of religious experience in the world of Greco-Roman polytheism.[9] At the origin of this tradition, we have the widely criticized Homeric theology with its epiphanies,[10] and near to the proximal end of the span of classical literature, in the first and second centuries of our era, we again have in Apuleius and Plutarch texts that explore religious experience but do so in ways that are remarkably evasive and elusive.[11] Plutarch tells us an enormous amount about the religious experience of others in his constant flight from one persona to another, while Apuleius (also a trained rhetor and teacher of rhetoric) gives us in the *Metamorphoses* a sustained, first-person narrative whose rich fantasy qualifies it as a fiction, yet at the same time the voice itself insists upon its confessional nature.

All of the many scholars who have written on Plutarch and religion have faced this problem, and a certain number of solutions have repeatedly emerged. One promising interpretive tool has been chronology (an area

---

[7] On the consolation literature in general, see Kassel (1958), and for further bibliography, Pomeroy (1999a) with Harvey (1999). On *Consolatio ad uxorem*, see Schorn (2009).
[8] Like many works in the corpus, the *Consolatio ad Apollonium* has raised doubts concerning its authenticity. See Cannatà Fera (1994).
[9] It should be kept in mind that Plutarch's cultural world was an entirely polytheist one, largely ignorant of what have been called the Abrahamic religions. He makes no mention of Christianity (which could easily be ignored during his lifetime), and his scant references to Judaism are hardly complimentary. It is quite possible that, like some of his contemporaries, he conflated the two. For an overview of Plutarch on the Jews, see Gallarte (2008).
[10] The earliest author to mention Homer by name, Xenophanes of Colophon, denounced Homeric (and Hesiodic) theology. He was followed by Plato in the *Republic*, but the issue seems to have been a dead one by the time of Aristotle, if not earlier.
[11] On the former, cf. Winkler (1985) and Shumate (1996).

that, along with prosopography, has been considerably advanced in the past generation by the work of C. P. Jones[12] and others). If we can agree that the essay *De superstitione*, with its rationalism, its hostility to most of what we think of as religious observance, and its rhetorical qualities, is "early" and that certain other texts, particularly *Non posse suaviter vivi secundum Epicurum* and *De sera numinis vindicta*, along with *De Iside et Osiride*, more accurately represent the mature Plutarch's attitudes toward religion, then a plausible picture emerges of the young rationalist maturing into a more conservative believer, drawn to mysticism. As Frederick Brenk, who has explored the relevant texts with care, observed,[13] this picture is too simple, and can be considerably refined. And in any case, the relative chronology of the items of the *Moralia* is still imperfectly understood, to say nothing of their absolute chronology.

Is there a core, a node of passages where we may credibly say that we are close to an account of Plutarch's own deeply held beliefs? Can we distinguish, in Plutarch, between pious traditionalism – a deep respect for ancestral forms of observance as the adhesive that binds culture and society together[14] – and traditional piety as such? If the former position – pious traditionalism – is understood to include within its range a philosophical rationalism, thinly disguised, then Plutarch might be mustered to that cause. On the issue of deeply held beliefs, however, an example will bring out the complexity of the problem and demonstrate the high level of generalization that must satisfy us if we are to reach any conclusions at all.

The character Aristodemus appears in two major dialogues against the Epicureans (whom Plutarch characterizes as virtual atheists) and is, to the best of our knowledge, Plutarch's own invention. Early on in *Adversus Colotem* Plutarch tells us what we are to expect from Aristodemus: he is "an ecstatic celebrant of Plato, and no Academician."[15] Based on what Plutarch tells us elsewhere about his own education and predispositions, this Aristodemus might, in fact, serve as a vehicle for at least one mode of religious thought to which Plutarch was sympathetic. So, when in *Non posse suaviter vivi secundum Epicurum* Aristodemus speaks of "the good cheer and delight" that should come to us "from the gods" (1100F) – assuming we are not deluded by the Epicureans into expecting nothing

---

[12] Beginning with Jones (1966).    [13] Brenk (1977: 14–15).

[14] Plutarch appeals repeatedly to such traditionalism. Cf. *Amatorius* 756B, where Plutarch himself (acting as mouthpiece for such ideas) asserts the adequacy of ancestral forms of observance as a foundation for piety. On the issue of myth and belief in the ancient world, see Veyne (1988). The issues in Plutarch, however, are more complex than Veyne acknowledged.

[15] The speaker who describes Aristodemus is identified as Plutarch (*Adversus Colotem* 1107F).

at all from the divine – we may perhaps take this as a tenet of Plutarch's faith. At the same time, we should remember that Plutarch places these ideas in the mouth of an enthusiast, distanced from his own (usually) sober, restrained tone. Plutarch might have been reluctant to put Aristodemus' words in his own mouth, but there is little reason to believe he would disagree with them.

Walter Burkert has rightly distinguished in the wide-ranging corpus of Plutarch between, on the one hand, the theologian, the philosopher of religion, and on the other, the "living reality of Plutarchan religion," perceptible in such passages – a vastly rarer and ultimately more precious thing than Plutarch's philosophical reflections on religion.[16] Burkert's treatment of the text is both delicate and meticulous, and one may well be inclined to agree with the general picture that emerges of a Plutarch for whom the gods and their rituals are, at least potentially, a source of joy. There are nevertheless pitfalls in every sentence, especially when one attempts to bring Plutarch's position on the specifics of religious observance and ritual into focus. Not only does the essay *De superstitione* appear to dismiss nearly all such observance as irrelevant or worse, but Plutarch at his own highest rhetorical pitch will trump even Aristodemus. A little later in *Non posse suaviter vivi secundum Epicurum* the latter praises the festivals and temple worship in general:

> There is no time spent anywhere that gives such joy as that spent in temples, no occasion that matches the joy of a festival, nor do any other sights or actions give us more joy than those we see or perform ourselves in the service of the gods, whether celebrating, dancing, or participating in sacrifices or initiations. (1101E)

But Plutarch "himself" in one of the most sermon-like of his ethical essays, *De tranquilitate animi*, approves of Diogenes the Cynic's question, "Doesn't a good man consider every day a festival?" and responds:

> Yes, and a very splendid one, if we view it reasonably. This world is a very holy temple and one perfectly suited to a god, and man is brought into it by birth, not as a spectator of man-made, unmoving statues, but rather of such perceptible imitations of the objects of mind as the divine mind has revealed (as Plato says), having within them the principle of life and movement, sun and moon and stars and rivers always pouring out new water and sending up nourishment for plants and animals. Life is a celebration of these things and a perfect initiation into them, and as such is necessarily full of tranquility and delight. (477C–D)

---

[16] Burkert (1996: 12).

He goes on explicitly to condemn the "many," who "wait for the Saturnalia, the Diasia, and the Panathenaia" to enjoy an alien, bought pleasure.

These two passages sum up very nicely the subtlety with which Plutarch explores the varieties of religious experience, as well as the reasons why it is so difficult to identify a given position as his own. There is always another perspective to be added to whatever has already been discovered, and in that perspective, what was once truth dissolves into a deceptive veil to be swept aside in order to discover the next, equally fragile, truth. Festivals are rewarding; enlightened indifference to festivals, more so.

How did all this affect Plutarch's performance as Priest of Apollo at Delphi (especially if his duties included the sacrifice of animals, about which he must surely have had misgivings[17])? It is our inability to reach this level of Plutarch's own experience – his own accommodations and compromises – that reminds us that what he does offer us, for all its richness, remains something far from confessional in the usual sense. The Plutarch whom Montaigne admired and imitated[18] is not an author who is about to deliver religious certainties.

## III   Interpretation of Symbol and Myth

Plutarch's position in the history of writers and thinkers about religion is secured by his essays on the interpretation of religious phenomena. Here again, the questions he raises far outnumber the answers he adheres to – or, rather, every answer implies new questions, whose answers may well supersede earlier ones, only to be themselves superseded as the inquiry continues. Perhaps the easiest way to understand this peculiar and very literary form of *epokhē* (philosophical suspension of judgment) is to emphasize the models provided by the *Quaestiones convivales*. In these mini-dialogues at the dinner table, which form such a large part of the corpus, the focus is on the conversation itself rather than any conclusions that might be reached.[19] In fact, to assert a definitive conclusion, an unqualified answer to the question at hand, would be the height of boorishness, a rejection of the rules of polite exchange. The *Quaestiones Graecae* and *Quaestiones Romanae*, many of which pose problems relating

---

[17]  See Mossman and Zadorojnyi's Chapter 14 in this volume.
[18]  See MacDonald's Chapter 19 in this volume.
[19]  Cf. Oikonomopoulou's Chapter 7 in this volume.

to myth and cult, regularly carry this evasiveness to the extreme of answering a question with a further question.[20]

The major Delphic dialogues (*De E apud Delphos*, *De Pythiae oraculis*, and *De defectu oraculorum*) all resemble the conversations in the *Quaestiones convivales* in their deliberate avoidance of closure, though in each dialogue a speaker brings the discussion to a close with an analysis that prevails, if only provisionally, over what has gone before.[21] The questions range from the very great (why have many oracular shrines ceased to function?) to the vanishingly small (what is the meaning of the dedications in the form of the letter epsilon at Delphi?). The common element that unites them is the interrogation of some phenomenon of religion, in the apparent belief that some truth of importance is concealed therein. The solutions, however, will point to the multiplicity, the polysemous quality of such signifiers, and to their capacity to stimulate thought and to be comprehended, however imperfectly, in multiple ways.

We may take *De E apud Delphos* as representative of the interrogation of small things (an undertaking echoed again and again in *Quaestiones Graecae* and *Quaestiones Romanae* as well as in the *Quaestiones convivales*). The dialogue is framed by a dedication[22] that offers a theoretical framework for such inquiries: Apollo, Plutarch asserts (in balanced phrases), gives us oracles to solve life's problems, and as for problems relating to intellect, Apollo poses them himself and inspires a craving in the soul that leads toward the truth. The dialogue then seems to begin to take place in "the school" at Delphi, whatever one may imagine that to have been. Here, in any case, the word seems to evoke Plutarch's own role as leader of discussions, a sort of Socrates long after the fact, himself "seeking" knowledge and interrogating others. But this in fact turns out to be only the frame of the frame, and instead of narrating the discussion at hand, the narrator "is reminded" of a discussion "a long time ago, when Nero was here" (385B), when Plutarch's teacher Ammonius and others explored this same issue.

---

[20]  This technique is pervasive in the two collections. *Quaestiones Romanae* No. 31 (271F–272B), "Why is the famous 'Talassio' sung in marriage ceremonies?", is a typical example. Plutarch's first answer is "Is it from spinning (*talasia*)?" and some material on brides, wool, and the distaff follows. The second answer, "Or is what the historians say true?", is followed by one of Plutarch's retellings of the story in Livy. On the other hand, some "questions" relating to iconography and other cultic matters are answered by anecdotal explanations reminiscent of Pausanias (e.g. *Quaestiones Graecae* 301F–302A on the iconography of Labrandean Zeus).

[21]  See Babut (1992) = (1994: 457–504). On Plutarch's triptych of Pythian dialogues, see Brouillette (2014) and Simonetti (2017).

[22]  To Sarapion, an Athenian poet who is also a character in *De Pythiae oraculis* and one of the many contemporaries of Plutarch mentioned in the *Quaestiones convivales*. See Puech (1992: 4874–4878).

This play with the time and place of the dialogue, and with the speaker's access to knowledge of it, is of course Platonic.[23] Plutarch's adaptation of the conventions of the Platonic dialogue, however, is his own and built on a new aesthetic in which the changes of direction are more unexpected and repeatedly result in a sort of thematic *mise en abîme*. Our attention focused now on this very specific past (67 CE, Nero's visit), we witness, as from a floating present, the speaker as a young enthusiast for mathematics, and the Socratic role taken over by Ammonius. The subject of the inquiry is a series of at least three Delphic dedications (the historicity of which is guaranteed by numismatic representations) that took the form of the capital letter epsilon (385F–386A). One, at least, was quite old, and known as "the E of the [Seven] Sages," and the others seemed to refer back to it, but the meaning of the original was apparently lost in time.

The first interpretation offered (by Plutarch's brother Lamprias) is a joke, generated by the nickname just mentioned. It is built on the assumption, however, that E is to be understood, in the standard fashion, as the numeral 5, and subsequently explores the necessity of explaining why the (Seven) Sages would dedicate a 5. Clearly, it was because five of them wished to dissociate themselves from the other two. This leads to discussion of the second amusing but unconvincing reading, attributed to a "Chaldean stranger" (in this complex play of mirrors a descendant of the Eleatic and Athenian strangers of Plato), which depends on ordinal rather than cardinal numbers: E is the second (of "seven") Greek vowels and Apollo (the Sun) is the second of the seven planets, therefore the letter is an appropriate dedication to the god. At this point, the voice of authority enters in the person of the priest Nicander, who expresses "the common and periegetic (tour-guide) opinion" (386B) on the matter – an ironic compromise between a hypothetical hegemonic Delphic account and what the guides tell the visitors.

Plutarch seizes this opportunity, though, to make a methodological point (not unlike the Platonic Diotima who incidentally teaches Socrates the difference between contraries and contradictories in the *Symposium*). The official line is posited on an important distinction: the claim is that neither the appearance (*opsis*) nor the sound (*phthongos*) of the E is symbolic, but only its name (*onoma*). And that name (spelled εἶ) is (when unaccented: εἰ) the word "if" in Greek, and this fact, according to the priestly and periegetic wisdom, refers to the formulas of wish and prayer.

---

[23] On the significance of the frames of Plato's dialogues, see the work collected in Michelini (2003).

The visitor to Delphi comes to ask *if* he should do x or y, and with a wish in his heart: "*If* only . . . ."

The response of Theon (a name of convenience not much different from "so and so") is swift. If E = "if," then surely the *if* in question must be the *if* of the syllogism, the foundation of all logic. Theon then delivers a short eulogy of the syllogism and its appropriateness as a dedication to Apollo, and the dialogue again changes direction. One Eustrophius claims the right, as a devotee of numerology, to make a serious claim for E = 5, a subcategory, presumably, within the group of interpretations that find the symbolic aspect of the E to be its appearance. The young Plutarch takes over for Eustrophius and delivers, over the next four pages (nearly half the length of the dialogue), a breathless list of the virtues of the number 5 and its appropriateness to Apollo. At the end of this peculiar exercise in self-parody, Plutarch's teacher Ammonius is given the last word, with another reading of the symbolism of the *name* of the E (εἶ), which is also (among other things) the second-person singular of the verb "to be"; that is, "You (sing.) are." Ammonius claims that this utterance, given substantial form in the E dedications, is the appropriate answer to Apollo's greeting to the visitor to the shrine. Apollo says to the visitor: "Know yourself," to which the visitor answers "You are," indicating that he does indeed appreciate his own fragmented, provisional existence, and the difference between that and the eternal and unchanging being of the god. This is the basis for an extensive lecture on being and becoming, which provides an adequate rhetorical closure for the piece, but hardly a definitive answer to the question at hand. The E – for all its substantiality (whether as wood, bronze, or gold) and its participation in the environment of the divine, which (as with oracular utterances) holds out the possibility of unity, or at least of univocality – belongs finally, along with ourselves, to the realm of becoming, not of being. The lines that link this dedication to the absolute are many, and their exploration is an end in itself, but any expectation that a single explanation will emerge as the true one to the exclusion of the others is doomed to frustration.

The E is a dedication, not a myth, but both belong to the class of phenomena that stand in a special relationship to the absolute, the realm of being. As an interpreter of myths and texts, Plutarch recapitulates the attitudes and qualities that appear clearly in *De E apud Delphos*: a pluralism that might itself be characterized as dogmatic, going hand in hand with the deliberate denial of the possibility of closure.

The essay *De Iside et Osiride* is a paradox in many ways.[24] The author who denounced the philobarbarism of Herodotus (*De Herodoti maligni-tate*, 857A) shows himself every bit as imaginatively engaged with Egypt as his predecessor.[25] The incidental information about Plutarch and religion that comes from the essay is rich. He addresses the essay to Clea, a friend who was a leader of the Thyades (roughly the equivalent of Maenads) at Delphi, and an initiate in the religion of Osiris (364E). Plutarch is charac-teristically reticent about his own relationship to this initiation, but he speaks (and refrains from speech) like an initiate, and most readers have taken this to mean he was a fellow initiate with Clea in these mysteries, just as he shared with his wife initiation into the Dionysiac mysteries (*Consolatio ad uxorem*, 611D). Once again, we find Plutarch constrained, in all probability by oaths of secrecy required of initiates, from a full revelation of his subject. The possibility cannot be excluded, however, that all of these gaps and silences are contrived for reasons more rhetorical than religious.

Plutarch's *De Iside et Osiride* is a vast *explication de texte*, but even the lengthy version of the myth that forms its basis (355D–358D) is explicitly bowdlerized, with the "particularly useless and excessive elements" removed (355D; cf. 358E). This tone of hostility, or at least impatience, with the story before him is heard again and again in the essay, and although Plutarch never adopts an explicitly defensive stance, it is clear that the Egyptian story is rich in pitfalls for those who lack proper guidance. Plutarch tells us (or rather, tells Clea) a great deal about how *not* to understand the myth, while offering a multitude of alternate readings of which he approves. It is one of the givens of the undertaking that this story, like any artifact (whether fashioned of gold, wood, or words) that refers to the divine, is both obscure and multivalent. In Egypt, the necessary hermeneutic tools resided with the priests, so that if a king was chosen from the warrior class, "immediately he became a priest and participated in the philosophy which is hidden for the most part in myths and accounts that contain murky reflections and glimmerings of the truth," a situation the Egyptians themselves express by putting sphinxes in front of their temples to represent the "enigmatic wisdom" of their the-ology (354B–C). Plutarch's final advice to Clea, before narrating and

---

[24] On Plutarch and myth, and particularly on this essay (4761–4763), see Hardie (1992) and Richter (2001).

[25] See J. G. Griffiths (1970: 103). This magnificently annotated edition of *De Iside et Osiride*, benefiting as it does from the skills of the Classicist along with those of the Egyptologist, is the first reference for anyone interested in the essay.

interpreting the myth of Isis and Osiris, makes clear the fact that this priest of Apollo has taken upon himself the role that was formerly the prerogative of the Egyptian priests, and that Plutarch the philosopher is the interpreter here, along with Plutarch the priest:

> When you understand the things concerning the gods [in the manner just indicated] and accept them from those who interpret the myth piously and philosophically, then as you go on performing and maintaining the traditional observances, in the realization that, in comparison with having correct ideas about the gods, nothing that you will sacrifice or do for them will please them more, you will escape superstition, which is no less an evil than atheism. (355C–D)

This last observation brings us back to the values of *De superstitione* and makes explicit the danger that lurks here. Egyptian theology, perhaps more than other traditions, is clothed in fantastic stories and so has given rise to error, which Plutarch proposes to expunge for Clea's benefit; once his task is done, the gain will be her ability to perform her own priestly duties unencumbered by that error. Correct understanding, that is, will banish all trace of superstition. This passage likewise sets one of the limits to Plutarch's hermeneutic endeavors: such stories must be interpreted not only philosophically but "piously." Clearly to be rejected are all interpretations that would tend to diminish belief in the gods, which we have seen Plutarch in his many voices asserting to be a source of joy.

The reading of the myth that Plutarch offers – of Typhon's dismembering of Osiris and of Isis' gathering up the parts and becoming impregnated with Horus/Harpocration – is in fact an account of the various modes of interpretation appropriate to myth. Interpretation by etymology – with Egyptian words notoriously sometimes explained by Greek ones (as Isis from *oida*, "I know")[26] – has already appeared and will come back again, but the first strategy to be tried and rejected is Euhemerism (360D). Along with the interpretation of these ostensibly divine myths as stories of men of the remote past, however, Plutarch simultaneously rejects the notion that this narrative is about gods at all. What they recount, he asserts, is to be understood as the actions of great *daimones*, some of whom (Isis and Osiris) later became gods, as Greek myth says that both Dionysus and

---

[26] J. G. Griffiths (1970) is particularly helpful here, and repeatedly emphasizes (106–110 and *passim*) that Plutarch's explanations of Egyptian words reveal a remarkable range of knowledge of hieroglyphics. Much of this may be owed to Manetho and to other earlier Greco-Egyptian authors, but it serves in any case to support the notion that Plutarch has done his homework. The explanation of the names of Egyptian gods based on Greek words is likewise far from naive. See also Richter (2001) on Plutarch's Hellenocentrism in this essay.

Heracles did (361E), while others remain *daimones* (Typhon). The elaborate "daemonology" of Plutarch is one of the most strikingly postclassical elements in his notions about religion and myth, but it is also firmly rooted in Plato.[27] The *daimon*, in the post-Platonic argument, is most simply the *tertium quid* between gods and men, the manifestation of the divine that penetrates this world, either disruptively (Typhon) or benevolently (the *daimones* that preside over oracles). In the hermeneutic traditions of Platonism, these beings often provide a means of explaining how myths both are and are not representations of the gods, and Plutarch's influential interpretive move here was echoed many times after him.

Once these basic principles are established, the essay evokes a series of allegories, many of which are rejected, but many more accepted, at least in a qualified way. It would seem that the many claims made about Osiris (e.g. that he "is" the Nile, or the principle of wetness or the Oceanus of *Iliad* 14.201, or Dionysus, or even the "sphere of the moon") all have something to contribute to "correct ideas about the gods." This is precisely the dogmatic pluralism referred to earlier, but again, it is far from naive. Plutarch says of the allegorists who make of Osiris and Typhon the causes or representations of various cosmic events, from weather to eclipses, that "individually they are all wrong, but taken together, they are right" (369A). Explaining this involves moving to another level of generality: there are, Plutarch asserts, two opposing powers in the universe (a position he attributes, credibly, to the Persians and Chaldeans, and less credibly to a series of Greek philosophers culminating in Plato, 370E–F). Here, we are very close to an issue of considerable importance in Plutarch's time. As a Platonist, Plutarch was committed to the idea that there is a first principle of good, but that evil is only imperfection and hence disruption of an essentially good order. We see over the subsequent centuries a gradual loss of this distinction, but Plutarch appears to hold firm. Many allegories may contribute to the picture of the world as a place of war between good and evil, but the gods themselves are all on the side of the good (cf. 377A), while, as we remember, Typhon is still a *daimon*.

Much of the latter part of the essay is devoted to stripping away mistaken interpretations. All those that see the gods of myth as designations of material principles are to be avoided, as inserting "terrible and atheistic

---

[27] Brenk (1977: esp. 85–112); for the broader picture, Timotin (2012). Some of Plutarch's most memorable passages involve *daimones* and their lore. *De defectu oraculorum* is particularly rich in such anecdotes, from the death of Pan (419A–D) to an account from Hesiod of the life-span of Nymphs (415C), itself an example of our debt to Plutarch for the preservation of many of the oddest as well as the most sublime passages from the lost pages of Greek literature.

notions" (377E) into the stories. Furthermore, even the readings that restrict the story to its Egyptian landscape are in some sense misguided, because, although they have different names and rites in different cultures, the gods are simply the gods, as the sun is the sun and the moon is the moon. What is important, therefore, in the Isis myth cannot be reduced to an evocation of Egyptian realities. Finally, rising to an even higher level of generalization (which, for a Platonist, is tantamount to a higher level of truth), Plutarch rejects a priestly interpretation said to be current "now," namely that Osiris is Hades (382E). Osiris is in reality transcendent and that is why "the ancient story" shows Isis loving the *absent* Osiris, pursuing him and becoming impregnated by him, to fill the world with good and beautiful things. "In this way these events are explained in the manner most fitting to the gods" (383A).

## IV   Plutarch's "Theosophical" Myths

Plutarch's dialogues represent a creative imitation of the dialogues of Plato, one in which the various elements of that rich mixture – the Platonic *poikilia* that posed difficulties for many interpreters of Plato[28] – are carefully and self-consciously developed in an aesthetic that is very much of Plutarch's own time. This process of creative adaptation is exceptionally clear in the myths that provide a rhetorical, if not a philosophical, closure to some of Plutarch's major dialogues, serving him as similar stories had served Plato.[29]

The Greek philosophical dialogue seems, as a genre, to have been largely a protreptic one, and there is some reason to believe that a pedagogical goal lies behind Plutarch's contributions.[30] This suggests in turn that the anticipated audience for Plutarch's dialogues may well be teenagers, boys of an age to be confronting decisions about their education. Plutarch says of such students that they derive pleasure and inspiration from "doctrines about the soul mixed up in mythology" (*Quomodo adolescens poetas audire debeat* 14E) and specifically mentions the lurid myths of Heraclides of Pontus, who may well be an essential link in the development of the protreptic dialogue and its myths between Plato and Plutarch.

---

[28] Iamblichus' principle that the interpreter of the Platonic dialogue must initially identify the specific goal or end, the *skopos* of that dialogue, is a characteristic late-Platonic reaction to this *poikilia*.
[29] Of the three "grands mythes" (Vernière 1977: 63), those in *De sera numinis vindicta* and *De facie quae in orbe lunae apparet* have a role similar to (e.g.) that of the Myth of Er in the *Republic*. The third, in *De genio Socratis*, is situated in the middle of the dialogue. On these myths, see Deuse (2010).
[30] Cf. Aristotle, *Protrepticus*, and Russell (2010: 3).

We have only scraps of Heraclides' myths, but Plutarch's reach us intact and surely constitute one of the most memorable parts of the corpus. The limits of the category of Plutarch's myths are not easy to set, because the fabulous often intrudes into the dialogues, particularly in the form of fantastic narratives by individuals of mysterious background.[31] The three core texts, however, tell a fairly consistent story.

In *De sera numinis vindicta*, one Thespesios is thought dead for two days, but wakes up (an echo of Plato's Er in *Republic* 10), reformed, to tell a tale of retribution after death for crimes, including punishments visited on the descendants of the actual perpetrator. This is the most mechanical of Plutarch's rewritings of Plato's myths,[32] but even here the imaginative range of the Platonic original is stretched, as the descendants on whom retribution has fallen cluster around their criminal ancestors "like bees or bats" (567E) enraged by what they have had to endure. In a final, comic twist, the soul of Nero appears, just as he is being prepared for rebirth in the body of a viper, but the powers governing this underworld intervene and substitute that of an aquatic "songster" – apparently a frog. There is, then, a term to retribution, and the operatic Nero did, after all, liberate the Greeks (567F).

Timarchus, in *De genio Socratis* where the myth is a rhetorical perform-ance in the middle of the dialogue, rather than a final resumption of themes, is likewise given up for dead, after an absence of two days inside the oracle of Trophonios at Lebadeia. He returns to tell a vertiginous tale of visions of the secret order of the universe, during which he enjoyed the services of a disembodied voice that served him as a guide (a motif that, again, may come from Heraclides and smacks of the pedagogic). A crack on the head leads, literally, to the freeing of Timarchus' soul through the cranial sutures – developmental time seems disrupted, as well as space and sequence – to witness a vision of a sea of islands above and a groaning abyss below. This latter is Hades, but in some sense also this world. Lights are seen floating on the water. These (Timarchus is told by his guide) are the *daimones* that enter the material universe, each with a little light composed of mind-stuff bobbing in the sea of matter. Some manage to stay afloat and others are pulled under, but the crucial point here, in terms of the larger

---

[31] See, for example, *De defectu oraculorum*, where the story of the demise of Pan is narrated (419C–D), followed by a passage echoing Sulla's myth in *De facie quae in orbe lunae apparet* and finally a lecture on demonology, attributed to a sort of *saddhu*, a *barbaros* who prophesies on a single day of the year on the shores of the Red Sea (420F–421E). This last "myth" has been read as a parody. Cf. Dörrie (1983) and the summary in Brenk (1986: 2121–2122).

[32] For discussion, see Taufer (1999).

discussion, is that everything depends on the bond (*syndesma*) that like a horse bit (*khalinos*) makes the embodied soul responsive to higher powers (592B). The soul's sensitivity to these guiding tugs and pulls is highly variable, and truly rebellious souls are swallowed up and lost. The point is never belabored – too much is happening too quickly in this dialogue to allow any real closure – but the model presented of human (and daemonic) existence clearly helps to explain Socrates' *daimonion*, and in turn the exceptional sensitivity of that particular embodied soul to directions from above.

Finally, the myth of *De facie quae in orbe lunae apparet* combines fantastic geography with a fabulous speaker: a "Stranger" (met in Carthage by one Sulla, a Carthaginian polymath) whose knowledge stems from thirty years in the service of the *daimones* who convey the prophetic dreams of the sleeping Cronus to an island in the sea, "five days' sail" from Britain. These dreams coincide in content with "everything previously thought in the mind of Zeus" (942A). This disorienting and beautiful tale is, finally, the basis of the claim to credibility of the Stranger's account, which is carefully tailored to the discussion about the moon.

The Stranger says, first of all, that the moon deserves high honor "among the visible gods" (942C). Kore (Persephone) presides over it, and it is made of soul-stuff, intermediate between the body-stuff of earth and the mind-stuff of the sun. As the body decays into earth after its "first" death, the soul retires to the moon. Most souls gradually separate themselves from life on earth and their associated mind – their immortal part – leaves the remainder of soul to decay into the moon, and itself goes off to become part of the sun. Some souls fall back into the terrestrial sphere – either because they are still drawn to it or from more philanthropic motives, for example to tend oracles. Some genuinely unruly souls (such as Tityas and Typhon) return to bring disruption and destruction to the affairs of our world. These are souls that, while in the moon, still dream of life in the flesh. We learn finally that the moon is central to the process of creation as well as that of destruction: when the sun imparts bits of mind to her, she produces new souls and earth contributes bodies, so that the world is repopulated.

There is a coherence to these visions of the relationship of soul to mind and to matter, but it is a coherence that has little to do with logic or analysis. The function of these stories is to stimulate the imagination of the reader, along with the impulse if not to engage, at least to stand in awe before the vast questions of being. If they are meant for teenage boys, that fact does not disqualify adults as spectators. At the same time, these formulations are sublime, disorienting, and vertiginous fictions that display the power of words no less than that of the imagination. They are models of rhetoric, easily confused with "theosophy" but really quite distinct from it. This is the theology of a writer acutely aware of the secondary, epiphenomenal status of language, and of the zeugma represented by the very term "theology." Plutarch is also a master of the use and manipulation of that epiphenomenon. The result is in some sense the intersection of two parallel lines, religion and rhetoric.

## Further Reading

For a variety of perspectives on issues relating to religion in Plutarch, the collection edited by Gallo (1996) is essential, and in particular Burkert (1996). For general orientation in the topic, the most useful short study is Hirsch-Luipold (2014). The essays in Hirsch-Luipold (2005) and Roig Lanzillotta and Muñoz Gallarte (2012) offer a rich gamut of studies on religion and afterlife in Plutarch. The work of Frederick Brenk over four decades (see especially Brenk 1977, 1998, and 2007) has thrown light on many aspects of Plutarch's engagement with religion.

On Plutarch's attitude to myth and its interpretation, see generally Vernière (1977); Hardie (1992). For *De Iside et Osiride*, see the commentary by J. G. Griffiths (1970) and the essay by Richter (2001). On divination in Plutarch, see Schröder (2010) and Simonetti (2017).

# CHAPTER 7

# Plutarch at the Symposium

## Katerina Oikonomopoulou

Plutarch's depictions and discussions of the symposium allow us to glimpse his extraordinary diversity of identities and roles in their full complementarity. In a uniquely vivid fashion, they shed light on Plutarch as a Platonic philosopher, priest and civic official, socialite and friend, Boeotian attached to his homeland and cosmopolitan traveler, Greek and Roman, writer, belletrist, and intellectual. The symposium is also a topic that enables us to capture the intellectual unity of his rich biographical, historical, moral, scientific, fictional, rhetorical, and philosophical oeuvre. References to and descriptions of symposia abound in Plutarch's corpus of *Lives* and *Moralia*: they may be scattered in passing comments on social life, or concentrated in lengthy descriptive scenes of convivial activity; they may feature in historical, biographical, or autobiographical narratives; they may be the focus of moral admonition, and the starting-points of reflection on the self, society, and politics; or they may be included because of their symbolism, in order to furnish a web of metaphors and associations that can be exploited for the purposes of moral evaluation, philosophical teaching, or cultural criticism. Last but not least, the symposium offered Plutarch the opportunity to hone his talent as a prose writer, by composing symposiastic works that broke new ground in terms of genre, and elevated antiquity's tradition of writing *Symposia* to new heights.

We should not be surprised. Scholarship has long stressed the importance of conviviality in Greek and Roman civic life, from Homer to the Christian era. Anthropology and sociology have furnished analytical tools for exploring the rationale(s) of communal sharing in food and drink as a key factor of societal bonding.[1] These also allow us to comprehend the symposium's ability, well inscribed within its wider social function, to

---

[1] Scholarship on the topic is vast. See especially Vetta (1983); Figueira and Nagy (1985); Murray (1990); Slater (1991); Bowie (1986; 1993); Gowers (1993); Murray and Tecuşan (1995); Donahue (2003; 2004); Roller (2003; 2006); König (2012); Hobden (2013); and Wecowski (2014).

reassert established communal divisions, between men and women, adults and children, citizens and slaves, citizens and foreigners, elite and non-elite.[2] In order to approach Plutarch's references to or descriptions of the symposium we need, with the necessary degree of caution, to treat them as historical testimonies of the ways in which his world of the High Roman Empire (late first and early second centuries CE, to be exact) practiced and reflected on conviviality. More specifically, we need to be concerned with the ways in which Greco-Roman elite culture, of which Plutarch is a key exponent, in this period treated the symposium as a space of class cohesion, as well as of distinction.[3]

As one might expect, the boundary between reality and representation in Plutarch's sympotic scenes is at best fuzzy (hence the earlier proviso of caution):[4] we cannot be sure that Plutarch is accurately or realistically depicting symposia of his lifeworld. His sympotic scenes are undoubtedly idealistic, serving purposes of literary self-presentation, even self-promotion. They may also selectively put the emphasis on specific aspects of the symposium (negative or positive) in order to achieve characterization or make a wider moral point. Their intertextual dynamic is potent too, for Plutarch writes within an established tradition of sympotic writing: this means that at least some of his sympotic scenes self-consciously serve as tributes to or emulations of his literary ancestors, especially Plato and Xenophon. We should not forget that Plato's and Xenophon's *Symposia* were works of lasting influence in the subsequent history of Greek writing on the symposium. More specifically, Plato and Xenophon are credited with the invention of the tradition of the philosophical symposium; that is, the drinking party that offers an opportunity for exercising philosophical reflection – and, indeed, gives it primacy over other aspects of conviviality, such as food, drink, and entertainment.[5] There is little doubt that Plutarch, who was a Platonist, treated the symposium as an ideal literary medium for (literally) giving voice to philosophical ideas, and exploring their validity. This further complicates the picture for historians wishing to take his banqueting scenes at face value.

---

[2] See Murray (1983); Schmitt Pantel (1990; 1999; 2003); Donahue (2004: 43–118); Roller (2003; 2006); König (2012: 3–13); Hobden (2013: 66–116); Wecowski (2014: 19–124).

[3] Ingenkamp (1999); Nikolaidis (1999); Stadter (1999c); König (2012: 13–29).

[4] See Pordomingo Pardo (1999). The problem has been especially relevant to scholarship on the *Quaestiones Convivales*. See Fuhrmann (1972: vii–xix); Teodorsson (1989: 12–15); Titchener (2009; 2011); Klotz and Oikonomopoulou (2011b: 3–12); König (2012: 20–29).

[5] See Relihan (1992); Romeri (2002: 61–106); Teodorsson (2009); Roskam (2010); König (2012: 6–13); Hobden (2013: 195–246).

Accordingly, the questions of historical relevance, symbolic manipulation, and literary stylization will structure my discussion of Plutarch's symposia and sympotic writing in the rest of this chapter. The reader should be aware that it is hard to disentangle them in a way that does not seem artificial. Yet each deserves separate treatment as a major parameter that gives raison d'être as well as resonance to Plutarch's writing on the symposium.

## Plutarch and Conviviality in the High Roman Empire

The world in which Plutarch lived afforded a spectrum of occasions for feasting and drinking, and embraced many different styles of sympotic practice, Greek and Roman, public and private. Rome has appropriately been termed an "empire of pleasures."[6] For someone like Plutarch, who was nurtured by the ideals of the aristocratic Greek symposium, deeply inspired by the philosophical *Symposia* of Plato and Xenophon, and at the same time was a privileged beneficiary of the luxuries enjoyed at rich Romans' *convivia*, this brought about tensions and conflicts detectable in his writing about the symposium. As a result, his work negotiates different types of sympotic activity and behavior, each tapping into specific realities of dining and drinking in imperial Rome.

Under the empire, the princeps' consumption habits could be scrutinized as symptoms of moral and political corruption. Suetonius' portraits of the gluttonous Claudius, "eager for food and drink at all times and in all places" (*cibi vinique quocumque et tempore et loco appetentissimus*), or Vitellius, "exceedingly devoted to luxury and cruelty" (*praecipue luxuriae et saevitiae deditus*),[7] illustrate the depravity associated with abuse of imperial power. In addition, Roman imperial poets offer us valuable glimpses of how the emperor's banquets were actually organized. By effecting the physical separation of the emperor from his guests, as well as by observing a hierarchical seating arrangement and providing different kinds or unequal portions of food to the participants, the imperial banquet sought to organize the ruler's grandeur and power over both his immediate subordinates (the members of the Roman senatorial class) and the larger society (the crowds that participated in these grand events).[8] Wealthy

---

[6] Dalby (2000).
[7] Suetonius, *Claud.* 33 and *Vit.* 13, respectively. Cf. *Tit.* 7, *Dom.* 4. See also Gowers (1993: 12–32) for the different ways in which individual consumption became linked with a concern about the fate of the state from republican Rome onwards.
[8] Statius, *Silvae* 1.6, with Donahue (2003; 2004: 16–29); Roller (2001: 129–212).

Romans replicated this dining style in their own *convivia*, thus attracting the satirists' caustic indignation.[9] Greek imperial authors were without doubt familiar with these practices, and found many ways to articulate a concern about the strain they put on the Greek ideal of sympotic equality.[10] Plutarch certainly makes the issue central in his *Quaestiones convivales*, if we are to judge by the fact that it emerges as early as the second chapter of book 1: 'Whether the host should arrange the placing of his guests or leave it to the guests themselves' (*Quaestiones convivales*, 1.2.615C ff.).[11] He is, however, characteristically unforthcoming if we scan his work for explicit references to Roman imperial dining practice. There is commentary on sympotic behavior of rulers closer to home, most notoriously of all Alexander the Great.[12] As far as the Roman side of things is concerned, however, Plutarch's case studies of a luxurious and excessive lifestyle (such as Lucullus and Marcus Antonius) are firmly placed in the republican era, eschewing any potentially dangerous allusions to his contemporary historical reality.[13]

If the sympotic practices of the Roman imperial court served as often unpleasant reminders of the Empire's unequal distribution of power, conviviality on the civic level, by contrast, emphasized that the internal solidarity of local communities continued to make political sense in the imperial context. We know from the epigraphic record that, throughout the imperial period, cities across the Roman Empire organized public feasts as an intrinsic part of their regular festival and religious practice. This tradition was particularly entrenched in the Greek East, where public feasting historically played a vital role in the life of the *polis*.[14] Plutarch's testimony in the *Quaestiones convivales* valuably complements this picture, showing how such occasions also offered the opportunity for the *polis* elites to strengthen their intercity ties by conducting mutual visits in order to celebrate one another's victories in athletic, musical, or poetic competitions,[15] or in order to attend local and panhellenic festivals (which often included such competitions) at which they or their friends

---

[9] Gowers (1993: 109–219, 126–179). On the *convivium* as a grander version of the Roman *cena* (evening meal), see Dupont (1992: 269–286; 1999).

[10] See Lucian, *De Merc.* 1off.; Alciphron, *Epist.* 3, especially 1–3, 5–6, 8–11, with König (2012: 247–265).

[11] Some of its aspects also crop up later on, in *Quaestiones convivales* 1.4 and 2.10. See Vamvouri Ruffy (2011; 2012: 163–214).

[12] For Alexander's *polyposia*, see later. See also Vamvouri Ruffy (2012: 195–196, 202–204).

[13] *Lucullus* 39–41; *Antony* 27–30, 56–57.

[14] Schmitt Pantel (1990; 1992; 1999; 2003); König (2007: 62–68; 2012: 23–25, 81–88, 109–112); Hobden (2013: 22–65); Wecowski (2014: 103–124).

[15] 1.10, 2.4, 5.1–3, 7.5, 8.4.

sometimes officiated.[16] Several such visits are mentioned in the *Quaestiones convivales*, to places such as Athens, Delphi, Elis, Corinth, Hyampolis, and, of course, Boeotia itself. Public functions and private relationships were inextricably enmeshed in this process, and Plutarch himself as the convenor of a symposium for his friends and relatives – in the context of a public feasting event also organized by him in the role of eponymous archon in his own city, Chaeronea – embodies the fusion of the elite's private and public roles (*Quaestiones convivales* 2.10).

Opportunities for feasting and drinking could also be provided in educational contexts in the High Roman Empire; this relatively late development undoubtedly owed much to the increased institutionalization of educational practice in the same period. Our best sources for this sort of activity are Aulus Gellius and Philostratus, both of whom describe symposia organized by teachers of philosophy and rhetoric in Athens – Calvenus Taurus and Herodes Atticus, respectively. Both teachers appear to have integrated conviviality into their educational program. Calvenus Taurus, as Gellius tells us, regularly gathered some of his students together for simple meals at his house, and these meals offered many opportunities for interactive training in philosophy, in the form of posing scientific questions, and logically speculating for answers.[17] Herodes Atticus, according to Philostratus (*VS* 585–586), organized an exclusive dining club (the *Clepsydrion*) for his most gifted students at Athens.[18] The practice was undoubtedly already in place in Plutarch's time, as it can be seen from his anachronistic tracing of its origins back to Plato himself.[19] What Plutarch particularly valorizes, however, is the coextensiveness of philosophical teaching with ordinary social interaction. As a result, several of the young characters in the *Quaestiones convivales* who can plausibly be thought of as pupils of philosophy attached to teachers such as Ammonius, Philinus, or Plutarch himself are also there qua sons who join their fathers at symposia as part of their normal socialization.

But Plutarch also lived in a world where private symposia reached unprecedented levels of lavishness.[20] The immense proportions and rich artistic decoration of the triclinia of private villas scattered across the Mediterranean indicate the scale of luxury and grandeur that sympotic events would have attained even in the seclusion of the countryside.[21] Not

[16] 2.2, 2.10, 3.1, 3.7, 4.1, 6.8–9. See König (2012: 81–88).
[17] *NA* 7.13, 17.8. See Lakmann (1995); Holford-Strevens (2003: 90–97); Roskam (2009a); Howley (2014).
[18] See König (2012: 15–16).   [19] *Quaestiones convivales* 6, preface, 686A–C.   [20] See Dalby (2000).
[21] See Dunbabin (1991) on triclinia and Dunbabin (1995; 2003) on Roman mosaics.

accidentally, the *Quaestiones convivales* contains some of the most vivid descriptions of the material setting of the Greco-Roman symposium when precisely such sympotic occasions are its point of focus. Thus, Plutarch speaks of outdoor symposia taking place in Soclarus' gardens by the river Cephisus, full of marvelous trees of all sorts (*Quaestiones convivales* 2.6), and indulges in description of the beauty of the spa resort at Aedepsus in Northern Euboea,

> which possesses many natural resources for the worthy enjoyment of leisure and is further embellished by villas and elegant apartment houses. Game and fowl are caught there in abundance, and the sea no less lavishly supplies the market with provisions for the table, producing many a fine, noble fish in the deep, clear waters close to the shore. This resort flourishes especially when spring is at its height, for many continue to come there all that season. They gather together, exempt from every want, and, having the leisure, engage endlessly in conversation. (*Quaestiones convivales* 4.4, 667C–D)

Other passages dazzle us with details of the foods offered at such symposia: abundance of fish, game, and fruits, giant truffles and wild boars.[22] Yet others speak of entertainment (often uncomfortably coexisting with intellectual conversation), which included music, singing, and dancing, recitations of New Comedy, mimic performances, and even dramatizations of select scenes from the Platonic dialogues.[23] In addition, these scenes invite us to share in some of the emotions involved: happiness for the wedding of relatives' or friends' children,[24] joy for the arrival or return of good friends after a long journey.[25] Through this colorful gamut and detail, Plutarch underlines the cosmopolitanism of his world, where people traveled widely within Greece as well as in the Mediterranean,[26] where Greeks fruitfully interacted with Romans and other foreigners, where goods and ideas circulated freely and were amiably shared, in accordance with the elite cultural code of *phisophrosynē*, material and intellectual generosity (*Quaestiones convivales* 7, preface, 697C).[27] The *Quaestiones convivales'*

---

[22] *Quaestiones convivales* 2.7, 3.10, 4.2, 4.4, 5.8. Refined eating and drinking habits, and elaborate preparations, often accompanied this abundance (4.4, 6.4, 6.7, 6.10). This urges for caution against Romeri (2002: 109–189), who argues that Plutarch's philosophical symposia suppress references to food. The picture is of course not so black and white.

[23] 1.1.615A–C, 5 preface, 673B, 7.5, 7.8, 9.15. See Beta (2009); Alikin (2009); D'Ippolito (2009).

[24] *Quaestiones convivales* 4.3, narrating the wedding feast for Plutarch's son Autobulus.

[25] The beneficiary in both instances is Plutarch himself: *Quaestiones convivales* 5.5, 8.7; compare 6.7.

[26] On the significance of travel within Greece, see König (2007: 66–67). On travels to Rome, compare the symposia hosted by Sosius Senecio, Mestrius Florus, and Sulla the Carthaginian in Rome (*Quaestiones convivales* 3.3, 5.7, 5.10, 7.4, 8.7).

[27] The concept of *philanthrōpia* is also intrinsic to this code. See especially Martin (1961); Becchi (2009a); and Nikolaidis (2009).

orchestrated, cumulative attempt to convey the rich material and intellectual exuberance of his era turns it into a cultural testimony of prime historical and ideological significance – indeed, into a monument for posterity that is in no way inferior to Pliny and Athenaeus' encyclopedic enterprises.[28]

## Plutarch's Symposia: Symbolic Aspects

If the historical practice of conviviality in the Roman Empire provides Plutarch's representations of symposia with a patina of realism (and helps us understand some of their most puzzling silences), the symbolic connotations the symposium carries in Plutarch's thought infuse them with special potency. I will here delineate some of the main conceptual strands that underpin Plutarch's discourse on the symposium and trace their cultural import.

Deeply embedded in Plutarch's thought, as well as in the Greek and Roman biographical tradition as a whole, is the idea that eating and drinking habits are manifestations of moral character. As a result, Plutarch's *Lives* and *Moralia* teem with narratives of symposia that recurrently highlight the same set of key features: the ambience of the symposium, the costliness of its preparations, the nature of the foods or wines consumed, the type of entertainment offered, the participants' styles of consumption, and the ways in which they interact with one another. These foci serve as ethical indexes, facilitating moral evaluation.[29] Thus in the *Life of Antony*, the contrast that Plutarch draws between Cleopatra's first *deipnon* for Antony, described rather tantalizingly as a "preparation that beggared description,"[30] and the "meagerness and rusticity" of the feast Antony organized for Cleopatra in return (*Antony* 26.3–27) serves to underline the cultural gap that separates the two protagonists (and Egypt and Rome more generally). Yet in the immediately following chapter (28), Philotas' description of Antony's extravagant dining style, after he has fallen prey to Cleopatra, alerts the reader to the swiftness with which such differences dissolve under the corrosive influence of seduction and pleasure.[31] Moreover, this development is subtly foreshadowed by the

---

[28]  This approach, it should be noted, does not imply a narrowly historicist "reading" of the *Quaestiones convivales*: its "authenticity" remains an open question (see earlier).
[29]  See detailed discussion in Paul (1991: 157–169); Titchener (1999).
[30]  Fortunately, we have a description of the feast in Athenaeus, *Deipnosophistae* 4.147e–148d.
[31]  On the notion of moderation in drinking in Plutarch, see Calderón Dorda (1999); Nikolaidis (1999); Pelling (1999a); Roskam (1999); Teodorsson (1999); Van der Stockt (1999a); Vamvouri Ruffy (2011; 2012: 97–124, 179–196).

preceding narrative stressing Antony's lack of self-control when it comes to drinking and expenditure (2.3–5). Symposia also play a central role to the characterization of Alexander both in his *Life* and in several anecdotes in the *Moralia* (as well as in other contemporary sources). The overall tone is decidedly more sinister, as Alexander's symposia are theaters of abuse and violence against his guests, in the case of Cleitus even leading to murder.[32]

Equally entrenched is the notion that dining and drinking styles illustrate ethnic character. Greek and Roman ethnographic and geographic writing had long shown fascination for such details, which it systematized for the purpose of classifying nations on a scale between Hellenism and barbarity, as well as to provide a ready measure of cultural difference.[33] However schematic or Hellenocentric, this system continued to play a key role in imperial Greeks' cultural self-definition by introducing a framework for understanding their continuously evolving relationship with a range of cultural "others": Persians, Egyptians, Celts, Jews, and, of course, Romans.[34] We recognize it in Plutarch's work as well: enquiries into why the Jews abstain from pork (*Quaestiones convivales* 4.5–6) or how the Persians and other nations regulate issues such as sympotic hierarchy, entertainment, and intellectual conversation (*Quaestiones convivales* 1.3, 2.1, 7.4, 7.9–10) can be used both to relativize the Greek convivial model, by pointing to the dazzling variety of convivial styles across cultures, and to reinforce it as the cultural paradigm, by employing stark contrasts between Greek moderation and barbarian excess, for example.[35] The Parthian dinner-party at the end of the *Life of Crassus* (33) evinces the latter: Crassus' head – a publicly displayed trophy of the Parthian victory – plays the role of protagonist in the symposiasts' entertainment that involves a grotesque reenactment of the scene in Euripides' *Bacchae* in which the frenzied queen Agave proudly exhibits the head of her slain son Pentheus as a trophy.[36] The theme comes back in the *Life of Titus Flamininus*, underlining Rome's precarious position between civility and barbarity:[37] Titus' brother, Lucius Flamininus, orders for a prisoner's decapitation to take place during

---

[32] *Alexander*, 50–51, 52–54, 70.1–2; *Quaestiones convivales*, 1.6 and 9.1.736F–737A. Yet compare *Alexander* 22.7–23 (for the king's self-control). See Mossman (1988); Beneker (2009); Gómez and Mestre (2010). The scenes effectively stress Alexander's problematic status as a model of Hellenism – see further Whitmarsh (2002); Vamvouri Ruffy (2012: 202–204).

[33] See Hobden (2013: 66–116).

[34] Cf. Athenaeus, *Deipnosophistae* (books 4 and 12); Philostratus, *VA*, especially 2.25–30, 3.1–5, 16–17; Chariton, *Call.* 4.3–5; Heliodorus, *Aeth.* 5.15–34, 7.27. See Almagor (2009); Tröster (2009); König (2012: 107–109); Oikonomopoulou (2013b).

[35] See Schmidt (1999: esp. 107–139); also Schmidt (2000; 2002; 2004); Meeusen (2017).

[36] Euripides, *Bacch.* 1170–1171, 1178–1179. See Zadorojnyi (1997a: esp. 180–181); Chlup (2009).

[37] See Swain (1990a).

a banquet in order to please his young lover. The gruesome act has repercussions for Titus, who is also subsequently drawn into questionable behavior.[38] But the oppositions between Greek and barbarian lifestyle feature in by far the most arresting juxtaposition in the image of the chameleonic Alcibiades: in Sparta he was all for bodily training, simplicity of life, and severity of countenance; in Ionia, for luxurious ease and pleasure; in Thrace, for drinking deep; in Thessaly, for riding hard; and when he was thrown with Tissaphernes the satrap, he outdid even Persian magnificence in his pomp and lavishness (*Alcibiades* 23.5).

Finally, the symposium is a loaded symbol in the context of Plutarch's prescriptive discourse on dietetics – a prestigious branch of imperial Greco-Roman medicine that he integrates into his Platonic system. Dietetical focus on the effects of nourishment on health necessitated considerable attention to the nature and effects of food and drink consumed at the symposium; it was not only the types of foods and drinks that were consumed themselves that mattered but also their combinations, and the processes of their assimilation by the human body. The extent to which Plutarch was concerned with such issues may be gleaned from his scientific interests in the *Quaestiones naturales* (wine: 10, 27, 31; fruits: 5, 30, 31; meats: 22)[39] but, most prominently, from his moralistic writings that issue prescriptions on health (especially the *De tuenda sanitate praecepta*),[40] as well as from those dialogues in the *Quaestiones convivales* that contain debate on whether variety of food is better than simplicity of diet (4.1), whether sexual intercourse ought to take place after eating and drinking or not (3.6), or whether new diseases can spring up as a result of dietary changes (8.9). Moral concerns about luxury and excess of consumption are often reframed as scientific problems in such contexts, pointing to the inter-complementarity of the two types of discourse.[41] In addition, Plutarch's Platonism suffuses these perspectives with philosophical insight. Platonic dualism underpins discussions of all aspects of material consumption, by presuming a sympathetic relationship between body and soul: only when the body is light, calm, and rested (a condition guaranteed through moderate consumption) can the soul remain untrammeled in its engagement with the world of the intellect.[42] The anxieties of the imperial

---

[38]  Through the unjust persecution of Cato; see *Flamininus* 18.2–19.4.
[39]  On this work, see detailed study and commentary by Meeusen (2016).
[40]  See Senzasono (1997); Van Hoof (2010: 211–254).
[41]  See Boulogne (1996: 2771–2776, 2783–2788); Vamvouri Ruffy (2011; 2012: 125–161).
[42]  *Quaestiones convivales* 5.7, 681D–F. This position originated in Plato, *Ti.* 86a–87b and was also popular in ancient physiognomical science. See Gleason (1995: 29); Vamvouri Ruffy (2012: 153–161).

phenomenon that Michel Foucault (1984) has broadly termed the "care of the self," with its new culture of introspection and self-scrutiny, are looming behind this nexus of preoccupations with food and luxury.

## Plutarch's Sympotic Writings: *Septem sapientium convivium* and *Quaestiones convivales*

Plutarch's exploration of the symposium reaches a creative pinnacle with his *Septem sapientium convivium* and with *Quaestiones convivales*. These two highly innovative sympotic dialogues are characteristic of the intellectual concerns and cultural preoccupations in the imperial Greco-Roman symposiastic tradition. Not accidentally, their resonance and influence are strongly felt in later imperial authors who wrote about the symposium, namely Aulus Gellius, Athenaeus and Macrobius.[43]

For both Plutarchan works, antiquity's rich philosophical tradition of writing *Symposia* played a catalytical role. In the fourth century BCE, Plato and Xenophon, with their (probably contemporaneous) *Symposia*, were the first to elevate the symposium to a prime site of philosophical exploration. Both did so as part of their wider interest in its social significance. Plato extensively dealt with key aspects of the educational and communal function of the symposium in his *Republic* and *Laws*; the *Laws* is particularly concerned about the correct management of the potentially uncontrollable effects of wine-drinking at the symposium, a preoccupation that runs through Plutarch's sympotic writing as well.[44] Xenophon's sympotic vignettes in the *Memorabilia* and *Cyropaideia* also testify to his steady interest in the topic.[45] But, as Luciana Romeri has argued, it was their *Symposia* in particular, with their privileging of the intellectual dimension of the symposium (suppressing its material aspect), that inspired a long, rich, and highly versatile tradition of sympotic writing in prose, primarily by philosophers.[46] From the fourth century BCE onwards, Academics, Peripatetics, Stoics, and Epicureans would all write sympotic works of various kinds: sympotic dialogues, but also collections of sympotic *Problemata* and of known civic regulations on dining and sympotic practice (most notably, Aristotle's *Syssitikoi*, or *Sympotikoi Nomoi*), works *On*

---

[43] See Harrison (2000: 197); Klotz and Oikonomopoulou (2011b: 12–18); Titchener (2011: 42–48).

[44] Plato, *Lg.* 638c–650b and 671a–674b, with Belfiore (1986); Noël (2002); Jouët-Pastré (2002). Cf. Plutarch, *Quaestiones convivales*, 1.4–7, 3.1.647C–F, 3.7. See n. 29 in this chapter.

[45] Gray (1992; 1998); Gera (1993: 132–191); Hobden (2004; 2005; 2013: 213–228).

[46] See Romeri (2002: 61–103, esp. 89–103) for details.

*Drunkenness* (*Peri methēs*), and deontological (especially Stoic) treatises *On Sympotic Duties* (*Peri sympotikōn kathēkontōn*). Last but not least, there were parodic anti-*Symposia*, the prose and anti-philosophical equivalent of the celebrated genre of epic parody, flaunting the obsession with food and consumption at the expense of intellectual entertainment and conversation.[47] Unfortunately, too little survives from this colorful variety of works (mere titles, some of them) to enable us to assess their significance for the imperial literature of the *Symposium* in a secure or reliable way. But there is no doubt that its diffusion was very wide, and its interests in some cases truly encyclopedic.

Of Plutarch's two sympotic writings only *Quaestiones convivales* can be approximately dated in terms of its composition (after 99 and before 116 CE, according to Christopher P. Jones).[48] By contrast, the archaic setting of *Septem sapientium convivium* and lack of explicit cross-references to its content in other Plutarchan works leave no reliable clues as to its dating. We ought, however, to be skeptical of the argument that the "repeated round-robin short answers given by the seven sages and the numerous riddles loosely stitched together ... point to an earlier date [sc. in comparison with Plutarch's other collections of *Problemata*, including the *Quaestiones convivales*], rather than a later one."[49] The work's peculiarly sententious format in fact tallies with its subject-matter (gnomic utterances were the intellectual trademark of the Seven Sages)[50] and hence, far from pointing to literary immaturity, testifies rather to Plutarch's nuanced choice of discursive style for the work. The issue of the chronological relationship between Plutarch's two sympotic works simply cannot, with the current state of evidence, be reliably settled.

Can the examination of formal and thematic affinities at least provide some clues as to how the two dialogues stand in relation to one another? At first glance, the differences in their respective choices of literary format, fictional setting, and content seem to point to distinct agendas. *Septem sapientium convivium* has been found overall to be more faithful to the model of sympotic dialogue set by Plato and Xenophon, both because it narrates a single sympotic occasion, taking place in the house of the Corinthian tyrant Periander sometime in the sixth century BCE, and because of the progression of its narrative according to the stages of the

[47] On this tradition, see Tecuşan (1993); Klotz and Oikonomopoulou (2011b: 13–15). On the theme of transgression in imperial Greco-Roman sympotic literature, see Romeri (2002: 23–106, 191–246); König (2012: 231–289).
[48] Jones (1966: 72–73).    [49] Harrison (2000: 198).
[50] See Snell (1954); Martin (1993); Morgan (2011: 61–68); Stamatopoulou (2014).

meal (in the style of Xenophon) and from lesser to greater intellectual substance (in the style of Plato).[51] As Judith Mossman has noted, the literary reconstruction of an earlier historical period reveals significant parallels with Plutarch's novelistic dialogue *De genio Socratis* set in the fourth century BCE.[52] Fittingly for its choice of dramatic characters, and without doubt as a result of its drawing from a vast pool of gnomic wisdom attributed to the Seven Wise men, the interests in *Septem sapientium convivium* are overwhelmingly political and moral.[53]

The *Quaestiones convivales*, on the other hand, is a collection of narrative snapshots of different symposia, featuring Plutarch himself and his circle of friends. The dramatic dates range from Nero's visit to Greece (67 CE) to Favorinus' years of adolescent study (early second century CE). The parties take place all over Greece, and, in a few instances, also at Rome.[54] The literary pedigree of the text is much more complicated, as, apart from Plato and Xenophon's *Symposia*, it also comprises sympotic works by philosophers of other schools, not all of which, as we have seen, would have been dialogues:

> To consign to utter oblivion all that occurs at a drinking-party is not only opposed to what we call the friend-making character of the dining-table, but also has the most famous of the philosophers to bear witness against it – Plato, Xenophon, Aristotle, Speusippus, Epicurus, Prytanis, Hieronymus, and Dio of the Academy, who all considered the recording of conversations held at table a task worth some effort. (*Quaestiones convivales* 1, preface, 612D)

What this statement emphatically displays is the self-conscious memorialization of the *entire* philosophical tradition of sympotic writing. Indeed, this tradition resonates in the work's content by means of allusions, thematic debts, and a critical filtering of what previous philosophers have said about the symposium and its paraphernalia.[55] In a similarly comprehensive gesture, use of the autobiographical mode in *Quaestiones convivales* echoes that of Plutarch's philosophical dialogues (*De E apud Delphos, De defectu oraculorum, Amatorius*),[56] while its miscellanistic subject-matter, ranging from moral and political reflection to

---

[51] Mossman (1997c); Jazdzewska (2016).    [52] Mossman (1997c: 121).
[53] See insightful analysis of *Septem sapientium convivium*'s historical frame and discursive format by Kim (2009). See also Jazdzewska (2013; 2016).
[54] See Jones (1966: 72–73; 1967: 206–207). Symposia at Rome: *Quaestiones convivales* 1, preface, 612E; 1.9, 5.10, 7.4, 8.7.
[55] On the role of philosophy in *Quaestiones convivales*, see Kechagia (2011a).
[56] On autobiography in *Quaestiones convivales*, see Klotz and Oikonomopoulou (2011b: 7–12).

natural science, from plants and zoology to human physiology, and from medicine to Homeric criticism, suggests a yet wider network of thematic interests and sources.

More careful examination, however, reveals some key common strands that point to the complementarity of *Septem sapientium convivium* and *Quaestiones convivales*. The first is their panhellenism: the gathering of the Seven Wise men, who come from different parts of the Greek world, at the tyrant Periander's table on the occasion of the sacrifice in honor of Aphrodite at Lechaeum (146D–E) parallels the gatherings Plutarch and his friends, people who come from different parts of the Roman Empire, hold at the table of eminent friends on various festival occasions. The vast chronological gap that separates the symposium described in *Septem sapientium convivium* from the symposia of *Quaestiones convivales* only serves to accentuate the diachronic continuity of the particular version of panhellenism that both works advocate – one that sees the "essence" of Greekness in the presence of multiple local Greek identities, and their harmonious interaction under the auspices of specific political, religious, or cultural institutions: Delphi, religious and athletic festivals, and, as far as Plutarch's era in particular is concerned, imperial Rome itself.[57] Tellingly, for what is a characteristically Plutarchan construction of the Greek past, in *Septem sapientium convivium* the rosiness of this ideal is somewhat marred by the presence of ominous premonitions of tyrannical violence (especially the scene of the portent, 149C–E, with Diocles' interpretation of it as a "sign of strife, *stasis,* and discord, *diaphora*"), thus pointing to the inherent instability of the (pan)hellenic model before the advent of Rome.[58]

Equally important is the question-and-answer technique, which plays a central role in both texts: the conversation takes the form of riddle-posing and riddle-solving, and of a series of intellectual challenges geared toward eliciting gnomic staccatos in *Septem sapientium convivium* (151E–152B; 153A–D), while in *Quaestiones convivales* it progresses as enquiries into the natural world or aspects of cultural life that invite lengthy argumentative expositions, in the style of Aristotle's *Problemata*.[59] It is significant that

---

[57] See König (2007: 62–68; 2012: 81–88). Compare *Quaestiones Graecae*, where the motif of the Greek world's interconnectivity is further explored. See Oikonomopoulou (2017a).

[58] See Jazdzewska (2013) on the theme of death and its political connotations in the work. See also references to despotism in 147A–E, with Aalders (1977). On the notion of *stasis*, see also *Praecepta gerendae reipublicae* and *De Pythiae oraculis*, 401C–D.

[59] Harrison (2000) is surely right in treating both works as parts of a unified project, aiming at the reinvigoration of the genre of *Problemata*.

both texts trace the origins of the technique further back into the past: in the case of *Septem sapientium convivium*, to the legendary contest between Homer and Hesiod (153E–154A), and in *Quaestiones convivales* to successive generations of Greek philosophers and intellectuals, whose own questions-and-answers are alluded to, cited, criticized, supplemented, or even taken up afresh in the dialogues.[60] By doing so, the two texts act in remarkable synergy in consecrating question-and-answer as a Greek intellectual activity par excellence – that is, as the technique that plays a vital role in the perpetuation of Greek historical and cultural memory and as the method that lies at the very heart of Greece's most celebrated cultural product, philosophy. The fact that it is the symposium that features as the natural site for this activity (religious sanctuaries such as Delphi play a similar role in Plutarch's Delphic dialogues) underlines its diachronic centrality in Greek cultural and intellectual life. Not accidentally, both Plutarch's texts construct an almost identical code of sympotic demeanor, discoursing on ways of ensuring harmonious interaction between the guests,[61] problematizing the principle of sympotic equality,[62] and exploring the relationship between the material and intellectual dimensions of the symposium.[63]

Judith Mossman and other scholars have comprehensively discussed the broader literary context, compositional structure, and key themes of *Septem sapientium convivium*, and I refer the reader to their work.[64] In my last section I will focus on Plutarch's *Quaestiones convivales* in an attempt to map out the intricacies and rich thematic horizon of this highly ambitious Plutarchan *Symposium*.

## The Dynamics of Erudite Drinking: The *Quaestiones convivales'* World of Knowledge

A reader approaching the *Quaestiones convivales* for the first time is likely to feel overwhelmed by its thematic range. The work's nine books contain a rich sampling of virtually every field of intellectual inquiry. Their topics include the symposium itself (its material aspects but also its values),[65] the natural world, the human body, animals, plants, culture (literary

---

[60] For example, 1.5 (Theophrastus), 1.9 (Aristotle), 3.6 (Epicurus). See Oikonomopoulou (2011).
[61] *Septem sapientium convivium* 147E–148E, with *Quaestiones convivales*, 1.1.
[62] *Septem sapientium convivium* 149A–B, with *Quaestiones convivales*, 1.2.
[63] *Septem sapientium convivium* 159B–160C.
[64] Mossman (1997c); Romeri (2002: 107–138); Kim (2009); Jazdzewska (2013; 2016); Stamatopoulou (2014).
[65] See especially the opening chapters of book 1 (*Quaestiones convivales*, 1.1–4), revealing of the work's sympotic philosophy.

interpretation, music, athletics, festivals, language), and philosophical disquisitions. Equally impressive is the number of characters paraded and the variety of their professions and specializations: doctors, grammarians, rhetoricians, philosophers of the main schools, assorted priests and officials, statesmen, artists and musicians, young pupils of philosophy.[66] This dazzling variety makes the work a veritable "sympotic miscellany" rather than simply a *Symposium*.[67] We can only get a sense of the intellectual importance of this project for its era, as well as for the overall history of Greek encyclopedic writing, if we think that the only subsequent sympotic project in Greek that surpasses it in its range of contents (though not in the variety of its fictional characters) is Athenaeus' *Deipnosophistae*.[68] Further, the fact that the *Quaestiones convivales* is mined by the later miscellanistic authors Gellius and Macrobius suggests a wide appeal beyond the strictly Greek cultural boundaries.[69] What, then, did Plutarch aim to achieve with this densely packed project, and how can we navigate through its meandering texture?

In his opening address to his Roman friend Sosius Senecio (*Quaestiones convivales* 1, preface, 612E), Plutarch speaks of his ambition to create a record of sympotic recollections, carefully selected according to the criterion of "suitability" (*ta epitēdeia*). The latter notion is not sufficiently glossed, but, given the overall context, Plutarch probably has in mind a criterion approximate to his (and other imperial miscellanists') favorite pair of "pleasure and usefulness" (see esp. *Quaestiones convivales* 1.1). Indeed, the various books' contents ingeniously fulfill this dual objective by introducing deceptively simple or trivial subjects – "Why do old men read from a distance?" (1.8), "Is it right to strain wine?" (6.7), "Which of Aphrodite's hands did Diomedes wound in the *Iliad*?" (9.4) – but drawing from a rich arsenal of empirical observation and background theoretical knowledge, making rigorous use of philosophical logic, and resorting to respected intellectual authorities for answers.[70] Where precisely does the usefulness of its contents lie, however?

An example from the text itself may help to answer this question. Chapter 1.8, as I have mentioned, is concerned with the reasons "why old

[66] See Puech (1992) for a prosopography of these characters.
[67] See Klotz and Oikonomopoulou (2011b: 22–27); Morgan (2011); König (2012: 60–89).
[68] See the essays in Braund and Wilkins (2000); also Romeri (2002: 247–321); König (2012: 90–120); Jacob (2013).
[69] On the *Quaestiones convivales'* reception by Gellius, see Klotz and Oikonomopoulou (2011c: 233–237).
[70] See König (2007; 2010: esp. 335–345; 2012: 75–81).

men hold writing at a greater distance for reading." A seemingly trivial problem, it is nevertheless introduced by means of two elegant quotations from Aeschylus and Sophocles (625C) and transformed into a rich intellectual exercise in the conversation that follows. Three different scientific theories are proposed as explanation, each deriving from a different philosophical authority: the theory of the joined vision rays, *augai* (unattributed in the text, though we know it goes back to the famous Greek astronomer Hipparchus), the theory of forms, *eidē*, shed by material objects, which penetrate the eyes through the body's pores, *poroi*, understood as openings or ducts in matter (attributed to the Peripatetic Hieronymus), and, finally, the theory of the mixture of a bright emanation (*pneuma*) streaming from the eyes with the light surrounding the perceived objects (attributed to Plato).[71] By expounding the basic principles of each theory, the speakers on the most straightforward level instruct the readers in *facts*, which in this instance involve knowledge of key theories in Greek scientific thinking. But this is by no means the whole picture. Rigorous scientific language accompanies the discussion, which makes use of fundamental concepts for understanding the material world (*poroi, pneuma,* mixture) and puts the emphasis on conclusions that follow from logical connections and strict adherence to causality (underlined through the recurrence of words such as "likely," *eikos* and "cause," *aition*, and connectives such as "thereby," *dio*).[72] Conceptual precision and the ability to argue clearly, coherently, and convincingly thus emerge as complementary objectives in the chapter, equally important to its factual dimension.

Looking at things from a broader perspective, the chapter vividly captures a particular style of intellectual engagement, reflecting a mindset that puts the emphasis on an aporetic outlook to the world (inquiry, *zētēsis* is universally valorized in the text),[73] intellectual pluralism (advocated through the use of the technique of multiple explanations), openmindedness, and civility of interaction (alternative opinions cannot be confidently articulated unless the company lays the ground open to differences of opinion). Elsewhere in the work Plutarch identifies this style with philosophy,[74] but it would be equally fruitful for us to think about it as a cultural code or system that is crucially inflected by philosophy (its history, concepts, methods, and discursive frame), and realized and tested

---

[71] For further details on the scientific background of this talk, see Teodorsson (1989, *ad loc.*).
[72] On the concept of *eikos* in *Quaestiones convivales*, see Kechagia (2011a: 99–104). On the importance of precision in speech (part of the broader prerequisite of brevity at the symposium), see König (2010: esp. 331–335; 2012: 66–71).
[73] See Kechagia (2011a: 93–97).    [74] Especially 1.2 and 5.7.680C–D, with Kechagia (2011a).

out in the intimate conditions of the symposium. It is this broader *culture* that the *Quaestiones convivales* ultimately seeks to instill in its readers, and which is the ultimate measure of both the allure and usefulness of its contents.[75]

The *Quaestiones convivales* has no systematic organizing scheme for its contents, in tune with the tradition of Greek and Latin miscellanistic and encyclopedic writing. Association plays a central role as an organizing principle, yoked as it is to Plutarch's patterns of memory as the author-narrator of his text (he himself admits in the preface to his second book that he organized its contents "as each came to mind," *hōs hekaston eis mnēmēn epēlthen*: 629D–E), as well as to the loose, associative twists and turns of the sympotic conversations that are purportedly the object of the author's recollection. This is a strategy that derives its potency and resonance from the world of ancient education (*enkyklios paideia*), which put the stress on the storage and retrieval of facts in and from memory on the basis of such associative schemes. It is joined by the aesthetic principle of *variatio* (Greek: *poikilia*), to which ancient education also attached pedagogical value: distaste for thematic monotony dictates the fragmentation of the material for the purpose of achieving often striking transitions.[76] These ensure the readers' constant engagement with the text, arousing their curiosity for what comes next, or allowing them to be pleasantly carried away by the unpredictable turns of the arguments and shifts of focus.

This pedagogical aspect is further enhanced by the choice of the sympotic theme, for the symposium (as we have already seen) was traditionally the key locus of Greek education. It is also promoted by the transparency of the logic followed for the solution of each problem, the ample provision of examples by the speakers, their use of analogies and metaphors for illustrating argument, and the encouragement to engage even with seemingly intractable, or hackneyed, topics for the purpose of intellectual exercise. As a concluding gesture that is meant to leave a lasting impression, the work pays homage to *enkyklios paideia* in its very last book (9), featuring a group of eminent teachers of young Athenian men as guests of honor of Plutarch's own teacher, Ammonius.[77]

One last question remains, and it concerns the intended effects of Plutarch's choice of narrative technique. The *Quaestiones convivales*

---

[75]  See Frazier (1998) on the *Quaestiones convivales*' code of sympotic entertainment.
[76]  See discussion by Small (1997: esp. 177–201). Also König (2007: 43–56; 2012: 88–89); Klotz and Oikonomopoulou (2011b: 24–27); Oikonomopoulou (2017b). On the Roman concept of *variatio*, see Fitzgerald (2016: esp. 149–195).
[77]  On Ammonius, see Jones (1967).

sometimes stages highly stylized narratives whose fictional exchanges exhibit an adherence to the patterns of factual citation and logical rigor I traced in my earlier example. Some of the chapters are narrated by Plutarch's voice throughout (such is incidentally the case of 1.8 mentioned earlier), the different opinions being cited in indirect speech (it is unclear whether this is paraphrase or summary). On other occasions Plutarch lets the characters' own voices take center stage, enlivening the narrative with humor, laughter, sharp irony, antagonistic friction, intellectual tension, and emotional affection, so that we can discern different discursive registers at play, which point to distinct professional and intellectual identities or cultural mindsets.[78]

These shifts certainly serve the aesthetics of *poikilia* on the level of rhetoric. But they also aim to diversify the dialogues in terms of their effect: while exchanges showing adherence to rhetorical rules seek to direct attention to method, the use of indirect speech may either aim at a greater focus on content or highlight Plutarch's distance from his material, with all the consequences this has for questions of credibility and truth. Direct speech, on the other hand, opens a window into the richness and multi-layered nature of the characters' interaction, and gives Plutarch the opportunity to hone his talents in character portrayal and psychological verisimilitude.[79] Here too Plutarch's sophistication as an author may be glimpsed in all its finesse; his creativity and versatility as a storyteller turn the *Quaestiones convivales* into a fine study of narrative technique and fictionalization on a par with the *Lives*.

## Further Reading

A considerable amount of scholarly work has been devoted to aspects of conviviality in Plutarch. Most important are the essays included in Montes Cala et al. (1999) and Ribeiro Ferreirra et al. (2009). Synthetic studies pursuing cultural readings are still lacking, however. Useful guidance into the sympotic scenes embedded in the *Lives* is offered by Brenk (1992) and Paul (1991). On *Quaestiones convivales*, the synoptic essay by Klotz (2014) is a good starting-point; Teodorsson's commentary (in three volumes: 1989; 1990; 1996) remains essential. Romeri (2002) and Klotz and Oikonomopoulou (2011a) offer sustained analyses of the work's literary

---

[78] See, once again, book 9, featuring different teachers: grammarians (1–3), rhetoricians (13), mathematicians (3, 12), and philosophers.

[79] Some of the implications of this play with voices are discussed by Klotz (2007; 2011a) and Brenk (2009).

background, philosophical character, key themes, and narrative texture. Nikolaidis (2017) calls attention to the enactment of elite sociality in *Quaestiones convivales*; Vamvouri Ruffy (2012) conducts a nuanced investigation of medicine and medical discourse within the work; König (2007; 2010; 2012) explores the intellectual and (inter)textual strategies. On the links of *Quaestiones convivales* with Greco-Roman imperial miscellanistic and encyclopedic writing, see König (2012); Klotz and Oikonomopoulou (2011a, esp. 2011b); and Oikonomopoulou (2017b). No full-length commentary in English as yet exists for *Septem sapientium convivium*, but Mossman (1997c) is a valuable guide into the text's literary backdrop and narrative coherence. Kim (2009) further explores key aspects of fictional technique and discursive style; Jazdzewska (2013; 2016) examines the function of laughter and the theme of death within the work, respectively, and Stamatopoulou (2014) discusses its treatment of Hesiodic poetry and wisdom.

CHAPTER 8

# Language, Style, and Rhetoric

## Donald Russell

As a good philosopher, Plutarch thought content infinitely more important than style.[1] He deprecated excessive attention to words by writer or by reader[2] and believed that the right way to read classical poetry was to concentrate on its moral lessons and not so much on information (*historia*) or brilliance of language.[3] Nevertheless, he was himself a master of the formal prose (*Kunstprosa* in the idiom of German philology) of his day and had enough versatility to vary his style not only according to genre but also sometimes even within a work, especially in dialogue. At the same time, his writing always shows two very marked characteristics: abundance, and richness of imagery and allusion. These features do not appeal to admirers of Greek prose who take its main virtues to be directness and simplicity. Plutarch was indeed no "Atticist."[4] What he produces is what Erasmus[5] very properly called a "mosaic" (*opus musaicum*). In the Renaissance, this had its attractions; and my own feeling for Plutarch is akin to my feeling for writers like Sir Thomas Browne and Jeremy Taylor, who owed much to him.

It is not easy to talk about Plutarch's style. There is no comprehensive study.[6] Editors generally do not concentrate on these matters; a notable exception is H. A. Holden in a series of nineteenth-century school editions of *Lives*,[7] each of which contains a word-index and notes on usage that are often useful, though sometimes misleading. For a lexicon, we are still dependent on Wyttenbach (1843), though this can now be supplemented

---

[1] This was written before Hutchinson (2018), which gives a fuller account.
[2] See, for example, *De recta ratione audiendi* 41E, *De gloria Atheniensium* 350D.
[3] *Quomodo adolescens poetas audire debeat* 30D.
[4] Schmid (1887–96), i.2 does contain much relevant to Plutarch; see especially iv.577–734. Compare Vela Tejada (2019).
[5] *Opus Epistularum* 1572: vi. 70 Allen: see Russell (1973a: 148).
[6] Weissenberger (1894) is slight; Ziegler (1949: 291–301) is very useful; but see also Russell (1973a: 18–41); J. G. Griffiths (1970: 10–16); Moles (1988: 12–16); Yaginuma (1992: 4736–4742); Hutchinson (2018).
[7] *Themistocles* (1881), *Gracchi* (1885), *Sulla* (1886), *Nicias* (1887), *Timoleon* (1889), *Demosthenes* (1893), *Pericles* (1894).

and sometimes replaced by computer searches on the Thesaurus Linguae Graecae (TLG). In these circumstances, the best approach is by means of commentary on particular passages, and the second part of this chapter takes this form. First, however, I formulate some general questions and try to define Plutarch's place in the history of Greek prose writing.

# I

There are four basic questions:

(i)   Where does Plutarch stand in relation to the classicism and Atticism that characterize Greek writing in the first and second centuries of our era? In other words, how should we describe the manner in which he combines his mimesis of the classics with his acceptance and development of the standards of Hellenistic prose?
(ii)  What part does formal rhetoric play in his writings, either as a set of structural principles or as a reservoir of techniques of ornament and force?
(iii) What are the special features of his abundance, imagery, and allusiveness?
(iv)  How far does his versatility go in providing him with a range of styles for various occasions?

Let us take these questions in turn.

(i)   There is an obvious difference between Plutarch, on the one hand, and his contemporary Dio Chrysostom and the second-century Atticists on the other.[8] Dio and the rest all aim to write the language of the fourth century BCE. Plutarch does not: he makes his claim to a place in the classical tradition not, on the whole, by linguistic and stylistic mimesis (there are exceptions to this, e.g. his "Platonic" myths) but by his "mosaic," the constant stream of allusion and quotations. Moreover, his enormous vocabulary – of the order of 30,000 words, perhaps twice that of Dio Chrysostom – includes many words that are not classical, especially compound verbs, many of which seem to be new in him, some no doubt his own coinage.[9] Later Atticist grammarians never regarded him as an authority, though he was much read throughout later antiquity.

---

[8] This is not to say that Plutarch is alone in his conservatism: Onasander, "Longinus," and "Heraclitus" come to mind as writers of the period who share many features with him.
[9] Teodorsson (2005).

Some syntactical features also are not classical, but they can hardly count as exclusively Hellenistic, because the Atticists too did not avoid them. They were too deeply ingrained in the literary language. For example, the use of μή for οὐ in participial phrases, whether or not they are conditional in sense, and in subordinate clauses of various kinds is clearly a change from classical Attic usage, but it was a change that was never reversed. Even Aelius Aristides[10] has no clear feeling for the classical rules. Similarly, Plutarch's use of the optative[11] has unclassical features: it is common in the protasis of conditions that have no sense of remoteness and have an indicative in the apodosis. He probably uses the optative less often than Lucian or Aristides, but his usage is not essentially different.

There are, of course, some features that are prima facie classicizing. Plutarch prefers πρίν to πρὶν ἤ. He rarely, if ever, uses διότι to introduce an indirect statement. His use of particles is richer than (for example) that of Diodorus, but still less varied than Dio Chrysostom's. He tends to use ὡς or ὅπως more than ἵνα in final clauses. (Why is this? Imitation of Xenophon? Or avoidance of the ambiguity resulting from the extended use of ἵνα in late Greek, especially in consecutive clauses?) He generally avoids juxtaposed τε καί – that is to say, he follows the practice of the Attic orators, not Plato. His use of the historic present is interesting. This was a feature of Xenophon (especially in the *Anabasis*)[12] but it disappeared from Hellenistic historical writing, to be revived by Atticists like Pausanias and Arrian. Yet it seems to have survived in ordinary speech, for it is common in the New Testament.[13] Plutarch[14] has two ranges of use: one confined to certain verbs (e.g. τρέπεται and verbs like κυροῦται, which denote proposal or ratification); and one in vivid narrative, as in the lively scenes at the end of *De genio Socratis*, where we have ἀφικνεῖται Χάρων, "Charon arrives" (595E); or παίει τὸν Κηφισόδωρον, "[Leontiades] strikes Cephisodorus" (597E). It is unclear – and perhaps an unmeaning question – whether these limited uses represent mimesis, say, of Xenophon or reproduction of contemporary speech.

Another important difference from most later Atticists is that Plutarch maintains the tradition of periodic prose, which (a) generally avoids hiatus except in certain specific conditions[15] and (b) has distinct

---

[10]  Boulanger (1923: 409).   [11]  Hein (1914).
[12]  Cf. "Longinus", *De subl.* 25; van Emde Boas et al. (2019: 430–431, 722–728).
[13]  E.g. Mark 14.66, ἔρχεται μία τῶν παιδισκῶν τοῦ ἀρχιερέως.   [14]  Stadter (1989: 115).
[15]  See Ziegler (1949: 295–297); Porter (1937: 90). He does this despite his ridicule of Isocrates: *De gloria Atheniensium* 350D.

rhythmical patterns, especially at the ends of periods and cola. The patterns he prefers come from Hellenistic rhetoric and are very similar to those commonly adopted by Cicero and other Latin writers. The commonest forms are variations of the double cretic (– ᵕ – – ᵕ –), cretic and spondee (– ᵕ – – –), and ditrochaeus (– ᵕ – –). They have been analyzed and studied in some detail,[16] but the most convenient way of learning to appreciate them may be to familiarize oneself with the classifications developed by Latin scholars.[17] We hear them everywhere, insistently repeated. They are an important determinant of word-order, and the reason for many common hyperbata. In the simple sentence ἐπὶ τῶν μεσημβρίνων καθεζόμεθα κρηπίδων, "we sat down on the southern steps" (*De Pythiae oraculis* 402C), the paean (i.e. resolved cretic) and spondee ending strikes the ear. This artifice (as we think of it, though to Plutarch it is surely second nature) affects even the most direct and vivid narrative. Cleopatra, about to die, orders a bath, bathes, and has a splendid dinner (*Antony* 85.1):

> ἐκέλευσεν λοῦτρον αὐτῇ γενέσθαι,
> λουσαμένη δὲ καὶ κατακλιθεῖσα,
> λαμπρὸν ἄριστον ἠρίστα.
>
> She ordered a bath to be prepared for her,
> and after the bath and after taking her place at table,
> she had a magnificent dinner.

Ditrochaeus; paean and spondee; cretic and spondee– and this on a passage marked as deliberately "simple" by the repetition λοῦτρον ... γενέσθαι, λουσαμένη δὲ, and the cognate accusative ἄριστον ἠρίστα.

(ii) Next, the rhetoric. We need first to distinguish a group of writings that show a very heavy use of rhetorical figures from the bulk of Plutarch's narrative and didactic writings. These are, first, the epideictic speeches on Rome, Athens, and Alexander (*Moralia* 316C–351B); secondly, a number of other short pieces that also seem highly rhetorical: *De superstitione*, *De primo frigido*, *Aquane an ignis sit utilior*, *De vitando aere alieno*, and *De esu carnium*.[18] The second

[16] Summary in Ziegler (1949: 298–299): Sandbach (1939) uses this topic to identify spurious works.

[17] See, for example, Nisbet (1990: 351); full treatment in Hutchinson (2018).

[18] On the style of both groups in general, see Krauss (1912); Kowalski (1918); on *De vitando aere alieno*, Russell (1973b).

group is in fact generically different from the first, as a pair of brief examples will show:

(a) *De fortuna Romanorum* 317E
Τῆς δὲ Τύχης ὀξὺ μὲν τὸ κίνημα
καὶ θρασὺ τὸ φρόνημα
καὶ μεγάλαυχον ἡ ἐλπίς,
φθάνουσα δὲ τὴν Ἀρετὴν ἐγγύς ἐστιν,
οὐ πτεροῖς ἐλαφρίζουσα κούφοις ἑαυτήν
οὐδ᾽ ἀκρώνυχον ὑπὲρ σφαίρας τινὸς ἴχνος καθεῖσα
περισφαλὴς καὶ ἀμφίβολος πρόσεισιν, εἶτ᾽ ἄπεισιν ἀειδής.

Fortune's movement is quick,
bold are her thoughts,
ambitious her hope;
outstripping Virtue she is close at hand,
not raising herself on light wings,
not resting the tip of her toes on a ball,
perilous and ambivalent she advances, then to vanish unseen.

There are many obvious tricks here: the short cola, the homeoteleuta, the insistent clausulae (almost all ditrochaei or cretic-spondee), and the bold and sometimes poetical compounds (esp. μεγάλαυχον, ἀκρώνυχον).

(b) *De vitando aere alieno* 831B
Ἤδη γάρ μοι πρὸς τοὺς εὐπορωτέρους καὶ μαλακωτέρους ὁ λόγος ἐστιν,
τοὺς λέγοντας
"ἄδουλος οὖν γένωμαι καὶ ἀνέστιος καὶ ἄνοικος;"
ὥσπερ εἰ λέγοι πρὸς ἰατρὸν ἄρρωστος καὶ ᾠδηκώς,
"ἰσχνὸς οὖν γένωμαι καὶ κενός;"
τί δ᾽ οὐ μέλλεις, ἵν᾽ ὑγιαίνῃς;
καὶ σὺ γενοῦ[19] ἄδουλος ἵνα μὴ δοῦλος ᾖς,
καὶ ἀκτήμων ἵνα μὴ κτῆμ᾽ ᾖς ἄλλου.

Now I must talk to the richer and softer living, those who say, "Am I to go without slaves, hearth, or home?" It is like a patient who is ill or swollen saying to the doctor "Am I to become thin and starved?" Why not, to secure your health? You too, go without slaves so as not to be a slave, go without property so as not to be the property of someone else!

The first passage was the full Gorgianic panegyric style: the second is what modern scholars often call "diatribe style,"[20] with its imaginary questions and answers, homely imagery, and vigorous appeal to the hearer. Even here,

---

[19] Note the unusual hiatus.  [20] See Moles (1996).

however, the rhythms are in evidence, and the abundance and alliteration of ἄδουλος . . . καὶ ἀνέστιος καὶ ἄνοικος would be at home in grander contexts. What is common to these passages – and to all these two groups of writings – is that they are the written versions of oral performances. This is not the case with Plutarch's other works, which are written for recipients or dedicatees, even if (as he sometimes tells us[21]) they began life as lectures (σχολαί) and were written up subsequently for friends.

It used to be commonly believed that these "rhetorical" works are all early, and that he abandoned this manner, and the practice of giving such performances, in later life. This cannot be proved. Our ignorance of Plutarchan chronology is profound.[22] We should indeed accept the view that the bulk of what we have dates from fairly late in his career, certainly after the death of Domitian in 96 CE. Such certainties as there are come from factual references or external evidence, not from consideration of style.[23] No doubt *An seni respublica gerenda sit* is late: only an elderly man would ask whether the elderly should take part in public life, and this text is indeed an excessively redundant, repetitive, and loosely structured affair.[24] But how far one should extrapolate from this to theorize on Plutarch's stylistic development is problematic.

Even in the "rhetorical" pieces, what may be called the "small-scale" rhetoric (figures of speech and thought) is much more conspicuous than the structural rhetoric. Plutarch seems happier composing single impressive passages than constructing a unity. This is something that is also noticeable elsewhere in his work. It is of course true that the comparisons that accompany the *Lives*[25] are a development of the common progymnasma of σύγκρισις.[26] Indeed, more generally, comparison, as we shall see, is one of Plutarch's principal tools of argument and persuasion. It is true also that the *Lives* display a fairly regular pattern of narrative and character description, but this pattern is of course essentially chronological. In the essays and dialogues, it is often difficult to see a scheme systematically worked out. *Quomodo adolescens poetas audire debeat* is instructive. It has two main themes: how to prevent students of poetry from acquiring bad moral principles from their reading, and how to find positive philosophical lessons in the poets. These themes are not always

---

[21] For example, *Quomodo adolescens poetas audire debeat* 15A, *De recta ratione audiendi* 37C, *Adversus Colotem* 1107F.
[22] Fuhrmann (1964) is far too optimistic.  [23] See especially Jones (1966).
[24] See Hubert's introductory note on 783A in the Teubner edition (20).
[25] Erbse (1956): Pelling (2002a: 349–364).
[26] See, for example, Theon 112–155 Spengel = 78–87 Patillon-Bolognesi.

clearly kept apart,[27] and the whole piece, with its strings of quotations, has an informal air. However, it does have a formal preface and an appropriate closing section, in which the student is solemnly escorted on his way from poetry to philosophy. Most strikingly, it has in the middle three chapters (10–12) of extraordinary formality. Each opens with an elaborate simile (a common introductory move, as we shall see) and two of these similes are about bees;[28] and each ends with an evident closure. What is the relation between these little compositions and the lecture (σχολή) that Plutarch tells us lies behind the treatise? Again, we get the impression of small-scale craftsmanship in a varied and more casually composed whole.

(iii)   Abundance, imagery, and allusion are the three elements of the rich "mosaic."

    (a)   The principal technique of abundance is binary (occasionally ternary) amplification (*Erweiterung*),[29] which demands an infinite supply of near-synonyms, nouns, and verbs as well as adjectives. The habit itself is classical (Demosthenes and Isocrates are both prone to it), but it is also characteristic of Hellenistic prose, both literary and official. It is not always clear whether the amplification is functional – that is, the words each make a contribution to the sense, and the couple defines the nuance better than either word would on its own – or a simple hendiadys, a single idea being artificially split in two, or even mere "tinsel" (*Flitterkram*, so Palm 1955: 145), introduced more for the sound of it or the balance of the clause than for any contribution to meaning. Examples will be seen in the passages discussed later. These *Erweiterungen* are not ubiquitous in Plutarch, but commoner in some works than in others, and often occur in clusters. Whether this is due to genre differences or to a change of habits is unclear.

    (b)   No Greek prose writer comes near Plutarch in richness of metaphor and simile. This aspect of his work has been much discussed.[30] Fuhrmann (1964) lists about 3,000 instances, discusses the various forms in which they are introduced, and enumerates the areas of experience from which they come. The

---

[27] Schenkeveld (1982), reprinted in Laird (2006: 313–322); Hunter and Russell (2011: 17–21).
[28] A common source of imagery in Plutarch: Dronkers (1892: 109–111), with some fifteen occurrences; Xenophontos (2013: *passim*).
[29] Rehdantz and Blass (1886: 13–18); Palm (1955: 143–145).
[30] See Dronkers (1892); Fuhrmann (1964).

*Moralia* are naturally richer than the *Lives*, and within the
*Moralia* the concentration is greatest in works that deal with
everyday morals and aim to convince a wide public, not just
professional philosophers. The extreme case is *Coniugalia
praecepta*,[31] which consists entirely of a series of likenesses
(ὁμοιότητες) designed to show what good marriage relationships are like.

All this does, I think, point to something fundamental in
Plutarch's way of thinking. Comparison is the key. We might
say he has a syncritical rather than a critical mind. Only too
often (e.g. in the crucial speech of Simmias in *De genio Socratis*
588B–589F) analogies altogether supplant reasoning and infer-
ence. It seems as if Plutarch never contemplates anything by
itself, but always in juxtaposition with something either like or
unlike it, and that he always wants to clarify his meaning by
pointing out the likenesses and the unlikenesses. This tendency
ends by making him something of a prose-poet, as Ralph
Waldo Emerson[32] clearly saw when he thought of him as
a writer who could give a lot of hints to poets, both in subject-
matter (the heroic tales of the *Lives*) and in the metaphorical
discourse that is the essence of poetry.[33] Again, the passages to
be discussed later will illustrate this.

(c)    Plutarch also excels almost every other prose writer in the
number and ubiquity of his quotations from the classics, especially the poets. This is of course part of the same "syncritical"
way of thinking. *Quomodo adolescens poetas audire debeat* discusses the ways in which poetical quotations may be used –
how, for instance, one passage may be refuted by another, or
a morally objectionable idea explained away by referring to its
original dramatic context – and it is often possible to see
Plutarch following his own principles in this way. There has
always been much discussion of his sources: how much comes
from first-hand reading, how much from anthologies and
collections of γνῶμαι?[34] This indulgence in quotation is an
important part of his way of claiming integration in the classical
tradition. The way in which he makes the characters in his

---

[31] Goessler (1962); Pomeroy (1999a).    [32] See Hirzel (1912: 143, 194).
[33] Cf. Aristotle, *Poetics* 1459a, b.
[34] Helmbold-O'Neil (1959: vii–ix). This index of quotations remains the best available guide for
further study.

dialogues (often members of his own family) scatter quotations around also indicates the importance attached in his cultural world to the display of this sort of knowledge.[35]

(iv) The most striking example of stylistic versatility within a single work is *De genio Socratis*.[36] Here the combination of philosophical discussion and historical narrative requires a good deal of variety. The frame-dialogue (ch. 1) is a mixture of a typical Plutarchan preface, with an elaborate simile, and a conversation-piece. The historical narrative itself (chs. 2, 4, 18–19, 25–34) bears comparison with the liveliest narratives in the *Lives* and is in addition carefully adjusted to the person of the young narrator, Caphisias. Within the antiquarian and philosophical discussions one can also detect some modulations. There is a miniature Socratic dialogue on benefits (ch. 14); Simmias' great speech (ch. 20) is grander than Galaxidorus' more rationalistic account (ch. 12), but less grand than the myth (ch. 22) and again distinct from the dogmatic statements of Theanor (ch. 24), which seem so rhetorical and Gorgianic, and at the same time so naïve in content compared with what went before, as to make one wonder how seriously Plutarch means us to take this rather conventional demonology. *Amatorius*, and to a certain extent the Pythian dialogues, also offer variety. But we should not exaggerate this. It is, I think, going too far to suggest that Plutarch uses stylistic variation to indicate the characters of his speakers (though Plato does, especially in *Symposium*). Plutarch has other ways of doing this.[37] Rather, the modulations are due to the varied content of the dialogues. These are all (and especially *De genio Socratis* and *Amatorius*) to a certain extent miscellanies that embrace a variety of material, often surprising to readers who look for unity of tone.

## II

I turn now to some examples. The first is one of the (not very numerous) passages in the *Lives* where we see Plutarch adapting an identifiable source. The subject is the reception at Sparta of the news of the disastrous defeat at

---

[35] Cf. in general Russell (1973a: 42–62).  [36] See Nesselrath (2010).  [37] Russell (1992).

Leuctra in 371 BCE. The source is Xenophon, *Hellenica* 6.4.16; Plutarch's adaptation is *Agesilaus* 29.3–6. Here is Xenophon:

Γενομένων δὲ τούτων
ὁ μὲν εἰς τὴν Λακεδαίμονα ἀγγελῶν τὸ πάθος ἀφικνεῖται,
γυμνοπαιδιῶν τε οὔσης τῆς τελευταίας
καὶ τοῦ ἀνδρικοῦ χοροῦ ἔνδον ὄντος,

5     οἱ δὲ ἔφοροι
ἐπεὶ ἤκουσαν τὸ πάθος
ἐλυποῦντο μέν (ὥσπερ οἶμαι ἀνάγκη)
τὸν μέντοι χορὸν οὐκ ἐξήγαγον
ἀλλὰ διαγωνίσασθαι εἴων,

10     καὶ τὰ μὲν ὀνόματα πρὸς τοὺς οἰκείους ἑκάστου τῶν
τεθνεώτων ἀπέδοσαν,
προεῖπαν δὲ ταῖς γυναιξὶ μὴ ποιεῖν κραυγήν,
ἀλλὰ σιγῇ τὸ πάθος φέρειν.
τῇ δ᾽ ὑστεραίᾳ ἦν ὁρᾶν
ὧν μὲν ἐτέθνασαν οἱ προσήκοντες

15     λιπαροὺς καὶ φαιδροὺς ἐν τῷ φανερῷ ἀναστρεφομένους,
ὧν δὲ ζῶντες ἠγγελμένοι ἦσαν,
ὀλίγους ἂν εἶδες,
τούτους δὲ σκυθρωποὺς καὶ ταπεινοὺς περιιόντας.

After this,
the messenger arrives at Sparta with news of the disaster,
it being the last day of the Gymnopaidia,
and the men's chorus was on stage,
and the ephors,
      when they heard of the disaster,
      were distressed – inevitably, I suppose –
      but they did not dismiss the chorus
      but let them finish the contest.
The names of the dead they reported to the relatives,
but they told the women not to raise a cry of mourning,
      but to bear their grief in silence.
Next day,
the relatives of the dead were to be seen walking around in public,
bright and cheerful,
while of the relatives of those reported alive
      you would have seen but few,
      and those going about grim-faced and humiliated.

And here is Plutarch:

ἔτυχε μὲν γὰρ ἡ πόλις ἑορτὴν ἄγουσα καὶ ξένων οὖσα μεστή
(γυμνοπαιδίαι γὰρ ἦσαν)
ἀγωνιζομένων χορῶν ἐν τῷ θεάτρῳ·
παρῆσαν δ᾽ ἀπὸ Λεύκτρων οἱ τὴν συμφορὰν ἀναγγέλλοντες.

5        οἱ δὲ ἔφοροι
καίπερ εὐθὺς ὄντος καταφανοῦς
ὅτι διέφθαρται τὰ πράγματα καὶ τὴν ἀρχὴν ἀπολωλέκασιν,
οὔτε χορὸν ἐξελθεῖν εἴασαν
οὔτε τὸ σχῆμα τῆς ἑορτῆς μεταβαλεῖν τὴν πόλιν,

10        ἀλλὰ κατ᾽ οἰκίαν τῶν τεθνεώτων τοῖς προσήκουσι τὰ ὀνόματα
          πέμψαντες,
αὐτοὶ τὰ περὶ τὴν θέαν καὶ τὸν ἀγῶνα τῶν χορῶν ἔπραττον.
ἅμα δὲ ἡμέρᾳ,
φανερῶν ἤδη γεγονότων πᾶσι τῶν τε σῳζομένων καὶ τῶν τεθνεώτων,
οἱ μὲν τῶν τεθνεώτων πατέρες καὶ κηδεσταὶ καὶ οἰκεῖοι

15        καταβαίνοντες εἰς ἀγορὰν
ἀλλήλους ἐδεξιοῦντο λιπαροὶ τὰ πρόσωπα, φρονήματος μεστοὶ καὶ ἤθους·
οἱ δὲ τῶν σῳζομένων, ὥσπερ ἐπὶ πένθει
μετὰ τῶν γυναικῶν οἴκοι διέτριβον·
εἰ δέ τις ὑπ᾽ ἀνάγκης προέλθοι,

20        καὶ σχήματι καὶ φωνῇ καὶ βλέμματι
ταπεινὸς ἐφαίνετο καὶ συνεσταλμένος.

It happened that the city was holding a festival, and was full of foreigners
(it was the Gymnopaidia);
the choruses were competing in the theater:
and there were the messengers from Leuctra with news of the defeat.
The ephors,
          though it was immediately obvious
          that the situation was disastrous and they had lost their empire,
neither allowed the chorus to go
nor the city to put off its festival look:
they sent the names of the dead to their relatives, house by house,
and themselves proceeded with the business of the spectacle and the choral
          competition.
When day broke,
and the survivors and the dead were known to all,
the fathers, kinsmen, and relatives of the dead
went down into the marketplace
and greeted one another with a cheerful face,
full of pride and good humor,
but the relatives of the survivors,

as though in mourning,
stayed at home with their women;
or, if any was absolutely obliged to go out,
he looked humiliated and shrunken
in posture, voice, and eyes.

The situation here has two paradoxical features, both indicative of Spartan courage and spirit: (i) Spartans do not panic, and the festival goes on; (ii) the bereaved are cheerful, the relatives of the survivors gloomy.

Xenophon's account is by no means without artifice. The paradoxes are reflected in balancing and antithetical clauses. Excluding the transitional γενομένων δὲ τούτων, the passage falls into three parts:

(i)   2–4: a μέν-sentence. The news arrives, it is the last day of the festival, and the men's chorus is ἔνδον, "inside" – rightly glossed by Plutarch by "in the theater."
(ii)  5–12: the answering δέ-sentence. This is quite elaborate. The main unit includes two μέν ... δέ/μέντοι units (7–9, 10–12), and in each of these the δέ-elements are amplified by adding together a negative and a positive description of the action related: this is the common figure κατ᾿ ἄρσιν καὶ θέσιν, "upbeat and downbeat"[38] (8–9, 11–12).
(iii) 14–18: the events of the next day make the paradoxes of Spartan behavior evident. Here again, there is a μέν ... δέ complex, with quite a close balance in length, and a noticeable pair of binary amplifications, λιπαροὺς καὶ φαιδρούς ... σκυθρωποὺς καὶ ταπεινούς.

What did Plutarch do with this? The structure he has chosen also falls into three parts.

(i)  1–4: a μέν ... δέ complex, but used differently from Xenophon's. The μέν-part gives the situation (the festival), the δέ-part gives the supervening event. This is a classic use of this sentence-form: the most celebrated model was Demosthenes, *On the crown* 169,[39] on the arrival at Athens of the news of the fall of Elatea: ἑσπέρα μὲν γὰρ ἦν, ἧκε δ᾿ ἀγγέλλων τις, "it was evening, and there came one with the news . . .." This may well be at the back of Plutarch's mind here; the situations are analogous.
(ii) 5–11: the reaction of the ephors. There is here more participial subordination than in the corresponding part of Xenophon (note the καίπερ-clause) but the two main points – the ephors' determination to continue the festival and the information given to the families – are the same.

---

[38] Rehdantz and Blass (1886: 1–10).
[39] Cf. "Longinus", *De subl.* 10–17; Wankel (1976: 646–648).

(iii)  12–21: the following day. Here again, there is much the same structure as in Xenophon, but with much more elaboration. Xenophon's vivid ἦν ὁρᾶν and ὀλίγους ἂν εἶδες are sacrificed, and a good deal of ornament is added. In place of Xenophon's two amplifications, Plutarch gives us (a) a triplet, πατέρες καὶ κηδεσταὶ καὶ οἰκεῖοι, (b) a new pair, φρονήματος καὶ ἤθους, "pride and good humor," (c) a Demosthenic tag (cf. *Against Meidias* 72), σχήματι καὶ φωνῇ καὶ βλέμματι (20), (d) a new partner for ταπεινός, viz. συνεσταλμένος, "shrunken" or "shrinking" (cf. Plato *Lysis* 210e4).

Plutarch has thus left out (1) the detail that it was the last day of the festival and (2) the positive order to the women not to raise the cry of mourning. He has added (1) the presence of foreigners, which clearly motivates the ephors' decisions; (2) the amplification of τὸ πάθος into the realization of the total loss of Spartan power; (3) the explicit statement that the ephors went on with the festival business; and (4) various explicit or suggested details in the last part – the disgraced stayed at home with the women as though they were in mourning (17–18), and if any went out it was only on necessary business.

There are, of course, a number of significant verbal differences. Plutarch has no hiatuses except two with καὶ (which is normal), while Xenophon has five in this short passage, at least three of which (οἶμαι ἀνάγκη 7, διαγωνίσασθαι εἴων 9, ὑστεραίᾳ ἦν 13) would be very strange in Plutarch. It is worth noticing that Plutarch does not follow the historic present ἀφικνεῖται.[40]

The clausulation is fairly typical:

| 1. | – ˘ – – | οὖσα μεστή |
| 2. | – ˘ – ≍ | γυμνοπαιδίαι **γὰρ ἦσαν** |
| 3. | – ˘ – – | τῷ θεάτρῳ |
| 4. | ˘ – – – ≍ | ἀναγγέλλοντες |
| 6. | – – ˘ ˘ – | ὄντος καταφανοῦς |
| 7. | – ˘ – ˘ ˘ | διέφθαρ**ται τὰ πράγματα** |
| 7. | – ˘ – ≍ | ἀπο**λωλέκασιν** |
| 9. | ˘ ˘ ˘ – – ˘ ≍ | μεταβαλεῖν τὴν πόλιν |
| 10. | ˘ ˘ ˘ – – ≍ | ὀ**νόματα πέμψαντες** |
| 11. | – ˘ – ≍ | χορ**ῶν ἔπραττον** |
| 16. | – ˘ – ≍ | ἐ**δεξιοῦντο** |
| 17. | – ˘ ˘ ˘ – ≍ | ὥσπερ ἐπὶ πένθει |
| 18. | – ˘ – – ≍ | οἶ**κοι διέτριβον** |
| 19. | – ˘ – ≍ | ἀνάγ**κης προέλθοι** |
| 21. | – ˘ – – ˘ ≍ | καὶ συνεσταλμένος |

---

[40] See Section I.

In a word: Plutarch's paraphrase is duller and fuller, but also more rhythmical and (in his echo of Demosthenes) more allusive.

My second example is the preface to *De curiositate* (515B–D):

Ἄπνουν ἢ σκοτεινὴν ἢ δυσχείμερον οἰκίαν ἢ νοσώδη
φυγεῖν μὲν ἴσως ἄριστον:
ἂν δὲ φιλοχωρῇ τις ὑπὸ συνηθείας
ἔστι καὶ φῶτα μεταθέντα
5      καὶ κλίμακα μεταβαλόντα
καὶ θύρας τινὰς ἀνοίξαντα
τὰς δὲ κλείσαντα
λαμπροτέραν εὐπνουστέραν ὑγιεινοτέραν μηχανήσασθαι.
καὶ πόλεις τινὲς οὕτω μεταθέντες ὠφέλησαν:
10     ὥσπερ τὴν ἐμὴν πατρίδα
πρὸς ζέφυρον ἄνεμον κεκλιμένην
καὶ τὸν ἥλιον ἐρείδοντα δείλης ἀπὸ τοῦ Παρνασσοῦ δεχομένην
ἐπὶ τὰς ἀνατολὰς τραπῆναι λέγουσιν ὑπὸ τοῦ Χαίρωνος.
ὁ δὲ φυσικὸς Ἐμπεδοκλῆς
15     ὄρους τινὰ διασφάγα
βαρὺν καὶ νοσώδη κατὰ τῶν πεδίων τὸν νότον ἐμπνέουσαν ἐμφράξας
λοιμὸν ἔδοξεν ἐκκλεῖσαι τῆς χώρας.
ἐπεὶ τοίνυν ἔστι τινὰ πάθη νοσώδη καὶ βλαβερὰ
καὶ χειμῶνα παρέχοντα τῇ ψυχῇ καὶ σκότος,
20     ἄριστον μὲν ἐξωθεῖν ταῦτα καὶ καταλύειν εἰς ἔδαφος
αἰθρίαν καὶ φῶς καὶ πνεῦμα καθαρὸν διδόντας ἑαυτοῖς:
εἰ δὲ μή,
μεταλαμβάνειν γε καὶ μεθαρμόττειν
ἁμωσγέπως περιάγοντας ἢ στρέφοντας.

A house that is airless, dark, poor protection against winter, or unhealthy
it is perhaps best to leave;
but if one is fond of the place out of habit
one can move lights
        alter a staircase
        open some doors and close others
and so make the house brighter, airier, and healthier.

Some have benefited cities by moving them in this way,
like my own native place,
which faced the west wind
and caught the evening sun's full force from Parnassus,
but was, so they say, turned round by Chaeron to face the east.
The scientist Empedocles,
by blocking a gorge in a mountain
which was causing an unpleasant and unhealthy south wind to blow into the
    plain,

was believed to have kept the plague out of the area.
Similarly, as there are certain unhealthy and harmful emotions
which bring storm and darkness to the soul,
the best thing is to drive them out and clear them to ground level,
giving ourselves clear weather and light and pure air;
but, if this is impossible,
we can at least change and refashion them,
by somehow reversing them or giving them a turn.

The argument here is meant to show that natural tendencies to vice may be turned to good use. It consists of a series of analogies: a house can be improved (1–8), a city can be relocated (9–13), an unhealthy natural feature can be engineered away (14–16). And so with πάθη, emotions, which are unhealthy or dangerous. Best to get rid of them altogether, second-best to modify them to serve a useful purpose (18–25). There is not much real argument in this; but the verbal structures in which the analogies are developed are very skillfully put together.

The first words are adjectives: airless, dark, poor protection against weather. The noun follows. We are talking about a house. But there is another adjective to come: unhealthy. This is a keyword in what follows, and in the analogy with emotions, which are the diseases of the mind. Indeed, each of the adjectives is picked up later: ἄπνουν in εὐπνουστέραν (8) and πνεῦμα καθαρὸν (21); σκοτεινήν in λαμπροτέραν (8), σκότος (19), and φῶς (21); χειμῶνα in δυσχείμερον (1) and αἰθρίαν (21); and νοσώδη in ὑγιεινοτέραν (8) and νοσώδη (16). The first period is conventionally structured. There is a brief μέν-clause (φυγεῖν μὲν ἴσως ἄριστον) picked up below, 20–21. The δέ-clause is much more elaborate; it is built up into a tricolon with homeoteleuton (4–7), the last and largest unit being split into two with the four crashing polysyllables λαμπροτέραν . . . μηχανήσασθαι (8). The clausulae also are notable: ἢ νοσώδη – ᵕ – –, ἴσ**ως ἄριστον** – ᵕ – ᵕ, ὑπὸ συνηθείας ᵕ ᵕ ᵕ – – –, φῶτα μεταθέντα – ᵕ ᵕ ᵕ – ≚, κλί**μακα μεταβαλόντα** ᵕ ᵕ ᵕ ᵕ ᵕ – ≚, τινας ἀνοίξαντα ᵕ ᵕ ᵕ – – ≚, τὰς δὲ κλείσαντα – ᵕ – – ≚, and μηχανήσασθαι – ᵕ – – –. Almost all are ditrochaei or cretic/paean with spondee.

It is tempting to see a change of rhythm in the next part (9–13). ὠφέλησαν is – ᵕ – ≚, τὴν ἐμὴν πατρίδα is either double cretic or – ᵕ – ᵕ ᵕ –, and there follow other forms that are less familiar.[41] We have ἄνεμον κεκλιμένην ᵕ ᵕ – ᵕ ᵕ ᵕ – (11), Παρνασσὸν δεχομένην – – – ᵕ ᵕ ᵕ – (12), ὑπὸ τοῦ Χαίρωνος ᵕ ᵕ – – – ≚ (13). This section also contains no reference back to the key adjectives of line 1. One might suspect that this is a lowering of the pretentious tone of the opening, to

[41] See Ziegler (1949: 298) for some of these.

which the third "movement" (14–17) seems perhaps to return. We notice here the involved word-order of 15–16, and the cretic-spondee clausula ἐμπνέουσαν ἐμφράξας with which this ends; also the run of long syllables (not common in Plutarch) in ἐκκλεῖσαι τῆς χώρας. The analogy has now to be drawn (18–24). The key adjectives are picked up, both in the ἐπεί-clause (νοσώδη, βλαβερά [ἄπνουν would be unsuitable], χειμῶνα, σκότος) and in the main sentence (αἰθρία, φῶς, πνεῦμα καθαρόν). The image of the house is taken up in καταλύειν εἰς ἔδαφος, "clear them to ground level." But whereas in the first section the "best" clause was short and the "second-best" long, here the two are more in balance. What is "best" is spelt out with some amplification, and the "second-best" with concise emphasis. The hypodochmius-type clausulae (18–20) (νοσ<u>ώδη καὶ βλαβερά</u> – – – ᵛ ᵛ ≍, ψυχῇ καὶ σκότος – – – ᵛ ≍) give way at the end to καὶ μεθαρμόττειν (– ᵛ – – –) and ἢ στρέφοντας (– ᵛ – –).⁴²

Such are the artifices of this preface.

My final example is a famous and much-discussed passage from *De Pythiae oraculis* (406D–F).⁴³

ἐπεὶ δὲ
τοῦ βίου μεταβολὴν ἅμα ταῖς τύχαις καὶ ταῖς φύσεσι λαμβάνοντος
ἐξωθοῦσα τὸ περιττὸν ἡ χρεία
κρωβύλους τε χρυσοῦς ἀφῄρει
5    καὶ ξυστίδας μαλακὰς ἀπημφίαζε
καί που καὶ κόμην σοβαρωτέραν ἀπέκειρε
καὶ ὑπέλυσε κόθορνον,
οὐ φαύλως ἐθιζομένων
ἀντικαλλωπίζεσθαι πρὸς τὴν πολυτέλειαν εὐτελείᾳ
10    καὶ τὸ ἀφελὲς καὶ λιτὸν ἐν κόσμῳ τίθεσθαι
μᾶλλον ἢ τὸ σοβαρὸν καὶ περίεργον,
οὕτω
τοῦ λόγου συμμεταβάλλοντος ἅμα καὶ συναποδυομένου
κατέβη μὲν ἀπὸ τῶν μέτρων ὥσπερ ὀχημάτων ἡ ἱστορία,
15    καὶ τῷ πεζῷ μάλιστα τοῦ μυθώδους ἀπεκρίθη τἀληθές,
φιλοσοφία δὲ
τὸ σαφὲς καὶ διδασκαλικὸν ἀσπασαμένη μᾶλλον ἢ τὸ ἐκπλῆττον
διὰ λόγων ἐποιεῖτο τὴν ζήτησιν,
ἀπέπαυσε δὲ τὴν Πυθίαν ὁ θεὸς
20    πυρικάους μὲν ὀνομάζουσαν τοὺς αὐτῆς πολίτας,
ὀφιοβόρους δὲ τοὺς Σπαρτιάτας

⁴² διδόντας ἑαυτοῖς (21) seems to be a hexameter ending, but if we read αὐτοῖς it becomes a ditrochaeus.
⁴³ See Schröder (1990: 51–54, 384–389).

ὀρεάνας δὲ τοὺς ἄνδρας
ὀρεμπότας δὲ τοὺς ποταμούς,
ἀφελὼν δὲ τῶν χρησμῶν
25    ἔπη καὶ γλώττας καὶ περιφράσεις καὶ ἀσάφειαν,
οὕτω διαλέγεσθαι παρεσκεύασε τοῖς χρωμένοις
ὡς νόμοι τε πόλεσι διαλέγονται
καὶ βασιλεῖς ἐντυγχάνουσι δήμοις
καὶ καθηγηταὶ διδάσκουσιν ἀκροατάς,[44]
30    πρὸς τὸ συνετὸν καὶ πιθανὸν ἁρμοζόμενος.

But when,
as life changed with the changes of fortunes and natures,
necessity, driving out superfluity,
        took away their gold hair-ornaments,
        stripped off their long soft cloaks,
cut short their luxuriant hair,
        and took off their high-heeled boots,
– now that they were becoming accustomed (and no bad thing)
to set the elegance of economy against the elegance of extravagance,
and to reckon the plain and simple an ornament
rather than the pretentious and elaborate –
so, likewise,
as speech changed at the same time and stripped itself bare,
history came down from her metre as from a chariot,
truth was distinguished from fable by being in prose,
philosophy, embracing the clear and informative in preference to the startling,
began to make her inquiries in prose,
        and the god stopped the Pythia
        calling her fellow-citizens fire-burners,
        the Spartans snake-eaters,
        men mountain-goers,
        and rivers mountain-drinkers,
and, taking away from her oracles
        verses, foreign words, periphrases and obscurity,
made her ready to converse with her clients
        as laws speak to cities
        kings meet their peoples
        and teachers instruct their pupils,
fitting her to be intelligible and persuasive.

The first half of this enormous sentence has personified χρεία, "need" or "necessity,"[45] as subject and four main verbs, three of them ἀπό-compounds and the fourth (ὑπέλυσε) the proper word for taking off your shoes. This core

----

[44]  The Greek text here follows Schröder (1990: 102).    [45]  Or "usefulness": Schröder (1990: 385).

is framed between two participial phrases, τοῦ βίου . . . λαμβάνοντος (2) and
οὐ φαύλως . . . περίεργον (8–11). These phrases are no less vital to the sense
than the main sentence, and this is quite characteristic of Plutarch. The content
of these lines comes from the tradition that the men who fought at Marathon
were a good deal more dandified and luxurious in their dress than their
successors at the time of the Peloponnesian War. This comes partly from
Thucydides (1.6: whence κρώβυλοι, apparently misunderstood by Plutarch as
"ornaments" rather than a type of hairstyle) and partly from comedy, but
especially (it seems) from Heraclides Ponticus' *On Pleasure* (fr. 55 Wehrli, from
Athenaeus 12.512a). In the interval between the wars, according to Heraclides,
times got harder and people's natures less ebullient. The second part of the
statement (8–11), in which the good side of the change is brought out, seems to
be an expansion of the idea in Pericles' funeral speech (Thucydides 2.40) of
"economical love of beauty" (φιλοκαλοῦμέν τε γὰρ μετ᾽ εὐτελείας).

The second half of our monster-sentence has been the subject of much
discussion.[46] It makes a connection, probably Plutarch's own, since it
seems tailor-made for the context, between a theory about the priority of
poetry over prose and a view of the oracles' social function. The theory
about poetry is probably Peripatetic, and Hirzel's guess[47] that it was in
Dicaearchus is a plausible one. It is Plutarch's business to link the two. His
words do this for him: μεταβολὴν . . . λαμβάνοντος (2) is taken up by
συμμεταβάλλοντος (13); ἀπημφίαζε (5) by συναποδυομένου (13); μᾶλλον ἢ
τὸ σοβαρὸν καὶ περίεργον (11) by μᾶλλον ἢ τὸ ἐκπλῆττον (17); and ἀφῄρει
(4) by ἀφελών (24).

The structure of the second part also begins with a participial phrase (so 13
corresponds to 2), and it then goes on to three coordinate clauses very much
larger in scale than those in the first half (4–7), and carefully balanced:
κατέβη . . . τἀληθές (14–15) and φιλοσοφία . . . ζήτησιν (16–18) are both
around forty syllables long, while the culminating pair of clauses (ἀπέπαυσε
δὲ . . . ἁρμοζόμενος, 19–30) is very much longer, and includes the descant on
bizarre words found in oracles (20–24), which is also roughly isocolic (11 + 11
+ 8 + 9) and produces something like the effect of the short cola early in the
first part (4–7).[48] The two main verbs of this part are ἀπέπαυσε and
παρεσκεύασε. Ἀπέπαυσε comes first in its unit, and its little descant follows
behind; παρεσκεύασε, on the other hand, is sandwiched between two
participial structures, ἀφελών . . . ἀσάφειαν (24–25) and πρὸς τὸ

---

[46] Well summarized in Schröder (1990: 54–55).    [47] Hirzel (1895: ii. 208 n. 4).
[48] Compare also lines 4–7 in the extract from *De curiositate* discussed earlier.

συνετόν . . . ἁρμοζόμενος (30) (compare the structure in 2–11 earlier).[49] Here, too, there is a little descant, in the roughly isocolic clauses of 27–29.

There are many other passages in which the same sort of formality, the same balances, the same repetitive movements could be seen. They are certainly not confined to the ostensibly "rhetorical" works. They are inherited partly from Gorgias and his pupils, especially Isocrates, partly perhaps from Hellenistic writers whom hostile critics called "Asianics." In any case, their use marks Plutarch off from, say, Dio Chrysostom and other more Atticizing writers. If one were to compare a purple patch in Plutarch with one in Dio – say, the "cosmos as a temple" topic in *De tranquilitate animi* 477C–F with Dio's *Olympicus* 33–34 – the difference would be plain. Dio's periods are looser, he has no taste for balances, rhymes, and echoes, his clausulae are different, he is indifferent to hiatus, and he has a much clearer grasp of classical usage. He marks a new phase in the development of Atticizing prose. Plutarch, in a sense, is at the end of an era, Dio at the beginning of another. But only in a sense: the picture is more complicated than that. Dio's manner had its antecedents, and Plutarch's its many successors in late antiquity, when he was much read, and where many echoes of him can be heard in Christian as well as pagan writers. But that is another subject.

## Further Reading

The stylistic fabric of Plutarch's prose is discussed by Russell (1973a: 18–41), Yaginuma (1992), Baldassari (2000), Teodorsson (2000), Duff (2010; 2015; 2017), Biraud (2014), and Hutchinson (2018). For the bigger picture of Greek stylistics, from classical Greece into the imperial age, see, for example, Dover (1997), Bers (2010), and Kim (2010; 2017); a particularly rich case study, with a Plutarchan focus, is Minon (2015). On Plutarch's ideas about literary language and verbal communication generally, see Van der Stockt (1990; 1992: 56–73) and Zadorojnyi (2014). Furhmann (1964) attempted to put together an exhaustive inventory of Plutarch's metaphors and similes. In *Quomodo adolescens poetas audire debeat* Plutarch uses elaborate imagery and complex syntax side by side with moralistic reflection on the challenges of literary language; on this work, see Hunter and Russell (2011).

---

[49] Plutarch's complex sentences are interestingly discussed and classified by Yaginuma (1992).

# CHAPTER 9

# Plutarch and Classical Greece

## Philip Stadter

### Plutarch's Relation to the Classical Past

Classical Greece, in particular the two centuries between the Persian Wars and the death of Alexander the Great, furnished Plutarch with an immensely rich cultural heritage that he admired and treasured. The famous cities, the men who led them, and the literature they produced captivated his imagination and exalted him with pride in his Greek identity.[1] Plutarch's description of the Periclean buildings compresses in a sentence his feeling toward that era:

> For in beauty each was ancient from the first, but in vigor each is recent and new-wrought even today: thus a kind of newness always flowers on them, preserving their appearance untouched by time, as if the monuments had mingled in them an ever-living breath and an ageless soul. (*Pericles* 13.4)

For him, as for his cultivated contemporaries, those ancient achievements in art, literature, and government were timelessly present, as inspiration, as model, and as proof of Greek greatness. Our very notion of the classical derives from this reverent attitude, so clearly present in Plutarch, toward something that is imagined as being a magnificent challenge to posterity from its very creation.[2] And yet, Plutarch did not flinch from noting and criticizing the faults of the classical past, especially in his *Parallel Lives*.

Education in rhetoric, especially the study of the great orators of fourth-century Greece, had long been a tradition for the Greek-speaking elite. However, a new affirmation of Greece's classical past began toward the end

---

[1] The attitudes of imperial Greek writers toward their classical past are addressed by Bowie (1974), Swain (1996), and Whitmarsh (2001). Cf. Tröster's Chapter 2 in this volume.

[2] See for an examination of the category of "classical" and its application to the ancient world Porter (2006a), as well as Porter (2006b: for Plutarch, esp. 329–333; 2006c). Bréchet (2003) gathers the evidence for Plutarch's respect for "the ancients," *hoi palaioi*.

of the first century CE, with the rise of orators performing declamations for an admiring public. Speeches on invented arguments, artfully delivered using carefully learned Attic Greek rather than contemporary idiom, revisited major moments of the classical period: Solon's opposition to Peisistratus, the battle of Marathon, the Athenian defeat at Aegospotami, or the charge against Demosthenes for bribery (to list some of the subjects of one younger contemporary of Plutarch, Polemo of Laodicea). Dio of Prusa, Plutarch's contemporary, used the figures of Philip II and Alexander to discuss monarchy (*Or.* 2 and 4), and authored a speech asserting, contrary to Homer, that Troy had never been captured (*Or.* 11). The fame, wealth, and rhetorical skill of these orators led them to serve as ambassadors to provincial governors and emperors; Herodes Atticus, one of the most famous, became consul and a friend of the emperor. This movement, given the title of "Second Sophistic" by Philostratus at the end of the second century, no doubt reflected the desire to affirm a cultural role for Greek speakers in the Roman Empire, exalting Greece's glorious past and asserting its continuing importance. Plutarch also shared to a limited extent in this activity. Several declamations of his survive, two on Greek topics: *De gloria Atheniensum*, arguing that Athens' military heroes outshone its poets and writers, and *De Alexandri magni fortuna aut virtute*, debating whether virtue or fortune was responsible for Alexander the Great's success. One speech, *De fortuna Romanorum*, turns from the Greek past to Roman history down to Augustus. These works cite abundant historical references to make their point and demonstrate Plutarch's familiarity with this type of declamation.[3] However, the body of his writing reveals major differences that set Plutarch apart from the orators of the Second Sophistic.

Unlike most Greek authors of the renaissance of the first and second centuries, Plutarch was a native of mainland Greece, proud of his native city Chaeronea and of his strong ties to nearby Delphi and Athens. Chaeronea was a crossroads and battlefield, the site of Philip of Macedon's victory over the Greeks in 338 BCE and Sulla's defeat of Mithradates' general Archelaus in 86 BCE. At Delphi, as priest of Apollo, Plutarch hoped to revive the sanctuary's ancient splendor (cf. *De Pythiae oraculis* 409A). He also had been made a citizen of Athens, where he had studied as a young man, and he speaks of his visits there and the resources of books and learned conversations it afforded (*De E apud Delphos* 384E; cf. *Demosthenes* 2). Moreover, the

---

[3] On Plutarch and the Second Sophistic, see Schmitz (2014) and Desideri (2017); cf. also Bowie (1974).

classical Athenian dialect, defined especially by the Attic dramatists, Thucydides, Plato, and the orators, had become in his day the language of the educated, a marker of elite status and culture, and had also furnished the substrate for the *koinē*, or standard language.[4] The cities with which he is most closely associated, Chaeronea, Delphi, and Athens, were "places of memory," to use Pierre Nora's (1984) term; that is, places filled with historical associations and monuments of the past: victories and defeats, artistic triumphs, and divine intervention.[5] Plutarch's familiarity with classical Greece derived not just from study of texts but also from walking the soil of Greece and marveling at the statues of generals and dedications of booty at Delphi (as do the interlocutors, e.g., in *De Pythiae oraculis*; cf. 397E, 398C, 399F, 401D), the walls and buildings of the Acropolis (*Pericles* 13), and the weapons recovered from the fields of Orchomenos near Chaeronea (*Sulla* 21). He saw the spear of Agesilaus preserved at Sparta and found in the city's archives the names of the king's wife and daughters (*Agesilaus* 19).[6] The past came alive in the stories of his grandfather, in inscriptions and shrines to local gods, in festivals and games, and even through his friends, among whom were descendants of Themistocles, Pindar, and Aratus (*Themistocles* 32.6, *De sera numinis vindicta* 557F, *Aratus* 1.5).

Most significantly, Plutarch read prodigiously in every sort of Greek literature. Among the poets he cites chiefly Homer, lyric, and Athenian drama. From the historians he often cites Herodotus, Thucydides, Xenophon, and Polybius, and the major lost historians such as Ephorus, Theopompus, and Phylarchus, but also numerous minor historical and antiquarian authors such as Charon of Lampsacus, Diocles of Peparethus, and Socrates of Argos (*FGrHist* nos. 262, 820, and 310). Innumerable historical anecdotes and citations of classical literature are scattered throughout Plutarch's works. He was thoroughly versed in the orators and especially the philosophers, with Plato taking pride of place, as demonstrated by the frequency of his citations and allusions. Whenever possible, he cited in the *Lives* sources contemporary to the events narrated, despite "the difficulty of hunting out the truth by investigation" caused by the favorable or hostile bias of contemporary authors (*Pericles* 13.6).[7]

Plutarch's acquaintances numbered many cultured philhellene Romans, for whom Greek literature, philosophy, and art were the touchstones of cultural achievement. A century earlier, Cicero and Caesar had studied

---

[4] Cf. Russell's Chapter 8 in this volume.
[5] Cf. Alcock (2002), Swain (1996 : 65–100), Jacquemin (1991), and Nora (1984).
[6] See Buckler (1992).
[7] Compare his observations on bias and distortion in *De Herodoti malignitate* 855A–856D.

rhetoric in Greece. In Plutarch's day noble Romans were urged by Quintilian to have their children learn Greek before Latin, and Pliny the Younger wrote to his friend Maximus, whom the emperor had just appointed to a special office in Greece: "You have been sent to Achaea, the pure and true Greece, where we believe civilization and literature began" (*Ep.* 8.24). In this context, Athens became the prime locale for all that the Romans admired of Greek culture, the centerpiece of an ideal Greece. Emperors such as Augustus, Domitian, Trajan, and Hadrian honored the city with buildings and privileges. Sparta was respected for its revived archaic rituals and stern educational system. The *Parallel Lives*, by comparing so many leaders of Athens and Sparta to famous Romans, play to this image of Greece.[8]

However, Plutarch also believed that he lived in a new era, in which political life as well as the general prosperity was superior to those of distant times. In considering the current status of the oracular cult at Delphi, for instance, he contrasted the metrical oracles on great themes of war and peace uttered in the classical period with the simple prose responses of the present times. But instead of taking this change as indication of a decline, he attributes it to the new era of peace and tranquility, in which it was no longer necessary to consult the god on grand matters (*De Pythiae oraculis* 408B–C). Plutarch himself exemplifies the preference in Roman Greece for prose literature over classical favoring of poetry.[9] Roman rule protected the cities of Greece from internal fighting and local tyranny, as well as from threats from Parthia or the northern barbarians. Plutarch might have one foot anchored in the Greek past, but the other he firmly planted in the contemporary Roman world. Looking back at the great years of Athens and Sparta, he admired their defense of their liberty against Persia, the wise men who had established the laws of their cities, the leaders who had led their citizens to great deeds, and the opponents of tyranny. But equally he knew that in his own time the fight for liberty and autonomy for Greek cities was neither possible nor desirable. "Marathon, the Eurymedon, Plataea, and all the other examples which exalt the crowd to empty prancing, should be left to the schools of the sophists." Rather, "the populace has as much of liberty as those in power [the Romans] grant, and more perhaps would not be better" (*Praecepta gerendae reipublicae* 814C, 824C, D).[10] What Greece – and therefore Plutarch himself – could

[8] On Roman Athens, see Rotroff and Hoff (1997); on Sparta, Cartledge and Spawforth (2001) and Kennell (1995); and on Plutarch's choice of heroes, Geiger (1981), Pelling (1989), and Desideri (1992).
[9] Compare Whitmarsh (2006a).
[10] See Trapp (2004), Swain (1996: 145–186), and Lo Cascio (2007).

contribute was the political experience of its great period, the cultural wisdom embodied in its literature, and the ethical-political teachings of the great philosophers, especially his beloved Plato.

Plutarch's interests extended well into the Hellenistic age, in contrast to the practice of most imperial Greek writers, who confined their historical references almost exclusively to the period ending with Alexander's death. Besides writing a separate *Life* of the Achaean commander Aratus (ca. 271–213 BCE), Plutarch included among the *Parallel Lives* those of Eumenes, Demetrius, Pyrrhus, Agis and Cleomenes, and Philopoemen, one fourth of the whole Greek series. Such breadth is found in his essays as well. His treatise *Mulierum virtutes* included stories from legendary times down to the mid-first century BCE. His collection of aphorisms, *Regum et imperatorum apophthegmata*, includes many anecdotes from the Hellenistic period, ranging from Ptolemy Lagus and Antigonus in the fourth century BCE to Antiochus VII in the second.[11] Plutarch's comprehensive vision, while centered on the classical period, encompassed Greeks of all periods. Moreover, as is evident from the *Parallel Lives*, he believed that there was a communality of political behavior that united the past and the present, Romans and Greeks. His proems to the *Lives* frequently call attention to these ties: the shared capacity of Pericles and Fabius to resist the follies of their fellow-citizens; the difficulties of Phocion and the younger Cato in pursuing a philosophically based course in a degenerate political world; and the joy Plutarch himself took in associating himself with heroes, Greek and Roman, as moral preparation for his encounters with his contemporaries.[12] Throughout his essay on civic politics under the empire, *Praecepta gerendae reipublicae*, anecdotes from classical Greece and republican Rome illustrate his points. Contemporary imperial administrators and civic leaders, whether Greek or Roman, could and should learn from the examples of the great men of the past.

## Classical Greece in the *Moralia*

Three works of the *Moralia* especially concern the classical period of Greece. A rhetorical showpiece, *De gloria Atheniensium*, argues that Athens' generals are more worthy of praise than its dramatists, poets, and painters. The theme allows Plutarch to recall all the great Athenian generals, with their battles and their victories. He opposes them to the

[11] The authenticity of this collection, sometimes doubted, has been defended by M. Beck (2002).
[12] See Duff (1999a: 13–51); *Pericles* 2.5, *Phocion* 2–3, *Aemilius Paulus* 1.

famous painters and historians, including Thucydides and Xenophon (who, he says, merely celebrated the military feats), and dismisses the great dramatists as producers of empty show. Still, the essay is far from a Platonic dismissal of the mimetic arts. In the guise of a contest, the essay celebrates the glory of Athens *both* in war and in the arts.

The essay *De Herodoti malignitate* denounces the historian for various faults, but especially for belittling the heroic Greek victory over Persia. The tone of Herodotus' work, Plutarch asserts, demonstrates bias against the Greeks, and especially toward Plutarch's Boeotian compatriots, the Thebans, because it does not present the Persian Wars as a noble struggle for Greek freedom, but reveals the frequent pettiness of Greek motives. Herodotus focused too much on the quarrels and jockeying for honor among the leaders of the Greek cities. Plutarch's book-by-book analysis of the historian reveals the care with which he had read the classic source for the conflict with Persia. His criticism conforms to the genre of such showpieces, which presuppose viewing the classical Greek past as the benchmark of noble valor and mix valid points with sophistic misdirection. On the other hand, his historical biographies of Themistocles and Aristides, written in a different genre, demonstrate much more confidence in Herodotus' account, and make much of the difficulty of achieving unity that Plutarch here ascribes to Herodotus' malice.[13]

The morality and practicality of tyrannicide receive an extraordinary analysis in *De genio Socratis*, which imaginatively recreates a pivotal moment in Theban history, the attack of Theban liberators against the Spartan-supported tyrants ruling Thebes in 379 BCE. In Plutarch's recreation, the liberators, as they wait to spring their attack, engage in philosophical discussions centering on Socrates' special sign and the role of the divine in human affairs. Plutarch's dialogue interacts suggestively with Plato's *Phaedo*, where Socrates, noting that his sign has not dissuaded him, defends his decision to die. The opening paragraph urges a sensitive and critical reading of this struggle of virtue with circumstances, of reason and passion (575C). The dialogue's complex structure calls attention to at least three levels of human behavior: that dominated by the passions and blind to divine influence, exemplified by the Theban tyrants; that in which reason exercises some control over the passions, seen in the Theban liberators; and that which is most rational and responsive to the divine, exemplified in Socrates and to a lesser degree in the Theban hero Epaminondas, who supports the liberators but does not join their violent

[13] Cf. Grimaldi (2004); Pelling (2007a).

action. Plutarch uses his account of this episode from the classical past to challenge his readers to evaluate the action of the conspirators as well as the decision of Epaminondas not to join them, and to feel the tension between the philosophical and the active life. Should a philosopher kill, or dare a political leader refuse to act?[14]

A fourth work, *Septem sapientium convivium*, goes back to the sixth century to consider the semi-legendary tradition of Greece's wise men, amusingly constructing character portraits of the sages participating in a dinner-party given by the Corinthian tyrant Periander, who himself was often numbered among the sages. Again, Plutarch explores the themes of divine influence expressed in signs and oracles and the human response found in politics and practical wisdom.[15]

## Classical Greece in the *Parallel Lives*

Plutarch's greatest achievement, and the one that succeeds best in bringing classical Greece alive to the modern reader, is the collection of *Parallel Lives*, twenty-two pairs of statesmen and generals, Greek matched with Roman. Plutarch chose not to present Greek statesmen in isolation but as part of a dual heritage, in which each component is understood in the light of the other. For Plutarch, however, the Greek heritage was a given, the Roman something external that he strove to incorporate into a larger whole. The fundamental issues that emerge from Plutarch's treatment of the heroes of classical Greece are, first, the struggle for liberty, independence, and freedom from tyranny; second, the qualities necessary in a leader to achieve these goals; and third, the destructive effect of ambitious striving for preeminence, both within and between states, on the concord that is the proper end of political life.

Plutarch is never specific on the overall criteria for inclusion in this collection, which grew gradually over a period of time, nor do we have a clear notion of the relative chronology of the composition of the *Lives*. Plutarch moved from hero to hero, following his own reading and interests, always alert to the best match with a Roman leader.[16] The selection of protagonists for the Greek *Lives* indicates Plutarch's understanding of the major themes of Greek history and the roles played by the major cities. As

---

[14] This sophisticated work has generated an extensive bibliography, listed in Nesselrath (2010). Besides the essays in Nesselrath, note Donini (2009), Markantonatos and Tsangalis (2008), Brenk (1996), Hardie (1996), and Babut (1984). The episode receives a different presentation in *Pelopidas* 7–13.

[15] See Busine (2002), Mossman (1997c), and Aalders (1977).

[16] On the principle of comparison underlying the *Parallel Lives*, see Beck's Chapter 10 in this volume.

has been noted, Plutarch's vision of Greece extended well beyond classical Athens, back into the mythical period and forward to Hellenistic kings and the struggle against Rome. Athens took pride of place, with a total of ten *Lives*; Sparta is second, with five, including the double set of the Hellenistic kings Agis and Cleomenes. Theseus of Athens, a counterpart to Romulus, founded the democracy as Romulus did the Roman Senate. His conflict with the demagogue Menestheus and the populace points forward to Athens of the classical period, as his private excesses recall those of Alcibiades.[17] The two lawgivers, Lycurgus and Solon, created the fundamental practices for the leading states, Sparta and Athens. While Lycurgus established the radical and rigorously disciplined simplicity of Spartan life, Solon's more pragmatic reform lay down the basic principles of Athenian democracy, in a context of give and take between the wealthy and the general populace.

When his sources permitted, Plutarch combined a framework derived from historical narratives with thematic, anecdotal, and topical material. We can recognize that the three preserved classical historians offered a basis for many *Lives*: Herodotus, the historian of the Persian Wars, for *Themistocles*, *Aristides*, and the Croesus episode in *Solon*; Thucydides, who celebrated the Peloponnesian War, for *Pericles*, *Nicias*, and *Alcibiades*; Xenophon, the continuator of Thucydides, for *Alcibiades* and the Spartans *Lysander* and *Agesilaus*. When possible, he incorporated contemporary sources apart from the historians, such as the laws and poems of Solon, the jibes of the comedians against Pericles, and the speeches of Demosthenes. Plato's writings, as we shall see, were especially important in exploring Alcibiades' relation to Socrates and Dion's hope for a philosopher king in Syracuse. Pride in his native land, Boeotia, and its leading city, Thebes, no doubt underlay the biography of Pelopidas and the lost biography of Epaminondas (who is believed to have been the first hero celebrated by the *Parallel Lives*).

The theme of Greek freedom and independence, a source of admiration and pride to those living under Roman rule, runs through the series. Themistocles and Aristides repelled a massive Persian attack and saved Greece from Asian domination by their victories at Salamis and Plataea; Cimon's success at the Eurymedon confirmed Greek freedom. Dion and Timoleon liberated Sicily from tyrants; Timoleon also defended against the Carthaginians. Epaminondas and Pelopidas expelled the tyrants from Thebes and upheld its independence from Sparta. Demosthenes and

---

[17] See Pelling (2002a: 171–195).

Phocion fought nobly but unsuccessfully to defend Athens and Greece from the encroachment of Macedon. Demosthenes' brilliant speeches opposed Macedon's growth and defended Athenian power: those speeches were still the focal point of Greek education in Plutarch's day.[18] His contemporary Phocion, whom the Athenians chose as general some forty-five times, attempted to reach an accommodation beneficial to the city. Alexander completed the defeat of Persia, but also ruled Greece as just one part of a Macedonian empire. A century and a half later, Philopoemen, "the last of the Greeks" (*Philopoemen* 1.7), vainly opposed Rome in the final war of Greek liberation.

Intermixed with these brilliant memories, however, Plutarch paints a darker picture of civic infighting and wars of Greek against Greek. The united front against Persia in the 480s BCE was fleeting. Although the Athenian Cimon attempted to persuade Athens and Sparta to work together at a time when they were becoming increasingly hostile, the following century saw constant conflicts among the Greek states, the bloodiest and longest of which was the Peloponnesian War.[19] In fact, with the exception of the famous battles against the Persians, "Greece fought all her battles against herself, to enslave each other, and every trophy stands as a shame and reproach" – the result, for the most part, of the wickedness and competitiveness of their leaders (*Flamininus* 11.6).[20] For Plutarch, perhaps influenced by the Roman civil wars of his youth, the worst evil was bloodshed within the state, whether individual cities or the Greek nation as a whole.

The victories of Alexander the Great introduce a different era and another perspective, that of kings and conquerors acting on an immense new stage. Alexander's *Life*, one of the longest, celebrates his conquests, but raises the fundamental question of imperial monarchy: can the monarch succeed in ruling himself, showing himself a true king rather than a tyrant? Alexander's ambition and success prefigured that of Caesar; his empire replaced civic independence. After Alexander, the theater of action is no longer cities but nations and continents, and Plutarch's perspective looks toward the Roman conquests that would soon sweep away the Hellenistic

---

[18] Kennedy (1972: 615): "The great model of style in this period is Demosthenes, whose works were the subject of many commentaries"; compare also 533–535 (Pliny the Younger), 554 (the second-century "cult" of Demosthenes), and 630 (Hermogenes), and Quintilian, *Inst.* 10.1.76, 10.2.24, 12.10.23, 26.

[19] *Nicias* 27.9: the Syracusans had won over the Athenians "the most complete victory of Greeks over Greeks."

[20] Compare *De Pythiae oraculis* 401C–D lamenting that so many of the offerings at Delphi came from wars among the Greeks.

kingdoms. The pair *Alexander–Caesar* is the focal center of other pairs in which late republican Roman commanders are paired with classical and Hellenistic kings and commanders.[21] The ambitions of the Greek protagonists become a backdrop to the performance of their Roman counterparts, as Rome moved toward the monarchy under which Plutarch and his readers lived.

## Plutarch and Athens

Given Plutarch's personal preference for aristocratic government and Plato's anti-democratic bias, the biographer's interest in democratic politics in Athens merits attention.[22] He admired both the Athenians' love of liberty and the humanitarian feeling they could show. At the end of *Aristides* (27.7), after describing their generosity toward that man's descendants, he notes, "the Athenians still today are admired and imitated for their many examples of compassion and nobility." In *Praecepta gerendae reipublicae*, he advises contemporary politicians to recall Athens' acts of generosity and reconciliation rather than the battles of Marathon or the Eurymedon (814B–C). His portraits of Athenian leaders reveal how they were able to unite the city and bring the populace, despite all its tendency to irrational impulses, to wise and even heroic action. Solon and Pericles exemplify the successful democratic leader.

Solon's law code arose out of political conflicts among rich landowners as well as between them and the impoverished farmers. Plutarch uses Solon's poems to document these struggles and the lawgiver's attempt to stand between the factions. Solon could have made himself a tyrant, Plutarch writes, but chose to introduce legislation that would set Athens on a new course, the primitive democracy that would mature during the classical period. Solon worked by compromise, giving neither side all they wanted. As Plutarch notes, Solon did not live in Lycurgus' Sparta and so had to work purely by persuasion, compromising, not dictating (*Solon* 6.1–2). He restructured personal debt, especially that for mortgaged land, with the famous "shaking off of burdens" (*seisakhtheia*) – a half-measure that pleased neither party. Other new laws, including a system of graduated property

---

[21] Among the successors of Alexander, Plutarch profiled Eumenes, Demetrius, and Pyrrhus, who were paired with late republican Romans: Sertorius, Antony, and Marius. The *Lives* also include the Spartan kings Agis and Cleomenes, paired with the Gracchi and the couple uniting Philopoemen with his conqueror Flamininus, when Greece was finally incorporated into Rome's growing empire. See Stadter (2010), Beneker (2005), and Harrison (1995).

[22] Cf. Saïd (2005b).

qualifications, the right of citizens to initiate lawsuits, and a council that would consider items to be presented to the assembly, were limited in the same way (*Solon* 16–20). The biographer sees Solon more as a sage counselor than a political leader: he advises through his poetry and his laws, but he refuses to assume tyrannical power, and he leaves the city upon completion of his code. In his travels Solon advises Croesus, as described by Herodotus (*Solon* 27; cf. Herodotus 1.29–33), then returns to warn of Peisistratus' aim to become tyrant at Athens. Solon's decision to advise Peisistratus "and approve many of his actions" (*Solon* 31.2) may reflect Plutarch's own position as a philosopher friend to leading members of the Roman imperial government.

Plutarch's Solon must steer the state between the unthinking enthusiasm of the populace and the selfish interests of a wealthy elite, while keeping clear of tyranny. This challenge continued in later Athenian *Lives*. At least as early as Aristotle's *Constitution of the Athenians*, fifth-century Athenian history had been presented as a competition between supporters of popular democracy – Themistocles, Pericles, Alcibiades – and aristocratic conservatives – Aristides, Cimon, Nicias. While making use of this schema, Plutarch also delves into the nuances of each leader's situation. Historical context and the individual gifts of each leader bring moments of success, but also of rejection. Pericles perhaps emerges as most able to rise above party to govern the city, at least for a time.

There is no doubt that *Pericles* is a very positive portrait. In the preface Pericles is presented as a model to imitate, outstanding for honesty and self-control. Pericles is above all calm and secure under pressure: after a heckler had hurled insults at him all day as he was transacting business, and even followed him to his house in the evening, rather than respond angrily, he delegated a slave to escort the man home with a torch (*Pericles* 5.2). Plutarch quotes Thucydides' judgment that the Periclean Athens was "nominally a democracy, but actually rule of the leading man" (*Pericles* 9.1; cf. Thuc. 2.65). Under Pericles' leadership the Athenians erected the Acropolis buildings, which Plutarch considers exquisite in their ever-blooming beauty, unequalled until the time of the Caesars (*Pericles* 13.1–4, *Comparatio Pericles–Fabius Maximus* 3.7). Plutarch admires Pericles as a cautious leader, who kept the Athenians out of Sicily, persuaded the Spartans with a bribe to abandon their invasion of Attica, and most importantly refused to lead the eager Athenians into an infantry battle with the greatly superior Spartans (*Pericles* 20.4–21.1, 22.2, 33.4–34.1). Moreover, in a time of crisis he reconciled with his opponent Cimon for the good of the city (*Pericles* 10). At his death, the Athenians realized he had been a bulwark of safety against the mean ambitions of other men. Plutarch concludes that he truly deserved the epithet "Olympian," considering how he had exercised power with forbearance and integrity (*Pericles* 39.2–4).

Yet on almost every page of the *Life* Plutarch reveals how this aristocratic, even kingly, Pericles was challenged by his opponents. He speaks of a deep division in the city, which separated it into two factions, "the people," led by Pericles, and "the few" (*Pericles* 11.3). Pericles was accused of using demagogic tactics to gain power, opposing good conservatives such as Cimon and – whether by his own intransigence, disgraceful compliance to his mistress Aspasia, or fear of political trials – triggering the Peloponnesian War (*Pericles* 9.2–5, 30–32). His enemies denounced him as a tyrant (*Pericles* 16.1). Looking back at his rule, Plato asserted that he corrupted the Athenians with financial handouts and festivals, making them extravagant and undisciplined (*Pericles* 9.1; cf. Plato *Gorgias* 515e, 518e). Although he led Athens for many years, the Athenians rejected his war policy and deposed him from office – only to reelect him shortly thereafter.

The *Lives* of Themistocles and Aristides show a similar division between popular and conservative leaders, with the difference that here, when faced with the crisis of the Persian attack, the two leaders joined forces and presented a united front against the invader. Themistocles' political opponent from his earliest years was said to have been Aristides. Eventually Themistocles succeeded in having him ostracized. But in the moment of crisis, he introduced a measure to recall Aristides and other exiles, so that all could fight for the city together. Later, he accepted Aristides' advice before the battle of Salamis, and again on the pursuit of Xerxes. In a larger context, Themistocles yielded to Spartan insistence that they must furnish the commander at Salamis, setting aside his own desire to lead the navy, although the Athenians had supplied the largest contingent. Despite his enormous ambition and pride, which aroused the envy that led to his exile, Plutarch's Themistocles demonstrates the nobility of seeking first the good of the city. It is fitting that, although living in Persia, by his suicide he makes common cause with Greece, not with the Persians who have honored him.

In his *Life*, Aristides is identified as a political opponent of Themistocles, but shown to be willing to support and contribute to Themistocles' initiatives in the defense of Athens. At a meeting at Salamis the two each renounce "vain and childish contention" (*kenēn kai meirakiōdē stasin*) and Aristides supports Themistocles' strategy (*Aristides* 8.3–4). Political opponents can and did work together for a common purpose, and so saved

Athens and Greece. They pursue this concord also in dealing with Sparta. Aristides yielded to the Spartan commander at Plataea, as Themistocles had at Salamis, and in the argument there over the position of honor on the left wing was willing to accept whatever position the Athenians were assigned: "We have come not to dispute with our allies, but to fight with our enemies'" (*Aristides* 12.3). Aristides, though favoring aristocratic government, did not let that preference interfere with the safety of his city. His integrity was such that despite his position of influence, he remained poor until his death.

The opposition of the two political tendencies is also apparent in the *Lives* of Nicias and Alcibiades, yet here Plutarch suggests that the character of each of the two leaders excluded not only united action but also the domination of one individual. Alcibiades, brilliant but vain and undisciplined, especially courted the favor of the populace, although he himself belonged to a distinguished family. Nicias instead was wealthy but also timid, fearful of the wrath of the people and the power of the gods. As Alcibiades appealed to the Athenians' emotions in urging the expedition against Syracuse, Nicias tried to recommend caution. Both were chosen commanders, Nicias against his will. Both lost, for Alcibiades' enemies mounted charges against him *in absentia*, and he fled for his life to Sparta, where he promptly recommended actions against his own city (*Alcibiades* 21–23). In Sicily, Nicias' superstitious caution after an eclipse precipitated the destruction of the army (*Nicias* 23). Alcibiades' personal ambition contributed to the defeat of the Sicilian expedition and the ensuing oligarchic revolution in Athens. Although Alcibiades later returned to help his countrymen, the damage had been done. He was exiled a second time, and finally died, hounded by his political enemies. Soon after, the city fell to the Spartans. The interplay of political opposition and personal flaws destroyed both the leaders and their city.

## Plutarch and Sparta

Sparta, according to Plutarch, did not suffer from the political tensions between elite and populace found at Athens, but over time declined from the ideal state projected by Lycurgus because of the ambition and competitiveness of its elite, their *philotimia* and *philonikia*, as exemplified by Lysander and Agesilaus. The Spartan law code and associated customs ascribed to Lycurgus fill the largest part of the lawgiver's *Life* (*Lycurgus* 5–28). Plutarch admired Lycurgus' comprehensive vision and conscious training from childhood in the values of the city. His account is our most complete source for this tradition. Three features stand out: (a) the radical simplicity of Spartan life, seen in the redistribution of land, rejection of convenient coinage, common messes, and limitations on display of wealth; (b) the creation of a council of elders, the *gerousia*, and later of a smaller body, the five ephors, to act as a restraint on the power of the two kings; and (c) the educational program that was meant to perpetuate the Spartan system. The harsh treatment of helots, which Plutarch deplores and attempts to disassociate from the lawgiver, and the unusual position of women were other special features. Plutarch admired Lycurgus' peaceable ideology, which he compared to that of the Roman Numa, and the stability of his constitution, which for so long kept the Spartans "free, independent, and disciplined." Indeed, he compares Lycurgus' state favorably with that of Plato's *Republic*: "Lycurgus didn't just leave words and ideas, but a real and unrivalled government" (*Lycurgus* 31.3). Perhaps most importantly, the well-defined educational system ensured continuity over the centuries, a lack Plutarch criticizes in Numa's attempt to turn the Romans to peace (*Comparatio Lycurgus–Numa* 4).

Lycurgus had consciously introduced competition into the Spartan system, Plutarch believed. But, he notes, "excessive competitiveness is not just bad, but dangerous for cities" (*Agesilaus* 5.5–7). The two *Lives* of classical Spartans, Lysander and Agesilaus, confirm the latter observation. Each man had noble qualities, but these were offset by less attractive features. Lysander's great achievement, the defeat of Athens in 404, not only brought the leading city of Greece to her knees but corrupted Sparta as well. In Plutarch's view, the Lycurgan laws trained his city to peace and virtue. Lysander's victory brought imperial rule over the Greek cities and a flood of destabilizing wealth to Sparta. There might have been a suitable outlet for Spartan combativeness in King Agesilaus' war against the Persians in Asia Minor in 396–394, which Plutarch believed was proper and glorious, like that of Cimon in the mid-fifth century. But Plutarch excoriates the war between Sparta and her sometime Greek allies, which forced him to return (*Agesilaus* 15.3–4). Nor was Agesilaus fitted for uniting the warring cities in a stable confederacy. Plato in the *Republic* (545a) had identified Sparta as a timocratic state, one that, having fallen from the ideal, produced men in whom the spirited element dominated, leading to competitiveness, eagerness for honors, and a love of warfare. The timocratic man, Plato writes, will "be excessively submissive to authority, and ambitiously eager for authority himself" (549a). Plutarch sees Agesilaus as just such a man.[23] Agesilaus'

---

[23] See, further, Stadter (1999b).

unrelenting efforts to humiliate Thebes and finally to exclude it from the common peace in 371 BCE manifested exactly the evils of Greek internecine warfare that Plutarch found so disturbing. The king's insistence on asserting Spartan preeminence in Greece led to its defeats at Leuctra and Mantinea and to the loss of Messenia, almost half its territory. For Plutarch, the defeat of Athens, caused in no small part by internal political rivalry, such as that between Nicias and Alcibiades, led also to Sparta's decline, through the inability of its leaders to put aside their desire for complete supremacy. Political concord in the early fifth century led to freedom from Persia; political strife a century later led to defeat and humiliation.

This appreciation of political concord and condemnation of factionalism and civil war is found often in Plutarch's works, but is especially prominent in his *Praecepta gerendae reipublicae*, written for his contemporaries, and in the *Parallel Lives*. Plutarch's fascination with the Greek past was much more than a Roman subject's nostalgia for the glory days of old or the freedom of autonomous cities. On the contrary, he recognized that the Roman conquest of Greece had brought stability to warring states and ended the fratricidal killing of Greek by Greek, what he calls "that envy, those alliances and cabals against each other" (*Agesilaus* 15.4). But he found in the Greek political experience the same difficulty of achieving concord, which he recognized in Roman republican history and in his contemporary world.

## Plato as Subtext

As has just been suggested, Plato's influence, as philosophical master and stylistic model, is obvious throughout Plutarch's works. In the *Parallel Lives*, there are constant suggestions that Plato's concepts provide a standard against which the protagonists are measured.[24] The Platonic subtext is especially apparent in *Alcibiades* and *Dion*. Thucydides and Xenophon provided the historical foundation for the *Life* of Alcibiades, especially his role in the Sicilian expedition, his exile and recall, and his command of the Aegean fleet. However, the first sixteen chapters that treat the years before Sicily, focusing on his ambition, his love of praise, and his many admirers, while drawing on many anecdotal traditions, are influenced especially by Plato's accounts in the *Symposium*, *Alcibiades I*, and, indirectly, the *Republic*.[25] Plutarch makes Alcibiades' choice between

[24]  On Plutarch and Platonic moral psychology, see Opsomer (Chapter 4) and Duff (Chapter 3) in this volume.
[25]  See Duff (1999a: 224–225), Verdegem (2010a: 137–141), Pelling (2005b: 116–125), and Gribble (1999).

Socrates and his many other lovers a choice between true virtue and the admiration of the many. He is greatly attracted, even mesmerized, by Socrates' call to virtue won by self-discipline, but finds it more pleasurable to seek popular approval. "Alcibiades had sufficient inborn nobility that Socrates' arguments touched him . . . and brought him to tears, but then he would surrender to the pleasures offered by his flatterers and flee from him like a runaway slave" (*Alcibiades* 6.1).

And so his life showed a constant tension between "statesmanship, eloquence, vision, and cleverness" and "luxury, excess in drink and sex, effeminacy . . . and unbelievable extravagance" (*Alcibiades* 16.1). Finally, he was abandoned by the populace, which had raised him up when they became fearful that his extreme behavior reflected a desire to betray them.

Dion, a student of Plato's who expelled the tyrant Dionysius II from Syracuse, was a fundamentally noble person – Brutus is the companion figure – in whom are revealed some of the weaknesses of Plato's utopian vision when applied to real life.[26] Encouraged by Dion, Plato traveled to Syracuse, hoping to educate the tyrants, especially young Dionysius II, to become philosopher kings. The job, of course, was impossible, and Plato lamented his treatment bitterly. Plutarch draws on Plato's own words in the *Seventh Letter* to document the philosopher's efforts and disappointments. Plutarch shows, however, that even Dion, after he seized power, could not rule effectively: his excessive rigidity alienated the populace and soon he was assassinated. In *Alcibiades* and *Dion*, then, Plutarch confronts Platonic ideals with historical experience, asserting his own evaluation of the classical past. That past, for all its greatness, revealed the human imperfections, the fault-lines of the political process. Like the *Lives* discussed earlier, these biographies realize the principal purpose of much of his work: to explore, through a loving but penetrating analysis of the classical past, the application of moral principles in political, social, and personal circumstances.

## Character in Fact and Anecdote

Granted that Plutarch expected his audience to be familiar with the basic texts of classical literature, including the major historians, what techniques did he employ to construct an entertaining, instructive, and morally challenging narrative? A passage from the preface to *Nicias* reveals how he hoped to increase his readers' knowledge and pleasure by drawing on his

---

[26] See Dillon (2008) and Pelling (2004: 91–97).

own extraordinary familiarity with the classical period. After protesting
that he has no intention to attempt to rival Thucydides' inimitable narrative of the Sicilian expedition, as other historians had foolishly hoped, he
notes that he must include events reported by him and by the Sicilian
historian Philistus, but will add less well-known facts from other authors or
from offerings and decrees. "My purpose," he writes, "has not been to
gather senseless historical facts, but record items that promote the understanding of character and personality" (*Nicias* 1.5). The narrative of Nicias'
life that follows includes, among many other particulars, a full description
of Nicias' lavish spending on a mission to Apollo's sanctuary on Delos,
apparently derived from an inscription erected by Nicias, and verbatim
quotes from comic poets attacking his pusillanimity (*Nicias* 4.4–8 and 8.3–
4). True to the biographer's declaration, these notices illustrate, in a way
that Thucydides does not, Nicias' timidity before the populace and his
hope to win divine favor with his great wealth, character traits that in turn
will shape Plutarch's own analysis of the failure of the Sicilian expedition,
when Nicias' fear of what the gods or the Athenians might do to him
prevented him from saving his army from total defeat.

   Certain that his audience will know the story and appreciate his reworking
of the standard account, Plutarch often omits or skims rapidly major sections
of earlier historians' narratives and shifts their emphases.[27] His narrative does
not include everything, but focuses on moments or anecdotes that illustrate
the subject's temperament or his motives. This process mutates narrative
into paradigm, shifting the emphasis from military campaigns and historical
continuity to character and interpretation, as the Alexander preface famously
asserted: "often an insignificant act, word, or joke displays character better
than bloody battles, massed armies, and sieges of cities" (*Alexander* 1). We
may return to the *Life* of Pericles for an example. Although Thucydides
furnishes the basic framework for its account of Pericles' role in the
Peloponnesian War, and echoes of his language are scattered throughout,
Plutarch makes fundamental changes. Passing over the brilliant Periclean
speeches found in Thucydides, he concentrates on a few episodes. Plutarch
alone attributes to Pericles the dispatch of ships to aid Corcyra, humiliating
the son of Cimon, his own rival, in the process (*Pericles* 29.1–2) – such
attribution of unassigned political decisions to the protagonist of a *Life* is
a common Plutarchan technique. He then offers additional material, not
found in Thucydides, on Pericles' opposition to reconciliation with Sparta
over the Megarian decree. These include an anecdote reporting a Spartan

[27] See, for instance, Pelling (1992) = (2002a: 117-141); (2007a).

witticism, the story of the herald Anthemocritus, and the famous lines of Aristophanes about the Megarians' abduction of Aspasia's whores. Earlier he had included a paragraph on Aspasia's relationship to Pericles (*Pericles* 24). Here he speaks of Pericles' problems defending his friends Phidias, Aspasia, and Anaxagoras, as well as himself, from political attacks (*Pericles* 30–32). These alternative stories of Pericles' motives and the political pressure upon him require the reader to reevaluate Pericles' behavior. Was he being merely stubborn, or distracting the public to protect himself and his friends? Thucydides had avoided these questions, yet Plutarch insists on interrogating the traditional classical narrative, probing motive and behavior. Returning to Thucydides' narrative, Plutarch concentrates on Pericles' wisdom in restraining the Athenians from battle and his role as doctor of the body politic, healing the frustration, suffering, and anger of the populace after the ravaging of the countryside and the effects of the plague. Thucydides had presented Pericles as close to an ideal, a statesman with foresight, courage, ambition, and eloquence. Plutarch's portrait is less consistently heroic, with more suggestion of the difficulties and tensions inherent in political leadership. While reading, we are forced to reconsider the justice of the attacks on him in all their unsavory detail – but then we are swept up by the praise of Plutarch's final paragraphs: "The man was extraordinary not only for his gentleness and self-possession ... but his greatness of spirit." The nickname "Olympian" was appropriate for a man with "such an even character and a life in power pure and undefiled" (*Pericles* 39.1–2). In a unique manner, Plutarch succeeds in blending unblinking questioning of the heroic past with a vibrant reassertion of its greatness.

Well-placed and suggestive anecdotes served Plutarch as a means to involve the reader in his recreation and reevaluation of the classical past. Aptly placed incidents retold and reinterpreted from a variety of sources bring the central characters vividly to the reader's imagination. Often an anecdote near the beginning of a *Life* will set the tone for what follows, as when Alexander alone is able to tame the spirited stallion Bucephalus (*Alexander* 6). The incident points to Alexander's superiority but also to the challenge he will face throughout his life in taming his own spirit through self-control. When Alcibiades is accused of biting during a wrestling match "as women do," his witty retort, "No, as lions," suggests the underlying tension of his whole life between his license and his ambition (*Alcibiades* 2.2). Clusters of anecdotes often bring out special characteristics of the hero and may contrast with historically recorded incidents. Such is the case when Plutarch narrates the battle of Issus in only one sentence but surrounds the battle with anecdotes that bring out

Alexander's character: his indifference to wealth, his sexual restraint in dealing with the captured Persian royal women, and his temperance in eating and drinking (*Alexander* 18–23). Thus the battle becomes an occasion for Plutarch to indicate the true kingliness of Alexander. Later in the same *Life*, a series of anecdotes present the king's generosity and care for his friends (*Alexander* 39–42) but precede the accounts of the quarrels that led to the killing of his close companions Philotas, Parmenio, and Cleitus. The effect is to portray two sides of the king and cause the reader to ponder in each case how friendship can turn to anger and distrust. In Plutarch's mind, the great figures of the classical age are not simply admirable or subjects of encomia but become problematic as he presents multiple aspects of their lives. The charm and flexibility of the biographer's anecdotes conceal his art in discovering and presenting the character of these heroes of the classical age within their historical context.

## Imperfections in the Classical Past

The *Parallel Lives* may be distinguished from most imperial rhetoric referring to the classical period by Plutarch's serious approach to historical tradition and his willingness to present negative aspects of his subjects' motives and actions. In the preface to *Aemilius Paulus* he speaks of his pleasure in writing the *Lives*, which seemed like "spending time in [his subjects'] company and living with them," and of the moral improvement to be derived from the process (*Aemilius Paulus* 1.1–3). However, in reviewing the great statesmen of the classical period, Plutarch was acutely aware of their inadequacies when measured against the severe standard of Plato's philosopher kings. These *Lives* are notable for the many negative brushstrokes in what he clearly intends to be positive portraits. He defends his approach in the preface to *Cimon*: "The faults and flaws, which, prompted by passion or by political necessity, stain a man's actions we should regard as lapses from virtue rather than evidence of vice. We should not be eager to overemphasize these defects but should write instead feeling shame that human nature fails to produce any character, which is absolutely noble or unquestionably virtuous" (*Cimon* 2.5).

Elsewhere, after recounting a particularly shameful action of the Achaean commander Aratus, he says:

> I write this not out of any design to disgrace Aratus, for in many things he showed himself truly Greek and a great man, but out of pity for the weakness of human nature, that, even in characters like these, so worthy

in so many ways and so remarkable in virtue, it cannot maintain its nobility unblemished by some envious fault. (*Agis/Cleomenes* 37.8)

The biographer accepts the imperfections of his protagonists, even those revealed in men of the most glorious age of Greece, as a fact of human nature. Far from attempting to impose a Platonic ideal on his subjects, he prefers to offer his readers portraits of men not so very different from themselves.

For Plutarch, the classical period did not represent some nostalgic and unattainable ideal, but a heritage, which could inspire his contemporary readers to similar acts of greatness in the quite different imperial context in which they lived. Plutarch, while noting the particularities of different historical moments, presents his subjects as people acting according to universal principles. For this reason his biographies seem timeless, and work on the modern reader as on his contemporaries. They allow the reader to evaluate each statesman as a living figure, set in a particular historical context and possessing both virtues and weaknesses, and to emulate his finest actions, "For anything noble actively attracts us to itself and implants in us an immediate stimulus to action, forming the spectator's moral character not merely through a representation, but by giving him moral purpose through the reasoned account of the (noble) deed" (*Pericles* 2.4).

The classical past, for Plutarch, offered a huge reservoir of history, art, and traditions, from which he drew examples of virtue for inspiration and encouragement. He expected that his readers should do the same. But he also insisted that the examples we draw from that reservoir must be carefully strained and tested, using investigative acumen and skeptical discussion and evaluation, to remove the inevitable debris, the inescapable outcome of human ambition, competition, greed, and desire. Internecine war and personal rivalries polluted those great times even as they did in his own day, and still do the present world. The best qualities of the classical past could be reacquired only by the constant exercise of prudent reason and controlled passion. Plutarch dared his readers to accept this challenge.

## Further Reading

For the cultural interaction between Plutarch's age and the classical past, see Bowie (1974); Swain (1996); Veyne (1999); Whitmarsh (2001; 2005; 2009); Connolly (2001); Webb (2006). On Plutarch's stance toward the past, see generally Stadter (2005a); on Plutarch's engagement with traditions and material evidence, see Buckler (1992); Payen (2014); Oikonomopoulou (2017a). Plutarch's *Lives* transform the Greek past into biographical exemplarity: see Frazier (1996), Zadorojnyi (2018b), Payen (2014), and especially Muccioli (2012). For Plutarch's treatment of classical political leaders, see, for example, the commentaries of Stadter (1989) on Pericles, Shipley (1997) on Agesilaus, and Verdegem (2010a) as well as Pelling (1996) on Alcibiades. For Plutarch's engagement with Herodotus, see Hershbell (1993), Marincola (1994), Inglese (2003), and Pelling (2007a); with Thucydides, Stadter (1973b) and Pelling (1992); with poetry, Zadorojnyi (2006b), Papadi (2008), and Mossman (1988; 2014); with Plato, Donini (1994a), Hershbell (2004), Opsomer (2005), and Pelling (2005b). Interesting case studies are galore: see, for example, Stadter (1992a); Casanova (2013); Gómez Cardó et al. (2014); Davies and Mossman (forthcoming in 2023).

CHAPTER 10

# Great Men
## Leadership in Plutarch's Lives

### Mark Alexander Beck

My aim in this chapter is to present Plutarch's salient thoughts on the topic of individual greatness, as represented in his biographical works, most notably in his magnum opus the *Parallel Lives*.[1] It goes without saying that his decision to include these men as his biographical subjects in the *Lives* presumes greatness in some form or other. What then is it that makes these men great in Plutarch's estimation? As a human quality, greatness itself is situational, elusive, and even evanescent. There is not one unified skillset or collection of attributes that invariably and consistently characterizes greatness. It therefore resists easy classification or categorization and appears to be contingent on time, place, and a multitude of other factors and variables. One work on the topic elects to uniformly identify greatness in historical figures with varieties of effective leadership.[2] This perspective closely approaches Plutarch's own viewpoint in the *Lives* on what constitutes greatness. All the men in the *Lives* are leaders, some more effective than others, and Plutarch is ostensibly concerned about the responsible wielding of power. Plutarch ranks human achievement hierarchically according to its degree of ontological dependence.[3] This means that he ranks those individuals engaged in political and military leadership roles more highly than historians who write about their exploits (*De gloria Atheniensium* 345F).[4] Ultimately, every civic-minded individual should strive to "be

---

[1] All citations of Plutarch's *Parallel Lives* follow the Loeb Classical Library edition, edited and translated by Bernadotte Perrin.

[2] Isaacson (2010).

[3] On the concept of ontological dependence, see the entry "Ontological Dependence" by T. E. Takho and E. J. Lowe in the *Stanford Encyclopedia of Philosophy* (revised 2015): https://plato.stanford.edu /entries/dependence-ontological.

[4] On the relation of this epideictic speech to Plutarch's thought, see Kidd's (1992: 146–153) perceptive introduction. Yet most of the past, as Plutarch was aware, can only be accessed through the medium of literature, since literature transmits to us the statements and actions of great and not so great individuals. Moreover, the preeminent Greek writers of the archaic and classical periods, Homer,

a speaker of speeches, and also a doer of actions" (quoting Homer, *Il.* 9.443, in *Praecepta gerendae reipublicae* 798B, *An seni respublica gerenda sit* 795E, and Plutarch affirms that we "possess no higher capacity than that for conducting cities or states" (*Comparatio Aristides–Cato Maior* 3.1). In his view, the achievements of a Julius Caesar or a Pericles surpass the literary or artistic accomplishments of myriad historians, poets, and painters. Equally, Lycurgus' achievement of designing an actual polis surpasses the literary representations of Plato, Diogenes, and Zeno that derive from it (*Lycurgus* 31.1–2).[5]

Plutarch wants us to perceive varieties of leadership, assess their efficacy and flaws, and learn from the lack of uniformity in a way that continuously supports our moral and intellectual development throughout our own lives, even if our station in life does not entail the wielding of great power. Each biography serves as a case study in potentialities and possibilities that offers the critical reader practical edifying value.[6] To this end, he deploys various literary techniques in representing individual aspects of leadership. These include his unusually complex and multifaceted application of *synkrisis*, intertextual references, and his use of *mimēsis* with its educational value.[7]

### Great Natures and Emotional Intelligence

Plutarch's conception of continuous moral improvement over time is consistent with most schools of thought in ancient philosophy and is based on the premise that an individual's character (*ēthos* or *tropos*) is not static and immutable from birth, but is capable of development and improvement (or conversely deterioration) in youth and adulthood.[8] His

---

Herodotus, the tragedians, Thucydides, Plato, and Xenophon, were all concerned with representing and exploring the qualities needed by a statesman, king, or general: see Schofield (1999: 4).

[5] The literary achievement of historians, for example, is derivative and ancillary, because without the great exploits of others they would have nothing to write about. The historian's account is but a reflection, as in a mirror, of another man's accomplishments and glory (*De gloria Atheniensium* 345F). Deeds that are ancillary include the accomplishments of craftsmen and musicians whose productions and performances may excite our admiration and appreciation but not necessarily our emulation. Phidias' role as architect of the temples on the Athenian Acropolis is sustained by and depends upon Pericles' political leadership. Plutarch thus allots Pericles full credit for the grandeur of the Acropolis (*Pericles* 13.6–7; *Comparatio Pericles-Fabius Maximus* 3). Philosophical discourse is therefore also evaluated against political action in the evaluation of Lycurgus' achievement (*Lycurgus* 31.1–2). See Liebert (2016: 97–146) for an elaborate treatment of Lycurgus' role in Plutarch's political philosophy.

[6] See Duff (2011b: 59–75).     [7] See now Schmidt et al. (2020) on intertextuality in Plutarch.

[8] See especially *De sera numinis vindicta* 551E–552D. See also Gill (1983; 2006: 415–419), Duff (1999a: esp. 48–49, 60–61, 72–98, 101, 156, 224–225; 1999b; 2004: 280–281; 2008b: 10) (with reference to

*Lives* reflect his ongoing concern with moral improvement and ethical training that is more directly represented in his ethical treatises.[9] In fact, he even thinks that those endowed with "great natures" (*megalai physeis*) – a concept he derives from Plato's *Republic* (491b–495b)[10] – are as susceptible to vice, when "corrupted by poor nurture and evil company," as they are to virtue (*De sera numinis vindicta* 551D). The possession of a great nature, or, we would say, great innate ability, simply magnifies the potential for doing great harm or great good: "For great natures bring forth nothing trivial, and the vigor and enterprise in them is too keen to remain inert" (552C). Plutarch employs an agrarian analogy that speaks to the discernment that must be exercised in perceiving those who could potentially become great under the right set of circumstances:

> Someone inexperienced in farming would not welcome the sight of land covered in dense undergrowth and wild plants, teeming with animals, and streaming with rivulets and mud; but exactly the same features show anyone who has acquired discrimination and discernment that the soil is rich, extensive and friable. Likewise great natures often bloom in odd and undesirable ways, and our initial reaction is to find their rough and prickly aspects intolerable, and to think we ought to cut them down and prune them; but a better judge recognizes even in these aspects the signs of stock which is good and valuable, and he waits for the time when they cooperate with reason and virtue, and the moment when their nature produces its particular fruit. (552C–D; trans. Waterfield)[11]

An individual's nature (*physis*) would therefore seem to bestow greater potentiality and not necessarily an innate predisposition toward goodness or badness. The "dense undergrowth and wild plants" to which this passage from *De sera numinis vindicta* refers is analogous to the strong passions (*pathē*) in youthful souls that require tempering (*De virtute morali* 451B–452D). The source of these passions is the *thymos*, which is frequently employed as a term for anger, and the goal of education is attainment of control over passions by reason.[12] Ultimately, reasoned restraint in one's

---

Plutarch's *Themistocles*), Verdegem (2010a: 119–121) (with reference to Plutarch's portrait of Alcibiades), and more recently Xenophontos (2016: 22–41).

[9] See Gill (2006: 414).

[10] See primarily Duff (1999a: 72–98; 1999b; 2004: 280–287). See also Beneker (2012: 7–17) and Becchi (2014).

[11] For the use of this agricultural analogy elsewhere in reference to talented individuals who lacked training, see *Aratus* 10.3–4, *Coriolanus* 1.2–4, *Alcibiades* 4.1, *Cato Maior* 2.3.

[12] On the different terms for anger including *thymos*, see Harris (2001: 50–70). On the *thymos* in particular, see Kalimtzis (2012: 34–72 and *passim*). See in particular Plutarch's treatises *De virtute morali* 440D–452D and *De cohibenda ira* 459B–E; Duff (1999a: 72–98; 2008b: 2); Gill (2006: 219–

dealing with others (*praotēs*) is the desired behavioral outcome of education. Thus to Plutarch the ideal man of action will be a passionate individual with a spirited nature (*thymoeidēs*), but prone to reasoned action subject
to the control exercised cooperatively by his rational intellect (*nous, dianoia, logos*). Ideally the rational component of the intellect (*logos*) should
exercise control over emotions "without extinguishing them."[13] Habitual
improvement in the assertiveness of the rational component is deemed
character development (*epanorthōsis*), with continuous alteration over time
viewed as character change (*metabolē*).[14]

   This powerful natural endowment may take an individual very far, even in
the absence of adequate early education (*paideia*). The full impact of deficient
education may only surface later in life, when a prominent individual's
character is tested, as the *Lives* of both Themistocles and Marius show.[15]
Their life stories represent the negative development of character (*metabolē*).[16]
The *Parallel Lives* is a series of case studies in the interaction of great natural
ability, experience, and education in the pursuit of power.[17] Sometimes, of
course, things went seriously wrong. The *Demetrius* and *Antony* pairing is
a case in point. Plutarch chooses these two men to illustrate in particular the
negative consequences arising from great natures (*megalai physeis*) deprived of
proper education (*Demetrius* 1.7) (see later in this chapter).[18]

## Modern Leadership

Modern influential theories of leadership echo these core elements. In
particular, the concept of "emotional intelligence," as described by
Daniel Goleman, corresponds considerably with the categories or traits
emphasized in Plutarch's description of the effective leader and the program of the *Parallel Lives* in general.[19] What Plutarch calls character (*ēthos,
tropos*), Goleman identifies as emotional intelligence.[20] Goleman discerns

---

238); Becchi (1999; 2014); Beneker (2012: 9–17; 2014). See further Opsomer's Chapter 4 in this
   volume.
[13] Xenophontos (2016: 26).     [14] See Xenophontos (2016: 29–41).
[15] See Duff (2008b) and Pelling (2014).
[16] Interestingly, as Xenophontos (2016: 30) notes, Plutarch employs *metabolē* in the *Lives* when
   referring to character deterioration.
[17] See especially Duff (1999a), Nikolaidis (2014), Liebert (2016), and Jacobs (2018).
[18] Duff (2004: 280–281), Monaco (2011–12), and Beck (2016). The *Alcibiades–Coriolanus* is another
   such pair. See also the *Lysander–Sulla*.
[19] See e.g. Goleman (2001). On the programmatic statements of the *Parallel Lives*, see Duff (1999a: 13–
   51) and Jacobs (2018: 94–107).
[20] This is my identification. Goleman (1995: 36) notes that the set of traits he identifies as emotional
   intelligence might be called "character" by some.

five components of emotional intelligence, "the *sine qua non* of leadership," as he says:[21] self-awareness, self-regulation, motivation, empathy, and social skill. *Self-awareness* is the ability to recognize and understand one's own "moods, emotions, and drives as well as their effect on others."[22] This correlates well with one of the stated primary aims of reading the *Lives*; that is, the acquisition of a clearer view of ourselves, as if through gazing at a mirror.[23] *Self-regulation* is "the ability to control or redirect disruptive impulses or moods" and "the propensity to suspend judgment."[24] This aligns perfectly with Plutarch's aim of attaining the behavioral self-control known as *praotēs*, a trait manifested most notably by Pericles who serves for Plutarch as the model statesman.[25] Goleman defines *motivation* as "a passion to work for reasons that go beyond money or status" and "a propensity to pursue goals with energy and persistence."[26] This concept accords well with the benefits conferred by the proactive *thymos* in Plutarchan psychology. The *thymos* is the source of the energy that translates into motivation and underlies the aggressiveness that does not shun conflict, an essential facet of leadership.[27] Next, Goleman identifies *empathy* as "the ability to understand the emotional makeup of other people" and "the skill in treating people according to their emotional reactions."[28] *Social skill* is defined as "the proficiency in managing relationships and building networks" and "an ability to find common ground and build rapport."[29] There is obviously a close relationship between *empathy* and *social skill*, as defined by Goleman. Both entail interpersonal skills that foster an atmosphere of sensitivity and cooperation. This includes, as Goleman notes in the case of *empathy*, "cross-cultural sensitivity."[30]

*Empathy* and *social skill* are less pronounced as key traits in Plutarch's psychology of leadership. Certainly *praotēs* (and also the terms *hēmerotēs*, gentleness, *philanthrōpia*, "people-liking," and *philophrosynē*, friendliness) would seem to overlap some of the semantic fields we associate with *empathy* and *social skill*.[31] Among Greeks, the presence of empathy is thematic in the *Lives* of Solon, Pericles, Cimon, and Agesilaus (to a fault!), while a certain lack of empathy is notable in the *Lives* of Agesilaus (toward Lysander), Demetrius, and Alcibiades. In the *Life of*

---

[21] Goleman (2001: 5). [22] Goleman (2001: 7).
[23] See later in this chapter. On the mirror analogy, see Stadter (2003–4), Zadorojnyi (2010), and Frazier (2011).
[24] Goleman (2001: 7). [25] See Beck (2004). [26] Goleman (2001: 7).
[27] Burns (1978: 36–41) is superb on the lack of conflict avoidance in leadership.
[28] Goleman (2001: 7). [29] Goleman (2001: 7). [30] Goleman (2001: 7).
[31] See Martin (1960; 1961), Alexiou (2008), Nikolaidis (2009), Van der Stockt (2011), and Roskam (2014).

*Alexander* the protagonist's level of empathy seems to decline or waver in the course of the *Life* from a high point evidenced in his breaking of the horse Bucephalus and the magnanimity and kindness with which Alexander treats Darius' captive wife and daughters, to a low point in the murder of his friend Cleitus and his brutal treatment of Callisthenes and Cassander.[32] In addition to conduct toward one's peers, the treatment of women, children, slaves, and animals figures strongly in Plutarch's assessment of what we would identify as empathy in his protagonists.

Furthermore, from the perspective of interactions of Greeks and Romans, empathy was obviously an important trait to have. Plutarch elucidates its importance in several Roman *Lives*, in which the protagonist displays notable restraint in his dealings with the subjugated Greeks during the republican era (e.g. Lucullus) or contempt and lack of restraint (e.g. Cato Maior[33] and Marius[34]). As one would expect, the *Lives* of Cato Maior and Cato Minor are both notable for the lack of sensitivity and empathy displayed by the protagonists, shared traits viewed by Plutarch almost as hereditary in origin. The lack of empathy in the *Life of Cato Maior*, or the Censor as he was called after the highest office he occupied, is represented prominently in his dealings with Greeks, his own slaves (many of whom were undoubtedly Greek), his horse, and his fellow politicians. In the *Life of Cato Minor* his relations with his wife, his (Greek) slaves, and his fellow politicians likewise come under scrutiny.[35] Plutarch's repeated examination of the Censor's treatment of slaves is interlocked with the theme of excessive frugality. He informs us that the Censor was accustomed to sell off the aged and infirm slaves, thus revealing his cool lack of attachment and loyalty to those who should have merited better treatment based on their long years of servitude (*Cato Maior* 4.5–6). Plutarch criticizes the unfeeling attitude (*atenous agan ēthous*) he thinks must be responsible for this practice (*Cato Maior* 5.1–7). The relatively rare adjective *atenēs* employed here generally indicates in Plutarch rigid, inexorable, or inflexible behavior, and is employed twice in the *Life of Cato Minor* (2.2; 4.1–2),[36] and is used to negatively characterize Cato's unbending pursuit of justice in association with the Stoic philosopher Antipater of Tyre. In the *Lives* of Coriolanus (15.3–5) and Dion (52.5–6) it is twice linked with the noun *authadeia*, which refers to "inflexibility," "willfulness," "haughtiness,"

---

[32]  See Beneker (2012: 103–152).    [33]  See *Cato Maior* 8.7, 9.1–3 and later in this chapter.
[34]  Duff (2008b: 16–18).    [35]  See Stadter (1995) on Cato's relations with women.
[36]  This same adjective is applied to Aristides' pursuit of justice (*Aristides* 2.2). Often it describes a negative trait that dovetails with stubbornness or haughtiness: *Dion* 52.5, *Coriolanus* 15.5, *Agesilaus* 35.5. See Duff (1999a: 210–211), Beck (2000), Ahlrichs (2005: 220–222), and Alexiou (2008: 371–378).

"rigidity," and "obstinacy," which in turn is associated with solitude (*erēmia*).[37] Naturally, such rigidity will negatively impact one's dealings with others both in foreign affairs and domestically. While Coriolanus does possess a "great nature" and the native talent that would have equipped him to accomplish great things, his lack of education (*paideia*) disallows proper moral development and explains his ultimate failure (*Coriolanus* 1.3).[38] His peers mistake his insensibility (*apatheia*) to pleasure, toil, and monetary gain as a sign of self-control, justice, and courage (*Coriolanus* 1.3). In both of the *Lives* of Cato Maior and Cato Minor, not coincidentally, the figure of Socrates is inserted as an extraneous foil to subtly bring out these characterological flaws in two men who were otherwise widely held to epitomize Roman ideals. We will return to this point later in the chapter when we explore the use of the Socratic paradigm.

## Transformational and Transactional Leadership

The distinction between *transformational* and *transactional* leadership is another aspect of modern leadership theory that finds resonance in Plutarch's *Lives*.[39] James MacGregor Burns is the originator of this fundamental dichotomy and articulates it as follows:

> I will identify two basic types of leadership: the *transactional* and the *transforming*. The relations of most leaders and followers are *transactional* – leaders approach followers with an eye to exchanging one thing for another: jobs for votes, or subsidies for campaign contributions. Such transactions comprise the bulk of the relationships among leaders and followers, especially in groups, legislatures, and parties. *Transforming* leadership, while more complex, is more potent. The transforming leader recognizes and exploits an existing need or demand of a potential follower. But, beyond that, the transforming leader looks for potential motives in followers, seeks to satisfy higher needs, and engages the full person of the follower. The result of transforming leadership is a relationship of mutual stimulation and elevation that converts followers into leaders and may convert leaders into moral agents.[40]

While it would be impossible to fully explore here the ramifications of this distinction in the *Lives*, it can certainly help to frame the Plutarchan views on

---

[37] Plutarch is here quoting the Platonic *Epistle* iv, 321b.
[38] On Coriolanus' leadership flaws, see Jacobs (2018: 183–226).
[39] Burns (1978: 141–369). Burns favors the term "transforming," but "transformational" has now come into widespread use to describe this variety of leadership and was introduced by Bernard Bass, who further developed Burns' work.
[40] Burns (1978: 4).

leadership. Thus, it is clear that Plutarch did not find transactional leadership only to be ideal. Bribing the people with games, banquets, gifts of money, and other lavish expenditures to acquire and keep political power was distasteful to him (*Praecepta gerendae reipublicae* 802D–E, 821F–822C, and 823C–E). The reputation derived from such uncultured forms of currying favor with the masses (euergetism) is flawed because it is "ephemeral and uncertain" (821F).[41] He envisions the ideal statesman as one who elevates, invigorates, and enlightens the civic body with his moral example and powerful intellect. Lycurgus, Solon, Aristides, Pericles, Numa, Fabius, and Aemilius Paulus all practice this elevated style of leadership.[42] They exert a lasting and beneficial influence on their cities. Dion, Cato Maior, Cicero, Cato Minor, and Brutus all strive to attain this goal, but each falls short in some way. Alexander is unquestionably a transformative leader in terms of his impact on Western history, but not so much in his *Life*. By contrast, Plutarch, in two epideictic speeches, *De Alexandri magni fortuna aut virtute* (326D–345B), portrays Alexander the Great as the true philosopher and a man of action, very nearly the ideal philosopher king, who uses military success and conquest instrumentally to unify Greek and barbarian in one cosmopolitan state guided by Greek laws and *paideia*. He is even represented as superior to Socrates and Plato in particular in that he more effectively promoted the dissemination of Greek *paideia* than Plato was capable of doing with his masterworks, the *Republic* and *Laws* (328A–E; 330F–331A; 333A). This brings us to the role of literature in the education of effective leaders.

## The Role of *mimēsis:* Leadership as Performance

Plutarch views literature as playing an important role in education (*paideia*) and thus character formation. Through exposure at an early age to representations of exceptional individuals, youngsters of talent and ability, with proper guidance, will be prompted to adopt a virtuous lifestyle and benefit their communities.[43] In fact, the assumption underlying Plutarch's views on education is that literary representations have formative value, are intellectually and

---

[41] Obviously not all forms of euergetism in the ancient world have the negative connotation alluded to here. Notably, both Cimon and Pericles engaged in positive forms of euergetism that won Plutarch's express approval. On the acquisition of power through euergetism and its maintenance in Plutarch, see Beck (2004; 2007b) and Roskam (2014).

[42] On the leadership qualities of Pericles, Fabius, and Aemilius Paulus, see Jacobs (2018: 128–179 and 283–305). On the statesman as a moral actor, see Stadter (1997) = (2015a: 215–230).

[43] See Zadorojnyi (2002: 299–306). On Plutarch's thought in general about literature in education, see Hunter and Russell (2011: 1–17), Bowie (2014), and Xenophontos (2016: 79–91). See also the important article by Duff (2008b) on models of education in Plutarch.

emotionally stimulating, and should therefore be incorporated into a curriculum that has as its aim the moral improvement and inspiration of the young.[44] Accordingly, literature is capable of providing us with accounts of appropriate role models for those who are endowed with the requisite natural ability (*physis, euphyia*) to profit from such guidance and instruction (*Quomodo adolescens poetas audire debeat, De recta ratione audiendi, Quomodo quis suos in virtute sentiat profectus*). The ultimate aim of this moral instruction is to equip young men for public office. For Plutarch, this process is not restricted to the young alone. Instead he envisions ideally a lifelong educational process whereby the continuous evaluation and analysis of experience, especially of greatness in action with its attendant successes and failures, leads to self-improvement, as we attempt to emulate[45] and adopt aspects of these behavioral paradigms in our own daily lives. Plutarch characterizes this as a gradual adaptive process whereby one divests oneself of some qualities or behaviors and assumes other more positive ones in their stead (*Quomodo quis suos in virtute sentiat profectus* 75D–E). *Mimēsis*, the concept that connotes both imitation and representation in Greek, is thus for Plutarch less ambiguous than it is for Plato.[46] *Mimēsis* (in its meaning as representation) therefore supplies yet another mode of experiencing the world, of which the reader of literature or the viewer of art may avail themselves so as to learn and eventually adopt corresponding modes of behavior in like situations (*mimēsis* as imitation).[47] Plutarch thus conceives of literature, properly appreciated, as capable of informing action. In the prologue to the *Life of Pericles* we are advised that simple imitation (*mimēsis*) without intellectual analysis is not sufficient: "For anything noble actively attract us to itself and instills in us an immediate urge to action; it does not build moral character in the spectator merely by means of imitation/representation (*mimēsis*), but by equipping him with a choice (*prohairesis*) through the investigation/account (*historia*) of the deed" (*Pericles* 2.3).[48]

---

[44] See Xenophontos (2016: 79–107).
[45] The noun *zēlos* and the associated verb *zēlousthai* are employed by Plutarch in the prologue of the *Pericles* (1.4, 2.2) to convey the desire to emulate implanted by admirable role models.
[46] On the complexity and function of mimesis in Plutarch's pedagogical program, see the stimulating observations of Zadorojnyi (2012). See also Goldhill (2002: 259). On mimesis in Plato, see Halliwell (2002: 37–147).
[47] See Duff (2001).
[48] Translation by Waterfield, with significant modifications. The negation of *mimēsis* is at issue here. For a thorough discussion, see Duff (2001), Goldhill (2002: 259), and also Beck (2010). Cf. Stadter (1989: xxix–xxx) for more elaborate translation: "For what is noble (*to kalon*) spontaneously draws us actively to itself and instills in us an immediate urge to action, not merely by building character in the observer through a representation but producing a moral choice by a reasoned account of the action."

An author qua narrator such as Plutarch, concerned with moral instruction, may therefore exploit the medium of literature to guide the narratee through accounts of actions that elicit from the narrator praise or censure, and promote in the narratee the kind of decision-making (*prohairesis*) reflective of positive character development.[49] As Philip Stadter notes in his commentary on this passage: "Plutarch sees the element of conscious choice as central to the life of virtue, both for his subjects and for his readers."[50] Informed decision-making is fundamental to greatness in leadership. In this prologue Plutarch drives home the point that the mind (*nous*) and the intellect (*dianoia*) must be engaged in this process (*Pericles* 1.2, 1.3). The visual faculty is appealed to and our admiration is stimulated and channeled into action. Simon Goldhill acutely observes in his analysis of this passage that "[R]eading the work of Plutarch makes your intellectual character by critical exercise. Reading *Pericles* is to make you imitate not so much Pericles as Plutarch."[51] The engagement Plutarch advocates is thus realistic, analytical, and pragmatic. We distill from our reading the essential greatness of Pericles' actions and endeavor to incorporate that into our own life plans.

This active application of our intellectual acuity to what we see happening in the world around us is pointedly exemplified in the very beginning of this prologue. Augustus, as Plutarch relates, witnessed some wealthy foreigners in Rome bestowing affection on young monkeys and puppies and was prompted to ask "whether their wives bear no children, thus reproaching them earnestly, in the manner of a leader (*hēgemonikōs*), for squandering (*katanaliskontas*) the innate capacity for love and affection that we humans have on animals when it is owed to humans" (*Pericles* 1.1). It is obvious from this that Augustus sees the world with elevated civic consciousness in his capacity as emperor,[52] and Plutarch is encouraging us, with his interpretive explanation, to do likewise – in our own more restricted way, of course. Literature not only affords the opportunity of "witnessing" great events as they happen but it also sensitizes our perception and guides our understanding of those seminal events in a way that conduces to positive behavioral outcomes in future

[49] On Plutarch's narrative persona and authorial guidance, see Beck (2000). Like Aristotle, Plutarch sees character as a manifestation of action. On the influence of the Peripatos on Plutarch, see Becchi (2014) (with the bibliography cited therein). Cf. Goldhill (2002: 259): "The reader is depicted as a spectator at a drama (*theatēs*), whose character is formed (*ēthopoiein*) by the experience of observation."

[50] Stadter (1989: 61).    [51] Goldhill (2002: 259).

[52] Augustus strove to encourage childbirth in Roman families with legislative measures (*lex Julia et Papia*).

situations.[53] In some ways, literature may be superior to firsthand experience. Instructive events and exemplary individual action may be perpetually (and vicariously) revisited by rereading. Another advantage of literature involves the exposure of young people safely to negative examples.[54] In narratological terminology this process may be described as focalization in the service of moralization.

Pericles is certainly an example in Plutarch of transformative leadership who left his impression on Athens and the Athenian people. We may also cite Numa as another. Perhaps the closest of Plutarch's heroes to a philosopher king, Numa redefined Roman priorities in the wake of Romulus' bellicose and morally corrupt rule.[55] These men differ in that their authority over their people derives primarily from the strength of their character and moral rectitude. They do not pander to the masses with acts of euergetism that aim to marshal support for their policies (e.g. Cimon, Caesar) – the modus operandi of transactional leadership in the ancient world.[56] Lawgivers are likely to be transformative leaders because they support change that very often brings them into conflict with elements in their society. As a result, they must, in some cases, develop strategies to succeed. Effective leadership is not rigid but instead mediates between competing claims to ensure a society's long-term viability and resolve dissent that may ultimately erode the fabric of society. Unquestionably exceptional communication skills are required and not just those of a great orator like Pericles. We will therefore explore the performative acts by which Solon and Lycurgus, the prominent examples of such transformational leaders/lawgivers in the *Lives*, moved their people.

Solon was the first champion of the people (Aristotle, *Ath. Pol.* 2.2; 28.2). He attempted to communicate with them in public settings and used poetry on occasion for that purpose. He also appears to have put on dramatic performances to capture their attention and marshal support for important issues. Plutarch, our best later source, recounts that he simulated madness, donned a herald's cap, and leapt upon the speaker's platform where he delivered a 100-verse-long poem to encourage the Athenians, who were wavering, to seize the island of Salamis from

---

[53] Plutarch himself offers a clear explanation of just what this approach implies. In this essay he emphasizes the ability to gather "what is congruent and useful, not just from the written or spoken word, but from any sight and any situation at all." See Beck (2010: 357–358).

[54] See Duff (2004: 276) and Gill (2006: 412–421); also Zadorojnyi (2002: 300–305).

[55] On Numa as philosopher king, see Boulet (2005; 2014). On Numa's redirection of Rome in the wake of Romulus, see Banta (2007a; 2007b). See also Stadter (2015a: 246–257) and Liebert (2016: 147–188).

[56] For a comprehensive view of this cultural phenomenon, see Veyne (1976) (abridged English translation 1990). See also Lomas and Cornell (2003).

Megara (*Solon* 8.1–2). By virtue of this "performance," Solon was able to induce the Athenians to break the law and wage war, with himself in command (*Solon* 8.3). The instance of rule-breaking associated with a performative act of an evidently charismatic individual should be noted here. The fact that the Athenians placed Solon in command indicates that they saw through his feigned insanity and trusted his leadership.[57] Solon's activities in the public sphere evoke comparison with the antics of the trickster figure qua culture hero of Greek mythology.[58] He uses deception, but in the service of the greater good. The authority and respect Solon wields eventually leads to his election as archon after Philombrotos and his appointment as mediator (*diallaktēs*) and lawgiver (*nomothetēs*) (*Solon* 14.4).

Lycurgus' leadership is also revealed in performative acts. One of the most compelling, in that it puts on display Lycurgus' character, comes early in the *Life*. Plutarch makes it clear that Lycurgus could have used the opportunity of the death of his brother, Polydectes, with the assistance of his brother's wife, to seize the throne, since she proposed to terminate her pregnancy to effect this. Lycurgus tricked her into bearing the child and immediately after his birth he had the boy brought to him, at which point "He took the child in his arms and said to the assembled company, 'Spartiates, a king has been born for you.' Then he laid him in the king's place and named him Charilaus because all the people were delighted, as well as being impressed by his high-mindedness and justice" (*Lycurgus* 3.3–4; trans. Waterfield).

The *Lycurgus* also contains an important episode that exemplifies the training of a *thymoeidic* individual by exposure to a positive role model and illustrates the power this positive example may have on the wider community. In the first half of the *Life*, Plutarch gives us an overview of the special circumstances that lead to Lycurgus' preeminence in the community and eventual renown, as the putative fashioner of the unique Spartan system of education (*agōgē*). Early in the *Life*, we are told that he is admired for his wisdom (*phronēma*) and justice (*dikaiosynē*) (*Lycurgus* 3.4). Plutarch reports that Lycurgus traveled extensively and brought back to Sparta the fruits of his experiences abroad (*Lycurgus* 4.1–2). He absorbed the political and military lessons from the people of Asia Minor and the Egyptians, whose

---

[57] Cf. Demosthenes *De falsa legatione* 19, Diogenes Laertius 1.46, and also Plutarch, *Comparatio Solon–Publicola* 4.2. The term ethnologists apply to this type of behavior is "play." See Conquergood (2007: 39).

[58] On the trickster figure and culture hero in Greek mythology, Hansen (2004: 141–143, 309–314). On Solon as an Odysseus-like figure, see Irwin (2006: 13–30) (I am indebted to Alexei Zadorojnyi for this reference).

professional military he is said to have admired (*Lycurgus* 4.4–5). Bolstered by this vast knowledge, Lycurgus then applied himself vigorously to the reform and reorganization of Spartan institutions and education, the main topic of the *Life*. At a crucial moment in the process, in his effort to curb luxury, Lycurgus is faced with open rebellion to the implementation of the common messes (*syssitia*) on the part of elite members of Spartan society (*Lycurgus* 11.1–4). During the ensuing riot, a young man named Alkandros, described as hasty (*oxys*) and passionate (*thymoeidēs*), assaulted and seriously wounded Lycurgus. As his punishment, Alkandros is compelled to serve in the house of Lycurgus where he comes "to know the gentleness (*praotēta*) of the man, the calmness (*to apathes*) of his spirit, the rigid simplicity of his habits, and his unwearied industry" (*Lycurgus* 11.3). With Lycurgus as a positive role model, Alkandros is able to gain self-mastery and becomes a most decorous (*emmelestatos*) and temperate (*sōphronikōtatos*) man (11.5–7). The community at large is in turn instructed by Lycurgus' example, as they witness both the lawgiver's compassionate restraint and Alkandros' transformation.

Richard Bauman explains how performance influences social control:

> It is part of the essence of performance that it offers to the participants a special enhancement of experience, bringing with it a heightened intensity of communicative interaction which binds the audience to the performer in a way that is specific to performance as a mode of communication. Through this performance, the performer elicits the participative attention and energy of his audience, and to the extent that they value his performance, they will allow themselves to be caught up in it. When this happens the performer gains a measure of prestige and control over his audience – prestige because of the demonstrated competence he has displayed, control because the determination of the flow of the interaction is in his hands. (2007: 35–36)

These examples place the protagonist on stage in a positive way, in a way that emphasizes greatness of character and conviction of purpose. We would emphasize that acts like these have an emotional impact that binds followers to leaders, an emotional experience shared to some degree by the reader as spectator (*theatēs*). These are uniformly positive examples. Yet Plutarch thought that negative examples could also have their utility.

The *Lives* of Demetrius and Antony are explicitly apotreptic. Most interpretations have focused on the tragic qualities of these lives.[59] In each case we are confronted with a hero with great potential who never

---

[59] See Duff (2004) for the relevant literature.

realizes his greatness, who falls short in the pursuit of his objectives, and eventually dies a tragic death. In the prologue of the *Demetrius*, as Tim Duff has shown, Plutarch is clearly responding to Plato in book 3 of the *Republic* (esp. 396c–409b), who argues against exposing young people to the corrupting influence of bad examples, including those presented on stage.[60] Both *Lives* are replete with stage terms used to guide the narratee's reading along lines of tragedy (*Demetrius* 18.3, 25.6, 28.1, 34.3, 41.3–4, 44.6–7, 53.1, 53.4, *Antony* 29.2, 45.2, 54.3, *Comparatio Demetrius–Antony* 6.2).[61] But there are references in both *Lives* to the comic as well, including an explicit reference that marks a turning point in the *Life of Demetrius* that brings the narrative "back from the comic to the tragic stage" (28.1).[62] In the prologue Plutarch describes how the Spartans used drunken helots as negative moral examples (1.5). Elsewhere (*Lycurgus* 28.4–5) these displays are described as somewhat comic (*katagelastous*).[63] This theme is taken up in the *Life of Antony*, where frequent reference is made to slaves, dressing like slaves, slave-like behavior, and laughter. The use of slaves as the presenters of undesirable behavior is mentioned with approval by Plato in a passage in the *Laws*, in which he turns to the topic of comedy (816d–e). Plutarch's description of ethical training that includes study of the opposite of moral behavior in the prologue is essentially an elaboration of Platonic thinking.[64] In the *Antony* Plutarch represents the protagonist's performative moments to discourage imitation.

The *Life of Demetrius* does not employ the motif of slaves as the objects of stage-managed ridicule in any overt way.[65] Development of this motif is reserved for the *Life of Antony*. It comes into play with the story of his unexpected return to Fulvia in the dress of a slave (*Antony* 10.4–5). Plutarch makes it clear at the outset that Antony's intentions were playful and that he desired to inject a bit of levity into their marriage (*Antony* 10.4). His proclivity to assume the dress of a slave resurfaces in the account of his actions immediately following the assassination of Caesar. Plutarch reports that Antony donned slave's clothes to avoid detection and went into hiding

[60] Duff (2004).     [61] Cited by Duff (2004: 284, n. 46).
[62] On the serio-comic elements in the *Antony*, see Beck (2016). On the comic versus the tragic elements in the *Demetrius*, see Monaco (2011–12).
[63] This example is used again by Fundanus in Plutarch's *De cohibenda ira* 455E. See Duff (2004: 273–277).
[64] See also Plato, *Philebus* 48c–49c. The echo of the words *agnoia* and *abelteran hexin* in the *Philebus* passage (48c) with the words in the prologue, *abelterian hēgountai kai agnoian* (*Demetrius* 1.3), is persuasive evidence that Plutarch had a reading of this dialogue in mind when composing this passage.
[65] But Plutarch does employ humor in the *Demetrius*. See Monaco (2011–12).

(*Antony* 14.1). There may be a hint of cowardice in this act, but no humor.[66] In another passage, based on Cicero's *Second Philippic* (67), Antony is represented furthermore as having created in his house, formerly the house of Pompey, a carnival-like atmosphere of theatricality complete with performers (*Antony* 21.2). After an interlude in Greece, during which time, we are informed, Antony's conduct improved, he crossed over to Asia and commenced a decidedly more luxurious lifestyle (*Antony* 23–24). Caesar comes into play this time as a foil (internal *synkrisis*) for Antony's extravagant and sensual living (*Antony* 24.2).

Plutarch tempers the harshness of his criticisms of Antony with an analysis of his character problems (slowness and simplicity), and notably his humorous and playful nature that allowed him to tolerate being laughed at (*Antony* 24.7–8). His susceptibility and submissive nature make him the perfect target for Cleopatra and his love for her is characterized as an evil, *kakon* (*Antony* 25.1). In his love for her, he "was taken captive" (*halisketai*). The implication is that he has lost his freedom. Theirs is not a relationship founded on mutual respect and admiration. Plutarch employs the verbs *kataphronein* (to look down upon, despise) and *katagelan* (to find laughable) in describing her attitude toward Antony and the motivation behind her decision to sail up the river Cydnus to meet him, adorned like Venus and accompanied by slave boys dressed like Erotes on either side of her (*Antony* 26.1–2).[67] Cleopatra is reported to have quickly divined the quality of the man from his ludicrous behavior and adapts her own behavior toward him accordingly (*Antony* 27.1).

In their nocturnal merrymaking they dress up like slaves and tour the streets of Alexandria at night (*Antony* 29.1–2). Interestingly, Plutarch relates how the cultivated Alexandrians are reported to have responded positively toward Antony's coarseness and vulgarity, likening him to a comic actor on stage (*Antony* 29.2). That the antics of Antony elicit laughter is further underscored in the well-known fishing episode, in which Cleopatra outdoes him by having one of her slaves attach a dried salted fish to Antony's line underwater. This comes, after Antony, trying to impress her with his angling ability, has had live fish attached to his line by his fishermen.

> Antony thought he had caught something, and pulled it in, to everyone's great amusement, of course. "Imperator," she said, "hand over your fishing

[66] See Pelling (1988a: 151) on Antony's fearfulness as represented in nearly all our sources.
[67] See Brenk (1992: 4391–4393, 4449–4457).

rod to the kings of Pharos and Canopus. It is your job to hunt cities,
kingdoms and continents." (*Antony* 29.4; trans. Waterfield)

Cleopatra's point is of course that this lowly pastime is unbecoming
of a man in his station and inconsistent with great leadership. At this
point in his life, at any rate, he appears to lack the motivation or
seriousness of purpose to take on great tasks. From approximately this
point on the humor in the *Life* and in Antony vanishes, as Antony
vainly attempts to expand his hold on the East in the Parthian War
and fails to win the West at Actium. His political and military leadership is shown to be as flawed as his character. He is the opposite of
a transformational leader. We must discern a sharp divide between the
trickster-like behavior of Solon and the ridiculous antics of Antony.
The former has his people's welfare in mind and is willing to go to
great lengths to protect them, while the latter clearly does not care
about that; he lacks empathy, motivation, and self-awareness, he does
not seem to respect himself and he is not respected by others, and he is
laughed at because he is laughable, all of which is brought out brilliantly by Plutarch's literary technique.

## *Synkrisis* and Characterization

One important way Plutarch brings home his intended lessons is via
contrast and comparison (*synkrisis*). Plutarch encourages us to evaluate
comparatively two complementary behavioral patterns in each of the
paired *Lives*. Their relative brevity (forty to fifty pages on average), the
comparative structure of the work, the nature of Plutarch's sources,
and his pedagogical aims insure a selection process that emphasizes the
representation of character.[68] Through the heuristic principle of comparison *synkrisis*, virtuous qualities or traits become more nuanced
when manifested in various individuals whose biographies evince an
instructive combination of similarities (*homoiotētes*) or differences
(*diaphorai*) so as to render a comparative analysis fruitful and edifying
(*Phocion* 3.4).[69] Themes, characteristics, and traits that surface in the
Greek *Life* are subjected to continued elaboration in the Roman

---

[68] Moles (1988: 9), Pelling (1988a: 10–12), Stadter (1989: li–lii), Duff (1999a: 243–286), and Pelling
(2011a: 13–19).
[69] Focke (1923), Erbse (1956), Stadter (1975), Pelling (1986b) = (2002a: 349–386) and (2005a), Larmour
(1992), Bosworth (1992), Swain (1992a), Duff (1999a: 243–286; 2011c: 253–259), H. Beck (2002),
Larmour (2014), and Jacobs (2018: 108–118).

*Life.*[70] Plutarch's choice of subjects is therefore, to some extent, guided by the didactic value their life histories afford.

In the proem to the *Lives* of Phocion and Cato Minor,[71] Plutarch alludes to alternate modes of comparison that exceed the bounds of individual pairs of *Lives*. He is intent here on explaining the comparative stance he is going to adopt with respect to Phocion's and Cato's particular brand of *aretē* that is designed to reveal subtle permutations of cardinal virtues:

> For there is surely a difference between the bravery (*andreia*) of one man and that of another, as, for instance between that of Alcibiades and that of Epaminondas; between the wisdom (*phronēsis*) of one man and that of another, as, between that of Themistocles and that of Aristides; between the justice (*dikaiosynē*) of one man and that of another, as, between that of Numa and that of Agesilaus. (*Phocion* 3.4–9; trans. Perrin)[72]

In his treatise *Quomodo quis suos in virtute sentiat profectus* Plutarch allows that there are various degrees of good and evil, "especially in the indeterminate and undefined kind that has to do with the soul" (76B; trans. Babbit).[73] This comparative stance may be extended beyond the strictly moral and characterological sphere to other realms of activity. In the *Life of Caesar*, for example, Plutarch favorably compares Caesar's generalship with that of other renowned Roman commanders such as Fabius, Scipio, Sulla, Marius, and Pompey (*Caesar* 15).[74] These examples indicate that, in evaluating leadership, Plutarch himself thinks beyond the overt parallel structure of his *Lives* in a comparative way that on occasion contrasts Greek with Greek and Roman with Roman. Some forms of comparison are more finely nuanced than this, however.

Hans Beck (2002) has pointed out the implicit intertextual comparisons inherent in neighboring *Lives* that share the same cultural

[70] There are some notable exceptions to this pattern, however. See, for example, the *Lives* of Alcibiades and Coriolanus and the explanations of Pelling (1986b: 94) = (2002a: 357) and Duff (1999a: 205–206). The *Aemilius Paulus–Timoleon* and *Sertorius–Eumenes* pairs are other examples. Ahlrichs (2005) has called this view into question.

[71] The comparative nature of this proem is noted by Trapp (1999: 487–488), who does not note the initial internal *synkrisis* of Demades with Phocion.

[72] See also *Demosthenes* 13.6 (comparison of Demosthenes with Cimon, Thucydides, and Pericles) and *Demosthenes* 14.1 (comparison of Phocion with Ephialtes, Aristides, and Cimon). This passage anticipates Plutarch's anti-Stoic stance vis-à-vis Cato in the *Life* as it attacks the Stoic doctrine of moral absolutism that disallows any gradations of virtue. See Duff (1999a: 155).

[73] See Roskam (2005b: 245).

[74] Compare also the comparison of Agesilaus, Lysander, Nicias, and Alcibiades with Flamininus (*Flamininus* 11.5–12.1) that is offered as the thoughts of the Greeks.

background.[75] In addition to several Greek *Lives*[76] that follow this pattern, he also cites the *Romulus* and *Numa*, *Caesar* and *Cato Minor*, and *Fabius Maximus* and *Marcellus*. He also observes that Plutarch employs foils to link thematically two or more *Lives* in which they appear.[77] The *Lives* of Marius, Sulla, and Lucullus provide exemplification of this technique wherein Sulla, in his better days, is contrasted, as a positive foil, with the harsh and brutal Marius. Later, both Sulla and Marius are used as negative foils to Lucullus. The *Lives* of Cimon and Lucullus display a very complex use of internal *synkriseis*, beginning in the proem, which serve to contrast the main protagonists positively with the likes of the ruffian Damon, the corrupt anonymous Roman commander, and the Spartan Pausanias, in developing the theme of euergetism.[78]

Moreover, Plutarch subtly and allusively inserts paradigmatic figures from literature and philosophy, such as Achilles, Odysseus, and Socrates, thus adding an additional intertextual or, one might say, metahistorical[79] dimension to the comparative interplay. The allusive interplay this creates further enhances and nuances characterization and serves as well to subtly guide the narratee's interpretation of the protagonist's behavior. The prologue to *Mulierum virtutes* (243C–D) includes mention of Achilles, Ajax, Odysseus, and Nestor among historical figures and clearly shows that Plutarch's aesthetics of exemplarity recognizes the value of fictional as well as historical figures.[80] The comparative interplay in the *Lives* is thus undertaken on a scale and to a degree of complexity that is truly breathtaking.

[75] Others have noted Plutarch's use of foils. See e.g. Pelling (1988b: 270) = (2002a: 293) (Lysander, Callicratidas, Callibius, Gylippus, and Pausanias), Duff (1999a: 170–182) (Lysander and Callicratidas), and Beneker (2005). See H. Beck (2002) for a very complete bibliography of prior work on this topic.

[76] Such as *Alcibiades* and *Nicias*. H. Beck cites (2002: 468 n. 7) Mossman (1992) on the correspondences in the *Life of Alexander* and the *Life of Pyrrhus*. Buszard (2008) studies the intertextual resonance between the *Alexander–Caesar* and *Pyrrhus–Marius* pairs as it relates to the topic of the interrelationship of *paideia* and ambition. See also Beneker (2005).

[77] H. Beck (2002: 468–470).

[78] See Beck (2007b). In terms of characterization, these internal *synkriseis*, as they are called, serve an important purpose in Plutarch's biographical technique in contrast to Suetonius' less dynamic *per species* method, in which the rubricizing of traits disallows refined and subtle portraiture. For a different view, see Pelling (1988b) = (2002a: 283–300) and Pelling (1990b) = (2002a: 301–338). Pelling believes that Suetonius' categorization method permits better presentation of the "many-sidedness" and "protean complexities" of human character and personality. On the two methods in general, see in particular Leo (1901), Bakhtin (1981: 140–143), and Wallace-Hadrill (1983).

[79] Zadorojnyi (2012) employs this term, popularized by Hayden White, in reference to Plutarch in his chapter on mimesis and the (plu)past in Plutarch's *Lives*.

[80] For more examples, see Muccioli (2012: 99–130).

Through study, evaluation, and appreciation of these biographies and their complex interrelationships, the Plutarchan reader is thereby enjoined to assimilate in some way or other their behavior to perceived models. This pragmatic approach to aesthetic appreciation of the *Lives* receives full articulation in the well-known prologue to the *Aemilius Paulus–Timoleon* pair in which Plutarch instances his own enjoyment and use of the *Lives* in character improvement and thus indicates the potential for character change into adulthood (*Aemilius Paulus* 1.1–4).[81] The metaphor of the mirror in this prologue underscores the visual aspect of his thinking on moral development, as the principle of *synkrisis* is then applied to oneself vis-à-vis the biographical subjects, with the formation of parallels thus occurring in multiple dimensions, as the narratee becomes cognizant of the interplay between the paired *Lives*, between the paired *Lives* and other *Lives* with similar themes in the corpus, and finally when the narratee seeks to align their own behavior with that represented in the biographies that their own analytical operations have deduced as being commendable and therefore worthy, on some level, of emulation and imitation.[82]

## The Thymoeidic Nature, Achilles, Odysseus, and *Paideia*

In part, understanding Plutarch's conception of greatness as it applies to human achievement and leadership ability is contingent upon understanding the evolution of the concept of the hero in ancient Greek culture. The Homeric epics, the *Iliad* and the *Odyssey*, focus on individuals, their characters and psychology, and the particular set of circumstances with which they must contend in the pursuit and attainment of goals. The main protagonists of these epics embody the ideals of human life in Homer's time and beyond. Achilles and Odysseus, as the main protagonists in the *Iliad* and the *Odyssey*, respectively, both represent notable behavioral paradigms. Achilles exhibits characteristics that are paradigmatic when viewed against the heroic code of values espoused by the society depicted in the *Iliad*. A list of outstanding qualities or characteristics (*aretai*) that bring honor and evoke admiration include: good looks, wealth, fighting ability (the most important characteristic for men to possess), athletic ability, good birth, intellectual ability (especially cunning intelligence as

---

[81] Discussed by Duff (1999a: 30–34) and Stadter (2000; 2003–4).
[82] See Stadter (2010) on the relationship between groups of *Lives* in *Parallel Lives* and the themes of "conquest, politics, kingship, and tragedy." Stadter sees three dimensions in the parallel biographies. On the relation of the *Aemilius Paulus–Timoleon* prologue to mimesis, see Duff (1999a: 30–34, 49–51) and Zadorojnyi (2012: 177).

exemplified by Odysseus), eloquence (both Nestor and Odysseus are notable for this quality), fidelity (for women and in a restricted sense for men), and age (a factor that may influence honor).[83] The Greek phrase that later comes into common parlance in the classical period and refers to the individual who epitomizes these traits is *kalos k'agathos*.[84] Achilles' main weakness is his difficulty in exercising restraint and curbing his anger (*thymos*).[85] Odysseus, on the other hand, is able to restrain himself. He is a master of dissimulation and displays a great deal of practical wisdom (*phronēsis*) combined with cunning intelligence in the process. He is a great warrior, but not the greatest warrior. His claim to greatness resides in his unique combination of physical ability coupled with a superior intellect. These two paradigms appealed to the Greeks and provided them with their early formative role models.[86]

Not surprisingly, in several of the *Parallel Lives* Plutarch evokes the images of Achilles and, to a lesser extent, Odysseus. But there is a catch.[87] Achilles was destructive to his own community and thus an ambiguous role model. Plato perceived this dilemma and, as Allan Bloom in his interpretation of the *Republic* observes, sought to replace these behavioral paradigms with another superior role model, Socrates.[88] Plutarch would appear to share the Platonic misgivings about Achilles, for in most instances allusions to Achilles in the *Lives* do not reflect positively on the protagonist and are more prominent in those *Lives* in which a lack of philosophical training and the resulting behavioral problems are most evident.

The most Achillean hero is of course Alexander the Great of Macedon, who, like Achilles, was invincible on the battlefield but had a significant anger problem.[89] This association is certain to date back to Alexander himself, who clearly emulated Achilles in a number of ways; nor has the vulgate historical tradition failed to transmit this aspect of Alexander's personality.[90] Arrian, for example, frequently employs the ambiguous term *oxytēs*, which can mean everything from alacrity to anger. Plutarch appears

---

[83] See e.g. van Wees (1992: 71–83) and Hobbs (2000: 60).
[84] For the definition of this term and its meaning to the Greeks, see Jaeger (1945: 13).
[85] See Harris (2001: 131–156 and *passim*) for a lucid discussion of Achilles as a paradigm for the failure of self-control.
[86] On Achilles and Odysseus as early role models for the Greeks, see e.g. Prior (1991: 6–21). For a broader perspective including Homer, see Raaflaub (2000: 23–59).
[87] See Nerdahl (2007; 2011–12).
[88] Bloom (1991: 354). See also Hobbs (2000: 59–136, 158–219).
[89] Harris (2001: 235–237); Beneker (2012: 103–152).
[90] Both Diodorus Siculus and Quintus Curtius Rufus, for instance, attribute Alexander's behavior to rage (*orgēlira*). See Beck (2013).

to take it one step further in a more philosophical direction. Early in the *Life* the adjectives "high-spirited" (*thymoeidēs*) and "lion-like" (*leontōdēs*) are proleptically applied to Alexander (*Alexander* 2.5).[91] This pair of adjectives initially calls to mind Achilles among those familiar with Homer and Plato. So Plutarch is directing the well-educated narratee toward Plato's view of Achilles, since both these adjectives are encountered in the *Republic* in conjunction with the description of the ideal guardian's nature. Such an individual is fearless and marked by the presence of a *thymos* that is unconquerable (*amakhon*) and invincible (*anikēton*); he will be gentle toward friends but harsh toward enemies, and possesses in addition a philosophic temperament (Plato, *R.* 375a–376c);[92] he will be a lover of victory and lion-like in nature (*R.* 586c–590b).[93] In Plutarch, as we shall see, it is possible to have a lion-like nature that is nevertheless under control and gentle.

Love of honor (*philotimia*) is closely coupled with spiritedness in the *Republic*.[94] Socrates states that the spirited part of the soul "honors and admires" (*R.* 553d4). Those who possess a spirited nature are compelled to imitate what they admire and this renders such individuals susceptible to education.[95] As Angela Hobbs notes, "the *thumos* looks for role models."[96] *Thymos* is a necessary component of courage but not courage itself.[97] In Plato it is education – that is, training in philosophy– that blunts the selfish egoism of *thymos* and renders those who possess this nature protective of, and not destructive to, their communities.[98] In the absence of the appropriate *paideia*, those of a spirited nature are capable of inflicting harm upon their communities.[99] Such formidable individuals, propelled to achieve greatness, could easily wax tyrannical by virtue of their innate power over others, as Thrasymachus in the *Republic* and Callicles in the *Gorgias* perceived.[100] How to manage this potentially destabilizing influence was

---

[91] On the symbolism of the lion and the epithet "lion-hearted" (*thymoleōn*) as applied to Achilles and Heracles in the *Iliad* (5.639; 7.228), see Hamilton (1969: 3f., ad loc. 2.4). See also Duff (1999a: 85–87), Beneker (2012: 133–139), and Beck (2013).

[92] On this passage containing the first use of *thymoeidēs* in Greek literature, see Adam (1905: 106 ad loc.). See also Kalimtzis (2012: 39–40).

[93] Bloom (1991: 405), in recognizing the close interrelationship between these terms, calls spiritedness "the lion in our souls." Bloom (at 349) also makes the key observation that "it is in the nature of spiritedness to be in the service of something."

[94] See the interesting discussion in Liebert (2016: 155–188).     [95] Rabieh (2006: 109).

[96] Hobbs (2000: 59).     [97] Rabieh (2006: 98).     [98] See Bloom (1991²: 348–365).

[99] See Rabieh (2006: 108).

[100] Cf. Callicles' description of the training of the best young men who are likened to lions in the *Gorgias* 483e–484a. On Thrasymachus and Callicles, see Hobbs (2000: 137–174). See also Duff (2003).

a key problem that Plato wrestled with in the *Republic*; that is, how to choose and educate leaders who were simultaneously vigorous and warlike in their dealings with enemies, yet mild and conciliatory in their associations with fellow-citizens and allies. This same issue is clearly of great concern to Plutarch too, who sees excessive love of honor (*philotimia*) and fame (*philodoxia*) as leading potentially to divisiveness and political discord.[101] The key is to place the *thymoeidic* individual in the service of the community. The danger of excessive ambition overwhelming altruism and producing civic discord and various other types of misconduct is thus thematic in Plutarch's *Lives*.[102]

Programmed by his philosophical allegiance to Plato, Plutarch alludes to Achilles in those *Lives* where reasoned restraint is lacking in some form or other and self-interest holds sway. In these *Lives* he explores the deleterious consequences the presence of a *thymoeidēs* spirit may have when unmitigated by *paideia*. *Thymos* is nonrational in origin and develops prior to reason. Plutarch regards *thymos* as a potential ally of virtue (*aretē*) (*De virtute morali* 445D, fr. 148.15–16). In describing Coriolanus as *thymoeidēs*, for example, he alludes to the source of his martial valor and the predominant characteristic that renders him a warrior to be feared on the battlefield (a good thing), but also a potential threat to his fellow-citizens in civic contexts (*Coriolanus* 15.4).[103] Coriolanus is an ambivalent figure because he received only military training but not the requisite Hellenic *paideia* that would have instilled some restraint. He is the raw form of the *thymoeidic* individual and that is perhaps why his *Life* is positioned atypically first in the pair.[104] In the corresponding Greek *Life*, Alcibiades' spirited nature is not designated with this adjective, but Plutarch twice alludes to his lion-like nature (*Alcibiades* 2.2, 16.2) and later quotes a verse from some unknown poet: "No child of Achilles, but Achilles himself" (*Alcibiades* 23.6).[105] His exposure to Socrates perplexingly failed to have a significant positive influence on his behavior, a topic taken up in the *Life*.[106]

In a most intriguing way, the Plutarchan Alcibiades is alluded to in ways that recall both Achilles and Odysseus.[107] Several scholars have remarked

[101]  Frazier (1988; 2014a); Roskam (2011a).
[102]  See Frazier (1988; 2014a), Duff (1999a: *passim*), Roskam (2011a), and Nikolaidis (2012) in Roskam et al. (2012).
[103]  Pelling (2002a: 344–346); Duff (2008b: 13–14).
[104]  See Verdegem (2010a: 87–91) for a good discussion with bibliographical references. See also now on the Coriolanus–Alcibiades pair Jacobs (2018: 180–226).
[105]  See Hobbs (2000: 254), Duff (2003), and Verdegem (2008; 2010a; 2010b).
[106]  See Pelling (2005b) and Beck (2014b: 466–468).
[107]  See Beck (2014b: 464–468) for an overview and bibliography.

that the characterization of Alcibiades is informed by the wily figure of Odysseus.[108] As Michael Nerdahl notes, Alcibiades, unlike Odysseus, is not a model of self-control. Less evident, and thus perhaps more tantalizing, are the references to Achilles.[109] Yet here again Alcibiades is no pure reflection of Achilles; he is somewhat feminine.[110] In short, Alcibiades fails to fully embody both of the early primary role models of the Greeks. He also fails to assimilate his behavior to Socrates who cannot draw Alcibiades away from the pernicious influence of that man's other male suitors.[111] He is susceptible to flattery, a feminine trait. The intertextual references here are to Plato's *Alcibiades I* and *Symposium*. In the *Symposium* Socrates is represented by Alcibiades himself as the ideal of manly courage and self-restraint.

Perhaps one of the clearest examples of the problems posed by the *thymoeidic* nature when it is not moderated by education can be found in the *Life of Pelopidas*. The rather Aristotelian prologue to the *Lives* of Pelopidas and Marcellus introduces the theme of recklessness in battle and the ensuing negative consequences this excess of courage or bravery may entail.[112] Both men, according to Plutarch, were "careless of their own lives" and "recklessly (*syn oudeni logismōi*)[113] threw them away at times when it was most important that such men should live and hold command" (*Pelopidas* 2.5). In the prologues to both *Lives* Plutarch cites Homer, the poet of war (*Pelopidas* 1.5; *Marcellus* 1.2); in the case of Marcellus, the Homeric citation (*Il.* 14.86–87) refers to his lifelong and narrowly exclusive devotion to warfare. Pelopidas is also not very well rounded. This is brought out in a key internal *synkrisis*, in which Plutarch contrasts Pelopidas' preference for physical pursuits, such as taking exercise in the *palaistra* and hunting, with Epaminondas' devotion to intellectual pursuits, such as listening to lectures and philosophy (*Pelopidas* 4.1). According to Plutarch, unnamed Theban lawgivers incorporated musical training on

---

[108] Gribble (1999: 269–270), Duff (2003: 96 with n. 30), and Nerdahl (2007: 140–151). On the Coriolanus-Alcibiades pair, see esp. Nehrdahl (2007: 131): "Odysseus-like cunning of Alcibiades" is contrasted with "the modeling of Coriolanus on Achilles."

[109] Beck (2014b).

[110] Gribble (1999: 265–266); Duff (2003: 95–100); Verdegem (2010a: 122–125).

[111] See especially Gribble (1999: 271–272), Duff (1999a: 224–227; 2009; 2011a: 28), Pelling (2005b: 116–125), and Verdegem (2010a: 137).

[112] See Georgiadou (1997: 45–65), who cites passages in the *Eudemian* and *Nicomachean Ethics* (*EE* 1228a27–1230a35-36, *EN* 1115a6–1117b22).

[113] The term resumes the earlier-mentioned adverb *paralogōs* (*Pelopidas* 2.5). With these terms Plutarch imputes an absence of rationality to the self-sacrifice of Pelopidas and Marcellus, who died unnecessarily when their cities needed them to live and lead. He reiterates this in the final *synkrisis* of both men's lives (*Comparatio Pelopidas–Marcellus* 3.1). See Georgiadou (1997: 45–46, 65).

the flute as a means to mollify and temper the *thymoeides* trait in young Theban men (*Pelopidas* 19.1). Apparently this training had little effect on Pelopidas, who is characterized, in another internal *synkrisis*, as more passionate in nature (*physei thymoeidesteros*) than his well-educated friend Epaminondas (*Pelopidas* 25.2). In the concluding *synkrisis* to the paired *Lives*, both Pelopidas and Marcellus are described as passionate (*thymoei-deis*), in addition to being courageous (*andreioi*), energetic (*philoponoi*), and magnanimous (*megalophrones*) (*Comparatio Pelopidas–Marcellus* 1.1). Neither appear to have assimilated the type of education or training that would have enabled them to tone down their passionate and fiery temperaments in critical situations.

Marcellus is employed as a foil in the *Life of Fabius Maximus*. In an internal *synkrisis* the Homeric nature of Marcellus' heroism is explicitly contrasted with Fabius' reasoned (*ekhomenos logismōn*) restraint (*Fabius Maximus* 19.1–3).[114] In the prologue of the *Fabius* the protagonist's deceptive psychological makeup is indicated and concludes with a reference to "his profound resiliency (*to dyskinēton hypo bathous*) and the magnanimous (*to megalopsykhon*) and leonine (*to leontōdes*) qualities of his nature" (*Fabius Maximus* 1.5).[115] While Fabius lived at a time that preceded the Hellenization of Roman culture, his speech, "rendered weighty by an abundance of maxims," nevertheless reflected an intellectual dignity and depth reminiscent of Thucydides (*Fabius Maximus* 1.8). This is high praise indeed coming from Plutarch, who greatly admired the great Greek historian, our key contemporary source of speeches delivered by Pericles, including the famous funeral oration (*Epitaphios*). This threefold *synkrisis* explicitly links Fabius with Thucydides and both men implicitly with Pericles.

## The Socratic Paradigm

As mentioned earlier, Plato sought to replace the traditional conception of the hero, as represented preeminently by the Homeric Achilles and Odysseus, with the example provided by his teacher and friend Socrates. The figure of Socrates provided the Greek and later Roman worlds with a fundamentally different type of hero. Physically he is not an ideal type, being likened to a Satyr/Silenus in appearance. In addition to lacking the

---

[114] Duff (2008b: 16).
[115] Pericles' lion-like quality is represented in the story relating the circumstances of his birth (*Pericles* 3.2). Cf. Stadter (1989: 64).

outward appearance of greatness, he is not a member of the elite class by birth (the son of a craftsman and a midwife). With Socrates comes the shift away from external to internal values, with an emphasis on the care of one's soul. Although he served bravely as a hoplite on the battlefield, he was not a military leader. He avoided politics but was capable of displaying great civil courage. For Plutarch, however, Socrates was exemplary in that he demonstrated that the precepts of moral philosophy could be enacted in daily life and in politics. We know from the Lamprias Catalogue and from his surviving works that Plutarch had a special interest in Socrates and was a staunch defender of the Athenian (Lamprias Catalogue, nos. 189–190).[116] For Plutarch, Socrates was not just a philosopher; he also served as a paradigm for the ideal statesman who enacts philosophy in every activity: "He was first to show that life at all times and in all parts, in all experiences and activities, universally admits philosophy" (*An seni respublica gerenda sit* 796D, trans. Fowler). In *De cohibenda ira* (458C–D) he mentions Socrates in the same breath with other political figures, most notably Aristides, as an example of moderation. Plato represents Socrates as famously stating that the unexamined life is not worth living (*Apology* 38a). This is one of the fundamental principles of education for Plutarch, who advises the application of the mind (*nous*) and intellect (*dianoia*) to the analysis of great deeds and works in the pursuit of greatness (*Pericles* 1–2; see earlier in this chapter).

Plutarch employs the Socratic paradigm prominently in the *Lives of Aristides–Cato Maior* and *Phocion–Cato Minor* to develop certain themes of morality and behavior. Most researchers have focused their attention on the *Phocion–Cato Minor* pair and have not shown awareness of the Socratic paradigm in the *Aristides–Cato Maior* pair.[117] There appears to be an intentional desire on Plutarch's part to link the *Lives* of Cato Maior and Cato Minor via the figure of Socrates. All four men are contrasted with Socrates and then with each other in a way that calls attention to the behavioral shortcomings of both Catos, but casts mostly favorable light on the two Athenians. In the *Life of Aristides*, the comparison with Socrates

---

[116] On Plutarch's attitude toward Socrates, see Hershbell (1988); Duff (1999a: 141–142); Pelling (2005b).

[117] Alcalde Martin (1999), Geiger (1999), Trapp (1999), and Zadorojnyi (2007). Sansone (1989: 228–229, ad loc. 50.1) notes in his commentary on *Aristides–Cato Maior* that "Socrates ... is an important element in the comparison between Aristeides and Cato." The main reason, as he sees it, hinges on the shared status of poverty between Aristides and Socrates, and on the Censor's rejection of Socrates. Pelling (2005b: 108) notes: "It is no coincidence that passing references to Socrates are especially frequent in pairs like *Aristides–Cato Maior* where virtue is particularly an issue."

serves to represent Aristides' poverty in a positive light initially.[118] While Plutarch later criticizes Aristides' poverty for its negative impact on his family, especially his daughters, he nevertheless condemns Cato's irrational acquisitiveness as one of the Censor's greatest flaws, a flaw inconsistent with the internalization of philosophic precepts, to which the Censor early in his life may well have attained (*Cato Maior* 2.3–4).[119] In a way, Aristides' just and moral behavior in the political sphere anticipates Socrates' ethical philosophy, much as, for the Romans at any rate, the Censor's supposed exemplary behavioral repertoire anticipates the Stoicism that eventually won the day in Rome. The Roman ideal that the Censor came to represent was rooted in the past and identified with the *priscae virtutes* and *mos maiorum*. It is impossible to separate the influence of this idealized paradigm and of Stoicism on Cato Minor.[120] Plutarch employs the Socratic paradigm in the *Life of Cato Maior* as well as the *Life of Cato Minor* to call into question the exemplary status of these two statesmen.

Both the Censor and Cato Minor have difficulties in leadership roles because of their lack of sensitivity or empathy that we referred to earlier. This is brought out in Plutarch's depictions of their relations with others; for Cato Minor, however, his commitment to Stoicism is palpably relevant too.[121] Cicero himself attacked Cato Minor's rigid and unrealistic brand of Stoicism in the *Pro Murena* (60–65).[122] According to Cicero, if Cato had received training from masters in Platonism and Peripatetic philosophy, he would have been "a little more disposed to kindness" (*Pro Mur.* 64; trans. Macdonald).[123] Yet in the rapidly shifting political landscape of the Roman Republic, Cicero changed his tune about Cato after that statesman's

---

[118] The topic of Aristides' indigence is broached in the proem of his *Life* (1), with reference to Demetrius of Phalerum's lost work *Socrates*. This suggests an Aristides/Socrates *synkrisis* in the work. Socrates was not always poor since we know that he served as a hoplite. He himself, according to Plato (*Apol.* 23b), attributes his poverty to his service to Apollo.

[119] Plutarch believes that a statesman must use his wealth for the benefit of the people. See e.g. *Pericles* 16.5–7. For the topic of euergetism as a major theme in the *Lives* of Cimon and Lucullus, see Fuscagni (1989: 47–58) and Beck (2007b). Plutarch may be responding here to the ancient view of the Censor as a *contemptor divitiarum* to such an extent that he came to embody the chief qualities of a Stoic sage, as represented in Livy's somewhat fanciful sketch (39.40.10–11). See Harris (1979: 76, n. 2).

[120] Afzelius (1941: 116).

[121] Plutarch takes an anti-Stoic stance vis-à-vis Cato Minor in his *Life* as he is generally critical of the Stoic doctrine of moral absolutism, which disallows any gradations of virtue; see Duff (1999a: 149–158); Zadorojnyi (2007); Beck (2014b).

[122] See in particular Craig (1986: 229–239). Cato's rigidity and political obtuseness are mentioned again by Cicero in *De officiis* 3.88.

[123] Cicero's attack hinges on paralleling Cato's philosophical stance with the unrealistic so-called Stoic paradoxes (*SVF* III 35–37, 41, 117–18).

"heroic" suicide, which became symbolic of the Stoic resistance to tyranny, and even went so far as to employ the Cato–Socrates comparison to embellish his remarks about the man in his *Tusculan Disputations* (1.71ff.) and to use him to exemplify the principle that the philosopher's way of life is really a preparation for death.[124] Cato's death, as represented by Plutarch, is antithetical to this portrait.[125] We must agree with Michael Trapp who suggests that Plutarch's intent in constructing such an unflattering image was not so much to criticize Cato himself as to criticize subtly "earlier (Roman) writing about Cato," such as Cicero's *Tusculan Disputations* and the writings of Seneca.[126] Cicero's lost work *Cato*, in response to which Caesar penned his scathing *Anti-Cato*, also lost to us, undoubtedly did much to perpetuate this idealization.[127] Seneca's frequent juxtaposing of the deaths of Cato with Socrates attests to the influence this *synkrisis* had on the literate a century later.[128] Much of the material critical of Cato that Plutarch presents in the *Life* appears to be drawn from the *Anti-Cato*.[129] The presentation of this material in the *Life* indicates, in my opinion, Plutarch's opposition to Cicero's and Seneca's idealized image of the man qua Stoic sage.

Plutarch thus employs the Socratic paradigm in the paired *Lives* of Aristides and Cato Maior and Phocion and Cato Minor to evaluate and finally discredit the ideologically influential image of the proto-Stoic Censor and his great-grandson Cato Uticencis, the paradigmatic Stoic sage of the outgoing Republic. The insertion of Socrates as a contrast figure

[124] See e.g. Wirszubski (1950: 126–147) and, with special reference to Plutarch, Geiger (1979b: 48–72). Dupont (1989: 15–17) vividly initiates her account of the daily life of the citizen in the Roman Republic with its symbolic end in the death of the younger Cato at Utica. Syme (1958, vol. 1: 28) traces the dissipation of Cato's ideological significance to the reign of Trajan: "The Republic died hard. It was not until the accession of Trajan that the ghost of Cato was laid to rest." The most comprehensive modern discussion of Cato's influence that I am aware of is Goar (1987), but Afzelius (1941) is still very useful. For Cicero, Cato in particular exemplified the principle that the philosopher's way of life is really a preparation for death. In a particularly telling passage, a comparison of Cato's and Socrates' deaths introduces a paraphrase of Plato's *Phaedo* (*Tusc.* 1.71–75). Cf. Plato, *Phaedo* 67d and 80e.

[125] See Geiger (1999); Trapp (1999); Zadorojnyi (2007); Beck (2009; 2014b).

[126] Trapp (1999: 496) (although Trapp himself does not in the end subscribe to this view). See also Geiger (1999) on the subsequent tradition of the Cato–Socrates coupling.

[127] See Goar (1987: 15).

[128] See Seneca, *Ep.* 67.7; 71.17; 98.12; 104.28f.; *Prov.* 3.4; 3.12ff.; *Tranq.* 16.1; *Cons. ad Marc.* 22.3 (collected by Geiger 1979b: 64–65, n. 61).

[129] See, for example, Geiger (1979b: 54–56). I disagree with Geiger's skeptical conclusion (56) that questions Plutarch's direct acquaintance with both the *Anti-Cato* and Cicero's *Cato*. Just the opposite would likely be true; that is, the availability and continued popularity of both works in Plutarch's own time (cf. *Caesar* 54.6) would virtually ensure that he read them. This remains a point of dispute, however. See Pelling (2011a: 407–408 ad loc.).

vis-à-vis both of these men had already been done by Cicero. Plutarch's use of the Socratic paradigm appears designed to lead the narratee to the opposite conclusion. It sets the flaws of both men in sharper relief in a way that to some extent explains their failures in leadership roles. This is especially true of Cato Minor, who was never able to be elected consul or fashion a lasting consensus.[130] Ironically, many of the Censor's positive qualities and attainments seem attributable to Greek influence, despite his avowed and notorious anti-Hellenic stance. His negative qualities and failings, most of which his great-grandson seems to have inherited, loom large against the urbane and conciliatory Socratic backdrop. In the end, neither the Censor nor Cato Minor can serve as serious exemplars of desirable conduct when measured against the paradigm of Socrates.

## Conclusion: Great Men, Leadership, and Literary Technique

Across the *Parallel Lives*, Plutarch presented greatness in leadership in sophisticated and insightful ways. Great men are great leaders, and the nature of what constitutes great leadership is constantly subjected to evaluation. The greatest men in the Plutarchan pantheon of leaders are the ones who combine empathy with innate greatness of character, who are ambitious and motivated individuals, but whose ambition is tempered by self-control and self-awareness. Plutarch utilizes a number of techniques to bring out, often subtly, the differences of character and psychological constitution in his protagonists. His aim is to assist us in becoming leaders ourselves, to the extent that we are able. The most powerful technique in his repertoire is obviously *synkrisis*. We are constantly invited to compare and contrast the protagonist with other individuals. On one level, this operation is undertaken with reference to the paired lives and is reinforced by shared themes and in many cases a formal *synkrisis* appended to the end of paired *Lives*, but it does not stop there. In the *Lives* of Aristides and Cato Maior, for example, we contrast the *Lives* of both men (a) with one another, (b) with other significant historical figures associated with their endeavors (e.g. Themistocles and Scipio), and (c) with Socrates, and, finally, Cato Maior is contrasted with Cato Minor. The Socratic paradigm is another much more elaborate, metahistorical type of *synkrisis*, one that brings to the fore issues of morality and character in a suggestive and allusive mode of exploration with a special view to Plutarch's Platonic

---

[130] On the political lessons to be drawn from this *Life* with an eye to Plutarch's political treatises, see Beck (2004).

leanings. These allusions, as well as those to heroes of the Greek literary past (Achilles, Odysseus), nuance Plutarch's portraits as he strives to distinguish subtle permutations of virtue, or what we could perhaps call personality. He wants us to recognize these men for who they are and evaluate ourselves against them in the way he evaluates them against others, and distill from this interaction something we can assimilate and use to make life better for ourselves and others. This is the essence of his programmatic mirror analogy, and this mirror is the creation of his literary technique, his power of representation or *mimēsis*. Plutarch has recognized here one of the essential facets of effective leadership: self-awareness. If we do not understand ourselves, then we cannot understand others, and that lack of understanding encourages suspicion, fear, and ultimately anger. With understanding comes empathy. This is the message that Plutarch promotes in the *Lives*, as true today as it was then.

## Further Reading

The most comprehensive account of the Plutarchan hero is still Duff (1999a); his chapter on *synkrisis* in that work is excellent. Jacobs (2018) is the most sustained exploration of Plutarch's biographical narratives as a matrix of pragmatic political advice. On internal *synkrisis* in the *Lives*, see H. Beck (2002). For the philosophical and educational underpinnings, see Duff (1999b; 2008b), Zadorojnyi (2002), Becchi (2014), the introduction in Hunter and Russell (2011), and Xenophontos (2016). On character, characterization, and individuality, see Pelling (2002a: 283–338) and Nikolaidis (2014). Zadorojnyi (2012) offers a fascinating perspective on mimesis and its role in Plutarchan biography. Duff (2004), Monaco (2011–12), and Mossman (2014) bring into focus specifically the elements of tragedy and comedy. Nerdahl (2007; 2011–12) studies the Homeric models – that is, Achilles and Odysseus – in the *Lives* and should be read with Bloom's (1991) interpretive essay and Hobbs (2000). The Socratic paradigm has been studied by (Trapp 1999), Pelling (2005b), Zadorojnyi (2007), and Beck (2014b). On modern theories of leadership, see in particular the works of Burns (1978) and Goleman (1995; 2001).

# CHAPTER II

# Thinking "Private Life"
## Plutarch on Gender, Sexuality, and Family

Françoise Frazier

Translated by Katherine Low

For approximately half a century our modern age has developed the notion of "gender"[1] in parallel with society's evolution, accorded an increasing importance to sexuality, and modified somewhat the definition of "family" as ways of thinking about relationships between men and women, parents and children, and brothers and sisters. Plutarch, the "philosopher for his own time"[2] who combined the attributes of man and thinker, did not imagine these relationships in terms of sexuality and gender. Rather, affection (*philostorgia*), love (*erōs* and *philia*), marriage, and the family were the key concepts in his study of "private life." He also lived, however, during an era of change. This change had consequences for the idea of marriage in particular,[3] a fact that justifies a more in-depth analysis of Plutarch's view of the subject, which he discusses both in the parenetic *Coniugalia praecepta* and in *Amatorius* – a Platonic-style dialogue where marriage is presented as Love realized in its most perfect form. In order to distinguish between contemporary attitudes and original ideas in his works, we must first clarify the notion of "private life," the philosophical tradition, and contemporary idea(s) of the family before reintegrating familial relations into Plutarch's view of human nature and code of ethics.

## The Philosophical Tradition: From the *Oikos* to the Family

When Xenophon in the *Oeconomicus* (fourth century BCE) describes Ischomachus and his young wife's life together, he does so as part of the "art of running a household" (*oikos*): "household" here includes all the

---

[1] In France, gender (*genre*) was until relatively recently only a grammatical category, whereas *sexe* was reserved for living beings. About the "feminist lens," and its advantages and inconveniences, see Nikolaïdis (1997: esp. 27–28 and 87).

[2] After the subtitle ("Un philosophe dans le siècle") of Sirinelli (2000).

[3] Foucault (1984: 174) = (1990: 148).

living things and all the goods belonging to the family. He explains how to manage capital and divide up tasks between the spouses.[4] Although Plutarch was a large-scale landowner who was certainly well informed about these matters,[5] he discusses them only very sporadically[6] as part of the broader ethical question of wealth and how to use it.[7] Social and political aspects[8] – preserving capital for one's descendants, being able to serve the state and bring relief to the most impoverished – stay outside Plutarch's study of the family, even though he is not unaware of them. In his *Coniugalia praecepta* he has no more interest in household management than the Stoics Musonius and Epictetus apparently do.[9] The active concepts in this sphere are "kinship" (*syngeneia*), "fellowship" (*koinōnia*), and "friendship," to revive the accepted but too narrow translation of *philia*, which "strictly speaking refers not to a romantic relationship but to the condition of belonging to a social group,"[10] and to links created by hospitality, kinship, or what *we* call friendship.

When thus venturing into the "private" sphere that belongs by right to all members of society, we must consider both social involvement and the impact on an individual in relative proportions that vary according to the period. The ancients defined the goal (*telos*) of life in its moral dimension in terms of "happiness" that entailed an absence of disturbance (*ataraxia*), and self-sufficiency (*autarkeia*). One might well wonder whether the aforementioned bonds threatened this. Aristotle was already asking that question, and it also underwent development in Plutarch's time. Paul Veyne and Michel Foucault[11] believed that they had identified in that period a "domestication" of civic moral values that sought to replace the idea of the good citizen fulfilling his civic duties with that of the good husband who respected his wife. So, as mentioned earlier, it is important to

---

[4] Xenophon's *Oeconomicus* and Plutarch's *Coniugalia praecepta* are accurately compared in Pomeroy (1999b: 33–42).

[5] See Chandezon (2005).

[6] The adjective *oikonomikos* is used only six times in his entire oeuvre: *De recta ratione audiendi* 40C and *De curiositate* 515E (both referring to Xenophon); *Comparatio Aristides–Cato Maior* 3.1; *Crassus* 2.8, *De Alexandri magni fortuna aut virtute* 332D, and *Adversus Colotem* 1126A (linked to *politikōs*).

[7] *Septem sapientium convivium* 157A and *Cato Maior* 4–5 and 20–21, with Frazier (1996: 154–156).

[8] *Pericles* 16.

[9] For example, *Discourses* 3.5.3: Epictetus, challenging a pupil ready to abandon philosophy, draws a contrast between it and domestic affairs, the man's wretched little piece of land, and matters relating to the *agora*.

[10] Chantraine (1980: 1204, s.v. "*philos*").

[11] The idea was mooted by Veyne (1978) and then taken up by Foucault (1984), who in turn is cited by Veyne (1985).

outline the philosophical tradition and the work of Plutarch's contemporaries.

From the Hellenistic era onwards, Epicureans and Stoics had been divided on two problematic issues: man's innate love for his offspring (which is a question of how human nature is viewed)[12] and the Sage's marriage, which pertains to the latter's social obligations.[13] It seems that Epictetus' master Musonius Rufus, following Antipater of Tarsus,[14] gave the study of marriage a sizeable role in his work: at least, three of the twenty-one essays preserved for us by his pupil Lucius, which focus on practical morality, are dedicated to it. One (XIV) discusses the Sage's marriage, and the other two (XIII.A and B) marriage in general. They extol marital fellowship (*koinōnia*) and add to the idea of the social necessity of marriage more "private" ethical considerations on how to live a good married life.[15]

However, there is also a much less favorable picture of people's experiences of family ties in Epictetus' *Discourses*. These are full of the remonstrances and grievances of individuals who complain about their father, their children, or, sometimes, their wife,[16] find fault with their brothers and think they have been wronged by them,[17] or else cannot bear the illness or loss of their close relatives.[18] The very fact that these themes recur indicates their importance in everyone's life: sometimes, when there are disputes over legacies and problems with inheritance,[19] one's interests in the wider community are affected, and at other times one's personal feelings, when for whatever reason close relatives become a source of distress. As our closest relations, they accordingly constitute the most immediate danger of dependency with regard to something external to us; they threaten our inner peace, but also give us an excuse for shifting the responsibility for our miscalculations onto others.[20] For all that, it should not be denied that the "communal creature" (*zōon koinōnikon*) that man is, according to Chrysippus,[21] is unavoidably entangled in a network of natural and

---

[12] Epictetus, 1.23.3: "What is the meaning of this sociability, if nature does not cause us to feel affection for the creatures born of us? Why do you [scil. Epicurus] advise the wise man not to have children?"

[13] This point is addressed by Plutarch in *Solon* 7. Thales of Miletus, who never married, tricks Solon into believing his son is dead, and uses Solon's grief as proof against all relationships and attachments – an argument that Plutarch proceeds to criticize at length.

[14] Quoted by Stobaeus (= *SVF* III 254, 5–257, 10) and discussed by Babut (1963).

[15] Foucault (1984: 178–180 and 187) = (1990: 151–153 and 159); Nussbaum (2002).

[16] 1.12.20–22; 1.28.7–9; 2.22; 3.3; 3.17.7; 3.18; 3.20.11; 4.1.43.      [17] 1.15.1–5; 2.10.12; 3.3; 3.8; 3.10.

[18] 1.11; 1.27.5; 2.21.18; 3.8; 3.13.2–4; 4.1.67.

[19] This is one reason to have recourse to divination (2.7). Plutarch also mentions questions about marriage: *De Pythiae oraculis* 408C.

[20] See e.g. 3.19.      [21] Diogenes Laertius 7.123 = *SVF* III 160.33–34.

supplementary social relationships (*skheseis*), and Epictetus fits them into his definition of philosophy's second sphere, that of moral action: "We should keep up our relationships with others, both natural and acquired (*tas skheseis . . . tas physikas kai epithetous*), as religious men, as sons, as brothers, as fathers, and as citizens" (3.2.4).

However, although they are important, these relationships only affect our social existence, and the roles that we must play.[22] Fulfilling our social duties, being a good son, good brother, or good father, and honoring divine worship and civic obligations does not mean forgetting that the "true self" is the spark of reason within us that makes us citizens of the universe,[23] and that there is a higher kinship that makes Zeus the father of men and gods and all humanity our brothers.[24] It is this kinship that is favored by the philosopher, embodied in the idealized figure of the Cynic, the only one permitted not to marry in order better to devote himself to the human race:

> Though a mere man, he is the sire of all humanity: men are his sons, and women his daughters; in this way he is beside them all and cares for them all. Do you think that he reviles everyone he meets because of a lack of restraint? He does it as a father, as a brother, as a servant of Zeus, who is father of us all. (3.22.81–82)

Plutarch too recognizes that familial relationships are necessary. But his Platonism and his life as a married man and father of a family,[25] as well as the diverse nature of his writings, mean that his ideas are appreciably different in tone from those of Epictetus. In the first place, the very fact that it is difficult to find an ideal philosopher-figure in the works of Plutarch clearly points to the importance for him of a life "for its own time," integrated into society.[26]

## *Philostorgia,* Familial *Philia,*and Social Morality

Plutarch and the Stoics are both convinced that affection for one's own family (*philostorgia*) is innate in man. This is the subject of Epictetus' *Discourse* 1.11, and Plutarch also discussed it in a work that remained

---

[22] See also 2.10; 1–6 discuss the fundamental role of man and world citizen, 7–9 the roles of son and brother, and 10–11 those of councilor (*bouleutēs*) and father.

[23] On this distinction and (Panaetius') Stoic theory, see Gill (1988).

[24] See 1.13.3–4 and the discussion of Hadot (1992:238–248).

[25] Epictetus mocks family life of this kind as being scarcely compatible with the Academy's skepticism: 2.20.27 and the discussion of Cuvigny (1969).

[26] See Van Hoof (2010: esp. 19–63); her analysis is thus a useful check on Foucault who emphasizes "the total heterogeneity of this type of [*sc.* philosophical] life compared with other forms of existence": (1990: 156) = (1984: 184).

unfinished (it may have been merely an unsuccessful draft, and is missing from the Lamprias Catalogue), *De amore prolis*.[27] It argues that this form of affection, although found in animals, is only fully realized in man as a social and rational creature (495B–C). Again, affection is the dominant theme in the treatise offered as a tribute to the two Nigrini brothers, *De fraterno amore*. Echoing the complaints in Epictetus' *Discourses*, Plutarch begins it with the bitter observation that "brotherly love is as rare today as brotherly hatred was in the past" (478C).[28] Accordingly, he has decided to promote an ideal that the dedicatees already exemplify (478B). This "protreptic" work is also the only systematic account we have of a question that philosophers seem to have problematized very little.[29] In *De fraterno amore* Plutarch endeavors first to find in our nature and our duties a basis for these bonds, before describing how they are dynamically manifested in everyday life.

The honors done to our kin (*to syngenes*, 479C) – that is, the first people with whom we have contact – should be linked to our innate need for *philia*, our inability to live alone. However, such a view is not enough and Plutarch, adapting for this context the *prōton philon* of the Platonic *Lysis*,[30] makes familial *philia* the prototype for all *philiai*. He adduces a fragment of Menander:

> Everyone deems he has found
> a matchless treasure in the shadow of a friend.

Most friendships are in fact shadows, imitations, images of this first (*tēs prōtēs*) friendship that nature has implanted in children toward their parents and in brothers toward their brothers (479C–D).

"Fraternal company" is foremost, coming before the *philia* "that binds companions together"[31] (*our* sense of "friendship"), which is here designated more vaguely as "most friendships" (*hai pollai*: there is perhaps a Platonic flavor here, hinting that after the "foremost friendship" there are many different sorts). It is also the only kind that can tolerate equality,

---

[27] See Babut (1969b: 74–79) and Roskam (2011c).

[28] See also *Aemilius Paulus* 5.9 on the decay of "modern" family life.

[29] Stobaeus only quotes Menander, Euripides, Sotion, Euclid, Hierocles, Musonius, and Xenophon on the subject. See Betz (1978).

[30] See the discussion in Fraisse (1974: 439 and n. 75).

[31] The Plutarchan *Amatorius* gives a list of four *philiai*: first of all, the kind that comes from nature (*physikon*), then that which brings together guests and hosts (*xenikon*), then that shared by comrades (*hetairikon*), and finally that of love (*erōtikon*) (758D). This list is confirmed as Platonic by Diogenes Laertius 3.81. See also *De fraterno amore* 481F, which lists "bonds with relatives or comrades or lovers" (*syngenikon, hetairikon, erōtikon*).

which, despite being demagogic and worthy of censure when instituted in the city, as it was by Solon, should prevail among brothers (484B–C). Since nature rarely makes them equal in all respects, they must strive to reduce all imbalances by mutual diligence (chs. 12–16).

How to conceptualize familial *philiai*, then? Aristotle, for example, pursues parallels with political constitutions (*EN* 8.13, 1161a 10ff.). As for Plutarch, he chooses to define the distinctive essence of *syngenikon*. Moreover, just as he does not posit the "pure" philosopher as the ideal human being, his "foremost friendship" is not the friendship between Wise Men (as beloved of the philosophical schools), but one that binds the members of the same family – not just brothers but also parents and children. For this innate character of fraternal love has a significant consequence: the honors done to one's parents, "which in the view of nature, and in the view of the law, that goes by nature, are fundamental and most great" (479F), are sacrosanct.[32] Fraternal love is thus revealed to be "a direct proof of love for both mother and father" (480F), while, on the contrary, hatred between brothers is "an evil sustainer of parents in their old age" and "a worse nurturer of children in their youth" (481B). When the progression to the next generation is flawed like this, the whole line of descent becomes involved. The gallery of case studies then begins with maintaining the correct attitude during the lifetime of one's parents and then at their death (chs. 9–11). It continues with the meticulous examination of all possible situations of inequality and disagreement, which must be continuously remedied (chs. 12–20), and ends with a comprehensive family portrait, in which Plutarch stresses the respect that should be shown to one's brother's relations by marriage and, especially, an uncle's duties in directing his nephews (ch. 21).

Although this family solidarity that Plutarch honors was not always put into practice by the society in which he lived, for him it was not merely a theory. Not only does he tell us of his affection for his brother Timon (*De fraterno amore* 487D–E) and affectionately depict his grandfather,[33] but the *Lives* also show that he saw this as an ethical feature worthy of being included in a representation of someone's character. Accordingly, he delights in evoking the fraternal love that bound Cato to his brother Caepio,[34] and Lucullus to his brother Marcus.[35] He dwells on the concord (exceptional for those troubled times) among the Antigonids: thus he

---

[32] Chapters 4–7 of *De fraterno amore* are devoted to parents.  [33] See Sirinelli (2000: 28–29).
[34] *Cat. min.* 3.8–9, 11.1–6, and 15.4 = *De fraterno amore* 487C.
[35] *Lucullus* 1.8–9 = *De fraterno amore* 484E.

brings out the mutual attachment of Antigonus the One-Eyed and
Demetrius (*Demetrius* 3), the father's simultaneously amused and culpable
indulgence toward his son's escapades (19), and then, in the next generation, Antigonus Gonatas' affection for his father (51.2 and 53). In
the Roman context, Plutarch also describes Cornelia's love for her sons
(*Gracchi* 1.6–7), which does not prevent her from enduring their death in
a most noble manner (*Gracchi* 40[19]), and equally Sertorius' and
Coriolanus' love and respect for their mothers (*Sertorius* 2.1 and 22.9–12;
*Coriolanus* 4.5–7). However, here the point of reference is Greek:
Epaminondas, the hero dear to Plutarch's Boeotian heart and philosophical soul. His *Life* is lost, but in the *Life of Coriolanus* he is said to "have
confessed to the same feeling" (*pathos*) as the Roman, who was so proud of
honoring his mother through his courage, and to have considered it "his
greatest piece of good fortune that his father and mother lived long enough
to see him serve as general and return home victorious from Leuctra"
(*Coriolanus* 4.6).

The word *pathos* is significant, for, in addition to its moral and social
dimension, the importance here attributed to familial bonds[36] is
a fundamental part of Plutarch's view of human nature. He is opposed
to the Stoic idea that man is a creature of reason, for whom passion was
believed to be mere misjudgment, and sees passion and reason as two
elements, different in type but both an integral part of human nature:[37]
"For who, even if he so wished, could separate or sever from friendship
a natural propensity toward affection, from humaneness pity and from true
benevolence (*eunoia*) the mutual participation in joy and grief?" (*De virtute
morali* 451E).

Emotions (*pathē*) determine the nature of our familial relationships as
well as those with our friends and, conversely, these bonds justify the price
set on them because they satisfy our *emotional* needs, provided one avoids
excesses of passion. The family circle thus gives us our first opportunity of
learning self-control:

> For either it is in vain and to no avail that Nature has given us gentleness and
> forbearance (*anexikakia*) which is the child of restraint (*metriopatheia*), or
> we should make the utmost use of these virtues *in our relations with our
> family and relatives*. And our asking and receiving forgiveness for our own
> errors reveals goodwill and affection quite as much as granting it to others
> when they err. (*De fraterno amore* 489C)

---

[36] The same applies to instances of conjugal devotion – see later in this chapter.
[37] See Babut (1969b: 319–333, 362–366); Opsomer (1994; 2006); further, Gill (2006).

When one is in mourning, too, one should be restrained. On this, Plutarch says nothing different from Epictetus, but as the father of a family he himself sorrowfully experienced it. So in the *Consolatio ad uxorem*[38] he begins by reminding Timoxena of the moderation in grief that it befits a sensible (*sōphrōn*) woman to maintain: "a continence that does not resist maternal affection, as the multitude believe, but the licentiousness of the mind. For it is yielding to a parent's love to long for and honor and remember the departed" (609A–B). Moreover, the best example of this attitude is none other than Timoxena. Previously, at the death of their little boy Chairon, whom she had breastfed herself, she had been able to display the emotions "of a noble and affectionate heart" (609E).

The *Lives* reaffirm the recommendations of the paraenetic treatises, and the biographer offers a staunch defense of Demosthenes, who lost his daughter shortly before Philip's death was announced, against Aeschines' attacks. While the latter, assuming that only floods of tears can mark true affection, condemned Demosthenes' *misoteknia*, Plutarch – who is more guarded about the expressions of joy to which the Macedonian's death gave rise – unreservedly approves the bereaved father's restraint:

> For leaving his domestic misfortunes and tears and lamentations to the women[39] and going about such business as he thought advantageous to the city, I commend Demosthenes, and I hold it to be the part of a statesmanlike and manly spirit to keep ever in view the good of the community, to find support for domestic sorrows and concerns in the public welfare. (*Demosthenes* 22.5)

A passage of this kind – which is not an isolated example[40] – shows that while one's family must be given its due place and while, beyond even familial solidarity, it is human nature to set a high value on the *philia* between close relatives, it cannot be claimed (as Paul Veyne wishes to) that in Plutarch's works the traditional civic ideal has given way to an idealization of private life. The author of the *Parallel Lives* and of *An seni respublica gerenda sit*, who himself served his city all his life even down to performing the most mundane tasks (*Praecepta gerendae reipublicae* 811B–C), does not call into question the idea that the public good comes first. He therefore thinks Timoleon worthy of censure because he felt remorse for allowing the assassination of the tyrant that his brother had become, even though he had

---

[38] See Pomeroy (1999c: 75–78).    [39] Who apparently lacked Timoxena's nobility of soul.
[40] See e.g. *Fabius Maximus* 24.6, *Cleomenes* 22, *Aemilius Paulus* 36.7–9, or, contrasting with Demosthenes' behavior, *Cicero* 41; Frazier (1996: 156–158).

warned the man and failed to make him change. His country's interest should have assured him that he had merely done his duty (*Timoleon* 3–5).

So, the civic ideal does not fundamentally change, and, at the same time, private life is still the preferred setting for womanly virtues. Women should be devoted above all to their father, husband, and children, and if they happen to be required to take part in public life, they should imitate Aretaphila of Cyrene. The tyrant Nicocrates compelled her to marry him; she helped to overthrow him, but "when she saw the city free, she withdrew at once to her own quarters among the women, and, rejecting any sort of meddling in affairs, spent the rest of her life quietly at the loom in the company of her friends and family" (*Mulierum virtutes* 257E). This outcome, which cannot help offending our modern way of thinking, calls on us to specify how Plutarch saw relations between men and women, in both the philosophical and practical spheres.

### The Marital Bond: Social Conformism and the Philosophical Ideal

The worth of women, the necessity of educating them, and the cross-gender universality of virtue have long been philosophical topics. Two of Musonius' discourses discuss the matter: one shows that women "also should do philosophy" (III), while the other asks whether daughters ought to be educated in the same way as sons (IV).[41] In Plutarch's case, there survive some fragments of a work entitled *That a woman should be educated as well* (frs. 128–133 Sandbach). This did not stop the admission of women to Epicurus' Garden being exploited when necessary by the opponents of the Epicureans (Plutarch among them) in order to reinforce the school's reputation as vulgar hedonists.[42]

Plutarch also put together a compendium of heroic deeds carried out by women (including Aretaphila's aforementioned actions):[43] the *Mulierum virtutes* was dedicated to his friend Clea, president of the Thyades at Delphi. This minor work is the result of a long conversation they had on the subject at the death of her relative Memma Leontis,[44] and he declares at the start that "men's virtues and women's virtues are one and the same" (243A).[45] The fact remains that in real life women could very rarely

---

[41] Translated in Nussbaum (2002: 314–318).

[42] See *Non posse suaviter vivi secundum Epicurum* 1089C, 1097D–E, *An recte dictum sit latenter esse vivendum* 1029B; Boulogne (2003: 141–144).

[43] On Aretaphila, see Blomqvist (1997).     [44] *Mulierum virtutes* 242F, with Stadter (1965: 3–10).

[45] He further explains (243B–D) how the realizations of virtue are different from one man to another, from one woman to another, and from a woman to a man, according to the circumstances and characters; these particularities are what he focuses on (see also *Phocion* 3.7–8 for the same idea). In all these cases, "virtue" (*aretê*) meant as "excellence" should not be confused with "manly courage"

distinguish themselves through service to the city other than in exceptional circumstances, and that Plutarch's "contemporary" parenetic works are not the place to develop this aspect of the question. However, it is noteworthy that *Amatorius*, in order to laud women's capacity for love and sacrifice, describes the revenge of Camma, who sacrificed her life to avenge the murder of her husband, and the secret existence Empona led for a long time after her husband was compromised in Civilis' conspiracy.[46] The *Lives* too supply some examples of fidelity, but also of the mediatory roles and efforts at reconciliation women can take on.[47] So in the *Life of Agis* we see Chilonis following her father into his unjust exile and, on his return, defending her husband from his vengeance (17–18). In the *Life of Romulus*, we also witness the Sabines intervening between their fathers and their husbands on the battlefield (19). However, no female distinguishes herself as much as Porcia, who is named in the preface of the *Mulierum virtutes* (243C) among those women whose valor can be measured against men's, and whose nobility of spirit (*phronēma*) should be compared with that of her husband Brutus. Through her exceptional virtue and her repeated appearances in the *Life of Brutus* she offers the best idea of female possibilities and limits.[48]

Her first appearance is at the point when Brutus, committed to the conspiracy, cannot hide his great anxiety from "his wife who slept by his side" (*Brutus* 13.2): in this way, Plutarch introduces us to the couple's intimacy. From the outset the description of Porcia is worthy of special mention: according to the manuscript reading, she was "in love with wisdom (*philosophos*), fond of her husband and full of sensible pride" (13.4). Despite the fact that she was no less than Cato's daughter, the first adjective was so surprising in the nineteenth century that the editor Karl Sintenis emended it to the much more traditional "affectionate" (*philostorgos*)![49] In any case, Porcia's great virtues lead her to prove to Brutus her resistance to pain before asking him to confide in her. After wounding herself in the thigh, she gives her husband a lecture on marriage that doubtless owes much to Plutarch: "Brutus, I am Cato's daughter, and I was brought into your house, not like a mere concubine, to share your

---

(*andreia*) – after the old Roman usage (cf. *Coriolanus* 1.6). So Plutarch's "brave women" are not necessarily "manly women," contra McInerney (2003).

[46] The first anecdote also occurs at *Mulierum virtutes* 20. On these *exempla*, see Frazier (2005).

[47] On these intercessions, see Goessler (1962: 125–129).

[48] Goessler (1962: 130–142) and the sensible conclusion of Stadter (1999a: 182).

[49] This point is addressed by Stadter (1999a: 181).

bed and board merely, but to be a partner (*koinōnos men*) in your joys and a partner (*koinōnos de*) in your troubles" (13.7).

The anaphora highlights what the Stoic Musonius extols as the very essence of marriage, *koinōnia*. Here Porcia and Brutus both attain sublimity, and Plutarch gives the admiring husband, who yields to his wife's request and confides in her, the touching prayer "that he might succeed in his undertaking and thus show himself a worthy husband of Porcia" (13.11).

We find the same harmony when the couple are separated after the Ides of March, and the biographer shows the same sensitivity by creating a kind of virtual farewell scene in which Hector and Andromache, the couple from epic, serve as a point of reference. While Porcia cannot restrain her tears before a painting depicting their farewells (23.2–4), Brutus' answer to Acilius, who has quoted to him Andromache's famous lines to Hector (*Il.* 6.429–30), is:

> But I, certainly, have no mind to address Porcia in the words of Hector [*Il.* 6.491]: "Ply your loom and distaff and give orders to thy maids," for though her body is not strong enough to perform such heroic tasks as men do, yet in spirit (*gnōmē*) she is valiant (*aristeuei*)[50] in defense of her country, just as we do. (23.6)

The couple are of one accord. Still, although Porcia is a brave woman and a worthy daughter of Cato, she cannot resist weeping – even less, join in her husband's action. Furthermore, on the Ides of March she shows herself unable to overcome her anxiety without fainting (15.5–8). But when, conversely, Brutus receives (false) news of her death, he "did not abandon his public duty, nor was he driven by his affliction (*pathos*) to dwell on his private concerns" (15.9). Likewise, Porcia's eventual death (whether she let herself die following an illness while Brutus was alive, or committed suicide after his death) again shows her agony (*pathos*) and her love for Brutus (53.7), while he dies for his country and for honor.

If such an imbalance remains even between exceptional spouses, it is clearly endemic to an "ordinary," contemporary couple relationship, such as that of the young Pollianus and Eurydice to whom Plutarch dedicates his *Coniugalia praecepta* as a wedding gift. Modern scholarship rarely misses the opportunity to denounce the conformist nature of a text that unquestioningly presupposes the husband's superiority over his wife and is matter of fact about adultery by the former. Plutarch calls upon the husband to

---

[50] The verb formed from the superlative *aristos* (best) assimilates Porcia's mindset to the *aristeiai* of the epic heroes.

avoid adultery in order not to make his wife unhappy (144C–D), and upon her to regard his misbehavior as mere drunken excesses, unworthy of her concern (140B).[51] The wife is also responsible for maintaining family unity[52] and has a duty to win the affection of her parents-in-law. There is also a warning against all the traditional female foibles: resorting to magic to beguile one's husband (139A), an excessive interest in appearance (141E), a readiness to listen to nasty rumors (143F), and a superstitious weakness for ecstatic cults (145C). This last danger is explained in a striking way. Drawing on a comparison between soul and body that is very much Platonically colored, Plutarch emphasizes that just as physical conception does not occur without a man's participation, one must be careful lest women's souls, "if they do not receive the seed of good doctrines and share with their husbands in intellectual advancement, [conceive] all kinds of un-toward ideas and low designs and emotions" (145D).

Rather than criticizing these "clichés,"[53] it is necessary to set them in the context of Plutarch's outlook and his commitment to championing marital *koinōnia*. The work is framed at the start "as a gift for you both to possess in common" (138C, *koinon amphoterois . . . dōron*); likewise, the way in which it proceeds, continually moving between one spouse's duties and the other's, points toward a sense of cooperation that is sustained by two powerful images. The first is that of "complete amalgamation," a notion borrowed from physics (142E–143A), the other of a "musical harmony" – albeit it falls to the husband (139C–D and 142D–E) to set the tone. It is for him to direct his wife along the path to morality by giving her an example of *aidōs* through his moderation and deference (139B–C and 145E), and along the path to philosophy. The conclusion, which is also the treatise's climax, juxtaposes the spouses' duties one final time. First, for Pollianus, Plutarch pleasingly adapts Andromache's lines:

> And for your wife you must collect from every source what is useful, as do
>   the bees, and carrying it within your own self impart it to her, and then
>   discuss it with her, and make the best of these doctrines her favorite and
>   familiar themes. For to her
> "Thou art a father and precious-loved mother,
> Yea, and a brother as well."
> No less ennobling is it for a man to hear his wife say, "My dear husband,

---

[51] More detailed studies are Patterson (1992); Chapman (2011: 13–45); note also Nikolaïdis (1997: 72–75) who aptly insists on "the most essential and radical adjustments" the husband is called to make at a time when he was not required to be sexually faithful.

[52] See also *De fraterno amore* 480Aff.

[53] On "the issue of superiority," Nikolaïdis (1997: 76–82); see further Chapman (2011: 1–5).

Nay, but thou art to me"
guide, philosopher, and teacher in all that is most lovely and divine.
(145B, with *Il.* 6.429–30)

Then, turning to Eurydice and reminding her of the previously offered
instruction, Plutarch calls on her to cover herself not only with the
adornment of virtue but also with the Muses' grace. Moreover, he has
Homer give way to Sappho:

> If Sappho thought that her beautiful composition in verse justified her in
> writing to a certain rich woman:[54]

> Dead in the tomb shall thou lie,
> Nor shall there be thought of thee there,
> For in the roses of Pierian fields
> Thou hast no share,

why, shall it not be even more allowable for you to entertain high and
splendid thoughts of yourself, if you have a share not only in the roses but
also in the fruits which the Muses bring and graciously bestow upon those
who admire education and philosophy? (146A)

Saliently, the work began with a prayer to the Muses that they may lend
their presence and cooperation to Aphrodite, and that they may feel that it
is no more fitting for them to provide a well-attuned lyre or lute than it is to
ensure that the harmony that concerns marriage and the household shall be
attuned with reason (*logos*),[55] concord, and philosophy (138C).

The reference to the Muses rewarding "education and philosophy" in
146A thus both achieves the effect of ring-composition and reinforces
Plutarch's overall message. It is also amid the peace of the Valley of the
Muses, but with Eros and not Aphrodite as chief deity,[56] that Plutarch
embarks on his most wide-ranging study of marriage,[57] which he recon-
siders in the light of the Platonic ideas on eros.

Amatorius is a Platonic-style dialogue where the plot is of great significance when paired with the theoretical discussion. The "original" conversation is narrated to friends by Plutarch's son, Autoboulus, and is meant to
have taken place during a voyage his parents made to Thespiae soon after
their marriage in order to attend the festival of Eros and thank the god for

---

[54] Opposition to luxury is also an important theme of the *Coniugalia praecepta*: on luxury, see
Teodorsson (2007–8).
[55] On *logos* and love, see Wohl (1997).
[56] On the hierarchy's inversion, see Frazier (2008d: 103–107).
[57] On *Amatorius* and the *Peri Gamou* literature, see Crawford (1999).

smoothing out a disagreement between their two families. So the discussion will take place with an image of the happy, loving couple that Plutarch and Timoxena were throughout their life (and inter alia gave birth to the dialogue's narrator!) in the background. The immediate pretext for the debate, even by Plutarch's admission, is "unusual" (749E, *paradoxou*). A young widow, Ismenodora, intends to marry the ephebe Bacchon, the son of one of her friends. Surely it is too early for such a young man to get married? Moreover, would not the difference in wealth and age give the wife an intolerable superiority? As in Plato's *Symposium*, with the guests' eulogies, and in the *Phaedrus*, with the two paradoxical speeches of Lysias and Socrates, Plutarch includes a "pre-philosophical" section.[58] First he takes up the traditional rhetorical debate over love for boys and love for girls (chs. 3–5);[59] the question pondered is not so much which love is superior, but what is *the* veritable and paramount love. Using Daphneus, a young man engaged to be married, as his mouthpiece, Plutarch from the outset assumes that love for women cannot be separated from marriage and rejects the exclusive claims of philosophical pederasty (751F). He then personally intervenes "as a devotee (*khoreutēs*) of conjugal love" (753C) and reasserts the basic themes of the *Coniugalia praecepta*. A husband should never degrade his wife. If he is her social inferior, it then falls to him to make up for this with moral superiority. And even though the didactic aspect remains, why not accept that in this case the wife tenderly guides her young, inexperienced husband (754D)?

From this opening section onwards, this extraordinary (and, as a consequence, ripe for philosophical study) case allows social conformism and the traditional division of tasks between the sexes to be left behind in order to bring to the fore the major demands of married life: mutual respect and the development "of the soul." Next, Ismenodora organizes the young man's abduction, following a custom employed in Crete by the *erastai* whom she imitates in taking, after a fashion, her opponents at their word (753B), but in a "good cause": marriage. This paves the way for further arguments: such an impulse in so sensible a woman can only come from a god. From now on, Eros' divine nature will hold sway at the heart of the text, like Diotima's revelations at the heart of the *Symposium*, or the myth of the soul's destiny in the *Phaedrus*. Plutarch takes from the latter dialogue the theory of *maniai*, the image of the "plain of Truth" (*Phaedrus* 248b =

---

[58] Rist (2001: 561).
[59] See [Lucian], *Amores* and Achilles Tatius, *Leucippe and Cleitophon*, 2.35–38; Goldhill (1995: 46–111, 144–160); Frazier (2008d: xix–xxiii).

*Amatorius* 765A), the wings of the soul and the procession formed by the god accompanied by pairs of true lovers (766B). He outlines the metaphysical horizon that Eros, "physician and savior," opens up to true lovers as he snatches away from the illusions of the physical world, "like the priest who aids initiates, those who have long desired to meet and be united with it" (765A) to bring them to the home of absolute, pure, and unadorned Beauty (*kallos*).

This language of mysteries and harmony recurs in the third section where, after a metaphysical discussion in which the lovers' gender is no longer taken into account but only love in the unified and "genuine" sense, the debate returns to the earthly realization of this ideal – just as in Plato's *Symposium*, after Diotima's revelations, Alcibiades embodies the philosophical love within Socrates. Plutarch goes on to refute the traditional idea, which Ismenodora's opponents support, that eros should be forbidden to respectable women (752B and 769D) and sets out to demonstrate that women are able to rouse as well as to feel what is a divine passion (chs. 21–25). Here on earth, time is of the essence and this is precisely what makes pederasty – in which relationships rarely endure – inferior (770B–C). In order to ensure that the union is permanent, the wife must "sacrifice to Eros" (769D). Love, forbidden by custom to a "sensible" (*sōphrōn*) woman, becomes on the contrary the source of "mutual restraint" (*sōphrosynē pros allēlous*, 767E). This almost untranslatable expression highlights, even more than the fidelity that results from the reciprocity of *sōphrosynē*, the moral worth of the couple that is born of their love. While *Coniugalia praecepta* considered that the marital bed was the ideal place for reconciliations (ch. 38) and that disputes were to be kept away from it (ch. 39), *Amatorius* emphasizes the part played by physical union in an intimacy that can only be experienced by a married couple, since philosophical pederasty precludes it: "Physical union with a wife is the source of mutual attachment, like a shared participation in the great mysteries. Pleasure is a small thing in itself, but it serves as a seed from which, day by day, mutual respect, kindness, tenderness and trust grow between husband and wife" (769A).

This highly moralistic idea, although it is given a mystic aura by the simile, stems once again from Plutarch's view of human nature and his belief that passion and worldly concerns are an integral part of our human condition. Tradition, drawing on religion, poetry, and laws, confirms the value of physical union (the *aphrodisia*):

> The Delphians were not wrong to call Aphrodite "Harmony," and Homer was right to designate such a union "friendship" (*philotēs*). It also proves that

Solon was a very experienced legislator of marriage laws. He prescribed that a man should consort with his wife not less than three times a month – not for pleasure surely, but as cities renew their mutual agreements from time to time, just so he must have wished this to be a renewal of marriage and with such an act of tenderness to wipe out the complaints that accumulate from everyday living. (769A–B)

Plutarch's ability here to take account of both trivial everyday matters and the spiritual meaning of love is particularly noteworthy and typical of his constant efforts to make philosophy a part of real life.

He may remain very unforthcoming about love's metaphysics ("great mysteries"), just as in the dialogue he is very reluctant to talk of such lofty subjects.[60] However, he lets us have a glimpse of what this could mean for him in *Consolatio ad uxorem*. It is his wife's "written advice addressed to Aristylla on the love of finery" that he counsels Eurydice to read in the *Coniugalia praecepta* (145A). And so the woman who shared her husband's intellectual interests, and with whom he had also partaken of the joy of producing, after four boys, a daughter, whom Plutarch was glad to call by the same name "Timoxena" (*Consolatio ad uxorem* 608C), also shared his metaphysical and religious beliefs. Plutarch builds up his conclusion by referring to the *koinōnia* of initiates of the Mysteries of Dionysus (611D), before enhancing that religious perspective with philosophical reflections on the greater possibility that a soul that has spent a short time on earth may escape the cycle of generations, and with a reminder of the customs that, in the case of such children who have died so young, forbid an impious mourning for "those creatures who have departed to an abode that is better and more divine." Lastly, he concludes: "Let us keep our outward conduct (*ta ektos*) as the laws command and keep ourselves within yet free from pollution and purer and more temperate" (612B).

This balance between the "external" and the self, to which Plutarch has recourse much less frequently than, say, Epictetus, here sums up perfectly the double perspective he employs to conceptualize marital and familial relationships. Within the subtle equilibrium between social attitudes and personal feeling that characterizes the study of private life, here the personal aspect, which grants religious purity the importance it deserves, is just as important as the other, if not more so. This is obviously due to the subject itself, which offers an insight into how Plutarch not only thought about his familial commitments but also experienced them in real life. However, it must be granted that they still remain to a great extent private

---

[60] *Amatorius* 762A, 763F, and Soclarus' reproaches (763F–764A, 766B).

and can only really be discerned in the background of his ethical and philosophical studies in *Amatorius* and *Consolatio ad uxorem*. But even though they are vague, these traces mean that Plutarch's texts are more than mere evidence of how an increased value was put on marriage and the family in his time, and more than the expression of a "philosophy, teacher of life." They give his work a deeply personal resonance that not only reflects his authorial personality but also allows his private self to show through.

## Further Reading

The historical frame and especially the move toward sexual symmetry are addressed by Foucault (1984) = (1990) and discussed by Goldhill (1995). Nussbaum (2002) focuses on Musonius Rufus, the Stoic contemporary of Plutarch. For a broader perspective on *philia*, see Konstan (1994).

An excellent synoptic study of Plutarch's views on eros against the background of his philosophical and psychological views is Opsomer (2006); see also Becchi (2007). Several studies address Plutarch's ideas on marriage and/or women: a comprehensive and fundamental discussion is Nikolaïdis (1997); Chapman (2011) treats the topic in a lucid way; see also Boulogne (2009–10) and the compact yet wide-ranging essay by Tsouvala (2014). Pomeroy (1999a) provides translations, commentaries, and a series of interpretive essays on *Coniugalia praecepta* and *Consolatio ad uxorem*. On the former work, see Wohl (1997). On feminine virtue according to Plutarch, a balanced discussion is offered by Patterson (1992) (revised 1999) and Stadter (1999a); further, Blomqvist (1997); McInerney (2003); McNamara (1999). On *De amore prolis*, see Roskam (2011c). The *Amatorius* is often discussed in light of Plutarch's Platonism, e.g. Rist (2001). On the ideas and compositional fabric of the dialogue, see Russell (1997); Crawford (1999); Brenk (2000); Görgemanns (2005); Frazier (2005–6; 2008d); Scannapieco (2007); Opsomer (2007a).

# CHAPTER 12

# *Wealth and Decadence in Plutarch's* Lives

## Christopher Pelling

## I

The bad are often rich, the good are poor; but still
We will ourselves take virtue over wealth.
For one stays firm for ever; as for wealth,
It slips through one man's hands straight to the next.

(Solon fr. 15 West, quoted at Solon 3.3 and<br>three times in Plutarch's other works)

Themistocles sneered, so the story goes, at the wonderful reputation that Aristides had won for his tribute-assessment: that's not fit praise for a man, he said, but for a moneybag. . . . Themistocles had once remarked that he thought a general's greatest virtue was the ability to read the enemy's mind in advance. "Yes, that's essential," said Aristides – "but the true mark of honor and generalship is to keep one's hands to oneself."

(Aristides 24.7)[1]

He was soon able to show off a treasury that never saw a dishonest informer but was always full of money. The lesson was clear, that it was possible for a city to be both wealthy and honest.

(Cato Minor 18.3)

Money talks, so they say. But, unfortunately, it is not always clear what exactly it says, or what people say about it. Plutarch was certainly interested in money and its role in public life, as that array of quotations shows, and he liked to put himself on the side of the virtuous angels. But there was more to it than that, and Paolo Desideri has brought out Plutarch's variety of mindset when it comes to wealth.[2] Sometimes the different voices start squabbling with one another, as in the *Comparatio* of Aristides and Cato

---

[1] On the important role played by money in *Themistocles*, see Zadorojnyi (2006b).
[2] In particular, Desideri (1985).

Maior (3–4). Was it so marvelous for Aristides to live in personal poverty, or did that simply give statesmanship a bad name? But why should Cato make such a business of wealth-acquisition if old-style asceticism is such an acknowledged good? More often, we get one voice at a time, all identifiably part of the same personality, but not always saying the same thing. There are moments when Plutarch develops a picture of primeval simplicity, when everything was marvelous and there was no acquisitiveness at all. One is reminded of all those Latin poets who pretend to think longingly of the time when one could get a girl with the gift of an apple, and one could save oneself so much bother. But just as those poets contrive to suggest that they would not really have been altogether at comfort in an apple-loving and easygoing world, Plutarch too clearly knows that money has its uses as well. His soft spot for the simple, moneyless, unacquisitive life comes out particularly in the *Lives* when he is talking about Sparta and Lycurgus' banishing of gold and silver coinage, and he certainly shows sympathy for the idea of equalizing whatever wealth there was: in one mindset he can wish that Numa had done what Lycurgus did and introduced an equality of wealth from the beginning, as this would have saved Rome from all the later evils that greed would bring (*Comparatio Lycurgus–Numa* 2.9). As so often with Plutarch, Plato is also in the background here, especially the insistence in the *Republic* on the difficulties of combining money-seeking with true virtue;[3] there is also that long history in Greek literature of alertness to the dangers of wealth (Solon fr. 4 West[2], Pindar *Ol.* 1.55–58, Aeschylus *Agam.* 376–384, 471–475, etc.), not to mention Roman satire (e.g. Juvenal 6.286–300) – and, indeed, as we will see (Section IV), historiography. But more usually Plutarch's emphasis falls on the need to use money well and not be enslaved to it, an emphasis close to that of the *De cupiditate divitiarum* and one that in the *Lives* is especially clear in *Solon–Publicola*; also perhaps in *Nicias–Crassus*, where the emphasis is less on the awfulness of riches in themselves and more on the bad ways in which money was acquired ("through fire and war," in Crassus' case; *Crassus* 2.4), the bad ways it could be used (Nicias' nervous attempts to placate the grim people), and the bad actions to which it can lead (Parthia).[4]

[3] On Plato's presentation, see Schriefl (2013); on Plutarch's response to Plato's thinking, Zadorojnyi (2006b: esp. 273–276). In *Republic* VIII–IX wealth, especially inequality of wealth, plays an important part in triggering each constitutional change: Schriefl (2013: 194–203, esp. 199–200). There are some differences here between *Republic* and *Laws*, where a limited degree of economic activity is allowed even to the virtuous.
[4] On this theme in the *Nicias–Crassus* comparison, see Duff (1999a: 269–271).

Paolo Desideri particularly stressed the difference in emphasis between the *Lives* and the political works. In *Praecepta gerendae reipublicae*, for instance, we are some way from the idealization of a distant, especially Spartan past, and Plutarch paints a much more realistic picture of how wealth might be used in a world of euergetism and private riches[5] (and we should remember that many of Plutarch's friends, especially his Roman friends, would count as very rich indeed). He may not like that public style much, and recommends a more enlightened "demagogy," based on *logos* and on caring more than on doles and games (esp. 802D–E; cf. 821E–822A, 823C–E, *An seni respublica gerenda sit* 787B); but he knows that it is the world in which an elite politician has to move.[6] Discussion centers on the *sort* of expensive disbursements and "honor-seeking gestures" (*philotimēmata*) that the rich politician needs to perform (822A–C; cf. 818C–E), not on whether he ought to do that sort of thing at all.[7] There are even opportunities for the wise politician to put a little discreet money-making in the way of a friend (808F–809B), such as recommending him to a rich man who needs someone to represent his interests. And Plutarch does not throw up his hands in horror.

This chapter will explore this variety of mindset even within the *Lives* themselves, and in particular its characteristic connection with moral decadence and decay. In particular, it will look at the ways in which Plutarch adapts his moralism to the rough world of Rome, where wealth played so large and often so corrupt a role, where decadence was not difficult to find, and where the loudest voices, those reveling most in talk about decadence, were so often those of the Romans themselves.

## II

One introductory point, and it is purely statistical. Of course there are more words than one for decadent luxury and this is not just a lexical game, but if there is one word that we would expect to find more than any other in this context it is *tryphē* – useful not least because it is so vague, with "a strong affective value but a very low descriptive one."[8] And we do. It is not

---

[5]  Desideri (1985: 397–398).
[6]  This too is Platonic: "Platon sieht also in Geld und Reichtum einerseits eine Gefahr, andererseits eine Notwendigkeit" (Schriefl 2013: 6). But Plato's emphasis falls on a more subsistence level of economic activity, at least in ideal cities.
[7]  Jones (1971: 110–121, esp. 111–112, 117) ("Plutarch is not delineating an ideal republic or legislating for an imaginary city").
[8]  Lenfant (2007: 52); cf. Gorman and Gorman (2014: 34–65). For the connection of *tryphē* with wealth, especially among non-Greek cultures, see Schmidt (1999: 107–139).

difficult to find cases where *tryphē* attaches to the cultures we would most expect, particularly Persia and the East but also Rome.[9] It is clear too that Plutarch is very familiar with the Roman historiographic *topos* of moral decline and its connection with reckless expenditure and excess. The very casualness of the way he introduces the idea at *Sulla* 1.5 is telling, just in a genitive absolute clause: "lifestyles having changed, and those upright and unblemished manners being a thing of the past, with decline bringing a taste for luxury and extravagance" – before he goes on to make the more pertinent point that *even in a society like that* Sulla ran into criticism for getting too rich too quick. Yet if one looks at where one finds *tryphē* as a theme, there is a good deal less of it in the Roman *Lives* than one would expect. Of course, there is some, especially in *Lucullus*;[10] but even there it is not so much a point about Rome as a whole as about the man himself, who figures also in one of the essays (*An seni respublica gerenda sit* 785F–786A, 792B) as the prime example of a man who collapsed into a reprehensible and luxurious retirement.

The *Lives* that really emphasize *tryphē* are the ones where we might least have expected it – the Spartan ones, where we are about three times as likely to come across a *tryphē* word than in the Athenian *Lives* (even though they include Alcibiades) or in the Roman.[11] There is something of the same phenomenon with "riches," *plout-* or *plousi-* words and compounds, though the discrepancy is less marked:[12] it is easy living, even more than wealthy living, that is in point. That is a very crude indication, of course, and quite often the point is not that Sparta is *tryphē*-ridden but that various Spartans were intent on stamping it out, especially Lycurgus at the beginning and Agis and Cleomenes at the end; yet it does reflect the way that *tryphē* is a *theme* in the Spartan *Lives*, much more so than in the Roman. But the most striking statistical point is that the most frequent occurrences of all come in the comparative epilogues. Wealth and luxury are so often important in weighing up the moral balance between the Greek and the

[9] Persia and the East: e.g. *Lycurgus* 4.3, *Themistocles* 16.3, *Artaxerxes* 20.1, *Eumenes* 6.3. Typifying Rome: besides *Sulla* 1.3, compare *Lucullus* 39.2 and *Marius* 34.5, noting the growth of such luxury through the late Republic and into the early principate. *Lucullus* 7.1 brings the Oriental and Roman suggestions together, with such Eastern manners corrupting a Roman army.
[10] On this, see Tröster (2008: ch. 3) and his Chapter 2 in this volume.
[11] The online Thesaurus Linguae Graecae (TLG) suggests twenty instances in Spartan *Lives* (once every 8.05 chapters); thirteen in Athenian *Lives* (once every 24.84 chapters); forty-five in Roman *Lives* (once every 21.67 chapters); and twelve in *synkriseis* (once every 6.42 chapters). The highest-scoring *Lives* are *Agis/Cleomenes* (eleven instances) and *Lucullus* (seven).
[12] Once every 4.12 chapters in Spartan *Lives*, once every 5.47 chapters in Athenian, once every 8.86 chapters in Roman, and once every 3.5 chapters in *synkriseis*. High-roller *Lives*: *Solon* (nineteen), *Agis/Cleomenes* (sixteen), *Lucullus* (thirteen), and *Gracchi* (twelve).

Roman, whether in terms of what they did for their states (*Lycurgus–Numa*) or of how they behaved themselves (*Cimon–Lucullus, Aristides–Cato Maior*).[13]

The statistical point does not in itself demonstrate much, but it does reflect the prominence of the theme of luxury and decadence in those Spartan *Lives* and the even more surprising muteness of the Roman *Lives*. What we do with that insight is another question. One tempting first bid would be to recall that Plutarch was a Greek under what has been called the Roman "occupation," and to think that he was sensible enough not to write anything too disapproving about "those most powerful men above," as he hauntingly calls the Romans in *Praecepta gerendae reipublicae* (814C). Yet that is unlikely to be the end of the matter, for often he is very pointed indeed about Romans and Roman values. Consider the bold remarks in the *Comparatio* of Lycurgus and Numa: "Did not Rome make her great advances through warfare? That is a question requiring a lengthy answer for men who define "advance" in terms of wealth, luxury, and empire rather than safety, restraint, and an honest independence" (*Comparatio Lycurgus–Numa* 4.12–13). And we shall see later (Section V) that Plutarch is scathing at the expense of the military men, Marius and Coriolanus, whose excesses can be explained by their lack of Hellenic culture.

Maybe, then, as a second, more nuanced pitch, we should wonder if the commentary on Sparta might also be an indirect way of suggesting, but only suggesting, points about Rome. It is interesting that this sharp remark about Roman militarism comes where it does, when the really military figure in the pair has been not the Roman Numa but the Spartan Lycurgus. This may be one oblique way (there are others too) in which Plutarch intimates reservations about Lycurgus' system but in a masked manner, in that case by seeming to talk about Rome when his point is really more about Sparta. Perhaps then we might think of the emphasis on *tryphē* as a sort of inverse procedure, where talking about Spartan excesses would suggest some thoughts about Rome as well.

In that case, though, we have to ask why he was so indirect, and one way or another it is more likely to be something to do with luxury in particular, not with any general reluctance to criticize Roman ways: that very passage from *Lycurgus* and *Numa* suggests that he can be direct enough in criticizing other prominent Roman values. Perhaps it was just that by now that theme of Roman moral decadence was simply so hackneyed that he could not do anything very interesting with it. There is something in that: in

---

[13] Duff (1999a: 261–262, 264, 269–271).

*Pompey*, as we shall see, when he talks about Roman decadence, he does not tie it only into easy living but more into other features of political ambition and ruthlessness (though still about greed). But there may be other reasons as well that lead him to tiptoe so delicately about Roman *tryphē*. We shall return to this later (Section V).

Enough has already been said to suggest that it will be especially interesting to look at those pairs that compare Romans with Spartans. The rest of this chapter will look at two particular test-cases, *Agesilaus–Pompey* and, first, the elaborate double pair *Agis/Cleomenes–Gracchi*.

## III

Love of riches, they said, will (or did) destroy Sparta, and nothing else (*philokhrēmosynē*, *Agis/Cleomenes* 9.1; *philokhrēmatia*, *Apophthegmata Laconica* 239E, etc.). Wealth comes into *Agis/Cleomenes–Gracchi* soon enough, with its disastrous impact on Sparta in the generations after the Peloponnesian War and the crisis this caused for the Lycurgan constitution, a theme also developed in *Lycurgus* itself (30.1) and *Lysander* (2.6, 16–17):[14] "When the eagerness for silver and gold first infiltrated the city, the acquisition of wealth brought with it greed and meanness, while its use and enjoyment brought luxury, effeminacy, and extravagance: so Sparta lost most of what was good, and suffered a time of unworthy humiliation" (*Agis/Cleomenes* 3.1).

The ancestral lots had become concentrated in the hands of perhaps 100 of the rich, and poverty became rife (5, 24.1, 31.7). Worse, the wealth had become concentrated in the hands of women (esp. 7.4–6): so, in a new step from *Lycurgus*, wealth becomes feminized. Indeed, the women of the royal house become key players, both for their wealth and for their willingness to be persuaded by the idealistic Agis (4.1, 7) and to persuade the young Cleomenes (22, 27.1–2, 28.1), finally for their exemplary behavior in crisis and in death (17, 20, 43–44, 50, 59).[15] (Eckart Schütrumpf has brought out that the presentation here owes a good deal to Plato,[16] and also to Book 2 of Aristotle's *Politics*, emphasizing the effect both of family

---

[14] Both *Lycurgus* and *Lysander* put stress on the theme not merely of wealth but also of coinage, and in *Lycurgus* this picks up on earlier themes, 9.2–5: it is the intrusion of coined money with Lysander that proves so disastrous. On this see Liebert (2016: 127–136). That theme is not absent from *Agis/Cleomenes* but comes in only incidentally (10.4). These *Lives* deal with the post-coinage world and are more concerned with the handling of the problem than with its genesis.

[15] On these women and Plutarch's presentation of them, see Powell (1999: esp. 397–401).

[16] Schütrumpf (1987) doubts the historicity of Epitadeus' rhetra (*Agis/Cleomenes* 5.3–7) for this reason. Schütrumpf throughout talks carefully of "Plutarch or his source" and ends (456–457) by speculating

lots passing to outsiders and of female wealth [1269b31–1270b6]: but
Aristotle had put in an important extra step, the resulting shortage of
manpower, *oliganthrōpia*, which Plutarch here ignores despite the obvious
thematic possibilities for the Gracchi comparison.) And in Plutarch wealth is
barbarized too:[17] one of the defenders of the new wealth-ridden order is
a certain Leonidas, who had picked up such decadent ways at the Eastern
courts of satraps and of Seleucus (3.9; cf. 7.2, 10.4, 11.6). Wealth is barbarized,
wealth is feminized (and one can trace both themes forward into *Cleomenes*
too): there are developments here of the idea of Sparta as a sort of "internal
Greek other," something that Paul Cartledge has analyzed interestingly for
Herodotus.[18] But there is more than one sort of "other"; Agis' program is to
confront this new Orientalized other with the older Lycurgan system, itself
so strange by normal Greek standards, and to turn the clock back.

  Even in *Agis/Cleomenes*, though, one can trace a more realistic strand as
well. Wealth may be the "imported curse of Sparta" (31.7; cf. *Lysander* 17.1),
but it is also very useful. It is in this *Life* that Plutarch elaborately expresses
his approval of the old proverb that "money is the sinews of affairs,"
especially in warfare (48). Cleomenes, never one to allow too many scruples
to stand in his way, knows how to offer money to Aratus to save
Acrocorinth (40.5), then to use Aratus' possessions politically too when
he takes Sicyon (40.7–9); just as Agis knew early on how to exploit the
wealth of the women in his family, not simply deride it (7.2–4). Still, even
if Cleomenes has something of the right realistic idea, he does not have
enough of it, and this is what finally allows Antigonus to defeat him at
Sellasia, "wearing down and outplaying Cleomenes, with his meagre and
barely adequate disbursement of wages to the mercenaries and supplies to
his citizens" (48.4). So it is eventually Cleomenes' *akhrēmatia*, the quality
of which he was so proud, that secures his defeat. It is a version of a familiar
Plutarchan schema, where the qualities that are a man's keynote, often his
strength, come round to destroy him: Coriolanus' unbendingness,
Antony's bonhomie, Caesar's friends, and here Cleomenes' attitude to
wealth. Sure enough, it is a bribed scout, one Damoteles, who sets up
Antigonus' victory (49.5); it is a gibe of Cleomenes at the court's luxurious

that this theme may be owed to Phylarchus, possibly drawing on the Stoic philosopher Sphaerus (cf.
*Agis/Cleomenes* 23.3: Sphaerus was Cleomenes' tutor). That may underestimate Plutarch's own
tendency to think in terms of *Republic* VIII–IX when dealing with constitutional change (Pelling
2014: 150–153); or, if Plutarch found a reference to Epitadeus in a source, we can at least see why he
would have found it natural to phrase the account in Platonic terms.
[17] There was already something of this in *Lysander* 6.8. Barbarizing and feminizing have a long classical
tradition of going together: Hall (1993), and more briefly (1989: 127, 209–210) and (1996: 13).
[18] Cartledge (1990; 1993).

lifestyle that triggers the move against him (56); and the final comeuppance is delivered by a Messenian exile who hates him because Cleomenes once bought his house but did not get around to paying him for it (56.2). Not everyone shares the king's own monetary insouciance.

Money, then, is a complicated theme in *Agis/Cleomenes*, and there has been a play between the idealized vision of the kings and the realities of the world in which they have to live. How will these complexities be revisited in *Gracchi*, and in the rough political world of Rome?

# IV

There are certainly some similarities in theme. In *Gracchi* too the women of the family are highlighted, and they are most laudable, especially the formidable Cornelia (1–2, 8.7, 25.3–6, 34.2, 40; also Licinia at 36).[19] Here too Eastern wealth becomes important, with the Pergamene legacy (14), and here too Oriental tastes become part of the rhetoric: the mudslinging optimates claim that Eudemus of Pergamum had given Tiberius "a diadem and some purple, as one who was going to be Rome's king" (14.3–4), then that Tiberius' gesture of scratching his head meant that he was "demanding a diadem" (19.3). Here too the support of the *dēmos* for its champions is critical in driving them on, but here too the *dēmos* becomes surly and fickle at the end (32.5, 37.7, 39.2–3). And there are certainly similarities in the predicament. At Rome too an initial public-minded gesture – the distribution of public land to the poor – had turned sour because the rich had been able to buy up the land (8.1–2). And in this case too it is put in financial terms: Tiberius' program is aimed at the "poor"; his opponents are, at least initially, the "rich" (8.4–5, etc.).

It is also arguable that Plutarch simplifies his source-material to make the themes even closer to those at Sparta, for he has played down a good deal of "Italian" material, so prominent in Appian, in order to present this as a particular problem for the urban *plebs*: so we have a clear contrast between rich and poor *citizens* in much the same way as we had in Sparta.[20] Tiberius' proposal is simplified to make it a stereotyped Greek *gēs anadasmos*, much more stereotyped and straightforward than it will be in Appian. But there is reason to think that Plutarch also knew of another stress that will be prominent in Appian, the drop in military manpower and Tiberius' concern to revive Italian *polyandria* (*BC* 1.7.28, 30, etc.). There is something of this in

---

[19]  Powell (1999: 399–401) again (above, n. 15) traces and discusses the importance of women in the pair.
[20]  Pelling (1986a: 170–171) = (2002: 215–216); esp. *Gracchi* 9.2.

Plutarch, enough to show that he knew the theme (8.4, *oligandria*; cf. 9.5), but distinctly less is made of it than in Appian. Yet there were evident possibilities here for developing this in comparison with the Spartan concern over *oliganthrōpia*; just as we saw Plutarch playing down the *oliganthrōpia* stress in *Agis/Cleomenes*, so he plays down the manpower element here.

There may be all sorts of reasons for this; one is, I think, Plutarch's tendency to collapse different types of conflict into a single, Greek-influenced pattern of *oligoi* against *dēmos*.[21] But one result of this simplification, whether or not it was a motive for it, is to make the wealth-theme and its moral implications more straightforwardly central to the *Life*. The law is aimed against "injustice and greed" (9.2); the opponents are avariciously selfish, and the Gracchi see the danger. We no longer need the further step in the argument of tracing the *pragmatic* reasons, the political and military ones, why some reform was a good idea.

All this makes it more interesting to see exactly how Plutarch treats this. The Gracchi do put their finger on a crucial problem; they may not get everything right – indeed, the book begins by stressing that they were carried away by ambition and went too far (*Agis/Cleomenes* 1–2; cf. *Praecepta gerendae reipublicae* 798F–799A)[22] – but there is no doubt that the rich are the ones who behave really badly. It is not difficult either to show that these *Lives* introduce themes that resonate through the rest of the republican *Lives* as well: the growth of violence, the bad behavior of the elite, the disaffection of the *dēmos*, and the unleashing of forces, especially the forces of the *dēmos*, that eventually even those who promote them cannot resist.[23]

So underlying a good deal of this is Plutarch's analysis of what is going wrong with Rome. In that case, what we might expect to find would be, again, a stress on the corrupting effect of wealth and luxury. It would have been so easy for Plutarch to tie the bad behavior of the rich into the familiar Roman theme of the disastrous impact of wealth. Private greed causes the problem; the influx of wealth and luxury makes it worse; then it is eventually the people's greed as well, and the immoral readiness of the rich to pander to that greed, that renders them bribable, and so things go further downhill. It is all very familiar, and it is what Sallust, for instance, would have said (partly, indeed, what he did say[24]). But it is not what

---

[21] As I argued in Pelling (1986a).

[22] On Plutarch's opinions about the Gracchi, cf. Sion-Jenkis (2000: 66 and n. 11), rightly distinguishing between admiration for the men and reservations about the program.

[23] Pelling (2011a: 34–35).

[24] But only partly. Sallust certainly stresses the catastrophic effect of Eastern wealth, the way the upper classes set the pattern, and the way in which soldiers and commons fell into that pattern themselves,

Plutarch says. Despite the setting up of the wealth-theme at the beginning
(and in *Agis/Cleomenes*) and despite that emphasis on "the rich," he is
strikingly reluctant to talk clearly of "bribery" when either Gaius Gracchus
or Livius Drusus turns to the *dēmos*, or even when he is dealing with the
problems they were facing. It is quite an achievement, for instance, to
explain the reasons for reforming the law-courts without mentioning
bribery at all (*Gracchi* 26[5].2–4); when the trial for Scipio's murder is
foiled, it is again violence rather than corruption that is in point (31[10].5–
6). One way or another, there is much more talk of bribery in Appian.[25]
Where riches become relevant in Plutarch's comparative epilogue, it is not
in any large worldview of what is happening to Sparta or to Rome: it is in
a more personal register, the stern determination of the men to forgo any
possibility of personal gain (*Comparatio Agis/Cleomenes-Gracchi* 1.6), so
different from those excesses of the "rich" opponents. Notice, too, the play
on the famous proverb "love of riches, nothing else, will destroy Sparta"
(above, p. 248) when "an excess of ambition, nothing else" is the disastrous
flaw of the Gracchi (5.5). The allusion is neat, but it also reflects the way in
which the *philokhrēmatia* theme is not, or is no longer, what it is all about.

# V

Here we have two points that are true not merely of the *Gracchi* but across
the *Lives* more generally. First, Plutarch is often strangely mealy-mouthed
about bribery and peculation in Rome, tending to avoid the d-words
(*dōrodokia* and *dekazesthai*) and the k-word (*klopē*). This is not because
he is naïve: there are times when he shows himself all too aware of what was
going on.[26] Why, he asks in *Coriolanus*, did the Romans insist on candidates coming down to the forum ungirt? It was not because they suspected
that they might be intending to disburse money; no,

> it was only at a late stage that buying and selling came in and money became
> mixed up with the voting in assembly; then it spread to jurors and armies,

but greed comes into the patterning more with the soldiers than with the commons: *BJ* 41–2, *BC* 10–
13 and 37–38, and *Hist.* frs. 11–13 and 16 Maurenbrecher. In the case of the commons, the emphasis
falls more on the way that they responded in kind to the elite's partisanship and violence.
[25] Thus for Appian the corn-legislation is one thing that renders the people *emmisthos* (*BC* 1.22.91);
there is a lot more talk too of the bribery that typified the law-courts; 1.22.92, 96–97.
[26] Other cases where Plutarch shows himself aware of the levels of corruption: *Sulla* 8.2, *Comparatio
Lysander-Sulla* 1.4, *Brutus* 22.3, 23.1, 39.1, *Cato Minor* 30.7, 35.6, 42.5, 43.7, 44, 47.1, 48.5–6, *Cicero*
29.7–8, and the passages in *Pompey* discussed later. Few of these tell directly to the disadvantage of
the main figure: notice the frequency of cases in *Cato Minor*, dealing with the stern *opponent* of
bribery. Cf. Desideri (1985: 397, 404 n. 68).

and bribery (*dōrodokia*) moved the city to monarchy, enslaving arms to cash. That person was right, whoever it was, who said that the first person to destroy democracy was the first to give banquets and bribes to the people. It appears that the evil crept in secretly and gradually, and was not immediately clear. (*Coriolanus* 14.3–4)

Not, it seems, the words of someone who is underplaying either the extent or the significance of bribery in the late Republic; and the same goes for such passages as *Caesar* 28.4–6, characterizing the *kakopoliteia* of the 50s:

It had reached the stage that candidates for office would set out their banking-tables in public and offer bribes shamelessly to the common people; the voters had been purchased before they came to the forum, and they gave their support not with their votes, but with their arrows and swords and slings. . . . Where would all this crazy turbulence end? Sensible people would be thankful if the outcome were monarchy, and nothing worse. Indeed, by now there were many who were ready to say in public that the state could only be cured by a monarchy, and the right thing to do was to take the remedy from the gentlest of the doctors who were offering it – meaning Pompey. (*Caesar* 28.4–6)[27]

Yet so many passages are indeed mealy-mouthed. Plutarch brings out that Caesar was deeply in debt before he became consul (*Caesar* 5.8–9). He knows too that this money was needed for elections: on the morning of the pontifical elections he tells his mother that "today you will see me either a high priest, or as an exile" (7.3–4). But he leaves it vague why all that money was wanted, vaguer than Suetonius (*Div. Iul.* 13, "not without the most extravagant largesse") and Cassius Dio (37.37.1–3, moralizing angrily about Caesar's tactics). Plutarch more usually speaks generally of "courting" the demos (*therapeuein*) or "fostering" or "taking them up" (*analambanein*), and when we can pin him down he seems to be thinking more of games and banquets and doles rather than upfront bribery (e.g. *Caesar* 4.5, 5.8–9, 57.8). Not that he approves very much of banquets and doles, but at least the indignation can take a milder form.

Why? Perhaps we should appeal to Plutarch's own historical principles, as he sets them out in *De Herodoti malignitate* (855B–856D, esp. 855B, 855E–856C): give your subject the benefit of the doubt, don't use harsher words when mild ones will do. We should still have to explain the strength of language in passages like those from *Coriolanus* and *Caesar*, but in neither of those passages is he complaining about the behavior of the men themselves: such conduct is a world away from anything Coriolanus

---

[27] On this passage, see also Pelling (2011a: 277–279).

will do, and anyway things have not got that bad yet; even in Caesar's case he is talking of the general malaise in Rome. That malaise requires a stern doctor, either Pompey as here or more usually Caesar himself (*Comparatio Dion-Brutus* 2.2, *Antony* 6.7, Pompey at *Pompey* 55.4), and Caesar becomes part of the remedy rather than the disease. So the mealy-mouthedness can still be made to fit the precepts of *De Herodoti malignitate*: don't use strong language when it tells to your man's discredit, but by all means use it when it points the crisis that your man has got to meet. Besides satisfying Plutarch's own historical conscience, it has the further advantage that it frees him to make different points. He wants to do more interesting things with Caesar and Pompey, not simply denounce them.

There is a wider point too, the second that we may generalize from the *Gracchi*. Despite Plutarch's intermittent readiness to idealize the distant past, he is reluctant to echo that "disastrous effect of foreign wealth" theme *at Rome*: at Sparta, as we have seen, things are different. So that is again the point the statistics suggested: he is far more ready to make such points about Sparta when we might expect them to be made about Rome. It is time, once again, to ask why, and look for an explanation that focuses on wealth and luxury in particular rather than Rome in general.

Part of the reason may be because the idea had traditionally become interwoven with a further anti-Hellenic and anti-cultural *topos*. The influx of wealth and growth of luxury could so easily be equated with the arrival of Greek statues and works of art and general intellectualism. Unsurprisingly, this is not Plutarch's way of looking at things.[28] He feels that Rome ought to have learnt a good deal more from Greece, and several of his military men, especially Coriolanus and Marius, would have done a good deal better if they had had the advantages of a Greek education (*Coriolanus* 1, *Marius* 2.3–4). The elder Cato is criticized strongly for the view that Greek influences would be so disastrous to Rome: "Time shows that he was wrong; for the time of Rome's greatest achievements was the time when it was most ready to welcome Greek studies and Greek culture" (*Cato Maior* 23.3, with interesting past tenses).

The nearest Plutarch gets to that theme of Eastern decadence is in two cases: first, *Marcellus*, where he catalogs the criticisms of Marcellus for bringing back the treasures of Syracuse: he was corrupting the Roman *dēmos*, turning them from farming and warfare to luxury and idleness, so that they spend most of the day discussing art and artists (*Marcellus* 21.6). That is hardly strong language, and a large part of Plutarch's sensibilities will surely have been on

---

[28] On this and what follows, Pelling (1986a: 185–187) = (2002: 224–225); Swain (1990a: 126–128).

Marcellus' side. He is civilizing these people more than he is corrupting them.[29]

Secondly, and more elaborately, *Sulla*, where a long passage dwells on the wealth that accrued from Sulla's conquests and its effect at Rome (ch. 12). One again thinks immediately of Sallust (*BC* 11). Yet in Plutarch it is not the case, as in Sallust, that Eastern experiences corrupt Roman tastes, instilling a taste for the easy life. The soldiers' taste for the easy life is there already, and all Greece does is offer an opportunity for the ruthless, self-interested generals to satisfy it. The relevant wealth comes from Greece, not from Asia, so for Plutarch it is not so barbarized; and it comes from the shrines that Sulla ransacked. All the blame falls on the Romans themselves; there was nothing wrong with the wealth in itself, certainly not when it was in the shrines. Not merely is this a different emphasis from Sallust, it is also different from that in the paired *Life of Lysander*, where it was indeed foreign wealth in itself that caused the problems. So we may have been set up here to expect the usual Roman *topos*, but we get it in a strikingly offkey way, and one that is much less derogatory about the wealth itself and the places it comes from.

We have also moved even further from that first-bid idea that Plutarch might be reluctant to be rude about the all-conquering Romans. It is just that their vices come from their own greed, and not from any sort of Eastern influence. They do not need any help along the decadent road.

## VI

In our last example, *Agesilaus–Pompey*, we see something of the same, except that the tuning is even more offkey. Certainly, moral decline plays a part in *Pompey*. That is clearest in the scene on the battlefield of Pharsalus on the evening after the battle (72.4–6). The victorious Caesar arrives in Pompey's camp, and is amazed by the luxury he sees: tents garlanded with myrtle, flower-strewn couches, tables brimming with goblets. No wonder the tough military man and his troops had won, hardened by all that fighting in Gaul and then in Spain. The intertextual suggestion of the similar scene after Plataea in 479 BCE is also hard to avoid (Herodotus 9.82).[30] Pompey and his aristocratic staff have come to play the role of Herodotus' luxurious Persians: that marks them as the losers, just as certainly as Antony and Cleopatra would be the Orientalized losers

---

[29] On this theme in *Marcellus*, see also Pelling (1989: 199–208, esp. 201–202); Swain (1990a: 140–141).

[30] Cf. Rossi (2000) on the original account of Caesar himself, *BC* 3.96, and Zadorojnyi (2012: 193–198).

seventeen years later. But so far there is no Eastern Cleopatra to do the corrupting. Just as in *Sulla*, the Roman elite has corrupted itself.

We have already heard something more elaborate about how and where Rome had gone wrong, and we heard it earlier on this same day. Before the armies clashed, some wise spectators had mused on the self-destruction of it all, spectators who include not merely "the best of the Romans" but also "some Greeks who were present as bystanders"; and Plutarch's Greeks may well know a lot about self-destruction, given that Greece itself had managed it pretty well.[31] Wealth certainly plays a part in those musings, as they reflect on

> the pitch to which greed and rivalry had brought the empire . . . . There were great tasks left to be fulfilled, Scythia and India, and greed even found a reasonable pretext there in civilizing the barbarian world: for what Scythian cavalry or Parthian bowmanship or Indian wealth could have checked seventy thousand Romans, advancing on them with Pompey and Caesar at their head? (*Pompey* 70.1, 4–5)

The Greek pair *Agesilaus* too had played with moral decline and linked it with wealth. That *Life* also developed many of the themes we have seen in *Agis/Cleomenes* and in *Lysander*, wealth as barbarized and Eastern (8.3, 10.6, 14.4, 23.1), an awareness of things going downhill at Sparta, and a picture of Agesilaus as an exception to the trend: in some ways it is more complex than in the other *Lives*, as Agesilaus' own personal life is more complex,[32] but at least in this traditional Spartan superiority to wealth Agesilaus comes out well (4.1, 10.7, 14.1–4, 20.1, 36.9–10). And here too the idealizing picture is moderated by Agesilaus' own shrewd awareness of the need to accommodate to the real world, especially when wealth is needed for warfare, even if it is just to keep his soldiers sweet: this is a man who "takes greater pleasure in making his soldiers rich than himself" (10.7; cf. e.g. 9.4–5, 11.1, 35.6, 36.6, *Comparatio Agesilaus-Pompey* 5.1).

*Pompey* initially looks as if it will develop a similar portrayal, with Pompey as the man who is superior to wealth. That is the point of contrast to his father in the first chapter ("There was only one cause of the hatred men felt

---

[31] Cf. especially *Flamininus* 11, *Agesilaus* 15.3–4, *Timoleon* 29.6, *De Pythiae oraculis* 401C–D. The musings in this passage have much in common with those at Appian, *BC* 2.77.320–4 and may well go back to Asinius Pollio, but Appian puts them in the minds of Caesar and Pompey themselves. One suspects that these Greek observers are an imaginative addition of Plutarch's own.

[32] 11.9 brings that out particularly well, where the punchline to the story of Spithridates and the kiss is "I rather think I would prefer to fight again that battle of the kiss rather than have all the gold I have viewed." That is not an unequivocally favorable anecdote, the moral issue being one of self-control rather than homosexuality; but it is not *wealth* that is Agesilaus' problem, if problem there is.

for the father, his insatiable lust for money, but there were many reasons for the son's popularity," 1.4). Again, as in *Agis/Cleomenes–Gracchi*, one point of contact between *Agesilaus* and *Pompey* is the influx of riches from the East (32.8, 35.4, 36.7, and esp. 45.4). So far, so symmetrical. But by the second half of *Pompey* it has all become more complicated. The Eastern riches have come; as we have seen, the effect of wealth on Rome itself becomes a theme; but the most interesting aspect is the way Pompey deals with it, or rather fails to. When he tries some sort of "corruption" or "bribery" – both metaphors are used – he gets it quite wrong: he tries to entice Cato with the offer of a marriage-alliance, and Cato turns him down flat (44.3). Immediately afterwards Pompey tries some further bribery to get Afranius elected consul; that is cack-handed too, going down badly with the public and affording Cato the opportunity for a smug told-you-so to his female relatives (44.4–6). More often it is his inaction rather than his action that is stressed. "When he saw the maladministration of the city magistrates and the bribery of the citizens, he *allowed anarchy to develop in the city*," he let it happen (54.3).[33] He is caught in a thematic crossfire: wealth is affecting everything all around him, and there is not much that he can do about it. When he is chosen to stem that anarchy and that bribery (54, 55.6), he does have some success, but it is qualified and temporary (55.6–11).

Wealth comes out in a different way with Lucullus and his retirement; Pompey is certainly contrasted with him there, but even the sluggish Lucullus manages to cause him embarrassment and drives him crucially and shamefully into the arms of Clodius (46.5–8). Another development is Caesar using his own wealth so shrewdly for widespread corruption, and thereby outmaneuvering him (46.4, 51.3, 56.4, 58.1–3). Pompey is very much the dumb partner in both those internal *synkriseis*, a man who is driven rather than drives. Pompey is out of his depth in a world managed by those who outdo him either in street-wisdom (Caesar) or on the high moral ground (Cato). He can manage them as little as he can manage the grandees who are responsible for all that luxury in his camp, and who, with their eye firmly on their projected postwar gains, bully him into adopting the wrong strategy (66.2–5, 67.4–7; cf. *Caesar* 41–42).

There are a lot of narrative themes being developed here, but Pompey himself is not directing any of them. That reflects the wider sense in which he is unable himself to grab his own *Life*'s narrative by the scruff of the neck and be himself the driving force. It is as if he finds himself in other people's movies.

---

[33] This is in line with his general policy of wanting to seem insouciant and turn a blind eye (54.2) to what was happening: on this, see Pelling (1980: 131–132) = (2002: 96–98).

## VII

What may we conclude?

1.  It may well be right to think of Plutarch as building the entire scheme of *Lives* as at least to some degree a unit, as Plutarch builds a big, comparative exercise not merely of individuals but of the Greek and Roman worlds.[34] Sparta is certainly an area where some themes come back non-coincidentally in a series of different *Lives*, and wealth and luxury are recurrently thematized both for their dangers and for the efforts to confront them.[35] But that unified vision of a whole series need not mean that Plutarch always says exactly the same thing; the variety of voices is also still important, especially when it comes to any idealizing picture of primeval simplicity. When Plutarch comes to the rough and tumble of the late Republic, he can still doubtless think that simple, equalized wealth and a non-acquisitive culture would be better – but it would be a bore if he kept on saying so. He usually finds rather more interesting things to do with his heroes than that, and for instance in *Agesilaus–Pompey* there are those unexpected twists and tweaks in the way he presents wealth.

2.  We have seen some ways in which a comparison between Sparta and Rome underlies several different pairs, together with the moral decline that wealth gives. The strategy of parallelism may be allowing him to make tactful and oblique suggestions here about Roman luxury, just as he does about Roman militarism. But that comparison does not always come out in the form we expect. In particular, we have seen several things that Plutarch does not say, even though we might have expected him to. Wealth is not simply corrupting at Rome, even though it might have been at Sparta; and the association with other vital themes of Greek identity (or at least Roman projections of Greek identity) may explain why. He is often mealy-mouthed about bribery and peculation, too, at least when that would redound to the discredit of his principal subjects.

3.  Still, Plutarch is all too aware that wealth *can* corrupt; his Spartan *Lives* make that plain; and many incidental characters get corrupted along the way – the friends of Alexander, the grandees and the troops whom Caesar pays so well (*Alexander* 41.3, *Caesar* 29.3–5, etc.). That makes it all the more striking that it is so seldom the *subjects* of the *Lives*

---

[34] The "to some degree" should be stressed: for fuller discussion, see Pelling (2010).
[35] On this, see the papers in Davies and Mossman (forthcoming in 2023).

themselves who get corrupted, even when their experiences might seem to offer prize instances of the excesses of the rich. That is not the way Plutarch does Antony, nor the way he does Crassus, nor even the way he does Lucullus, disapprove though he might of the man's final descent into decadence. In each case he finds something else to do, some way of linking the excesses to other, pre-wealth flaws or characteristics of the man: and that is especially interesting in the case of Lucullus, for even the final excesses are there linked with his earlier and wholly creditable taste for Greek culture (*Lucullus* 1.6),[36] and the denunciation is not wholly unrelieved. We might again stress the generosity that is a feature of the historiographic principles of *De Herodoti malignitate*; we might find a sidelight here too on the way in which Plutarch views character-change; we might certainly see a typically Plutarchan close linkage of a figure's strengths and vulnerabilities. I should myself again stress the way that Plutarch tends to find more interesting things to say about his figures than simply the *topos* of corrupting wealth. This chapter has shown what a variety – a wealth, even – of ideas he has in his characterizing repertoire.[37]

## Further Reading

Except for Desideri (1985), Plutarch's treatment of wealth has attracted little detailed attention. Various cases in the *Lives* are collected and discussed by Wardman (1974: 79–86); his emphasis falls on the good use of wealth, especially for the benefits of the community, and the need to regard it as a means rather than an end. Similar themes emerge in Frazier (1996: 149–156), who gives particular attention to the issues raised by wealth at Sparta and at Rome. The association of excessive wealth with barbarians is explored in Schmidt (1999: 107–139). Tröster (2008: 48–76) discusses the treatment of luxury (*tryphē*) in *Lucullus*. *Agis–Cleomenes–Gracchi* has been the subject of several treatments (Roskam 2011a; De Pourcq and Roskam 2016; Pelling in press), and so has *Agesilaus–Pompey* (Hillman 1994; Trego 2012–13; Nevin 2014).

---

[36] Admittedly, Plutarch treads very carefully in those final chapters, and the worst aspects appear as "barbarian" (41.7) rather than Hellenic: Tröster (2008: 28–33, 56–58).
[37] Some parts of this chapter rework a paper referred to as "forthcoming (b)" in Pelling (2002a) but long abandoned. Others have their origin in the Helen North Memorial Lecture, which I had the honor of giving in Swarthmore in March 2014 after a preliminary airing in Leiden the previous November.

From the more panoramic discussions of wealth in antiquity, Gorman and Gorman (2014) give a synoptic discussion of *tryphē* in Greek literature. Edwards (1993) explores the Romans' own taste for denouncing luxury. Wallace-Hadrill (2008: ch. 7) subtly shows how luxury objects became "an important way of talking about Roman society," with its various anxieties and tensions. The most extraordinary ancient collection of relevant material is that of Athenaeus in Book 12, well discussed by Lenfant (2007) and by Gorman and Gorman (2007; 2014: ch. 3).

CHAPTER 13

# Plutarch and the Barbarian "Other"

## Eran Almagor

Greek preoccupation with the traditional ethnic and cultural "others," namely the barbarians,[1] does not disappear in imperial literature. On the contrary, it is still a prevalent theme and a constant concern.[2] It is not surprising, therefore, to find numerous references to the barbarians in Plutarch's wide-ranging corpus.[3] Although the only Plutarchan title that explicitly mentions barbarians is the lost work *Quaestiones barbaricae* (*Aitiai barbarikai*, no. 139 in the Lamprias Catalogue),[4] they figure prominently in his writings. Not only in the Greek biographies, such as *Themistocles* (1.4; cf. 3.4), *Cimon* (1.2), *Lysander* (3.2), or *Timoleon* (1.3), but also in the Roman ones (*Sertorius* 1.10, *Aemilius Paulus* 4.2; *Marcellus* 4.6), barbarian ethico-political "otherness" is introduced early on, preparing the reader for a major clash involving Eastern or Western nations. However, while barbarians do appear in Plutarch as the traditionally stereotyped and denigrated "others" of classical literature, providing a cultural and ethical matrix that continues to generate the sense of Greek identity, they also have other roles to play, which reflect the more specifically Plutarchan agendas. Thus, on the one hand, it would seem that Plutarch's access to the barbarians in the imperial age is circumscribed both by Roman political contexts wherein the Greeks are merely passive participants and by memories of old Hellenic valor that is filtered only through texts and oratory. Yet Plutarch can also use barbarians artistically to create an intricate and nuanced portrait of the hero, making them a means of characterization as well as being

---

[1] Standard studies on the concept and image of *barbaros* are Wilken (1906); Jüthner (1923); Opelt and Speyer (1967); Funck (1981); Lévy (1984); Hall (1989); Hall (1997: esp. 44–47).

[2] Cf. Livy 31.29.15, Philostratus, *VS* 553, with Whitmarsh (2001: 105–108; 2005: 35); Pausanias 10.19.5, with Jones (2004: 17–18). On the barbarians and Greek identity in Strabo, see Almagor (2005). On the importance of barbarians in the Second Sophistic period, see, for example, Anderson (1993: 101–133); Gleason (1995: 142–144); Swain (1996: 68, 78, 87–89); Saïd (2001: 286–295); Holmes (2008: 93, 96, 100–101); Fontanella (2008: 207, 213); Schmidt (2011).

[3] The most comprehensive discussion to date is Schmidt (1999); see also Nikolaidis (1986); Mayer (1997); Pelegrín Campo (1997); Strobach (1997: 47–54, 115–141, 142–170); Brenk (2005); Schmidt (2002; 2004).

[4] On which see Jones (1971: 124–125); for speculation about its contents, see Schmidt (2008).

part of the plot. This chapter explores, first, the collective profile of barbarians in Plutarch's works; second, his play with the established stereotypes, employed to characterize the protagonists in the *Lives*; third, Plutarch's oscillation between a twofold (barbarian vs. Greek/Roman) and threefold (Greek vs. Roman vs. barbarian) ethnic taxonomic schemes, and the subtle moral and political implications thereof, as shown through the example of the Persians; fourth, the complexities of cultural confrontation and hybridity; and finally, the "deep," all but allegorical role of barbarians in Plutarch's ethico-political cogitation. Given the vastness of the theme, only a general overview and several examples are presented.

The important studies of Nikolaidis (1986) and Schmidt (1999) have demonstrated that, to a large degree, Plutarch's portrayal of the barbarians follows the classical Greek stereotypes, in effect representing non-Greek individuals and ethnic communities as stock figures. Overall, the negative as well as positive traits of barbarians found in Plutarch's works reflect the two clichés of the barbarian in classical literature; that is, overly (decadently) refined or exceedingly wild. This corresponds to Aristotle's succinct and well-known classification of barbarians into two types (*Pol.* 7.1327b18–38; cf. *De aër. aqu. et loc.* 22–23). The tribes living in the cold climate of Europe are full of spirit and therefore remain free. However, lacking in understanding and skill, and bereft of political organization, they are incapable of ruling over others. Conversely, the population of Asia is intelligent but wanting in spirit, and hence is always in a state of subjection and slavery. The Greeks, situated geographically between them, are also intermediate in character, avoiding excess and combining the good features of both types – something the barbarians could never do (*Pol.* 7.1327b29–33).[5] Aptly, Plutarch would normally characterize the Western and Northern nations as possessing courage, audaciousness (*thrasytēs*), and boldness (*thymos*)[6] that knows no bounds, while it is mostly Eastern groups that are depicted as holding back because of their softness (*malakia*).[7]

---

[5] This image of Greece as positioned between uncivilized and lawless nations of Europe and the overrefined, soft peoples of Asia is not a simple binary picture, as one might infer from the discussion of Greek Orientalism: cf. Said (1978: 2–3, 21, 56, 97); Hall (1989: 99–100). It also betrays attributes of what may be termed a rudimentary *occidentalist* prejudice. See Schmidt (2004: 228) and later in this chapter on the lack of discipline among the Western tribes. This complex picture was adapted in imperial times to accommodate Rome: Vitruvius 6.1.10–11.

[6] *Marius* 11.13, 16.5, 19.4, 9, 23.3, 7; *Caesar* 18.1, 19.6–7, 24.5–7; *Camillus* 23.1, 36.3; *Crassus* 9.8, 25.8; *Sertorius* 16.1–2, 9–11. Examples from the East are remarkably fewer: *Aristides* 14.5 (~ Herodotus 9.20), 18.3–4 (~ Herodotus 9.62); *Crassus* 23.2, 27.1; *Lucullus* 21.2, 5–6, 26.6; and, of course, *thymos* is regularly ascribed to Greeks and Romans as well. Cf. n. 23 in this chapter; Schmidt (1999: 69–104, 240–244).

[7] *Lucullus* 11.7–8, 25.5, 28.5–6, 31.7–8, 36.7; *Cimon* 12.7; *Themistocles* 16.6; *Aristides* 10.1, 16.4–5; *Alexander* 33.8, 63.4–5. See Schmidt (1999: 212–219); Almagor (2017b: 133).

The aforementioned two studies (in particular that of Schmidt) outline an elaborate system of rhetorical antitheses by which Plutarch contrasts Greek virtues and barbarian vices. For instance, typical of barbarians are the traits of *agrios/agriotēs* (savage/savagery),[8] *thēriōdēs* (bestial),[9] *ōmos/ōmotēs* (cruel/cruelty)[10] – which also includes harsh treatment of defeated enemies[11] or mutilation of bodies – and lawlessness (*anomia*).[12] By contrast, to the Greeks are attributed features of *dikaiosynē* (justice),[13] *nomimos* (being lawful),[14] *praos/praotēs* (gentleness, mildness), and *philanthrōpia* (humaneness, clemency).[15] Typically, civilization/civility (*hēmeros* and cognates) properly belong to the Greeks (*Timoleon* 35.1–4; *De Alex. fort.* 328A–329A) and Romans.[16] Though not exclusively barbarian, the vices of *tolmē* (audacity, rashness)[17] and *hybris* (insolence, impudence)[18] are associated with them, as well as *thrasos/thrasytēs* (overconfidence)[19] and *phronēma* (arrogance).[20] Barbarians characteristically lack discipline[21] and are clamorous.[22] Unlike them, the Greeks display courageous valor (*thymos*

---

[8] *Cato Minor* 63.6; *De fortuna Romanorum* 320C; *De genio Socratis* 578D; *De vitando aere alieno* 828F; *De Stoicorum repugnantiis* 1049B; *De communibus notitiis adversus Stoicos* 1075A. See Nikolaidis (1986: 241–242); Schmidt (1999: 36–45).

[9] *Sertorius* 14.1; *Aemilius Paulus* 20.4; *Marius* 6.2; *Artaxerxes* 19.7; *De superstitione* 170C; *De Alexandri magni fortuna aut virtute* 328E; cf. *Quaestiones convivales* 7.4, 703D–E. See Schmidt (1999: 29–35). Cf. *Pompey* 12.7–8, 51.2. Greekness contrasted with bestiality: *Non posse suaviter vivi secundum Epicurum* 1099B.

[10] *Crassus* 26.4–7; *Artaxerxes* 18.4, 30.3.

[11] Chasing and killing men on the run is explicitly said to be neither noble nor Greek (*Apophthegmata Laconica* 228F); compare the Achaean treatment of the Mantineans (*Aratus* 45.6).

[12] Cf. *De Alexandri magni fortuna aut virtute* 328B; *Dion* 35.3; *De Herodoti malignitate* 866F–867B (~ Herodotus 7.238); *Crassus* 33.7. Cf. Nikolaidis (1986: 234 n. 23, 235 n. 28). See Schmidt (2004: 228–229).

[13] For example, *Aristides* 6.1; *Agesilaus* 15.5.

[14] Cf. Nikolaidis (1986: 240 n. 46); *Pelopidas* 26.3; *Phocion* 29.5; *Comparatio Lysander–Sulla* 2.1.

[15] For example, *Marcellus* 3.6; *Philopoemen* 8.1; *Flamininus* 5.7; *Lysander* 27.7; *Pyrrhus* 1.4; *De sollertia animalium* 964A; see Hirzel (1912: 23–32); Martin (1961: 167, 175); de Romilly (1979: 279, 299, 303–305); Nikolaidis (1986: 239–240); Schmidt (1999: 53–65); traits opposed to *agrios* (in animals): *Quaestiones convivales* 8.7, 727C; *Pompey* 28.5; *An seni respublica gerenda sit* 787C.

[16] *Pompey* 33.2; *Cato Minor* 63.6; see de Romilly (1979: 280, 304).

[17] Not always negative; cf. *Alexander* 58.2; *Themistocles* 8.1; *Marius* 20.10. See Schmidt (1999: 170–172 and 70–72).

[18] *De vitando aere alieno* 828F; cf. *Eumenes* 6.3; *Lucullus* 35.6; *Lysander* 6.6–8 (~ Xenophon, *Hell.* 1.6.6–7); *Pompey* 24.11–13.

[19] *De defectu oraculorum* 418E; *Quomodo adolescens poetas audire debeat* 29D-F (Trojans as barbarians); Frazier (1996: 200–207). Cf. *Crassus* 27.1.

[20] *Lucullus* 21.3; *Cimon* 12.1; *Comparatio Cimon–Lucullus* 3.4; *Fabius Maximus* 27.1; though this word and its cognates could have a positive sense as well, for instance when said of Cyrus the Great: *De Alexandri magni fortuna aut virtute* 343A; *De Herodoti malignitate* 858D.

[21] Cf. *Sulla* 16.6–7; *Marcellus* 10.1; *Camillus* 41.6.

[22] Cf. *Dion* 30.6; *Marius* 15.6, 19.4. See Schmidt (1999: 29–30, 46–47, 87–89, 157–159).

and *aretē*),[23] skill and ability,[24] foresight and disciplined silence.[25] Plutarch also ascribes to the barbarians the unflattering traits of *mokhthēria* (baseness),[26] *ponēria* (wickedness),[27] *apistia* and *apatē* (treachery, duplicity, deceit),[28] *anandria* (cowardice),[29] and *zēlotypia* (jealousy).[30] One distinguishing feature of the barbarians is their excess in wealth,[31] set against the Greek virtue of simplicity.[32] Barbarians practice human sacrifice and have many superstitious religious beliefs (*deisidaimonia*),[33] while the Greeks have *eusebeia* (piousness).[34] Last but not least, barbarians tend to turn up in the text as immense multitudes.[35]

Still, it would be exaggerated to see this dichotomy as strict and watertight. Plutarch's barbarians may also have positive traits.[36] It is evident that he makes capital out of these stereotypes for the sake of biographical characterization. The negative features of the barbarians bring out the good qualities of the protagonist, while their positive traits, like martial valor, sometimes demonstrates the hero's unique virtue when he is able to

---

[23] *Dion* 30.6–10; cf. *Agesilaus* 18.4–5; *Apophthegmata Laconica* 225B–C; also *Aristides* 14.3–4 (~ Herodotus 9.20–22); see Schmidt (1999: 89–100).

[24] *Timoleon* 27.6 and cf. the parallel scene at *Aemilius Paulus* 4.3. See Schmidt (1999: 166–174).

[25] *Quomodo adolescens poetas audire debeat* 29D–F; *Pericles* 34.1. See Nikolaidis (1986: 232–233 and n. 16); Schmidt (1999: 157 n. 110). Cf. *De fraterno amore* 487C; *De cohibenda ira* 456A (Romans).

[26] *Mulierum virtutes* 246B; *Agesilaus* 10.5; *Artaxerxes* 24.9. Cf. pseudo-Plutarch, *De liberis educandis* 3F–4B. See Schmidt (1999: 213, 219–223, 234–237).

[27] Cf. *Lysander* 4.2; *Sulla* 24.3.

[28] *Marius* 10.3–6; *Sulla* 3.5; *De Alexandri magni fortuna aut virtute* 341E–F. Cf. *Timoleon* 11.1; *Pompey* 76.8; *Agesilaus* 9.3–4 (~ Xenophon, *Hell.* 3.4.5–12, *Ages.* 1.10–14); *Crassus* 21.1–9, 30.2–3; *Artaxerxes* 18.1. See Schmidt (1999: 203–212).

[29] *Aristides* 16.4–5; *De Alexandri magni fortuna aut virtute* 338E–F. Cf. the sentiment in *Cimon* 12.7; *Themisocles* 16.6 (~ *Aristides* 10.1 ~ Herodotus 8.110–120); *Lucullus* 36.6–7; *Crassus* 18.4. See also *Alexander* 63.4–5; *Alcibiades* 39.5–6; *Lucullus* 17.5, 25.5, 28.5–6, 31.7–8; *Comparatio Cimon–Lucullus* 3.2 (fleeing).

[30] *Themistocles* 26.4 (cf. *Artaxerxes* 27.1); cf. *Alexander* 9.5, 77.6; *Lucullus* 16.2; *De fortuna Romanorum* 324D; also *Themistocles* 31.2.

[31] Cf. *Cimon* 10.9; *Sulla* 16.4; *De Alexandri magni fortuna aut virtute* 342B. Western riches: *Marcellus* 8.1; *Caesar* 25.3.

[32] *Solon* 28.2–6. Spartan: *Apophthegmata Laconica* 214D–E; *Agesilaus* 14.4, 23.9; *De sera numinis vindicta* 558A. Cf. *Numa* 3.7–8 (Roman). Nikolaidis (1986: 237–238).

[33] See *Sertorius* 11.6; *De superstitione* 166A–B, 169C, 171B–C; *Caesar* 19.8; *Lucullus* 24.3; *De communibus notitiis adversus Stoicos* 1075A; *De Stoicorum repugnantiis* 1051E; cf. Nikolaidis (1986: 234–235); Pérez-Jiménez (1996); Schmidt (1999: 224–226, 229–234).

[34] *De superstitione* 166B.

[35] Cf. *Timoleon* 27.6; *Crassus* 18.3, 23.6; *Cimon* 12.8; *Agesilaus* 39.9; *Alexander* 60.10; *Caesar* 15.4, 26.4; *Lucullus* 25.1, 26.4; *Themistocles* 9.5; *Camillus* 15.2, 40.1; *Marius* 20.2; *Sertorius* 3.2.

[36] For example, *Lysander* 24.1; *Antony* 41.1–6; *Sertorius* 14.5–6; *Marius* 11.3; cf. *Caesar* 18.1; *Pyrrhus* 26.6; *Numa* 12.11; *Crassus* 8.3, 11.10, 21.6–9, 25.8; *Aristides* 5.4 (~Herodotus 6.111–113), 18.3–4 (~Herodotus 9.62); *Lucullus* 16.1–3; *Fabius Maximus* 15.2–4; *Flamininus* 21.1; *Alexander* 59.2–3, 64.1; *Septem Sapientium Convivium* 148C–D; also *Praecepta gerendae reipublicae* 821D–E. See later in this chapter and Schmidt (1999: 263–267, 294, 328).

surpass them.[37] A more complex character in terms of ethno-ethical qualities is the Persian King Artaxerxes II Mnemon. In fact, the Persians are generally a kind of special case in classical literature in that both "archetypes" of barbarity mentioned earlier (i.e. boldness and softness) are applied to the Persians: often presented as submissive slaves, they may at the same time be viewed as uninhibited – a feature that climaxes in the figure of their master, the Great King.[38] For the Greeks, a time-honored rhetorical or philosophical compromise to accommodate such contradictory stereotypes[39] is to insist on the decadence and decline of the Persian kingdom,[40] or to explain them as the enslaving effects of unconstrained luxury.[41] Plutarch skillfully combines these two familiar solutions in his *Artaxerxes*. While the king is unreserved in his murderously violent conduct (*Artaxerxes* 25.3, 29.11), anger (16.1, 29.11), cruelty (14.9, 16.3–7, 17.7, 19.9, 30.3), and unbridled sexual behavior (23.5, 27.2), his restrained side can be seen in scenes where he is hesitant and kind-hearted (4.4), when he humbly prostrates himself (twice: before Hera, 23.7 and the sun, 29.12), and when he is willing to endure toil – notably when he steps down from his horse and undergoes hardships like an ordinary disciplined soldier (24.10–11).[42]

Given such ingenious play on ethnic stereotypes,[43] the character of Plutarchan Greek and Roman heroes engaged with barbarians becomes increasingly harder to pin down – just like the barbarian nature itself. For example, Sertorius is reported to have armed his Iberian followers and

---

[37] Function of negative traits: Schmidt (2002: 58); cf. Hood (1967: 14–15, 16, 18, 34, 87, 99, 136, 148); positive features: Schmidt (1999: 144); Hood (1967: 30, 36). See also Beck's Chapter 10 in this volume.

[38] See Hall (1989: 80) on "hierarchicalism" and "immoderate luxuriousness and unrestrained emotionalism," respectively. On the licentiousness of the Great King, evidenced by his luxury, see Herodotus 1.188; Xenophon, *Ages.* 9.3; Polyaenus 4.3.32; Athenaeus 4.144bc, 146c, 12.513ef, 514f, 528d, 539b, 545d–f; Curtius Rufus 3.3.17. See Briant (2002a: 286–297). Schmidt (2004: 229) lists as the negative components of barbarian monarchy in Plutarch "absence of law" and "absence of freedom," which are precisely the two stereotypes that contradict each other.

[39] Consider how in Aelian (*VH* 10.14) Socrates describes the Persians as idle and hence the most free (*sic!*), as opposed to the slavish Phrygians and Lydians.

[40] So Plato, *Laws* 3.693c–698a; Xenophon, *Cyr.* 8.8.15–16; Isocrates *Paneg.* 150–152. Cf. Briant (2002b: 193–196).

[41] So Isocrates, *Paneg.* 150–151. Cf. Briant (2002b: 197–198); Almagor (2017b: 133–134).

[42] Siding with either of the Greek stereotypes about the Persian national character, scholars have read Plutarch's portrayal of the king differently. Orsi (in Manfredini and Orsi 1987: xxvii–xxviii) stresses positive characterization focusing on chapter 24; Hood (1967: 68–85), on the other hand, emphasizes a negative image, based on chapter 25. Cf. Mossman (2010: 156–157) on chapter 24. Schmidt (1999: 318–324) advances a balanced approach; see further Almagor (2014a: 282–284; 2018: 29–30, 190).

[43] Cf. Almagor (2013).

changed their military habits by introducing fancy weapons and armor
decorated with gold and silver (*Sertorius* 14.2).[44] While instilling into them
advanced ways of warfare, Sertorius also ironically makes the Western
Iberians adopt features typical of the flamboyant, "decadently" Eastern
warriors; by contrast, Sertorius' ally Mithridates VI Eupator of Pontus
chooses at about the same time to do away with armor inlaid with gold and
precious stones, and fashions his swords in the Roman manner (*Lucullus*
7.5).[45] After Sertorius' death, contrary to what we are told earlier about the
Iberians' custom to die rather than survive their leader (*Sertorius* 14.5), his
troops surrender to Pompey and Metellus (27.1) – an act suggesting that
Sertorius may have over-orientalized them.[46] The change of the Iberians'
*ēthos* is paralleled by the unexpected description (*Sertorius* 10.5–7) of
Sertorius' own (reversed) change of *ēthos*, from mild to brutal.[47] This
transformation of Sertorius mirrors (and inverts) that which the hero
himself brings about in his foreign soldiers.

Doubtless, Plutarch works from a longstanding discursive tradition of
casting the Eastern barbarians as arch-enemies of Greece. His narratives
about Athenian and Spartan heroes and Alexander the Great go back to
a period when the clash with Persia and eventual Greek victory helped
create a Hellenic sense of shared belonging, essential to the process of
"inventing" Greekness itself.[48] As such, Plutarch's narratives tally with
nostalgia for the former glories of Hellas as seen in near-contemporary
declamations and texts of the Second Sophistic, where barbarians are
treated as that perpetual enemy against whom Greek affairs have been
conducted.[49] Plutarch's sustained interest in Persia from this angle is
patent. Eleven of the extant Greek *Lives* have confrontations with the
Persians as an integral part of their plots, or take place during an era

---

[44] Konrad (1994: 141).
[45] An acknowledgment of the superiority of the Roman army's organization, according to Schmidt (1999: 92).
[46] Compare the Characitani, who have become uncharacteristically afraid of war (*Sertorius* 17.4) – a trait we would expect to find in the East.
[47] See Russell (1966a: 146); Gill (1983: 478–479); Swain (1990a: 134); Konrad (1994: xxxvii, 119–122, 206–208).
[48] See Hall (1989: 57–62); cf. Cartledge (1993: 36–62); Nippel (2002: 288–293); Isaac (2004: 278–283). In fifth-century Athens, Persia was construed as a different, parallel universe, devoid of freedom or equal right of speech (*parrhēsia, isēgoria*) (cf. Herodotus 5.78, 7.101.3, 104.1, 105, 8.69.1) but kept in a state of natural slavery (Aeschylus, *Pers.* 50; Euripides, *Hel.* 276; Aristotle, *Pol.* 1.1252b7–9, 1254a15–20, 3.1285a20; Plutarch, *Ad principem ineruditum* 780C; cf. Hall 1989: 193–197), ruled by the arbitrary whims of one man, namely the Great King, and not by law (Aeschylus, *Pers.* 241–243 vs. 584–594; Herodotus 7.103.4, 104.4).
[49] See Bowie (1970: 7, 14, 27); Swain (1996: 95–96); Whitmarsh (2005: 68 n. 43); cf. Philostratus, *VS* 519–520, 541, 595.

when the Achaemenid Empire posed a threat to Greek liberty.[50] The unwritten *Leonidas* (*De Herodoti malignitate* 866B) should also be mentioned in this context,[51] as well as Plutarch's *Life* of Artaxerxes.[52] The use of a clear-cut differentiation of Hellenes and barbarians[53] in a period when ethnological taxonomies are more intricate and must include the Romans[54] bespeaks an effort to return to the bygone, glorious, and ideologically simple times. Similar nostalgia underwrites Plutarch's criticism of Medism (*Aristides* 13, 18.4–6) and his negativity about Persians of the Achaemenid era,[55] as well as his deprecating use of the term *barbaros* as reflected in the coined epithet *philobarbaros.*[56] The latter term is found in two Plutarchan passages, once to brand Herodotus for acquitting the Egyptian Busiris from the guilt of trying to sacrifice Heracles (*De Herodoti malignitate* 857A), and once applied to fate, which disfavored Alexander in his clash with the Achaemenids (*De Alexandri magni fortuna aut virtute* 344B).

Indeed, the complexity of ethnic designations during the Hellenistic period can be seen in the two declamatory essays on Alexander (in particular the first), which display both the universalist aspect of Greek *paideia* and its restricted, chauvinistic/racist features. This ambivalent presentation appears in the laudatory image of the Macedonian king as a "philosopher in arms" or educator of the barbarians.[57] It is thus possible to mine the essays for

---

[50] The eleven *Lives* are those of Themistocles, Alcibiades, Aristides, Lysander, Cimon, Agesilaus, Alexander, Pelopidas, Demosthenes, Pericles, and Nicias. The lost Epaminondas would tip the scale to make it more than half of the Greek biographies that are part of the *Parallel Lives*; Almagor (2017b: 124–126; 2018: 16). Cf. Geiger (1981: 90). On the Persian Wars in Plutarch, see Pelling (2007a: esp. 150–162).

[51] Hood (1967: 20–24) is an interesting attempt to write a literary analysis of a work that in all probability was never even composed. On the *Leonidas*, see Almagor (2022: 27–28).

[52] Plutarch almost certainly did not compile a series of biographies of the Persian kings similar to that of Roman emperors, and the *Artaxerxes* was not a part of a sequence of Achaemenid *Lives*. There is no evidence for such a series in the Lamprias Catalogue, nor does this biography disclose its existence, let alone that the idea was ever contemplated. See Almagor (2014a: 278).

[53] As in *Themistocles* 15.4; *Pericles* 15.1, 17.1; *Alcibiades* 26.8; *Cimon* 18.6, 19.3; *Pelopidas* 17.11; *Aristides* 19.4; *Lysander* 6.7; *Pyrrhus* 14.6; *Eumenes* 16.6; *Agesilaus* 15.2; *Alexander* 74.2; *Phocion* 17.7; *Demetrius* 8.2; *Artaxerxes* 16.2; *Quaestiones convivales* 3.2, 649E. Cf. Schmidt (1999: 133–137, 236–237).

[54] Even in the Roman *Lives*, there is the division of nations into Greeks and barbarians: *Numa* 18.4; *Sulla* 19.5; *Caesar* 55.3; *Lucullus* 26.1, 29.3, 32.4; *Cato Maior* 23.4. On Plutarch's attitude to Rome and Romanness, see Tröster's Chapter 2 in this volume.

[55] Hood (1967: 10, 16, 18, 26), Almagor (2017b: 126). Cf. Schmidt (2002: 58) on Plutarch's "nationalistic statements" (e.g. *De defectu oraculorum* 412A).

[56] The word later appears in Pollux, *Onom.* 6.166, but Plutarch may have invented the compound form. See Schmidt (1999: 40 n. 90).

[57] On this image as more straightforward than the alleged more complex and ambivalent picture seen in the *Life* of Alexander, see Duff (1999a: 65, 267), Schmidt (1999: 273, 287), Lamberton (2001: 44, 97), and Whitmarsh (2002: 179–180).

sophisticated tongue-in-cheek insights into the relation between political theories and action, as well as the very concept of Greek *paideia*. One may note the contrast between the emphatic insistence on Alexander's humanity in not treating barbarians as plants and animals (329B) – and the persistent similes describing education and acculturation (328E: sowing Asia with Greek magistracies; 330B: taming warring nations as dealing with animals).[58]

On another level, the barbarians signify the real political adversaries of the Roman Empire and what it stands for, and are employed by Plutarch to produce a sense of shared civilization common to the Greek and Roman readers, especially in relation to the Greco-Persian wars.[59] Here, the nostalgic references to the barbarians of old are laden with additional significance. There are allusions attesting to Plutarch's familiarity with the imperial attempt to draw parallels between the Greco-Persian wars and Roman operations in the East, by way of establishing a shared great past and a common cultural heritage.[60] This trend culminated with the campaigns of Trajan (114–117 CE) and Verus (162–166 CE) and inspired Greek authors such as Arrian in both his *Parthica* (*FGrH* 156 F 30–53) and *Alexander's Anabasis*, or the anonymous writer on Verus' expedition (*FGrH* 203). One result of this tendency was the depiction of Arsacid Parthia through several motifs and themes used to describe the Achaemenid kingdom; that is, as a decadent Oriental court[61] (Plutarch seems to adopt this very approach in the second half of his *Crassus*), or to conflate allusions of the distant past with the present Roman-Parthian rivalry.[62] There are echoes of Greek action against "Asia" in the Roman *Lives* (*Comparatio Aristides–Cato Maior* 2.3; *Comparatio Nicias-Crassus* 4.4). There may be a sarcastic variation of this identification in Antony's comparison of his

---

[58] Schmidt (1999: 33 n. 40) brands this ironic discrepancy as "paradoxalement." For Alexander's appearance as philhellene and not as a Hellene and the view of Greekness as partially not-Greek (i.e. Roman) in these essays, see Asirvatham (2005: 118–121).

[59] On the barbarians in Roman propaganda and how they are represented in literature, see Zanker (1988: 50–51); Hardie (1997); Schmidt (2002: 64–67).

[60] On this identification, see Cicero, *Pro domo sua* 60; Vergil, *Georg.* 4.290; Propertius 2.13.1–2, 3.3.11.21; Horace, *Od.* 1.2.22, 51; 1.21.14; 2.2.17; 3.3.44; 3.5.4; 4.14.42; Ovid, *AA.* 1.225; Seneca, *Apoc.* 12. See Seager (1980), Rosivach (1984: 2–3), Spawforth (1994: esp. 237–243), and Hardie (1997) on Augustan appropriation of fifth-century images of the Persian Wars. Cf. Isaac (2004: 375–380); Jung (2006); Lerouge (2007). Aiding this association was the fact that the Parthians considered themselves successors of the Persians: cf. Tacitus, *Ann.* 6.31.

[61] Seneca, *De constant.* 13.4; Martial, 10.72.5–7; Justin, 41.3.9. Yet, cf. Isaac (2004: 376–380) on the different stereotypes from those attributed to the Persians.

[62] Almagor (2017b: 126; 2018: 17; cf. 2023: 97). For example, Lucian in *How to write history*, when dealing with historians of the Parthian wars, also cites *Anabasis* 1.1.1 at 24.

failed venture in the East with that of the Ten Thousand and in his admiration of Xenophon's army (*Antony* 45.12).[63]

Another way, albeit a subtle one, in which Greco-Persian wars have contemporary political resonance is possible. The Achaemenid kingdom frequently figures in Greek descriptions of Roman imperial institutions by dint of terminology used by classical authors to portray the Persian system, such as "satraps" or "Great King";[64] that is to say, the language itself is programmed to recall a time when the Greeks were confronting a dominant non-Hellenic political system.[65] Plutarch shares in this trend, as is evident in his choice of terminology and, more generally, in his use of analogy and juxtaposition. He employs the word "up" (*anō*) when he refers to going to Rome (*Praecepta gerendae reipublicae* 814C), just as the writers of old would denote the way to Persia.[66] Achaemenid references are also embedded in the structure of the *Parallel Lives* in a manner that creates intriguing parallelism between the Eastern, Hellenistic enemies of Rome and the Persian opponents of the Greeks. For example, the war between Rome and Antiochus III is comparable with the Persian Wars (*Cato Maior* 12–14 – *Aristides* 5, 8–20), yet it is not immediately obvious whether the Persians resemble their successor kingdom of the Seleucids or rather the Romans, and whether Antiochus III as a Macedonian-Greek ruler is a champion of Hellenic culture in its fight against barbarians or not – he invades Greece, yet is defeated at Thermopylae.[67] Awareness of the contemporary, potentially delicate subtexts of the Greco-Persian wars in the Roman Empire may be detected in Plutarch's advice given to a local statesman to beware of the imperial power, which is closely juxtaposed to his admonition to refrain from stirring up the masses by mention of past glories (*Praecepta gerendae reipublicae* 814B–C):

> there are many acts of the Greeks of former times by recounting which the statesman can mold and correct the characters of our contemporaries ... but

---

[63] Note that ironically, Plutarch begins the Parthian sequence in the biography by having Antony equate himself with the Persian king Artaxerxes I (*Antony* 37.1). Cf. Pelling (1988a: 221–222).

[64] Mason (1970: 157); Bowie (1970: 33 n. 95); Swain (1996: 176 with n. 125, 321 n. 80). Cf. Dio Chrysostom 7.66, 7.93, 33.14, 50.6; *Philostratus, VS* 524. See Almagor (2017a: 339; 2017b: 125).

[65] For this trend in the Greek novel, see Schwartz (2003) on Chariton's *Chaereas and Callirhoe*.

[66] Cf. Epictetus, *Disc.* 1.10.2. Another allusion may be *Comparatio Cimon–Lucullus* 1.5, where Lucullus' table is described as "satrap-like," in correspondence with the Greek name for Persian provincial governors; cf. Tröster (2008: 56 n. 31); Almagor (2017b: 127; 2018: 18; 2023: 101, 103). In the dedication of *Regum et imperatorum apophthegmata*, Emperor Trajan is explicitly compared to Artaxerxes II (172B–E). According to M. Beck (2002), this dedication is authentically Plutarchan, but see Almagor (2018: 269-273).

[67] Note that Cato remembers (from Herodotus surely) that the Persians used a circuit of the pass (13.1) and leads the Romans in the same rout. Cf. Almagor (2019).

Marathon, the Eurymedon, Plataea, and all the other examples which make
the common folk vainly to swell with pride and kick up their heels, should
be left to the schools of the sophists.[68]

If this juxtaposition, like the analogies alluded to before, points at an
association of Rome and Persia otherwise prominent in the minds of
contemporary Greeks, then another facet to the Plutarchan Persians may
be added. While overtly speaking about the fifth-century kingdom,
Plutarch may be implicitly referring to the Rome of his own day and
concealing his ambivalent attitude toward the real empire by projecting it
onto the former monarchy.[69] This fact may explain the choice to recount
the *Life* of an Achaemenid monarch who was in a position to settle political
disputes in Greece. In particular, it might be said that from the Hellenic
point of view, Greece's submission to the conditions of Artaxerxes II in the
King's Peace (387/6 BCE) was broadly analogous to its position under
Rome, with Persia symbolizing the imperial system. Thus, in view of the
ultimate downfall of the Eastern empire, the biographer may also be
hinting at a possible dire course of events in the West.[70]

This association of Persians and Romans is clearly presented from
a Hellenocentric perspective. In conformity with the standard Hellenic–
barbarian dichotomic classification, the Romans are to a certain degree
viewed as "others" by Greek authors.[71] One strand in Plutarch's thought
admittedly portrays them as such; although the biographer does not
explicitly describe the Romans as barbarians, this is sometimes
insinuated.[72] The intricacy of the situation can be appreciated by zooming
in on one of the hallmark features of the classical barbarians. In Greek
thought, barbarians are identifiable by their rough speech and in particular
by their alien enunciation, hence the onomatopoetic term *barbaroi*.[73] To

[68] Loeb Classical Library translation. See Jones (1971: 113–114); Spawforth (1994: 245–246); Whitmarsh
(2005: 66–70); Gascó (1990). Cf. Aelius Aristides 42.1 on the inappropriateness of speaking about
a war against the barbarians. There may be an allusion here to the claim of Aristophanes' Aeschylus
that the *Persae* arouses the audience's patriotism (*Ra.* 1026–1027).

[69] The association of the Persian Wars and the Trojan Wars, dating back to the classical period – cf.
Hall (1989: 21–25); Pelling (2007a: 148) – is also worthy of note, given the Romans' professed
ancestry in Troy. Nevertheless, Erskine (2001: 6–7, 225–253) points to the subtleties of the Romans'
alignment with the Trojans and that this identification does not automatically cast the Romans as
barbarians in the Greek perspective.

[70] Cf. Almagor (2014a: 284–285; 2023: 101–102).

[71] See Champion (2000) on several passages in Polybius. Cf. Marincola (2011).

[72] See *Flamininus* 2.5, 11.7: *allophyloi.* Cf. *Pyrrhus* 16.7: *barbaron.* The indigenous population of Latium
appears barbaric before the civilizing impact of Heracles: cf. *Quaestiones Romanae* 272B-C. For the
view that Plutarch's readers were not imagined as Romans, see Pelling (2002a: 270–271); Duff
(2007–8: 7–11). See further Almagor (2023: 91–94).

[73] The *locus classicus* is Strabo, 14.2.28. Cf. Almagor (2005: 44–48).

the insiders of Greek discourse these linguistic and phonetic characteristics of barbarians were tantamount to natural traits, and the classification of human societies based on such traits would also be considered natural, indeed commensurate with the disparity between humans and beasts.[74] On several occasions Plutarch equates the voices of barbarians with sounds of brutes. In one memorable scene from the *Life of Cimon* (18.2–3), just before the hero's departure to what will be his final battle – indeed in his very final hours – he has a dream in which a bitch barks at him, and baying with a mixed-in human voice tells him to be a friend both to her and her whelps. According to Cimon's diviner-friend, the dog symbolized the Medes, since the mixture of speech points to the composition of the Persian army, made up of Hellenes and barbarians. Thus, barking represents barbarians and their elocution. The same biography also depicts the enmity between Greeks and barbarians as *natural* (*Cimon* 18.1).[75] In the biography of Marius, the lamentation of the Northern tribe of Ambrones is likened by the narrator not to "the wailings and groaning of men, but to howling and bellowing with a strain of the wild beast in them" (*Marius* 20.2–3).[76] The ethnic distinction, albeit less overt, is paralleled here with the natural divergence between man and beast, which at the very end of the *Life* is brought out in the saying attributed to Plato (*Marius* 46.1). Plato praises his guardian genius and Fortune for being born a man and not an irrational animal, and a Greek rather than a barbarian.[77] Moreover, in the final episode of the *Life* Marius is reported to have been swept into a strange delusion, which has made him believe he was still a commander in the Mithridatic War and has caused him to indulge in the gestures he used to employ in warfare, specifically the shrill battle-cry (*Marius* 45.10: *kraugē*). Marius' screams literally echo the shouts of the barbarian Ambrones described earlier (*Marius* 19.3: *kraugē*; cf. 21.2). These examples from *Cimon* and *Marius* show us how complex Plutarch's ethnic/ethical references can be. We are not sure whether it was a particular development that made the heroes lose restraint and let their character display features of the very "other" against whom they were fighting, or whether in their final

[74] For this rhetorical motif, see Hall (1989: 126); Isaac (2004: 196–207). Cf. Aristotle, *EN* 7.1145a30; 7.1149a11; also Dio Chrysostom 38.46. People dwelling at the marginal zones of the inhabited world are often envisioned as imaginary creatures and not as human: Nippel (2002: 282–283); Herodotus 4.105.2; Tacitus, *Germ.* 46.4. Cf. Wiedemann (1986).

[75] This theme recurs elsewhere (*Aristides* 16.3). Cf. Schmidt (1999: 236 and n. 167). See also *Agesilaus* 16.6; Plato, *Rep.* 5.470c; Isocrates, *Paneg.* 158, 184; *Panath.* 163.

[76] Loeb Classical Library translation, slightly adapted. Cf. *Marius* 16.3. Plutarch's notion of screaming in warfare as barbarian: Nikolaidis (1986: 232–233).

[77] Cf. Schmidt (1999: 33–34).

hours the barbarian that was naturally lurking inside Marius (as a typical uneducated Roman) or Cimon (half-Thracian on his mother's side: *Cimon* 4.1) is finally revealed.

Related is the question whether the distinctions among Romans, Greeks, and barbarians are due to nature or to nurture.[78] The ancients acknowledged that the barbarians could not be reduced to qualities prede-termined by origin and birth: they were also molded by certain habits and customs that were, typically, savage.[79] As *cultural* categories, barbarism and Greekness are defined by and dependent on education (or a lack thereof). Indeed, Plutarch sometimes uses the term *barbaros* simply to mean "unciv-ilized." For instance, in *Amatorius* (756C), a superstitious belief about Eros is declared "barbaric"; that is to say, "primitive." Greek behavior can be described as "barbarian,"[80] and Plutarch plays on this particular meaning when the concept is applied to non-Hellenes. Thus Pyrrhus considers the Romans to be barbarians, yet notes that their battle formation is "not barbaric" (*Pyrrhus* 16.7).[81] Olympias, the mother of Alexander, discharges her divine inspirations in a manner the narrator labels "rather more barbaric" (*Alexander* 2.9: *barbarikōteron*).[82] Note the comparative degree of the adverb – barbarity can be quantified, it seems. If there is a grading scale for evaluating barbarism, it follows that the classical ethnic dichotomy that determines whether a person could be either Greek or barbarian has evolved in a decidedly different direction.[83] Still, one cannot escape the impression that the application of the epithet here is also meant to allude to Olympias' ethnic origin and consequently to problematize Alexander's identity (*Alexander* 2.1).

Ambiguity remains in the case of Greeks swayed completely in the direction of barbarians. Thus, the Carthaginian occupation of Syracuse in 343 BCE raised the fear that Greek Sicily would be barbarized (*Timoleon* 17.2: *ekbarbarōsis*).[84] Here, Plutarch might be tacitly drawing on influen-tial intertexts, such as the Platonic *Eighth Epistle*, which talks of the Carthaginian impact on the barbarization of the Greeks in Sicily by the Carthaginians (8.353a: *ekbarbarōtheisa*), or Isocrates' account of how Salamis in Cyprus lost its Hellenic character before Evagoras

---

[78] Duff (1999a: 73–74); Pelling (2002a: 283–347).
[79] And hence can be applied to Greeks as well. Cf. Saïd (2002: 62, 87–100) on the Greek–barbarian opposition contested, blurred, or reversed in Euripides.
[80] Cf. Nikolaidis (1986: 241) on *Dion* 35.3 and *Phocion* 35.2.      [81] See Mossman (2005b).
[82] "In a wilder fashion" (Loeb Classical Library); "more zealously" (Nikolaidis 1986: 235). Cf. also *De defectu oraculorum* 418E ("rather barbaric" is the idea that daemons sin or die).
[83] See Saïd (2001: 291) on Dio Chrysostom 36.25; Almagor (2005: 52) on Strabo, 4.5.2.
[84] On this vocabulary, see Bowersock (1995).

(*Evag.* 20–21, 47: *ekbebarbarōmenē*).[85] Yet, in Plutarch, this instance of cultural change is not free from irony, for the barbarization of Sicily would have been brought about by Greek mercenaries, as the following scene makes apparent (*Timoleon* 20.7).[86]

Further curious combinations are possible, especially if Greekness is no longer attached to ethnicity. At the outset of *Numa* (1.2), the legendary lawgiver is presented by the narrator as having been influenced by a certain barbarian. However, in the *Comparatio* (*synkrisis*) with *Lycurgus* (1.9) Numa is said to be far more Hellenic a lawgiver than his Greek counterpart. One of the explicitly mentioned sources in the *Numa* is Juba. The latter was led by Caesar in a triumphal procession (*Caesar* 55.3) and turned "from being a barbarian and a Numidian to be counted among the most learned historians of Hellas." In his writings Juba apparently insists on a Greek etymology for the Latin word *ancilia*, bucklers (*Numa* 13.6). Plutarch describes Juba's claim as literally "keen to Hellenize the name." So we have the barbarian Juba Hellenizing a Roman name and the Roman Caesar Hellenizing a barbarian, with a narrator both "barbarizing" and "Hellenizing" a Roman (Numa).

Corresponding to contemporary cultural currents of Greek imperial literature and the growing phenomenon of public declamations, Plutarch was also engaged in a game of inclusion and exclusion with his prospective readers. Greek writers and orators relied on the audience's familiarity with their examples and themes, language, and style.[87] At the same time, however, the authors and rhetors had to be innovative and creative and thus present original deviations from tradition, resulting in a blatant self-display of an outsider figure.[88] The obvious cases were those of foreigners, who became "Greek" while still considered barbarians – the well-known figures being Favorinus of Arelate (Arles)[89] and Lucian of Samosata.[90] Both presented themselves as moving between the barbarian and Greek worlds and between center and periphery.[91] Paradoxically, their foreignness

[85] See now Schmidt et al. (2020) on intertextuality in Plutarch in general.

[86] "You, who are Greeks, are eager to barbarize" (*hymeis Hellēnes ontes ekbarbarōsai prothymeisthe*). Perhaps an allusion to Euripides, fr. 719 Kannicht-Snell: "shall we, who are Greeks, be slaves to barbarians?" (*Hellēnes ontes barbarois douleusomen*).

[87] Cf. Russell (1983: 74–86, 106–127); Anderson (1989: 89–103; 1993: 47–67); Swain (1996: 94–96, 193–194); Schmitz (1997: 156–159); Whitmarsh (2005: 24–32, 38–39).

[88] Cf. Swain (1996: 81–87); Whitmarsh (2005: 34–37), Almagor (2016a: 117; 2023: 96).

[89] See Gleason (1995: 8–20, 145–158); Whitmarsh (2001: 119–121, 167–178).

[90] See Anderson (1976); Swain (1996: 70, 298–312, 329); Whitmarsh (2001: 116–129, 247–294; 2005: 82–83).

[91] Cf. Bowersock (1969: 43–58); Bowersock and Jones (1974); Jones (1978: 104–131); Desideri (1991b); Swain (1996: 69–79, 192–197, 225–241). See Almagor (2016a: 118) on Josephus (cf. *BJ* 1.16: *allophylos*).

guaranteed better integration into the elite Greek literary community. Lucian uses the figure of the barbarian wise man Anacharsis (*Anach.* 17: "a Scythian, yet also a *sophos*")[92] to display his own peculiar "outsider" position.[93] This device enables him to reverse the roles of the Greek spectator and the "other" as spectacle (*Anach.* 1–4, 9, 13, 23).[94] This interplay between inclusion and exclusion was first and foremost relevant to the unique accultural process embodied in Hellenization or the possession of *paideia*: the very education that marked the boundaries between Greeks and barbarians could have been mastered so as to enable people to traverse the very borders it preserved.[95] This play was also pertinent to the special situation of Imperial Greeks under Roman rule: they were insiders in terms of possessing a dominant culture, yet they were outsiders in that they lacked political power.[96] Thus, for instance, Plutarch's self-presentation as a latecomer in the non-Greek language of Latin (*Demosthenes* 2.1–2), echoing a similar self-display of Dionysius of Halicarnassus (*AR* 1.7.2–3), is merely a variation of this theme with respect to the acquisition of Greek by barbarians (cf. Josephus, *AJ* 20.263).[97]

Signally, Plutarch operates with a threefold division of humanity, with the Romans being placed between Greeks and barbarians.[98] Two texts mentioned earlier, namely the lost *Quaestiones barbaricae* and the extant *Artaxerxes*, triangulate with, respectively, the *Quaestiones Romanae* and *Quaestiones Graecae* and the *Parallel Lives* of Greek and Roman heroes.[99] It should be possible to speculate on the moral rationale behind this triadic scheme.[100] The Romans, in Plutarch's opinion, share some of the unsavory traits of the barbarians, such as cruelty and uninhibited ambition, but are

---

[92] Cf. Armstrong (1948); Ungefehr-Kortus (1996); Mestre (2003).

[93] Cf. Goldhill (2001a: 2, 4); König (2005: 74). On Lucian and Anacharsis, see *Scyth.* 9–10 and Branham (1989: 83). Similarly, Lucian uses the figure of the Gaul who speaks in eloquent Greek (*Her.* 4–6).

[94] Cf. Saïd (1994: 163–170).    [95] See Whitmarsh (2001: 90–130) on the concept of *paideia*.

[96] Cf. Swain (1996: 139–145); Whitmarsh (2001: 62–67).

[97] See Almagor (2016a: 115–116). On Plutarch's presumed actual knowledge of Latin, see Barrow (1967: 151); Jones (1971: 20, 28, 30, 84–86); Russell (1973a: 54); Strobach (1997: 32–46); Zadorojnyi (2006a); Pelling (2011a: 43–44, 55–56).

[98] Cf. Aelius Aristides 14 (*Roman Oration*) 11, 14, 41, 96, 100; Swain (1996: 350–352); Saïd (2001: 287–288). On similar threefold division in post-classical authors, see Almagor (2005: 51). Cf. also Cicero, *Fin.* 2.15.49; Quintilian, *Inst.* 5.10.24. See Almagor (2023: 93–94).

[99] Cf. Mossman (2010: 145, 147), who claims there is no *Greek* context that could be used as a parallel to the unique atmosphere of the Persian court of the *Artaxerxes*; also at 159. Stronk (2010: 99) proposes Nero as a *Roman* counterpart to the Persian king.

[100] This may also stem from the Greek practice of allotting a special place to nations that received the Hellenic culture but were still considered foreign, and also from the Roman reluctance to be regarded as either Greek or barbarian. In the main Latin taxonomy, the Romans are opposed to the *exter(n)i*, literally "from outside (the community)", a concept that does not have the negative

also capable of adhering to the same set of values as the Greeks. The upshot of this is that without the restraining impact of proper Hellenic education, the Romans might surrender to their passionate ambition (cf. *Flamininus* 20–21, *Marcellus* 28.6).[101] The Roman/barbarian association can be insinuated via subtle narrative technique too. The alleged demand Pelopidas saw in his sleep, that he should sacrifice a maiden in order to be victorious is decried by his entourage as "barbarous and lawless" (*Pelopidas* 21.5–6)[102] and therefore is viewed as inconceivable. In the parallel biography of Marcellus, the narrator points out that though the Romans have no barbarous or unnatural practices, at the time of the war with the Insubrians (ca. 225 BCE), they were forced to obey certain oracular commands from the Sibylline books, and so buried alive two Greeks and two Gauls (*Marcellus* 3.6). The fact that Pelopidas refused to perform human sacrifice (and offered a mare as a substitute) while the Romans did not is suggestive: whereas the narrator explicitly denies the adoption of any barbarous practices by the Romans (the latter are framed as distinct from both Greeks and Gauls), their barbarity is implicitly underlined in the story.[103] The narrator's claim that apart from this act of human sacrifice (of Greeks!), the religious matters of the Romans were done "in a hellenic manner (*Hellēnikōs*) ... and mild towards the deities" is ironic; the image of Roman piety is further destabilized by the fact that they perform human sacrifice in an attempt to avert invasion of the barbarian Gauls, who in their turn are known to sacrifice their children to propitiate the gods (*De superstitione* 171B–C).[104]

Plutarch's attitude toward the Romans is different from his approach to another borderline case, namely the Egyptians. He is more appreciative of the ancient non-Greek culture (and wisdom) of the Egyptians[105] than of the Romans. This can be seen in the philosophical work *De Iside et Osiride*,

---

connotations of *barbaros*. Cf. Lévy (1984). This division can be seen, for instance, in the structure of the book of Valerius Maximus (the term *externa* refers to both Greek and barbarian deeds and sayings) and in most of the extant biographies of Nepos, depicting the illustrious political leaders of the *exterae gentes*, meaning Greeks as well as barbarians; see Nepos' short appendix on foreign kings (*de regibus exterarum gentium*) with Geiger (1979a).

[101] See Russell (1966a: 145 n. 1; 1973a: 132); Swain (1990a; 1996: 140–144).

[102] Compare the story in *Agesilaus* 6.6–9 and Xenophon, *Hell.* 3.4.3–4; Georgiadou (1997: 169). Cf. Almagor (2023: 94–95).

[103] Yet cf. Schmidt (1999: 42), who insists that the Romans are not to be considered as barbarians here for they were forced to act in this manner. Cf. Pelling (1989: 200–201).

[104] Cf. *Themistocles* 13.3 depicting the sacrifice of Persians (with Swain 1990a: 142, who presents the Greeks as barbarous as well). On human sacrifice in Plutarch, see also Schmidt (1999: 40–44). Compare Achilles' sacrifice of Trojan prisoners in *Iliad* 23.174ff.

[105] Cf. Alston (1996: 103).

dealing with an Egyptian myth of the good god Osiris, his enemy the evil god Seth-Typhon, and Isis, Osiris' sister and wife (*De Iside et Osiride* 355D–358E). According to the myth, Osiris is locked by Seth-Typhon inside a chest and thrown into the Nile. Isis discovers the body and hides it (356B–357F), but Seth-Typhon cuts it into fourteen parts (358A, 368A). Isis is able to reassemble Osiris, and the latter instructs Horus, their joint son (358B–D, 367A). Horus clashes with Seth-Typhon and triumphs over him (358D, 367B), but Isis releases him (358D). While the fanciful Egyptian myth and accompanying cult are admittedly alien to the Greeks, Plutarch attempts in this treatise to present their philosophical significance in a version of *interpretatio Graeca*.[106]

After suggesting several strategies to understand the myth (atheistic Euhemeristic: 359E–360D, daimonological: 360E–363B, simplistic allegorical: 363D–367C, and through theories associating it with celestial bodies: 367D–368F, or materialistic and monistic explanations: 369A–D),[107] Plutarch reaches the true interpretation, based on his brand of metaphysical, Platonic,[108] dualism (369A–B). This theory postulates a third, intermediate, nature between the opposite principles, exemplified in the figures of Isis and Horus.[109] Isis is interpreted as the orderly matter (372E–F) or rather the world-soul embodied in matter.[110] Thus, while Romans are portrayed by Plutarch as essentially barbarians, despite their attempts to conceal their true nature by adopting Greek education, the Egyptian myths are conversely seen as principally transmitting Greek ideas, regardless of their external barbarian coloring. It would appear that for Plutarch the Egyptians are absorbed into the Greek world and mind frame more than the Romans.[111]

Barbarians as an ethnological and ethical category seem to facilitate a great deal of nuanced rhetorical and conceptual experimentation across the *Lives*. The Eastern "others" of the *Crassus* adopt Greek culture: Artavasdes the Armenian composes tragedies, orations, and histories, and

---

[106] *De Iside et Osiride* 351E, 352C, 354B, 355D, 377F–378A. See Richter (2001: 198–200, 206–208); Petrucci (2016: 227–229). On the work, see Hopfner (1940); J. G. Griffiths (1970); Froidefond (1988). See Alston (1996: 104).

[107] See Richter (2001: 202–205); Petrucci (2016: 230–232).

[108] *De Iside et Osiride* 372E, 373E–374A, alluding to Plato, *Ti.* 49a, 51a, 50c–e, *Rep.* 7.546bc. Cf. Petrucci (2016: 241–242).

[109] Petrucci (2016: 234, 238–240).

[110] That is, the soul with reason, order, form, and concord (cf. *De animae procreatione in Timaeo* 1015F–1016C, 1017A–B, 1024A, 1027A). This is the second stage of the Platonic pre-cosmic soul (see *De Iside et Osiride* 370C–371A, *De animae procreatione in Timaeo* 1014E, 1016B, *Platonicae quaestiones* 2.1001C, 4.1003A). Cf. Plato, *Polit.* 272e–273c, Baltes (2000: 248–250), and Opsomer (2004: 143, 149).

[111] See, however, Juvenal 15 and Alston (1996: 100–103, 105).

the knowledge of Euripides displayed in the last chapter of the biography (*Crassus* 33), where a scene of the *Bacchae* is acted out, can be considered indicative of Hellenic inculturation.[112] The use of Euripides is suggestive, as he is the tragedian best known for giving the "others" a voice.[113] But in Parthia there is a different, more resistant sort of "otherness" at work. As shown by Zadorojnyi (1997a: 180–182), the barbarians enjoying the *Bacchae* lack the sophistication necessary for seeing it as a fiction, and consequently fulfill the gruesome potentiality of the play. In this *orbis alter* of the Parthians,[114] the more they display Hellenic traits, such as the ability to perform Greek drama, the more they show themselves to be barbarians. Conversely, it should also be observed that the more they act in a barbarous way, the more they become true Greek interpreters of the play, stressing features that increase its shocking effect and enhance the artistic merit of the Greek tragedy.[115]

In a different example, during another Eastern banquet, described in the *Artaxerxes* (15.1–7), a eunuch of the queen mother, who wishes to avenge the death of her son Cyrus the Younger, lures the man who actually delivered the fatal blow to the prince into relating his part of what happened.[116] The man, called Mithridates, instantly causes his own downfall since the facts revealed by him contradict the official version that hailed Artaxerxes as the unaided slayer of Cyrus, and is led away to a brutal execution (*Artaxerxes* 16.3–7). One of the successful ploys used by the eunuch is to pretend that the banquet follows the Greek sympotic ethical code, enfolded in his introduction of the proverbial phrase: "for as the Greeks say: wine, and there is truth" (*Artaxerxes* 15.4). The outcome of Mithridates' gullible belief that there is indeed full understanding and trust at the drinking table, and that his vulnerable inebriated condition will not be abused by any other participant, foregrounds the mismatch between the Hellenic institution of the *symposium* and the barbarian context.[117] However, the fact that Mithridates is so easily tricked shows how elusive

---

[112] Cf. *De Alexandri magni fortuna aut virtute* 328D.

[113] See n. 79 in this chapter. Cf. Saïd (2002: 62), who asks whether Euripides does not question the very distinction of Greek and barbarian.

[114] To borrow the phrase of Manilius, 4.674–5.

[115] Note that the parallel *Life of Nicias* (29.5) has a short anecdote about a ship that is only allowed entry into the Caunian harbor after its sailors declare they know Euripides' songs – if the Caunians are to be seen as barbarians, their fondness for Euripides depicts them as Hellenized barbarians, thus this is both a foil to the finale of the *Crassus* and an ironic allusion to Euripides, *Cycl.* 654 (Carians). Cf. Schmidt (1999: 49, 312–313) on the *Crassus* scene.

[116] What follows elaborates on one particular direction explored in Almagor (2009).

[117] Cf. also Bowie (2003). On Plutarch's model of symposium, see Oikonomopoulou's Chapter 7 in this volume.

ethnic labeling can be. The eunuch's presentation of the Greek way of drinking as involving no restraint on free speech and as a model to be followed is at once Greek and barbarian. The very instant the eunuch feigns Greek characteristics, he also displays his barbarian nature, which is uncommitted to the Hellenic rules of the proper behavior during the banquet and is also stereotypically presented as uncontrolled and unreliable. Indeed, the eunuch actually betrays the trust of his fellow symposiast. The Greek borderline between temporary audacity and outrageous intoxicated misbehavior, which defines lack of self-control at a *symposium*[118] as the negative foil to the good, truly "Hellenic" paradigm, is completely missed by Mithridates, highlighting the barbarian character of the recipient. Yet, a more reserved demeanor does not necessarily mean espousal of Greek values. The silent acceptance of Mithridates' calamity by the other symposiasts (*Artaxerxes* 15.7) is typically un-Hellenic, and is related to the barbarian slavish behavior, lacking the essential Greek characteristic of *parrhēsia*.

Another interesting case of cross-examination of values is the story of the meetings between Themistocles and Artaxerxes I (*Themistocles* 28–29.5). Plutarch presents both figures as stimuli against which the stereotypic images of each ethno-ethical group are displayed and tested. Language plays a major role, as it does throughout this biography.[119] The Great King allows Themistocles to show himself as a typical Greek, enjoying free speech (28.2–5, 29.3–5), speaking with boldness (28.6), and craftily using stylized arguments (28.2–4). As for Themistocles, he prompts Artaxerxes to behave like a typical Oriental despot, namely to act on whims (29.3, 5), show his generosity (28.1, 29.3), and be affected by sycophancy (29.4–5). It may be argued, however, that both men also bring out in each other uncharacteristic features that transcend their respective stereotyped profiles. Themistocles puts forwards a very sophisticated and clever argument before the king (28.2–5), but nowhere is it said that his words are translated by an interpreter (who only asks the question at 28.1). It would be interesting to entertain the thought that no part of Themistocles' elaborated argument is understood by the king at their initial meeting, and that it is indeed all Greek to him. In this scenario, it is Themistocles who is the "other" speaking an incomprehensible language – the default constituent

---

[118] See examples in Paul (1991).

[119] Mayer (1997); Gera (2007) notes the irony involved when Themistocles needs to learn Persian in order to engage in the Greek activity of *parrhēsia*. *Pace* Hood (1967: 18–19), who believes that only the Persians prove the setting for the display of Themistocles' traits, like the hero's cunning or his pursuit of honor; characterization clearly goes both ways. See also Almagor (2017b: 144–147).

of a barbarian, as it were. This foreshadows his subsequent absorption in the Persian court (29.3–7, 31.2).[120] In the next chapter of the biography the roles are reversed: not only does Artaxerxes appreciate free speech (29.3) in the Greek fashion, but he also values a fellow speaker in the same language when granting Themistocles a year to learn Persian (29.5); it is in perfect accordance with the Hellenic outlook, which values the use of a common tongue by the Greeks.[121]

There is a twofold rationale for the strong presence of barbarians[122] at almost every turn in Plutarch's works. Plutarch's ethical interests call for negative or positive models as well as foils, individual as well as collective; at the same time, the *Lives* deal with eminent statesmen and generals, who *qua* politicians are in constant need of some concrete "other" to engage with. But barbarians are a tool of Plutarchan characterization not just on the level of the historical action (e.g. as opponents to be defeated) but also as a reflection of the hero's emotions and values, effectively translating the clash of Greeks (or Romans) with the barbarians into an allegory of the struggle between the rational and irrational parts of the hero's (Platonically structured) soul.[123] For example, after Darius' harem falls into the hands of Alexander, Plutarch depicts the Macedonian king as generously refraining from harming or disgracing the captive women. Yet Alexander jokes that these Persian women are "sores to the eyes" (*Alexander* 21.10). This phrase, which obviously indicates the passionate side Alexander wishes to repress, alludes to an episode from Herodotus (5.17–19), where the Persian ambassadors in Macedonia complain at a banquet held in their honor that the women present are placed too far away from them, and are thus "pains for their eyes" (Hdt. 5.18.4), since they cannot be touched. The Plutarchan Alexander does not accept the Persian practice of taking advantage of his newly acquired harem,[124] and displays Greek restraint – contrary to the barbarian licentiousness as evoked by the literary allusion and perhaps expected of him. However, by quoting Herodotus' Persians, Alexander

---

[120] Cf. Almagor (2017b: 144–145).

[121] One of the criteria of Greek ethnic identity: e.g. Herodotus (8.144: *homoglōsson*) or Isocrates (*Epist.* 9.8). The attitude of Artaxerxes also marks Themistocles' conduct previously in the *Life* (*Themistocles* 6.2) as a barbarian act. When Themistocles kills an interpreter speaking in Greek on behalf of the enemy, he thereby sets limits to *parrhēsia* and, even though he comes across as anti-Persian, is at fault for disregarding the common language that unites the Greeks. Note that in both cases Themistocles has no need for an interpreter. Cf. Gera (2007: 454–455).

[122] Cf. Schmidt (1999: 329–330; 2002: 57; 2004: 227).

[123] On the Platonism of Plutarch's psychology, see Opsomer's Chapter 4 in this volume.

[124] Cf. Stevenson (1997: 50) and similar Eastern practice: 2 Samuel 3:7, 12:8; 1 Kings 2: 22. Compare the legend of Solomon and Ashmodai: Krappe (1933: 260). Also cf. Curtius Rufus 6.6.8 on Alexander and the Persian harem. Yet, see Almagor (2017b: 143 n. 133).

reveals that he shares their sentiment. In the very moment of restraint, Alexander discloses his passionate side, which can be characterized as barbarian,[125] thus prefiguring his later course of Medizing and his claim to be the rightful successor of the Great King.[126]

In a similar vein, the portrayal of Lucullus as "Xerxes Togatus" (*Lucullus* 39.3)[127] presents his sumptuous extravagance as an emulation of the East.[128] The wealth so recklessly used by Lucullus is typically likened by the narrator to a barbarian prisoner of war (*Lucullus* 41.7).[129] This imagery insinuates not only that Lucullus' riches come from the East but perhaps also that they are a compensation for the barbarian adversary he failed to capture, namely Mithridates (*Comparatio Cimon–Lucullus* 3.2). While the barbarians were eventually not subdued by the Roman general in their own territory, having been only temporarily checked by Roman presence (cf. *Lucullus* 20, 23.1, 29.5–6), Lucullus did succeed in incorporating them, as it were, into his own estate and gardens. In Rome, the outward signs of an Eastern luxury betray oriental vices, only thinly veiled by the Roman outer garment.

In Plutarch's writings, the barbarians are not simply an inheritance from classical literature that he passively accepts. Plutarch rather adopts, restructures, and remodels the cultural and rhetorical construct of *barbaros* to the point where there is nothing simple or straightforward about the way barbarians function in his corpus. Because the barbarians uniquely enjoy both a quasi-essentialist existence and a potential of being "acculturized," Plutarch is able to let them play several roles in the literary presentation of political figures and events. On the one hand, they accentuate the framework of the narrative in that they represent the adversaries, act as the very agents of the hero's downfall, or characterize the main figure by serving as his foil. On the other hand, they can problematize the relation of Romans to Greek *paideia* or the very notion of "Greekness." The barbarians are thus one of Plutarch's devices by which he turns political history into literary art (through characterization and narrative techniques) and literary texts into

---

[125] Cf. Whitmarsh (2002: 191) on Alexander as aptly embodying East and West, since Macedonian identity is set between Hellenism and barbarism.

[126] Medizing: *Alexander* 20.7–8, 28.2–3, 45, 50.4–51.3, 54.3, 69.1, 70.2; claim to the throne: 29.4, 33.2, 34.1, 37.7.

[127] A saying attributed by Plutarch to the Stoic Tubero, but in Velleius Paterculus 2.33.4 ascribed to Pompey apropos of Lucullus' grandiose building projects, which recall Xerxes' bridge and canal. See Tröster (2008: 60–61 n. 50, 63); Almagor (2023: 103).

[128] On the stereotype of oriental riches, cf. Aeschylus, *Pers.* 842, Hall (1989: 80–83, 126–129, 206–207) and in Plutarch, *Regum et imperatorum apophthegmata* 173A–B; Schmidt (1999: 107–140).

[129] On the stigma of barbarism applied to Lucullus, see Tröster (2008: 29, 42 n. 76, 52 n. 15, 56–57).

politically charged documents (implying an understated ambivalence toward the Roman Empire). Plutarch brings the ethnic labels into play with a subtlety and skill that allows the narrative and the barbarians therein to move between the past and the present, to shift between moral concerns and historic interests, and indeed to roam between the worlds of Greece and Rome.

## Further Reading

Studies on the concept and image of *barbaros* in Greek and Latin literature are numerous. See especially Weidner (1913); Sinor (1957); Bovon (1963); Müller (1978). For treatments of the "other" in classical literature, see also the useful discussions by Schwabl (1962); Salmon (1984); Speyer (1989); Dihle (1994); Heath (2005: 192–201); Papadodima (2010); and the engaging book of Vlassopoulos (2013). For the Persian view of Greeks, see Sancisi-Weerdenburg (2001).

The staple study of the portrayal of barbarians in Plutarch is Schmidt (1999). On the *Life of Artaxerxes*, see Mossman (2010); Almagor (2016b). For Plutarch's *Crassus*, see Chlup (2009); for the relevant passages in *Alexander*, Hamilton (1969) is still helpful, although the comments are brief and the perspective appears today to be narrow; for Cimon, see also Blamire (1989); for Lucullus, see the scholarly study of Keaveney (1992); for a combined reading of several of the biographies mentioned, see Buszard (2008).

# CHAPTER 14

# Plutarch and Animals

## Judith Mossman and Alexei V. Zadorojnyi

Plutarch is often seen nowadays as a champion of the animal cause, virtually as a precursor of the modern pro-animal argument.[1] It is important, however, to recognize that the prominence of animals in Plutarch's work is symptomatic of the widespread and vibrant textual experimentation with animals in imperial Greco-Roman literature. The trend peaks in the second century CE. Plutarch's younger contemporary Arrian wrote a treatise *On Hunting with Dogs*;[2] Oppian's poem *On Fishing* (*Halieutica*) uses fishes as a frame for exploring morality, education, and knowledge itself;[3] Apuleius' *Metamorphoses* and the pseudo-Lucianic *Donkey* (*Onos*) blend burlesque with sociopolitical and ethical (at the least) symbolism;[4] in the *Characteristics of Animals* by Claudius Aelian there is overt moralism but also latent political and cultural commentary;[5] the list could go on.[6] Animals were relevant within imperial philosophical thought, too. Philo of Alexandria composed a dialogue[7] in which much evidence for animal intelligence and ethics is presented yet turned down. The third-century

---

[1] This approach is maintained by Newmyer (2006); his book builds on a series of earlier articles, notably Newmyer (1992; 1997; 1999; 2003). To Hindermann (2011: §8), Plutarch is "erster antiker Denker mit einem sympathetischen Verständnis für Tiere" ("the first ancient thinker with a sympathetic understanding for the animals"); Lhermitte (2015: 22) describes Plutarch as "sans doute le partisan le plus connu de l'intelligence animale" ("without doubt, the best-known defender of animal reason"). For orientation in the modern debate on the moral and cognitive status of animals, see e.g. Taylor (2003); Steiner (2005).

[2] Arrian of course had in mind Xenophon's essay *On Hunting*: see Stadter (1976); the two texts are offered together in Phillips and Willcock (1999). On the contemporary cultural context of Arrian's essay, see Kasulke (2000).

[3] Kneebone (2008; 2017: esp. 213–222).

[4] Bradley (2000); Hall (1995). For the link between the donkey's long ears and the all-important motif of curiosity in Apuleius, see Hijmans et al. (1995: 150).

[5] Fögen (2009b); Smith (2014); Lhermitte (2015: 90–95, 235–243, 325–327, 463–475, and *passim*).

[6] See Anderson (1993: 185–188); Dumont (2001: 375–384).

[7] Goguey (2003: 24–28); Gilhus (2006: 42–44); Jazdzewska (2015a: 46–50). The text survives in Armenian translation; the standard English translation and commentary is Terian (1981). The date of composition is probably the mid-30s CE.

Neoplatonist Porphyry advocates vegetarianism as a way to improve one's spiritual well-being.[8] Like all these authors (and their ancient readers), Plutarch draws upon and responds to (a) the rich and abiding literary tradition of mobilizing animal imagery and themes,[9] as well as (b) the long-established philosophical debate on animal psychology and rationality, with far-reaching ethical implications about how animals should be treated.[10]

It is no overstatement to say that the main role of animals in ancient philosophy, from Plato onwards, is to facilitate understanding of human nature[11] and to put into sharp(er) relief the normative benchmarks for human life.[12] In other words, the Platonist intellectual Plutarch[13] inhabits a fundamentally anthropocentric discursive world,[14] wherein the animals are given consideration not so much for their own sake but as a learning resource:

> philosophers . . . refer some of their questions to the nature of irrational animals, as though to a foreign polity, and submit the decision to their affects and characters as to a court that cannot be either influenced or bribed. (*De amore prolis* 493B; trans. Helmbold, modified)

This mindset is at work behind, for instance, Plutarch's construal of animal worship among the Egyptians (*De Iside et Osiride* 380F–381A, 382A–C),[15] or when he argues that in the essential familial relationships animals meet nature's brief rather better than humans do (*De amore prolis* 493B–495C);[16]

---

[8] Steiner (2005: 103–111); Osborne (2007: 224–238); yet see Edwards (2016), who argues against taking Porphyry's pro-animal outlook in *Abstinence* at face value.

[9] See Hawtree (2014); Lefkowitz (2014); Thumiger (2014a; 2014b); Pütz (2014); Kitchell (2017); Korhonen and Ruonakoski (2017: 42–60, 66–70, 106–186); Goguey (2003: 53–71, 107–121); Tutrone (2012: 57–72, 90–98, 251–263). Payne (2010) serves a delicious smorgasbord of readings in the ancient and modern animal-related poetics.

[10] Ancient philosophical ideas about animals are accessibly mapped out in Dierauer (1997); Sorabji (1997); Gontier (1999: 19–54, 71–102); Gilhus (2006: 37–63); Lorenz (2013: 226–245, 331–334, 340–342); Newmyer (2008; 2014b); Lhermitte (2015: 13–21, 52–261); more panoramic discussion in Newmyer (2017a). The most comprehensive account is still Dierauer (1977); especially searching interpretations are Sorabji (1993) and Osborne (2007).

[11] So, for example, Plato, *Statesman* 263c5–d8; Diogenes Laertius 6.40; Sextus Empiricus, *Against the Professors* 8.87: "if we want to learn (*mathein*) what man is, we must first comprehend (*egnōkenai*) what an animal is."

[12] Consider how the famous Cynics are credited with preachy juxtapositions of humankind with animals: e.g. Dio of Prusa 6.21–23; pseudo-Diogenes, *Epistles* 39.4, 40.2; pseudo-Crates, *Epistles* 11 and 24.

[13] See Opsomer's Chapter 4 in this volume.

[14] Cf. Renehan (1981), but also Korhonen and Ruonakoski (2017: 33–39).

[15] Boulogne (2005a); for the bigger picture, see Pfeiffer (2008).

[16] This gambit of moralistic pedagogy in *De amore prolis* is combined, however, with the insistence on superiority of human reason and emotional life: Becchi (1993: 71–72, 75; 2000: 212–213, 221); Newmyer

the story about Brasidas' encounter with a mouse (*Quomodo quis suos in virtute sentiat profectus* 79E)[17] is a transferable lesson in both practical wisdom and ethical self-awareness. And yet Plutarch's anthropocentric philosophical agenda is inclusive and allows for poignant insights into animal suffering,[18] as well as for some witty challenges to the human complacency vis-à-vis animals.

## Animals in the *Lives*

The *Life of Pericles* opens with endorsement of a reproachful remark by Augustus (called here "Caesar") about wealthy pet-owners in Rome:[19] just as the soul's potential for affection should not, says Plutarch, be misspent on animals because it is "owed to humans" (*anthrōpois opheilomenon*),[20] so our learning faculty ought to prioritize when handling the data supplied by the senses (*Pericles* 1.1–2). The Plutarchan analogy between animals and experiences "unworthy of serious concern" (*mēdemias axia spoudēs*, 1.2) is not altogether surprising. To Plutarch, people matter more than animals by default. Thus, it is a welcome resolution to a sacrificial scenario that the victim is a horse rather than a maiden (*Pelopidas* 22);[21] a child's grief over the death of her pet dog does not stop the father hailing the situation as a good omen, because the dead dog happens to share its name with the enemy king (*Aemilius Paulus* 10.6–8); it makes sense to assume that the divine holds dear humans (*ton theon … philanthrōpon onta*) rather than an animal species, whether horses or birds (*Numa* 4.4).[22] But in terms of the narrator's self-fashioning in the *Lives*, anthropocentrism can coexist with the creation of a persona kindly toward animals. The following passage from *Cato Maior* epitomizes such self-characterization.[23]

> Some ascribed this to the man's miserliness (*mikrologia*), but others took it as the sign of a man keeping himself within his means for the correction and moderation of others. However, I for my part consider that to drive off

(2006: 39, 61–62); Jufresa Muñoz (2007: 267–268). Cf. Tutrone (2012: 163–195) on the tension in Seneca's *Epistles* between the ideology of anthropocentric rationality and the references to animals as "natural" agents.

[17] Also told in *Regum et imperatorum apophthegmata* 190B and *Apophthegmata Laconica* 219C; Agesilaus replaces Brasidas in *Apophthegmata Laconica* 208F.

[18] As shown by Plutarch's quotation of the dictum by the Hellenistic philosopher Bion of Borysthenes about the frogs "dying for real" (*De sollertia animalium* 965B). See more later in this chapter.

[19] Stadter (1989: 53–54); Duff (1999a: 34).    [20] Cf. *De fraterno amore* 482C.

[21] Yet see *Agesilaus* 6.4–6; Petropoulou (2008: 103); González González (2019: 171–174).

[22] The same point is made by the Pythagorean visitor in *De genio Socratis* 593A; see Van der Stockt (2007: 201–203).

[23] Beck (2000: 19–23); cf. Calder (2011: 106–107).

slaves and sell them in their old age[24] is to treat them like yoke-animals and the mark of an excessively unbending nature, and one which holds there is no common bond between one man and another apart from utility. And yet we see that kindness (*khrēstotēs*) has a wider scope than justice (*dikaiosynē*): for we naturally apply law and justice only to men, but as far as acts of kindness and goodwill are concerned, sometimes these flow down from our gentleness (*hēmerotēs*) as from a rich spring even as far as irrational animals. And the nourishment of horses who have failed from old age, and not only the whelping years of dogs, but also their care in old age, are the proper business of the good man. ... We should not treat those who have life (*psykhē*) like sandals or chattels, throwing them away when they are broken and worn out by their services, but if for no other reason, for the sake of practice (*meletēs houneka*) in kindness to men (*philanthrōpia*) we should train ourselves to be gentle and kind with them. I certainly would not sell even a working ox because of its age, let alone an elderly man, uprooting him from the place where he had grown up and his accustomed daily round, as though from his fatherland, for the sake of small change, useless as he will be to those who buy him just as to those who have sold him. But Cato as it were swaggers like a young man about this and says that he left behind in Spain even the horse which he used on campaign when he was consul,[25] so that he might not impose the expense of its passage on the city. It is possible for someone to argue either that these things are to be set down to greatness of spirit (*megalopsykhia*) or to miserliness (*mikrologia*). (*Cato Maior* 5.1–2, 5.5–7)

An understandable desire to point to the exceptional qualities of the thought of this striking passage,[26] which clearly suggests that kindness might substitute for justice in dealing with animals, has sometimes obscured its artfulness. Animals are important here, but so are humans. Slaves warrant more, not less, kindness than animals. Kindness to animals is a technique to be practiced not for its own sake, but to refine one's dealings with other humans.[27] Indeed, there is an important blurring here between real animals and the use of animals in imagery, simile, and metaphor so common in ancient discourse of all kinds, and certainly elsewhere in Plutarch. Slaves are treated by Cato

---

[24] Cf. Cato, *On Farming* 2.7.     [25] In 195/194 BCE. Cf. Apuleius, *Apology* 17.9.

[26] Sorabji (1993: 118, 125): "I have not found this argument anywhere else"; Newmyer (2006: 54); further, Santese (1994: 141–145) and de Fontenay (1997: 282–286). Marcus Aurelius (6.23) also demands kindness for animals from a reasoning being, but unlike Plutarch he equates them, being irrational, with lifeless objects. Marcus shows none of the spontaneity conveyed by Plutarch's spring metaphor in *Cato Maior* 5.2 and makes no link between kindness to animals and kindness to humans.

[27] Compare the rationale for kindness toward animals in Philo, *On the Virtues* 140, on which see Berthelot (2002).

"like yoke-animals";[28] the metaphor then becomes semi-realized when Plutarch (at least the narrated Plutarch) contrasts his own actions with Cato's: "I certainly would not sell even a working ox because of its age, let alone an elderly man."

Not only humans generally, but Greeks and Romans are at issue here: the Roman Cato is compared unfavorably not only with the Greek Plutarch himself (the biographer thus intruding into the biography) but also, in the intervening section of the chapter (5.3–4), with the Athenians, who publicly honored the laudable eagerness of a particularly diligent mule during the building of the Parthenon;[29] with Cimon, whose horses are buried close to his own tomb;[30] and with a dog that swam alongside Xanthippus' trireme during the evacuation of Athens at the approach of the Persians and was honored by him with burial on a headland that is named the Dog's Tomb "to this day." The three examples are taken from classical Athenian history, receding from the nearer to the more remote past.[31] Only one of them actually involves caring for an animal in old age rather than honoring an animal after death; but the cumulative effect is to recall that Cato is paired with Aristides the Just, a figure from the Golden Age of Athenian history (the comparison with the age of Cronus is used at *Aristides* 24.2). Even more importantly, *Aristides* is a *Life* where justice, gratitude, and the memory of past service are central, right up to the closing chapter, where Athens is praised for her kindness to the families of her benefactors (*Aristides* 27). Cato's meanness is exposed by contrast, as part of his complex and uncomfortable relationship with things Greek in the *Life*. Not many readers at the end of *Cato* 5 conclude that these economies point to greatness of soul: the weight of the narrative is heavily in the other direction.

Aristides, famously, is the Just, and Plutarch contrasts him with statesmen whose sobriquets are more aggressive (including "the Eagle" Pyrrhus and "the Hawk" Antiochus: *Aristides* 6.2).[32] Justice, Plutarch argues at 6.3–5, is the divine attribute that makes men love the gods and without which human

---

[28] Cf. 21.1, where Cato's young slaves are "still able to bear rearing and training like puppies or colts."

[29] See further Griffith (2006: 151–152); Korhonen and Ruonakoski (2017: 78–79).

[30] That is, Cimon the grandfather of the Plutarchan hero. Note that Plutarch obscures the fact that these horses were most likely sacrificed before receiving such prestigious interment; cf. Herodotus 6.103.3; Aelian, *Characteristics of Animals* 12.40; Papakonstantinou (2014: 109–113).

[31] The story of the mule also features in *De sollertia animalium* 970A–B. On Plutarch's engagement with the Greek past, see Stadter's Chapter 9 in this volume.

[32] Contrast the appreciative mention of these royal sobriquets by Aristotimus in *De sollertia animalium* 975B.

power becomes "bestial" (*thēriōdē*).[33] Justice in the *Cato* passage may not be extended to (domestic) animals,[34] but the reader who recalls the *Aristides* might consider here that Cato's harshness to both men and beasts risks his own humanity. This is not the only passage in the pair where men and beasts are blurred through imagery: collectively, both the Greeks and the Romans become animalic. The Spartan phalanx at Plataea "suddenly had the look of one fierce animal (*henos zōou thymoeidous*) turning to fight and bristling" (*Aristides* 18.2); the Romans at *Cato* 8.2 are like sheep as they follow their leaders; the Firmians must be like lions falling on their prey in Cato's speech at 13.6. Kings are carnivorous beasts (8.8 *zōon ... sarkophagon*); luxury is like the Hydra (16.5). Just as Cato's attitude to Greek *paideia* fluctuates and complicates his moral standing,[35] so animal imagery throughout the pair transforms his little economies into an important index of character. What looks at first sight to be a passage about animals is really about people in general and Cato in particular.

In general in the *Lives*, animals perform the function of displaying the character of the subject, whether used figuratively (as when the young Alcibiades bites a companion in a boyish scuffle: "You bite like a woman!" says his opponent. "No, like a lion!" affirms Alcibiades)[36] or as actors in anecdotes that reveal the subject's character. Alexander's horse Bucephalus is the most elaborate example.[37] Sertorius controls the superstitious Spaniards by shrewdly deploying his tame and trained white fawn (*Sertorius* 11 and 20).[38] In two anecdotes from the *Alcibiades*, which are

---

[33] The comparison between bad men and beasts is also Platonic: see e.g. *Republic* 586a–b; Dierauer (1997: 9); Burgess (2008: 21–22). "Bestial" (*thēriōdēs*) is an epithet that Plutarch frequently applies to barbarians: see Schmidt (1999: 27–35) and Almagor's Chapter 13 in this volume; for subtle discussion of the animal motifs in the *Artaxerxes*, see Almagor (2009–10; 2014b). But ultimately "beastliness" in Plutarch is a moral, not an ethnic quality: the trope "beast(s)" may be used, for instance, about a nasty Greek tyrant (*Pelopidas* 29.3), or Julius Caesar's hard-as-nails soldiers (*Caesar* 39.3). Sometimes the metaphorical beast is the victim rather than the perpetrator of brutality. Thus, Caesar is overwhelmed by the assassins "like a beast" (66.10); see Pelling (2011a: 481).

[34] Elsewhere Plutarch refers to the tradition, attested both in Greece and in Rome, of punishing animals for transgressive behavior, but also of showing gratitude to certain animals for their service to the community (*Solon* 24.3; *De fortuna Romanorum* 325D; *Quaestiones Romanae* 287C); see further Calder (2011: 110–111); Lhermitte (2015: 430–435, 445–447).

[35] Swain (1990a: 126–128, 136); Pelling (2002a: 312).

[36] *Alcibiades* 2.2–3; see Russell (1966b: 39); 194); Duff (1999a: 231; 2003: esp. 99–100 and 112–113); Pelling (2002a: 302); Salcedo Parrondo (2005); Verdegem (2010a: 122–125). The proverbial images of fox and lion are repeatedly mobilized in the paired *Lives* of Lysander and Sulla: see Duff (1999a: 174–176, 200–201). For more examples of figurative references to animals as an element of characterization in the *Lives*, see Jufresa Muñoz (2007: 276); further, Fuhrmann (1964: 58–59, 145–148); also n. 42 in this chapter.

[37] Frazier (1992: 4496–4499); Stadter (1996: 291–296); generally, Calder (2011: 87); Fögen (2017b: 107–113) looks at Bucephalus as a case study in quasi-biographical ancient interest in animals.

[38] The parallelism between animal-taming and ruling over the natives is noteworthy: Xenophontos (2016: 164–165).

juxtaposed (9.1–10.2), the protagonist interacts with an animal in front of "internal" observers, but the narratees are of course implicitly invited to read between the lines, and beyond. Plutarch first tells how Alcibiades cut off the tail of his magnificent and expensive dog.

> When his companions scolded him and told him that everyone was pained (*daknontai*: literally, "bitten") on account of the dog and was abusing him, he laughed and said, "Then what I wanted is coming about; for I want the Athenians to chatter about this so that they may say nothing worse about me." (9.2)

It seems not to be anachronistic to see this as a rebarbative story, even if Plutarch's contemporaries (and Alcibiades') would have seen the tail's removal more as an act of vandalism than of cruelty.[39] Alcibiades' hint that there might well be worse to say of him looks forward uncomfortably to a time when there certainly will be; his manipulation of public opinion and the cynical means chosen to do so epitomize Alcibiades at his most incalculable and his most unattractive.[40] And then immediately afterwards, as part of his technique of confusing the reader about Alcibiades' moral status,[41] Plutarch relates how Alcibiades was passing by the Assembly, heard the applause for someone contributing money to the state, and decided, apparently on impulse, to make his own contribution. When the crowd's applause for him frightened his pet quail into flying off, there was a general rush to recapture it; Antiochus succeeded in doing so, "on account of which he became very dear to Alcibiades" (10.2). Here, instead of the cynicism of the previous chapter of the *Life*, is an (apparently) spontaneous desire to benefit the city – and receive the applause for doing so – and an illustration of the huge affection in which he is held by the Athenians. But there is, again, foreshadowing of trouble to come – Antiochus' folly in 35.4–6 will provide Alcibiades' enemies with ammunition to send him into his last exile. Animals in the *Alcibiades*, then, contribute to the texture of the characterization of this biographical subject in a colorful and provocative manner.[42]

---

[39] So Calder (2017: 78): "The act threatens that this is not a man to trifle with, if he will casually injure innocent familiars."

[40] See Verdegem (2010a: 161–162). The story made an impression on later readers: when Henry Constantine Jennings bought a handsome Roman statue of a Molossian guard dog with a docked tail from a workshop in Rome in the 1750s, he had no hesitation in calling it "the dog of Alcibiades." The dog is now in the British Museum (reg. no. 2001,1010.1).

[41] Duff (1999a: 229–240).

[42] On the quail story, see Verdegem (2010a: 167–168). It may be that animals are particularly prominent in *Alcibiades*, perhaps underlining his moral indeterminacy in the same way that gender destabilization does (on this see Duff 1999a: 231). Apart from the lion image (reprised at 16.3) and the

## Animals in the *Moralia*

More complex still are Plutarch's writings on animals in the *Moralia*,[43] most prominent among which are two dialogues (*De sollertia animalium*; *Bruta animalia ratione uti, sive Gryllus*)[44] and the two-part discourse *De esu carnium*. It will become clear that in common with many, perhaps most, other ancient writers about animals, Plutarch in these essays, as in the *Lives*, is really more interested in discussing people than animals per se. Of these essays, *De esu carnium* is textually problematic, with neither section surviving complete and with at least one passage (994B–D) that has intruded from another work. It is also possible that the end of *Bruta animalia ratione uti, sive Gryllus* may be missing, since the program of discussion advertised is not ultimately carried through.[45] To some extent it is feasible to see all three works as part of Plutarch's broader attack on Stoic philosophy, since the Stoics are the most prominent deniers of rationality to animals,[46] and the first two works directly or indirectly address the rationality of animals, while *De esu carnium* touches on it (997E) and comes close to granting animals linguistic ability:

> Then we decide that the cries and squeaks they make are inarticulate sounds, not pleas and entreaties and appeals to justice from each one saying "I do not beg to be spared your necessity, but your arrogant violence (*hybris*)! Kill me to eat me, but do not slaughter me to eat more enjoyably!" (994E)[47]

---

other examples discussed, Alcibiades is compared with a chameleon at 23.4 and a gadfly (*myōps*) at 21.6, which might be an intertextual salute to Plato's *Apology of Socrates* 30e; see, respectively, Duff 1991a: 231, 235) and Verdegem (2010a: 257 n. 121); on Socrates as gadfly, see Naas (2015) – yet the time-honored translation of *myōps* in the Platonic passage as "gadfly" is not unchallengeable: see Marshall (2017).

[43] In addition to Newmyer's work (n. 1 in this chapter), useful synoptic discussions are Becchi (1993; 2000); Santese (1994: 146–168); Steiner (2005: 93–103); Gilhus (2006: 45–52); Newmyer (2014a); Volpe Cacciatore (2017). Dumont (2001: 351–364) provides an interesting assortment of passages, although analysis is superficial; Ditadi (2000: 25–223) is a feat of high-minded yet tendentious exegesis.

[44] The dual title is the only one in the Plutarchan corpus, and neither appears in the Lamprias Catalogue. Both titles entail wordplay: for Gryllus = "grunter," "oinker," see later in this chapter, and in Greek the collocation *ta aloga logōi* ("irrational... reason)" creates an irony hard to capture in English.

[45] Russell (1993: 348); Ziegler (1951: 740).

[46] So Russell (1973a: 68); Becchi (2000); Steiner (2009–10); Newmyer (2014a: 226–228). On the Stoic view on animals, see e.g. Dierauer (1977: 199–243); Steiner (2005: 77–92; 2008: 36–44); Newmyer (2006: 24–29).

[47] The passage is not at all trivialized by its embeddedness in the rhetorical matrix of *prosōpopoeia*: see Korhonen and Ruonakoski (2017: 66–67). On the central importance of language to the Stoic *scala naturae*, see Labarrière (1997: 263–264, 272–273 with n. 18); for a similar move in the modern controversy, see e.g. Dennett (1996: 10–24, 196–201); also Osborne (2007: 64–70) for incisive critique of language-based definition of intelligence. On views about animal language in antiquity, see further

However, the methods Plutarch uses to discuss human relations with animals are subtle and do not permit us to read any of these works as a straightforward anti-Stoic polemic.

This subtlety of argument is partly created by the textual setting in which animal rationality is discussed. The complex texture of *De sollertia animalium* and *Bruta animalia ratione uti, sive Gryllus* in particular makes crafting a consistent "Plutarchan" worldview a dangerous game[48] if it is done by taking passages out of their context. One may seek to identify certain speakers as more or less likely to be conveying a view the author wishes to validate, and some passages do closely mirror others elsewhere in the Plutarchan corpus; but no unambiguous overall "message" emerges. For Plutarch does not even always assert the rationality of animals: in *Cato* 5, for example, beasts are explicitly without reason and not entitled to justice.[49] Likewise, the plea for vegetarianism in *De esu carnium*[50] can be contrasted with acceptance of moderate consumption of meat in *De tuenda sanitate praecepta* (131F–132A)[51] and the level-headed inquiry into the reasons for the exquisite taste of the bear's paw (*Quaestiones naturales* 917D); in *De sollertia animalium* vegetarianism is not on the radar at all. Even in the homiletic *De esu carnium*, notwithstanding the gruesome depictions of cruelty to animals (993B, 997A),[52] Plutarch is prepared to regulate meat-eating, instead of banning it outright:

> But if, by Zeus, freedom from error is impossible for us because of our habitual ways, let us transgress with shame and accountably. We shall eat flesh, but from hunger, not as a luxury. We shall kill an animal – but with pity and in distress, not abusing or torturing it as many do these days. (996E–F)[53]

---

Sorabji (1993: 78–86); Gera (2003: 11–17, 36–37, 57–67, 208–212); Heath (2005: 5–17, 317–325); Fögen (2007; 2014); Tutrone (2012: 133–139); Kleczkowska (2014); Lhermitte (2015: 215–232); Clark (2017). Plutarch's stance is analyzed by Santese (2005).

[48] *Pace* Becchi (2000); Newmyer (2006: 6–8 and esp. 119 n. 109). Cf. Santese (1994: 165–168).

[49] See also Billault (2005: 41) on *De fraterno amore* 478E and *De fortuna* 98B (the latter text is possibly not by Plutarch); Becchi (2000: 209–210 and n. 32) on Plutarchan contradictions, which he is intent on reconciling (e.g. 211).

[50] On Plutarch and vegetarianism, see Tsekourakis (1987); Jufresa (1996); Becchi (2005); also de Fontenay (1997: 294–295) on the *Quaestiones convivales* 729E. For other writers of the Second Sophistic on food, see Wilkins (2008). Compact surveys of ancient vegetarianism: Gilhus (2006: 64–69); Dombrowski (2014); Lhermitte (2015: 367–383).

[51] Newmyer (2006: 100–101). Compare the irony of Philo the physician about strict vegan diet in *Quaestiones convivales* 660E–F. Pythagoras is invoked as the arch-vegetarian at *De esu carnium* 993C, yet elsewhere in Plutarch there are suggestions that the Pythagorean diet was not totally vegetarian (fr. 122; *Quaestiones convivales* 670D, 728D–E).

[52] Many scholars are convinced that Plutarch was genuinely opposed to animal suffering: Becchi (1993: 59; 2000: 207); Sorabji (1993: 209); Santese (1994: 141); Newmyer (2006: 17–18, 72–74).

[53] Cf. the sobering conclusions in Calder (2011: 58, 108, 118).

The arguments in favor of vegetarianism gravitate toward its advantages from the "secular"[54] human perspective: a meat-free diet is more appropriate for human beings both physically (994F–995E) and ethically (994E–F, 995F–997E, 998B–C) – indeed, it is a "training in humaneness" (995F–996A).[55] Eating choices are thus foregrounded in the concept of habituation, which operates on a sliding scale from bad (996E) to positive. Another topic where Plutarch's judgment appears flexible is sex. Among animals, sexuality is straightforward and therefore pure (*De amore prolis* 493E–F; *Bruta animalia ratione uti, sive Gryllus* 990C–D), whereas humans are guilty of decadence and debauchery (990D–991A). Sex with animals is flagged up as an abomination (990F–991A) – yet the zooerastic incident in Periander's household does not, for all its sinister overtones, cause an outcry (*Septem sapientium convivium* 149C–E),[56] and in *De sollertia animalium* there is no negativity attached to the stories about animals who pursued erotic relationships with humans (972D–F).[57]

Turning to *De sollertia animalium* and *Bruta animalia ratione uti, sive Gryllus*, the interpretive premise has to be that some characters in a dialogue may take up positions, and use particular arguments, which are at least partly dictated by rhetoric. *De sollertia animalium* is a case in point.[58] In this dialogue two speakers, one of whom (Autobulus), is probably Plutarch's father,[59] initially discuss animal rationality between themselves before preparing the way for a rhetorical competition between two much younger speakers whose arguments are much more anecdotal and less philosophically sophisticated than those of their elders. The rhetorical competition is then collapsed into a draw at the end of the dialogue. The main purpose of the rhetorical competition is paideutic: the two young men are given a theme on which they can dilate enthusiastically and with the authority of a keen huntsman and fisherman, respectively. Autobulus in fact begins to argue that hunting (and presumably fishing) is cruel, but he abandons this position at the approach of the younger members of the party for fear of

---

[54] Saliently, Plutarch stops short of committing to belief in reincarnation (996B–C, 998C–F) and avoids (*pace* Jufresa 1996: 224) talking about the role of meat in religious sacrifice.

[55] Cf. *De capienda ex inimicis utilitate* 91C and *De sollertia animalium* 959D–F, 964E–F. For the general principle, compare *Quaestiones convivales* 703B–C: "habit teaches humaneness" (*philanthrōpias didaskalia to ethos estin*), Pompey 28.5.

[56] On this text, see Mossman (1997c: 128–129); Li Causi (2009–10: 51–54).

[57] Further on sex and affection between humans and animals in antiquity, see Hindermann (2011); Korhonen (2012); Franco (2017).

[58] See Mossman (2005a); Mossman and Titchener (2011: 274–289); Li Causi (2010: 192–195).

[59] Alternatively, this Autobulus would have to be Plutarch's oldest son: Horky (2017: 106–107, 114).

hurting their feelings (965B).[60] Already on the previous day all parties have agreed (960A) that all animals are to some extent rational; and that consensus is the backdrop to the debate in the rest of the dialogue. This has the effect of moving the debate away from the Stoic agenda of denying rationality to animals and directing it on to examining in more detail the rationality that animals are held to have.[61] Signally, when Autobulus lays the groundwork for the rhetorical competition, his phraseology is indebted to the Aristotelian idiolect: animal intelligence is viable within a quantitative evaluative model[62] that turns on the principle of "more" and "less" (963A *kata to mallon kai hētton*; cf. 962B–D).[63] This quantitative approach might appear generous toward the animals, yet the intellectual superiority of humans remains secure – the animals' reason is, according to Autobulus, "weak and muddled" (963B).[64]

The dialogue is full of charming anecdotes and displays considerable art in the way it manipulates and explores various uses of anthropomorphism,

---

[60] The dialogue's attitude to hunting is somewhat ambivalent. Soclarus in 959C praises it as a "clean spectacle of skill and intelligent courage pitted against stupid and violent force" (*katharan . . . thean tekhnēs kai tolmēs noun ekhousēs pros anoēton iskhyn kai bian antitattomenēs*), whereas Autobulus notes the violent and sadistic aspects of hunting (959D, 965B); however, he also admits (964F) that it is "not unjust to chastise and kill" beasts who are "unsociable and dangerous (*amikta kai blabera*)." See further Martin (1979); Tovar Paz (1996); Mossman (2005a: 143–146); Li Causi (2010: 195–208); Volpe Cacciatore (2017: 384); an ingenious solution has been proposed by Jazdzewska (2009–10). Hunting as part of the daily routine of Plutarch's target readership: *De exilio* 603E. In the *Lives*, hunting is a suitable pastime for leaders: e.g. *Alexander* 23.3–4, 40.4; *Pompey* 12.7–8, 51.2; *Pelopidas* 4.1; *Sertorius* 13.2.
[61] Mossman (2005a: 143, 146).
[62] Or, inclusive "spectrum": so Horky (2017: 106–120). See also Newmyer (2017b: 249–250).
[63] Cf. Aristotle, *History of animals* 588a25, *tōi mallon kai hētton*, 608b4–6, 612b18–21; also Philo, *On Animals* 29. See Dierauer (1977: 259, 268–269); Becchi (1993: 66; 2000: 207–208); Santese (1994: 153, 165); Ditadi (2000: 212); Newmyer (2006: 34, 40). Plutarch also employs the "more and less" formula in ethical treatises: *Quomodo quis suos in virtute sentiat profectus* 75F–76B, especially 76B; *De virtute morali* 449D–F. The presence of Aristotle in *De sollertia animalium* is not an open-and-shut case. The two young speakers both quote Aristotle's zoological research (973A–B ~ *HA* 535b17, 608a18; 978D ~ *HA* 622a1; 981B ~ fr. 354 Rose; 981F ~ *HA* 621a21–27); more instances of animal behavior could be unacknowledged borrowings from Aristotle: 974B ~ *HA* 612a24–25 (tortoise's self-cure); 971C ~ *HA* 613b17–21, 30–33 (the cunning of the mother-partridge); 961D–E ~ *HA* 604b10–15, compare 611b26–27, 597b21–25 (animal reaction to music). Earlier on, however, Autobulus invites the company to judge "from experience" and not "give trouble to the books of Aristotle" (965D–E). Moreover, Soclarus brackets together the Stoics and the Peripatetics (963F *hoi . . . apo tou Peripatou*) as deniers of animal rationality (cf. Porphyry, *Abstinence* 3.24.6). Still, it is significant that Aristotle's name is not mentioned in 963F; indeed the implied target of the reference could be, for example, Heraclides of Pontus (cf. Porphyry, *Abstinence* 1.13, 1.26.4). The most sustained attempt to reconcile *De sollertia animalium* with the Aristotelian views is Becchi (1993: 76–83; 2000: 218; 2001: 121–124, 126–128), yet there is no agreement in scholarship on how uncompromising and consistent was Aristotle's denial of rationality to animals.
[64] Cf. Lhermitte (2015: 140–141).

and contains critique of the Stoic position that animal perception is distinct from rationality.[65] At the same time, various ironies created by the structure of the piece should make us wary of the assumption that Autobulus' characterization of the Stoics' arguments is necessarily a fair one;[66] or that we might be in a position to reconstruct Plutarch's own view in any straightforward way from the speeches of the four main characters of the dialogue. One hypotext for *De sollertia animalium* may be Xenophon's *Cynegeticus*.[67] Another, potentially more important, may be the conclusion of Plato's *Timaeus*. Here Plato describes the descent via metempsychosis of imperfect men into women, birds, and animals:

> But the race of birds was created out of innocent light-minded men, who, although their minds were directed toward heaven, imagined, in their simplicity, that the clearest demonstration of the things above was to be obtained by sight . . . . The race of wild pedestrian animals, again, came from those who had no philosophy in any of their thoughts, and never considered at all about the nature of the heavens, because they had ceased to use the courses of the head, but followed the guidance of those parts of the soul which are in the breast. In consequence of these habits of theirs they had their front-legs and their heads resting upon the earth to which they were drawn by natural affinity . . . . And the most foolish of them, who trail their bodies entirely upon the ground and have no longer any need of feet, he made without feet to crawl upon the earth. The fourth class were the inhabitants of the water : these were made out of the most entirely senseless and ignorant of all, whom the transformers did not think any longer worthy of pure respiration, because they possessed a soul which was made impure by all sorts of transgression; and instead of the subtle and pure medium of air, they gave them the deep and muddy sea to be their element of respiration; and hence arose the race of fishes and oysters, and other aquatic animals, which have received the most remote habitations as a punishment of their outlandish ignorance. (91d–92b; trans. Jowett)

Clearly the Plutarchan debate as to whether the land animals are cleverer than the sea animals, and the inclusion of birds among both land and sea animals, is in stark contrast with Plato's hierarchical system.[68] Still,

---

[65] The most important passage is Autobulus' speech at 961C–F (which can be linked with the similar argument at *De esu carnium* 994E): interpreting such data as quasi-traces (*hōsanei*) of reason is perverse, he says. See Ditadi (2000: 211–216); Goguey (2003: 87–88); Lhermitte (2015: 97–99).

[66] Wildberger (2008) suggests that quantitative evaluation of animals was not precluded for the Stoics; her caveat on *De sollertia animalium* 961C–F is that "we need not necessarily believe that 'quasi' is as empty a term as Plutarch wants us to believe" (58–59).

[67] Mossman (2005a: esp. 144–145, 155–157).

[68] So Ditadi (2000: 219): "Nel difendere il mondo marino Plutarco sembra tradire la lezione platonica" ("In his defense of the marine world Plutarch appears to betray the Platonic lesson").

Timaeus' account of the descent of man into animals of various kinds fits well with Plutarch's argument that animals have some reason, even if not as much as men (see especially 962A–C). It appears to weaken any distinction between human and animal reason, just as it blurs the distinction between human and animal bodies: animals are as they are because as men they failed in (human) reason.[69] *De sollertia animalium* employs rhetorical strategies that are reminiscent of this blurring and that assist in the overall argument of the dialogue: animals are constantly described in anthropomorphic terms, while people are not infrequently described as beasts.[70] *Timaeus* is not directly quoted in the dialogue (though *Phaedo* 81a7 is, by Aristotimus at 972D), but as the subject of Plutarch's only surviving exegetical work it was evidently a text Plutarch knew intimately and highly valued;[71] both the overall structure of the Plutarchan dialogue and number of individual passages recall it for the alert reader. Both Plato's and Plutarch's texts fall into two parts; in both a conversation from the day before is revisited (in *Timaeus* the content of *Republic* is summarized) before, in the second part, two different characters put on a performance for the first speaker (Socrates) or (in Plutarch) speakers. In both texts there is stress on the second part of the dialogue as performance or entertainment (*Timaeus* 17a–c and 20b–c; *De sollertia animalium* 960A–B). As to individual passages, near the start of the dialogue, at 959E–963F, Autobulus creates his own version of the Platonic descent of bad men into animals: an account of the descent of man measured by his treatment of different kinds of animals until "the murderous and bestial in [man's] nature flourished and were kept immovable by pity."[72] This moral descent is compared to the process by which the Thirty Tyrants at Athens began by murdering people who were seen to deserve it but then moved on to more controversial victims (959D–E; cf. *De esu carnium* 998B); this may recall that one of the speakers in *Timaeus* is Critias. Aristotimus' argument against the intelligence of sea-creatures (975B–C) recalls the reasoning of *Timaeus* 92a–c,[73] as does the overall contrast he makes between birds and fish at 975A–C, particularly through identification of the

---

[69] Burgess (2008: 17): "It is nowhere stated that the animals . . . do not possess all three parts of the soul and specifically the reasoning soul; it is rather the case that the reasoning soul of these animals, though present, is unable to function at an appropriate level because of the adapted physical structures of animals or because of their environment." On Plato's ideas about metempsychosis, see Brisson (1997); Burgess (2008); Lhermitte (2015: 58–60, 428–430).

[70] See e.g. 962D, 982C, 959E, 984C; Mossman (2005a: 151, 153–154).

[71] See Hershbell (1987: 234–247); Opsomer (2004).

[72] See de Fontenay (1997: 291), though she does not connect this passage with the *Timaeus*.

[73] Aristotimus states, "We call stupid and thoughtless (*tous amatheis kai anoētous*) people 'fish' when we abuse or make fun of them." In *Timaeus* 92b1–2 the fish are said to come from "the most entirely senseless and ignorant of all beings" (*ek tōn malista anoētatōn kai amathestatōn*).

aquatic animals' "soul" with their habitat.[74] Phaedimus' counterargument at 975F–976A focuses instead on the ability of the sea-creatures to receive whatever instruction from man they come across, and represents a neat reversal of the Platonic explanation of the origins of fish: Plato's fish came from men who would not learn, for Phaedimus, fish learn when they can. Thus in different parts of the dialogue, Plato's account is both asserted and challenged. Phaedimus is the less confident speaker,[75] but intertextuality with *Timaeus* does not force the reader to reject his argument. His section on dolphins alone is a good corrective to Aristotimus' excessively negative view and the inconclusive end to the competition strongly suggests that there is right on both sides. The ideas of this text are anything but devalued by being tested and problematized by the dialogue form in which they are expressed.[76]

*Bruta animalia ratione uti, sive Gryllus* is an equally sophisticated piece that presents some of the same themes but uses a Homeric episode much beloved of ancient philosophers, the Circe-story from *Odyssey* 10, to query the relationship of man and beast.[77] Speech as a marker of rationality is the most obvious area where the dialogue plays on established thought about the distinction between animals and humans.[78] Plutarch's dialogue shows Odysseus asking Circe to transform back into men any Greeks she may have turned into beasts. But the eponymous character, a pig who was once a Greek, is adamant that he does not wish to be turned back into a man and explains why at length.[79] The relationship between Plutarch's text and his Homeric model is a complex one.[80] In Homer, the scouting-party sent by Odysseus into the mysterious hinterland of the island of Aeaea discovers the magical palace of Circe. When the sailors eat the food she has prepared, they are turned into pigs who have no power of speech and are externally as bestial as the wolves and lions that tamely greet them when they arrive,

---

[74] The "deep" intertext for Aristotimus' points about the closeness of birds to the gods (975A–B) and the impoverished mental faculties of aquatic creatures (975B–C) could be *Timaeus* 47b–c, where Plato links human rationality with observation of the supremely regular heavenly phenomena; Burgess (2008: 18–19 and n. 29). The fish are thus handicapped by their distance from heaven.

[75] Mossman (2005a: 155–159).

[76] This work clearly had considerable influence, considering the unacknowledged quotation by Porphyry in his *Abstinence* (3.20–4 = *De sollertia animalium* 959E–963F). See Newmyer (2006: 105 n. 4).

[77] This dialogue too seems to have had some influence, most palpably on Lucian's *Gallus*: Wälchli (2003: 230–237); for bolder speculation, see Jazdzewska (2015b).

[78] 986B, 988F, "verbalizing from swinishness" (*ek tēs syēnias phthengomenos*); further, Kirk (2017). See n. 47 in this chapter.

[79] The trope of the talking animal locates him in a tradition that goes back to the talking horses of Achilles (*Iliad* 19.397–423); Tozza (2012: 194–197).

[80] Casanova (2005a; 2005b); Tozza (2008–9; 2012); Hunter (2018: 173–180). Odysseus' profile in Greek tragedy may be intertextually relevant too: see Casanova (2006–7).

even though (we are told) they retained their human minds (*Odyssey* 10.239–240). In Homer, Odysseus' men are retransformed (and rejuvenated and beautified into the bargain) only a short time afterwards at Odysseus' behest (10.382–396). Gryllus, though he claims to know Odysseus (see later in this chapter on this intriguing claim), has clearly been a pig for some time, and cannot therefore be one of his companions.

Plutarch's reading of this narrative has been interpreted in a number of ways, and the influence of a number of different philosophical schools and philosophical purposes has been detected.[81] Gryllus himself, though his arguments recall many philosophical trends[82] and notwithstanding the label "sophist" (989B; cf. 988F, 992C), is characterized broadly as a Cynic.[83] He employs many overtly Cynic arguments, and a Cynic tone, against Odysseus. The keynote argument, that animals are wiser than humans, is widely seen as Cynic. The use of *parrhēsia*, frank speech, by a Cynic philosopher (in this case a porcine one) to a social superior (Odysseus the king of the Cephallenians, 986E: a punning title),[84] the use of puns, and more generally the adaptation of Homer can all be associated with Cynic thought.[85] Further, the setting on the island of Aeaea might

---

[81] See Indelli (1995); Bréchet (2005). Gryllus is frequently seen as an Epicurean (cf. Horace, *Epistles* 1.4.16, "a pig from the Epicurean herd"): e.g. Usener (1887: 70); Hunter (2018: 177). Horky (2017: 122–130) is a thoughtful and balanced reading of the Epicurean strand in Gryllus' argument. See later in this chapter for the perceived Stoicism of Odysseus.

[82] Notably, his definition of temperance (*sōphrosynē*) as "curtailing and ordering channeling" of desires (989B) resembles the standard Middle-Platonic formula of ethical virtue as *metriopatheia*: *De virtute morali* 443C–D, 444B–C; 451C; 451E–452B; *De tuenda sanitate praecepta* 127A; *De genio Socratis* 584D–F; Aulus Gellius 1.26.11; Apuleius, *On Plato* 2.5; "Alcinous," *Handbook of Platonism* 30.3–6. Cf. Konstan (2010–11: 380–381).

[83] Often suggested: see especially Bergua Cavero (1991); also Stanford (1954: 46); Dierauer (1977: 187–193); Sorabji (1993: 160–161); Indelli (1995: 25–33); Bréchet (2005: 46). Perhaps a Cynic ought to be represented by a dog; but dogs only form part of Circe's menagerie at Horace, *Epistles* 1.2.26, on which see Eidinow (1990). By preserving Gryllus' identity as a pig but giving him a Cynic air and many Cynic arguments, Plutarch may be allowing him to represent an amalgam of Cynicism and Epicureanism: so Bréchet (2005: 51, 54–55). The fact that Plutarch is indifferent or quite likely unsympathetic toward contemporary Cynics adds some more weight to the view that Gryllus does not speak for Plutarch – see later in this chapter.

[84] Mossman and Titchener (2011: 291) render Cephallenians as "Brainiacs."

[85] Animals wiser than humans: Dio of Prusa 6.18; Goulet-Cazé (1996: 61–64); Desmond (2008: 150–161). *Parrhēsia*: Diogenes Laertius 6.69 and *passim* in Book 6. Puns: see, for example, Branham (1996: 94), citing Diogenes Laertius 6.37, 68; Desmond (2008: 123–124). Adaptation of Homer: Antisthenes wrote a number of works based on Homer; see Diogenes Laertius 6.17–18; see also immediately later in this chapter on Crates' reworking of Homer. The tapestry of associations is too rich to be gone into fully here: as Helmbold notes in Cherniss and Helmbold (1957: 489–490), the dialogue comes close to instantiating a proverb: "The sow teaches Athena" (*Demosthenes* 11.5, *Praecepta gerendae reipublicae* 803D). In this case, the hog teaches a favorite of Athena. Still, the cumulative effect is to characterize the pig as essentially Cynic.

encourage the reader to recall Crates' poetic description of the Cynic paradise Pera (knapsack):

> There is a city, Pera, in the middle of wine-dark smoke (*typhos*), beautiful and with rich soil, washed by dirt, possessing nothing. To it sail no fools or parasites or lechers drooling at some whore's behind. Instead it brings forth thyme and garlic and figs and loaves of bread. For such things nobody fights wars, and here they do not arm themselves to battle for coin or glory. (Diogenes Laertius 6.85, trans. Desmond)

Crates alludes specifically to Homer's description of Crete (19.172–180), which is mentioned later by Gryllus, but it could also apply to Aeaea. Plutarch wrote a *Life of Crates* (a fellow Boeotian; Lamprias Catalogue no. 37), and is highly likely to have been familiar with this poem, and with Crates' other literary works, which included more parodies of Homer and other *paignia* (jokes),[86] so any reference to him would not be surprising in this context. The *ad hominem* insult with which the Plutarchan dialogue currently ends should be read as a Cynic-style snub along the lines of many others recorded as characteristic of those wittiest, and rudest, of the ancient philosophers. Dio of Prusa also reconfigures and gives a Cynic slant to the Circe-episode at *Oration* 6.62, where he makes Diogenes say:

> I shall find all the food I need in apples, millet, barley, vetches, the cheapest of lentils, acorns roasted in the ashes, and cornel-berries, on which Homer says Circe feasted Odysseus' comrades and on which even the largest animals can subsist. (trans. Cohoon)

The allusion is ironic, though not particularly intended to undermine Diogenes: this is the fare Circe fed the crew when they had become pigs, not the food she gave to them (mixed with the magical substance which transformed them) as men; but Diogenes the Cynic sage is wise enough to see it as sufficient for men too.[87]

If Gryllus is a Cynic, is Odysseus a Stoic?[88] Odysseus is the great Stoic hero, after all (though, along with Heracles, he is a great Cynic hero

---

[86] The term was used as a staple tag for (light) verse; Julian, *Oration* 6.199d applies it specifically to Crates' poetry.

[87] Contrast the clear distinction made by Galen (*On the Powers of Foods* 1.14 and 2.38) between human and animal food: see Wilkins (2008: 321).

[88] E.g. Bréchet (2005: 49). In another Plutarchan reworking of the Circe episode (*De communibus notitiis adversus Stoicos* 1064A) Odysseus faces a choice of magical potions: one potion would make him insane; the other would transform him into an ass, with his human reason intact. The personified Stoic *phronēsis* urges him to drink the former potion. See Bettini and Franco (2010: 346 n. 165). In his eagerness to one-up the Stoics, Plutarch distorts their idea that humans (and other animals) are psychophysical units, so that the rational qualities and capacities inherent in human

too).[89] This view would site *Bruta animalia ratione uti, sive Gryllus*, like *De sollertia animalium*, as anti-Stoic. But there are difficulties: animal virtue rather than rationality is the issue for most of the text as we have it, and the hallmark Stoic terminology is absent.[90] Still, if a pig not only speaks to you but beats you into submission in the argument, not even a hardened Stoic is likely to be able to deny the beast reason. As in *De sollertia animalium*, the big question about rationality is figured as already resolved and a further stage in the argument occupies the dialogue instead. But Odysseus in the text as we have it says little that marks him as a Stoic (he does not get much of a say anyway). And let us not forget that Gryllus is cheating: he used to be a man and has kept his human mind; indeed, for much of the extant dialogue he reduces Odysseus to virtual silence.[91] Of course, there is a joke here: the eloquent Odysseus is all but silenced by a pig.[92] And the pig reads Homer, though not always as carefully as he might. Indeed, it is partly his misreading of Homer that prompts the reader to ask: is the pig really winning the argument?

For instance, the admission that he extracts from Odysseus, that the island of the Cyclops surpasses Ithaca because it is naturally fertile, and the further admission that the soul is the same as the soil (986F–987B), while a neat twist, demands from the reader a different response: Ithaca, famously a good nurse of youths (*Odyssey* 9.27), produces better creatures than the island of the Cyclopes can boast (although in some ways the Cynics, anti-social as they were and sometimes accused of cannibalism, might have seen that differently).[93] Odysseus should have resisted this very dubious use of metaphor as argument.

At 989E, Gryllus claims to have seen Odysseus in Crete once and to have admired his clothes (a worldly attitude he is now above, for sure). But the

---

nature are inseparable from being physically human: *SVF* I 518; II 885; Long (1996: 227–231, 235–244); Couloubaritsis (1986: 110–118).

[89] Odysseus in Stoicism and Cynicism: Stanford (1954: 121–127); Höistad (1948: 94–102); Montiglio (2011: 66–94).

[90] There is a serious question as to whether the dialogue is complete. If there is a large lacuna in 991D, and/or the end is missing, which the omission of the virtue of justice from the discussion might suggest, then anything could have happened: Odysseus might have responded more intelligently than he does in the extant text. Yet see Casanova (2012).

[91] Odysseus' fatal error is to accept Gryllus' suggestion that naturally virtuous souls are better than those who have to work at acquiring virtue (987A–B). Elsewhere Plutarch talks of animal nature as static and primitive: *De amore prolis* 493C–E, *Adversus Colotem* 1125A.

[92] See also Billault (2005: 36–37).

[93] See Diogenes Laertius 6.73; Branham (1996: 103) (Diogenes as "a defender of freaks," based on Dio of Prusa 10.30); Desmond (2008: 86). This is not a characteristically Cynic argument, however: Antisthenes, at least, thought that virtue could be taught (Diogenes Laertius 6.10).

incident referred to is *Odyssey* 19.172–235, where Odysseus tells Penelope a long and circumstantial story about meeting himself in Crete. No fool, she asks for further details and is given a description of what Odysseus was wearing, which is recalled here.[94] Donald Russell suggests that "in making Gryllus be witness to a fiction, Plutarch perhaps intended to stress the fantasy of his imagined dialogue."[95] José Antonio Fernández Delgado puts the reference down to the creation of general Homeric atmosphere and sees the *Gryllus*-episode as "atemporelle".[96] But details from the Homeric passage are closely recalled, though not in the same order:[97] the purple cloak, the wonderful chiton, and the clasp on the cloak. The shape of the clasp, however, dwelt on in Homer, is referred to rather airily by Gryllus as *paignion*, a frivolity.[98] The reason is clear: the subject is a hound throttling a fawn. In Gryllus' account of animal courage he asserts (987D–E) that "lion is never enslaved to lion, nor horse to horse through unmanliness." A picture of an animal killing one of another species does not help his rhetoric and so is dismissed. Gryllus, in short, describes himself as a minor character in a lying narrative from the epic named after his dialogical opponent, which hardly sits well with the scorn he pours on Odysseus' glory (987B–C). And Gryllus has not been studying his Homer with enough attention if he is inserting himself into the wrong part of Odysseus' narrative.[99]

Gryllus' language and his critique of Homeric similes reinforce the impression that his argument is flawed.[100] Gryllus sums up his argument that animal courage is superior to human by using Homeric compound words to illustrate that poetic comparisons indicating courage are made with animals, not with humans. However, the word used most for courage (for which there would have been alternatives) is *andreia*, "manliness,"

---

[94] *Odyssey* 19.225–231 (trans. W. Shewring): "King Odysseus wore a thick double mantle; it was crimson and had a clasp of gold with two sheaths. In front was a cunning piece of work – a hound had a dappled fawn between its forepaws, holding it firm as it struggled. Everyone was amazed to see how the hound and the fawn both were gold, yet the one was gripping and throttling the fawn, and the other striving to break away and writhing with its feet."

[95] Russell (1993: 387).      [96] Fernández Delgado (2000: 175). See also Casanova (2005: 108–109).

[97] Hunter (2018: 178–180).

[98] The Greek word may serve as a metaliterary clue to Plutarch's text too: Hunter (2018: 179 n. 5); compare the closure of Gorgias' *Helen* (fr. B11.21 Diels-Kranz).

[99] The portrayal of Circe also surrounds her with slightly offkey re-readings of Homer: for example, she uses Calypso's argument (*Odyssey* 5.203–213) that it is pointless to go back to Penelope rather than stay with her, a goddess, to suggest that Odysseus is wrong to want to turn the animals back to men at 985F–986A. See Billault (2005: 34–36); Casanova (2005a: 104–105).

[100] According to Herchenroeder (2008: 372–373), the pig uses too many Atticisms and does so inconsistently. This not very convincing; Odysseus, after all, has two instances of double tau for double sigma in his third speech (985D).

which works to undermine Gryllus' point.[101] It seems the ex-man cannot help using a metaphor from men to express virtue.

There are other flaws in Gryllus' argument on courage, too. It is not obvious that he is right that courage blended with reason is inferior to the undiluted courage shown by animals. There is more than one passage of Plato that is relevant here: not only *Phaedo* 68d, where brave men are said to endure death for fear of something worse, which could be seen as supporting Gryllus' argument, but especially *Laches* 196d–e, where courage is cross-examined and Nicias insists on wisdom as a component of courage. Socrates subsequently leads Nicias away from this definition, but his contention here is not in fact directly refuted. Certainly the examples given by Gryllus of brave female animals are not encouraging: like Socrates in the *Laches*, he brings up the Crommyonian sow, then adds the Sphinx, the Teumessian vixen (see Pausanias 9.19.1), and the Python. They may or may not all be brave, but they are all mythological and all monstrous.

All this casts doubt on the regular view that the pig is a mouthpiece for Plutarch.[102] To be sure, in some places Gryllus' views are consistent with arguments Plutarch elsewhere gives to characters who are favorably drawn (for example, *De sollertia animalium* 964F–965A). Then, too, in Plato's *Republic* 2 (372d4–5) Socrates, as his first attempt at envisaging the perfect city, describes a simple-living community, which Glaucon dismisses as "a city of pigs." Socrates, on the other hand, calls it the Healthy City, and Glaucon's preferred more comfortable one is a city with an inflammation.[103] So perhaps Gryllus' arguments for the simple life might strike a chord with Plutarch's readers and his own Platonism.[104] But the consistency game, as suggested earlier, is a dangerous one to play: other passages of Plutarch suggest a very different view. Consider *Marius* 46.1, where Plutarch rebukes Marius' discontent by recalling that Plato had blessed himself on his deathbed that he had been born a man, not an animal, and a Greek, not a barbarian. And nowhere else in Plutarch is it argued that it is better to be an animal than a person.[105] Compare fr. 200 (from Porphyry), plausibly identified as Plutarchan.[106] The fragment picks

---

[101] 986F, 987C, 988A (*andreia* used of the female Sphinx), 988C, 988D, especially 988B, "men have no natural claim to courage" (*tois andrasin ou physei metesti tēs andreias*) – a pun, rather than a self-contradictory slip.

[102] Major exceptions to this consensus are Bréchet (2005), Herchenroeder (2008), and Konstan (2010–11).

[103] Herchenroeder (2008: 369–370).

[104] Further on Platonic influence in *Bruta animalia ratione uti, sive Gryllus*, see Bréchet (2005: 55–58).

[105] Herchenroeder (2008: 362); Calder (2011: 114).      [106] Helmig (2008).

up on the same Homeric conception as Odysseus does at 986E when he accuses Gryllus of having lost his intelligence as well as his shape when he drank Circe's potion. But in fr. 200 the argument is clearly interpreting and building on the Odyssean passage to suggest that being a beast would be bad for your soul:

> The story [of Circe and the pigs] is a riddling version of what Pythagoras and Plato said about the soul, how although imperishable in nature and eternal, it is by no means incapable of suffering or change, but at its so-called destruction and death it undergoes a change and reordering to other bodily shapes; pursuing according to its inclination the one which suits it and is appropriate in its habitual similarity to its way of life.

In the light of this fragment, Odysseus' remark at 986E "Or was it rather an inclination to swinishness that magicked you into this body?" seems more serious than the mere abuse Gryllus dismisses it as.[107] Furthermore, Plutarch knows well that the *Republic*'s Kallipolis ends up not looking very like the "city of pigs" at all – the thrust of Plato's argument is not that everyone in the ideal city should live at a basic animal level, or that only natural and untaught virtue is worth having.

Even Gryllus' name may suggest a problem with his moral position. "Gryllus" not only puns on the Greek for grunting and evokes grotesque visual art,[108] it is also the name of Xenophon's father and his son. Xenophon's son died fighting bravely at Mantinea (362 BCE); Plutarch writes movingly about Xenophon's dignified reaction to the news of his death in the *Consolatio ad Apollonium* (118F–119A). Animals may have reason, and Gryllus certainly does, but he is after all a rather exceptional animal who used to be a man. Animals may have virtues – indeed, the argument that their virtues are superior to human ones is not necessarily unpersuasive.[109] The animals do not have a monopoly on either virtues (think Gryllus, son of Xenophon) or reason, though, and Gryllus, an unimpressive man and a domesticated pig, is not much of an exponent

---

[107] "Swinishness," *syēnia* (cf. 988F), is editorial conjecture for the manuscripts' *synētheia*, "customary habit," which would mean "Or was it rather an inclination in your habitual way of life which magicked you into this body?" Konstan (2010–11: 374–375 n. 8) opts for *syēnia*, but *synētheia* (preferred by Indelli 1995: 118–119) certainly reflects Plutarch's ideas about character (*De amore prolis* 493C, *Quaestiones convivales* 682C), and specifically in the context of reincarnation (fr. 200); compare Plato, *Republic* 620a2–3: "the majority were choosing by habit" (*kata synētheian*). This word can also mean "herding together" of animals, rather a neat pun, but *syēnia*, as an unambiguously insulting word, suits the context better.

[108] Herchenroeder (2008: 348–359) discusses the name at length.

[109] See Mossman and Titchener (2011: 294); Lhermitte (2015: 52, 101); Newmyer (2017b: 236–242). Yet see n. 91 in this chapter.

of animal virtue. Unlike Nicias, Laches, and Socrates in Plato's *Laches*, the pig seems to have little or no experience of courage, for all he harangues Odysseus about it.[110] The Underworld, and Scylla and Charybdis (referred to with splendid obliquity in the first line of the dialogue as "these things," *tauta*),[111] are out there waiting for Odysseus and those who sail with him, and the journey will not be easy. But Odysseus will get home to Ithaca, as Circe said at 985F he was bent on doing, whereas in the end a pig is just bacon. For some readers, then, the joke becomes a rather different one from the sophisticated Odysseus being beaten by a beast in argument: in fact, the joke is on the pig.

In conclusion, while it is true that Plutarch is perhaps the clearest example of an ancient author who found animals good to think with, it is far from easy to pin down his texts about animals, and still harder to be sure what, if any, settled views he held about the respective roles that should be played by animals and humans in the world order. What is clear is that animals provided him with a focus for thinking about people, about human nature. Human flaws and human virtues could be explored and expressed with reference to animals through metaphor, through anecdote, and through rhetoric. The humanity with which Plutarch succeeded in investing his texts about animals is thus a very large part of his point.

## Further Reading

The best general starting point is Campbell (2014); superb bibliography in Fögen (2017a).

Standard, if slightly too benign, overviews of Plutarch's attitude to animals: Newmyer (2006; 2014a). For more in-depth examination of the philosophical issues, see Santese (1994); Becchi (2000); Horky (2017). On *De Sollertia animalium*, see especially Mossman (2005a). There has been a veritable explosion of scholarly interest in *Bruta animalia ratione uti, sive Gryllus* over the last two decades; Bréchet (2005) and Herchenroeder (2008) are must-read studies.

---

[110] Herchenroeder (2008: 373–374) stresses that the pig's inveighing against the domestication of animals at 987E is inconsistent with his own choice of life at Circe's.
[111] See also Casanova (2005a: 100–101).

CHAPTER 15

# Plutarch in Byzantium

## Noreen Humble

I have decided to copy out Plutarch's works
because I greatly like the man, as you know.[1]

Maximus Planudes (ca. 1255–1305)

The influence of Plutarch on Byzantine literature and the course of transmission of his texts from late antiquity to the Renaissance are vast subjects. Even the parameters of such a study are subject to discussion.[2] The fact that more scholarly work has been carried out on the manuscript tradition of Plutarch's works[3] than on direct inquiry into Plutarch's reception by Byzantine authors[4] reflects a general approach to Byzantium that has only recently begun to lose its grip; that is, the view that the Byzantines are interesting solely as "transmitters of classical learning for the benefit of the West."[5] But even the copying of

* I would like very much to thank the editors for their patience, encouragement, and excellent editorial guidance. Thanks are also due to Katie Cupello for her work as my research assistant and to Jeff Beneker, Lucas McMahon, Przemyslaw Marciniak, Ingela Nilsson, Charlotte Roueché, and Keith Sidwell for casting their learned eyes over various drafts and offering illuminating advice. They are not to be held responsible for any shortcomings herein.
[1] Leone (1991: 169, #106).
[2] For example, does the Byzantine period start in 330 with the foundation of Constantinople or in the seventh or even eighth centuries after the Arab invasions? Important discussions on the implications include Ljubarskj et al. (1998: 59–60); Cameron (2006: 5–6); Shepard (2008: 21–26); and Odorico (2009).
[3] The manuscript tradition both of the *Lives* and the *Moralia* has been examined closely. For the *Moralia*, the most comprehensive overview is Irigoin (1987) (with references to earlier bibliography). Also Gallo (1988), Harrison (1991: 4667–4669), and the introductions to all the Budé editions of the *Moralia* treatises. For the *Lives*, see, for example, Flacelière, Chambry, and Juneaux (1964: xxxii–l), Irigoin (1976; 1982–3), and again commentaries on individual, or pairs of, *Lives*.
[4] Studies dealing specifically with Plutarch and Byzantium are few: Hirzel (1912: 98–101) is brief; Ziegler (1964: 309–315) – (1951: 948–953) is still useful; building on these are Tartaglia (1987: 341–346), Garzya (1998), and Pade (2007: I.37–59); Baldwin (1995) deals solely with the sixth to eighth centuries; the entry on Plutarch in Kazhdan (1991), and likewise, Payen (2001) and Pade (2014: 535–536) are very brief; Harrison (1991: 4677) skips from late antiquity to the Renaissance in his survey. Oikonomopoulou and Xenophontos (2019) is a recent welcome antidote.
[5] Cameron (2006: 198); see also discussions about approaches to Byzantine literature such as Ljubarskj et al. (1998) and Mullett (2002).

a text (an expensive and lengthy process) is rarely done simply for purposes of preservation, and the case of Plutarch is doubly of interest because his writings were not studied in schools and he does not write in the pure Attic style so favored for imitation by many of the Byzantine authors.

What I want to do in this chapter, then, is first to trace the state of our knowledge about the transmission of the texts. Then I want to look at some specific examples of reception in the period extending from the ninth to the fourteenth centuries.[6] The survey is of necessity selective but will nonetheless show how much still we have to investigate and discover on this topic.

## Transmission

Of the extant works today attributed to Plutarch, there are the twenty-two pairs of *Parallel Lives*, plus *Lives* of Aratos, Artaxerxes, Otho, and Galba, and approximately eighty treatises, the latter collectively referred to as the *Moralia*, some of which are now considered spurious.[7] That this does not comprise all that Plutarch wrote can be seen from fragments of lost works preserved in other authors,[8] and from comparison of titles with the list known as the Lamprias Catalogue. The Catalogue first appears in a tenth-century manuscript but is generally agreed to date to the third or fourth centuries and to be an inventory of Plutarchan works in a late antique library.[9] As the list (among other problems) includes works we now consider spurious as well as omitting works we now consider Plutarchan, comparison is not straightforward, but in general when we consider the fragments and the Catalogue it looks as if there is extant less than half of what Plutarch originally wrote.[10]

The loss and the preservation belong to different periods of the Byzantine era. A recognized watershed comes with the work of the Byzantine monk Maximos Planudes (ca. 1255–ca. 1305), a teacher and scholar,[11] who spent a

---

[6]  The more neglected period in recent studies. Garzya and Pade (see n. 4 in this chapter), for example, have far more examples from (late) antiquity than from the ninth century onwards.

[7]  Opinion is always shifting on this point: for example, the *Regum et imperatorum apophthegmata* and *Apophthegmata Laconica* are considered spurious in Russell (1968: 132), but see Beck (2002) for arguments in favor of authenticity; see also Stadter (2008: 53–54) for a brief overview.

[8]  The most accessible collection is Sandbach (1969).

[9]  On the Catalogue, see Irigoin (1986; 1987: ccciii–cccxviii) and Garzya (1988: 12).

[10]  Irigoin (1987: ccxxxvi–ccxxxvii) provides a good assessment of how much has probably been lost.

[11]  On Planudes, Wegehaupt (1914) and Wendel (1950) are still useful; also see Wilson (1996: 230–241) and Fryde (2000: 226–267). Constantinidis (1982: 66–89) concentrates on Planudes' role as a teacher.

great deal of time and energy collecting, editing, and copying all the works of Plutarch he could find.[12] Two autograph manuscripts exist: one, dating to 1294–6, contains *Moralia* #1–69 and the *Lives* of Otho and Galba; the other, dated July 11, 1296, contains these, as well as twenty-three pairs of *Parallel Lives* (with *Aratos–Artaxerxes* here counted as a pair).[13] Treatises #70–78 were added to the corpus shortly after Planudes' time.[14] Note that the numeration of *Moralia* treatises followed in this paper is that found in the manuscript Parisinus graecus 1672, which is traditionally referred to as Planudean. Modern numeration follows the order used in the printed edition of 1572 by Henri Estienne.[15]

Planudes, however, was not working in a vacuum, and it is still evident even to us that interest in Plutarch had already burgeoned during the tenth to twelfth centuries.[16] Early manuscripts exist that (a) combine some *Lives* and some treatises, (b) contain *Lives* only, and (c) contain treatises only.[17] Patterns are hard to discern and standardization appears to have been established earlier for the *Lives* than for the treatises.[18] So, for example, by the tenth century we can see two separate ways of presenting the *Lives*: (a) a two-volume edition ordered chronologically by the Greek subject and (b) a more popular three-volume edition ordered chronologically by the Greek subject within geographical location (e.g. Athens, Syracuse, Sparta).[19]

The period of loss, as far as we can ascertain, seems to occur between the sixth and early ninth centuries. Not only does the Lamprias Catalogue supply the names of numerous treatises that do not appear in circulation after this period, but most of the fragments or references to now lost works can be firmly located prior to the sixth century, even when notice is made of them in later periods. So, for example, the Byzantine patriarch Photios

---

[12] On Planudes' editing skills, see Wilson (1996: 235–236); on the extent of his scholarly activity, see Diller (1937).

[13] Ambrosianus graecus 895 (= C 126 inf.) and Parisinus graecus 1671 respectively. See Constantinidis (1982: 74–75), Manfredini (1988b: 123), and Wilson (1996: 235). Garzya (1998: 17–18) is a good overview.

[14] Wilson (1975) has shown that a codex previously attributed to Planudes and dated ca. 1302 (Parisinus graecus 1672), which is the earliest copy of treatises #70–78, should be dated a half-century later and connected with followers of Planudes. See Hillyard (1977: 35–36) for a useful synopsis. See also later in this chapter for traces before the fourteenth century of knowledge of *Moralia* #73 (*Adversus Colotem*) and #76 (*De Herodoti malignitate*).

[15] See the first volume in the Budé edition of *Moralia* (Flaceliére et al. 1987: cccxix–cccxxi) for a concordance between the two lists. The first volume in the Loeb series, Babbitt (1927: xxi–xxiii), also provides the Planudean numeration.

[16] Wilson (1996: 151).     [17] Irigoin (1987: ccxxxiv–ccxxxv); Garzya (1988); Manfredini (1988a).

[18] Scholars often talk of treatises #1–21 becoming canonic early on (e.g. Wilson 1996: 235), but Irigoin (1987: cclvi) expresses caution on this front, though elsewhere he suggests we might have traces of an attempt at an edition of Plutarchan treatises as early as the tenth century: Irigoin (1976).

[19] Irigoin (1982–3) is good on the establishment of these patterns.

(ca. 810–93; on him see later in this chapter) in his summary of the *Excerpta* of the fourth-century Neoplatonic philosopher Sopater of Apamea (*Bibliotheca* 161) provides evidence that in the fourth century, Plutarch's *Lives* of Crates, Daiphantus, Pindar, and Epaminondas were still in circulation. Further, only just over half the Plutarchan treatises that Stobaios (fl. fourth/fifth century) excerpts for his *Anthology* (compiled for the moral training of his son) are now extant.[20] It is not necessary to posit some anti-Plutarchan movement to explain the loss; a brief overview of the general political situation in the Byzantine world will suffice. War, albeit successful for the empire, dominated the sixth century, but gains were swiftly followed by losses in the seventh century as Arab invasions cut into Byzantine territory. The economy then spiraled downwards for at least a century and consequently access to education declined. Further, leading scholars, who were invariably churchmen or civil servants, were involved in the bitter debate over iconoclasm, leaving less time for pure learning and philosophizing. The period (roughly speaking the seventh to ninth centuries) is, in fact, often referred to as the "dark ages,"[21] and Plutarch is not the only author to have suffered losses to his oeuvre during this time.

It is worth noting that although most of the evidence for what has been discussed above comes from the Byzantine East and that it is likewise from the East that Plutarch's texts penetrated into the West starting in the fourteenth century (see later in this chapter), there are traces of Plutarch to be found in the Greek-speaking West too after the period of the dark ages.[22] It is difficult to know, however, if the manuscript tradition is independent or linked somehow to what is happening in the East. An argument has in fact been made in favor of the Lamprias Catalogue representing the contents of a library in Southern Italy or Sicily.[23] Henricus Aristippus (died ca. 1162), archdeacon of the Latin church in Catania, who served the Norman rulers in Sicily and is known to have participated in an embassy to the Byzantine emperor,[24] mentions in a letter that Plutarch is among the authors represented in Sicilian libraries, but

---

[20]  On Stobaios and Plutarch, see Piccione (1998).

[21]  See Auzépy (2008) and the more detailed reassessment of the core of this period, particularly with respect to the impact of iconoclasm, in Brubaker and Haldon (2011).

[22]  When we move north out of the Greek-speaking area, knowledge of Plutarch before the end of the fourteenth century appears dependent solely on notices in classical Latin authors, but also via the probably forged (though when is debated) *Institutio Traiani*, excerpts of which first feature in John of Salisbury's *Policratus* (completed in 1159). See Pade (2007: I.62–66, with earlier bibliography) and Pade's Chapter 16 in this volume.

[23]  See Irigoin (1986: 323–324).

[24]  On Aristippus, see Canart (1978: 148–149), Garzya (1988: 19), and Wilson (1996: 213–214).

gives no hint of the manuscript's content.[25] Whether this particular manuscript was, like others we know of during this time, a gift from a Byzantine emperor to a Norman king is difficult to tell.[26] Indeed, we likewise have no way of knowing whether or not the manuscript Aristippus refers to is actually, or is related to, the extant twelfth-century manuscript of Southern Italian or Sicilian origin that contains twenty-one Plutarchan treatises.[27] Knowledge of one of these twenty-one treatises (*Quomodo adolescens poetas audire debeat*) is found roughly a century later in a philosophical work of the poet-scholar-notary Giovanni Grasso of Otranto (fl. ca. 1215–50),[28] but he also appears to know Plutarch's *Adversus Colotem*, and the earliest extant copy of that work comes from the mid-fourteenth century and the environs of Constantinople (see n. 14 in this chapter).[29]

The first trace we have of a Plutarchan text in the Latin-speaking West is undoubtedly from the East. It is a Planudean codex of *Moralia* #1–69 that appears in the early fourteenth century in Padua in the possession of Pace of Ferrara. It is tempting to connect the appearance of the codex with Planudes' diplomatic mission in Venice in 1296–7.[30] The ability to translate ancient Greek, however, remains confined to the South of Italy essentially for another century, despite the establishment of a chair of Greek in Avignon in the early 1300s and (abortive) efforts by figures such as Petrarch to learn the language.

But Avignon does play an important role in the transmission of Plutarchan texts from East to West.[31] It is there in 1373 that the first translation into Latin is made of a work of Plutarch. Simon Atumanus, who was a monk in Constantinople but later, having converted to Catholicism, became archbishop of Thebes, translated *De cohibenda ira* for, and at the request of, Cardinal Pietro di Tommaso Corsini.[32] From where precisely Atumanus got hold of the Greek text of the work is unclear: was it copied for him by a friend in Constantinople? Was it part of his

[25] See Pade (2007: I.62) for the text and translation of this part of the letter.
[26] Garzya (1988: 19) leans toward placing it in a purely Italian tradition.
[27] Vindobonensis phil. gr. 129 (W), on which see Irigoin (1987: ccxlix–ccl) and Manfredini (1987: 1002), following Cavallo (1980: 192). See also Pade (2007: I.62).
[28] See Romano (1994) on Grasso's *Lysis*; and further on Grasso, Gigante (1979: 19–53, 103–144).
[29] Sandbach (1941: 110–111) and others have noticed that the title page of the eleventh-century manuscript, Marcianus 250, contains a reference to *Moralia* #70–77 and #38, but the dating of the hand of the title page is under dispute and may in fact belong to the fourteenth century (see Manton 1949: 98 n. 3 and Manfredini 1988b: 134–135).
[30] See Stadter (1973a). The manuscript is Ambrosianus C 126 inf.
[31] Weiss (1953) is still an excellent overview. See also Di Stefano (1968) and Pade (2007: I.66–87).
[32] See Di Stefano (1968: 132–133) and Pade's Chapter 16 in this volume.

personal, or his Episcopal, library?[33] Likewise unknown is the origin of the Greek manuscript of thirty-nine *Lives* that Juan Fernandez de Heredia had translated in the last decades of the fourteenth century. Heredia was the Grand Master of the Hospitallers on Rhodes from 1379 to 1382, and then spent the rest of his life in Avignon (1382–96), and it is generally assumed that he came into possession of the manuscript on Rhodes where he had it translated first into modern Greek, then into Aragonese.[34] But our knowledge of the exact origin and movement of manuscripts of Plutarch in the fourteenth century (other than that it seems likely to be primarily from East to West) is hazy at best.[35]

## Reception

Plutarch's influence was both immediate and continuous.[36] Though over half his oeuvre does not survive the dark ages and though examples of knowledge of his work are few and far between in this period,[37] there is a constant presence from the late ninth century of what does survive. Assessing how he was received by the Byzantines is, however, still far from easy because of the simple fact that there remains much basic work to be done editing Byzantine texts, let alone contextualizing them.[38]

That said – and keeping in mind that Byzantine culture over this period is far from static – Plutarch's wide appeal ensured continued interest. Opinion, when given, is invariably positive and seems to be so because of

---

[33] The manuscript he used remains unidentified (Manfredini 1987: 1003, followed by Stok 1998: 120) and this question is not usually addressed. Pade (2007: I.73) argues for the likelihood that the manuscript was in Atumanus' possession, not Corsini's. Di Stefano (1968: 27) does note that Thebes was an intellectual center at the time, so perhaps the manuscript was to be found there? On Atumanus, see further Setton (1956: 47–52) and Fedalto (2007).

[34] On Heredia, see Luttrell (1960) and Clare (1968). See Pade's Chapter 16 in this volume (as well as Pade 2007: I.76–80) for the most recent overview. See Pérez Jiménez's Chapter 17 in this volume on the tradition of Spanish translation; also Álvarez Rodríguez (1984) for the *fortuna* of the Aragonese translation.

[35] It is in Florence where interest in Plutarch blossoms at the end of the fourteenth century. Pade (2007) is the best place to take up the reception of the *Lives*; see her compact discussion in this volume (Chapter 16). There is no comparable monograph on the reception of the *Moralia* as a whole, though Stok (1998) and Becchi (2009b) give good overviews; and there are many articles on individual treatises and/or groups, e.g. Guerrier (2008) and Volpe Cacciatore (2009).

[36] See Ziegler (1964: 309–312), Irigoin (1987: ccxxvii–ccxxxvii), Garzya (1998: 21–22), and Pade (2007, I.37–54) for examples from late antiquity.

[37] In contrast to Ziegler's (1964: 312) contention that Plutarch disappears from the record in these years, see Baldwin (1995) and Pade (2007: I.54–55).

[38] A point repeatedly noted in Ljubarskij et al. (1998), Duffy (2006), and Kaldellis (2007). In the last half-century many fine volumes have been produced in Brill's Teubner Series and in the Corpus Fontium Historiae Byzantinae series from Walter de Gruyter, all with excellent indices, which will greatly aid coming to grips with Byzantine literature and its reception of antiquity.

the basic but important fact that in many ways Plutarch's moral outlook was compatible with that of orthodox Christianity. This observation, found repeatedly in late antiquity, reappears regularly from the ninth century onwards.[39] For example, in the fifth century Bishop Theodoret surmised that Plutarch must have read the Gospels, so compatible with Christianity did he find Plutarch's thought.[40] And in the eleventh century Ioannes Mauropous, a teacher, court rhetorician, and later a monk, composed the following *Epigram on Plato and Plutarch*:

> If ever you should want to remove from your wrath
> some of the pagans, oh Christ of mine,
> you could raise up Plato and Plutarch for me;
> for both, in word and in manner,
> adhere most closely to your laws.
> If they did not recognize that you are God of all things,
> then there is a need only of your goodness,
> through which gift you are willing to save all.[41]

Citation of Plutarch is made both explicitly and implicitly, both exactly and by paraphrase, both firsthand and through intermediaries. In particular, the popularity of florilegia and epitomes in transmitting knowledge of Plutarch's thought needs greater investigation,[42] despite the fact that the difficulty of tracing influence and transmission in this way is compounded because excerpts are not always acknowledged and are frequently altered or paraphrased in order to suit better their new context.[43] But some trails have already been discovered: for example, John of Antioch, who in his (?sixth-century)[44] *Chronicle* uses Plutarch's *Life of Sulla* (sometimes with acknowledgment, but mostly without and through paraphrase), is then used in turn as a source by those compiling excerpts for Constantine VII

---

[39] See La Matina (1998) on Plutarch and Christian authors in late antiquity; also Garzya (1998: 24–25) provides a long list of Christian admirers. Also see Valgiglio (1975) and Beneker (2011) on St. Basil of Caesarea's engagement in his *Address to Young Men* with Plutarch's *Quomodo adolescens poetas audire debeat*.

[40] See Tartaglia (1987: 342–343).    [41] de Lagarde (1882: 24, #43).

[42] Jenkins (1963: 47) makes the general point about their importance for compilers and anthologizers like Stobaios (and later Photios and Constantine VII Porphyrogenitos' encyclopedic projects, the *Souda* and *Eustathios*) in the dissemination of classical literature. On Stobaios possibly using an earlier collection of excerpts, see Piccione (1998); on the possibility of Photios' dependence on excerpts for his knowledge of Plutarch's *Lives*, see later in this chapter; on the eleventh-century writer Kekaumenos and his dependence on florilegia for his *Strategikon*, see Roueché (2002), especially 116–117 and 126 (for Plutarch through Stobaios).

[43] See e.g. Helmig (2008), who revisits and argues for the ascription to Plutarch of an excerpt Stobaios had attributed to Porphyry (Plutarch fr. 200 Sandbach = Porphyry fr. 382 Smith).

[44] At least according to Mariev (2008: 5–9), though dating is an extremely vexed issue.

Porphyrogenitos in the tenth century, and by Planudes for his own late thirteenth-century collection of excerpts.[45] Or consider the proposal of Mario Manfredini that Zonaras (fl. second quarter of the twelfth century) in his *Epitome historiarum* and the anonymous compiler of a thirteenth-century collection of Plutarchan excerpts both used an earlier collection of excerpts and an earlier epitome of the *Alexander* and *Caesar*.[46] At times also it seems that Plutarch's general approach and moral outlook, particularly with regard to biographical writing, has been internalized (see further later in this chapter). Certainly the scholar Ioannes Tzetzes (ca. 1110–80/5), in his *Histories*, seems to have held up the Plutarchan mirror and seen parallels with his own life in both of Plutarch's *Catos* (seeing his own situation in that of Cato Maior's son but also in that of Cato Minor);[47] and it is he who, though forced because of financial pressure to sell some of his library, kept hold of his copy of Plutarch's *Lives*.[48]

Though there is much to choose from, I want to look a little more closely at the reception of Plutarch by six figures who are representative of the higher echelons of Byzantine literary discourse: a patriarch, an archbishop, an emperor (or, more strictly, his scholars), a professor of philosophy, the daughter of an emperor, and a Grand Logothete (i.e. head of the civil service). The choice reflects not just the reality that, in general, higher education was the privilege of the (primarily male) elite but also that it was essential for a career in the civil service as well as in the church. Rhetorical skill was highly desired, and that included imitating Attic Greek; prestige was attached to the ability to display this skill in administrative and church documents.[49]

Probably the most important intellectual to emerge out of the late eighth-century revival is Photios (ca. 810–93).[50] From a well-off family, he was a central political and religious figure and was twice Patriarch of Constantinople (858–67, 877–86).[51] We have numerous letters and

---

[45] Mariev (2008: 37) on Plutarch as a source; also Walton (1965).

[46] See Manfredini (1992; 1993). See also Pelling (1973) for an argument that Zonaras preserves two excerpts from these *Lives* that had disappeared in the main textual tradition of Plutarch's *Alexander–Caesar*.

[47] Noted long ago by Hirzel (1912: 100) and by Kaldellis (2007: 305–306).

[48] Wilson (1996: 190).

[49] For brief overviews, see Wilson (1996: 1–4) and Cameron (2006: 133–134). On classical learning and the church, see Wilson (1970). See also the following more detailed studies on higher learning: Lemerle (1986) (origins to tenth century), Browning (1975), Kazhdan and Wharton Epstein (1985: 120–166) (eleventh to twelfth centuries), and Constantinides (1982) (thirteenth to fourteenth centuries). On literary mimesis, see Hunger (1969–70).

[50] His dates are a matter of debate. Kazhdan (2006: 8) prefers 820–91.

[51] See Lemerle (1986: 207–211). Wilson (1996: 89–119) and Kazhdan (2006: 7–41) are judicious and complementary overviews of the man and his works. Whether or not Photios taught is a matter of debate; Lemerle (1986: 211–214) argues strongly against the possibility.

homilies from his pen along with two works that even more patently show his wide reading of classical literature: the *Lexicon* and the *Bibliotheca*. Photios' own title for the latter work reveals its purpose more accurately than our modern shorthand: *Inventory List and Enumeration of the Books I have read and of which my Beloved Brother Tarasios has asked for my Evaluation in Summary: these are 281 in all.*[52] Plutarch crops up several times in the *Bibliotheca*. First, as noted earlier, numerous Plutarchan works (both biographies and treatises, including some that were certainly lost even in the patriarch's day) are mentioned in Photios' epitome of Sopater's excerpts (*Bibliotheca* 161).[53] And at the end of the epitome, in his judgment of Sopater's collection (104b5–14), Photios remarks on its value as a spur toward virtue and nobility and for the practice and teaching of rhetoric – both points are Byzantine preoccupations, though the former is more particularly pointed in view of the Plutarchan excerpts.[54] Later in the work can be found extracts (with varying degrees of alteration and para-phrasing) from nineteen *Lives* (*Bibliotheca* 245). In contrast to Photios' discussions of, for example, Arrian (92) or Lucian (128), there is no summary or comment on Plutarch's style or any programmatic statement to help us understand the significance of these passages. Finally, *Bibliotheca* 259–268 bear a close, though far from identical, resemblance to the (pseudo-)Plutarchan *Vitae decem oratorum* and do contain stylistic analysis to varying degrees for each of the orators.

Scholarship that has examined Plutarch in Photios has tended to focus on two intertwined areas: what Photios reveals about the textual tradition of Plutarchan works and, when he differs from Plutarch, what his sources must have been. So, for example, *Bibliotheca* 161, in addition to providing information we would not otherwise have about Sopater, helps determine a better *terminus post quem* for the disappearance of certain Plutarchan works. *Bibliotheca* 245 provides the crucial piece of evidence for the circulation of the less popular bipartite edition of the *Lives*.[55] And finally, the differences between *Bibliotheca* 259–268 and the (pseudo-)Plutarchan *Vitae decem oratorum* allow for the suggestion of a third, now lost, version of these biographies that Photios is deemed to have copied.[56] In most of

---

[52] The translation is from Kazhdan (2006: 10).

[53] There is nothing to suggest that Photios read the works Sopater excerpts. He likewise summarizes other anthologies (e.g. *Bibliotheca* 167 and 186).

[54] As Wilson (1996: 103) notes. He also comments specifically on the utility of the *Moralia* excerpts (104a36–38), on which see Garzya (1988: 17).

[55] See discussion and nn. 18–19 earlier in this chapter. Schamp (1995: 183 and n. 137) is skeptical about the existence of the bipartite edition.

[56] So Schamp (2000).

this scholarship there is a tendency to disallow any real agency on the part of Photios: he is a copyist who has thankfully preserved this material for us and our job is to discover his sources. Yet it is notable in scholarship that focuses more on Photios himself that a different picture, one of a strong and opinionated agent, emerges.[57]

Most striking perhaps on this front has been Rebekah Smith's reassessment of *Bibliotheca* 259–268. She argues persuasively in favor of Photios actively editing and adding stylistic commentary (as opposed to copying from an intermediary source) to the material he found in (pseudo-) Plutarch, on the basis of his own reading and predilections.[58] Her view, therefore, is that *Bibliotheca* 259–268 is very much more a product of Photios' own world and preoccupations than an uncritical copying of some now lost work.[59] *Bibliotheca* 245 also needs to be reexamined in light of Photios' broader concerns. Whether or not we view the passages as preparatory excerpts for a summary that was never completed, and whether we believe Photios read the whole *Lives*[60] or simply a collection of excerpts from them,[61] there still needs to be an explanation for why he chose these particular passages. Certainly some of the frequently observed oddness of the collection can be accounted for if Photios was only looking at excerpts, but other concerns need to be considered. For example, it has been argued that elsewhere Photios' summaries of historians "reflect concerns that truly moved him," such as his hostility toward tyrants, the relationship between emperors and their wise advisers, the nature of imperial power, and so forth.[62] Numerous passages in *Bibliotheca* 245 show similar preoccupations. For example, the only passage from the *Cicero* is less about Cicero than about Caesar's abandonment of him in favor of keeping the triumvirate together, with Photios' salutary warnings about the excesses of the power-hungry (cf. *Cicero* 46 with *Bibl.* 245.395a1–21). And one of the passages from *Phocion* is

<hr>

[57] For example, Kazhdan (2006: 6–36).

[58] Smith (1992), along with Kazhdan (2006: 10–36), holds a more generous view of Photios' critical ability than, for example, Treadgold (1980) and Wilson (1996: 89–119), though both of the latter make important observations.

[59] Schamp (2000) strongly disagrees with Smith and reasserts the view that divergences from the (pseudo-)Plutarchan work belong to Photios' source, not to Photios' own editing. Kazhdan (2006) expresses more sympathy with Smith's approach. Heath (1998), though primarily concerned with Photios' sources, also acknowledges Smith's findings.

[60] For example, Treadgold (1980: 80–83) argues that the excerpts in *Bibliotheca* 245 were made while Photios was reading the *Lives* (and that they were later copied out by a secretary without further input from Photios).

[61] This view can be found in Schamp (1995: particularly 175–177 and 183), who argues that the introduction to *Bibliotheca* 245 points to this reading: "I have read diverse stories from the *Parallel Lives* of Plutarch, of which my edition picks out in epitome a varied selection."

[62] See Kazhdan (2006: 15–16), who also finds these concerns in Photios' letters and homilies.

about how difficult a job giving political advice is (cf. *Phocion* 10.3–4 with *Bibl.* 245.395a37–b3). Further, Doron Mendels has observed that Photios has a preoccupation with material on the "downfall of the Macedonian Kingdom and the tragic end of its dynasty."[63] And though she specifically excludes from consideration the Plutarchan excerpts (on the grounds that they are not really history), it is striking how many of them focus on the Macedonian dynasty and the Successors.[64] Thus the Plutarchan excerpts may also have been chosen at least partly because of Photios' more general interest in dynastic succession and continuity in the East.

It is difficult to determine decisively the issue of how much Photios learned about Plutarch through older florilegia and how much through direct reading, given that we must primarily work within the realm of speculation when talking about the movement and production of manuscripts of Plutarch in the ninth century – though if there had been a manuscript in Constantinople, as patriarch he surely would have had access to it.[65] However, it is certain that Arethas (born ca. 850), who rose to be archbishop of Cappadocian Caesarea,[66] had in his possession a manuscript of the *Lives*. It is to him that the earliest scholia on the *Lives* can be attributed (on a manuscript dating ca. 917–22).[67] Scholia were common on school texts – and, indeed, on Plato, for example, Arethas seems to be copying older scholiastic notes[68] – but rarer on other authors, so what little we have on Plutarch in this regard is important to consider. While Arethas' notes do little to enlighten us about Plutarch's world, they do provide insight into his own.[69] And it is particularly clear that Plutarch's moral stance is, on the whole, attractive to the archbishop. Thus on *Cato Maior* 5.6 where Plutarch speculates on whether or not an action of Cato's was due to noble or base thoughts, Arethas remarks, "good for you, Plutarch!" And he adopts an apologetic tone in the note on *Solon* 1.6

---

[63] Mendels (1986: especially 202).

[64] In addition to extracts from the *Alexander, Eumenes, Demetrius,* and *Pyrrhus,* the passages from *Demosthenes* are all concerned in one way or another with Philip, Harpalos, or Alexander, the *Aemilius Paulus* passage and two of the five passages from *Agis/Cleomenes* are about Antigonus, and one of the *Phocion* passages concerns Antipater.

[65] See Mango (1975: 37–43) for a discussion of the availability and location of books in Photios' day; more generally Wilson (1967).

[66] He may have been a pupil of Photios; see Wilson (1996: 120) for a brief overview.

[67] Arethas is in fact the only individual scholiast on Plutarch who has been identified thus far. See Manfredini (1975) for Arethas on Plutarch and Manfredini (1979) for a collection of the most important scholia on Plutarch. For summaries, see Wilson (1996: 128) and Garzya (1998: 19–20).

[68] See Wilson (1996: 120).

[69] Manfredini (1975: 350; 1979: 83–84) is slightly more positive about the value of Arethas' notes than Wilson (1996: 128).

(regarding Solon's attraction to beautiful boys and promotion of pederasty through his laws and poems), saying:

> Don't be angry with Plutarch because of this capricious story. The Greeks are of such a sort concerning this depravity [i.e. homosexuality] that even Plato who has yoked his winged chariot to the counsellor of his own gods and speaks in elevated language about divine matters ... was caught thinking and saying in a crack-brained way worse things than these in the *Charmides*.[70]

Arethas' apologetic stance here mirrors what we find a century or so later in the often-quoted plea of Mauropous (see earlier):[71] Plutarch attracts and holds the attention of the Christian world because of the general compatibility of his moral outlook with theirs.

A few decades later, in the mid-ninth century, we see an explosion of literary activity connected with the emperor Constantine VII Porphyrogenitos, who ruled from 913 to 959. Though the prefaces to a large number of compositions suggest Constantine wrote extensively, it is generally now agreed that the works are, rather, the product of scholars at his court; so in this case we are looking at reception on a broader scale – that is, under his rule. Since it is from this time that we start to see a proliferation of copies of Plutarch's *Lives*, and since a convincing argument has been made for identifying the source of a particular group of manuscripts of Plutarch as a scriptorium attached to the library and court of Constantine VII,[72] we might expect to see some signs of interest in and exploitation of the Plutarchan material and methodology among the compositions of those with access to these manuscripts. Encouraging this line of thinking is the fact that there is a clear and growing tendency in the tenth century toward historical writing centering on specific individuals (as opposed to chronicle or annalistic writing).[73] So, for example, Romilly J. H. Jenkins has argued that the influence of Plutarch can be seen in the Constantine-commissioned *Continuation of Theophanes*: four books of

---

[70] For these two scholia, see Manfredini (1979: 97, #72 and 92, #27). Wilson (1996: 128) draws attention to Arethas' comments in the same vein on the *Charmides*.

[71] On Mauropous more generally, see Karpozilos (1990: 9–27) and Wilson (1996: 151–153).

[72] Irigoin (1976) bases the argument on codicological considerations.

[73] See e.g. Markopoulos (2003; 2009). Indeed, Németh (2010: 47–48) has suggested intriguingly that the very absence of Plutarchan material from the Constantine VII-commissioned *Eklogai* (a vast compilation of selected passages of which only a portion has survived but that had a clear moral aim) was because the biographical style of writing was favored in this period and it was, therefore, other less-favored genres that were excerpted for this project; on this, see also Humble (2013). On the *Eklogai* in general, see further Lemerle (1986: 323–331) for a good overview, and Németh (2010) for a detailed reassessment.

historical narrative, each centered around the life of one emperor, covering the period 813–67. The key features are the organization of the material by individual reign and the "noticeable effort . . . to paint the character as that of a living man, compounded of good and evil."[74] Jenkins also argued that in the *Life of Basil* (emperor Basil I, 867–86, Constantine VII's grandfather)[75] the internal *psogos* (speech of blame) of Michael III, Basil's predecessor, was drawn specifically from Plutarch's *Life of Antony* and the (now lost) *Life of Nero*.[76] It has been too easy to dismiss Jenkins because of his argument regarding the lost *Life of Nero*,[77] but Alexander Kazhdan, in his informative counterarguments that the literary influences in the *Life of Basil* are more recent (ninth and tenth centuries) or original to the author, also highlights some aspects that could equally be explained as Plutarchan.[78] The structure of the *Life of Basil* is thematic within the broad chronological sweep; portents during Basil's childhood foretell future brilliance (e.g. Bekker, p. 225.17–21; Ševčenko 10); throughout he shows concern with lifelong learning and reading; he possesses all the virtues Plutarch would hope to see in his subjects – piety, statesmanship, bravery, wisdom, moderation, and justice (e.g. Bekker, p. 315.7–9; Ševčenko 72.27–31) – yet he is not perfect. He is inconsolable when his son dies, though soon regains control (Bekker, p. 345.11–19; Ševčenko 98.9–21), and more than once he falls victim to sycophantic slanderers, causing him to turn on trusted advisers or family members (Bekker, p. 286.15–18, pp. 349–351; Ševčenko 50.48–64, 100.1–53). That the author of the *Life of Basil* was doing something new in this composition should not, I think, be doubted, but that need not preclude him having imbibed some of the principles of Plutarchan biographical writing from his own reading and having reworked them for his own purposes.[79]

[74] Jenkins (1954: 15), who is followed by Scott (1981: 70).
[75] The *Life of Basil* was for a long time considered the fifth book of the *Continuation of Theophanes* and the 1838 edition by Bekker the standard text, until Ševčenko's greatly improved edition of the *Life of Basil* was finally posthumously published (2011). Traditionally, the *Life of Basil* has been considered the work of Constantine (e.g. Alexander 1940; Jenkins 1948; Lemerle 1986: 318), but for the view that it was written by an anonymous ghost-writer in Constantine's court, see Ševčenko (1992); Mango concurs in his introductory comments in Ševčenko (2011: 13). On the fence is Kazhdan (2006: 137). See also Markopoulos (2009: 698–700 n. 6 on the debate and n. 10 on the need for a "holistic study" of the *Life*).
[76] See Jenkins (1948). Lemerle (1986: 318) sees broader Plutarchan influence in the *Life of Basil* but does not elaborate.
[77] "Wishful thinking," as Ljubarskij (1993: 132) judiciously points out; Kazhdan (2006: 144, 324) focuses on this point. Note, however, that Payen (2001: 1972) reports Jenkins' view as fact.
[78] See Kazhdan (2006: 137–144).
[79] The same questions can be posed about the roughly contemporary hagiographical writing of Symeon Metaphrastes (fl. 980s, on whom see Høgel 2002 and Kazhdan 2006: 231–247).

The question is: how detailed a knowledge of the *Parallel Lives* and the other treatises did the educated elite at this time have? Did their awareness initially come through excerpts and epitomes (as perhaps was the case earlier with Photios), prompting them to search out and copy complete works? Or were the Plutarchan works being read from beginning to end? The answer is probably a combination of the two, although sometimes it is hard to be certain which is the answer from the type of evidence we have. For example, in a letter of ca. 937/8 by the court official Niketas, we learn that he had borrowed some Plutarch from Alexander, Metropolitan of Nicaea. Since in a later letter (ca. 938–40) Niketas comments on the stories told about Alcibiades' chameleon-like quality (cf. Plutarch, *Alcibiades* 23.4), the manuscript must have contained at least excerpts, which included this anecdote, if not the whole *Alcibiades*.[80]

By the eleventh century there is no longer any question that persons of great learning with access to an excellent library would be able to lay their hands on manuscripts of Plutarchan works, both the *Lives* and many of the treatises. Indeed, one of the leading intellectual figures in this century, Michael Psellos (1018–ca. 1078/96?), a high-ranking civil servant and government-sponsored professor of philosophy, has wide-ranging knowledge of Plutarch and is well disposed toward him. In this perhaps we are to view the influence of Mauropous, whose pupil Psellos was.[81] In his short treatise *On the character of certain writers*, he writes:

> I single out ... the whole works of Plutarch ... in my opinion Plutarch has traversed not only every charm of vocabulary but also all thoughts expressed in periods or aphoristically; he enchanted me also by narrating both simply and with complexity, expounding his thoughts in different ways.[82]

Metraphrastes redacted the *Menologion* (a collection of biographies of saints ordered by when they are celebrated in the church calendar), updating the style from previous versions and adding prologues (which his encomiast, Psellos, singled out for notice). Høgel (2002: 137–145) discusses the themes in these new prologues and argues that they were meant to "enhance the status of the menologion as a collection." Høgel does not, however, consider whether Metaphrastes might have been spurred to add these by exposure, for example, to Plutarch's *Lives*, where the prologues also serve to reiterate the common purpose and themes of the overall biographical project. On Plutarch's prologues, see Stadter (1988) and Duff (2008a). Indeed, Metaphrastes' prologues resemble Plutarch's in their addresses to the audience, their intention to provide readers with a virtuous example to follow, and their inclusion of themes such as the comparison between the biographer and a painter. The *Life of St Nicholas*, for example, contains the painter/biographer comparison (cf. *Alexander* 1) and the point about the beneficial imitative purpose of the *Lives* (cf. *Demosthenes* 1); for the Greek text, see *Patrologia Graeca*, vol. 116, col. 317.

[80] Westerink (1973: 77 [letter #9] and 87 [letter #12]). Kazhdan (2006: 171) draws attention to the former.
[81] See Karpozilos (1990: 11) and Kaldellis (2007: 202).    [82] Boissonade (1964: 50–51).

This favorable opinion is reflected in various, often indirect, ways across a wide range of Psellos' works, from his orations[83] to his major historical work, the *Chronographia*, which is structured around the lives of individual rulers.[84] In the *Chronographia* Psellos does not refer to himself as a biographer but as a historian. Often, however, he appears to justify the content by using Plutarchan principles adapted to his own needs. Book 6, on the reign of Constantine IX (1042–55) – the first emperor whom Psellos himself served and about whom he also composed panegyrics (6.25) – is filled with such instances. For example, Psellos makes a clear allusion to Plutarch's judgment of Herodotus in *De Herodoti malignitate*, when he says that if he chose to eulogize Constantine but then left out praiseworthy deeds and only dealt with blameworthy ones, he would be "most malicious, like the son of Lyxes, who employed the worst deeds of the Greeks in his histories" (6.24; cf. *De Herodoti malignitate* 655C–E).[85] His comments about the need to summarize some events (6.73) and choosing intimate facts over public facts for revealing character (6.167), and using anecdotes that other historians might reject (6.173), all recall Plutarch's programmatic statements at the beginning of the *Alexander*.[86] And there is a marvelous internal *synkrisis* at 6.163–4 that shows awareness of Plutarch's moral purpose and is very reminiscent of Plutarchan *synkriseis*. After first commenting that such renowned leaders as Alexander, Caesar, Augustus, Pyrrhus, Epaminondas, and Agesilaos are shown by their biographers to incline sometimes even more toward vice than virtue and speculating on what the result of imitating such lives would be, he says: "So when I compare this very great emperor with those famous men, I know that he is inferior to them in bravery, but he is greater with respect to other good qualities." Among the good qualities that are then listed are the very Plutarchan virtues of gentleness (164) and clemency (167).[87]

---

[83] See under 'Plutarchus' in the *Index Auctorum* in Littlewood (1985: 163).

[84] Tellingly entitled, in the Penguin translation, *Fourteen Byzantine Rulers*. Wilson (1970: 73), Scott (1981: 70–71), Lauritzen (2005: 162–167), and Pietsch (2005) all talk briefly of Plutarchan influence on this work, but no major study has been undertaken on this point. On the *Chronographia* in general, see Kaldellis (1999).

[85] Lauritzen (2005: 162–163) notes the allusion, without reference to the earlier and more subtle discussion of McCarthy (1940–1: 297–298), who points out the reversal of Plutarchan points of criticism and the conflation that suggests Herodotus' intention was eulogy. It is worth noting, too, in view of the discussion earlier, that this reference provides evidence for some sort of knowledge of *De Herodoti malignitate* (*Moralia* #76) for which our earliest manuscript is post-Planudean; see n. 14 in this chapter and also Sandbach (1941).

[86] See Lauritzen (2005: 163–166) for other points regarding the importance of *Alexander* 1 for Psellos' approach.

[87] For a brief overview of both virtues, see Duff (1999a: 77–78) with earlier bibliography.

Psellos also uses a Plutarchan work as a structural basis in his *De omnifaria doctrina*,[88] a work that summarizes various scientific, theological, and ethical ideas and shows a similar kind of relationship to the (pseudo-)Plutarchan *De placitis philosophorum*[89] to that which Photios' *Bibliotheca* 258–269 showed to the *Vitae decem oratorum*: a number of the headings have been taken over (but the order rearranged) and only a small portion of the content (and then again generally rearranged). The content, not surprisingly, reflects Psellos' own philosophical predilections and so is more heavily weighted toward his favorite philosophers, above all Plato and the Neoplatonists, particularly Proclus.[90] So, for example, in the section making use of the (pseudo-)Plutarchan title "On beginnings, what they are" (*De omn. doc.* 83 W), Psellos quotes only Plato as an authority, compared to the much longer piece in (pseudo-)Plutarch (*De placitis philosophorum* 1.3), which includes the views of numerous pre-Socratic philosophers prior to only a brief mention of Plato near the end.

To whatever degree one believes Psellos' own rhetoric about his achievements, particularly regarding the revival of the study of philosophy,[91] he certainly had a wide influence on others, one of whom was the princess Anna Komnene (1083–ca. 1148–55).[92] She is of interest not least because she is the first extant female historian and her *Alexiad*, a lengthy history of the reign of her father, Alexios I Komnenos, is a key historical document for the period.[93] As the emperor's daughter, Anna clearly led a privileged life, although she presents her parents as only encouraging her scholarly ambitions to a point. Though it is clear that the *Iliad* is an influence and though the general laudatory bent of her work might suggest that encomia or hagiography are more likely models than Plutarch, Anna specifically calls the *Alexiad* a history of her father's deeds, thus continuing the

[88] Westerink (1948) provides a thorough modern edition. Anastos (1949) is a useful overview.
[89] This work, like the *Vitae decem oratorum*, was considered a genuine Plutarchan text in the Byzantine era; it is attributed to Plutarch early on by Eusebius but does not appear in the Lamprias Catalogue. See further Lachenaud (1993).
[90] On Psellos' philosophical background, see Kaldellis (2007: 193–202).
[91] Kaldellis (2007: 191–224) defends Psellos' own high opinion of himself; Wilson (1996: 156–166) is a touch more skeptical.
[92] On Anna's admiration of Psellos, see Macrides (1996) and Ljubarskij (2000).
[93] Howard-Johnson (1996) argues persuasively that Anna likely used unpublished material written by her husband, Nikephoros Bryennios, for the detailed military passages in the work. His attempt to downplay Anna's agency in the overall arrangement of the material, however, has been soundly refuted; see Neville (2016: 181 n. 1) for bibliography. Neville (2012: 43–44) shows that Nikephoros, likewise, was familiar with Plutarch's corpus. On Anna Komnene, see also the volume of essays edited by Gouma-Peterson (2000).

trend of centering historical writing on a single individual. Since, however, some scholars have commented on the centrality of Plutarch to her work,[94] it is worth briefly examining what this comprises. Georgina Buckler draws attention particularly to Anna's use of Plutarchan vocabulary. In connection with one example she shows Anna reworking a Plutarchan scene in a rather sophisticated manner. When Alexios is shown reluctantly suggesting using church treasures to augment the war fund (*Alexiad* 5.2), Anna appears to have in mind Plutarch's description of Pericles' approach to finances (*Pericles* 23.1); later, Alexios is given a speech in his own defense regarding this action, in which he says he is following the example of Pericles (*Alexiad* 6.3).[95]

The one passage that shows the lengthiest undoubted borrowing of Plutarch's words is *Alexiad* 12.3.3.[96] Here it is quite clear that Anna is quoting a passage from Plutarch's *Coniugalia praecepta* (142C), where the philosopher Theano remarks that her bare elbow is not for public show. Anna compares her mother to the philosopher to make the point that a virtuous woman ought modestly to conceal her body and thoughts in public. The quote is, to be sure, not exact – it has been shortened and the clarification that Theano was a philosopher has been added – but it is still apparent that Plutarch is her source. Was Plutarch's *Coniugalia praecepta* proper reading for an imperial princess? Did she stumble upon the work by accident in her zealous studying? Did she come across it in a collection of excerpts? For example, the Plutarchan anecdote is reproduced even more closely in Stobaios *Anthology* 4.23.49a. Once again, we need a closer examination of the path of individual treatises through the hands of Byzantine authors in order to provide firmer answers to such questions.[97]

The final figure in this brief survey is Theodoros Metochites (1270–1332), a man who reached the highest position in the civil service, the position of Grand Logothete under the emperor Andronikos II Palaeologos (1282–1328).[98] When he first gained familiarity with

---

[94] Buckler (1929: 515): "her favorite Plutarch"; Runciman (1970: 15): "much of her information about Greek learning seems to come from Plutarch."

[95] Buckler (1929: 86, 201–203, 488–490, 515) on Plutarchan vocabulary; *ibid.* 206 on the passage from the *Pericles*, conflated by Anna with Thucydides 2.13.3–5.

[96] At least as far as can be determined from the *conspectus fontium* in Reinsch and Kambylis (2001).

[97] See Catanzaro (2013) on Niketas Choniates (ca. 1155–1217) and Xenophontos (2014a) on Nikephoros Basilakes (ca. 1115–82) for other examples of direct appropriation of Plutarchan passages in twelfth-century Byzantine texts; also Simpson (2019).

[98] For a thorough overview of Metochites and his times, see Ševčenko (1975). See also Wilson (1996: 256–264), Fryde (2000: 322–336), and, in addition, Bazzani (2006), who compares Metochites to the Italian humanists.

Plutarch is difficult to tell,[99] but it is from his pen that we have the most comprehensive overall assessment of Plutarch available to us from the Byzantine period: the essay *On Plutarch* (#71 of 120 essays comprising his *Miscellanea*).[100] In his assessment, Plutarch has "an abundance of wisdom" (71.1.1) and "a natural talent for the whole of wisdom … able to write with the greatest ease about everything" (71.1.2), and

> if someone wants to know anything that happened before Plutarch's entry into life, his work and studies, that person must either try to get hold of all the books written before Plutarch or in his time … or he can content himself with acquiring *his* books, there to find all the material for every need … the man is a complete treasure-house of the whole of history and knowledge and like a market-place of wisdom. (71.8.5–7)

And so on in this vein. Ševčenko easily demonstrates that this is no empty rhetoric and cites numerous examples that show that Metochites drew on both the *Lives* and various treatises, both by direct citation and paraphrase.[101]

Plutarch's general influence can also be seen in the structure and form of Metochites' own compositions, as is evident, for example, in his *Comparison between Demosthenes and Aelius Aristides* (*Miscellanea* #17). The very form of the work and the fact that one of its themes is the effect of the type of political constitution under which the two men are constrained to act remind us immediately of concerns of Plutarch's *Lives*.[102] For example, Metochites notes that Demosthenes lived in a democracy and so his rhetoric had real and immediate consequences, whereas Aristides lived under an absolute monarchy, which paradoxically allowed him to have greater freedom of speech in

---

[99] It seems certain there was a complete Plutarch at the Chora monastery (which Metochites restored in 1316–20 and where he lived for the last two years of his life), but how it got there is a matter of debate: Ševčenko (1975: 41–42) argues that it was left there by Planudes, but Constantinidis (1982: 68–70) raises some questions about this evidence and suggests it is equally plausible that Metochites had the manuscript brought to Chora when he refounded the monastery and restocked the library. Arco Magrí (1991: 468) casts doubt on the notion that Planudes and Metochites were even on friendly terms.

[100] For analysis, see Tartaglia (1987) and Bydén (2002: 218–243), and more briefly Wilson (1996: 262) and Garzya (1998: 26–27). Hult (2002) provides a modern edition with English translation (from which all quotations below come). See also Arco Magrí (1991) and Xenophontos (2019) on Metochites' engagement with the (pseudo-)Plutarchan *On Homer* at the end of his essay on Plutarch.

[101] Ševčenko (1975: 41 n. 170 in particular; but also 48 n. 216, where he shows Metochites drawing on Plutarch's views about Epicureanism generally but probably using a florilegium as a source of an anecdote).

[102] Contra Wilson (1996: 262), who views this as a potential original contribution of Metochites.

his compositions, though they had no political consequences.[103] Further, it seems absolutely clear that Metochites composed his *Miscellanea* in imitation of Plutarch's *Moralia*.[104] The list of titles of topics[105] and their moral and didactic bent, and the "eclecticism" and "preference for ethics to natural philosophy and mathematics," are points Metochites makes about Plutarch himself but that can just as well be made of the contents of the *Miscellanea*.[106]

But the imitation is not quite as straightforward as all this suggests. It has been well observed that Metochites was somewhat self-obsessed. For example, his essay *Reflection on the expression "Live unknown"* (*Miscellanea* #72), though "inspired by Plutarch's piece on the same subject," consists mainly of Metochites talking about himself.[107] And if we consider closely some of his observations in the essay on Plutarch, we might note that they do not always match our own, and thus we might consider whether or not they reflect more the way Metochites himself wished to be viewed rather than any acute and carefully thought-out judgment on Plutarch. For example, his assertion that Plutarch did not belong to any particular philosophical school (71.4.4) is scarcely the conclusion a modern reader would reach, and it has been suggested that Metochites' comments about Plutarch's style (i.e. that smooth rhetoric is not always appropriate for philosophy, 71.9–10) are more apt as a description of his own style than as an understanding of Plutarch's style or thoughts on style.[108] Self-identity is thus merged with the model. That Metochites was promulgating this vision of himself, and that it was successfully received in some quarters, can be seen in a letter one of his pupils, Nikephoros Gregoras, wrote to him. In this letter Gregoras praises Metochites and his *Miscellanea* in precisely the same way that Metochites praises Plutarch within the same *Miscellanea*.[109]

The preceding survey only scratches the surface of the reception of Plutarch in Byzantium. It shows, however, that the Byzantine intellectuals

[103] See Ševčenko (1975: 47–48) for a summary of the *synkrisis*, though he does not note Plutarchan themes. Gigante (1969: 13–14) pays some attention to Plutarchan influence here but only in a general sense. Arco Magrí (1991: 466) argues that Metochites' comparison of Homer and Plutarch at the end of *On Plutarch* was written in homage to Plutarchan *synkriseis*.
[104] Bydén (2002: 270, 286).
[105] For example, #3 *That everyone suffers from intellectual vanity*, #11 *On Aristotle and his fame in natural science and logic*, #37 *Lament on the decline of Rome and the reversal of its great prosperity*, and #85 *That it is not proper to devote oneself entirely to getting rich*. See Hult (2002: 5–15) for the full list.
[106] See Tartaglia (1987: 339) and Bydén (2002: especially 286–287) for the quotations.
[107] See Ševčenko (1975: 48).     [108] See Russell's Chapter 8 in this volume.
[109] Tartaglia (1987: 339) notes this; Bydén (2002: 269–271) provides the Greek text of the letter and analyzes it in more detail.

were not merely interested in Plutarch for the purpose of pedestalizing and preserving him (however grateful we might be to them for the latter). Above all, they were attracted to him because of the compatibility of his outlook with Christian morality.[110] This fact is central to understanding the wide appeal of his works, whether they were read in their entirety or accessed only through florilegia. Plutarch's methodology, philosophical concepts, opinions, and stories were all adapted in various ways to support and promulgate ideas and opinions that Byzantine intellectuals wanted to disseminate. Their reception is never slavish. There are certainly many questions that we may never have enough information to answer, but continuing access to good modern editions of the Byzantine authors under discussion and of the collections of letters from the period will help in time to increase our understanding of the richness of the Byzantine reception of Plutarch.

## Further Reading

On Plutarch in Byzantium, there is now an impressive lineup of essays in Oikonomopoulou and Xenophontos (2019); a valuable earlier survey is Garzya (1998). On Photios and Plutarch, see the compact overview by Németh (2019: 189–190); for interesting opposing positions, see Smith (1992) and Schamp (1995; 2000). On Arethas and Plutarch, Manfredini (1975) is indispensable. Jenkins (1948; 1954) is still the starting point for a discussion of Plutarch and the Constantinian *Life of Basil*. On Psellos and Plutarch, see McCarthy (1940–1); Lauritzen (2005); Delli (2019); Reinsch (2019). Anna Komnene's interest in Plutarch is addressed, albeit rather briefly, by Buckler (1929) and Grünbart (2019: 270–271). There is substantially more on Metochites and Plutarch, the most profitable starting points being Ševčenko (1975), Hult (2002) (who includes the Greek text and a translation of Metochites *Miscellanea* #71 on Plutarch), and now Xenophontos (2018; 2019). On the manuscript tradition, Irigoin's body of work (especially Irigoin 1982–3; 1987) is second to none. To it, regarding the *Moralia* treatises in particular, should be added Martinelli Tempesta (2013) and Pérez Martín (2019).

---

[110] There is no suggestion, for example, that anyone was ever prosecuted for promulgating Plutarchan ideas, as John Italos was for his lectures on Plato (see Wilson 1996: 153–154).

# CHAPTER 16

# Plutarch in the Italian Renaissance

## Marianne Pade

Like most Greek authors, Plutarch had been almost unknown in Western Europe during the Middle Ages, but when Renaissance humanists rekindled interest in Greek language and culture, he became one of the most widely read authors of the period. This chapter will discuss how Plutarch's name first came to the attention of the early Renaissance humanists, then how his works gradually became accessible to Western readers, in Latin translation, and finally how Plutarch's ideas influenced Renaissance ethico-political thought.

### Petrarch and the Fourteenth Century

By the middle of the fourteenth century, Plutarch was known in the Latin West almost exclusively as the author of the so-called *Institutio Traiani*, a didactic treatise on the theory of government allegedly written by Plutarch for his imperial pupil Trajan. Our earliest immediate source for this otherwise unknown work is the group of sixteen extensive Latin fragments in John of Salisbury's *Policraticus*, completed in 1159.[1] Some scholars have argued that the *Institutio Traiani* is John's invention, but others believe he may have had access either to a genuine classical or late antique text attributed to Plutarch, or to a medieval work that he believed to be ancient and by Plutarch. However, the treatise itself is known only from the *Policraticus* and from the many works depending on it. The first of the sixteen fragments of the *Institutio*, a letter from Plutarch to Trajan, was often transmitted independently.[2]

The transmission of the letter to Trajan during the thirteenth and the first half of the fourteenth centuries could in itself be interpreted as an

---

[1] For literature on the *Policraticus*, see the bibliography in Kloft and Kerner (1992: 127–130); the latest edition of the *Institutio Traiani* is Kloft and Kerner (1992: 8–31).
[2] Elsmann (1994: 112–134, 249–275); Pade (1999: 63–65).

indication of some interest in Plutarch. However, there is little other evidence to support this theory, and in fact the first writer after John to mention Plutarch at some length was Petrarch (Francesco Petrarca, 1304–74). Though he always maintained the superiority of Latin culture, he was interested in the Greek world and wished to become acquainted with the writers that Cicero and Virgil had emulated.[3] Petrarch mentions Plutarch several times from the 1340s onwards, and, surprisingly, apparently derived his information from sources other than John's *Policraticus*. In the *Letter to Seneca* (1348) Petrarch describes Plutarch as having compared Greek and Roman achievements in literature and statesmanship, which evidently refers to the *Lives*.[4] Furthermore, in a passage in the *Secretum* (1342/3, revised between 1353 and 1358) Petrarch writes about the competition between Greeks and Romans to achieve supremacy in eloquence, a strife that also existed among the Romans themselves; there were Latin-speaking people who favored the Greeks, and Greeks who were of the opposite opinion – among them, some said, the philosopher Plutarch. Here, again, it seems as if Petrarch had some idea of the contents of the *Lives*. Both passages point to a knowledge of Plutarch independent of John of Salisbury, in my opinion probably derived from some of Petrarch's Greek acquaintances, such as his teacher Barlaam or Nicholas Sigeros, the learned Byzantine ambassador who was later to present him with a manuscript of Homer.[5]

Although Petrarch may have known more about Plutarch than anyone else in the Latin West at the time, he continues to talk about him as the

---

[3] Weiss (1977: 170–171).

[4] Momigliano (1949: 189–190). The passage discussed (*Le Epistole familiari* XXIV 5.3) is as follows: *Plutarchus siquidem grecus homo et Traiani principis magister, suos claros viros nostris conferens, cum Platoni et Aristotili – quorum primum divinum, secundum demonium Graii vocant – Marcum Varronem, Homero Virgilium, Demattheni Marcum Tullium obiecisset, ausus est ad postremum et ducum controversiam movere, nec eum tanti saltem discipuli veneratio continuit. In uno sane suorum ingenia prorsus imparia non erubuit confiteri, quod quem tibi ex equo in moralibus preceptis obicerent non haberent; laus ingens ex ore presertim hominis animosi et qui nostro Iulio Cesari suum Alexandrum Macedonem comparasset* ("When Plutarch, a Greek and teacher of the emperor Trajan, compared our famous men to those of his own country, he held Marcus Varro up against Plato and Aristotle – the first of whom the Greeks call divine, the second almost so – Virgil against Homer, and Cicero against Demosthenes. In the end he had the courage also to start a contention between generals; not even respect for his exalted pupil held him back. In one instance he was not ashamed to acknowledge the genius of his own people as inferior: they do not have anyone comparable to you when it comes to moral philosophy. High praise indeed, especially coming from someone who is biased, someone who compared his own Alexander the Macedonian to our Julius Caesar" – my translation). It should be noted that only Demosthenes and Cicero and Alexander and Caesar are actually Plutarchan pairs. Judging by the rest of the names Petrarch mentions here, it seems he wished to attribute to Plutarch comparative *Lives* also of the greatest representatives of ancient philosophy and poetry.

[5] For Petrarch's relationship with Barlaam, Sigeros, and Pilatus, see Pertusi (1964) and Fyrigos (1989).

teacher of Trajan; in fact, at the time, "Plutarch" had become a household name for the preceptor of a prince. In the letter to Trajan the relationship between teachers and their illustrious pupils is discussed, and Plutarch admonishes Trajan, with reference to Nero, Seneca, and Quintilian, that the wrongs committed by pupils tend to be blamed on their teachers. This becomes almost a topos for Petrarch. In the *Trionfi*, for instance, published in 1349, we find Plutarch associated with Seneca and Quintilian. The three are merely mentioned together as illustrious teachers, but the connection of the names must itself be an allusion to the letter to Trajan.[6]

## The First Translations: *De Cohibenda Ira* and the Aragonese *Lives*

Petrarch's interest in the Greek world may be one of the reasons why Plutarch's name was not completely unknown in the Latin West by the second half of the fourteenth century, although still no genuine work of his was available to Latin readers. This only changed when the Greek scholar Simon Atumanus[7] translated *De cohibenda ira* into Latin at the request of Cardinal Pietro Corsini, as Simon informs us in the letter of dedication, dated Avignon, January 20, 1373.[8] He, or perhaps Petrarch, with whom he was acquainted, may have become interested in this particular treatise because of the passage where Aulus Gellius mentions that Plutarch had written about the sad effects of anger.[9]

Between 1373 and 1395 Corsini sent Simon's translation to the Florentine chancellor Coluccio Salutati (1331–1406).[10] He was an ardent admirer of Petrarch, so it was probably because of his influence that Salutati developed the interest that made him eager to acquire new translations of works of Greek literature. When Salutati received the Latin *De cohibenda ira*, he read it avidly but, in his own words, was appalled to see that the Latin of the translation was too obscure to attract the reader, and that it was impossible to guess the sense intended by Plutarch: Simon's version followed the Greek

---

[6]  *Ivi era il curioso Dicearco / ed, in suo' magisteri assai dispari, / Quintiliano e Seneca e Plutarco* ("There was the curious Dicaearchus, and, so different as teachers, Quintilian, Seneca, and Plutarch"): *Trionfi* 3.88–90. For other passages where Petrarch quotes pseudo-Plutarch, see Pade (2007: vol. 1, ch. 2.2, nn. 180–183).

[7]  Di Stefano (1968: 11–16) and Weiss (1977: 11).    [8]  Weiss (1977: 41 n. 179).

[9]  Aulus Gellius, *NA* 1.26.7: *non ita esse Plutarchum, ut philosophum deceret; irasci turpe esse; saepe eum de malo irae dissertauisse, librum quoque* περὶ ἀοργησίας *pulcherrimum conscripsisse* ("[he said] that Plutarch had not behaved as a philosopher ought to; it was disgraceful to be angry, he had often discussed the evils of anger and even written a beautiful book *On control of anger*").

[10]  For the life of Salutati, see Ullman (1963: 3–16) and Witt (1976; 1983; 2000: 292–337).

text *ad verbum*;[11] in fact, Salutati would have attributed the coarseness to Plutarch's own style, had he not known the passages from the *Institutio Traiani* quoted by John of Salisbury. Simon's preface, moreover, was ample proof that the translator's Latin was insufficient. Salutati decided to rewrite Simon's text to make it good Latin, dedicating his version, too, to Cardinal Corsini.[12] Simon's original translation is extant in a single fourteenth-century manuscript (see n. 11 in this chapter), whereas at least four copies of Salutati's version have survived.[13] It is far more elegant and lively than Simon's but, as might be expected, often far removed from the sense of the original.[14]

Salutati is also responsible for bringing the first Western translations of the *Lives* to Italy: around 1380 the Aragonese Juan Fernández de Heredia, Master of the Knights Hospitallers of Rhodes, had a number of Greek, Latin, and French histories translated into Aragonese, among them thirty-nine of Plutarch's *Lives*. They were first translated into demotic Greek, on Rhodes,[15] and then into a form of Aragonese by the Dominican Bishop Nicholas of Drenopolis (the ancient Adrianopolis in Epirus). The translation seems to have been finished by 1387 or 1388,[16] and Coluccio Salutati had heard about it already at the beginning of the 1390s, when he wrote to Heredia to obtain a copy, explaining that he was thinking of preparing a Latin version from the Aragonese.[17]

Salutati received a copy of the Aragonese *Lives* ca. 1395 and began to study it immediately.[18] He never carried out his plan to prepare a Latin version of

---

[11] Weiss (1977: 207–210) compared the Greek original with Simon's translation, transcribed from the sole surviving manuscript, cod. 8.55.34 of the Biblioteca Colombina in Seville.

[12] Salutati *Epistolario* 11.480–483: *sentiebam altas solidasque sententias inculto dicendi genere et obscuritate profundissima non traditas, sed obstrusas; putassemque totum hoc de Plutarchi stilo procedere nisi quedam sua venustissime translata comperissem apud magistrum Iohannem de Saberiis anglicum … accessit etiam ut translatoris id vitio factum esse cognoscerem, proemialis epistola, … cogitavi mecum opusculum illud de suae translationis obscuritate planiore dicendi genere in lucem intelligentie revocare; … denique pro semigreca translatione remitto tibi latinum tractatum* ("I felt how [Plutarch's] deep and substantial sentences were not rendered, but rather smashed by an uncouth manner of speaking and the profoundest obfuscation. I would have believed all this was due to Plutarch's style if I had not found something of his translated in the most delightful way in the English John of Salisbury … moreover, I was persuaded that it was the fault of the translator because of his prefatory letter … I decided to call back the treatise from his translation's darkness into the light of understanding by using a more intelligible style; … at last, instead of a half-Greek translation I return to you a Latin treatise"). Witt (1978: 336–342) discusses the problems surrounding the dating of Salutati's letter.

[13] Ullman (1963: 35).

[14] Weiss (1977: 216–218). See also Di Stefano (1968: 40–55), with the edition of the text at pp. 134–170.

[15] Clare and Jouan (1969: 568–569).

[16] For the Aragonese *Lives*, see Luttrell (1960; 1970); Clare and Jouan (1969); Álvarez Rodríguez (1983). The Aragonese *Lives* have been edited by Álvarez Rodríguez, first in his (1983) doctoral thesis and now in (2009). See also Pade (2007: I.76–80).

[17] For this translation, see Pertusi (1964: *passim*).     [18] See Pade (2007: I.81 and n. 218).

the *Lives* from the Aragonese; instead they were translated into Tuscan,[19] probably before 1397. The Tuscan version is extant in at least fourteen manuscripts,[20] the majority of which are found in Florentine libraries. Despite its relative success, the Tuscan version seems to have been ignored very soon by the learned world of the humanists – who preferred the Latin versions, made directly from the Greek, which began to be produced after 1400. However that may be, Salutati's efforts to have Simon Atumanus' *De cohibenda ira* and Heredia's Aragonese version of the *Lives* retranslated meant that at the end of the fourteenth century there was a direct knowledge of Plutarch in Italy; we are no more dealing with pickings from miscellanies, such as those of Gellius, or encyclopedias, such as John of Salisbury.

## The *Aetas Plutarchiana*

Roberto Weiss once named Italian humanism of the late fourteenth and early fifteenth centuries the "Plutarchan Age," referring to the fervent interest in Plutarch's writings that manifested itself for the first time since antiquity among a Latin readership.[21] As we have seen, Plutarch was not completely unknown in Italy by the end of the fourteenth century, but it was the teaching of Manuel Chrysoloras (ca. 1350–1415) that more than any other factor made Plutarch one of the most widely studied Greek writers in Italy.

A high-ranking Byzantine diplomat and scholar, Chrysoloras had been invited by Salutati to teach Greek in Florence. Among his motives for accepting the invitation must have been the hope that his cultural embassy would influence the West to help defend Constantinople against the Turks.[22] As we now know, he failed in this, but otherwise his tenure at Florence, where he held the chair of Greek from 1397 to 1400, was an immense success and marks the beginning of a stable tradition of Greek studies in Italy.[23]

Chrysoloras used Plutarch's works in his teaching and emphasized the importance of Plutarch in a famous letter to Salutati, written during his years in Florence. Chrysoloras praised Salutati's work on Plutarch, whose writings were proof of the very close relationship that once existed between

---

[19] Weiss (1977: 218–220).
[20] Compare Resta (1962: 10 n. 1); to the twelve manuscripts listed by him should be added *Biblioteca Medicea Laurenziana, Acquisti e Doni* 786 and *Biblioteca Nazionale Centrale di Firenze, Panciat.* 59 (65). Very few copies seem to have existed of the Aragonese *Lives*; in his chapter on the *fortuna* of this translation in Spain, Álvarez Rodríguez (1983: 146) was able to find references to only two or three.
[21] Weiss (1977: 226).   [22] See, for instance, Hankins (2002: 175–177) and Humble (2010a).
[23] For Salutati's invitation to Chrysoloras, see Cammelli (1941: 28–42) and Witt (1983: 303–305). The official invitation to Chrysoloras of March 28, 1396, written by Salutati, has been edited by Garfagnini (1984: 86–87) and again by Reeve (1991: 134–136).

Greeks and Romans; indeed, for many great Romans it could be said that his *Lives* had contributed more to their fame than any Latin book.[24] The letter shows how Chrysoloras saw Plutarch as central to his cultural enterprise;[25] his pupils, and eventually their pupils as well, were responsible for most of the translations of the *Lives*.

From the beginning of the fifteenth century we increasingly find references to Plutarch and to Plutarch manuscripts in humanists' letters; we also find the first humanist translations of Plutarch, most of them of the *Lives* and all of them into Latin. The earliest were all done in Florence or by humanists connected to the Florentine intellectual milieu.[26] Thematically, they reflect the republican interpretation of history and the concern with the republican origins of the city. *Brutus*, *Cicero*, *Antony*, and *Cato Minor* all concentrate on the last years of the Roman Republic and are also new sources for the much-debated question of Caesar's murder. The translation of *Brutus* by Iacopo Angeli (ca. 1360–1410/11), a close friend of Coluccio Salutati,[27] is probably the first published Latin translation of any of Plutarch's *Lives* made directly from the Greek. After *Brutus*, Angeli translated *Cicero* (1400/1), *Pompey*, and *Marius* (both probably before 1406). About the time of Salutati's death in 1406, Angeli came into contact with the Greek Peter Philargus, later Pope Alexander V. From Philargus he got the manuscript he used for his translations (both done before 1409) of Plutarch's *De Alexandri magni virtute aut fortuna* and *De fortuna Romanorum*. These are the first of Plutarch's essays to be translated after Simon Atumanus' fourteenth-century version of *De cohibenda ira*. In a period and in a cultural environment in which the focus was on the *Lives*, it is no surprise that Angeli chose essays that deal with the relative merits of some of the heroes described there.

The next humanist to produce translations from Plutarch was Leonardo Bruni (1370–1444), one of the most widely read contemporary writers in the fifteenth century and chancellor of Florence from 1427 until his death in 1444.[28] Since Hans Baron's work on fifteenth-century Florentine humanism (see section on "The Impact of Plutarchan Ethics upon Renaissance Ethico-Political Thought" later in this chapter),[29] Bruni has been considered the embodiment of the "civic humanist," a man who, like Cicero, was both

[24] Salutati *Epistolario* IV.341–343, Appendice prima; see also Cammelli (1941: 88).
[25] Rollo (2002: 74–75 and n. 156) emphasizes the connection between Chrysoloras' letter to Salutati, his teaching, and his cultural and diplomatic endeavors.
[26] For the study of Plutarch in early fifteenth-century Florence, see Pade (2007: I, ch. 3).
[27] The best account of Angeli's life is Weiss (1977: 255–277).
[28] There is a good biography of him in Griffiths, Hankins, and Thompson (1987: 21–46); see also Vasoli (1972).
[29] Baron (1955; 1966).

statesman and man of letters, and who used his classical learning in the service of his city. Bruni's original works comprise dialogues, orations, treatises on education and translation, biography, and historiography; and he translated, or adapted, works by, among others, St Basil, Xenophon, Demosthenes, Aristotle, Plato, Polybius, Procopius, and Plutarch. It has been said that his Greek scholarship was primarily influenced by Petrarch's humanism and intended, first and foremost, to restore and renew Latin culture.[30] This "Latin" bias is expressed in numerous ways in Bruni's original writings, and we encounter it in several of his translations and adaptations, for instance in the *Commentary on the First Punic War* (*Commentaria de primo bello punico*), which is based on Polybius, whose narrative Bruni supplemented with portions of various classical writers in order to correct Polybius' account and make it less anti-Roman.[31] Bruni's work on Plutarch may be seen as a manifestation of the same tendency. Most of his Plutarchan translations are of the lives of famous generals and statesmen from the Roman Republic: Mark Antony (*Antonius*, 1404–5), Cato Minor (1405–8), Aemilius Paulus (1408–9), the Gracchi (1410), Quintus Sertorius (1408–9 or 1410), and Cicero in the *Cicero novus*, his adaptation of Plutarch's *Cicero* (1413). His translation of the *Life* of King Pyrrhus of Epirus (before 1413) was surely motivated by his interest in Roman republican history, and his *Demosthenes* (1412) was intended as a foil for the *Cicero novus*, which reversed Plutarch's judgment and portrayed Cicero as the greater man, the ideal "civic humanist".

A central theme in the preface to *Antonius* is the ability of the Latin language and literature to rival Greek.[32] Bruni laments the great loss of Latin authors that had taken place since antiquity. Reading Plutarch, he became aware that neither the deeds nor even the names of the men who had won Italy a glorious name throughout the world were known any longer – among the Latins, it must be understood. Therefore he had resolved, if time allowed, to translate all of Plutarch's *Lives*. Bruni did not carry out this plan, but his preface probably explains what to many Westerners was the attraction of the *Lives*: their subjects, the great heroes of the Roman past. In his preface to the *Cicero novus*, Bruni explains that he was dissatisfied with the Plutarchan *Life* because it left out many things that were pertinent to the portrayal of the Roman; and Plutarch's treatment of Cicero was not always impartial, because he wanted Demosthenes, the other half of the pair, to emerge as the greater of the two. Bruni therefore proceeded to read all that had been written about Cicero in both Latin and

---

[30] Hankins (2002: 192).    [31] Reynolds (1954).    [32] Partial translation in Hankins (2002: 189).

Greek in order to write a new life with a more mature appreciation and fuller information.[33] If the *Cicero novus* was still closely based on Plutarch's life, later in life Bruni composed original biographies. In the *Life of Aristotle*, completed by April 1430, Bruni to some extent follows the structure of Diogenes Laertius' account, which he often refutes using information from other sources, among them Plutarch.[34] However, the *Lives* (*Vite*) *of Dante and Petrarch*, published in 1436, in some ways mark a return to the Plutarchan model; the two lives, written in Italian, are clearly conceived as parallel biographies, and are followed by a *synkrisis/ comparatio*.[35] It is interesting that Bruni here adapts the Plutarchan technique of "paired" *Lives* that as a translator he largely ignored (with the partial exception of his *Demosthenes* and *Cicero novus*).[36]

The third humanist to work on Plutarch in Florence was Guarino Guarini of Verona (1374–1460),[37] one of the most famous teachers of the Italian Renaissance. He was invited to succeed Chrysoloras in Florence in 1410. By then he had worked and studied for five years (1403–8) in Constantinople, staying in Chrysoloras' household, and during that time he had translated Plutarch's *Alexander*, which he probably only published some years later together with the other half of the pair, *Caesar*. In Florence Guarino translated the pseudo-Plutarchan *De liberis educandis* (1411), which enjoyed considerable popularity. However, he mainly continued doing what Angeli and Bruni had done, namely translating *Lives* of interest for Roman history; that is, *Flamininus* (1411), *Marcellus* (probably before June 1412), *Coriolanus* (before 1414), and *Caesar*, which was published together with his earlier version of *Alexander* (ca. 1411–13).

Dissatisfied with the atmosphere in Florence, Guarino left the city for Venice in 1414.[38] Guarino was an ardent admirer of Venice's stable, patrician constitution and he probably also sympathized with the city's cultural orientation toward the East. It is hardly a coincidence that it was during the period Guarino was teaching in Venice that we see for the first time a number of translations of Plutarch's lives of Greek heroes. Guarino

---

[33] I have used Griffiths' English translation of Bruni's preface in Griffiths, Hankins, and Thompson (1987: 184–185).

[34] Compare Fryde (1983: 33–53; 1988). There are partial or complete editions of Bruni's *Vita Aristotelis* in Baron (1928: 41–44); Düring (1957: 168–178); Griffiths, Hankins, and Thompson (1987: 283–292); and Viti (1996: 501–529).

[35] Baron (1928: 50–69) and Viti (1996: 537–560).

[36] On the humanists' interest, or lack of interest in the concept of parallelism, see the discussion in Humble (2010a).

[37] For a biography of Guarino, see Verger (1997).

[38] For the study of Plutarch in Venice, see Pade (2007: I. ch. 4).

himself translated six lives of Greek statesmen between 1414 and 1418 (*Dion, Themistocles, Phocion, Eumenes, Pelopidas*, and *Philopoemen*). Two of them, Dion and Phocion, were pupils of Plato and known for their non-populist policy. Guarino translated the life of the former for his pupil, the patrician Francesco Barbaro, who undoubtedly cherished the implicit comparison with Dion, the aristocrat who tried to realize Plato's ideal of the philosopher-ruler; there are some indications that Barbaro liked to see his city as Plato's ideal state come true – and by implication himself and his class as its philosophically trained aristocratic rulers.[39] Two years later Barbaro himself published his translation of the pair *Aristides and Cato*, while his fellow pupil, Leonardo Giustinian, translated *Cimon and Lucullus* and, almost twenty years later, *Phocion*. Guarino would return to Plutarch on several occasions. In the 1430s in Ferrara, he dedicated his Latin version of *Lysander and Sulla* (1434) and a compendium based on the *Quomodo adulator ab amico internoscatur* to his pupil and patron Leonello d'Este.

## The 1430s: The Medici and the Roman Curia

Florence again became a center for the study of Plutarch in the 1430s, in humanist circles close to the Medici or those seeking patronage from the curial grandees who stayed in the city during Pope Eugene IV's exile from Rome. If one can interpret Florentine interest in Plutarch in the early years of the century as related to the republican impetus so markedly expressed by contemporary Florentine humanists, then we may also see the renewed interest in the *Lives* as somehow reflecting the constitutional crisis of Florence during these years and in the last instance, of course, the position of the Medici. Moreover, the powerful presence of the Curia in the city and its ideological needs are reflected in the scholarly work of a number of humanists.[40]

The Medici, the wealthiest banking family of Florence, were exiled in November 1433, to be recalled less than a year later in September 1434. Cosimo de' Medici became the de facto ruler of Florence, like Augustus seemingly preserving the constitutional system of the old regime. Artists and intellectuals seeking Medici patronage did well to go along with the pretense.[41] A whole series of translations from the *Lives* were dedicated to the Medici, carefully chosen to express various elements in Medici

---

[39] See Pade (2013).
[40] For the study of Plutarch in Medici Florence and among curial humanists, see Pade (2007: I. ch. 7).
[41] Cf. Brown (1992: 2–52).

self-presentation by more or less subtle historical parallels. The heroes of these *Lives* saved their country from great peril or liberated it, and some, like Cosimo, suffered exile. Antonio Pacini's translation of *Timoleon*, dedicated to Cosimo (after 1434), is perhaps the first of these. Timoleon was the general who liberated Sicily from tyranny (like Cosimo freed Florence from the Albizzi) and introduced a moderate democracy in Syracuse. Shortly afterwards, Pacini dedicated the *Camillus* to Cosimo's brother Lorenzo, implicitly addressing Cosimo himself (who was frequently compared to Camillus after his return from exile) too. In the preface Pacini emphasizes the theme of Camillus' return to the utterly ruined state, which he then rebuilt. And like Camillus, Cosimo would eventually be hailed officially as *pater patriae*.[42] Themistocles is another of Plutarch's heroes known for his prudent and valiant behavior in exile. The Florentine humanist Lapo da Castiglionchio dedicated a translation of *Themistocles* to Cosimo (1434–6), dwelling on the similarities between the two great men.

Francesco Filelfo (1398–1481), on the other hand, was one of the Florentine intellectuals who had not supported the winning side in these turbulent years, and he had to look elsewhere for patronage. He saw ancient Sparta with her stable constitution as a model Florence ought to study in her troubled situation. In the early 1430s he translated three works related to Sparta, Xenophon's *Agesilaus*, *Spartan Constitution*, and Plutarch's *Life of Lycurgus*, together with Lycurgus' Roman counterpart, the Roman king Numa (1430). He dedicated all these works to the influential Cardinal Nicola Albergati, stressing in his preface to the Plutarchan pair how the example of Lycurgus could help in the present situation of Florence:

> *Intueberis enim tum ex Lacedaemoniorum illa re publica tum ex hac praesenti uita iis militiae praeceptis et institutis prudentissimum et fortissimum regem illum semetipsum instruxisse et egregie confirmasse, quibus florentissimae respublicae clarissimaque imperia et lautissime augentur et pacatissime conseruantur et pulcherrime exornantur.*

> You will see, both in the treatise on the Spartan constitution and in this *Life*, that Lycurgus, a most wise and resourceful king, created for himself a military system which decidedly strengthened him. And you will also notice that it is similar to the one which helps blossoming cities [a pun on the Latin name of Florence, *Florentia*] and great empires grow to splendor, survive in peace and shine with beauty.[43]

---

[42] For these themes in Medici propaganda, see again Brown (1992).
[43] Pade (2007: II. ch. 2.1 [§15]). See also Resta (1986: 20–21).

Filelfo later translated the *Lives* of Galba and Otho (1454) and the two *opuscula*, *Regum et imperatorum apophthegmata* (*Apophthegmata ad Traianum*) and *Apophthegmata Laconica*.

In the 1430s Florence also experienced the presence of the Roman Curia and the Council of Ferrara–Florence. Exiled for almost a decade, Pope Eugenius IV spent long periods in Florence with the Curia, planning for the return of the papacy to Rome. Eugenius' project stressed the importance of the city of Rome, and during these years humanist writings bear witness to a growing interest in the history and topography of Rome as a city, identifying the church as the heir to the empire and the popes as successors of the Roman emperors. In the humanist interpretation, the return of the popes to Rome would somehow be equivalent to a second founding of the city, echoing the first one by Romulus. This is reflected also in the humanists' work on Plutarch. Lapo da Castiglionchio (1406–38) dedicated translations of *Lives* of early Roman kings and statesmen to important members of the Curia: *Publicola* to Cardinal Giordano Orsini (ca. 1435)[44] and *Romulus*, together with *Theseus* to Cardinal Prospero Colonna (1436). Lapo moreover dedicated a Latin version of *Solon* to Eugenius IV (1435), since the wisdom of the Athenian lawgiver resembled that of Eugenius, one of *Pericles* (1436/7) to Giovanni Vitelleschi, who led Eugenius' war to restore papal power in central Italy, and one of *Aratus* (1437) to Cardinal Giovanni Cesarini.[45]

## Completing the Corpus

By the end of the 1430s the majority of Plutarch's *Lives* circulated in Italy in Latin translations. Manuscripts reveal how readers would commission copies of *Lives* that reflected their specific interests and often combined texts of Plutarch with texts by other authors focusing on a specific theme, such as the history of the late Roman Republic. We also increasingly see manuscripts containing large collections of *Lives*, in Latin translation, possibly preserving the original pairs and arranged according to the chronological order of the Roman heroes, as would later be the case with the printed editions of the Latin *Lives*.[46] While some *Lives* received attention from more than one humanist translator, all in all scholarly work on

---

[44] Orsini also received a Latin version of *Timoleon* from Giovanni Aurispa (1438).

[45] Other translations from Plutarch by Lapo were *Fabius Maximus* (1436), dedicated to Alfonso of Naples and *Artaxerxes* (1437), of which we possess dedications both to Duke Humphrey of Gloucester and to Alfonso of Naples. Cf. Pade (2007: I. ch. 7.9).

[46] Cf. Pade (1995).

Plutarch was directed toward making the entire corpus of *Lives* accessible in Latin translation. In 1458 or 1459 the Florentine *cartolai* Vespasiano da Bisticci started preparing a collection of the *Lives* for Piero de' Medici, who wished to own all forty-eight biographies, in Latin. Accordingly, translations of the remaining *Lives* were commissioned: Alamanno Rinuccini, who had already translated *Nicias* and *Crassus* for Piero in 1454/5 now produced Latin versions of *Agis* and *Cleomenes*, again dedicated to Piero (1458), and *Agesilaus*, which he dedicated to Lorenzo di Piero de' Medici in 1462. Rinuccini's fellow Florentine, Donato Acciaiuoli, translated *Demetrius* and *Alcibiades*, again as part of Vespasiano's project. Piero's collection is now Ms. Laur.lat. 65,26–27 in the Biblioteca Medicea Laurenziana in Florence.[47]

By the spring of 1470 Giovanni Antonio Campano was able to collect Latin translations of almost the entire corpus of the *Lives*, which he printed in Rome;[48] the edition became the basis for nine incunabula and innumerable sixteenth-century editions.

Though we know that Greek manuscripts of Plutarch circulated in Italy,[49] his works were primarily read in Latin translations. The printed vulgate of the *Lives* created by Campano was superseded only in 1559 by Amyot's French translation.

The *Moralia* largely enjoyed a separate fortune from that of the *Lives*. In general, the two corpora were neither translated nor transmitted together. At least in the earlier generations, there was a marked preference for the *Lives*, whereas the *Moralia* were often seen as supplements to them.[50] A good example of this is *De Alexandri magni fortuna aut virtute*, twice

[47]	Cf. Pade (2007: I. ch. 8 and vol. II, which contains a list of all manuscripts of the Latin translations of the *Lives* and transcriptions of the letters of dedication). Vespasiano's edition is described in nos. 87 and 88 of the list. Other fifteenth-century Latin translations of *Lives* are: *Camillus* by Ognibene da Lonigo (1433?); *Agesilaus* by Carlo Gonzaga (1430s); *Timoleon* by Andrea Biglia (after 1425); *Marius, Theseus, Pelopidas* and *Fabius Maximus* by Antonio Pacini (after 1437); *Romulus* by Giovanni Tortelli (1438); *Pelopidas* (1441–2) and *Alcibiades–Coriolanus* by Antonio Beccaria (before 1456); and *Artaxerxes* by Lampugino Birago (before 1460).
[48]	2 vols. in 2° – BMC 4,21; HC *13125; IGI 7920. Campano's edition is described in Giustiniani (1961). In the cases where more than one translation existed, Campano used: Antonio Pacini's *Theseus* and Giovanni Tortelli's *Romulus*, both substituted by Lapo's version in the 1478 and later editions; Donato Acciaiuoli's *Alcibiades* (with the *comparatio*) and Guarino's *Coriolanus*; Lapo's *Themistocles* and Pacini's *Camillus*; Pacini's *Fabius Maximus* (in the 1499 and later editions the *comparatio* is printed in Lapo's translation), *Pelopidas, Timoleon, Marius,* and Leonardo Giustinian's *Phocion*. Instead of Plutarch's *Life of Agesilaus*, Campano printed Battista Guarino's translation of the encomium by Xenophon; cf. Pade (2007: I. ch. 12).
[49]	Manfredini (1987).
[50]	For a short discussion of the relative popularity of the two corpora among Italian humanists, see Bevegni (1993: 33–35).

translated in the first half of the fifteenth century and often transmitted together with the life of Alexander. Most of the earliest translations from the *Moralia* are in fact of *opuscula* concerned with the same themes we find in the *Lives*; that is, the description of character and personality.[51] Of the few humanists who showed a special interest in the *Moralia*, I shall only name two here: the Sicilian Antonio Cassarini (1390/6–1447) who translated nine *opuscula* between 1439 and 1447,[52] and Niccolò Perotti (1430–80), who as a young man translated *De Alexandri magni fortuna aut virtute*, *De invidia et odio* (both ca. 1449), and *De fortuna Romanorum* (1453/4) for Pope Nicholas V.[53]

## The Impact of Plutarch on Renaissance Biography: Some Examples

In his seminal article on the fourteenth-century reception of Suetonius and Plutarch, Walter Berschin maintained that from the beginning of the fifteenth century, Plutarch became the prime model of Renaissance biographers.[54] Though I am not absolutely convinced that there was an awareness of the characteristics of Plutarch's biographical form at that early date, the intense exposure of the reading public to the Latin translations of the *Lives* did in time leave its mark. I shall not here attempt to provide an overview of the typologies of Renaissance biography. Instead I shall discuss a few examples where we see the influence of (a) Plutarch's biographical form; that is, the comparative element; (b) the structure of his *Lives*; that is, chronology as the main organizing principle governing the arrangement of the material, as opposed to the arrangement of the material by topic (*per species*) that Suetonius preferred; (c) the thematic nature of his *Lives*; that is, the public life and character of person portrayed, as opposed to the intimate details of private life related by Suetonius; (d) his biographical technique, the use of the significant detail or saying; and (e) the Suetonian model – even on Plutarchan material.

We do see that humanist writers imitated Plutarch's comparative form, even though they found it difficult to imitate Plutarch's biographical style in detail, as is shown for instance by Leonardo Bruni (see earlier in this

---

[51] For instance, *De liberis educandis* (ca. 1411) and *Parallela minora* (1428) both by Guarino, 1428; *Ad principem ineruditum* (1423) by Rinuccio da Castiglione. See Giustiniani (1979: 48–49).

[52] Becchi (2009b: 25–26).

[53] Becchi (2009b: 27–28). Becchi lists all fifteenth-century Latin translations of the *Moralia* produced in Italy.

[54] Berschin (1983a: 40–42).

chapter on his *Vite di Dante e Petrarca*). Apart from Bruni's Italian *Lives*, we find examples of this in Gianozzo Manetti's *Lives of Socrates and Seneca* (ca. 1440).[55] In spite of the comparative overall structure, the *Life of Socrates*, which has recently been studied by Manuela Kahle, is actually rather Suetonian, with sections on Socrates' physical appearance, character, private life, and public offices.[56] Another humanist who composed parallel lives is the Florentine Donato Acciaiuoli, whose *Lives of Hannibal and Scipio* (1467–8) supplemented the existing series by Plutarch.[57] Like Manetti's *Lives*, they were regularly copied and printed together with the Latin translations of Plutarch's *Lives*.

The earliest attempt known to me to compose the life of a contemporary using the Plutarchan structure is Tito Livio Frulovisi's *Life of Henry the Fifth* (1438). A student of Guarino's, Frulovisi wrote the *Life* while secretary to Humphrey of Gloucester, Henry's brother. We know that Frulovisi studied Plutarch's *Life of Pericles* in order to imitate it in his own composition, but in the eyes of a modern critic he failed badly.[58] We also see writers experimenting with biographical form: Pier Candido Decembrio's early *Life of Filippo Maria Visconti* (1448) is a perfect Suetonian biography. The work is divided into seventy-one chapters, each devoted to a specific topic. As did his model, Decembrio puts Visconti's private life and habits under the microscope. The result is an all-too-honest analysis of the ruler's character that caused quite an uproar in Renaissance courts. Understandably, Decembrio chose Plutarchan biography, with its focus on the character and public persona of its hero, for his next *vita*, that of Francesco Sforza (1461–2), which is also strictly chronological in the organizing of its material. Admittedly, Lorenzo Valla's *Gesta Ferdinandi regis* (1445) is not a biography, strictly speaking, but it has some Suetonian traits. It was criticized, by Bartolomeo Facio, for relating the salacious details drawn from the private lives of the earlier kings of Aragon. Facio's attack on Valla may be seen as signaling a shift in humanist priorities, from the production of Suetonian biographies of contemporary princes to highly embellished royal historiography, or to biographies following the Plutarch model. A telling example of this is Donato Acciaiuoli's reworking of Einhard's very Suetonian *Vita Karoli* into a Plutarchan chronological narrative (1461).[59]

In the preface to his *Life of Alexander*, Plutarch famously said that he wrote *Lives*, not histories, explaining that "in the most illustrious deed

---

[55] The two lives are edited in Baldassari and Begemihl (2003).    [56] Kahle (2017b: 49).
[57] Affortunati and Scardigli (1992).    [58] Blackwell (1986: 431-434); Pade (2007: I. 299).
[59] Ianziti (2016).

there is not always a manifestation of virtue or vice, nay, a slight thing like a phrase or jest often makes a greater revelation of character than battles when thousands fall" (1.2). In his *De dictis et factis Alphonsi regis Aragonum* (ca. 1455), modeled on the *Apomnemoneumata*, Xenophon's recollections of Socrates, Antonio Panormita actually makes use of the Plutarchan technique, relying on "sayings" to demonstrate the virtue of his subject.[60]

We see a clash between the new Plutarchan model and traditional medieval biography where the material is arranged by topic in the work of the learned John Whethamstede, Abbot of St Alban's. Whethamstede composed several encyclopedias, among them one entitled *Granarium* (before 1440) that contains a number of biographical articles, based on the Latin translations of Plutarch's *Lives*, which he quotes verbatim and at length. Even so, the material is presented by topic; that is, the Plutarchan narrative is rearranged into a biographical form reminiscent of medieval hagiography – or of a Suetonian life.[61]

## The Impact of Plutarchan Ethics upon Renaissance Ethico-Political Thought

As I described at the beginning of this chapter, it was in the (historically incorrect) guise of Trajan's educator that Plutarch became known in the Latin West during the late Middle Ages. This was how he was still seen in the fourteenth century, when Petrarch repeatedly mentioned him as a great teacher and as a writer of *Lives*. Humanist educators generally subscribed to Cicero's principle *historia magistra vitae* ("history teacher of life," *De or.* 1.2.36) and taught that learning through examples by far surpasses learning via precept; in other words, that history and biography are far more effective in a person's education than moral philosophy. Thus Petrarch's description alone or coupled with Plutarch's fame as the educator of a prince could have made Western readers wish to become acquainted with his writings. One who pursued this course was Coluccio Salutati, who greatly influenced the next generations of humanists. According to Salutati, *humanitas* is the combination of moral excellence and practical experience with learning. Learning is acquired through the study of literature – Greek and Latin, that is – and the different genres are valued in proportion to their ability to convey moral lessons.[62] Thus the disciplines that seem most indispensable to the *studia humanitatis* are: moral philosophy; history, which teaches the reader through examples; and rhetoric, without which profound thoughts or great events cannot be properly

[60] Schadee (2016: 100–103).  [61] Pade (2017).  [62] See Kessler (1968).

expressed. Plutarch's *Lives* are written with the explicit aim of teaching through the examples of great men, of conveying a moral lesson in a style that would make it irresistible, of forming the reader's character. In short, they should recommend themselves to anyone interested in the *studia humanitatis*. The very educational program expressed by Plutarch in the *Lives* coincides perfectly with the theories of Renaissance educators and that in itself, one might say, was enough to secure his popularity. Plutarch's educational zeal has been seen as one of the reasons why the *Lives* remained one of the "bibles" of Western civilization. For instance, his work was one of the three books used for civilizing the monster in Mary Shelley's *Frankenstein* – the other two being Milton's *Paradise Lost*, which was to convey religious understanding, and Goethe's *Sorrows of Young Werther*, meant to educate feeling. The *Lives* were an education in politics and "high thoughts" – and the *opuscula* that dealt with the same themes were definitely the most popular.[63]

If Plutarch's moral and pedagogical project assured him the attention of Renaissance readers, then his method of forming the reader's character through the examples of great public figures also made the reception of his works dependent on ideological factors. For more than forty years Hans Baron's concept of "civic humanism," his analysis of how especially Florentine intellectuals responded to the demands and needs of the surrounding society, has dominated scholarly discussions of the subject. Baron described the new humanism of the fifteenth century, which stressed the importance of civic life and active political participation, governed by the wisdom imbibed from the ancients. According to Baron, it was the struggle between Florence and Milan from 1389 to 1402, leading almost to the demise of Florence as an independent state, that made Florentine intellectuals realize the value of their civic, republican culture.[64] Though often criticized, Baron's books have given the next generations of scholars a very useful, and much used, interpretive framework, which has been applied not only to Florentine humanism but also, *mutatis mutandis*, to political conditions and intellectual life in Venice and other Italian cities. As I tried to demonstrate earlier, the focus on Plutarch's works differed in various centers of the Italian Renaissance. Not only was the study of Plutarch influenced by ideological factors; the way he was translated and transmitted also became part of a political discourse that changed from republican Florence to patrician Venice and the Roman Curia.

---

[63] Goldhill (2002: 246–247).
[64] Cf. Baron (1955; 1966). The impact and criticism of Baron's thesis are amply documented in Hankins (2000).

## Further Reading

The fullest and most systematic account of the "rediscovery" of Plutarch by Italian humanism is Pade (2007). Weiss (1977) remains generally valuable. Important essay-length studies are Humble (2010a), Becchi (2019), and Giustiniani (1979). The reception of Plutarch during the Renaissance should be explored alongside the reception of other ancient life-writers, such as Suetonius (Berschin 1983a; Ianziti 2016) or Diogenes Laertius (Kahle 2017b), as well as the overarching tendency to draw upon classical texts in the various guidebooks for statesmen (e.g. Schadee 2016). On John Whethamstede's engagement with Plutarch, see Pade (2017).

# CHAPTER 17

# Plutarch and the Spanish Renaissance

*Aurelio Pérez Jiménez*

Spanish humanism anticipated general Western knowledge of Plutarch by nearly a century. After Juan Fernández de Heredia (ca. 1310–96) commissioned the translation of the *Parallel Lives* into Aragonese (ca. 1380), aside from some notices referring to the pseudo-Plutarch preceptor of Trajan, there is a long gap until the second half of the fifteenth century. At that time, the translation of the *Parallel Lives* from Latin by Fernández de Palencia invigorated Plutarch's reception in Spain and opened the door to his growing influence on the Spanish Renaissance.

From this time on, scholarly attention to the works of Plutarch went beyond simple translation by Spanish humanists. Indeed, both the *Lives* and *Moralia* proved to offer a wealth of material for historians and theologians in their defense of Catholicism, to philosophers in the formulation of their doctrines, to scholars in their erudite commentaries, and in general to a large number of moralists, compilers, and literary creators. The increasingly widespread availability of the Chaeronean's works not only in Latin and Castilian translations but also in the original Greek text, available since the first Aldine editions of the *Moralia* (1509) and *Parallel Lives* (1505), reinforced the educational potential of Plutarch's works. By the time of the Renaissance, Plutarch had achieved a permanent place in Spanish universities, and his works could be found in public and private libraries.[1]

After the translation of the *Parallel Lives* by Fernández de Palencia (Seville, 1491), some pairs of *Lives* were translated by Francisco de Enzinas (*Cimon–Lucullus*, 1547 and *Theseus–Romulus, Lycurgus–Numa, Solon–Publicola*, and *Themistocles–Camillus* – one pair attributed to him or to Gracián de Alderete has been questioned – (Strasbourg, 1551); in the seventeenth century the *Brutus* of Quevedo (Madrid, 1654) and the *Numa* of Antonio Costa (Barcelona, 1693) were published, both in paraphrase format, with commentary.[2] The *Moralia*

---

[1] Bergua Cavero (1995: 4–9); Pordomingo Pardo (1996: 463).
[2] See on translations Pérez Jiménez (2009); only key names and dates are listed here.

fared better, called on to support the moral and theological interests of Spanish intellectuals in the sixteenth and seventeenth centuries. Representative translations include those of Gracián de Alderete, who translated *Apothegms* (Alcalá, 1533) and *Moralia* (Alcalá, 1548; Salamanca, 1571); perhaps Alonso Ruiz de Virués, *De cupiditate divitiarum* (Valladolid, 1538); Diego de Astudillo, *De cohibenda ira* and *Coniugalia praecepta* (Antwerp, 1551); and Pedro Simón Abril, *Apothegms* (Saragossa, 1590).[3] Also preserved is a manuscript translation of *De capienda ex inimicis utilitate* by Gaspar Hernández (ca. 1554) and another, albeit partial, of *De vitando aere alieno* by Juan Páez de Castro (1556).

This translation activity, nearly always from the Greek text, was due in part to the increasingly wide knowledge of ancient Greek after the creation of Chairs in Spanish universities, and the consequent rise of philologists, who often used Plutarch's works for readings and commentaries. Key figures and their dates follow. Elio Antonio de Nebrija (1441–1522), not very generous in his *Commentary on Persius* (1503) in quoting Greek authors, cited Plutarch more than four times, an honor he shared only with Plato and Aristotle. Fernando de Herrera (1534–97) used various *Moralia* treatises together with the *Lives* of Sulla and Pyrrhus for his commented edition of Garcilaso (Seville, 1580). Francisco de Vergara (+ 1545) in *De graecae linguae grammatica libri quinque* (Alcalá, 1537) referred to the *Lives* and *Moralia* as useful books. Sebastian Fox Morcillo (ca. 1526–ca. 1548) quoted the *Moralia* (and once *Solon*) in his *In Platonis Timaeum commentarii* (Basel, 1554); he relied on these texts to support his interpretation of the *Timaeus*, to confirm his own ideas, and to reconcile Plato and Aristotle via the Chaeronean;[4] furthermore, he mentioned Plutarch among the sources of his *De imitatione seu de informandi styli ratione* (1554). Juan Luis de la Cerda (1569–1607) also profited from Plutarch (sometimes reproducing the Greek text) for his commentary (Madrid, 1609) on Virgil's *Eclogues*[5] and *Georgics*.[6] Although Juan Lorenzo Palmireno (1524–79) does not inform us about his sources in *Phrases and Patterns Loquendi of War* (1568), relying on linguistics, we can assume he used Plutarch; in fact, in *The Student of the Village* (1568) he advised his readers

> to create nicknames or similes that are useful for persuading if you are a preacher, and relieving the suffering, if you are a doctor, and helping to understand a precept, if you are a teacher .... You should not pay any attention to whether they are in Latin or in a Romance language. For me, I prefer those of Plutarch. (194–195)

---

[3] Morales Ortiz (2000: 139–145).   [4] Martínez Benavides (1999).   [5] Iglesias Montiel (1991).
[6] Ortega Castejón (1991).

Pedro Simón Abril (1530–95) in *Greek Grammar Written in Spanish* (Madrid, 1587) proposed that his students read Plutarch both as an historian and a moralist.[7] Simón Abril's familiarity with the Chaeronean is evident also in other works where he quotes Plutarch's titles and passages, for example in the *Philosophy Called Logic or Part Rational* (Alcalá, 1587): he refers here to the *Demosthenes* and to *Regum et imperatorum apophthegmata* in the "Note to the Reader," where he placed Plutarch among the most serious philosophers, namely Plato, Aristotle, and St Basil. Even the chronology and the *Life* he wrote to introduce a translation of Cicero's *Letters to His Friends* (Barcelona, 1592) are taken largely from Plutarch. There are a few references to Plutarch in Juan and Alonso de Valdés' (1490–1532) *Dialogues*: his name appears once in Juan's *Dialogue on Language* (1535), when Valdés himself speaks about books not as valuable as those of Demosthenes, Xenophon, Plutarch, and Lucian; and in Alonso's *Dialogue of Mercury and Charon* (1528/30), Plutarch is cited as authority for the consideration of the Prince as an image of God.

The cases of Francisco Cascales' (1565–1642) *Poetic Manual* and *Philological Letters* and of Pedro Juan Núñez's (1522–1602) *De recta atque utili ratione conficiendi curriculi Philosophiae* (Barcelona, 1594) are different: they are rich in references to the *Moralia* especially. Cascales invoked the authority of Plutarch to reinforce his own literary theories;[8] Núñez inserted Plutarch's name among his sources, calling him *Plutarchus gravis in primis philosophus* (2v). Alfonso García Matamoros (+ 1572) recalled the school founded by Sertorius in Huesca in *Pro adserenda Hispanorum eruditione* (Alcalá, 1553) and included Plutarch among writers who dealt with love. Juan Huarte de San Juan (1529–88) in *The Examination of Men's Wits* took examples from Plutarch (e.g. Archimedes' death, Hannibal, and Fabius Maximus). And Antonio Agustín (1516–86), with the help of Núñez, tried to resolve a textual problem in *De defectu oraculorum* on behalf of the Italian scholar Latinio Latini.[9]

The admiration of these humanists for our author is clear from the entry "Plutarco" in the *Treasury of the Castillian or Spanish Language* (Madrid, 1611) by Sebastián de Covarrubias y Orozco (1539–1613):

> PLVTARCO is from the Greek proper name *Ploutarchos*. We derive this name from this so-called "grauissimo auctor." It means *Princeps diuitiarum*, a title that this man deserved on account of the richness he left us in his writings.

So it was natural enough that Plutarch, whose name was linked in the Middle Ages to the *Institutio Traiani* and who in various treatises

[7] López Rueda (1973: 247–248).    [8] Alemán Illán (2005).    [9] Pérez Jiménez (2007: 684–686).

evidenced pedagogical interests, opened the way to a new Europe preoccupied with the theory of education. In Spain, there were three pillars to this theory: first, Elio Antonio de Nebrija in his *De liberis educandis* (1509) displayed his own classical and scholarly inspiration via examples from Plutarch's works, which even provided him the title of his book; second, Juan Luis Vives (1492–1540) in the *Introductio ad sapientiam* (1524) shared with Plutarch the duty of the wise to assume a heightened social commitment and contribute to the common good; furthermore, he relied on the *Coniugalia praecepta* when in *De institutione feminae christianae* (1523) he analyzed female values;[10] and third, Juan Lorenzo Palmireno in such works as *The Scholar Courtier* (1573) takes advantage of Plutarchan doctrines when calling for active social participation of the wise and presenting models of behavior to teachers.

The privileged position of Plutarch in the Spanish Golden Century was based on his moral and theological treatises, philosophical diatribe, and miscellaneous writings. In fact, several factors contributed to the acceptance by the Roman Catholic Church of a pagan author, such as Plutarch was: his conservative Platonic doctrines, always advocating Providence and human responsibility (that is, the two basic principles of Catholic thought); the evidence of ancient Fathers such as St Basil and St John Chrysostom, who frequently cited Plutarch's works – this alone was sufficient to include him as an authority in this genre of writings; also, the belief that Plutarch had been baptized in antiquity and even that he was a martyr, according to Eusebius and despite more than some reasonable doubts. Last but not least, the admiration of Erasmus for Plutarch helped promote a certain popularity even among more heterodox Spanish intellectuals.

Indeed, a list of Spanish theologians and moralists who used or cited *Moralia* in the sixteenth and seventeenth centuries would be a long one. *Coniugalia praecepta*, for example, provided the pattern for Luis Vives' *De institutione feminae christianae*, for Fray Luis de León's (1527–91) *The Perfect Marriage*, and perhaps for Pedro de Luján's *Conversations about Marriage* (Seville, 1550) – in all these treatises, Plutarch's ideas are relevant. As far as philosophical diatribe is concerned, Pedro de Valencia (1555–1620) inserted many quotations from Plutarch in his *Academica* (Antwerp, 1596), using them to affirm a position against the Stoics; he knew Greek and often quoted in that language.[11] Some of these works show the philological competence of their authors, but others also have literary value, making them basic classical references for Spanish literature. This is true in the case

---

[10] Narro Sánchez (2011).    [11] Nieto Ibáñez (2005:794–795).

of Cristóbal de Villalón (1510–ca. 1562), who in the second song of his
*Crotalón* imitated the dialogue between Ulixes (Odysseus) and Gryllus of
*Bruta animalia ratione uti, sive Gryllus*;[12] another valuable example is the
Toledan Luisa Sigea de Velasco (1522–60), who in his *Colloquim de vita
privata et aulica* put in the mouths of Flaminia and Blesilla whole passages
from *De capienda ex inimicis utilitate* and *Quomodo adulator ab amico
internoscatur*, taken from the Latin translations by Erasmus.[13]

Plutarch's works were also of interest to the Christian theorists – the moral,
philosophical, and theological richness of his texts made them a valuable
companion to biblical exegesis. Theoretical assumptions for this practice are
found in the writings of the Dominican fray Luis de Granada (1504–88), the
Cistercian Lorenzo de Zamora, and the Jesuit Gil González Dávila (1570–
1658). The former refers several times to Plutarch in his famous *Sinners' Guide*
and shows predilection for him in the preface to the *Collectanea moralis
philosophiae* (Lisbon, 1571), an anthology of suitable passages for preaching;
here Plutarch is worthy of filling in Greek literature the place reserved for
Seneca among the Latin authors. According to the tradition, Fray Luis
considered him *Christianissimum instituendae vitae magistrum*,[14] and structured all the thematic parts of his work according to the ethical *Moralia*.[15]
Lorenzo de Zamora in the course of the *Mystical Monarchy* (Madrid, 1598 and
Alcalá, 1601) went to Plutarch for examples suitable for theological and moral
questions.[16] Furthermore, he proclaimed the utility of the classics for reading
the Scriptures; the chapter "Defense of Human Letters" invokes Plutarch
several times: first, by vindicating the poets against the opinion of such
philosophers as Plato and Plutarch himself; next, by using him as an authority
for three of the five rules that should control reading of classical texts; and
finally he upholds not only the value of Plutarch's doctrines but also his
literary artistry as a model for religious discourse.[17] Finally, González Dávila
gives us in his *Talks about the Rules of the Company of Jesus* further clues to
Plutarch's role in the religious life of the Jesuits; concerning penance (7th talk,
4th rule), he makes use of the biographer to confirm a judgment of St. Paul:
"Plutarch knew it [sc. the Christian message], saying that it is a sign of
humility to take pleasure in correction." In the same way, for the examination
of conscience (10th talk), the opinions of Church Fathers are complemented
by references to Plutarch, Seneca, and Epictetus.[18]

[12] Indelli (1992: 322, 344–352); Bergua Cavero (1995: 196–263).    [13] Pérez Jiménez (1998).
[14] Bergua Cavero (1995: 27–29).    [15] Correia Martins (2011).    [16] Nieto Ibáñez (2007: 649–662).
[17] Nieto Ibáñez (2007: 644–648).
[18] The treatises most quoted by Dávila are *De capienda ex inimicis utilitate, Quomodo quis suos in virtute
sentiat profectus*, and *De cohibenda ira*.

Such theoretical proposals found immediate application in the practice of preaching. Like Fray Luis de Granada, the Jesuit Juan Bonifacio in *De sapiente fructuoso* (Burgos, 1589) reserved second place (after Seneca) for Plutarch among authors recommended for use in sermons; he referred usually to the usefulness of the *Moralia* in general, but he preferred the educational treatises.[19] There are many other authors who used Plutarch in this way.[20] Fray Hernando de Santiago preached at the funerals of Philip II (*Sermones funerales*, Madrid, 1599) and Philip III. In a funeral discourse referring to the latter (Granada, 1621), he pointed out that the biblical statement *vanitas vanitatum et omnia vanitas* reduced the king of so vast an empire to "seven feet of land in San Lorenzo"; and to reinforce his argument he quoted an apothegm attributed by Plutarch to the Macedonian Philip: *O quam minimam partem, natura fortiti, appetimus orbem terrae.* This example alone would suffice to illustrate the connection to Plutarch in the works of Spanish preachers of this time, but three more names are worth mentioning: Fray Hernando de Zárate (+ ca. 1597), Francisco Terrones del Caño (+ 1601), and Juan Pérez de Montalbán (1602–38). The first, in his *Speeches on the Christian Patience* (Alcalá, 1593) regarding the sources of historical examples, underlined the figure of Plutarch as a compiler of "very sharp and eloquent statements"; furthermore, he bolstered his own statements with material from treatises such as *De capienda ex inimicis utilitate, Regum et imperatorum apophthegmata, Consolatio ad uxorem,* and *De cohibenda ira,* as well as from *Lives* such as *Phocion* and *Alexander.* Terrones del Caño, in the *Art or Instruction Necessary for the Preacher* (1617), reminded us that Fray Luis de Granada and Juan Bonifacio also recommended the use in sermons of sayings taken from Plutarch and other philosophers. Of course, he himself provided examples of such examples, referring specifically to *Quomodo adolescens poetas audire debeat.*[21] Finally, Montalbán in *Moral, Human and Divine Examples, for Everyone* (1661) suggested that the library of every preacher should include the works of Seneca and Plutarch (fol. 288).

If the *Moralia* were a major source for theologians and moralists, the *Parallel Lives* performed the same function for teachers of political theory and historians. Among the former, Spanish humanism has left us authentic jewels of erudition such as the work of Castillo de Bovadilla. The two thick volumes of his *Politics for Corregidores* (1595) are rich in classical quotations, reserving a privileged place for Plutarch, at least in the first part; its body

---

[19] E.g. *De liberis educandis, Quomodo adulator ab amico internoscatur, De cohibenda ira,* and *Coniugalia praecepta.*
[20] Cf. Herrero Salgado (1994).   [21] Herrero Salgado (1994).

text and marginal notes quote from practically every Plutarchan *Life* and also some of the *Moralia* in order to aid the moral instruction of rulers. The most often cited work is, of course, *Praecepta gerendae reipublicae*, but also frequently cited are other ethical treatises, as well as the collections of apothegms and the pseudo-Plutarchan *Institutio Traiani*.[22]

After Castillo de Bovadilla, the art form of Spanish political essays reached its peak in the works of authors such as Francisco de Quevedo Villegas (1580–1645), Diego de Savedra Fajardo (1584–1648), and the Jesuit Baltasar Gracián (1601–58). The familiarity of the first with Plutarch's works is well known;[23] he translated *Brutus* and included many quotations from the *Lives* and *Moralia* in his essays, but because of his admiration for Seneca and Epictetus, he defended Stoicism against Plutarch (1634). He would repeat this innovative critical attitude a year later in a defense of Epicurus, although in that case Quevedo was limited to arguments put forward in the previous century by the Italian Nicola Agelli.[24] Saavedra, in *The Royal Politician Represented in One Hundred Emblems* (Munich, 1640), referred to or quoted from *Aristides, Themistocles, Timoleon, Alexander, Lysander, Solon*, and *Numa*; furthermore, in *The Literary Republic* (1665) he presented Plutarch as a teacher of rulers.[25] And finally, Baltasar Gracián cites Plutarch in all of his most known works,[26] especially *The Complete Gentleman* (1646), *Acuteness and Art of Ingenuity* (1648), and the romance *The Critic* (1651–7). Gracián was an enthusiastic admirer of the *Parallel Lives* whose imitative method he adopted. This is evident in the "Primor XVIII" of *The Critic*, where sentences such as the following seem almost dictated by the moralist of Chaeronea:

> Prominent men are animated textbooks about glory; from them the wise man must learn lessons of greatness, repeating their deeds and enhancing their exploits.

In his works Gracián quotes generously from the *Lives* and *Moralia*; in his presentation of the Critic as a passionate admirer of Plutarch as well as of Plato and Epictetus, he transfers to the Critic what appears to have been his own experience, in the prologue to the work:

> I have tried to borrow from each brilliant author what I most liked: Homer's allegories, Aesopus' fictions, Lucian's good sense, Apuleius' descriptions, Plutarch's moralities, etc.

---

[22] Pérez Jiménez (2002: 358–359).    [23] Díaz Martínez (2002).    [24] Bergua Cavero (1995: 30–31).
[25] Pérez Jiménez (2002: 361).    [26] Bergua Cavero (1995: 32).

Spanish historians often mined the *Lives* for local color, as in the *Chronicle of Valencia* (1538–46) by Pere Antoni Beuter (1490–1554), who quoted from *Sertorius* and *Pompey*, as well as from the spurious *Hannibal*.[27] Naturally, Plutarch was also the model for biography and literary portraits, as Hernán Pérez del Pulgar (1451–1531) stated in the introduction to his *Famous Men of Spain* (1500). He was also important for those writing biographical sketches of conquerors: Juan Ginés de Sepúlveda (1490–1573) adapted his portrait of Hernán Cortés in *De orbe novo* using Plutarchan methods;[28] the Vallisoletan Agustín de Zárate (1514–60) declared it explicitly in his comparison of Pizarro's and Diego de Almagro's heroic deeds (IV 9); and Fernando Pizarro y Orellana in *Famous Men of the New World* (Madrid, 1623) cited specific passages of the *Lives* some twenty times. Finally, Plutarch's *Lives* and *Moralia*, besides other classical works, gave a Greco-Roman flavor to historiographical accounts about the New Continent: Fernández de Oviedo (1478–1557), who published in Seville (1535) the first part of his *General and Natural History of the Indias*, compared the deeds of Cortés to Caesar's exploits and to other historical characters from Justin, Suetonius, and Plutarch; he cited several *Lives*, comparing Phocion and Pizarro at the beginning of book XLIX. Pedro Cieza de León (1520–54) mentioned Plutarch several times in his *Chronicles of Peru* (Seville, 1553), referring usually to the *Lives* – for example, in I.3 he linked the Vestals' fire in the *Numa* with Indians' religious customs. The Dominican friar Bartolomé de las Casas (1484–1566) used a Latin edition of the *Moralia* (Lugduni, 1548) for his polemical *History of the Destruction of the Indias* (1552), in which he also cited the *Lives*.[29] The Jesuit José Acosta (1539–1600) found examples in Plutarch's works to illustrate his own reflections on the conduct of conquerors or to explain customs of the indigenous peoples, both in *De procuranda Indorum salute* (Salamanca, 1577) and the *Natural and Moral History of the Indias* (Seville, 1590). Plutarch was also quoted by seventeenth-century historians, such as Antonio de Solís y Rivadeneyra (1610–86), a historian of the conquest of Mexico.

But among Spanish historians, Melchor de Ortega and Juan de Pineda (ca. 1513–ca. 1593) deserve special mention: the latter is the author of a general history in thirty books, the *Ecclesiastical Monarchy* (1588), in which the name of Plutarch appears nearly a hundred times; his *Familiar Dialogues about Christian Agriculture* (Salamanca, 1589) also owe much to our author (more than 300 references, especially to the *Moralia*), whom de Pineda considers a predecessor of Christian theologians.[30] Melchor de

[27] Sancho Montés (2005).   [28] Ramírez de Verger (1990).   [29] Pérez Jiménez (1990: 244–245).
[30] Ramón Palerm (2011).

Ortega, in his *First Part of the Large History of the Very Courageous and Valiant Prince Felixmarte from Hyrcania* (Valladolid, 1557), occupies a special place because of the book's unusual narrative style, midway between historiography and tales of chivalry. To lend credibility to this fictional history (whose authorship is attributed to an Athenian historian called Philosio), the author resorted to Plutarch and Petrarch: the former would presumably have translated the book from Greek into Latin, and the latter from Latin into the Tuscan language, from which de Ortega claimed to have translated his story. Verisimilitude is also enhanced by the fact that the work begins with a fragment of the *Lives* of Cimon and Lucullus, taken certainly from the Spanish translation of 1547.[31]

This work, somewhere between history and literary fiction, allows us to analyze the importance of Plutarch's works as a pattern for imitative and miscellaneous writers. Fray Antonio de Guevara (1480–1545), whose work is considered in Spain to be a precursor of the essay form, followed Plutarch faithfully in one of the *Familiar Epistles* (Valladolid, 1539), the "Letter to don Pedro de Girón when he was exiled in Oran," which recalls the Plutarchan *De exilio*,[32] but he also often invents citations from Plutarch, crediting him with references of his own. This happens in the most well-known essays, such as in *Contempt for the Court and Praise of the Village* and *Princes Relox*, both published in Valladolid in 1539.[33] More authentically Plutarchan are the numerous quotations evident in the miscellaneous *Silva of Various Lessons* (1540), through the pages of this text its author Pedro Mexía (1497–1551) paraded citations from both the *Lives* and *Moralia*.[34] Bernardino Gómez Miedes (ca. 1520–89) in his *Commentariorum de sale libri V* (Valencia, 1579) repeatedly cited the *Quaestiones convivales*, including a large number of direct quotations, or quotations mediated by Erasmus, and likewise in his other works.[35] Francisco Fernández de Córdoba (+ 1626) in his *Didascalia multiplex* (Lyon, 1615), apart from general references, cited passages from *Brutus*, *Marcellus*, *Cleomenes*, and several *Moralia* treatises.[36] During this period, examples of Plutarchan paremiological and apothegmatic literature are numerous: Juan de Timoneda (1518/20–83), in his well-known *Good Advice and Portfolio of Yarns* (Valencia, 1564) and *After-Dinner and Walkers' Relief* (Saragossa, 1563), appropriated anecdotes and apothegms from Erasmus and Plutarch.[37] But especially significant is Juan de Mal Lara's (1524–71)

---

[31] Aguilar Perdomo (1999).　　[32] García Gual (1988).　　[33] García Gual (1991; 1998; 2000).
[34] Cuartero Sancho (1981: 21–74); Cherchi (1993: 54–59).　　[35] Ramos Maldonado (1999).
[36] Pérez Molina and Guzmán Arias (1991).　　[37] Cuartero Sancho (1981: 77–101, 125–147).

*Everyday Philosophy* (Seville, 1568), where (fol. 214 r) the author specifically names among his sources Plutarch's *De liberis educandis* and Seneca's *De ira*. Plutarch's collection of apothegms was the model for the *Spanish Anthology of Apothegms and Judgements, Wise and Gracefully Told by Some Spaniards* (Toledo, 1574), as its author Melchor de Santa Cruz de Dueñas (1505–85) confessed in the dedication to Don Juan de Austria. The sixteenth century closed with *The Six Hundred Apothegms* (Toledo, 1596) of the Cordovan Juan Rufo (1547–1620), where we again see Seneca and Plutarch cited together.

In any case, Plutarch was not unknown to the great masters of Spanish literature of the Golden Century. Plutarch's *Lives* and *Moralia* provided them with themes, citations, and anecdotes for the greater illumination of their characters. Miguel de Cervantes (1547–1616)[38] refers to the *Life of Alexander* in the prologue to the *Quixote* – "Plutarch will give you a thousand Alexanders" – showing his admiration for the Chaeronean. But that allusion to the *Alexander* was not Cervantes' only reference to Plutarch: in the *Quixote*, 1st Part, ch. 33 (= "The Curious Impertinent"), *The Jealous Extremaduran*, in Latin, and *The Gallant Spaniard*, in Spanish, we can read the adage put by Plutarch into the mouth of Pericles: "usque ad Aras," which could come directly from Plutarch, or via Aulus Gellius or Erasmus.[39]

In *Quixote*, 1st Part, ch. 33, reminiscent of the Herodotean Gyges and Candaules tale, the Narrator's affirmation that Anselmo "had got as a wife a second Portia" could be Plutarchan; the allusion invokes implicitly Plutarch's Portia, who injured her thigh to convince her husband that she could keep the secret of the conspiracy against Caesar; in Cervantes, Camilla, by pretending to perform the same act, affirms her fidelity to Anselmo. It is more difficult to attribute Cervantes' other references to historical figures (among them Theseus, Lycurgus, Numa, Solon, Cato, Horace, Curtius, Caesar, and again Alexander) directly to Plutarch. The story told by the priest in *Quixote* about Alexander's intention to use Darius' box as container for the copy of the *Iliad* seems to be taken from Plutarch's *Alexander* 26.[40] The dramatist Lope de Vega (1562–1635) also used Plutarch's name as a cultural touchstone. His knowledge of the Chaeronean was extensive: some dedications of his dramatic pieces began with quotations from Plutarch, such as in the second part of *The Perfect Prince*, addressing the Marquis de Alcañices. Here Lope attributes to Don John II of Portugal the following phrase from Plutarch: "Kings were

---

[38] Menéndez Pelayo (1905: 329).    [39] Ramírez-Araujo (1954).    [40] López Férez (2008: 122).

Ministers of God for the care and health of men, and, as it concerns the goods He gave them, to keep a part and to distribute the other."

Other references in such dedications are more direct citations, as in *The Real Lover* addressed to his own son and quoting *Brutus*. The same *Life* is alluded to in the dedication to Marcia Leonarda of the novel *The Prudent Revenge*, and mentions of Plutarch both by name and by references to passages taken from his work are present in another novel, *The Unhappiness Because of dishonor*; in this case, one of the characters supports his views against predetermined fate by invoking Plutarch vis-à-vis the orthodoxy of the Church:

> When he writes as an insult that the statement "no one can avoid his fate" is womanish, Plutarch of Chaeronea well understood Catholic thinking, as if Plutarch himself was in fact Catholic, because free wills are free to justify their judgements to the Heavens.

References to Plutarch and his works can also be found in Lope's verses, as for instance in the *New Art of Writing Comedies in This Time*, offering a critical position vis-à-vis the literary assessment of Menander by Plutarch (vv. 168–170):

> God knows that I regret to confirm,
> that Plutarch, speaking about Menander,
> did not understand ancient comedy.

He does the same in poems and other verse and prose comedies such as *The Avenging of Women*, vv. 751–752; *To Serve a Discreet Lord*, vv. 778–787; *The Cats' War*, vv. 49–51; *The Dorothea* (in which he refers to Leena (Leaina), Portia, Laodamia, Clelia (Cloelia), Alexander, Crassus, and the Milesian women); *To Love without Knowing Who* (II, 64); *The Man of His Word* (III, 383b); *The Secretary of Himself* (II, 324a); *The Pilgrim in His Own Country* (book II, p. 164); and *The Human Seraphim*. Finally, in Act II of *The Felisarda* there is a reference to the satyr and the fire that recalls in part the Plutarchan *De capienda ex inimicis utilitate*.

Calderón de la Barca had Plutarch frequently in mind, although not to such an extent as did Lope. Indeed, *The Weapons of the Beauty* is a recreation with much license of Plutarch's *Coriolanus*; furthermore, we find Pan (an image of Christ) in *The True God*, a sacramental mystery play, via *De defectu oraculorum* 17. Concerning other poets, one must mention here the *Odes* of Fray Luis de León that imitate the *Lives' synkrisis* and even include direct quotations from the Spanish translation of the *Moralia* by Gracián de Alderete.[41] Fray Luis also

---

[41] Martínez Fernández (1994).

mentioned Plutarch – with admiration – in his prose works; for instance, he included in *The Perfect Married Woman* a passage from *Coniugalia praecepta* (32, 142D), which was an excellent topic for Alciato (see Figure 17.1) and his followers:

> Plutarch says that Phidias, a noble sculptor, made for the Eleans an image of Venus with her feet on a tortoise, a mute animal that does not ever abandon its shell; he thus instructs women to stay at home and to keep silent.

Fray Luis' quotation is a good transition to the last topic of this review of Plutarch's influence in the Spanish Renaissance: emblematic literature. Plutarch was inserted into this genre by its creator, the Italian scholar Alciato; but since then, the *Moralia* and *Lives,* on account of their symbolic and moral strength, continued to be common features of that genre. It should not surprise us that commentators of Alciato such as Juan de Valencia (1550) or El Brocense (1571) displayed their knowledge of Plutarch in explicating emblems (Figure 17.1). This was a common practice in sixteenth-century Europe, as the writings of Julius Hadrianus and Joachim Camerarius clearly show. Most original is the proposal of Juan de Mal Lara, another commentator on Alciato (Selig, 1956), regarding the iconography of the galley of Don Juan de Austria. Partly referencing Alciato, partly the *Lives* and the *Moralia,* his erudite comments make of this work a rich lode of exempla for war and good governance, for moral education and even popular wisdom.[42] Naturally, among the works of Alciato and his commentators, pride of place is given to the books of Spanish emblems, where there are numerous iconographic motifs, mottos, and epigrams inspired by the *Parallel Lives*[43] and *Moralia,*[44] examples of which can be seen in Figures 17.2 to 17.4. These references, while not very numerous, are sufficient to prove that Plutarch was an invaluable presence in the libraries of their creators, inspiring them like other Greek and Latin writers. In the sixteenth century this is clear from the *Moral Impresse* (Prague, 1581) of Juan de Borja (1533), from the *Moral Emblems* (Segovia, 1589, 1591) of Juan de Horozco y Covarrubias (1589–1608), and from the *Moralized Emblems* (Madrid, 1599) of Hernando de Soto (Figure 17.2).

The seventeenth century opens with Sebastián de Covarrubias (Figure 17.3), who admits other Plutarchan topics in his *Moral Emblems* (Madrid, 1610) and the more religiously oriented *Moral and Spiritual Impresses* (Baeza, 1613) of Juan Francisco de Villava;[45] this approach also

---

[42] Pérez Jiménez (2006: 234–246).   [43] Pérez Jiménez (2003a).   [44] Pérez Jiménez (2003b).
[45] Pérez Jiménez (2005).

**ALCIATI EMBLEM.** *533*

*Parcite,ait,Danai,leuis sene gloria rapto,*
*At non erepto gloria patre leuis.*

Adorea id est,gloria vel decus.Plinius lib.18. *Adorea.*
cap. 3 Gloriam (inquit) ipsam à farris honore
adoream appellabant.Similia exempla filiorum
qui pij fuerint in parentes , habes apud Aristotelem in lib.de Mundo ad Alexandrum in ipso
fine.Et apud Herodotum in prima historia, de
Bithone.Nemo enim Deum rectè colere potest,
si impius in parentes fuerit.

Mulieris famam , non formam vulgatam esse oportere.

DIALOGISMVS.

EMBLEMA CXCV.

Ll 3

Figure 17.1 Francisco Sánchez, El Brocense, *Commentarium in Andr. Alciati
Emblemata,* Lugduni, 1573, p. 535 ~ *Coniugalia praecepta* 142D.

# MORALIZADAS. 43

## *Ex hoste aliquando bonum.*

## Del daño, a vezes prouecho.

*Fereo fin esperança*
*De ſaludde vna hinchazon;*
*Obra haziendo a ſu intencion,*
*Entre vn eſquadron ſe lança.*
*Fue de vna flecha paſſado*
*con que la hinchazon ſe aplaca,*
*Que a vezes del mal ſe ſaca-*
**Prouecho nunca eſperado.**

F 3 Ningu-

Figure 17.2 Hernando de Soto, *Emblemas moralizadas,* Madrid, 1599, fol. 43v ~ *De capienda ex inimicis utilitate.*

Figure 17.3 Sebastián de Covarrubias Orozco, *Emblemas morales*, Madrid, 1610, cent. III 45, fol. 245r = *Quomodo adulator ab amico internoscatur* 58F–59A.

informs the *Sacred Impresses* (Valencia, 1689) of the Jesuit Francisco Núñez de Cepeda (1616–90), whose work has played an important role in the diffusion of this illustrated Plutarch; in fact, the Society of Jesus afforded

him the opportunity to cross the Atlantic and fill with Plutarchan echoes many American cathedrals and commemorative monuments. But the development of Spanish emblematic literature reaches its peak in the *Emblemata centum: Regio politica* (Madrid, 1653) by Juan de Solórzano Pereyra (1575–1655). In this beautiful book Plutarch not only inspires structural elements but is above all the main source of authority for the erudite comments explaining the hundred emblems (Figure 17.4) that comprise this work.[46]

## Further Reading

The Anglophone reader should get their bearings on the reception of Plutarch in Spain from Pérez Jiménez (2014; 2019). To date, the most comprehensive discussion of how Plutarch was read during the Spanish Renaissance is Bergua Cavero (1995), while Morales Ortiz (2000) concentrates on translations of the *Moralia*. For a compact overview of Spanish translations, see also Pérez Jiménez (2009).

---

[46] Pérez Jiménez (2002: 364–365; 2003c: 389).

CHAPTER 18

# Plutarch and Shakespeare
## Reviving the Dead

*Julia Griffin*

*Julius Caesar*, Act I, scene ii. The sardonic Casca is describing for Brutus and Cassius, and the audience, the abortive scene of Caesar's coronation. Cassius asks a question:

| | |
|---|---|
| CASSIUS | Did Cicero say anything? |
| CASCA | Ay, he spoke Greek. |
| CASSIUS | To what effect? |
| CASCA | Nay, an I tell you that, I'll ne'er look you i' th' face again. But those that understood him smiled at one another and shook their heads; but for mine own part, it was Greek to me.     (I.ii.278–284) |

This whole conversation is Shakespeare's invention.[1] Plutarch, the principal source for the play, spends much time, in two of his *Lives*, on the beginnings of the conspiracy against Caesar, but Casca – Gaius Servilius Casca – does not appear in either of them until the moment of the killing itself. Then, according to the *Life of Brutus* (in the version Shakespeare read),

> Casca … drew his dagger first, and strake Caesar upon the shoulder … Caesar feeling him selfe hurt, tooke him straight by the hande he held his dagger in, and cried out in Latin: O traitor, Casca, what doest thou? Casca on thother side cried in Graeke, and called his brother to helpe him. (Bullough V.102; cf. *Brutus* 17.5)[2]

Plutarch's *Caesar* gives the same sequence; Casca, speaking for the only time in either *Life*, does so in Greek (*Caesar* 66.8). Why, then, should

---

[1] All quotations from Shakespeare are taken from Evans (1997) also known at The Riverside Shakespeare.

[2] When quoting from North's translation of Plutarch, I have, where possible, used Bullough (1957–79) for the reader's convenience; when the text does not appear there, I have quoted from the 1579 edition. The 1595 edition contains more *Lives* than the 1579, which Bullough follows, but the text is not otherwise substantially changed.

357

Shakespeare give his Casca this odd, offhand little denial?[3] In the play's
own terms, it fits in with the "blunt" persona he is presenting here; but this
only moves the question back, as Shakespeare chose to invent this persona
for him. So perhaps the explanation is to be found outside the play, or
behind it. "For mine own part …": it sounds like a moment of private
humor, a nod from the playwright to the biographer, his predecessor and
ally, and to the medium of language that divided them. Shakespeare's
alliance with Plutarch, the intermediaries between them, and the divergences between them all are the subject of this essay.

## The Renaissance Plutarch

> you may prove yourselves, that there is no prophane studye better
> than Plutarke. All other learning is private, fitter for Universities than
> cities, fuller of contemplacion than experience, more commendable
> in the students themselves, than profitable unto others. Whereas
> stories are fit for every place, reach to all persons, serve for all tymes,
> teach the living, revive the dead …[4]

Thus Sir Thomas North, introducing, for the first time in English, the
work he called *The Lives of the Noble Grecians and Romans*. The date was
1579; enthusiasm for Plutarch was in the air. Translation and editing had
begun in the late fourteenth century, but the first complete translations
appear between 1559 and 1572: three of them, two into Latin, one into
French. The most significant of these, both for scholarship and influence,
were the work of Jacques Amyot: the *Vies Illustres* in 1559; the *Oeuvres
Morales* in 1572. Amyot was the great conduit of Plutarch into the vernacu-
lars in France and England: he was read, zealously, by Montaigne, and also
by the French dramatists;[5] North had probably encountered his work when
visiting France, on diplomatic business, in 1574. Amyot's version was the
basis of North's English *Lives*, which first appeared in print when
Shakespeare was fifteen years old.[6] North's title page speaks of "that

---

[3] Bullough, reprinting Plutarch's two *Lives* and so encountering the problem twice, deals with it differently
each time; the first time he is neutral: "Contrast I [ii] 281" (Bullough V.86, n. 2); the second time he offers
an explanation: "Casca *pretended* not to know Greek, I [ii] 277–82" (Bullough 102, n. 4; italics mine).
Why Casca should so pretend remains a question. Perhaps he is still pretending when, in Shakespeare's
scene of the assassination (III.i.76), he speaks English (see discussion later).

[4] North (1579). Richard Field brought out a second edition in 1595: see later in this chapter.

[5] See MacDonald's Chapter 19 in this volume.

[6] North claimed to have translated the work "out of French into Englishe" (title page); scholars have
debated whether he was in fact being too modest. Matthiessen (1931: 73) observantly notes that in the
*Life of Pompey* North's Caesar, about to cross the Rubicon, utters Greek words, as Amyot's Caesar
does not; we should note, though, that the Greek is also supplied by a Latin translator, Hermannus

great grave learned Philosopher and Historiographer"; part of Plutarch's great attraction for the Renaissance was that combination. North did not himself translate the other half of the oeuvre, the *Moralia*, though Amyot had done so. In 1603, however, Philemon Holland, availing himself of Amyot's help (and that of the Latin translators), brought out a complete version. Thus, by halfway through Shakespeare's career, all of Plutarch was available in English – all, and then some more.

Like many classical authors, Plutarch, at that date, was a partly fictional figure: some of the most popular that the *Lives* and *Moralia* include are spurious. North, in 1579, translated two *Lives* that Amyot had rightly discounted (*Scipio* and *Hannibal*, discussed later); in 1603 he added more apocrypha, including a spurious comparison of Caesar and Alexander. The text of Plutarch was, in part, the conscious creation of his intermediaries: besides the new *Lives*, they added glosses within the text (explaining, for example, what a "Nereid" is) and marginalia: the early editions of Amyot confine these to strictly factual explanations, for example of the currency; but later ones become much more opinionated, distributing praise and blame.[7] Generally, North's margins provide only summary, but sometimes he too adds more: "See the fickle minds of common people" (p. 245 = Bullough V.518, n. 8), he directs, when the plebs turn against Coriolanus. This direction was part of the text that Shakespeare read; his Plutarch was not unmediated, and not quite our own.

## How Did Shakespeare Read Plutarch?

North, on his title page, described Plutarch as a philosopher as well as historian. Was Shakespeare familiar with the philosophical side of his work – the *Moralia*? The answer is not certain, but the question is easy to sum up. The first English translation appeared in 1603; Shakespeare could thus have drawn on it during the second half of his career. There is no certain proof that he used it, but it is likely he drew on some of the best-known essays (this probability is discussed briefly later). Whatever the situation with the *Moralia*, however, Plutarch influenced Shakespeare much more obviously and certainly through the *Lives*.

Cruserius, in 1564. Anyone considering North's procedure needs to take account of the Latin versions; a pioneer in this is John Denton (see references later).

[7] The sententious marginalia are the work of Amyot's later editor, the Huguenot pastor Simon Goulart de Senlis: see Pineaux (1986). The first edition so affected is that of 1587 – later than the one used by North. Although Amyot rejected the spurious *Lives* of Hannibal and Scipio, he allowed them to be included, in the French translation of Charles de l'Escluse, in the 1567 edition and onwards (attributed to l'Escluse on the title page). They were thus present in the edition that North used (see later).

"Source," "influence," "intertext": the terminology changes, but the significance for Shakespeare of Plutarch's biographies remains indisputable. The importance of the intermediary has been stressed in recent criticism.[8] North's version was widely influential in England: it is clear that even good classicists used it, such as George Chapman (translator of Homer) and perhaps Francis Bacon.[9] As far as the *Lives* are concerned, Shakespeare's Plutarch is North's Plutarch – complete with its distinctive verbal vividness and occasional confusion. A quick example of this, rarely noted, is Cleopatra's reference in the play to "my birthday" (III.xiii.184): Plutarch, and Amyot, make it quite clear that Antony's birthday is the one being celebrated; North's translation misled his reader.[10]

Did Shakespeare own a copy of North, and if so, which edition? There is no direct evidence; only deduction. The first edition (1579) was produced by the Huguenot printer Thomas Vautroullier; this is the edition Shakespeare must have used before 1595, when his friend Richard Field, who married Vautroullier's widow, brought out a new edition, largely unchanged except for the title page. A copy of the 1579 edition survives with an inscription from Alice, Countess of Derby, to a "William"; the sheet is damaged, and we cannot be sure who this William was, but there is a connection between the countess' family and Shakespeare.[11] In 1603 a third edition appeared, with extra, spurious lives added: these included

---

[8] Some interesting discussion (varied in approach and not limited to the recent) includes: MacCallum (1910); Matthiessen (1931); Miles (1996: esp. ch. 6); Worth (1986) in a volume that contains other fine essays on Amyot; and the essays of Denton on *Coriolanus*, especially Denton (1993).

[9] For Chapman, see Ure (1958); for Bacon, see his unpublished essay "Of Tribute" in Vickers (1996: 50), which shows signs of North's wording in its account of Caesar's assassination: as Casca attacks, Caesar calls him "traitor" – North's word (from Amyot), quite different from the Plutarchan Greek, in either *Caesar* or *Brutus*, or the contemporary Latin translations of Xylander (1561) and Cruserius (1564).

[10] The Greek draws a contrast between the quiet way she had celebrated *her* birthday (*tēn heautēs genethlion*) and the lavish way she was now celebrating *his* (*tēn ekeinou*) (*Antony* 73.5); North writes: "where she did solemnise the day of her birth very meanely and sparingly ... she now in contrary maner did keepe *it* with such solemnitie, that she exceeded all measure of sumptuousnes and magnificence" (Bullough V.306; italics mine). Pelling (1988a: 299) suggests that Shakespeare reduced the two birthdays to one because "two birthdays would be clodhopping on stage"; in fact, North had made the reduction for him. This seems not to be noticed in any modern edition of *Antony and Cleopatra*; but see the underrated work by Green (1979: 91). Something similar happens with Octavius' rejection of Antony's offer to meet in single combat. In Plutarch, Octavian replies that Antony has other ways to die (*Antony* 75.1); in North's translation, "Caesar aunswered him, that *he* had many other wayes to dye then so" (Bullough V.307; italics mine). North's vague use of the pronoun again seems to have misled Shakespeare – to wonderful effect: "Let the old ruffian know / I have many other ways to die ..." (IV.i.4–5). Plutarch's Octavian refuses while implying that he would win; Shakespeare's contemptuously rejects the whole idea of personal heroics as something barbaric, obsolete.

[11] This copy is the property of the Shakespeare Birthplace Trust, catalog no. SR OS 93.1.

a *Life of Octavius Caesar*, which some think Shakespeare used in writing *Antony and Cleopatra*. All three editions, in any case, were single, folio volumes, handsome and expensive, in roman typeface (the kind thought appropriate for classical works) and adorned with engravings: medallions of heroic heads at the beginning of each *Life*.[12]

The plays that take the *Lives* as a basis are *Julius Caesar, Antony and Cleopatra*, and *Coriolanus*. Other plays draw on them for part of the plot or general context (*Titus Andronicus, A Midsummer Night's Dream, Timon of Athens, Two Noble Kinsmen*); others reveal a possible debt (*King Lear, Othello, The Merchant of Venice*, the *Henry IV* plays) – the same applies to the long poem *The Rape of Lucrece*.[13] The *Lives* Shakespeare used are, primarily, those of Theseus, Caesar, Brutus, Antony, and Coriolanus; he also drew on the pairs to those *Lives*, the comparisons between the pairs, and some others in addition.[14] This list represents a range of uses: from careful historical detail to general atmosphere and turns in the plot. Shakespeare combined Plutarch with other sources, classical and beyond; traces turn up where they might least be expected.

Unfortunately, there is no room here to discuss all this. Most of this chapter will be devoted to the three great tragedies of republican Rome, but I shall follow Shakespeare by beginning and ending with a brief discussion of the plays, earlier and later, in which Plutarchan characters, or at least their names, appear.

## Shakespeare's Early Use of Plutarch: "Antique Fables"

Duke Theseus, told of the fantastical goings-on in the first four acts of *A Midsummer Night's Dream*, is incredulous:

> I never may believe
> These antique fables                                    (V.i.2–3)[15]

---

[12] North himself seems to have used the 1574 edition of Amyot. See Gentili (1991: 36 n. 22): the medallions introduced in that edition of Amyot are the same as those in North. North was in France in 1574, so this seems very plausible.

[13] For the last category, see, respectively, Teague (1992); Graves (1973); Honigmann (1959); Mossman (1997b). For *Lucrece*, Shakespeare may have looked at the *Life of Publicola* and, in *Moralia, Mulierum virtutes*.

[14] For the use of parallel *Lives*, see Honigmann (1959); also Cantor (1997) and Braden (2004).

[15] The Riverside prints "antic" ("grotesque"); many other modern editions read "antique," the reading I have preferred here. The first Folio (1623) has "anticke," the first Quarto (1600) "antique." The two words, or spellings, are regularly interchanged in early modern texts; it is likely here that a pun is intended.

The *Dream* is one of Shakespeare's first plays to make use of the *Lives*; for a reader of Plutarch, the remark has an extra resonance. Theseus is the first of Plutarch's noble Grecians and Romans, chronologically and in the order of all printed editions, and in writing his biography Plutarch confronted directly the problem of "antique fables" obfuscating the truth.

> I would wish that the inventions of Poets, and the traditions of fabulous antiquitie, would suffer themselves to be purged and reduced to the forme of a true and historicall report: but when they square too much from like-lyhode, and cannot be made credible, the readers will of curtesie take in good part that, which I could with most probability wryte of such antiquities. (North, p. 2; cf. *Theseus* 1.5)[16]

How much could be "purged," and how? In the *Theseus* and the *Dream*, the warlike Amazons are allowed in, along with Heracles (in the play, he is just a reminiscence from Theseus). The fantastic Minotaur is excluded; and yet he turns up, transfigured, in the *Life*, and perhaps the play too. Plutarch rationalized him into a man named Taurus (16.1); Shakespeare has a man with a donkey's head (not a bull's), and also a "changeling boy," the source of dispute between a king and his queen – North, unlike Plutarch or Amyot, calls the Minotaur "a boy, a bull," a description that might well have sparked Shakespeare's imagination. Plutarch says that Attica suffered a blight, which could only be relieved by sending Attican children as sacrifices to the Minotaur; in the play, blight results from the fairies' fight over the "changeling" and is lifted (presumably) when Titania surrenders the boy to Oberon.

Clearly Plutarch's *Lives* were not the principal source for the *Dream*, with its cast of English fairies and English mechanicals (Athenian, in theory, but with names like Snout and Bottom); nevertheless, it may be that its very heterogeneity derives something from North's text. There may also be a visual influence, more or less conscious. The first page of the Theseus *Life*, in all the editions of North published in Shakespeare's lifetime, shows the hero, in profile and a helmet, with putti and wild curlicues all around him; they form a pleasing unit without interacting, like the Duke and the fairies in the play.

At the other end of North's volume Shakespeare will have found a life that stretches historical integrity in a different way. Scipio Africanus, the last subject in the 1579–95 editions of North, is a non-mythical hero with a spurious biography – the work of the fifteenth-century scholar Donato

---

[16] See, on this, Pelling (1999c), expanded in Pelling (2002a: 171–195).

Acciaiuoli, supplied to replace a supposedly lost original, and paired by him with a *Life of Hannibal*.[17] Shakespeare may have drawn on this for his first (and coauthored) Roman play, *Titus Andronicus*, whose fictional, or composite, hero seems to owe something to the famous Roman general: like Scipio, Titus defeats a dangerous enemy but is treated ungratefully by Rome.[18] The Scipio *Life*, though not Plutarchan, draws parallels between its subject and one of Plutarch's own: that earlier Roman general, Coriolanus. In *Titus*, the hero's son threatens to take revenge "As much as ever Coriolanus did" (IV.iv.68): providing thus Shakespeare's first mention of the hero whose story would form the last of his Plutarchan plays.

But this was in the future. These earlier plays show traces from Plutarch, but his influence is not central or unifying. Later, in *Julius Caesar, Antony and Cleopatra*, and *Coriolanus* – following the order of their composition, not the chronology of their subjects – Shakespeare made much larger and deeper use of Plutarch: as an ordering principle as well as a source for brilliant details – details that together create the life of the whole.

## Plutarch, Shakespeare, and Rome (I): *Julius Caesar*

For English playwrights of Shakespeare's time, ancient Rome was a more attractive subject for serious drama than ancient Greece. The educational system, based on Latin writers, made it a more familiar world: a world in which students learned to write and to debate.[19] Plutarch's Romans were likely to be more attractive than his Greeks; by a very influential coincidence, those Roman *Lives* that survived from antiquity are almost all set during the Republic. Perhaps, had more of his imperial *Lives* survived than those of Galba and Otho (neither of them very inviting subjects), the Roman world of Renaissance drama would look rather different. Other versions of Rome were available, of course, even without those lost *Lives*, and in general the historians were more attracted by the Empire; for English dramatists, however, the late Republic was the most popular area. Though not all used Plutarch, many did, more or less – Ben Jonson's *Catiline* (1611), George Chapman's *Caesar and Pompey* (?1612), and Samuel Daniel's two versions of *Cleopatra* (1594, 1607).

---

[17] For a full discussion of this, see Humble (2010a). Shakespeare will have known that this *Life* was not original only if he read North's translation of Amyot's introduction, which explicitly rejects it.

[18] This idea was first put forward by Law (1943). See the discussion in Bullough VI.23–26.

[19] Greek, on the other hand, appears predominantly in pastoral fantasy – shepherds and shepherdesses always have Greek names.

No playwright made more concentrated use of this material than Shakespeare. In his first republican play, *Julius Caesar*, we see him engaging with Plutarch to create a picture of Rome characterized by density, coherence, and a strong sense of identity.[20] At the time of Caesar's assassination, four of Plutarch's subjects – Caesar, Cicero, Brutus, and Antony – were all senators in Rome. Shakespeare responds to this biographical community: his Roman plays acquire an extra appearance of solidity by occasional quick allusions to characters not in the scene or the play – as with Casca's reference to Cicero in *Julius Caesar* I.ii, or Sextus Pompey's to Apollodorus in *Antony and Cleopatra* II.vi.68. The remarkable naturalness, and knowingness, with which characters refer to each other also strengthens our sense of their reality. "Who offered [Caesar] the crown?" Cassius asks Casca (*JC* I.ii.233). "Why, Antony" is the reply; and that "Why" carries the unmissable implication: "Of course; as we would all expect."

At the same time, Shakespeare responded to the *wideness* of Plutarch's picture. Almost without exception, plays on Caesar's assassination begin just before it and end immediately afterwards; their setting is Rome.[21] Shakespeare begins his with Caesar offered the crown – at the height of his dangerous power – and ends with the deaths of his killers, in another country. English drama written for the public theater was not dominated by the classically derived conventions so influential on the Continent: the "unities" and the idea that violent action should not be shown on stage. Much more action was thus available to Shakespeare than to most non-English dramatists of the topic. This means that he had much more freedom to represent Plutarch's action directly on the stage rather than through narration by a character. He seems to have been the second playwright to show the death of Caesar on stage, and the first or the second to show the death of Cleopatra.[22]

But Plutarch offered more than the sum of his material. As the work of Christopher Pelling has so well demonstrated, the *Lives* are also artfully organized: "many of his scenes might already seem shaped for the theatre."[23] What an English play set in the Roman Republic might look like may be seen from the anonymous, chaotic *Caesar's Revenge*, which

---

[20] The date of this play is generally agreed to be late 1599. Like *Antony and Cleopatra* and *Coriolanus*, it was first published in the first Folio of 1623.
[21] For more on this, see Griffin (2009).
[22] The first, for the former character, and the second, or possibly first, for the latter, were also English: the anonymous author of *Caesars Revenge* (?early 1590s) and Samuel Daniel, in the revised version of his *Cleopatra* (1607).
[23] Pelling (1997e), reprinted in Pelling (2002a: 387–411); see also Cook (1996).

Shakespeare probably knew, and Thomas Lodge's *The Wounds of Civil War* – neither of which shows much, if any, sign of Plutarchan influence. Plutarch offered both abundance and a sense of shapeliness. Shakespeare based the events of his play primarily on two lives, *Caesar* and *Brutus*: respecting the structure of each, he divided his play in the middle, placing the assassination at the very center – a powerful, and very unusual, dramatic decision.

Relying on a second-hand translation of a Greek source, Shakespeare's picture of Rome is foreign at several removes.[24] Some blurriness in his picture can be traced back through his predecessors. What did Roman dress look like? In *Julius Caesar*, we are told that Caesar wears a doublet (I. ii.265); in *Coriolanus*, the hero appears in a "gown" (II.ii.137, etc.): both represent the Greek "himation," as rendered by North (who uses the word "doblet" only in that one instance: Bullough V.80). The Latin behind all this is "toga," which perhaps neither Shakespeare nor North was visualizing very clearly.[25] The long historical distance between Plutarch and his English followers might make itself felt in other ways too. Occasionally, North contributes something that indicates a wholly different worldview from that of Plutarch. A famous example is the declaration he adds to a speech by Brutus: "I shall live in another more glorious worlde" (Bullough V.120 = *Brutus* 40.8). Shakespeare does not follow North here – his Brutus says only: "whether we shall meet again I know not" (V.i.114); when he is anachronistic, it is generally in his characters' physical world (clocks, doublets) rather than the intellectual.[26] He does not correct their religion; nor is it clear what he thinks of their political system, subject as he was of two monarchs with strong views about the virtues and rights of monarchy.[27] What is clear is the sense that his characters, Roman and not Roman, have of what "Rome" means: an ideal of uncompromising rectitude, hard for Romans to live up to and for foreigners to oppose. This sense has been contagious: anachronisms and all, writers from the seventeenth century onwards testify to the power of Shakespeare's vision of Rome. It is a vision that Shakespeare derived, in large part, from Plutarch; and he used Plutarch also to explore its tensions, and its cost.

[24] See Miles (1989), Braden (2014), and the work of Denton, e.g. (1997) and (1993).

[25] Amyot has "robbe" throughout. See Denton (1993). There are two occurrences of the word "toge" in modern editions of Shakespeare's plays, *Othello* I.i.25 and *Coriolanus* II.iii.110: neither appears in the Folio, and only one ("toged" – *Othello*) in a quarto, so it would be rash to base conclusions on it.

[26] For a fine discussion of Shakespeare and anachronism, see Martindale and Martindale (1990: ch. 4).

[27] For a summary and discussion of divergent modern views, see Chernaik (2011: 244–248).

## "Can You See Your Face?"

To pass directly from Plutarch's to Shakespeare's Caesar is to confront a big difference. Next to Plutarch's vigorous hero,[28] Shakespeare's seems reduced, static. We are given little sense of an inner, hidden life: the character never entrusts the audience with a soliloquy, as do the Caesars of most Renaissance tragedy. The effect is to make his grandeur seem hollow: we see a tremendous public front, but something of a blank behind it. Shakespeare picks up Plutarch's indications of Caesar's sharpness – he recognizes the dangerousness of Cassius, which the less observant Antony denies (I.ii.190–210; cf. Plutarch, *Caesar* 62.10) – but juxtaposes them with indications of weakness, either adopted from Plutarch or invented by the playwright himself. Plutarch reported that Caesar was subject to epilepsy (17.2, 60.7); Shakespeare created from this the scene, reported by the hostile Casca, in which Caesar, offered the crown, "fell down in the market-place, and foam'd at mouth, and was speechless" (I.ii.252–253); this closely follows Caesar's own demonstration of his deafness, an affliction Shakespeare invented for him. The play heightens Caesar's role in his own fate: paradoxically, his powerful will takes the form of unwitting self-destruction. In the scene in which Decimus Brutus Albinus (Shakespeare calls him Decius Brutus) persuades Caesar to attend the Senate, Shakespeare stays close to the narrative of the *Caesar*, but while Plutarch gives Caesar no speech, the play supplies it – heroic, in the ears of the speaker, but, in the circumstances, pathetic, as he first declares that "The cause is in my will: I will not come," and then yields rather than show fear: "I will go" (II.ii.71, 107). Well-wishing Artemidorus, in a last-minute attempt to warn him, hands him a scroll: Plutarch says that Caesar tried to read it but was prevented by the pressing crowd (*Caesar* 65.2–3); Shakespeare's Caesar grandly puts it by: "What touches us ourself shall be last served" (III.i.8).[29] His consciousness of self, of his appearance, continues to the end: his last word is his own name – a talisman that no longer protects.[30]

Something similar happens with the play's other hero, Brutus. The play juxtaposes, or even combines, heroic statements of identity with inadvertent displays of weakness. After Caesar's death, Brutus adopts Caesar's own

---

[28] For the dynamism of Plutarch's Caesar, see, for example, *Caesar* 17.2–7, 36.2, 49.7–8, 58.4–10.
[29] According to Suetonius, Caesar passed the scroll to his left hand with a sheaf of others, intending to read it later: *Iul.* 81.4. Shakespeare invents his grand gesture.
[30] Plutarch's word is *phylaktērion* (*Caesar* 57.8). On the talisman-metaphor in Plutarch's *Caesar*, see Pelling (1997d: 223–224). (Pelling's whole essay is of the highest interest for Shakespeare's play.)

habit of "illeism," referring to himself in the stately third person; we see him also succumbing to his own reputation. "I can raise no money by foul means," he proclaims (IV.iii.71), reproaching Cassius for not doing so on his behalf – a moment considerably distorted from Plutarch, where he merely asks Cassius for money (*Brutus* 30.1–2).[31] In one striking case, North's language may have suggested a certain hollowness in Brutus.[32] Shortly before the last battle, Plutarch makes him expound to Cassius his ideas about suicide. In his youth, he says, he deplored it; but he has come to feel differently (40.7–8). Amyot conveys the sense clearly;[33] but, as several scholars have noted, North translates here clumsily, in a way that blurs the temporal sequence:

> Brutus aunswered him, being yet but a young man . . . I trust, (I know not how) a certaine rule of Philosophie, by the which I did greatly blame and reprove Cato for killing of him selfe . . .. But being nowe in the middest of the daunger, I am of a contrary mind. (Bullough V.119–120)

In Shakespeare's version of the scene, Brutus proclaims his disapproval of the act (V.i.100–107); then, asked by Cassius if he is prepared to be led in triumph, he answers simply, grandly:

> No, Cassius, no. Think not, thou noble Roman,
> That ever Brutus will go bound to Rome;
> He bears too great a mind.           (V.i.110–112)

Simple and grand; but also wholly inconsistent, as it seems, with the speech before. Shakespeare's Brutus, enjoying the sound of his own name, seems not to have noticed what he has been saying. At the end of the play Antony, his old enemy, delivers what seems to be a narrative comment, summing Brutus up as "the noblest Roman of them all": his speech draws from Plutarch's comments at the beginning of the *Life of Brutus*, as well as from

---

[31] Because the scene has been so much debated, on textual and other grounds, I omit here the case that seems to me the strongest of all: Brutus' double use of Portia's death – first to excuse himself for losing his temper with Cassius, then to impress the Roman delegation with his philosophical calm (IV.iii.147–195). Plutarch makes his Brutus react philosophically to a false rumor of her death that he received just before the assassination (*Brutus* 15.5–9); the end of the *Life* gives an odd double account of her death – either she died *after* Brutus or she died first, and he reproached his friends for not caring for her (*Brutus* 53.5–7). Shakespeare seems to have used this clutch of stories to produce a different sort of doubleness – one that does not redound to Brutus' credit. But some take a more sympathetic view of his behavior: see Clayton (1983).

[32] See, for a fuller discussion of this, Miles (1996: 113–114).

[33] "Brutus luy respondit, Estant encore ieune & non assez experimenté es affaires de ce monde, ie feis, ne sçay comment, un discours de philosophie, par lequel ie reprenois & blasmois fort Caton de s'estre desfait soymesme . . . mais maintenant me trouvant au milieu du peril, ie suis de toute autre resolution" (Amyot 1565: fo. 698$^{r-v}$).

comments Plutarch attributes to Antony himself (*Brutus* 29.7). But there is an inevitable difference between true narrative and pronouncement by a character who has been shown already to be capable of both generous responsiveness and deft opportunism. The nobility of Brutus, like the greatness of Caesar, is stated but not quite guaranteed.

Shakespeare's Brutus and Caesar meet only once, in the central scene of the assassination. Shakespeare seems to have combined, for this, the accounts of Plutarch (*Caesar* 66 and *Brutus* 17) and that of Suetonius (*Iul.* 82); the two authors differ in their details, but both evoke a curious linguistic theatricality.[34] Plutarch, in both the *Lives*, *says* that Caesar, when first attacked, speaks Latin, thus seeming to set off the words linguistically from the narrative without actually doing so (the words appear in Greek); Suetonius makes him, at the point of death, speak Greek, in the middle of the narrative's Latin. Drawing on both accounts, Shakespeare makes the dying dictator speak a different language, and makes that language Latin: *Et tu, Brute?* The sudden burst of foreign speech suggests the character's self-consciousness; also that of the author, who inherited this scene many times over – and primarily from a source written in a language that he, like his character Casca, could not understand. (Casca, as we have seen, speaks Greek in Plutarch's accounts of the scene; in Shakespeare's, he speaks English.)

Although the characters come out rather differently, Shakespeare's picture is not only filled with Plutarchan details but also responsive to his larger vision. Plutarch approached Julius Caesar from different biographical viewpoints, as he told the stories of the men whose lives clustered around his. The last comment on Caesar in his own biography is bleak: that he gained only "a vaine name only, and a superficiall glory" (Bullough V.88 = *Caesar* 69.1). In the play Caesar appears, throughout, as a character observed both by others and by himself, and that public identity is what makes him vulnerable. Going further than Plutarch, Shakespeare applied the same lesson to Brutus. The life of the "Noble Roman" also directs the form of his death.

### Plutarch, Shakespeare, and Rome (II): *Antony and Cleopatra*

For Caesar's assassination, playwrights had a variety of sources to draw on, Plutarchan and other. Plays about Antony and Cleopatra, by contrast, focus much more on one of Plutarch's *Lives*, the *Antony*, than on any other

---

[34] Nyquist (2022) argues persuasively that Shakespeare was influenced here also by the *Life of Publicola*, in which the sons of Lucius Junius Brutus engage in a blood-pact against the new republic.

ancient source. This has an effect on the presentation of the central figures. Plutarch's account reveals a generous attitude toward Antony and Cleopatra, history's losers, which is not present in other classical sources.[35] Renaissance historians who write about the pair are generally not sympathetic either;[36] but the dramatic tradition is kinder. Whereas Julius Caesar excited a range of responses among dramatists, Antony and Cleopatra appear, generally, as attractive – despite the disapproval expressed by their fellow characters, rather as Plutarch's own reproving comments stand in contrast to his increasingly sympathetic representation of the two in action.[37]

In *Antony and Cleopatra*, more even than in *Julius Caesar*, we see the unusual sweep of Shakespeare's dramaturgy, responding to the broad scope of Plutarch's biography.[38] Whereas almost all other sixteenth- and seventeenth-century plays on the subject begin after Actium (and often after Antony's death), Shakespeare chooses to start nine years earlier, in 40 BCE, with the lovers at the height of their joint glamor.[39] Other playwrights confine their action to Alexandria; Shakespeare's play spreads from Alexandria to Rome and back, via Syria, Macedonia, and Athens. But – again, still more than in his earlier play – he also mined Plutarch for details. Many of the high points of *Julius Caesar* derive from or are suggested by other classical sources – such as Antony's great speech, which has an analogue in Appian, but nowhere else; or they combine classical accounts – for example, the assassination itself, which fuses Plutarch's versions with that of Suetonius; or they are improvised by Shakespeare himself – as with the conspirators' scene after the killing. But in *Antony and Cleopatra*, the most memorable moments, either integral to the grand narrative or incidental to it, all derive directly from Plutarch. Three such moments are Cleopatra's first appearance to Antony, on her barge (*Antony* 26 = *Antony and Cleopatra* II.ii.190–226); the God abandoning Antony (75.4–6 = IV. iii); and the deaths of Cleopatra and her servants (85 = V.ii.280–327).

---

[35] Pelling (1988a: 12–16).

[36] See Barroll (1958: 238): "When [Antony] then united with Cleopatra, a malicious schemer hungry to gain control of the Roman Empire, there was little question in the minds of most writers as to which side they supported."

[37] Plutarch's sympathetic treatment of Antony's death, in the *Antony*, makes a rather shocking contrast with his description of it in the *Comparatio* with Demetrius as cowardly and disgraceful: free from the pull of his own biographical narrative, his disapproval of the collapsing Roman warlord reasserts itself. For a discussion of many of Shakespeare's predecessors, see Morrison (1974). Besterman (1926) has an impressive "Bibliography of Cleopatra."

[38] The date of this play is probably late 1606/7. See, more recently, Dimitrova (2019: 501–505).

[39] The exception is Thomas May, whose *The Tragedy of Cleopatra, Queen of Egypt* (1626) is comparable to Shakespeare's play in the scope of its action.

*"I Will Tell You . . ."*

So Enobarbus introduces the scene of Cleopatra's first appearance, transformed from direct narrative into reminiscence and the play's most famous
speech. To stage the scene directly would have been beyond the resources of
Shakespeare's stage;[40] later versions also find a way to include the barge in the
form of a narration. Thomas May, in his *Tragedy of Cleopatra, Queen of Egypt*
(first performed 1626), has his Antony remind Cleopatra of a happier past:
"down the silver stream of *Cydnus,* thou / In *Venus* shape cam'st sayling" (Act I,
sig. [B6]). John Dryden, in *All for Love* (1678), has the much more interesting
idea of making Antony remind not Cleopatra but Dolabella, the younger
Roman now urging him to leave the Queen but once himself in love with her:

> Her Nymphs, like *Nereids,* round her Couch, were plac'd;
> Where she, another Sea-born *Venus,* lay.
>
> DOLABELLA   No more: I would not hear it.
> ANTONY         O, you must!
> She lay, and leant her cheek upon her hand,
> And cast a look so languishingly sweet,
> As if, secure of all beholder's hearts,
> Neglecting, she could take 'em:
>
> (III.i.167–171)[41]

Both May and Dryden are inspired by Shakespeare's version, but neither
follows the boldness of his setting. He alone gives the speech not to
Antony, her lover, but to Enobarbus, the sardonic observer (Plutarch
makes Cleopatra actually his enemy – 63.3); his audience is public –
a group of titillated Romans, in holiday mood. By so framing the scene,
Shakespeare shows us Cleopatra's effect on Rome: "Oh rare for Antony!"
responds Agrippa, audibly licking his lips.

The speech is not only the most famous in the play but the most famous
example in all Shakespeare's plays of the direct use of Plutarch. The Greek is
a wonder of description, and Shakespeare followed the wording of North's
translation very closely, reproducing some phrases verbatim: the oars that
"kept stroke" to the flutes; Cleopatra's dress, "cloth of gold of tissue"; even
the gloss that North (following Amyot) added to Plutarch's text:

> Nereides (which are the mermaides of the waters) (Bullough V.274)
> Nereids / So many mermaids     (II.ii.206–207)

---

[40] Consider the stage directions for the Battle of Actium (III.x): "Canidius marcheth with his land
army one way over the stage, and Taurus, the Lieutenant of Caesar, the other way. After their going
in is heard the noise of a sea-fight. Alarum. Enter Enobarbus."
[41] John Dryden, *All for Love: or, The World Well Lost* (London, 1678), p. 35.

Plutarch's scene (*Antony* 26) is, as Pelling says, "extremely sensuous";[42] Shakespeare heightens its sensuality. He adds the sense of heat – the fans that both heat and cool Cleopatra's cheeks (a far more erotic evocation than Dryden's pretty "leant her cheek upon her hand"); and the luxurious participation of the waves, "amorous" of the beating oars. But Enobarbus' speech owes more to Plutarch than its contents alone. As far as the play is concerned, Cleopatra's dazzling entry was her own idea; Plutarch, however, says it was suggested by another Roman, Quintus Dellius, who took one look at her and saw "that within few dayes she should be in great favor with [Antony]" (Bullough V.273 = cf. *Antony* 25.3). Plutarch's shrewd, voyeuristic Roman finds a place transformed, in Shakespeare's account, from the scene's originator to its narrator, and its audience.

### *"Peace, What Noise?" (IV.III.12)*

The barge scene shows Shakespeare converting a passage of narrative into flashback, a speech; in the strange little scene where the God abandons Antony, the narrative is directly dramatized, with speakers invented for the purpose.[43] In Plutarch's account, Antony has lost at Actium and is about to fight the final battle against Octavius when the city of Alexandria, "full of feare and sorrowe" (Bullough V.308), hears "a marvelous sweete harmonie of sundrie sortes of instrumentes of musicke, with the crie of a multitude of people, as they had bene dauncing, and had song as they use in Bacchus feastes"; the "troupe" parades invisibly through the city and leaves by the gate "that opened to the enemies." Clearly this is an omen, of some sort:

> Now, such as in reason sought the depth of the interpretacion of this wonder, thought that it was the god unto whom Antonius bare singular devotion to counterfeate and resemble him, that did forsake them. (Bullough V.308 = *Antony* 75.6)

In Plutarch's account, this phantom parade is a sort of echo to something earlier and real: the Bacchic celebrations that greeted Antony, pre-Cleopatra, when he entered the city of Ephesus (24.4). Shakespeare, who omits any mention of that earlier scene, recreates the later one into something rather different. He changes its timing: Antony, in the play, is in fact about to win a temporary victory. Alexandria is reduced to four soldiers; the festive noise becomes music "under the earth" – that is (for the audience), the stage. The soldiers interpret what they have heard:

RST SOLDIER        What should this mean?
SECOND SOLDIER     'Tis the god Hercules, whom Antony loved,
                   Now leaves him.                                    (IV.iii.15–17)

Why does Shakespeare change the identity of the immortal, from Bacchus to Hercules? Plutarch makes it clear that both are patrons and avatars of Antony; perhaps, as critics have suggested, Shakespeare chose Hercules, really a demi-god, because he, unlike the full god, Bacchus, was also a figure of vulnerability and suffering. Plutarch compares Antony, a brave soldier enslaved by a woman, to Hercules in the power of Omphale, who put him into female dress (*Comparatio Demetrius–Antony* 3.4); Shakespeare's Cleopatra remembers putting her "tires and mantles" on her lover (II.v.22).[44] In the Ephesus scene, Plutarch comments that Bacchus is a god of two natures, kind to some but cruel to most (24.4–5); Shakespeare, as we shall see, edits out the cruelty of both Antony and Cleopatra, and this may be another reason for the Hercules-substitution. And finally, that substitution is brilliantly suitable for the speakers in the scene: to Antony's soldiers, the laboring Hercules might well be a better patron for their commander than Bacchus, the capricious, exotic god of wine.

With the change comes a new starkness. Plutarch's scene is sinister for its very cheerfulness – the unconcern with which the god and his entourage depart; Shakespeare's voiceless, underground music suggests rather an eerie melancholy. Hercules leaves alone, as if himself defeated in his wish to protect his follower. Shakespeare may also have been influenced by a Plutarchan scene he had dramatized earlier in the play: the Soothsayer's warning to Antony that his "genius" cannot resist that of Octavius (II.iii.11–31; cf. *Antony* 33.2–3, also *De fortuna Romanorum* 319F–320A). Hercules, departing, is perhaps the embodiment of that defeated genius. Both scenes, the Greek and the English, are haunting, and haunted, in different, complementary ways.

### "Charmian, Is This Well Done?" (V.II.325)

Almost all plays about Cleopatra end with her death;[45] a messenger of some sort (often the Roman Proculeius) narrates the events so vividly described by Plutarch. Shakespeare may have been the first dramatist to show the

---

[44] See, on this rich subject, Waith (1962: 113–121).
[45] The exception is Robert Garnier's *Marc Antoine* (1578), translated into English by the Countess of Pembroke in 1592.

death on stage. The audience, dependent on Enobarbus' narration for Cleopatra's grand entry into Antony's life, are shown for themselves the matching scene, as she is dressed again in her finery to meet him: perhaps Shakespeare had in mind the two "synodoi" or societies that the lovers made in Plutarch, the *amimētobioi* and the *synapothanoumenoi*, "Those Who Live Inimitably" and "Those About to Die Together" (71.4). The play's Cleopatra, in her last hours, is preoccupied with the way she may appear in Octavius' triumph, which seems to evolve in her mind into the Jacobean theater: "Some squeaking Cleopatra boy my greatness" (V. ii.220). Shakespeare entrusted her last hours to his own unknown boy-actor, or rather boy-actors. They were required to manage comedy, as well as tragedy: Shakespeare seized on the Plutarchan figure of the "country-man" (*tis . . . ap' agrou*, 85.2), who "smiles" at the guards – that hint was enough to make him a comic figure,[46] joking about the "worm." He bumbles in and out; then Cleopatra and her two servants apply the asps to themselves. The last to die is Charmian. Plutarch's description of her death is magnificent; here is North's rendering:

> Her death was very sodaine. For those whom Caesar sent unto her ran thither in all hast possible, and found the souldiers standing at the gate, mistrusting nothing, nor understanding of her death. But when they had opened the dores, they founde Cleopatra starke dead, layed upon a bed of gold, attired and araied in her royall robes, and one of her two women, which was called Iras, dead at her feete: and her other woman called Charmion halfe dead, and trembling, trimming the Diademe which Cleopatra ware upon her head. One of the souldiers seeing her, angrily sayd unto her: Is that well done Charmion? Verie well sayd she againe, and meete for a Princes discended from the race of so many noble kings. She sayd no more, but fell downe dead hard by the bed. (Bullough V.316; cf. *Antony* 85.5–8)

North's imagination was clearly fired by this scene; he makes one signifi-cant change, not anticipated by his direct source, Amyot. Plutarch says nothing about a "soldier." He speaks only of "someone": *eipontos de tinos orgēi*, "when someone spoke angrily" (85.7). Shakespeare's version follows North, and then adds something more:

FIRST GUARD  What work is here, Charmian? Is this well done?
CHARMIAN     It is well done, and fitting for a princess
           Descended from so many royal kings.
           Ah, soldier!                          (V.ii.325–328)

---

[46] The word "clown," by which he is identified in the dramatis personae to the Folio text, means "rustic person" in Shakespeare's English.

With those last two words, Shakespeare opens up the world of suggestion that North's wording had created. She is not just declaiming but speaking – to an individual, a man who somehow knows her name; upon him she bestows her final breath. The effect is of a strange, teasing intimacy: the Roman soldier and the elusive Egyptian enact, in this final moment, an epitome of the whole tragedy. "I will tell you . . ."

## Gipsy Cleopatra

Shakespeare's Cleopatra is the result, in part, of careful omission. Shakespeare continues Plutarch's tendency to edit out her cruelty. Plutarch had suppressed the ugly story about her sister Arsinoë – that Antony had her dragged from sanctuary, on Cleopatra's insistence, and put to death.[47] Shakespeare goes further, cutting stories that Plutarch tells. Octavius, in the play, remarks that she had "pursu'd conclusions infinite / Of easy ways to die" (V.ii.355–356); Plutarch explains how she pursued them, that is, by experimentation on prisoners (71.6). The cruelty of Shakespeare's Cleopatra is comic – except, perhaps, as directed toward Antony. Her erotic techniques, though based on those of her original, are also lighter, more whimsical. Plutarch describes her contriving to be caught by Antony weeping, or hastily wiping her eyes "as if she were unwilling that he should see her weepe" (53.7 = Bullough V.289); Shakespeare's Cleopatra prefers to take him off guard: "if you find him sad, / Say I am dancing . . ." (I.iii.3–4).

Exploiting etymology, Shakespeare uses the word "gipsy" for the Queen. Mercutio, in the much earlier *Romeo and Juliet*, had offered the description as an absurdity: so love-blinded is Romeo, he says, that to him "Cleopatra [is] a gipsy" (II.iv.41); in *Antony and Cleopatra*, the term is applied to her seriously, by an angry Roman – almost at the beginning of the play, when the audience is still waiting to meet her (I.i.10). Shakespeare's England dealt harshly with "gipsies," "counterfayte Egypcians," seen as vagabonds, shifty strangers;[48] applied to Cleopatra, a real Egyptian and a queen, the term has the frisson of double-paradox. Shakespeare's Cleopatra is "tawny," "with Phoebus' amorous pinches black" (I.v.28 – that erotic violence again). The whole idea of a beauty that was not blond had a paradoxical air in Shakespeare's time, at least for the poets, and her

---

[47] See Pelling (1988a: 192), citing Appian, *BC* 5.9 and Josephus, *AJ* 15.88–93.
[48] This is the wording of an Act passed against them in 1597, quoted in Vaughan and Vaughan (1991: 35). For more on this, see Beier (1985: esp. 58–62).

dark gipsyishness fits with her other contrarieties: a "royal wench," a "lass unparalleled."[49] Her attractiveness is thus very differently conveyed from the way it is in Plutarch to whom she is a "flatterer" (29.1) – a category interesting to him – but not a "lass" or a "wench": Plutarch emphasizes her intellectual ability, her language skills, the sweetness of her voice. We cannot be sure whether Shakespeare's Cleopatra possesses anything so definite. She is always elusive; the safe, capacious word "beauty" is applied to her only once, and that by Sextus Pompey, who may never have seen her (II.i.22). This is a departure from Plutarch; still more from North, who uses the word some seven times. North, in fact, uses the word more often than the Greek, which has more variety; and it is another of her paradoxes that Shakespeare's Cleopatra seems somehow to have more in common with the Greek original than with the English translation.[50] Plutarch does not, like Shakespeare, imagine Cleopatra as "tawnier" than Antony, but still he finds her exotic, her appeal unique: he likes to call her "the Egyptian," and he does so more times than his vernacular translators represent (31.3 = Bullough V.278; and again in Greek but not in English or French – 25.3, 29.5). Throughout the *Antony*, he goes to some lengths to explain that her beauty is not the point; and in this Shakespeare follows his meaning, his spirit, more faithfully than his translators.[51]

Central to Plutarch's account of Cleopatra is the idea that she is a riddle, her power over Antony mysterious. Readers of Plutarch, and watchers and readers of Shakespeare, argue over the central question of her real feelings for Antony; they also argue over whether Plutarch or Shakespeare presented her more favorably, in a morally better light. Approaching the comparison from the Plutarchan side, Christopher Pelling thinks Plutarch's Cleopatra more reliably faithful; approaching from the Shakespearean, David Green thinks the reverse.[52] The disagreement, in

---

[49] Shakespeare's idea of a dark Cleopatra was by no means inevitable: *Caesar's Revenge* speaks confidently of her "goulden yellow lockes" (ed. Boas 1911: sig. B4ᵛ).

[50] Plutarch speaks of her *kallos* (27.3, 57.5, 73.3) but also *hōra* (25.5, 57.5, 83.3), *opsis* (25.3), and – more vividly – *kharis* (83.3): North renders all of them as "beauty."

[51] It may be that Shakespeare picked up an idea of exoticism in Plutarch's Egypt by reading his essay on Isis and Osiris (*De Iside et Osiride* 351C–384B). Neill (1994: 232) observes that he uses the rare word "habiliment" for Cleopatra, dressed as Isis – a word that occurs in Holland's translation of the essay rather than North's translation of the *Life*. For more speculation on Shakespeare and *Moralia*, see later in this chapter.

[52] Pelling (1988a: 44): "Plutarch's figure is sometimes enigmatic, but far less so than Shakespeare's"; Green (1979: 114): "Shakespeare makes a consistent character out of the ambiguous personage presented by Plutarch." See also Morrison (1974: 120): "Plutarch does not ever say that Cleopatra loved Antony; it is only after Antony's death that he suggests an emotional attachment, by her mourning and her request to be buried with him. The Renaissance writers, however, all make Cleopatra quite as devoted to Antony as he is to her."

this case, confirms the basic similarity between the two accounts; the deep sympathy between them.

## From Domitius to Enobarbus

Perhaps the play's largest single addition to the *Life* is the character of Enobarbus, worked up from a few brief mentions to the status of shrewd commentator, guide to the audience, and secondary tragic hero. His Plutarchan prototype, Lucius Domitius Ahenobarbus, appears only three times in the narrative: when Antony is thinking of giving up his Parthian campaign, he leaves it to Domitius to tell the men (40.8); before Actium, Domitius persuades Antony to send Cleopatra back to Egypt – and he does so, briefly (56.3); and finally, Domitius deserts – Antony sends his possessions after him, though Cleopatra opposes it, and Domitius dies shortly after of fever (63.3–4: Plutarch dispatches him in a few lines). From these sparse hints, Shakespeare creates a character who sees through both Cleopatra and Antony; is driven, in despair, to leave his floundering commander; then dies, almost immediately after, of sheer remorse. The fact that a character as apparently level-headed as Enobarbus, so sardonic in his responses to the lovers' theatrics, still dies as he dies is one way of communicating the extraordinary resilience, the robustness of their glamor.[53]

## Plutarch, Shakespeare, and Rome (III): *Coriolanus*

### *Roman Virtue*

The choice of Coriolanus as dramatic subject indicates, in itself, the depth and particularity of the relationship that Shakespeare, by 1610, had developed with North's Plutarch.[54] For this story, Plutarch's *Life of Coriolanus* was much the most extensive source easily available to him.[55] And, unlike Caesar and Cleopatra, this hero was an unusual choice, especially in England (in France he was more popular, but Shakespeare's *Coriolanus* is the only one in English until Nahum Tate's revision of it in 1681).

---

[53] Morrison (1974: 119–120) notes that penitent traitors are a regular feature of Renaissance Antony and Cleopatra plays; usually the penitent traitor is Proculeius, or Rhodon, the tutor to Cleopatra's little son who betrayed him to Octavius. But Shakespeare's choice of Antony's friend for the role is unique.

[54] The date is a matter of dispute, but most critics put it shortly after *Antony and Cleopatra*, sometime around 1608/9.

[55] Plutarch's narrative derives from that of Dionysius of Halicarnassus, but this, though available in Latin (1586), was not translated into English until the eighteenth century.

Shakespeare follows Plutarch's storyline and at times echoes his language, as mediated through North: at one point, a line has clearly dropped out of the play, and editors have been able to patch it up confidently with a line from North (II.iii.243: the line was first restored by Nicolaus Delius). Plutarch's explanation of *virtus*, the word that means both "virtue" in general and the virtue of courage in particular (*Coriolanus* 1.6), is paraphrased closely by the general Cominius in II.ii, and becomes the central paradox of the play – though Shakespeare, like Plutarch himself, uses two words in his own language ("virtue" and "valor" – Plutarch has *aretē* and *andreia*), making the paradox less striking than the Latin translators, who use the single Latin word. But Shakespeare also opens up his source in a distinctive way. As I shall argue, he uses Plutarch's details, and North's language, to create a rather different, darker story.

## *"The Most Noble Mother of the World"*

In contrast to other ancient writing on Coriolanus, Plutarch, as biographer, emphasizes Coriolanus' early years as the son of a widow.[56] He thus gives Volumnia (as he is the first to call her) a significant role in the story. Coriolanus married in accordance with her wishes, we are told, and continued afterwards to live in her house (*Coriolanus* 4.7). Considering all this, however, she turns out to be rather a disappointing character. Plutarch says that she overindulged her son, and her single appearance before the final scene confirms that idea, as she weeps passively, wordlessly, over his exile (21.3); even her final appearance in Corioles is not her own idea, but that of her friend Valeria. In the play, the same premise is developed very differently. We are not explicitly told, as in Plutarch, that Coriolanus lost his father young; instead, Shakespeare internalizes the idea to show a woman who has completely elided the memory of her husband (see her whole conversation with her daughter-in-law in I.iii). Plutarch made her overindulgent; but the playwright followed the logic of Plutarch's own story and made her, as Coriolanus' only parent, the driving force behind his heroic overachieving. Shakespeare may have been inspired in this also by another of Plutarch's Roman widows – Cornelia, mother of the Gracchi. Unlike Cornelia, however, Volumnia is an outspoken enemy of the plebs: the sort of mother who "holp to frame," as she says (V.iii.63), this particular hero.

---

[56] See Pelling (1997e) and Russell (1963).

*The "Gown of Humility"*

Plutarch's Coriolanus is a declared enemy to the plebs and their new political leaders, the tribunes, and is driven into exile by them. This climactic scene follows his attempts, in the aftermath of a successful war, to become consul – attempts that take the established form of appearing in a toga without a tunic beneath in order to display wounds incurred in Rome's defense. Plutarch's Coriolanus goes through this process without demur; not so Shakespeare's Coriolanus, for whom the candidacy itself is the climactic scene. Unlike his Plutarchan prototype, Coriolanus, though he dresses in the manner required – in what the play calls a "gown of humility" – refuses to display his wounds. It may be that this refusal was prompted by the wording of North's transla-tion. As we saw earlier, North regularly translates as "gowne" the Greek word Plutarch uses for "toga"; perhaps, as John Denton brilliantly suggests, Shakespeare imagined that this alone, without the garment beneath (translated by North as "coate"), would leave Coriolanus far more exposed than he would in fact have been in a toga's drapes; the "gown of humility" may also have seemed, to Shakespeare, something like the white sheet worn by an English penitent.[57]

Other reasons may also have played their part in Coriolanus' refusal. Following Plutarch, Shakespeare had made the sight of Caesar's wounds and torn clothing crucial in moving the hearts of the crowd toward him (*JC* III.ii.169–205: see *Caesar* 68.1; *Brutus* 20.4–5; *Antony* 14.7; *Cicero* 42.4); in Shakespeare's dramatization, that display became a grand example of cynical manipulation by the displayer, Antony. Coriolanus, the man who hates the crowd, reverses that scene, shunning both the exploitativeness of Antony and the exposure of Caesar, his flesh laid bare before "Hob and Dick" (*Coriolanus* II.iii.116).[58] Later in the play, his rival, Aufidius, suggests that Coriolanus' behavior is motivated by "nature, / Not to be other than one thing": as unflinching in peace as in war (IV.vii.41–42). The point is confirmed by North's marginalia: on the same page, juxtaposed, we find: "Coriolanus constant minde in adversitie" and "The force of anger" (North 1579: 248 = Bullough V.525–526). Coriolanus' constancy *is* his anger: in a world where virtue and valor share a word, his weaknesses are inseparable from his strengths.[59]

---

[57] Compare, for example, the humiliation of the Duchess of Gloucester in *2 Henry VI* II.iv.

[58] For the "feminization" of the bleeding body, see Paster (1989) and the influential discussion by North (1579).

[59] For a fine discussion of "constancie" here and elsewhere in *Coriolanus*, see Miles (1996: esp. at 118).

## *"Ladyes, Ye Have Devoutely Offered Me Up"*

Shakespeare's alteration of Volumnia creates a different introduction to the great scene where she appeals to her vengeful son on behalf of Rome.[60] Whereas Plutarch says that she was persuaded to do so by Valeria, herself convinced by a dream, Volumnia in the play simply appears, without warning, accompanied by the two other women (Valeria and Virgilia, Coriolanus' wife) in a wholly subordinate role. The appeal scene reveals both the closeness and the great creative energy with which Shakespeare read Plutarch's account. As Volumnia speaks, elements of North's language emerge, but altered, dislocated. Plutarch's Volumnia reproached her son: "No man living is more bounde to shewe him selfe thankefull in all partes and respects, then thy selfe; who so unnaturally sheweth all ingratitude" (Bullough V.540 = *Coriolanus* 36.2). Shakespeare's version echoes her, to different, booming effect:

> There's no man in the world
> More bound to's mother; yet here he lets me prate
> Like one i'th'stocks.
>
> (V.iii.158–160)

"More bound to shewe" is here tightened up, "more bound to's mother": not merely more obliged, but more tied to her. According to Plutarch, her last words were defeatist in tone: "to what purpose doe I deferre my last hope?" (Bullough V.540; *Coriolanus* 36.3). In the play, she ends very differently:

> I am hush'd until our city be afire,
> And then I'll speak a little.        (V.iii.181–182)

Presumably she plans to deliver a rousing curse; but her words echo, in distorted form, Plutarch's account of Coriolanus' surrender: "he spake a litle apart to his mother and wife." Plutarch gives a powerful visual image of him surrendering, "holding her hard by the right hande" (Bullough V.541 = *Coriolanus* 36.5). Rather than finding a way of translating that moment into dialogue, Shakespeare takes it directly in the rare form of a stage direction: "He holds her by the hand, silent."

"I see myself vanquished by you alone," says Plutarch's hero to his mother (Bullough V.541 = *Coriolanus* 36.5). Shakespeare's goes further: "Most dangerously you have with [me] prevailed" (V.iii.188). He yields to Volumnia in the

---

[60] For more on Shakespeare's development of this great scene, bringing out different points of language, see Heuer (1957). In his appendix B, MacCallum (1910) usefully prints four versions: Plutarch's Greek, Guarino's Latin, Amyot's French, and North's English – though he does not compare them.

realization that this may be fatal to him. It is the culmination of a suicidal pattern of behavior, which is clinched in the final scene. Plutarch's Coriolanus, surrounded by the angry Volsces, says nothing – silent, like Plutarch's dying Caesar. Shakespeare gave his Caesar a final outburst of heroic self-consciousness; his Coriolanus dies as a heroic suicide: "Cut me to pieces, Volsces" (V.vi.III). As for Volumnia, Plutarch says that, after Coriolanus' death, "the women" of Rome asked for the longest possible period of mourning for him (39.5). Not so Shakespeare's Volumnia, who is never heard from again after she has won from her son her final, fatal demand. "Ladyes, ye have devoutely offered me up": the words are spoken, in North's Plutarch, by the statue of Fortune, dedicated by the women on their return from Corioles (Bullough V.542 = *Coriolanus* 37.3). They are not spoken in the play; and yet they resonate. Shakespeare found his story in the events and the characterization that Plutarch showed him, and in North's words.

## Coriolanus, Antony, and Enobarbus

Part of the inspiration for Shakespeare's hero was probably the Plutarchan comparison between Coriolanus and Alcibiades, which emphasizes Coriolanus' inflexibility in contrast with Alcibiades' shiftiness. The story of Alcibiades himself threads through Shakespeare's *Timon of Athens*; he and Timon together form a link between *Antony and Cleopatra* and *Coriolanus*.[61] Plutarch tells us that Antony, after Actium, affects the life of a disgruntled hermit like Timon, whose story is then told (69.4–70). Timon's story is one of disillusionment: a man who sees too late through his false friends' flattery. Was it, in part, from the Timon story that Shakespeare developed, by reverse, his picture of Enobarbus?

It may well also be that that picture was encouraged by the Plutarchan essay *Quomodo adulator ab amico internoscatur*, which spends much time on the danger of apparent frankness. To quote Philemon Holland's translation:

> this counterfeit liberty of plaine dealing and plaine speech, may be well likened to the wanton pinches and bitings of luxurious women, who tickle and stirre up the lust and pleasure of men by that which might seeme to cause their paine.[62]

The context of this is Cleopatra's court: flatterers pretend to reproach Antony for underrating her love, knowing that this is what he wants to

---

[61]  See, for more on this, Bullough's discussion V.454–455 and Cantor (1997).
[62]  Holland (1603: 99) = *Quomodo adulator ab amico internoscatur* 61B.

hear. Enobarbus, by contrast, offers genuine "plaine speech" – and when he tries to act like a false friend, it destroys him. The pinching, luxurious women, of course, recall Cleopatra herself. Perhaps even in *Antony and Cleopatra*, Shakespeare's full debt to Plutarch is yet to be recognized.[63]

## Conclusion

The vision of the Republic that emerges from Shakespeare's plays is a tragic one: fought over and lost in *Julius Caesar* and *Antony and Cleopatra*; perhaps, in *Coriolanus*, just too hard to live with. At the end of Shakespeare's dramatic career he left all this behind, and he returned to a fanciful, allusive use of Plutarch – the Greek *Lives*, rather than the Roman. We find Plutarchan names cut loose from their histories: Pericles Prince of Tyre (in the sources the character was called "Apollonius"); Cleomenes and Dion, courtiers in *The Winter's Tale*. In the last play of all, the collaboratively written *Two Noble Kinsmen*, Duke Theseus returns, together with the Cretan labyrinth: the play suddenly, decisively echoes North's wording from the *Theseus*.[64] There may also be other Plutarchan echoes in that play: the name of the mysterious "Flavina," a dead friend tenderly remembered (I.iii.49–85), suggests Flavianus, an interlocutor in *Amatorius* – the essay translated by Philemon Holland as *Of Love*. Plutarch has ceased to be a deep "source"; he is now, again, a fund to dip into, a resource; perhaps, by this time, an old friend.

In the late comedy *Cymbeline*, the heroine, Imogen, alone and far from home, identifies herself to a stranger by a name chosen apparently at random: she is the page, she says, of one "Richard du Champ" (IV. ii.377). Critics have long recognized in this a gallicization of Richard Field, Shakespeare's friend, publisher of Shakespeare's own poems and of North's Plutarch. Perhaps this odd little moment is the nearest thing we have to an acknowledgment by Shakespeare of that book on the stage. Montaigne has left abundant testimony to his feelings for Plutarch, and for the translator who brought them together:

> I doe with some reason, as me seemeth, give pricke and praise unto *Iaques Amiot* above all our French writers ... above all, I kon him thankes that he hath had the hap to chuse, and knowledge to cull-out so worthy a worke, and a booke so fit to the purpose, therwith to make so unvaluable a present unto his Country.[65]

---

[63] Evans (2001) suggests that this essay gave Shakespeare an idea for *Othello*, in which the villainous Iago deceives through seeming to be blunt. The essay thus forms a link between the two tragedies.
[64] Arcite, in the play, speaks of "The cranks and turns of Thebes" (I.ii.28); compare North, "the turnings and cranckes of the *Labyrinth*," p. 9 = Plutarch, *Theseus* 19.1.
[65] Florio (1603: 210–211 [Essay II.4]).

– to quote the rather ungainly English version of John Florio. Shakespeare, by contrast, left no direct tribute: no personal declarations, no prefaces (as other dramatists did – for example Daniel and Dryden, before their Cleopatra plays). But the intimacy of his involvement is no less, though so differently, apparent. We can only assume that he would have "konned thanks" to Thomas North, and concurred with him: "I must needes love him with whome I have taken so much payne."

## Further Reading

North's translation of Plutarch (1579 edition) was published complete in the Tudor Translations series, with an introduction by George Wyndham (1895–6, six volumes). A minimal selection – the *Lives* of Caesar, Brutus, Antony, and Coriolanus – based on the 1595 edition is available, in modernized spelling, in Spencer (1964). Bullough (1957–79: esp. vols. 5 and 6) provides selections from a much wider range of *Lives*, reprinted from the 1579 edition in the original spelling – none, unfortunately, complete. On North, Matthiessen (1931) remains valuable, even though his approach is not to the taste of all modern theorists of translation.

Martindale (2004) and Burrow (2013) are first-rate introductions to classical reception in Shakespeare; in both volumes attention is given to Shakespeare's use of Plutarch, and López Rueda (1973) is an especially interesting essay on creative forgetting of classical texts. McGrail (1997) is a fine collection of essays. Miles (1996) is an excellent study of Shakespeare's Roman characters and the burdensome ideal of Rome. MacCallum (1910) is still the most useful single work on the Plutarchan Roman plays, full of treasures (reprinted in 1967 with a rather condescending preface by T. J. B. Spencer). The work of Christopher Pelling is typically rich in insights that shed light on Shakespeare: see especially Pelling (1997e; 2011a: 64–76). The more recent compact surveys of Shakespeare's handling of Plutarchan material are Braden (2014) (with emphasis on the perception of Romanness), Dimitrova (2019), and Kingston (2022: 321–336).

CHAPTER 19

# Plutarch in France
## Sixteenth to Eighteenth Centuries

### Katherine MacDonald

Michel de Montaigne (1533–92) credited his contemporary Jacques Amyot's (1513–93) translations of Plutarch (*Lives*, 1559; *Moralia*, 1572) with lifting him out of the mire of ignorance and inspiring him to write the *Essays*.[1] Together, Amyot and Montaigne ensured the tremendous cultural importance of Plutarch in France from the late sixteenth century onwards.[2] After a decline during the Enlightenment when the *Encyclopédistes* deemed his ideas obscure, Plutarch again rose to prominence at the close of the eighteenth century thanks to Jean-Jacques Rousseau (1712–78) and the revolutionaries. A republican Plutarch had replaced Plutarch as the "mirror for princes" whose works the playwright and historiographer Jean Racine (1639–99) had read to an ailing Louis XIV.

This chapter will begin by considering the French reception of Plutarch's *Moralia* in this period. Against a backdrop of violent civil unrest in the late sixteenth century, the *Moralia* provided a social ethics that emphasized gentle humanity. In the following century, the *Moralia* became a key text for those involved in articulating the concept of *honnêteté* ("politeness," an ideal of refined behavior in an elevated social context): for these writers, Plutarch was a valued guide to graceful comportment in polite society. By the eighteenth century, however, the *Encyclopédistes* had dismissed Plutarch's contribution to moral philosophy as superficial.

The second section will look at the vigorous responses Plutarch's *Lives* elicited from French theoreticians of historiography. It will consider the *Lives* as the inspiration behind numerous works of biography, both in collections and pairs of parallels, including those between ancients and

---

[1] First published in 1580 (books 1 and 2) and 1588 (book 3). All further references to Montaigne are to M. A. Screech's translation = Montaigne (1987). All further references to Amyot's translation of Plutarch's *Lives* (*Les Vies des hommes illustres*) are to the Pléiade edition: Gérald Walter, ed. (Paris, 1951 [1977]).
[2] See more recently Guerrier (2014); Frazier and Guerrier (2019).

moderns. These works formed an important intervention in the seventeenth-century "Quarrel of the Ancients and the Moderns." Finally, I will examine the *Lives'* formative influence on French classical tragedy from its sixteenth century beginnings, through its adolescence under Louis XIII and his chief minister Richelieu (1585–1642), to its full flowering with Pierre Corneille (1606–84) and Jean Racine.

## Moralia

In the sixteenth and the first half of the seventeenth centuries, Plutarch's *Moralia* was important to its French audience at different social levels for several interconnected reasons. First, it was valued as a mirror for princes; the shaping of the royal character was of vital national importance since it was held to determine that of the subjects.[3] As for its non-royal readers, they looked to Plutarch's text for practical wisdom that might be useful as much in the domestic sphere as in polite society. Robert Aulotte notes that French readers and writers in this period overwhelmingly gravitated to the treatises on practical morality, rather than those on religion, cosmology, or abstruse philosophical problems.[4] Of abiding popularity were the works on friendship (e.g. *Quomodo adulator ab amico internoscatur* and *De amicorum multitudine*) and the consolations (the spurious *Consolatio ad Apollonium*, as well as *Consolatio ad uxorem* and *De exilio*). The lawyer François Le Tort's selection of abstracts, the *Trésor des morales de Plutarque* (1577), bears out Aulotte's observation in that it privileges works on social ethics, such as *De garrulitate* and *De cohibenda ira*.[5] In the next century, the moralist and literary critic Charles de Saint-Évremond (1614?–1703) cited *De genio Socratis, De facie quae in orbe lunae apparet,* and *De animae procreatione in Timaeo* as works he found difficult and consequently had no taste for.[6] Moreover, the *Moralia* helped to further develop a taste for psychological and moral investigations in writers such as Montaigne.[7] Plutarch's moral writings also provided a stylistic model for these inquiries into the human condition.[8]

François Rabelais' (ca. 1494–1553) satirical novel *Pantagruel* (1532) provides an example, albeit fictional, of a royal reader of Plutarch's *Moralia*. In King Gargantua's letter to his son Pantagruel, he confesses that he struggled to learn Greek in his mature years, since in his youth the educational climate

---

[3] Cf. Amyot's dedicatory epistle to Charles IX in his translation of the *Moralia, Les Oeuvres morales et meslees,* 1572.

[4] Aulotte (1965: 263).    [5] Frazier (2008b: 85).

[6] "De Plutarque," in Saint-Évremond (1962: 160).    [7] Aulotte (1965: 264).

[8] Aulotte (1965: 266).

was unpropitious. Having mastered the language, he now delights in reading "les *Moraux* de Plutarque." He recommends the *Moralia* to his son as "celestial manna of good knowledge."[9] Gargantua's discussion of his education precedes the curricular advice to his son. Plutarch is thus not explicitly on the young prince's syllabus but features as the leisure reading of the seasoned monarch. Rabelais himself owned three copies of the *Moralia*, including a Greek Plutarch.[10] Indeed, Plutarch's *Moralia* is the source for more quotations and borrowings in Rabelais' works than any other text, including the *Lives*.[11] Although Rabelais' giant kings are fictional creations, they evoke their real counterparts. As Rabelais reminded Cardinal Odet de Chatillon in the dedication to the *Quart livre* (1552), the late François I had *Gargantua* and *Pantagruel* read out to him.[12] So, we can imagine François I identifying himself with the king Gargantua and thereby being discreetly encouraged by Rabelais to consider Plutarch's *Moralia* as suitable royal reading material. At the same time, Plutarch's presence in Rabelais' text, through his borrowings from the *Moralia*, ensured that the Greek philosopher's message was transmitted to a royal audience.

Pierre de Saint-Julien (1519?–93), who translated *De cohibenda ira* and *De curiositate* into French in 1546, followed Erasmus in his opinion of Plutarch as an observer of intimate family life whose works could provide counsel for private life to the ordinary man.[13] Like Erasmus, Saint-Julien initially situates the utility of the *Moralia* in the private sphere. However, he also emphasizes the transferable nature of Plutarchan wisdom to public life:

> Now Plutarch says that one must accustom oneself, and learn patience little by little in one's home, with one's wife, children and servants so that, when outside, it should be entirely within our power to make use of this patience . . .. For Plutarch judged the man to be unworthy of command over others who did not know how to control himself.[14]

---

[9] Rabelais (1994: 244). [10] Rabelais (1994: 1271 n. 7).
[11] One of the most interesting is Rabelais' transposition, in his "Quart livre," chapters 26–28, of the death of Pan in *De defectu oraculorum* (419B–E) into a Christian context, comparing it to that of Christ: Rabelais (1994: 599–605); see Hirzel (1912: 123).
[12] Rabelais (1994: 520, 1483 n. 4).
[13] In Erasmus' dedication to the Hungarian royal treasurer Alexius Turzo of his 1525 Latin translation of the same two works he had emphasized the practical, accessible nature of Plutarch's wisdom and placed it squarely in a domestic context: "Socrates made philosophy come down from the heavens to earth; Plutarch introduced it into the bedroom, the alcove, the bed of everyman . . .. Indeed, in these books, Plutarch writes about things that anyone, at any time, can soon put to use." Cited in Méniel (2008: 110).
[14] *Deux opuscules . . . l'un de non se courroucer et l'autre de curiosité* (Paris: Jacques Bogard pour Gilles Corrozet, 1546), 36. Saint-Julien based his translation on Erasmus' Latin version; Méniel (2008: 117).

Saint-Julien picks up here on the stress laid by Plutarch on practical exercises designed to form good moral habits progressively over time.[15] Later in the sixteenth century, Simon Goulart (1543–1628), editor of several pirate editions of Amyot's translation of the *Moralia*, presented Plutarch as an exemplary active philosopher whose works should be read by those in authority: theologians, jurists, and statesmen.[16]

By the third quarter of the sixteenth century the wars of religion were raging across France. Religious extremism generated atrocities that horrified contemporary observers such as Montaigne and the Protestant soldier and poet, Agrippa D'Aubigné (1552–1630).[17] Amyot too acknowledged the unsettled nature of his times when he wrote in his dedication of the *Oeuvres morales et meslees* of his regret that Charles IX's reign had thus far been "very tumultuous and calamitous." It is an intriguing coincidence of history that the royal privilege for Amyot's translation of the *Moralia* was issued on August 26, 1572, just two days after the beginning of the St. Bartholomew's Day massacre in which some 3,000 Protestants were killed in Paris alone.[18] In this context, we may suppose that Plutarch's message of mildness and humanity was a welcome counterbalance to violent fanaticism.[19] Another aspect of the *Moralia*'s usefulness in such troubled times is suggested by the full title of Le Tort's *Trésor des morales* (1577). In it, Le Tort advertises Plutarch's text as "containing precepts and lessons that each man should adhere to in order to live virtuously [*honnêtement*] and *according to his status and profession*." For Le Tort, Plutarch's *Moralia* had the important merit of safeguarding the social order by keeping its readers in their proper place.

By dedicating the *Oeuvres morales et meslees* to Charles IX and reminding him of his own former role as royal tutor, Amyot presented Plutarch's text as containing an ideal course of instruction in morals for kings. Amyot reinforced this notion by referring to the tradition that Plutarch had served as preceptor to the Roman emperor Trajan. Amyot discussed wisdom, perfection of understanding, and control of the will as necessary for those who wished to rule. He suggested that reading the *Moralia* might give Charles IX access to these things: "Because true greatness is not being able to do anything one wants but wanting to do only what one should."

[15] Russell (1973a: 88).
[16] Simon Goulart, "Avis au lecteurs," in *Oeuvres morales et mesless*, tr. J. Amyot, F. Estienne (ed.), 1581. Méniel (2008: 115).
[17] See Montaigne, *Essays – passim*, especially "On physiognomy" (3.12, 817); D'Aubigné, *Les Tragiques* (1618).
[18] Legros (2008: 275–276).   [19] Russell (1973a: 90).

Furthermore, echoing *Quomodo adulator ab amico internoscatur*, Amyot asserted that through reading books like the *Moralia*, kings might learn things that their courtiers would otherwise keep from them, for fear of displeasing them. However, Amyot acknowledged that kings could not shut themselves away in a study to read their Plutarch as a scholar would. Rather, he proposed, they should gather learned men around them to talk to them at table. Amyot thus incited Charles IX to follow in his grandfather François I's footsteps by extending patronage to men of letters. But, at the same time, Amyot significantly set Plutarch in a context of polite sociability as would Montaigne, along with several others in this period.

Montaigne made no secret of his indebtedness to Plutarch, whom he read in Amyot's translation. As he wrote in his chapter "In Defense of Seneca and Plutarch" (*Essays* 2.32): "my intimacy with these two great men and the help they give to me in my old age, as well as to my book which is built entirely out of their spoils, bind me to espouse their honor."[20]

Typically for Montaigne, who often associated his book with himself,[21] he here points out the ancient moralist's usefulness to him as he endeavors to face old age philosophically; at the same time, he notes the extent of Plutarch's contribution to the construction of his book. There are indeed more than 500 direct borrowings from Plutarch's works in the *Essays*, and just over half of these come from the *Moralia*.[22] But Plutarch's influence on Montaigne goes well beyond these borrowings to color his very approach to writing.

Montaigne explains the special attraction Plutarch's writing in the *Moralia* holds for him in several passages in the *Essays*. He admires Plutarch as a writer because: "he would rather leave us craving for more than bloated."[23] Plutarch's patchwork style of writing is like a stimulating mosaic that suits Montaigne as a reader, since he claims that he is incapable of sustained mental application.[24] The format of Plutarch's *Moralia*, which he describes as containing knowledge in "pieces not sewn together,"[25] is just right for him because he could take the text up and leave it off as he wished. Montaigne values this brevity not merely because of its suitability for the sporadic reader. He remarks that the compact quality of Plutarch's writing coincides with a density of content that can provide subsequent

---

[20] Montaigne (1987: 817).
[21] For example, "a book of one substance [*consubstantiel*] with its author": "On giving the lie," *Essays* 2.18 = Montaigne (1987: 755).
[22] Konstantinovic (1989); Kingston (2022: 279–280).
[23] "On educating children," *Essays* 1.26 = Montaigne (1987: 176).
[24] See "On books," *Essays* 2.10 = Montaigne (1987: 459).
[25] "On books," *Essays* 2.10 = Montaigne (1987: 463).

generations of writers with infinite material for further elaboration. As he
writes in "On educating children" (*Essays* 1.25), there are many places in
Plutarch's writings where he merely indicates with his finger where we
might go. Montaigne then cites an example from Plutarch's *De vitioso
pudore* to which he attributes the genesis of his friend Étienne de La
Boétie's (1530–63) treatise against tyranny, *On voluntary servitude*: "that
one saying of his, 'that the inhabitants of Asia were slaves of one tyrant
because they were incapable of pronouncing one syllable: NO'."[26]

Montaigne values Plutarch's *Moralia* for the stimulus it provides to
further writing. This applies to his own writing as well. If Montaigne has
ventured to put pen to paper, it is because he, like his compatriots, has been
subject to Plutarch's civilizing influence, thanks to Amyot's translation.[27]
Only having read Plutarch's book does Montaigne himself dare to write:
"thanks to it, we now dare to speak and to write."[28] Significantly, Plutarch
informs not only Montaigne's writing but also his speech.[29] The presence
of the spoken word, and thus the suggestion of conversation here, is in
keeping with Montaigne's appreciation of Plutarch for "his opinions which
are gentle [*douces*] and well-suited to public life."[30] This perception of
Plutarch as a good conversation guide for the *gentilhomme* who wished to
learn how best to conduct himself in polite society would find an echo in
Nicholas Faret's manual, *L'honneste homme ou l'Art de plaire à la Cour*
("The Gentleman or the Art of Pleasing at Court," 1630).[31] Faret recommends Plutarch as a teacher of *honnêteté* who illuminates the way not only
to virtue but also to practical good sense (*prudence*).[32]

In addition to Plutarch's beneficent civility, Montaigne appreciates the
philosopher's gentle, inquiring way of expressing his views.[33] Plutarch's willful
ambiguity and lack of dogmatism resonated with Montaigne, who himself
renounced any ambition to prescribe a behavior to his readers: "Others form
Man; I give an account of Man."[34] On a stylistic level, too, Montaigne
recognized the influence of Plutarch's *Moralia*, with their non-programmatic

[26] Montaigne (1987: 459).
[27] "Ignorant people like us would have been lost if that book had not brought us up out of the mire":
*Essays* 2.4 = Montaigne (1987: 408).
[28] Montaigne (1987: 408).
[29] In his writing, Montaigne cultivated a conversational style, hence the equivalence he makes between
speaking and writing. See *Essays* 1.26 = Montaigne (1987: 171).
[30] *Essays* 2.10 = Montaigne (1987: 464).
[31] Aulotte (1965: 266). Faret borrowed extensively from the *Moralia*, in particular the various
*Apophthegmata*, *De garrulitate*, and *Mulierum virtutes*.
[32] Cited in Aulotte (1965: 266).    [33] *Essays* 2.12 = Montaigne (1987: 568).
[34] *Essays* 3.2 = Montaigne (1987: 907).

composition, on his own writing. In "On vanity" (*Essays* 3.9), he notably compares his own wandering (*vagabondant*) style to Plutarch's "flights of fancy" (*gaillardes escapades*): "There are works of Plutarch in which he forgets his theme, or in which the subject is treated only incidentally, since they are entirely padded out with extraneous matter."[35] A tendency to digress and frequent quotations such as those Montaigne notes in Plutarch's *Moralia* are conspicuous stylistic features of the *Essays*.

Finally, in a time of extremism and intransigence, Montaigne identified in Plutarch a humane acceptance of the mixed nature of our existence. It is significant that a key passage in "On experience" (*Essays* 3.13) that encapsulates Montaigne's view of the conditions of human life is an extended borrowing from Plutarch's *De tranquilitate animi*:

> Our life is composed, like the harmony of the world, of discords as well as of different tones, sweet and harsh, sharp and flat, soft and loud. If a musician liked only some of them, what could he sing? He has got to know how to use all of them and blend them together. So too must we with good and ill, which are of one substance with our life. Without such blending, our being cannot be.[36]

Agrippa d'Aubigné's (1552–1630) epic poem the *Tragiques* presents the horrors of the civil wars of religion from the perspective of a Protestant soldier and man of letters. Here, too, Plutarch's gentle humanity serves as a guide to conduct in the midst of generalized vice. Against a backdrop of blood-curdling violence, the poem's second book, "Princes," contains an allegorical depiction of the arrival at the Valois court of a young man traditionally identified with d'Aubigné himself.[37] In a dream, Fortune and Virtue impart conflicting advice on behavior when faced with the general iniquity of the court. Aulotte has noted that Virtue's discourse contains many echoes of Plutarch's *Moralia*. For example, Virtue exhorts the young man: "turn your curiosity inwards" and "spy on yourself rather than on your neighbors" (1407). Virtue's advice follows the question in Plutarch's *De curiositate*: "Why do you see so clearly into other people's business and so little into your own?"[38] Virtue's counsel, "Reproach the person who has been found wanting without ire and without recrimination" (1407), could be taken as a summary of *De cohibenda ira*.[39]

Plutarch again became important as a mirror for princes with the advent of Louis XIV. In his 1643 ideal library for the young monarch, the libertine

[35] Montaigne (1987: 1125); for fuller analysis of "On vanity", see Kingston (2022: 280–286).
[36] Montaigne (1987: 1237). See Amyot (1572: f. 74B) and Konstantinovic (1989: 513–514).
[37] "Princes," vv. 1175–1485 in *Les Tragiques* = D'Aubigné (1995: I.2).     [38] Aulotte (1965: 264).
[39] Aulotte (1965: 264).

poet Nicholas Vauquelin des Yveteaux reserved a privileged place for Plutarch as *maistre des bonnes mœurs* ("teacher of good morals"), whose works might furnish the sovereign with "examples of magnanimity, justice and *galanterie*."[40] Vauquelin's mention of *galanterie* chimes with Montaigne's and Faret's view of Plutarch as an easygoing, companionable philosopher uniquely suited to polite society. The French academician François de La Mothe de Vayer, who himself wrote several texts for the future king's instruction and eventually served as tutor to Louis XIV, gained the accolade of being "the Plutarch of France" from several of his contemporaries.[41] Even as a mature king, Louis XIV continued to enjoy Plutarch. During an illness in 1696, Louis had Racine stay with him through the night and read Plutarch to him, although the king's preferred reading by this time was clearly the *Lives* rather than the *Moralia*.[42]

Robert Aulotte notes a waning in the cultural importance of the *Moralia* in the second half of the seventeenth century. From this time onwards, Plutarch's moral writings furnished decorative motifs rather than direct and true nourishment for intellects in the way they had for Montaigne.[43] Still, there continue to be scattered reminiscences of the *Moralia* in the greatest writers of the age, including Corneille, Molière, and Racine.[44] Jean de La Fontaine (1621–95) too made use of examples from the *Moralia* in several of his *Fables*. In *The Old Man and His Children* La Fontaine takes from Plutarch's *De garrulitate* (511C) the image of concord represented by darts or spears that cannot be broken when bundled together but can easily snap when separated. In Plutarch, it is the dying king of the Scythians who uses the image to impart his final advice for good governance to his eighty sons.[45] La Fontaine, typically, has transposed the example into a bourgeois context: in his fable, a rich old man speaks from his deathbed to his three sons about how to best to administer his estate. (Needless to say, they do

---

[40] Aulotte (1965: 255). Vauquelin had been preceptor to Louis XIII, but he was thrown out of court for licentious conduct.

[41] See, for example, G. Naudé, *Jugement de tout ce qui a esté imprimé contre le Cardinal de Mazarin* (1650), 375; Hirzel (1912: 135).

[42] Hirzel (1912: 136).    [43] Aulotte (1965: 272).

[44] Aulotte (1965: 271). See Corneille, "Epître dedicatoire," *Médée* and Plutarch's citation of Simonides' analogy between the verbal and the visual arts (*Quomodo adolescens poetas audire debeat* 17F; also *De gloria Atheniensium* 346F–347A and *Quomodo adulator ab amico internoscatur* 58B); Molière, *Ecole des femmes*, vv. 447–452 and *Regum et imperatorum apophthegmata* 207C; Racine, *Bérénice*, Préface, and *Quomodo adulator ab amico internoscatur* 68A.

[45] Aulotte (1965: 271). La Fontaine, *Fables*, "L'Education" 8.24 and *De liberis educandis, Apophthegmata Laconica*; "Le renard et la cicogne" 1.18 and *Quaestiones convivales* 1.1; "Le vieillard et ses enfants" 4.18, v. 12 and *De garrulitate* 511C; "Discours Madame de la Sablière" 9, vv. 82–91 and *De amore prolis* 494E.

not follow his wise words, and they soon squander their legacy.) In 1680, the epistolarian Marie de Sévigné (1626–96) judged Plutarch's *Moralia* to be "admirable."[46] Her son Charles de Sévigné (1648–1713) wrote to his sister Françoise de Grignan (1646–1705) to recommend to her Plutarch's *Quomodo adulator ab amico internoscatur*, a work to which he often returned.[47]

From the beginning of the eighteenth century, there is a growing distrust of Plutarch as a source of moral wisdom. Thus, in the *Encyclopédie* (1751) article "Morals" (vol. 10, p. 701), Louis Jaucourt (1704–80) cites Montaigne's favorable judgment of Plutarch from "On books." Jaucourt then diverges from Montaigne when he concludes dismissively: "the subjects of Plutarch's *Moralia* are, in general, treated very superficially."[48] Rousseau is a notable voice of exception to the eighteenth-century contempt for Plutarch's *Moralia*. Rousseau's thought on education in his *Discourse on the Arts and the Sciences* (1750) – as well as in the *Émile* (1762), where he emphasizes the pedagogical importance of virtue, physical training, and the Spartan simplicity of language – shows the influence of Plutarch.[49]

## *Lives*

From the sixteenth to the eighteenth century Plutarch's *Lives* sparked numerous critical discussions among French historiographers and theoreticians of history. At stake were Plutarch's use of anecdotes from his heroes' private life (the famous "signs of the soul" of *Alexander* 1.3), his exactitude, his capacity for psychological analysis, and the neutrality of his comparisons. In his 1566 treatise *Methodus ad facilem historiarum cognitionem* ("Method for the Easy Comprehension of History") the political philosopher and jurist Jean Bodin (1530–96) acknowledged that Plutarch was qualified to write the history of illustrious persons because he had experienced palace life as Trajan's tutor.[50] Bodin in turn deemed Plutarch's *Lives* to be a form of history suitable for imitation by contemporary princes, since its sections could be easily read in between other activities. However, Bodin chastised Plutarch for relating "unbelievable and clearly preposterous" things, although he was careful to insert "they say" to prevent his readers from incautiously believing the tale.[51] Bodin further criticized Plutarch's comparisons of Greeks and Romans, accusing

---

[46] Hirzel (1912: 136).    [47] Hirzel (1912: 136).    [48] Aulotte (1965: 272).    [49] Aulotte (1965: 272).
[50] Bodin (1969: 63).    [51] Bodin (1969: 64); see Kingston (2022: 258–259).

him of nationalist bias, although he reckoned the Plutarchan parallels of fellow countrymen to be acceptably neutral.

Montaigne took issue with Bodin's criticisms in "In Defense of Seneca and Plutarch" (*Essays* 2.32). In particular, Montaigne blamed Bodin for attacking the judgment of "the most judicious author in the world."[52] Montaigne disagreed with Bodin's assessment that Plutarch "wrote things which are incredible and entirely fabulous." He cited Bodin's example of the Spartan boy in *Lycurgus* 18.1 who chose to be flogged to death rather than be exposed as a thief when he concealed a fox under his cloak. Montaigne found this example ill-chosen, since it presumes to limit "the powers of the faculties of our souls." We can more or less know the limits of our physical strength because that is governed by natural laws, but Montaigne, relativist as ever, considers it foolish to circumscribe the capacities of the human will. Montaigne used Plutarch's *Lives* as a guide to "the true diversity" of humankind's "inward qualities." Among historians, Montaigne preferred biographers such as Plutarch who treated motives rather than events and "what comes from the inside more than what happens outside."[53]

Saint-Évremond's essay *On Plutarch* (1664) uses Montaigne's support of Plutarch in "On books" as its starting point.[54] Here, Saint-Évremond stated his strong preference for the *Lives*, which he considered Plutarch's masterpiece, and far superior to the *Moralia*. Like Montaigne, Saint-Évremond appreciated Plutarch's attention to the private lives of his heroes. Still, Saint-Évremond was not as impressed as Montaigne was by Plutarch's capacity for subtle psychological analysis in the *Lives*.[55] In Saint-Évremond's estimation, Plutarch would not have been able to deal with a complex, contradictory character like the Roman conspirator Catiline. Saint-Évremond did not share Montaigne's admiration for Plutarch's comparisons either. Perhaps thinking to improve upon the original, he wrote a couple of his own, taking both ancient and modern subjects: a "Parallel of Condé and Turenne" (1652) and "On Alexander and Caesar" (ca. 1653).[56]

It was Plutarch's predilection for anecdote that divided critical opinion on the *Lives* in the eighteenth century. Voltaire (1694–1778) is notably trenchant in his criticism of Plutarchan biography in his *Century of Louis*

---

[52] Montaigne (1987: 818).    [53] *Essays* 2.10 = Montaigne (1987: 467).
[54] Saint-Évremond (1962: 159–164).    [55] Saint-Évremond (1962: 161).
[56] Saint-Évremond (1969: 415–421 and 1962: 200–228). Saint-Évremond assumed Goulart's comparison of Alexander and Caesar in his edition of Amyot's translation (possibly Paris: A. Robinot, 1645) was by Plutarch.

*XIV* (1751). For Voltaire, the *Lives* were little more than a collection of agreeable but dubious anecdotes. After all, how could Plutarch have accessed "faithful memoirs" of the lives of Theseus or Lycurgus?[57] Voltaire considered the *Lives* to be not history but a frivolous collection of moral maxims supposedly uttered by Plutarch's heroes. As such, Voltaire esteemed that Plutarch was not a fitting model for contemporary historians, who ought to be striving to reach higher standards of truthfulness.

Still, eighteenth-century writers did not universally share Voltaire's skepticism of the Plutarchan anecdote and history of private life. Rousseau writes in the *Confessions* (1782–9) of his childhood passion for the *Lives* and the profound effect they had on him. Reading about Agesilaus, Aristides, or Brutus inspired him to imaginatively transform himself into these great men, going further in his imitation than Plutarch had said of his own use of history as a mirror for self-fashioning in the preface to the *Aemilius Paulus*.[58] The young Rousseau even had to be restrained from thrusting his hand into a stove in imitation of Scaevola.[59] In his treatise on education, *Émile* (1762), Plutarchan-style biography occupies an important place in Rousseau's curriculum for the young pupil. Here, he suggests that private biography, because of its naturalism, is more suitable for the study of the human heart than public history, where artifice reigns.[60]

The radical egalitarian Abbé Gabriel Bonnot de Mably (1709–85) also held Plutarch in high esteem, not for his exactitude, which Mably acknowledged was not perfect, but for his truthfulness in moral matters, which he considered more important for a historian.[61] In *On the Manner of Writing History* (1783), Mably singles out Plutarch as the perfect model for biographers. Mably acknowledges that Plutarch might lack some technical knowledge (for instance, Latin), but writes that he could forgive everything of a historian who possessed "the secret of winning my confidence and my friendship." Echoing Montaigne's assessment of Plutarch's amiable persona, Mably stated that his charm lay in the fact that he did not seem to obviously instruct but instead to simply converse with his reader.[62] Unlike Saint-Évremond, Mably judged Plutarch to be excellent at delving into the human heart and exposing its complexities. Like Rousseau, Mably admired Plutarch for his naturalism in portraying his subjects' human failings: "He never presents us with fantasy men like those historians who fear to degrade their heroes by sometimes allowing them to be men."[63]

---

[57] Voltaire (1957: 889).  [58] Rousseau (1964: 8–9); further, Kingston (2022: 384–399).
[59] The famous episode found in Livy (2.12) as well as in Plutarch's *Publicola* 17.2–8.
[60] Rousseau (1969: 531).  [61] Mably (1988: 338).  [62] Mably (1988: 345).  [63] Mably (1988: 345).

Plutarch's humanism meant that he was still useful as a guide to understanding Mably's fellow-citizens. However, the republican Mably regretted that France's "political constitution" had diminished the genius of contemporaries by classing the population in hierarchical orders.[64] In Mably's estimation, a contemporary Plutarch would find that there were no longer any men great enough for him to write about.

Despite Mably's pessimism about the dearth of subjects for the would-be French Plutarch, the *Lives* inspired numerous imitations in the genre of biography. Plutarchan biography, which combines lively description and analysis of moral character with often dramatic narrative organized in a roughly linear progression from birth to death, proved more appealing to French life-writers than the comparatively static Suetonian model, whereby virtues and vices appear in separate sections exemplified by a list of actions and anecdotes.[65] The first attempts at Plutarchan-style biography in France appeared in editions of the *Lives* themselves, and took ancient personalities as their subjects. French publishers took their cues from their Italian counterparts who regularly included extra biographies, written by humanists, in their editions of the *Lives*.[66] Thus, the 1470 collection of Latin *Lives* contained Leonardo Bruni's *Life* of Aristotle and Guarino Veronensi's account of Plato.[67] The 1520 first Paris edition (J. Bade) of the Latin *Lives* followed suit by including these humanist biographies. The first edition of Amyot's translation contained only biographies by Plutarch. However, subsequent editions did contain new *Lives* to replace the "lost" originals, such as those by Donato Acciauoli of Hannibal and Scipio translated by Charles de l'Écluse (1526–1609).[68] In addition to supplying the "missing" comparisons, Simon Goulart appended *Lives* of Plutarch and Seneca, Epaminondas, Philip, Dionysius, and Augustus Caesar to his editions of Amyot's translation.[69]

Once the vogue for *Lives* was definitively established, French writers set about producing collections of biographies of their own. They were initially careful to suggest their works' similarity with Plutarch's by including both ancient and contemporary subjects. These books were lavishly illustrated with engraved portraits, often in the form of "antique" medallions, as in turn were editions of Amyot's Plutarch. Such were the

---

[64] Mably (1988: 346); see further Kingston (2022: 378–384).
[65] Leo (1901); see Pelling's Chapter 1 in this volume.    [66] Pade (2007: I. 385–391).
[67] It also contained Nepos' *Life of Atticus*, pseudo-Herodotus' *Life of Homer* (thought to be by Plutarch), and a biography of Virgil (Rome: C. Sweynheim and H. Pannartz). Girolamo Squarciafico's 1502 edition of Plutarch's biographies contained a *Life* of Socrates (Venice).
[68] E.g. Paris: M. Vascosan, 1567.    [69] E.g. Dijon, 1583 and Paris, 1587.

collections by Antoine Du Verdier (1573), Guillaume Roville (1578), and André Thevet (1584).[70] Thevet elaborately placed himself in Plutarch's shadow when he acknowledged his predecessor's unsurpassable contribution to the development of biography in his life of Plutarch (*Vrais pourtraits*, f. 91 v°).

By the turn of the century, French writers were confident enough in the appeal of biography to produce collections of *Lives* with only modern subjects. Furthermore, they began to concentrate on subjects who were demonstrably different to Plutarch's statesmen and generals. Thus Scévole de Sainte-Marthe published his conspicuously modern and exclusively literary *Eulogies of Illustrious Men of Learning Who Flourished in France in This Century* (1598).[71] Women were the subject of biography collections by Brantôme (composed after 1584 but published in 1665–6), Madeleine de Scudéry (1642, in her brother Georges' name), and Jacquette Guillaume (1665).[72] Sometimes these works set themselves up to rival Plutarch. Charles Perrault (1628–1703) published his proudly all-modern *Illustrious Men of France in This Century* (1698) shortly after André Dacier produced his exploratory first volume of his new translation of Plutarch's *Lives*.[73]

The influence of Plutarch's *Lives* extended beyond biography to shape the development of French tragedy in this period. Certainly a preponderance of plays on historical topics in the sixteenth century contain borrowings from Plutarch, whom, at least after 1559, the tragedians generally read in Amyot's version.[74] The declamatory style of these plays and even their conception of tragedy attest to the *Lives*' influence. Rather than to Greek tragedy, with its dialogues geared toward advancing the dramatic action, sixteenth-century playwrights looked to Plutarch (as well

---

[70] Antoine Du Verdier, *La Prosopographie* (Lyon: A. Gryphius); Guillaume Roville, *Promptuaire des Medailles* (Lyon: G. Roville); André Thevet, *Les vrais pourtraits et vies des hommes illustres* (Paris: veuve J. Kerver and G. Chaudiere). See Eichel-Lojkine (2001: 30).

[71] *Virorum doctrina illustrium qui hoc seculo in Gallia floruerunt Elogia* (Poitiers). Sainte-Marthe may also have been following the alternative classical tradition of biographies of intellectuals represented by Diogenes Laertius' *Lives and Opinions of Philosophers* or Philostratus' *Lives of Sophists*.

[72] In Brantôme's *Lives* of French and foreign generals, he acknowledges "this great Plutarch ... of whom a pen stroke would be worth more than all my writings." Cf. Hirzel (1912: 131). Brantôme, *Vies des dames illustres de France de son temps* (Leyde: J. Sambix le jeune); Scudéry, *Les Femmes illustres* (Paris: A. de Sommaville); Guillaume, *Les Dames illustres* (Paris: T. Jolly).

[73] Perrault, *Les hommes illustres qui ont paru en France pendant ce siècle* (Paris: A. de Sommaville); Dacier, *Les vies des hommes illustres de Plutarque* (Paris: C. Barbin, 1694).

[74] Jodelle, *Cléopâtre captive* (1553); Jacques Grévin, *La Mort de César* (1561); Robert Garnier, *Porcie* (1568), *Cornélie* (1574), *Marc Antoine* (1578); Jacques de la Taille, *La Mort d'Alexandre* and *Daïre* (1573); Anon., *Pompée* (1579); Nicolas de Montreux, *Cléopâtre* (1595); Pierre Thierry de Mont-Justin, *Coriolanus* (1600); Margarit Pageau, *Monime* (1600); Antoine de Montchrestien, *Les Lacènes* (1601); Jean Behourt, *Hypsicratée, ou la magnanimité* (1604). List from Lavoine (1986: 273).

as, of course, Seneca) for rhetorical set speeches they could insert into their historically themed works. Thus Antoine de Montchrestien's (1561–1621) *Les Lacènes* (1601) opens with a speech by the ghost of Therycion, a friend of Cleomenes, still very much alive when he speaks in Plutarch's text. Therycion's speech is a paraphrase of the most prominent set speech in the *Life of Cleomenes*, regardless of the fact that in Plutarch's biography this occurs long before the play's action.[75] As such, it provides the spectator/reader of Montchrestien's play with little in the way of helpful exposition.[76] These plays also share a didactic conception of tragedy that owes much to Plutarch's view of history as a source of exemplars of virtue.[77] For example, Jacques Grévin (1539–70) summarized the moral of his play *César* (1561): "Here, Sirs, you see the piteous end of this courageous soldier and how fortune finally turned her back on him having elevated him to the greatest dignity and to the top of her wheel."[78]

Montchrestien similarly presented his *Les Lacènes* as a lesson in fortitude when faced with fortune's vicissitudes.[79] The play's interest is located not so much in its events as in the Spartan men and women's constancy in facing the catastrophes that befall them.[80] The objective of imparting a clear moral lesson could also lead playwrights to deviate from Plutarch, though, in particular by simplification. For instance, Montchrestien's Cleomenes is a purely admirable Stoic hero whose soul is consistently shown to be stronger than any misfortune, whereas Plutarch's had an element of rashness.[81]

Structure is another level on which Plutarch had both provided sixteenth-century French playwrights with inspiration and forced them to innovate. In composing his biographies, Plutarch generally adopts a three-part division – education, entry into political life, death – which does not fit well with the structure of tragedy (protasis–epistasis–catastasis–catastrophe, beginning *in medias res*).[82] As a consequence of this difficulty, French tragedians at the time tended to be very selective in their borrowings, usually concentrating on the spectacle of the hero's behavior in the face of death. This phenomenon could also constitute a historically motivated response to Plutarch on the part of French tragedians in the unstable preclassical period.[83] The link between tragedy and its historical circumstances is made in editions of

[75] Montchrestien, *Les Lacènes* 1.1; Amyot, *Les Vies: Cleomène*, chapter 53 – Plutarch, *Agis/Cleomenes* 52. See Calkins (1943: 29–42).
[76] R. Griffiths (1970: 75–76).
[77] See e.g. Amyot's *Paul–Émile* (1–2) and *Périclès* (1–2). Lavoine (1986: 274).
[78] Grévin (1971: 97).
[79] Montchrestien, *Les Lacènes*, "Epigramme," and "Au Lecteur" in *Œuvres completes* (Rouen, 1604).
[80] Calkins (1943: 26).     [81] Amyot, *Les Vies: Cleomène*, chapter 25.     [82] Campangne (2012).
[83] Campangne (2012).

Montchrestien's *Oeuvres completes* in some prefatory verses that describe tragedy as a genre especially appropriate to a country that has been a "bloody Theatre of every kind of cruelty." Indeed, instead of seeking to efface the horrors of civil war, tragedians were consistently drawn to the most horrifying and bloody passages in Plutarch. Thus Montchrestien based his *Lacènes* only on the final chapters of *Cleomenes*[84] that describe the "piteous tragedy" of the Spartan women, rather than being inspired by the *Life* of the Spartan king for its political reflection on ambition and the dangers of a quest for popular glory.

In the 1630s, under Louis XIII and his first minister Cardinal Richelieu, dramatists continued to turn to Plutarch as a source of historical tragedies, concentrating on his Roman *Lives*. However, at this time, Plutarch, because he conspicuously refrained from flattering those who had overthrown the Republic and inaugurated the Empire, raised problems for dramatists seeking favor with Richelieu, who was then attempting to establish an absolute monarchy in France and to extend French power in Europe by military force.[85] Nonetheless, several dramatists close to Richelieu rose to the challenge when they composed plays with Plutarchan sources, adapting their material judiciously in ways designed not to offend the Cardinal.[86] For example, in their treatments of Julius Caesar, both dedicated to Richelieu, Georges Scudéry (1601–67) and Guyon Guérin de Bouscal (1613–57) omit Plutarch's frank account of Caesar's motives and instead cast him as a kindly figure betrayed by ungrateful friends. Guérin transforms Plutarch's Brutus from an admirable defender of the Republic into an old-fashioned Stoic, out of touch with contemporary political realities, as Charles Chaulmer (d. 1680) does with his Pompey. Plutarch's highly equivocal Mark Antony becomes, in the hands of Scudéry, a much more monolithic character who serves as a mouthpiece for Richelieu when he advocates incarcerating anyone suspected of conspiring against Caesar's centralization of power. Two Coriolanus plays by François Chapoton and Urbain Chevreau (1613–1701) likewise simplify Plutarch to convey a straightforward cautionary lesson to any nobles bent on sedition.[87]

---

[84] Amyot, *Les Vies: Cleomène*, chapters 72–73 – Plutarch, *Agis/Cleomenes* 59.

[85] My account of these dramatists' politically motivated transformations of Plutarch follows Clarke (1994: 41–42).

[86] See e.g. Georges de Scudéry, *La Mort de César* (1636); Guyon Guérin de Bouscal, *La Mort de Brute et de Porcie ou Vengeance de la mort de César* (1637); Charles Chaulmer, *La Mort de Pompée* (1638); François Chapoton, *Le Veritable Coriolan* (1638); and Urbain Chevreau, *Coriolan* (1638).

[87] Plutarch's original *Coriolanus* is a deterrent example that insists on the harm his excessive nature did to the Roman state. Yet in his *Comparatio* of Coriolanus and Alcibiades, Plutarch also drew attention to Coriolanus' "strong and vigorous nature" – unfortunately untamed by

Plutarch's *Lives* also contributed to the works of the two greatest French classical tragedians: Corneille and Racine. Nicolas Boileau (1636–1711), the chief supporter of the ancients in the "Quarrel of the Ancients and the Moderns," highlighted Plutarch's importance to Corneille when he wrote in about 1700 to his opponent Charles Perrault:

> Can you deny that M. de Corneille found in Livy, Cassius Dio, Plutarch, Lucan and Seneca his most beautiful features, that he derived from them the great ideas which led him to invent a new type of tragedy unknown to Aristotle?[88]

As for Corneille, his own account of his debt to the ancients, and in particular to Plutarch's *Lives*, is more nuanced than Boileau's. There are only two direct references to Plutarch's *Lives* in Corneille's writings on his plays, one in the preface to *Sertorius* (1662) and the other in the preface to *Agésilas* (1665). In each case, Corneille refers to Plutarch in almost the same breath as he justifies the liberties he has taken with his source. Thus in the preface to *Sertorius*, he uses the lack of a clear chronology in Plutarch's *Life* of the Roman general, and his public's superficial knowledge of history, to authorize his decision to make Sulla outlive Sertorius.[89] (In fact, the dictator had died some years before Sertorius' assassination in Spain in 72 BCE.) He also acknowledges that, since the *Life* of Sertorius had no female characters, he had fabricated two: Aristie, whose name resembles that of Antistia, the real ex-wife of Pompey, and Viriate, the fictional queen of Lusitania, both of whom figure as possible brides for Sertorius. In the preface to *Agésilas*, after first referring his reader to Plutarch, Corneille emphasizes the originality of his drama. Corneille then advocates that writers should stray from the paths already well trodden by the ancients.[90] And indeed, although the political rivalry between King Agésilas (Agesilaus) and the general Lysander to whom he owes his throne has its basis in Plutarch, Corneille's play revolves primarily around a romantic plot involving fictional characters: Lysander's daughters whose marriages he seeks Agésilas' permission to arrange.[91] The ending also deviates from Plutarch: Agésilas, having sacrificed his love for a Persian princess and having magnanimously declined to use incriminating

---

a philosophical education – and his "good and praiseworthy qualities" including "temperance and clean hands." See Russell (1973a: 108–112); Wardman (1974: 98–99, 122–123); Duff (1999a: 206–221).
[88] Boileau, "Lettre à Charles Perrault," *Oeuvres complètes*, ed. by Berriat-Saint-Prix, vol. 4 (Paris, 1837), 89. Cited in May (1967: 148).
[89] Corneille (1965: 160).   [90] Corneille (1965: 169).   [91] Knight (1991: 96–101).

evidence of Lysander's plotting against him, decides to marry one of the general's daughters and thus secure his loyalty.

So Corneille by no means felt beholden to the letter of Plutarch's text, but instead sought in the *Lives* a source of inspiration that could serve his own dramatic ends: with Sertorius and Agesilaus, that interweaving of love and politics typical of French classical tragedy. Intriguingly, it is where Corneille is not following any single declared source in Plutarch that his drama shows the greatest debt to the *Lives*, most notably at a thematic level. For example, it seems likely that Corneille artfully blended the themes and characterizations he found in the *Lives* of Romulus, Numa, and Coriolanus when concocting his play about the legendary combat between the Roman Horatii and the Alban Curiatii, *Horace* (1640).[92] In particular, *Horace* dramatizes the contrast Plutarch develops in the *Lives* of these first two Roman rulers between the warlike Romans and the gentle Sabines – similar in this respect to Corneille's Albans.[93] Moreover, Plutarch inspired the invention of a new female character, Horace's Alban wife Sabine, who articulates Romulus' and Numa's qualms about the nascent imperial ambitions of Rome. Together with Horace's sister Camille, Sabine repeatedly intervenes in a vain attempt to dissuade the men from fighting. In so doing, she is also reminiscent of the women in *Coriolanus*.[94] It can be said that *Horace* transcends the propagandism of plays by contemporary rivals discussed earlier partly because Corneille aspired to Plutarch's balance and moral comprehensiveness when it came to characterizing his heroes and their situations.[95] Although similarly dedicated to Richelieu, *Horace* thus dares to express the immorality of wars of conquest and the human sufferings they necessarily entail.

In contrast to Corneille, who came to the *Lives* exclusively through Amyot's version, Racine first read his Plutarch in Greek when he was a schoolboy at the Jansenist school at Port Royal. We can follow the traces of this early reading in Racine's 1655 annotations on the *Lives*. Racine made these notes, many of which attempt to reconcile Plutarch with Jansenist teaching, under the careful supervision of his teachers. Thus, in a note on the *Lives* of Agis and Cleomenes, Racine wrote: "A man is never perfect

---

[92] Corneille cited only Livy's *Roman History* (1.24) in his dedication to Richelieu. My account of Corneille's use of Plutarch in this play follows Clarke (1994: 39–49).

[93] See e.g. *Horace* II.3, ll. 480–482.

[94] In Plutarch's *Coriolanus* (33.5–6), the women rally to Rome's defense on the example of the Sabine women who are Corneille's heroine's namesake. Clarke points out that according to seventeenth-century dramatic naming conventions, we should have expected the Alban Sabine to be called Albine. By naming her Sabine instead, Corneille draws attention to this parallel.

[95] See e.g. Amyot, *Les Vies: Cimon*, Chapter 5 – Plutarch, *Cimon* 2. Cited by Clarke (1994: 47–49).

even if he is very virtuous."[96] Such reflections would have been an important corrective to the prideful humanistic admiration Racine might have
experienced when reading about the triumphs of Plutarch's heroes. Racine
also made comparisons between contemporary figures and Plutarch's
protagonists. For example, he compared Romulus with Saint Louis,
Coriolanus and Alcibiades with Condé (Louis II de Bourbon), who allied
himself with France's enemy Spain during the civil wars of the Fronde, and
Aratus with Cardinal Richelieu.[97] In at least one place, Racine glossed an
expression of Plutarch's that would later turn up as a line in one of his
plays.[98]

    But such close quotations from Plutarch are rare in Racine's work.
More typical is the kind of selective adaptation of a character we see in
*Mithridate* (1673), where Racine cites Plutarch as his authority for the
main female character, Monime, who is to marry the king of Pontus.
Here, like Corneille, he is openly casual in his treatment of his historical
source, which he says he has only partially followed.[99] Racine writes
that he was moved to make Monime his heroine by Plutarch's evident
pleasure in describing her in the *Life of Lucullus*. To support this
statement, he quotes a lengthy passage on Monime from Amyot's
translation, which he admires as more "gracious" than modern
French.[100] However, in order to create a purely virtuous heroine,
Racine omits some phrases from Amyot's version that suggest
Monime may have hoped to gain materially from her union with
Mithridate. For the same reason, Racine omitted to mention the passage in *Pompey* where Pompey discovers "lascivious letters" exchanged
between Monime and Mithridates.[101]

    Like tragedy, French painting of the seventeenth century also attests to
the influence of Plutarch's *Lives*. In the 1630s, Eustache Le Sueur (1616–55)
produced several works with Plutarchan themes, including paintings of
Alexander and his physician (lost but known through an engraving and
a drawing) and of Volumnia and Veturia before Coriolanus (Paris,
Louvre).[102] Many of Nicolas Poussin's (1594–1665) drawings and paintings
of the 1630s and 1640s and later were inspired by his readings in the works

[96] Racine (1966: II.938).     [97] Racine (1966: II.934–937).
[98] In Racine's notes on Plutarch's *Alexander*, he wrote: "Alexander never stole a victory" (1966: II.941).
    Cf. Racine's *Alexandre* 4.2.1062; Plutarch, *Alexander* 31.2.
[99] Racine (1966: I.602); Kingston (2022: 345–346).
[100] Amyot, *Les Vies: Lucullus*, chapter 32 ~ Plutarch, *Lucullus* 18.3–6.
[101] Amyot, *Les Vies: Pompée*, chapter 55 ~ Plutarch, *Pompey* 37.3.
[102] Le Sueur also used the *Moralia* (*Mulierum virtutes* 257E–258C) for the theme of his *Camma and Synorix in the Temple of Diana* (pre-1645; Boston Museum of Fine Arts). Mérot (1987: 93, 168, 180).

of the ancient historians and moralists, and in particular of Plutarch, whom he also frequently quotes in his letters.[103] In particular, he illustrated incidents from the lives of Pyrrhus, Mucius Scaevola (*Publicola* 17.1), Coriolanus, and the suicide of Cato Minor.[104] These works emphasize the Stoic values of devotion to country and duty over personal desires. Poussin also used Plutarch's heroes as themes for his landscape paintings, most notably in his two images of Phocion: *Landscape with the Body of Phocion Carried Out of Athens* (1648, National Museum of Wales, Cardiff) and *Landscape with the Ashes of Phocion Collected by His Widow* (1648, Walker Art Gallery, Liverpool).[105] Anthony Blunt observes that Phocion's austere yet gentle character as depicted by Plutarch would have appealed to Poussin. Furthermore, the brevity of speech attributed to him by Plutarch parallels Poussin's principle of economy in his art.[106]

In the late eighteenth century, Jacques-Louis David (1748–1825) turned to Plutarch's early Roman *Lives* in addition to Livy for the themes of several of his great history paintings, which seem to extol personal sacrifice for the good of the state: *The Oath of the Horatii* (Louvre, 1784) and *The Lictors Bringing Brutus the Bodies of His Sons* (Louvre, 1789). Although these paintings have been endowed with significance for the French Revolution with which David was closely associated, the *Brutus* in particular has a subversive quality that made it ultimately unsuitable as an icon of republicanism. Norman Bryson discusses how the grieving figure of Brutus, enveloped in shadow on the far left of the painting, has a "sinister quality" that recalls Plutarch's ambiguous description of him as "either divine or brutish" (*Publicola* 6.5).[107] David's painting leaves unresolved the contrast between Brutus' male world of hero-ism and political action and the emotionalism of the female relatives behind the curtain in such a way that the image cannot be taken as a straightforward republican symbol. Likewise, Bryson terms David's *The Intervention of the Sabine Women* (Louvre, 1799), painted after his incarceration as a partisan of Robespierre, a "public work of recantation" of his politics during the Terror. In this image, David depicts the women with their emotionalism and loyalty to family over the state as being finally in the right.[108]

In sum, then, Plutarch's works lent themselves to a rich variety of interpretations, thus vouchsafing their author's extraordinary cultural leg-acy in pre-revolutionary France. Against the backdrop of civil unrest in the

---

[103] Blunt (1995: 161–168).

[104] *The Saving of the Infant Pyrrhus* (1634, Louvre); *Mucius Scaevola* (drawing, St. Petersburg, Hermitage); *Coriolanus* (ca. 1650, Musée municipal, Les Andelys); *Cato* (drawing, 1638–40, Windsor Castle, Royal Library). Blunt (1995: 161).

[105] Blunt (1995: 165).    [106] Blunt (1995: 166).    [107] Bryson (1981: 235).    [108] Bryson (1981: 246).

sixteenth century, the *Moralia* became a facilitator of social order that provided a model for more humane interaction. If only princes would read their Plutarch, his advocates argued, a more peaceable kingdom would result. Dramatists could find in the *Lives* a wealth of material to suit patrons who aimed at absolutism, as well as to satisfy their audience's craving for horrifying spectacle or outstanding virtue. The greatest playwrights were inspired by Plutarch in their creation of complex characters facing moral dilemmas. By the end of the period, the revolutionaries espoused Plutarch for his models of republican virtue. Thus, in her prison journal, Jeanne-Marie Roland (1754–93), a victim of the Terror, wrote that reading Plutarch was what turned her into a republican: "he awoke that strength and pride that makes the republican character; he inspired true enthusiasm in me for public virtues and liberty."[109]

At around the same time, though, a young Napoleon at military college in Champagne was also eagerly devouring his Plutarch in Amyot's translation. As his English schoolfellow, known only as C. H., who was in charge of the library at Brienne wrote in his memoirs, Napoleon would spend hours in the "concealed retirement" of the college gardens "feasting on the example of those great men which he was preparing himself to surpass."[110] His favorite hero was, unsurprisingly, Caesar, whose constant striving to surpass himself (cf. Plutarch, *Caesar* 58.5) appealed to the ambitious future emperor, who was frequently seen standing on the tabletops acting out scenes from Plutarch with his friend Fauvelet de Bourienne.

## Further Reading

On Plutarch's cultural legacy in France (alongside other European countries), see the classic work by Hirzel (1912) and now Kingston (2022). On the *Moralia*, Aulotte (1965) provides a wealth of information. Aulotte's study is excellently complemented by Guerrier (2008). On Amyot's translation, see Guerrier (2014) and especially Frazier and Guerrier (2019). Konstantinovic (1989) provides an in-depth examination with an exhaustive catalog of Montaigne's borrowings from Plutarch; see also Edelman (2019), Mack (2016), and the entry on Plutarch in Desan (2007). Important studies of Plutarch's influence on the development of different genres can be found in Lavoine (1986) and Eichel-Lojkine (2001). On Plutarch's presence in French culture up to the mid-nineteenth century, see further Guerrier (2012); Frazier (2014b); Manzini (2019).

---

[109] Roux (1986: 312).     [110] Carrington (1988: 152).

# Bibliography

Aalders, G. J. D. (1977) "Political thought in Plutarch's *Convivium Septum Sapientium*", *Mnemosyne* 30: 28–39.

(1982) *Plutarch's Political Thought*. Amsterdam.

Adam, J. (ed.) (1905) *The Republic of Plato. Vol. I.* Cambridge.

Affortunati, M. and B. Scardigli (1992) "La vita 'plutarchea' di Annibale: Un'imitazione di Donato Acciaiuoli", *A&R* 37: 88–105.

Afzelius, A. (1941) "Die politische Bedeutung des jüngeren Catos", *C&M* 4: 100–203.

Aguilar, R. and I. Alfageme (eds.) (2006) *Ecos de Plutarco en Europa: de fortuna Plutarchi studia selecta.* Madrid.

Aguilar Perdomo, M. (1999) "La utilización de la *Vidas paralelas* de Plutarco en el *Felixmarte de Hircania*: a propósito de su autor, Melchor de Ortega", *Thesaurus: Boletín del Instituto Caro y Cuervo* 54: 289–306.

Ahlrichs, B. (2005) *Prüfstein der Gemüter: Untersuchungen zu den ethischen Vorstellungen in den Parallelbiographien Plutarchs am Beispiel des Coriolan* [Beiträge zur Altertumswissenschaft 16]. Hildesheim.

Alcalde Martín, C. (1999) "Rasgos socráticos de la personalidad de Foción en la *Vida* de Plutarco", in Pérez Jiménez, García López, and Aguilar (1999), 159–172.

Alcock, S. (2002) *Archaeologies of the Greek Past: Landscapes, Monuments, and Memories.* Cambridge.

Alden, M. (2005) "Lions in paradise: lion similes in the *Iliad* and the lion cubs of *Il.*18.318–22", *CQ* 55: 335–342.

Alemán Illán, J. (2005) "Plutarco y Aristóteles en Francisco Cascales: Evolución del concepto de διάνοια en la teoría literaria del Humanismo", *Myrtia* 20: 255–264.

Alexander, P. (1940) "Secular biography at Byzantium", *Speculum* 15: 194–209.

Alexandridis, A., M. Wild, and L. Winkler-Horaček (eds.) (2008) *Mensch und Tier in der Antike: Grenzziehung und Grenzüberschreitung: Symposon vom 7. bis 9. April 2005 in Rostock.* Wiesbaden.

Alexiou, E. (1999) "Zur Darstellung der ὀργή in Plutarchs Bioi", *Philologus* 143.1: 101–113.

(2008) "*Eunoia* bei Plutarch: von den *Praecepta Gerendae Reipublicae* zu den *Viten*", in Nikolaidis (2008), 365–386.

(2010) "Plutarchs *Lysander* und *Alkibiades* als 'Syzygie'", *RhM* 153: 323–352.

Alikin, V. (2009) "The reading of texts at the Graeco-Roman symposium and in the Christian gathering", in Ribeiro Ferreira et al. (2009), 103–112.

Almagor, E. (2005) "Who is a barbarian? The barbarians in the ethnological and cultural taxonomies of Strabo", in D. Dueck, H. Lindsay, and S. Pothecary (eds.), *Strabo's Cultural Geography*. Cambridge, 42–55.

(2009) "A 'barbarian' symposium and the absence of philanthropia (*Artaxerxes* 15)", in Ribeiro Ferreira et al. (2009), 131–146.

(2009–10) "Characterization through animals: the case of Plutarch's *Artaxerxes*", *Ploutarchos* 7: 3–22.

(2013) "'But this belongs to another discussion': exploring the ethnographic digressions in Plutarch", in Almagor and Skinner (2013), 153–178.

(2014a) "*Aratus* and *Artaxerxes*", in Beck (2014a), 278–291.

(2014b) "Hold your horses: characterization through animals in Plutarch's *Artaxerxes*. Part II", *Ploutarchos* 11: 3–18.

(2016a) "Josephus and Greek imperial literature", in H. Chapman and Z. Rodgers (eds.), *A Companion to Josephus*. Malden, MA, 108–122.

(2016b) "Parallel narratives and possible worlds in Plutarch's *Life of Artaxerxes*", in De Temmerman and Demoen (2016), Cambridge, 65–79.

(2017a) "The empire brought back: Persianism in imperial Greek literature", in R. Strootman and M. Versluys (eds.), *Persianism in Antiquity*. Stuttgart, 327–343.

(2017b) "Plutarch and the Persians", *Electrum* 24: 123–168.

(2018) *Plutarch and the* Persica. Edinburgh.

(2019) "Echoes of the Persian Wars in the European Phase of the Roman-Syrian War (with an Emphasis on Plut., *Cat. Mai.* 12–14)", in A. A. Coşkun and D. Engels (eds.), *Rome and the Seleukid East: Selected Papers from Seleukid Study Day V, Brussels, 21–23 August 2015*. Brussels, 87–133.

(2022) "When Hermes enters: towards a typology of the silences of Plutarch's narrator and their uses in characterization", in J. Beneker, C. Cooper, N. Humble, and F. B. Titchener (eds.), *Plutarch's Unexpected Silences: Suppression and Selection in the Lives and Moralia*. Leiden, 11–35.

(2023), "Plutarch's parallelism and resistance", in D. Jolowicz and J. Elsner (eds.), *Articulating Resistance under the Roman Empire*, Cambridge, 89–111.

Almagor, E. and J. Skinner (eds.) (2013) *Ancient Ethnography: New Approaches*. London.

Alston, R. (1996) "Conquest by text: Juvenal and Plutarch on Egypt", in J. Webster and N. Cooper (eds.), *Roman Imperialism: Post-Colonial Perspectives*. Leicester, 99–109.

Álvarez Rodríguez, A. (1983) "Las 'vidas de hombres ilustres' (Nos. 70–72 de la Bibl. Nac. de París), edición y estudio", Colección Tesis doctorales; n. 107/83, Departamento de Filología Románica, Facultad de Filología, Universidad Complutense de Madrid.

(1984) "Plutarco romanceado en el siglo XIV: suerte e importancia de la traducción aragonesa", *Cuadernos de Filología* 4: 143–158.

(1985) "Los helenismos en las traducciones de Juan Fernández de Heredia", *Cuadernos de Filología* 5: 99–110.

(ed.) (2009) *Plutarco de Queronea: Vidas semblantes. Versión aragonesa de las Vidas paralelas, patrocinada por Juan Fernández de Heredia.* Vols. I–II. Zaragoza.

Amyot, J. (1559) *Plutarque: les vies des hommes illustres.* 2 vols. Paris.

(1565) *Les vies des hommes illustres, Grecs et Romans, comparées l'une avec l'autre par Plutarque de Cheronee.* Paris.

(1572) *Plutarque oeuvres morales et meslees.* 2 vols. Paris.

Anastos, M. (1949) Review of Westerink (1948) *Speculum* 24: 446–450.

Anderson, G. (1976) *Lucian: Theme and Variation in the Second Sophistic.* Leiden.

(1989) "The *Pepaideumenos* in action: Sophists and their outlook in the early Roman Empire", *ANRW* II.33.1: 79–208.

(1993) *The Second Sophistic: A Cultural Phenomenon in the Roman Empire.* London.

Andrei, O. (1989) "Introduzione", in O. Andrei and R. Scuderi (eds.), *Plutarco: vite parallele, Demetrio – Antonio.* Milan, 35–93.

Arco Magrí, M. (1991) "Una pagina de Metochite sul Περὶ Ὁμήρου di Plutarco", in D'Ippolito and Gallo (1991), 461–473.

Armstrong, A. (1948) "Anacharsis the Scythian", *G&R* 17: 18–23.

Ash, R. (1997) "Severed heads: individual portraits and irrational forces in Plutarch's *Galba* and *Otho*", in Mossman (1997a), 189–214.

(2008) "Standing in the shadows: Plutarch and the emperors in the *Lives* and *Moralia*", in Nikolaidis (2008), 557–575.

Ash, R., J. Mossman, and F. B. Titchener (eds.) (2015) *Fame and Infamy: Essays for Christopher Pelling on Characterization in Greek and Roman Biography and History.* Oxford.

Asirvatham, S. (2005) "Classicism and *Romanitas* in Plutarch's *De Alexandri Fortuna Aut Virtute*", *AJPh* 126: 107–125.

Astin, A. E. (1978) *Cato the Censor.* Oxford.

Aulotte, R. (1965) *Amyot et Plutarque: La tradition des Moralia au XVI^e siècle.* Geneva.

Auzépy, M. (2008) "State of emergency (700–850)", in Shepard (2008), 251–291.

Averintsev, S. (2002) "From biography to hagiography", in French and St Clair (2002), 19–36.

Babbitt, F. (ed. and trans.) (1927) *Plutarch's Moralia: Vol. I.* Cambridge.

Babut, D. (1963) "Les Stoïciens et l'amour", *REG* 76: 55–63.

(ed.) (1969a) *Plutarque, De la vertu éthique.* Paris.

(1969b) *Plutarque et le stoïcisme.* Paris.

(1984) "Le dialogue de Plutarque sur le démon de Socrate: essai d'interpretation", *BAGB* 1: 51–76. Reprinted in Babut (1994), 405–430.

(1992) "La composition des *Dialogues Pythiques* de Plutarque et le problème de leur unité", *Journal des Savants* 2: 187–234. Reprinted in Babut (1994), 457–504.

(1994) *Parerga: choix d'articles de Daniel Babut.* Lyon.

Baker, P. (ed.) (2017) *Biography, Historiography, and Modes of Philosophizing: The Tradition of Collective Biography in Early Modern Europe.* Leiden.

Baker, P., R. Kaiser, M. Priesterjahn, and J. Helmrath (eds.) (2016) *Portraying the Prince in the Renaissance: The Humanist Depiction of Rulers in Historiographical and Biographical Texts*. Berlin.

Bakker, E. J. (ed.) (2010), A *Companion to the Ancient Greek Language*. Malden, MA.

Bakhtin, M. (1981) *The Dialogic Imagination: Four Essays*, ed. M. Holquist. Trans. C. Emerson, and M. Holquist. Austin, TX.

Balard, M. (ed.) (1986) *Fortunes de Jacques Amyot: actes du colloque international*. Paris.

Baldassari, M. (2000) "Osservazioni sulla struttura del period e sulla costruzione ritmica del discorso nei Moralia di Plutarco", in Van der Stockt (2000b), 1–13.

Baldassarri, S. and R. Begemihl (eds.) (2003) *G. Manetti: Biographical Writings*. Cambridge, MA.

Baldwin, B. (1995) "Plutarch in Byzantium", *Byzantion* 65: 525–526.

Baltes, M. (2000) "La dottrina dell'anima in Plutarco", *Elenchos* 21: 245–270.

(2005a) "Mittelplatonische ἐπιτομαί zu den Werken und der Philosophie Platons", in Baltes (2005c), 155–169.

(2005b) "Plutarchs Lehre von der Seele", in Baltes (2005c), 77–99.

(2005c), *ΕΠΙΝΟΗΜΑΤΑ: Kleine Schriften zur antiken Philosophie und homerischen Dichtung von Matthias Baltes*, ed. M.-L. Lakmann. Munich.

Banta, J. (2006) *Imperium cum finibus: Plutarch's Archaic Rome*. Diss., State University of New York at Buffalo.

(2007a) "Who gives a fig (tree a name)? Chronotopic conflicts in Plutarch's *Romulus*", *Intertexts* 11: 25–41.

(2007b) "The Gates of Janus: Bakhtin and Plutarch's Roman *meta-chronotope*", in Larmour and Spencer (2007), 238–270.

Baragwanath, E. (2008) *Motivation and Narrative in Herodotus*. Oxford.

Barchiesi, A. (2000) "The crossing", in S. Harrison (ed.), *Texts, Ideas, and the Classics*. Oxford, 142–163.

Barigazzi, A. (1984) "Plutarco e il corso futuro della storia", *Prometheus* 10: 264–286. Reprinted in Barigazzi (1994), 303–330.

(ed.) (1993) *Plutarco. Se la virtù si debba insegnare (La fortuna, Se la virtù si possa insegnare). Se siano più gravi le malattie dell'animo o del corpo, Se il vizio sia sufficiente a rendere infelici, La virtù e il vizio (CPM 17)*. Naples.

(1994) *Studi su Plutarco*. Florence.

Barnwell, H. (ed.) (1965) *Pierre Corneille: Writings on the Theatre*. Oxford.

Baron, H. (1928) *Leonardo Bruni Aretino: Humanistisch-Philosophische Schriften; mit einer Chronologie seiner Werke und Briefe*. Leipzig.

(1955) *Humanistic and Political Literature in Florence and Venice at the Beginning of the Quattrocento. Studies in Criticism and Chronology*. Cambridge.

(1966) *The Crisis of the Early Italian Renaissance*. Cambridge.

Barroll, J. (1958) "Shakespeare and Roman history", *Modern Language Review* 53: 327–343.

Barrow, R. (1967) *Plutarch and His Times*. London.

Barzanò, A., C. Bearzot, F. Landucci, L. Prandi, and G. Zecchini (eds.) (2003) *Modelli eroici dall'Antichità alla cultura Europea.* Rome.

Bauman, R. (2007) "The emergent quality of performance", in Monaghan and Goodman (2007), 35–37.

Bazzani, M. (2006) "Theodore Metochites, a Byzantine humanist", *Byzantion* 76: 32–52.

Bearzot, C. (ed.) (1993) *Plutarco vite parallele: Focione* (introduzione, traduzione e note di Cinzia Bearzot), *Catone Uticense* (introduzione di Joseph Geiger, traduzione e note di Lucia Ghilli). Milan.

Becchi, F. (1975) "Aristotelismo ed antistoicismo nel 'De virtute morali' di Plutarco", *Prometheus* 1: 160–180.

(1978) "Aristotelismo funzionale nel 'De virtute morali' di Plutarco", *Prometheus* 4: 261–275.

(1981) "Platonismo medio ed etica plutarchea", *Prometheus* 7: 125–145.

(1990a) "La nozione di ὀργή e di ἀοργησία in Aristotele e in Plutarco", *Prometheus* 16: 65–87.

(ed.) (1990b) *Plutarco: la virtù etica. Introduzione, testo critico, traduzione e commento (CPM 5).* Naples.

(1993) "Istinto e intelligenza negli scritti zoopsicologici di Plutarco", in M. Bandini and F. Pericoli (eds.), *Scritti in memoria di Dino Pieraccioni.* Florence, 59–83.

(1999) "Plutarco tra platonismo ed aristotelismo: la filosofia come *paideia* dell'anima", in Pérez Jiménez, García López, and Aguilar (1999), 25–43.

(2000) "Irrazionalità e razionalità degli animali negli scritti di Plutarco", *Prometheus* 26: 205–225.

(2001) "Biopsicologia e giustizia verso gli animali in Teofrasto e Plutarco", *Prometheus* 27: 119–135.

(2005) "Éthique et régime alimentaire dans les écrits plutarquiens de psychologie animale", in Boulogne (2005b), 145–156.

(2007) "Para una interpretación unitaria de la doctrina del eros en Plutarco", in Nieto Ibáñez and López López (2007), 95–103.

(2009a) "La notion de *philanthropia* chez Plutarque: contexte social et sources philosophiques", in Ribeiro Ferreira et al. (2009), 263–273.

(2009b) "Le traduzioni latine dei *Moralia* di Plutarco tra XIII e XVI secolo", in Volpe Cacciatore (2009), 11–52.

(2014) "Plutarch, Aristotle, and the Peripatetics", in Beck (2014a), 73–87.

(2019) "Humanist Latin translations of the *Moralia*", in Xenophontos and Oikonomopoulou (2019), 458–478.

Beck, H. (2002) "Interne *synkrisis* bei Plutarch", *Hermes* 130: 467–489.

(2003) "Parallele Karrieren – *Parallele Leben*? Plutarchs *Fabius Maximus* und *Marcellus*", in Barzanò et al. (2003), 239–263.

Beck, M. (1998) *Plutarch's Use of Anecdotes in the Lives.* Diss., University of North Carolina at Chapel Hill.

(2000) "Anecdote and the representation of Plutarch's ethos", in Van der Stockt (2000b), 15–32.

(2002) "Plutarch to Trajan: the dedicatory letter and the *Apophthegmata* collection", in Stadter and Van der Stockt (2002), 163–173.

(2004) "Plutarch on the statesman's independence of action", in de Blois et al. (2004), 105–114.

(2005) "The presentation of ideology and the use of subliterary forms in Plutarch's works", in Pérez Jiménez and Titchener (2005), 51–68.

(2007a) "Plutarch", in I. J. F. de Jong and R. Nünlist (eds.) *Time in Ancient Greek Narratives: Studies in Ancient Greek Narrative. Vol. II*. Leiden, 397–411.

(2007b) "The story of Damon and the ideology of euergetism in the *Lives* of Cimon and Lucullus", *Hermathena* 182: 53–69.

(2009) "*Cena apud Catones*: ideology and sympotic behavior", in Ribeiro Ferreira et al. (2009), 147–163.

(2010) "Plutarch's *hypomnemata*", in Horster and Reitz (2010), 349–367.

(2012) "Plutarch", in I. J. F. de Jong (ed.) *Space in Ancient Greek Literature: Studies in Ancient Greek Narrative. Vol. III*. Leiden, 441–462.

(2013) "Alexander for the Romans: the ideology of anger control in Plutarch and Arrian", in Pace and Volpe Cassiatore (2013), 47–61.

(ed.) (2014a) *A Companion to Plutarch*. Chichester.

(2014b) "The Socratic paradigm", in Beck (2014a), 463–478.

(2016) "The serio-comic *Life of Antony*", in Opsomer, Roskam, and Titchener (2016), 137–146.

Beier, A. (1985) *Masterless Men: The Vagrancy Problem in England, 1560–1640*. London.

Bekker, I. (ed.) (1838) *Theophanes Continuatus*. Bonn.

Belfiore, E. (1986) "Wine and catharsis of the emotions in Plato's *Laws*", *CQ* 36: 421–437.

Bellanti, A. (2003) "Aristotele pitagorico? La concezione della medietà nel *De virtute morali* di Plutarco", *RFN* 95: 3–36.

Beneker, J. (2005) "Thematic correspondence in Plutarch's *Lives* of Caesar, Pompey, and Crassus", in de Blois et al. (2005), 315–325.

(2009) "Drunken violence and the transition of power in Plutarch's *Alexander*", in Ribeiro Ferreira et al. (2009), 193–200.

(2011) "Plutarch and Saint Basil as readers of Greek literature", *SyllClass* 22: 95–111.

(2012) *The Passionate Statesman: Eros and Politics in Plutarch's Lives*. Oxford.

(2014) "Sex, eroticism, and politics", in Beck (2014a), 503–515.

Bergua Cavero, J. (1991) "Cinismo, ironía y retórica en el *Bruta ratione uti* de Plutarco", in García López and Calderón Dorda (1991), 13–19.

(1995) *Estudios sobre la tradición de Plutarco en España (siglos XIII–XVII)*. Zaragoza.

Bers, V. (2010) "*Kunstprosa*: philosophy, history, oratory," in Bakker (2010), 455–467.

Berschin, W. (1983a) "Sueton und Plutarch im 14. Jahrhundert", in A. Buck (ed.), *Biographie und Autobiographie in der Renaissance*. Wiesbaden, 35–43.

(ed.) (1983b) *Biographie zwischen Renaissance und Barock*. Heidelberg.

Berthelot, K. (2002) "Philo and kindness towards animals (*De virtutibus* 125–147)", *The Studia Philonica Annual* 14: 49–65.

Besterman, T. (1926) "Bibliography of Cleopatra", *Notes Queries* 150.6: 93–97, 111–114.

Beta, S. (2009) "Riddling at table: trivial *ainigmata* vs. philosophical *problemata*", in Ribeiro Ferreira et al. (2009), 97–102.

Bettini, M. and C. Franco (2009) "La notion de *philanthrōpia* chez Plutarque: contexte social et sources philosophiques", in Ribeiro Ferreira et al. (2009), 263–273.

(2010) *Il mito di Circe: Immagini e racconti dalla Grecia a oggi*. Turin.

Betz, H.-D. (ed.) (1978) *Plutarch's Ethical Writings and Early Christian Literature*. Leiden.

Bevegni, C. (1993) "Teodoro Gaza traduttore del 'Maxime cum principibus philosopho esse disserendum' di Plutarco: primi appunti per un'edizione critica con particolare riguardo alla lettera dedicatoria ad Andrea Bussi", in S. Feraboli (ed.), *Mosaico: Studi in onore di Umberto Albini*. Genova, 33–42.

Billault, A. (2005) "Le modèle animal dans le traité de Plutarque", in Boulogne (2005b), 33–42.

Biraud, M. (2014) "Usages narratifs des clausules métriques et des égalités syllabiques dans *l'Eroticos* de Plutarque", *Ploutarchos* 11: 39–55.

Blackwell, C. (1986) "Humanism and politics in English royal biography: the use of Cicero, Plutarch, and Sallust in the 'Vita Henrici Quinti' (1438) by Titus Livius de Frulovisi and the 'Vita Henrici Septimi' (1500–1503) by Bernard André", in I. McFarlane (ed.), *Acta Conventus Neo-Latini Sanctandreani: Proceedings of the Fifth International Congress of Neo-Latin Studies*. Binghamton, NY, 431–440.

Blamire, A. (ed.) (1989) *Plutarch, Life of Kimon*. London.

Blomqvist, K. (1997) "From Olympias to Aretaphila: women in politics in Plutarch", in Mossman (1997a), 73–97.

Bloom, A., (ed.) (1991) *The Republic of Plato*, 2nd ed. New York.

Blunt, A. (1995) *Poussin*. London.

Boas, F. (ed.) (1911) *Caesar's Revenge by Anon. (1611)*. Oxford.

Bodin, J. (1969) *Methodus ad facilem historiarum cognitionem*. Trans. B. Reynolds. New York.

Boissonade, J. F. (ed.) (1964) *Michael Psellus: De operatione daemonum*. Amsterdam.

Bonazzi, M. (2003) *Academici e Platonici: Il dibattito antico sullo scetticismo di Platone*. Milan.

(2007) "Plutarco, l'Academia e la politica", in Volpe Cacciatore and Ferrari (2007), 265–280.

(2009) "Antiochus' ethics and the subordination of Stoicism", in Bonazzi and Opsomer (2009), 33–54.

(2016) "The perfidious strategies, or, the Platonists against Stoicism", in Weisser and Thaler (2016), 166–184.

Bonazzi, M. and J. Opsomer (2009) *The Origins of the Platonic System: Platonisms of the Early Empire and Their Philosophical Contexts* (Collection d'études classiques, 23). Louvain.

Bosworth, A. (1988) *From Arrian to Alexander: Studies in Historical Interpretation.* Oxford.

  (1992) "History and artifice in Plutarch's *Eumenes*", in Stadter (1992b), 56–89.

Boulanger, A. (1923) *Aelius Aristide.* Paris.

Boulet, B. (2005) "Is Numa the genuine philosopher king?" in de Blois et al. (2005), 245–256.

  (2014) "The philosopher king", in Beck (2014a), 449–462.

Boulogne, J. (1992) "Les 'Questions Romaines' de Plutarque", *ANRW* II.33.6: 4682–4708.

  (1994) *Plutarque: Un aristocrate grec sous l'occupation romaine.* Villeneuve d'Ascq.

  (1996) "Plutarque et la Médecine", *ANRW* II.37.3: 2762–2792.

  (2000) "Les ΣΥΓΚΡΙΣΕΙΣ de Plutarque: Une rhétorique de la ΣΥΝΚΡΑΣΙΣ", in Van der Stockt (2000b), 33–44.

  (2003) *Plutarque dans le miroir d'Épicure.* Villeneuve d'Ascq.

  (2005a) "Le culte égyptien des animaux vu par Plutarque: Une étiologie égyptienne (*Isis et Osiris*, 71–76, 379D–382 C)", in Boulogne (2005b), 197–205.

  (ed.) (2005b) *Les Grecs de l'antiquité et les animaux: Le cas remarquable de Plutarque.* Villeneuve d'Ascq.

  (2009–10) "La philosophie du mariage chez Plutarque", *Ploutarchos* 7: 23–34.

Bovon, A. (1963) "La représentation des guerriers perses et la notion de barbare dans la première moitié du cinquième siècle", *BCH* 87: 579–602.

Bowen, A. (ed.) (1992) *Plutarch: The Malice of Herodotus (de Malignitate Herodoti).* Warminster.

Bowersock, G. W. (1969) *Greek Sophists and the Roman Empire.* Oxford.

  (1995) "The barbarism of the Greeks," *HSCPh* 97: 3–14.

Bowersock, G. W. and C. P. Jones (1974) "A guide to the sophists in Philostratus' *Vitae Sophistarum*", in G. W. Bowersock (ed.), *Approaches to the Second Sophistic.* University Park, PA, 35–40.

Bowie, A. (2003) "'Fate may harm me, I have dined today': near-eastern royal banquets and Greek symposia in Herodotus", *Pallas* 61: 99–109.

Bowie, E. (1970) "Greeks and their past in the Second Sophistic", *P&P* 46: 3–41. Reprinted in M. Finley (ed.) (1974) *Studies in Ancient Society.* London, 166–209.

  (1986) "Early Greek elegy, symposium and public festival", *JHS* 106: 13–35.

  (1993) "Greek table-talk before Plato", *Rhetorica* 11.4: 355–373.

  (2008) "Plutarch's habits of citation: aspects of difference", in Nikolaidis (2008), 143–157.

  (2014) "Poetry and education", in Beck (2014a), 177–190.

Boys-Stones, G. (1997) "Thyrsus-bearer of the academy or enthusiast for Plato?" in Mossman (1997a), 41–58.

(1998) "Plutarch on *koinos logos*: towards an architecture of the *De Stoicorum Repugnantiis*", *OSAPh* 16: 299–329.

(2001) *Post-Hellenistic Philosophy: A Study of Its Development from the Stoics to Origen*. Oxford.

(2018) *Platonist Philosophy 80 BC to AD 250: An Introduction and Collection of Sources in Translation*. Cambridge.

(2019) "Difference, opposition, and the roots of intolerance in ancient philosophical polemic", in G. H. van Kooten and J. van Ruiten (eds.), *Intolerance, Polemics, and Debate in Antiquity: Politico-Cultural, Philosophical, and Religious Forms of Critical Conversation*. Leiden, 259–281.

Boys-Stones, G., B. Graziosi, and P. Vasunia (eds.) (2009) *Oxford Companion of Hellenic Studies*. Oxford.

Braden, G. (2004) "Plutarch, Shakespeare, and the alpha males", in Martindale (2004), 188–205.

(2014) "Shakespeare", in Beck (2014a), 577–591.

Bradley, K. (2000), "Animalizing the slave: the truth of fiction", *JRS* 90: 110–125.

Branham, R. Bracht (1989) *Unruly Eloquence: Lucian and the Comedy of Traditions*. Cambridge, MA.

(1996) "Defacing the currency: Diogenes' rhetoric and the invention of Cynicism", in Branham and Goulet-Cazé (1996), 81–104.

Branham, R. Bracht and M.-O. Goulet-Cazé (eds.) (1996) *The Cynics: The Cynic Movement in Antiquity and Its Legacy*. Berkeley, CA.

Braund, D. (1993) "Dionysiac tragedy in Plutarch's *Crassus*", *CQ* 43: 468–474.

Braund, D. and J. Wilkins (eds.) (2000) *Athenaeus and His World: Reading Greek Culture in the Roman Empire*. Exeter.

Bréchet, C. (2003) "Les *palaioi* chez Plutarque", in B. Bakhouche (ed.), *L'Ancienneté chez les anciens, vol. II: Mythologie et Religion*. Montpellier, 519–550.

(2005) "La Philosophie de Gryllos", in Boulogne (2005b), 43–62.

(2007) "Vers une philosophie de la citation poétique: écrit, oral et mémoire chez Plutarque", *Hermathena* 182: 101–134.

Brélaz, C. (2008) "L'adieu aux armes. La défense de la cité grecque dans l'Empire romain pacifié", in C. Brélaz and P. Ducrey (eds.), *Sécurité collective et ordre public dans les sociétés anciennes*. Geneva, 155–196.

Bremer, J. (2005) "Plutarch and the 'liberation of Greece'", in de Blois et al. (2005), 257–267.

Brenk, F. (1977) *In Mist Apparelled: Religious Themes in Plutarch's Moralia and Lives*. Leiden.

(1986) "In the light of the moon: demonology in the early imperial period", *ANRW* II.16.3: 2068–2145.

(1987) "An imperial heritage: the religious spirit of Plutarch of Chaironeia", *ANRW* II.36.1: 248–349.

(1992) "Plutarch's life 'Markos Antonios:' a literary and cultural study", *ANRW* II.33.6: 4347–4402.

(1996) "Time as structure in Plutarch's *The Daimonion of Sokrates*", in Van der Stockt (1996), 29–51. Reprinted in Brenk (1998), 59–81.

(1998) *Relighting the Souls: Studies in Plutarch, in Greek Literature, Religion, and Philosophy and in the New Testament Background.* Stuttgart.

(2000) "All for love: the rhetoric of exaggeration in Plutarch's *Erotikos*", in Van der Stockt (2000b), 45–60.

(2002) "Religion under Trajan: Plutarch's resurrection of Osiris", in Stadter and Van der Stockt (2002), 73–92.

(2005) "The barbarian within: Gallic and Galatian heroines in Plutarch's *Erotikos*", in Pérez Jiménez and Titchener (2005), 93–106.

(2007) *With Unperfumed Voice: Studies in Plutarch, in Greek Literature, Religion and Philosophy, and in the New Testament Background.* Stuttgart.

(2009) "In learned conversation: Plutarch's symposiac literature and the elusive authorial voice", in Ribeiro Ferreira et al. (2009), 51–61.

Brennan, T. (1998) "The old Stoic theory of emotions", in J. Sihvola and T. Engberg-Pedersen (eds.), *Emotions in Hellenistic Philosophy.* Dordrecht, 21–70.

(2003) "Stoic moral psychology", in Inwood (2003), 257–294.

Briant, P. (2002a) *From Cyrus to Alexander: A History of the Persian Empire.* Trans. P. T. Daniels. Winona Lake, IN.

(2002b) "History and ideology: the Greeks and 'Persian decadence'", in Harrison (2002), 193–210.

Brisson, L. (1997) "Le corps animal comme signe de la valeur d'une âme chez Platon", in Cassin and Labarrière (1997), 227–245.

Brittain, C. (2001) *Philo of Larissa: The Last of the Academic Sceptics.* Oxford.

Brouillette, X. (2014) *La Philosophie delphique de Plutarque. L'itinéraire des Dialogues pythiques.* Paris.

Brouillette, X. and A. Giavatto (eds.) (2011) *Les dialogues platoniciens chez Plutarque: Stratégies et méthodes exégétiques.* Leuven.

Brown, A. (1992) *The Medici in Power: The Exercise and Language of Power.* Florence.

Browning, R. (1975) "Enlightenment and repression in Byzantium in the eleventh and twelfth centuries", *P&P* 69: 3–23.

Brubaker, L. and J. Haldon (2011) *Byzantium in the Iconoclast Era c. 680–850: A History.* Cambridge.

Bryson, N. (1981) *Word and Image: French Painting of the Ancien Régime.* Cambridge.

Bucher-Isler, B. (1972) *Norm und Individualität in den Biographien Plutarchs.* Bern.

Buckler, G. (1929) *Anna Comnena: A Study.* Oxford.

Buckler, J. (1992) "Plutarch and autopsy", *ANRW* II.33.6: 4788–4830.

Bullock, A. (1991) *Hitler and Stalin: Parallel Lives.* New York.

Bullough, G. (ed.) (1957–79) *Narrative and Dramatic Sources of Shakespeare* (8 vols.). London.

Burgess, S. (2008) "Plato's *Timaeus* on clever and non-clever creatures", in Alexandridis, Wild, and Winkler-Horaček (2008), 13–26.

Burkert, W. (1996) "Plutarco: Religiosità personale e teologia filosofica", in Gallo (1996), 11–28.

Burns, A. (2015) *Diatribe and Plutarch's Practical Ethics*. Diss., University of Iowa.

Burns, J. M. (1978) *Leadership*. New York.

Burridge, R. (2004) *What Are the Gospels? A Comparison with Graeco-Roman Biography*, 2nd ed. Ann Arbor, MI.

Burrow, C. (2013) *Shakespeare and Classical Antiquity*. Oxford.

Busine, A. (2002) *Les sept sages de la Grèce antique: Transmission et utilisation d'un patrimone légendaire d'Hérodote à Plutarque*. Paris.

Buszard, B. (2005a) "The decline of the Roman republic in *Pyrrhus–Marius*", in de Blois et al. (2005), 281–296.

(2005b) "The decline of Roman statesmanship in Plutarch's *Pyrrhus–Marius*", *CQ* 55: 481–497.

(2008) "Caesar's ambition: a combined reading of Plutarch's *Alexander–Caesar* and *Pyrrhus–Marius*", *TAPhA* 138: 185–215.

(2010) "The speech of Greek and Roman women in Plutarch's *Lives*", *CPh* 105: 83–115.

Bydén, B. (2002) "The nature and purpose of the *Semeioseis gnomikai*: the antithesis of philosophy and rhetoric", in Hult (2002), 245–288.

Byl, S. (1977) "Plutarque et la vieillesse", *LEC* 45: 107–123.

Caballos Rufino, A. (1990) *Los senadores hispanorromanos y la romanización de Hispania (Sigla I al III p.C). I: Prosopograifia* (Monografías del Departamento de Historia Antigua de la Universidad de Sevilla). Écija.

Cacciari, A. (1995) "Plutarco", in U. Mattioli (ed.), *Senectus: La vecchiaia nel mondo classico. Vol. I: Grecia*. Bologna, 361–395.

Caiazza, A. (ed.) (1993) *Precetti politici* (*CPM* 14). Naples.

Calder, L. (2011) *Cruelty and Sentimentality: Greek Attitudes to Animals, 600–300 BC*. Oxford.

(2017) "Pet and image in the Greek world: the use of domesticated animals in human interaction", in Fögen and Thomas (2017), 61–83.

Calderón Dorda, E. (1999) "El vino, la medicina y los 'remedia ebrietatis' en los *Moralia* de Plutarco", in Montes Cala et al. (1999), 119–128.

Calkins, G. (ed.) (1943) *Antoine de Montchrestien: Les Lacènes*. Philadelphia, PA.

Cameron, A. (2006) *The Byzantines*. Chichester.

Cameron, A., J. Herrin, A. Cameron, R. Cormack, and C. Roueché (eds.) (1984) *Constantinople in the Early Eighth Century: The Parastaseis Syntomoi Chronikai*. New York.

Cammelli, G. (1941) "Manuele Crisolora", in *I dotti bizantini e le origini dell'umanesimo: Vol. I*. Florence.

Campangne, H.-T. (2012) "Poétique de l'instant tragique: la place et l'influence des *Vies* de Plutarque dans la définition du tragique en France, 1600–1645", in Guerrier (2012), 55–68.

Campbell, G. (ed.) (2014) *The Oxford Handbook of Animals in Classical Thought and Life*. Oxford.

Canart, P. (1978) "Le livre grec en Italie méridionale sous les règnes Normand et Souabe: aspects matériels et sociaux", *Scrittura e civilta* 2: 103–162.

(1982) "La collection hagiographique palimpseste du Palatinus Graecus 205 et la passion de S. Georges BHG 670 g", *AB* 100: 87–109.

Candau Morón, J., F. González Ponce, and A. Chávez Reino (eds.) (2011) *Plutarco Transmisor*. Seville.

Cannatà Fera, M. (1994) "Plutarco e la *Consolatio ad Apollonium*", *AncW* 25: 171–189.

Cantor, P. (1997) "Shakespeare's *Parallel Lives*: Plutarch and the Roman plays", in McGrail (1997), 69–82.

Carrara, P. (1988) "Plutarco ed Euripide: alcune considerazioni sulle citazioni euripidee in Plutarco (*De aud. poet.*)", *ICS* 13: 447–455.

Carrière, J. C. (1977) "A propos de la *Politique* de Plutarque", *DHA* 3: 237–251.

(ed.) (1984) *Plutarque: Oeuvres morales. Vol. XI.2*. Paris.

Carrington, D. (1988) *Napoleon and His Parents: On the Threshold of History*. London.

Cartledge, P. (1990) "Herodotus and 'the Other:' a meditation on empire", *EMC/CV* 9: 27–40.

(1993) *The Greeks*. Oxford.

Cartledge, P. and A. Spawforth (2001) *Hellenistic and Roman Sparta: A Tale of Two Cities*, 2nd ed. New York.

Casanova, A. (2005a) "Il Grillo di Plutarco e Omero", in Boulogne (2005b), 97–110.

(2005b) "The time setting of the dialogue *Bruta animalia ratione uti*", in Pérez Jiménez and Titchener (2005), 121–132.

(2006–7) "Il *Grillo* di Plutarco e la tradizione della figura di Ulisse", *Ploutarchos* 4: 19–28.

(2012) "La giustizia nel *Grillo* e la conclusione del dialogo", in Ribeiro Ferreira, Leão, and Martins de Jesus (2012), 181–189.

(ed.) (2013) *Figure d'Atene nelle opere di Plutarco*. Florence.

Cassin, B. and J.-L. Labarrière (eds.) (1997) *L'animal dans l'antiquité*. Paris.

Castelnérac, B. (2007) "The method of 'eclecticism' in Plutarch and Seneca", *Hermathena* 182: 135–163.

Catanzaro, A. (2013) "Plutarch at Byzantium in XII century: Niketa Choniates and Plutarchean political *areté* in the *Chronikè Diéghesis*", in Pace and Volpe Cacciatore (2013), 111–117.

Cavallo, G. (1980) "La trasmissione scritta della cultura greca antica in Calabria e in Sicilia tra I secoli X–XV", *Scrittura e civilta* 4: 157–245.

(ed.) (1982) *Libri e lettori nel mondo Bizantino: Guida storica e critica*. Rome.

Cazals, R. (2001) "Plutarque a-t-il menti?" in S. Caucanas, R. Cazals, and P. Payen (eds.), *Retrouver, imaginer, utiliser l'Antiquité*. Toulouse, 141–146.

Champion, C. (2000) "Romans as ΒΑΡΒΑΡΟΙ: three Polybian speeches and the politics of cultural indeterminacy", *CPh* 95: 425–444.

Chandezon, C. (2005) *Plutarque en sa terre*. Diss., Sorbonne University.

Chaniotis, A. (2010) "Illusions of democracy in the Hellenistic world", *Athens Dialogues*, November.

Chantraine, P. (1980) *Dictionnaire étymologique de la langue grecque. Vol. IV.2.* Paris.

Chapman, A. (2011) *The Female Principle in Plutarch's Moralia.* Dublin.

Cherchi, P. (1993) "Plutarch's letter in Mexia's *Silva*", *Modern Philology* 91: 54–59.

Chernaik, W. (2011) *The Myth of Rome in Shakespeare and His Contemporaries.* Cambridge.

Cherniss, H. (1954) "The sources of evil according to Plato", *PAPhS* 98: 23–30.

    (ed. and trans.) (1976a) *Plutarch's Moralia. Vol. XIII.1. 999C–1032F.* Cambridge, MA.

    (ed. and trans.) (1976b) *Plutarch's Moralia. Vol. XIII.2. 1033A–1086B.* Cambridge, MA.

Cherniss, H. and W. C. Helmbold (eds. and trans.) (1957), *Plutarch's Moralia. Vol. XII. 920A–999B.* Cambridge MA.

Chlup, J. (2009) "Crassus as symposiast in Plutarch's *Life of Crassus*", in Ribeiro Ferreira et al. (2009), 181–190.

Chrysanthou, C. (2017) "The proems of Plutarch's *Lives* and historiography", *Histos* 11: 128–153.

    (2018) *Plutarch's Parallel Lives: Narrative Technique and Moral Judgement.* Berlin.

    (2020) "Plutarch and the 'malicious' historian", *ICS* 45: 49–79.

Clare, L. (1968) "La première traduction en Occident des *Vies Parallèles* de Plutarque", *BAGB* 27: 405–426.

Clare, L. and F. Jouan (1969) "La plus ancienne traduction occidentale des *Vies* de Plutarque", in *Actes VIIIe Congrès de l'Association G. Budé.* Paris, 567–569.

Clark, G. (2017) "Philosophers' pets: Porphyry's partridge and Augustine's dog", in Fögen and Thomas (2017), 139–157.

Clarke, D. (1994) "Plutarch's contribution to the invention of Sabine in Corneille's *Horace*", *The Modern Language Review* 89.1: 39–49.

Clayton, T. (1983) "'Should Brutus never taste of Portia's death but once?' Text and performance in *Julius Caesar*", *Studies in English Literature* 23: 237–255.

Colonnese, C. (2007) *Le scelte di Plutarco: le vite non scritte di greci illustri.* Rome.

Connolly, J. (2001) "Problems of the past in imperial Greek education", in Y. L. Too (ed.), *Education in Greek and Roman Antiquity.* Leiden, 339–372.

Connors, S. P. (ed.) (2014) *The Politics of Panem: Challenging Genres.* Rotterdam.

Conquergood, D. (2007) "Poetics, play, process, and power: the performative turn in anthropology", in Monaghan and Goodman (2007), 38–40.

Constantinidis, C. (1982) *Higher Education in Byzantium in the Thirteenth and Early Fourteenth Centuries: 1204–ca 1310.* Nicosia.

Cook, A. (1996) "The transmutation of heroic complexity: Plutarch and Shakespeare", *CML* 17: 31–43.

Cook, B. (2004) "Plutarch's 'many other' imitable events: *Mor.* 814b and the statesman's duty", in de Blois et al. (2004), 201–210.

Corneille, P. (1965) *Writings on the Theatre*, ed. H. Barnwell. Oxford.

Correia Martins, A. I. (2011) "O binomio felicitas vera & falsa nas sentencas de Plutarco no tratado de filosofia moral de Frei Luis de Granada", in Candau Morón et al. (2011), 533–544.

Coulobaritsis, L. (1986) "La psychologie chez Chrysippe", *Entretiens Hardt* 32: 99–142.

Craig, C. (1986) "Cicero's Stoicism and the understanding of Cicero's speech for Murena", *TAPhA* 116: 229–239.

Crawford, M. (1999) "*Amatorius*: Plutarch's Platonic departure from the *peri gamou* literature", in Pérez Jiménez, García López, and Aguilar (1999), 287–298.

Cuartero Sancho, M. (1981) *Fuentes clásicas de la literatura paremiológica española del siglo XVI*. Zaragoza.

Cuvigny, M. (1969) "Plutarque et Épictète", in *Association G. Budé: Actes du VIII^e Congrès (5–10 mai 1968)*. Paris, 565–566.

Dalby, A. (2000) *Empire of Pleasures: Luxury and Indulgence in the Roman World*. London.

D'Aubigné, A. (1995) *Les Tragiques*, ed. J.-R. Fanlo, 2 vols. Paris.

Dauge, Y. A. (1981) *Le barbare: Recherches sur la conception romaine de la barbarie et de la civilisation*. Brussels.

David-de Palacio, M.-F. (2012) "'L'Anti-Plutarque': variations Germanique, Américaine et Française entre 1860 et 1925", in Guerrier (2012), 319–335.

Davies, P. and J. Mossman (eds.) (forthcoming in 2023) *Plutarch and Sparta*. Swansea.

de Blois, L. (1992) "The perception of politics in Plutarch's Roman *Lives*", *ANRW* II.33.6: 4568–4615.

de Blois, L., J. Bons, T. Kessels, and D. Schenkeveld (eds.) (2004) *The Statesman in Plutarch's Works. Vol. I: Plutarch's Statesman and His Aftermath: Political, Philosophical, and Literary Aspects*. Leiden.

(2005) *The Statesman in Plutarch's Works. Vol. II: The Statesman in Plutarch's Greek and Roman Lives*. Leiden.

de Fontenay, E. (1997) "La *philanthrôpia* à l'épreuve des bêtes", in Cassin and Labarrière (1997), 281–298.

de Jesus, C. (2009) "Dancing with Plutarch: dance and dance theory in Plutarch's *Table Talk*", in Ribeiro Ferreira et al. (2009), 403–414.

De Lacy, P. (1952) "Biography and tragedy in Plutarch", *AJPh* 73: 159–171.

de Lagarde, P. (ed.) (1882) *Iohannis Euchaitorum metropolitae quae in codice Vaticano graeco 676 supersunt*. Göttingen.

Delli, E. (2019) "The reception of Plutarch in Michael Psellos' philosophical, theological and rhetorical works: an elective affinity", in Xenophontos and Oikonomopoulou (2019), 205–233.

Dennett, D. (1996) *Kinds of Minds: Towards an Understanding of Consciousness*. London.

Denton, J. (1993) "Wearing a gown in the market place or a toga in the forum: Coriolanus from Plutarch to Shakespeare via renaissance translation", in G. Caliumi (ed.), *Shakespeare e la sua eredità*. Parma, 97–109.

(1997) "Plutarch, Shakespeare, Roman politics and Renaissance translation", in McGrail (1997), 187–210.

Depew, M. and D. Obbink (eds.) (2000) *Matrixes of Genre: Authors, Canons, and Society*. Cambridge, MA.

De Pourcq, M. and G. Roskam (2016) "Mirroring virtues in Plutarch's *Lives* of Agis, Cleomenes, and the Gracchi", in De Temmerman and Demoen (2016), 163–180.

de Romilly, J. (1979) *La douceur dans la pensée grecque*. Paris.

(1994–5) "Cruauté barbare et cruautés grecques", *WS* 107/108: 187–196.

Desan, P. (ed.) (2007) *Dictionnaire de Montaigne*. Paris.

Desideri, P. (1985) "Ricchezza e vita politica nel pensiero di Plutarco", *Index* 13: 391–405.

(1986) "La vita politica cittadina nell'impero: lettura dei *Praecepta gerendae rei publicae* e dell'*An seni res publica gerenda sit*", *Athenaeum* 64: 371–381. Reprinted in Desideri (2012), 111–123.

(1989) "Teoria e prassi storiografica di Plutarco: una proposta di lettura della coppia Emilio Paolo – Timoleonte", *Maia* 41: 199–215. Reprinted in Desideri (2012), 201–218.

(1991a) "Citazione letteraria e riferimento storico nei 'Precetti politici' di Plutarco", in D'Ippolito and Gallo (1991), 225–233.

(1991b) "Dione di Prusa fra ellenismo e romanità", *ANRW* II.33.5: 3882–3901.

(1992) "La formazione delle coppie nelle 'Vite plutarchee'", *ANRW* II.33.6: 4470–4486. Reprinted in Desideri (2012), 229–245.

(1995a) "'Non scriviamo storie, ma vite' (Plut., *Alex.* 1.2): la formula biografica di Plutarco", *Testis Temporum. Aspetti e problemi della storiografia antica*. Como, 15–25. Reprinted in Desideri (2012), 219–227.

(1995b) "Plutarco e Machiavelli", in Gallo and Scardigli (1995), 107–122. Reprinted in Desideri (2012), 283–297.

(2011) "Greek *poleis* and the Roman Empire: nature and features of political virtues in an autocratic system", in Roskam and Van der Stockt (2011), 83–98. Reprinted in Desideri (2012), 125–139.

(2012) *Saggi su Plutarco e la sua fortuna*, ed. A. Casanova. Florence.

(2017) "Plutarch's *Lives*", in Richter and Johnson (2017), 311–326.

Desmond, W. (2008) *Cynics*. Stocksfield.

De Temmerman, K. (ed.) (2020) *The Oxford Handbook of Ancient Biography*. Oxford.

De Temmerman, K. and K. Demoen (eds.) (2016) *Writing Biography in Greece and Rome: Narrative Technique and Fictionalization*. Cambridge.

Deuse, W. (1983) *Untersuchungen zur mittelplatonischen und neuplatonischen Seelenlehre*. Wiesbaden.

(2010) "Plutarch's eschatological myths", in Nesselrath (2010), 169–197.

Díaz Lavado, J. (1996) "Poesía y educación en Plutarco a través del testimonio de 'De audiendis poetis'", in F. Lisi y Bereterbide, J. Ureña Bracero, and J. Iglesias Zoido (eds.), *Didáctica del Griego y de la cultura clásica: IX Jornadas de Filología Griega (Cáceres, Mayo de 1993)*. Madrid, 113–120.

Díaz Martínez, E. (2002) "Notas sobre las referencias a Plutarco en la prosa de Quevedo", *Boletín de la Biblioteca de Menéndez Pelayo* 78: 69–79.

Dierauer, U. 1977. *Tier und Mensch im Denken der Antike*. Amsterdam.

(1997) "Raison ou instinct? Le développement de la zoopsychologie antique", in Cassin and Labarrière (1997), 3–30.

Dihle, A. (1956) *Studien zur griechischen Biographie*. Göttingen.

(1994) *Die Griechen und die Fremden*. Munich.

(2000) "Ein Streit um die rechte Sokrates-Nachfolge", in A. Haltenhoff and F.-H. Mutschler (eds.), *Hortus Litterarum Antiquarum: Festschrift für Hans Armin Gärtner zum 70. Geburtstag*. Heidelberg, 93–105.

Diller, A. (1937) "Codices Planudei", *Byzantinische Zeitschrift* 37: 295–301.

(1954) "Pletho and Plutarch", *Scriptorium* 8: 123–127.

Dillon, J. (1977) *The Middle Platonists: A Study of Platonism 80 B.C. to A.D. 220*. London.

(1988) "'Orthodoxy' and 'eclecticism': Middle Platonists and neo-Pythagoreans", in Dillon and Long (1988),103–125.

(1996) *The Middle Platonists: A Study of Platonism 80 B.C. to A.D. 220*. Ithaca, NY (updated edition).

(1997) "Plutarch and the end of history", in Mossman (1997a), 233–240.

(2002) "Plutarch and god: theodicy and cosmogony in the thought of Plutarch", in D. Frede and A. Laks (eds.), *Traditions of Theology: Studies in Hellenistic Theology, Its Background and Aftermath* (Philosophia antiqua 89). Leiden, 223–237.

(2008) "Dion and Brutus: philosopher kings adrift in a hostile world", in Nikolaidis (2008), 351–364. Reprinted in L. J. Trudeau (ed.) (2012) *Classical and Medieval Literary Criticism* 146: 184–191. Detroit, MI.

(2010) "Aspects de l'exégèse dualiste de Platon par Plutarque", in Brouillette and Giavatto (2010), 65–74.

Dillon, J. M. and A. A. Long (eds.) (1988) *The Question of "Eclecticism": Studies in Later Greek Philosophy*. Berkeley, CA.

Dimitrova, M. (2019) "Taking centre stage: Plutarch and Shakespeare", in Xenophontos and Oikonomopoulou (2019), 493–511.

D'Ippolito, G. (1991) "Il Corpus plutarcheo come macrotesto di un progetto antropologico: modi e funzioni della autotestualità", in D'Ippolito and Gallo (1991), 9–18.

(1996) "Stilemi ilomorfici nel macrotesto plutarcheo", in Fernández Delgado and Pordomingo Pardo (1996), 17–29.

(2009) "Plutarco e la lettura nel simposio", in Ribeiro Ferreira et al. (2009), 113–121.

D'Ippolito, G. and I. Gallo (eds.) (1991) *Strutture formali dei 'Moralia' di Plutarco: Atti del III Convegno plutarcheo*. Naples.

Di Stefano, G. (1968) *La découverte de Plutarque en Occident: aspects de la vie intellectuelle en Avignon au XIVe siècle*. Turin.

Ditadi, G. (2000) *Plutarco: L'intelligenza degli animali e la giustizia loro dovuta*. Este.

Dmitriev, S. (2005) *City Government in Hellenistic and Roman Asia Minor*. Oxford.

Dodds, E. (1933) "The portrait of a Greek gentleman", *G&R* 2: 97–107.

Dognini, C. (2007) "Il *De Herodoti malignitate* e la fortuna di Erodoto", in Y. Perrin (ed.), *Neronia VII. Rome, l'Italie et la Grèce. Hellénisme et philhellénisme au premier siècle après J.-C. Actes du VIIe Colloque International de la SIEN (Collection Latomus 305)*. Brussels, 481–502.

Dombrowski, D. (2014) "Philosophical vegetarianism and animal entitlements", in Campbell (2014), 535–555.

Donahue, J. F. (2003) "Toward a typology of Roman public feasting", *AJPh* 124: 423–441.

(2004) *The Roman Community at Table during the Principate*. Ann Arbor, MI.

Donini, P. (1974) *Tre studi sull' aristotelismo nel II secolo d. C.* (Historica, Politica, Philosophica. Il Pensiero Antico). Turin.

(1982) *Le scuole, l'anima, l'impero: la filosofia antica da Antioco a Plotino*. Turin.

(1986) "Lo scetticismo academico, Aristotele e l'unità della tradizione platonica secondo Plutarco", in G. Cambiano (ed.), *Storiografia e dossografia nella filosofia antica* (Biblioteca storico-filosofica, 2). Turin, 203–226.

(1988) "The history of the concept of eclecticism", in Dillon and Long (1988), 15–33.

(1994a) "Plutarco e la rinascita del platonismo", in *Lo spazio letterario della Grecia antica* I. Pt. 3. Rome, 35–60.

(1994b) "Testi e commenti, manuali e insegnamento: la forma sistematica e i metodi della filosofia in età postellenistica", *ANRW* II.36.7: 5027–5100.

(2002) "L'eredità academica e i fondamenti del platonismo in Plutarco", in M. Barbanti, G. R. Giardina, and P. Manganaro (eds.), Ἕνωσις καὶ φιλία. *Unione e amicizia. Omaggio a Francesco Romano*. Catania, 247–273.

(2009) "Il silenzio di Epaminonda, i demoni e il mito: il platonismo di Plutarco nel *De genio Socratis*", in Bonazzi and Opsomer (2009), 187–214.

(2011) *Commentary and Tradition: Aristotelianism, Platonism, and Post-Hellenistic Philosophy* (Commentaria in Aristotelem Graeca et Byzantina, Quellen und Studien, 4). Berlin.

Döring, K. (1979) *Exemplum Socratis: Studien zur Sokratesnachwirkung in der kynisch-stoischen Popularphilosophie der frühen Kaiserzeit und im frühen Christentum*. Wiesbaden.

Dörrie, H. (1969) "Le platonisme de Plutarque", *Association Guillaume Budé. Actes du VIIIe congrès (Paris, 5–10 avril 1968)*, 519–530.

(1971) "Die Stellung Plutarchs im Platonismus seiner Zeit", in R. Palmer and R. Hamerton-Kelly (eds.), *Philomathes: Studies and Essays in the Humanities in Memory of Philip Merlan*. The Hague, 36–56.

(1983) "Der 'Weise vom Roten Meer': Eine Okkulte Offenbarung durch Plutarch als Plagiat entlarvt", in P. Händel and W. Meid (eds.), *Festschrift für Robert Muth*. Innsbruck, 95–110.

Dörrie, H. and M. Baltes (1998) *Die philosophische Lehre des Platonismus. Einige grundlegende Axiome/Platonische Physik (im antiken Verständnis). Vol. II. Bausteine, 125–150. Text, Übersetzung, Kommentar.* Stuttgart.

Dover, K. J. (1997) *The Evolution of Greek Prose Style*. New York.

Dronkers, A. (1892) *De comparationibus et metaphoris apud Plutarchum*. Utrecht.

Dryden, J. (1678) *All for Love: or, The World Well Lost*. London.

Duff, T. E. (1997) "Moral ambiguity in Plutarch's *Lysander–Sulla*", in Mossman (1997a), 169–187.

(1999a) *Plutarch's Lives: Exploring Virtue and Vice*. Oxford.

(1999b) "Plutarch, Plato and 'great natures'", in Pérez Jiménez, García López, and Aguilar (1999), 313–332.

(2000) "Plutarchan *synkrisis*: comparisons and contradictions", in Van der Stockt (2000b), 141–161.

(2001) "The prologue to the *Lives* of Perikles and Fabius", in Pérez Jiménez and Casadesús Bordoy (2001), 351–363.

(2003) "Plutarch on the childhood of Alcibiades (*Alk.* 2–3)", *PCPhS* 49: 89–117.

(2004) "Plato, tragedy, the ideal reader and Plutarch's *Demetrios and Antony*", *Hermes* 132: 271–291.

(2005) Review of Stadter and Van der Stockt (2002), *CR* 55: 462–465.

(2007–8) "Plutarch's readers and the moralism of the *Lives*", *Ploutarchos* 5: 3–18.

(2008a) "How *Lives* begin", in Nikolaidis (2008), 187–207.

(2008b) "Models of education in Plutarch", *JHS* 128: 1–26.

(2008c) "The opening of Plutarch's *Life of Themistokles*", *GRBS* 48: 159–179.

(2009) "Plato's *Symposium* and Plutarch's *Alcibiades*", in Ribeiro Ferreira et al. (2009), 37–50.

(2010a) "Il linguaggio della narrazione in Plutarco", in G. Zanetto and S. Martinelli (eds.), *Plutarco: lingua e testa*. Milan, 207–224.

(2010b) "Plutarch's *Themistocles and Camillus*", in Humble (2010b), 45–86.

(2011a) "Platonic allusion in Plutarch's *Alcibiades* 4–7", in P. Millet, S. Oakley, and R. Thompson (eds.), *Ratio et Res Ipsa: Classical Essays Presented by Former Pupils to James Diggle on His Retirement* (*PCPhS* suppl. vol 36). Cambridge, 27–43.

(2011b) "Plutarch's *Lives* and the critical reader", in Roskam and Van der Stockt (2011), 59–82.

(2011c) "The structure of the Plutarchan book", *ClAnt* 30: 213–278.

(2014) "The prologues", in Beck (2014a), 333–349.

(2015) "Aspect and subordination in Plutarch's narrative", in Ash, Mossman, and Titchener (2015), 129–148.

(2017) "Plutarch and tense: the present and imperfect", in Georgiadou and Oikonomopoulou (2017), 55–66.

(ed.) (forthcoming) *Oxford Readings in Ancient Biography*. Oxford.

Duff, T. E. and C. Chrysanthou (eds.) (forthcoming) *Generic Enrichment in Plutarch's Lives*. London.

Duff, T. E. and L. E. Fletcher (eds.) (forthcoming) *Herodotus and Plutarch*.

Duffy, J. (2006) "Dealing with the Psellos Corpus: from Allatius to Westerink and the Bibliotheca Teubneriana", in C. Barbour and D. Jenkins (eds.), *Reading Michael Psellos*. Leiden, 1–11.

Dumont, J. (2001) *Les animaux dans l'Antiquité grecque*. Paris.

Dunbabin, K. (1991) "Triclinium and Stibadium", in Slater (1991), 121–148.

(1995) "Scenes from the Roman convivium: *frigida non derit, non derit calda petenti* (Martial XIV.105)", in Murray and Tecuşan (1995), 252–265.

(2003) *The Roman Banquet: Images of Conviviality*. Ann Arbor, MI.

Dupont, F. (1989) *La vie quotidienne du citoyen romain sous la république*, Paris.

(1992) *Daily Life in Ancient Rome*. Oxford.

(1999) "De l'oeuf à la pomme: la *cena* romaine", in Flandrin and Cobbi (1999), 59–86.

Düring, I. (1957) *Aristotle in the Ancient Biographic Tradition*. Gothenburg.

Edelman, C. (2019) "Plutarch and Montaigne", in Xenophontos and Oikonomopoulou (2019), 479–492.

Edwards, C. (1993) *The Politics of Immorality in Ancient Rome*. Cambridge.

Edwards, G. (2016) "The purpose of Porphyry's rational animals: a dialectical attack on the Stoics in *On Abstinence from Animal Food*", in R. Sorabji (ed.), *Aristotle Re-Interpreted: New Findings on Seven Hundred Years of the Ancient Commentators*. London, 263–290.

Ehlers, W. (ed.) (1998) *La Biographie antique*. (Entretiens Hardt, XLIV). Geneva.

Eichel-Lojkine, P. (2001) *Le siècle des grands hommes: les recueils de vies d'hommes illustres au XVIème siècle*. Louvain.

Eidinow, J. (1990) "A note on Horace, *Epistles* 1. 2.26 and 2. 2.75", *CQ* 40: 566–568.

Elsmann, T. (1994) *Untersuchungen zur Rezeption der Institutio Traiani*. Stuttgart.

Engberg-Pedersen, T. (1996) "Plutarch to Prince Philopappus on how to tell a flatterer from a friend", in J. Fitzgerald (ed.), *Friendship, Flattery and Frankness of Speech: Studies on Friendship in the New Testament World*. Leiden, 61–79.

Erbse, H. (1956) "Die Bedeutung der Synkrisis in den Parallelbiographien Plutarchs", *Hermes* 84: 398–424.

Erikson, E. (1958) *Young Man Luther*. New York.

Erskine, A. (2001) *Troy between Greece and Rome: Local Tradition and Imperial Power*. Oxford.

Evans, G. Blakemore (1997) *The Riverside Shakespeare*, 2nd ed. Boston.

Evans, R. C. (2001) "Flattery in Shakespeare's *Othello*: the relevance of Plutarch and Sir Thomas Elyot", *Comparative Drama* 35: 1–41.

Fedalto, G. (2007) *Simone Atumano: Monaco di Studio, arcivescovo latino di Tebe. Secolo XIV*. Brescia.

Fernández Delgado, J. A. (2000) "Le *Gryllus*, une éthopée parodique", in Van der Stockt (2000b), 171–182.

Fernández Delgado, J. A. and F. Pordomingo Pardo (eds.) (1996) *Estudios sobre Plutarco: Aspectos Formales*. Madrid.

Fernoux, H. (2011) *Le demos et la cité: communautés et assemblées populaires en Asie Mineure à l'époque impériale*. Rennes.

Ferrari, F. (1995) *Dio, idee e materia: La struttura del cosmo in Plutarco di Cheronea*. Naples.

(1996) "Dio: padre e artefice. La theologia di Plutarco in *Plat. Quaest.* 2", in Gallo (1996), 395–409.

(1998) "Plutarco in Siriano, in Arist. *Metaph.* 105,36ss.: lo statuto ontologico e la collocazione metafisica delle idee", in Gallo (1998a), 143–159.

(2000) "Platonismus und Tradition", in M. Erler and A. Graeser (eds.), *Philosophen des Altertums*. Darmstadt, 109–127.

(2002) "La trascendenza razionale: il principio secondo Plutarco", in F. Calabi (ed.), *Arrhetos Theos: L'ineffabilità del primo principio nel medio platonismo*. Pisa, 77–91.

(2003) "Causa paradigmatica e causa efficiente: il ruolo delle idee nel *Timeo*", in C. Natali and S. Maso (eds.), *Plato physicus: Cosmologia e antropologia nel Timeo*. Amsterdam, 83–96.

(2005) *Dottrina delle idee nel medioplatonismo*, in F. Fronterotta and W. Leszl (eds.), *Eidos – Idea. Platone, Aristotele e la tradizione Platonica*. Sankt Augustin, 233–247.

(2007–8) "La chora nel *Timeo* di Platone: Riflessioni su 'materia' e 'spazio' nell'ontologia del mondo fenoménico", *Quaestio* 7: 3–23.

Ferrari, F. and L. Baldi (eds.) (2002) *Plutarco: La generazione dell'anima nel* Timeo *(CPM 37)*. Naples.

Fields, D. (2008) "Aristides and Plutarch on self-praise", in Harris and Holmes (2008), 151–172.

Figueira, T. and G. Nagy (eds.) (1985) *Theognis of Megara: Poetry and the Polis*. Baltimore, MD.

Fitzgerald, W. (2016) *Variety: The Life of a Roman Concept*. Chicago, IL.

Flacelière, R. (1934) "*De pythiae oraculis* 409bc", *RPh* 8: 56–66.

(1936) "Avec Plutarque à Delphes", *BAGB* 51: 47.

Flacelière, R. and E. Chambry (eds.) (1972) *Plutarque Vies. Vol. III: Périclès-Fabius Maximus – Alcibiade-Coriolan*. Paris.

Flacelière, R., E. Chambry, and M. Juneaux (eds.) (1964) *Plutarque Vies. Vol. 1: Thésée-Romulus – Lycurgue-Numa*. Paris.

Flacelière, R., J. Irigoin, J. Sirinelli, and A. Philippon (eds.) (1987) *Plutarque. Oeuvres morales. Vol. I.1* (Paris).

Flandrin, J. and J. Cobbi (eds.) (1999) *Tables d'hier, tables d'ailleurs: Histoire et ethnologie du repas*. Paris.

Fletcher, L. E. (2017) "Narrative time and space in Plutarch's *Life of Nikias*", in Georgiadou and Oikonomopoulou (2017).

Fletcher, L. E. (forthcoming) "History and tragedy in Plutarch's *Nicias*", in Duff and Chrysanthou (forthcoming).

Fletcher, R. and J. Hanink (eds.) (2016) *Creative Lives in Classical Antiquity: Poets, Artists and Biography*. Cambridge.

Florio, J. (trans.) (1603) *The Essayes or Morall, Politike and Militarie Discourses of Lord Michaell de Montaigne*. London.

Focke, F. (1923) "Synkrisis", *Hermes* 58: 327–368.

Fögen, T. (2007) "Antike Zeugnisse zu Kommunikationsformen von Tieren", *A&A* 53: 39–75.

(ed.) (2009a) *Tears in the Graeco-Roman World*. Berlin.

(2009b) "The implications of animal nomenclature in Aelian's *De natura animalium*", *RhM* 152: 49–62.

(2014) "Animal communication", in Campbell (2014), 216–232.

(2017a) "Animals in Greco-Roman antiquity: a select bibliography", in Fögen and Thomas (2017), 435–474.

(2017b) "Lives in interaction: animal 'biographies' in Graeco-Roman literature?" in Fögen and Thomas (2017), 89–138.

Fögen, T. and E. Thomas (eds.) (2017) *Interactions between Animals and Humans in Graeco-Roman Antiquity*. Berlin.

Follet, S. (1972) "Flavius Euphanès d' Athènes, ami de Plutarque", in F. Bader (ed.), *Mélanges de linguistique et de philologie grecques offerts à Pierre Chantraine*. Paris, 35–50.

Fontanella, F. (2008) "The encomium on Rome as a response to Polybius' doubts about the Roman Empire", in Harris and Holmes (2008), 203–216.

Foucault, M. (1984) *Histoire de la sexualité. Vol. III: Le souci de soi*. Paris.

(1990) *The History of Sexuality. Vol. III: The Care of the Self*. Trans. R. Hurley. London.

(2001) *Fearless Speech*. Trans. J. Pearson. Los Angeles, CA.

Fox, M. (1993) "History and rhetoric in Dionysius of Halicarnassus", *JRS* 83: 31–47.

Fraisse, J.-C. (1974) *Philia: La notion d'amitié dans la philosophie antique*. Paris.

Franco, C. (2017) "Greek and Latin words for human–animal bonds: metaphors and taboos", in Fögen and Thomas (2017), 39–60.

Frazier, F. (1988) "A propos de la 'philotimia' dans les *Vies*: quelques jalons dans l'histoire d' une notion", *RPh* 62, 109–127.

(1992) "Contribution à l'étude de la composition des Vies de Plutarque: l'élaboration des grandes scenes", *ANRW* II.33.6: 4487–4535.

(1996) *Histoire et Morale dans les Vies parallèles de Plutarque*. Paris.

(1998) "Théorie et pratique de la παιδιά symposiaque dans le *Propos de Table* de Plutarque", in M. Trédé and P. Hoffmann (eds.), *Le Rire des anciens: Actes du Colloque International (Université de Rouen, École normale supérieure, 11–13 janvier 1995)*. Paris, 281–292.

(2005) "La 'prouesse de Camma' et la fonction des *exempla* dans le *Dialogue Sur l'Amour*", in Pérez Jiménez and Titchener (2005), 197–212.

(2005–6) "L'*Érotikos*, un éloge du Dieu Éros? Une relecture du dialogue de Plutarque", *Ploutarchos* 3: 63–102.

(2008a) "Éros, Arès et Aphrodite dans l'*Érotikos*: Une reconsidération de la réponse à Pemptidès (ch. 13–18)", in J. Ribeiro Ferreira, L. Van der Stockt, and M. do Céu Fialho (eds.), *Philosophy in Society. Virtues and Values in Plutarch*. Leuven & Coimbra, 117–136.

(2008b) "Le *Trésor des Morales de Plutarque* de François Le Tort", in Guerrier (2008), 71–86.

(2008c) "Philosophie et religion dans la pensée de Plutarque: Quelques réflexions autour des emplois du mot πίστις", *Éplaton* 5: 41–61.

(2008d) *Plutarque. Érotikos. Dialogue sur l'Amour*. Paris.

(2011) "Autour du miroir: Les miroitements d'une image dans l'oeuvre de Plutarque", in Roskam and Van der Stockt (2011), 297–326.

(2014a) "The perils of ambition", in Beck (2014a), 488–502.

(2014b) "The reception of Plutarch in France after the Renaissance", in Beck (2014a), 549–555.

(2020) *Quelques aspects du platonisme de Plutarque. Philosopher en commun, tourner sa pensée vers Dieu.* Ed. L. Roig Lanzillotta. (Brill's Plutarch Studies, vol. 4). Leiden.

Frazier, F. and O. Guerrier (2019) "Plutarch's French translation by Amyot", in Xenophontos and Oikonomopoulou (2019), 421–435.

Frede, M. (1999) "Epilogue", in K. Algra, J. Barnes, J. Mansfeld, and M. Schofield (eds.), *Cambridge History of Hellenistic Philosophy.* Cambridge, 771–797.

French, P. and W. St Clair (eds.) (2002) *Mapping Lives: The Uses of Biography.* Oxford.

Froidefond, C. (ed.) (1988) *Plutarque: Oeuvres morales. Vol. V.II: Isis et Osiris.* Paris.

Fryde, E. (1983) *Humanism and Renaissance Historiography.* London.

(1988) "The first humanistic life of Aristotle: the 'Vita Aristotelis' of Leonardo Bruni", in P. Denley and C. Elam (eds.), *Florence and Italy: Renaissance Studies in Honour of Nicolai Rubinstein.* London, 285–296.

(2000) *The Early Palaeologan Renaissance (1261–c.1360).* Leiden.

Fuhrmann, F. (1964) *Les Images de Plutarque.* Paris.

(ed.) (1972) *Plutarque: Oeuvres Morales. Vol. IX.1: Propos de Table (Livres I–III).* Paris.

(ed.) (1978) *Plutarque: Oeuvres Morales. Vol. IX.2: Propos de Table (Livres IV–VI).* Paris.

Funck, B. (1981) "Studie zu der Bezeichnung *bárbaros*", in E. Welskopf (ed.), *Soziale Typenbegriffe im alten Griechenland und ihr Fortleben in den Sprachen der Welt.* Vol. IV. Berlin, 26–51.

Fuscagni, S. (ed.) (1989) *Plutarco Vite Paralle: Cimone* (introduzione, traduzione e note di S. Fuscagni), *Lucullo* (introduzione e note di B. Scardigli; traduzione di B. Mugelli). Milan.

Fyrigos, A. (1989) "Barlaam e Petrarca", *Studi Petrarcheschi* 6: 179–200.

Gallarte, I. M. (2008) "El judaísmo en las *Vitae* y *Moralia* de Plutarco", in Nikolaidis (2008), 815–830.

Gallo, I. (ed.) (1988) *Sulla tradizione manoscritta dei Moralia di Plutarco.* Salerno.

(ed.) (1992) *Plutarco e le scienze.* Genoa.

(ed.) (1996) *Plutarco e la religione: Atti del VI Convegno plutarcheo (Ravello, 29–31 maggio, 1995).* Naples.

(ed.) (1998a) *L'eredità culturale di Plutarco dall'Antichità al Rinascimento.* Naples.

(1998b) "Forma letteraria nei *Moralia* di Plutarco: Aspetti e problemi", *ANRW* II.34.4: 3511–3540.

Gallo, I. and C. Moreschini (eds.) (2000) *I generi letterari in Plutarco. Atti del VIII Convegno plutarcheo, Pisa, 2-4 giugno 1999.* Naples.

Gallo, I. and B. Scardigli (eds.) (1995) *Teoria e prassi politica nelle opere di Plutarco: Atti del V Convegno plutarcheo (Certosa di Pontignano, 7–9 giugno 1993).* Naples.

García Gual, C. (1988) "Cartas de consuelo al desterrado: Plutarco y fray Antonio de Guevara. Imitación al contraste", *1616: Annuario de la Socieded Española de Literatura General y Comparada* 6–7: 37–41.

(1991) "Plutarco y Guevara", in García López and Calderón Dorda (1991), 127–142.

(1998) "El Plutarco de Fray Antonio de Guevara", in Gallo (1998a), 367–375.

(2000) "El Plutarco de Fray Antonio de Guevara", in N. Castrillo Benito (ed.), *La herencia greco-latina en la lengua y literatura castellanas.* Burgos, 67–73.

García López, J. and E. Calderón Dorda (eds.) (1991) *Estudios sobre Plutarco: Paisaje y naturaleza.* Madrid.

García Moreno, L. (1995) "Roma y los protagonistas de la dominación romana en Grecia en las *Vidas paralelas* de Plutarco", in E. Falque and F. Gascó (eds.), *Graecia capta: De la conquista de Grecia a la helenización de Roma.* Universidad de Huelva, 129–147.

(2002) "Filohelenismo y moderación: Garantías según Plutarco de una dominación estable del mundo griego por Roma", in Ribeiro Ferreira (2002), 261–280.

García Valdés, M. (ed.) (1994) *Estudios sobre Plutarco: ideas religiosas: actas del III simposio internacional sobre Plutarco, Oviedo 30 de abril a 2 de mayo de 1992.* Madrid.

Garfagnini, G. (1984) "Lo Studium generale regie civitatis Florentie: 1321–1472 (Antologia di documenti)", *Storia dell' Ateneo fiorentino: Contributi di studio. Vol. I.* Florence, 57-107.

Garzya, A. (1988) "La tradizione manoscritta dei *Moralia*: linee generali", in Gallo (1988), 9–54.

(1998) "Plutarco a Bisanzio", in Gallo (1998a), 15–27.

Gascó, F. (1990) "Maratón, Eurimedonte y Platea (*Praec. ger. reip.* 814A–C)", in Pérez Jiménez and del Cerro Calderón (1990), 211–215.

Gefen, A. (2012) "Les écrivains contre Plutarque: détournements, critiques et réécritures des *Vies Parallèles* aux XIX^e^ et XX^e^ siècles", in Guerrier (2012), 337–349.

Gehrke, H.-J. (1976) *Phokion: Studien zur Erfassung seiner historischen Gestalt.* Munich.

Geiger, J. (1979a) "Cornelius Nepos, *de regibus exterarum gentium*", *Latomus* 38: 662–669.

(1979b) "Munatius Rufus and Thrasea Paetus on Cato the Younger", *Athenaeum* 57: 48–72.

(1981) "Plutarch's *Parallel Lives*: the choice of heroes", *Hermes* 109: 85–104. Reprinted in Scardigli (1995), 165–190.

(1985) *Cornelius Nepos and Ancient Political Biography*. Historia Einzelschriften 47. Stuttgart.

(1999) "Plato, Plutarch, and the death of Socrates and of Cato", in Pérez Jiménez, García López, and Aguilar (eds.) (1999), 357–364.

(2017) "Greeks and the Roman past in the Second Sophistic: the case of Plutarch", in Georgiadou and Oikonomopoulou (2017), 119–125.

Gentili, V. (1991) *La Roma antica degli elisabettiani*. Bologna.

Georgiadou, A. (1988) "The *Lives of the Caesars* and Plutarch's other *Lives*", *ICS* 13: 349–356.

(1997) *Plutarch's* Pelopidas: *A Historical and Philological Commentary*. Stuttgart.

(2014) "The *Lives of the Caesars*", in Beck (2014a), 251–266.

Georgiadou, A. and K. Oikonomopoulou (eds.) (2017) *Space, Time and Language in Plutarch*. Berlin.

Gera, D. (1993) *Xenophon's* Cyropaideia: *Style, Genre and Literary Technique*. Oxford.

(2003) *Ancient Greek Ideas on Speech, Language and Civilization*. Oxford.

(2007) "Themistocles' Persian tapestry", *CQ* 57: 445–457.

Giannattasio Andria, R. (2000) "*Galba* e *Otone* tra biografia e storia", in Gallo and Moreschini (2000), 81–91.

(2006) "Il proemio del *Galba* e *Otone* di Plutarco", in G. de Gregorio and S. Medaglia (eds.), *Tradizione, ecdotica, esegesi: miscellanea di studi*. Naples, 59–77.

Gigante, M. (1969) *Teodoro Metochites, saggio critico su Demostene e Aristide*. Milan.

(1979) *Poeti Bizantini di terra d'Otranto nel secolo XIII*. Naples.

Gilhus, I. (2006) *Animals, Gods and Humans: Changing Attitudes to Animals in Greek, Roman and Early Christian Thought*. London.

Gill, C. (1983) "The question of character development: Plutarch and Tacitus", *CQ* 33: 469–487.

(1985) "Plato and the education of character", *Archiv für Geschichte der Philosophie* 67: 1–26.

(1986) "The question of character and personality in Greek tragedy", *Poetics Today* 7: 251–273.

(1988) "Personhood and personality: the four *personae* theory in Cicero, *De officiis* I", *OSAPh* 5: 169–199.

(1990) "The character–personality distinction", in Pelling (1990c), 1–31.

(1996) *Personality in Greek Epic, Tragedy, and Philosophy: The Self in Dialogue*. Oxford.

(2006) *The Structured Self in Hellenistic and Roman Thought*. Oxford.

Giustiniani, V. (1961) "Sulle traduzioni latine delle 'Vite' di Plutarco nel Quattrocento", *Rinascimento* 1: 3–62.

(1979) "Plutarch und die Humanistische Ethik", in W. Rüegg and D. Wuttke (eds.), *Ethik im Humanismus*. Boppard, 45–62.

Gleason, M. (1995) *Making Men: Sophists and Self-Presentation in Ancient Rome*. Princeton, NJ.

(2006) "Greek cities under Roman rule", in D. Potter (ed.), *A Companion to the Roman Empire*. Oxford, 228–249.

Glucker, J. (1978) *Antiochus and the Late Academy (Hypomnemata, 56)*. Göttingen.

Gnauk, R (1936) *Die Bedeutung des Marius und Cato maior für Cicero*. Berlin.

Goar, R. (1987) *The Legend of Cato Uticensis from the First Century B.C. to the Fifth Century A.D.* Brussels.

Goessler, L. (1962) *Plutarchs Gedanken über die Ehe*. Zürich. English translation of 44–69 in Pomeroy (1999a), 97–115.

Goguey, D. (2003) *Les animaux dans la mentalité romain*. Brussels.

Goldhill, S. (1995) *Foucault's Virginity: Ancient Erotic Fiction and the History of Sexuality*. Cambridge.

(1999) "Body/politics: is there a history of reading?" in T. Falkner, N. Felson, and D. Konstan (eds.), *Contextualising Classics: Ideology, Performance, Dialogue. Essays in Honor of John J. Peradotto*. Lanham, MD, 89–20.

(2001a) "Introduction: setting an agenda – 'everything is Greece to the wise'", in Goldhill (2001b), 1–25.

(ed.) (2001b) *Being Greek Under Rome: Cultural Identity, the Second Sophistic and the Development of Empire*. Cambridge.

(2002) "The value of Greek: Why save Plutarch?" in S. Goldhill, *Who Needs Greek? Contests in the Cultural History of Hellenism*. Cambridge, 246–293.

(2008) *The End of Dialogue in Antiquity*. Cambridge.

Goleman, D. (1995) *Emotional Intelligence*. New York.

(2001) "What makes a leader?" in W. Rosenbach and R. Taylor (eds.) *Contemporary Issues in Leadership*, 5th ed. Boulder, CO, 5–18.

Gómez, P. and F. Mestre (2009) "The banquets of Alexander", in Ribeiro Ferreira et al. (2009), 211–222.

Gómez Cardó, P., D. Leão, and M. de Oliveira Silva (eds.) (2014) *Plutarco entre mundos: visões de Esparta, Atenas e Roma*. Coimbra.

Gomme, A. (1945) *A Historical Commentary on Thucydides: Vol. I*. Oxford.

Gontier, T. (1999) *L'homme et l'animal. La philosophie antique*. Paris.

González González, M. (2019) "Who should be sacrificed? Human sacrifice and status in Plutarch: *Themistocles* 13, *Pelopidas* 21–22, *Philopoemen* 21", *Arethusa* 52: 165–179.

Görgemanns, H. (2005) "Eros als Gott in Plutarchs *Amatorius*", in Hirsch-Luipold (2005), 169–195.

(ed.) (2006) *Plutarch: Dialog über die Liebe*. Tübingen.

(ed.) (2011) *Plutarch: Dialog über die Liebe*, 2nd ed. Tübingen.

Gorman, R. and V. Gorman (2007) "The *tryphê* of the Sybarites: a historiographical problem in Athenaeus", *JHS* 127: 38–60.

(2014) *Corrupting Luxury in Ancient Greek Literature*. Ann Arbor, MI.

Gossage, A. (1967) "Plutarch", in T. Dorey (ed.), *Latin Biography*. London, 45–77.

Goulet-Cazé, M.-O. (1996) "Religion and the early Cynics", in Branham and Goulet-Cazé (1996), 47–80.

Gouma-Peterson, T. (ed.) (2000) *Anna Komnene and Her Times*. New York.

Gowers, E. (1993) *The Loaded Table: Representations of Food in Roman Literature.* Oxford.

Grassl, H. (1982) "Arrian im Donauraum", *Chiron* 12: 245–252.

Graves, W. (1973) "Plutarch's *Life of Cato Utican* as a major source of *Othello*", *Shakespeare Quarterly* 24: 181–187.

Gray, V. (1992) "Xenophon's *Symposion*: the display of wisdom", *Hermes* 120: 58–75.

(1998) *The Framing of Socrates: The Literary Interpretation of Xenophon's Memorabilia.* Stuttgart.

Graziosi, B. (2002) *Inventing Homer.* Cambridge.

Gréard, O. (1880) *De la morale de Plutarque*, 3rd ed. Paris.

Green, D. (1979) *Plutarch Revisited: A Study of Shakespeare's Last Roman Plays and Their Source.* Salzburg.

Grévin, J. (1971) *César*, ed. E. Ginsberg. Geneva.

Gribble, D. (1999) *Alcibiades and Athens: A Study in Literary Presentation.* Oxford.

Griffin, J. (2009) "Shakespeare's *Julius Caesar* and the dramatic tradition", in M. Griffin (ed.), *A Companion to Julius Caesar.* Oxford, 371–398.

Griffith, M. (2006) "Horsepower and donkeywork: equids and the ancient Greek imagination. Part Two", *CPh* 101: 307–358.

Griffiths, G., J. Hankins, and D. Thompson (1987) *The Humanism of Leonardo Bruni.* Binghamton, NY.

Griffiths, J. G. (ed.) (1970) *Plutarch's De Iside et Osiride.* Cardiff.

Griffiths, R. (1970) *The Dramatic Technique of Antoine de Montchrestien: Rhetoric and Style in French Renaissance Tragedy.* Oxford.

Grimaldi, M. (ed.) (2004) *Plutarco: La Malignità di Erodoto.* Naples.

Gruen, E. (1992) *Culture and National Identity in Republican Rome.* Ithaca, NY.

Grünbart, M. (2019) "Plutarch in twelfth-century learned culture", in Xenophontos and Oikonomopoulou (2019), 265–278.

Guerrier, O. (ed.) (2008) *Moralia et Oeuvres Morales à la Renaissance: Actes du Colloque International de Toulouse (19–21 mai 2005).* Paris.

(ed.) (2012) *Plutarque de l'age Classique au XIXᵉ siècle: presences, interferences et dynamique. Actes du colloque internationale de Toulouse (13–15 mai 2009).* Grenoble.

(2014) "The Renaissance in France: Amyot and Montaigne", in Beck (2014a), 544–558.

Guilland, R. (ed.) (1967) *Correspondance de Nicéphore Grégoras.* Paris.

Guillén Selfa, L. (1997) "Plutarco: moralidad y tragedia", in Schrader, Ramón, and Vela (1997), 241–253.

Hadot, P. (1992) *La citadelle intérieure: Introduction aux Pensées de Marc Aurèle.* Paris. (1995) *Qu'est-ce que la philosophie antique?* Paris.

Hägg, T. (2012) *The Art of Biography in Antiquity.* Cambridge.

Haldon, J. (1990) *Byzantium in the Seventh Century: The Transformation of a Culture.* Cambridge.

Halfmann, H. (1979) *Die Senatoren aus dem östlichen Teil des Imperium Romanum bis zum Ende des 2. Jahrhunderts n.Chr.* Göttingen.

(2002) "Die Selbstverwaltung der kaiserzeitlichen Polis in Plutarchs Schrift *Praecepta gerendae rei publicae*", *Chiron* 32: 83–95.

Hall, E. (1989) *Inventing the Barbarian: Greek Self-Definition through Tragedy.* Oxford.

(1993) "Asia unmanned: images of victory in classical Athens", in Rich and Shipley (1993), 108–133.

(1995) "The ass with the double vision: politicizing an ancient Greek novel", in D. Margolies and M. Joannou (eds.), *Heart of the Heartless World: Essays in Cultural Resistance in Memory of Margot Heinemann.* London, 47–59.

(ed.) (1996) *Aeschylus: Persians.* Warminster.

Hall, J. (1997) *Ethnic Identity in Greek Antiquity.* Cambridge.

Halliwell, S. (1990) "Traditional Greek conceptions of character", in Pelling (1990c), 32–59.

(2002) *The Aesthetics of Mimesis: Ancient texts and Modern Problems.* Princeton, NJ.

Hamilton, C. D. (1992) "Plutarch's 'Life of Agesilaus'", *ANRW* II.33.6: 4201–4221.

(1994) "Plutarch and Xenophon on Agesilaus", *AncW* 25: 205–212.

Hamilton, J. (1969) *Plutarch, Alexander: A Commentary.* Oxford.

Hankins, J. (ed.) (2000) *Renaissance Civic Humanism: Reappraisals and Reflections.* Cambridge.

(2002) "Chrysoloras and the Greek Studies of Leonardo Bruni", in Maisano and Rollo (2002), 175–197.

Hansen, W. (2004) *Classical Mythology: A Guide to the Mythical World of the Greeks and Romans.* Oxford.

Hardie, P. (1992) "Plutarch and the interpretation of myth", *ANRW* II.33.6: 4743–4787.

(1996) "Sign language in 'On the Sign of Socrates'", in Van der Stockt (1996), 123–136.

(1997) "Fifth-century Athenian and Augustan images of the barbarian Other", *Classics Ireland* 4: 46–56.

Harris, W. (1979) *War and Imperialism in Republican Rome 327–70 BC.* Oxford.

(2001) *Restraining Rage: The Ideology of Anger Control in Classical Antiquity.* Cambridge, MA.

Harris, W. V. and B. Holmes (eds.) (2008) *Aelius Aristides between Greece, Rome, and the Gods.* Leiden.

Harrison, G. (1991) "The critical trends in scholarship on the non-philosophical works in Plutarch's *Moralia*", *ANRW* II.33.6: 4646–4681.

(1995) "The semiotics of Plutarch's Σύγκρισις: the Hellenistic lives of Demetrius – Antony and Agesilaus – Pompey", *RBPhH* 73: 91–104.

(2000) "Problems with the genre of problems: Plutarch's literary innovations", *CPh* 95: 193–199.

Harrison, T. (ed.) (2002) *Greeks and Barbarians.* Edinburgh.

Hartog, F. (2005) *Anciens, Modernes, Sauvages.* Paris.

Harvey, D. (1999) "Bibliography of Plutarch's *Advice* and *Consolation*", in Pomeroy (1999a), 197–215.

Hastings, M. (2009) *Finest Years: Churchill as Warlord 1940–45*. London.

Hawtree, L. (2014) "Animals in epic", in Campbell (2014), 73–83.

Heath, J. (2005) *The Talking Greeks: Speech, Animals, and the Other in Homer, Aeschylus, and Plato*. Cambridge.

Heath, M. (1998) "Caecilius, Longinus and Photius", *GRBS* 39: 271–292.

(2008) "Aristotle on natural slavery", *Phronesis* 53: 243–270.

Hein, A. (1914) *De optativi apud Plutarchum usu*. Trebnitz.

Helmbold, W. (ed. and trans.) (1939) *Plutarch's Moralia. Vol. VI. 439A–523B*. Cambridge, MA.

Helmbold, W. and E. O'Neil (1959) *Plutarch's Quotations*. Baltimore, MD.

Helmig, C. (2008) "Plutarch of Chaeronea and Porphyry on transmigration – who is the author of Stobaeus I 445.14–448.3 (W.-H)?" *CQ* 58: 250–255.

Herchenroeder, L. (2008) "Τί γὰρ τοῦτο πρὸς τὸν λόγον; Plutarch's *Gryllus* and the so-called *grylloi*", *AJPh* 129: 347–379.

Herrero Salgado, F. (1994) "Plutarco y la oratoria sagrada del siglo de oro," in García Valdés (1994),371–380.

Hershbell, J. (1987) "Plutarch's *de animae procreatione in Timaeo*: an analysis of structure and content", *ANRW* II.36.1: 234–247.

(1988) "Plutarch's portrait of Socrates", *ICS* 13: 365–381.

(1992a) "Plutarch and Epicureanism", *ANRW* II.36.5: 3353–3383.

(1992b) "Plutarch and Stoicism", *ANRW* II.36.5: 3336–3352.

(1993) "Plutarch and Herodotus: the beetle in the rose", *RhM* 136: 143–163.

(2004) "Plutarch's political philosophy: Peripatetic and Platonic", in de Blois et al. (2004), 151–162.

Heuer, H. (1957) "From Plutarch to Shakespeare: a study of Coriolanus", *Shakespeare Survey* 10: 50–59.

Hijmans, B. Jr., R. Van der Paardt, V. Schmidt, B. Wesseling, and M. Zimmerman (eds.) (1995) *Apuleius Madaurensis. Metamorphoses Book IX: Text, Introduction and Commentary*. Groningen.

Hillman, T. (1993) "When did Lucullus retire?" *Historia* 42: 211–228.

(1994) "Authorial statements, narrative, and character in Plutarch's *Agesilaus – Pompeius*", *GRBS* 35: 255–280.

Hillyard, B. (1977) "The medieval tradition of Plutarch, *de audiendo*", *RHT* 7: 1–56.

Hindermann, J. (2011) "Zoophilie in Zoologie und Roman: Sex und Liebe zwischen Mensch und Tier bei Plutarch, Plinius dem Älteren, Aelian und Apuleius", *Dictynna* 8. https://doi.org/10.4000/dictynna.717.

Hirsch-Luipold, R. (ed.) (2005) *Gott und die Götter bei Plutarch: Götterbilder – Gottesbilder – Weltbilder*. Berlin.

(2014) "Religion and myth", in Beck (2014a), 163–176.

Hirzel, R. (1895) *Der Dialog*. Leipzig.

(1912) *Plutarch*. Leipzig.

Hobbs, A. (2000) *Plato and the Hero: Courage, Manliness and the Impersonal Good*. Cambridge.

Hobden, F. (2004) "How to be a good symposiast and other lessons from Xenophon's *Symposium*", *The Cambridge Classical Journal* 50: 121–140.

(2005) "Reading Xenophon's *Symposium*", *Ramus* 34.2: 93–111.

(2013) *The Symposion in Ancient Greek Society and Thought*. Cambridge.

Høgel, C. (2002) *Symeon Metaphrastes: Rewriting and Canonization*. Copenhagen.

Höistad, R. (1948) *Cynic Hero and Cynic King: Studies in the Cynic Conception of Man*. Uppsala.

Holford-Strevens, L. (2003) *Aulus Gellius. An Antonine Scholar and His Achievement*. Oxford.

Holland, P. (1603) *The Philosophie, commonlie called, The Morals [. . .]*. London.

Holmes, B. (2008) "Aelius Aristides' illegible body," in Harris and Holmes (2008), 81–114.

Holtorf, H. (1913) *Plutarchi Chaeronensis studia in Platone explicando posita*. Diss., University of Greifswald.

Honigmann, E. (1959) "Shakespeare's Plutarch", *Shakespeare Quarterly* 10: 25–33.

Hood, D. (1967) *Plutarch and the Persians*. Ph.D. diss., University of Southern California.

Hopfner, T. (1940) *Plutarch über Isis und Osiris*. Darmstadt.

Horky, P. (2017) "The spectrum of animal rationality in Plutarch", *Apeiron* 50: 103–133.

Horster, M. and C. Reitz (eds.) (2010) *Condensing Texts – Condensed Texts*. Stuttgart.

Howard-Johnson, J. (1996) "Anna Komnene and the *Alexiad*", in M. Mullett and D. Smythe (eds.), *Alexios I Komnenos*. Belfast, 260–301.

Howley, J. (2014) "*Heus tu rhetorisce*: Gellius, Cicero, Plutarch and Roman study abroad", in J. M. Madsen and R. Rees (eds.), *Roman Rule in Greek and Latin Writing: Double Vision*. Leiden, 163–192.

Hult, K. (ed.) (2002) *Theodore Metochites on Ancient Authors and Philosophy: Semeioseis Gnomikai 1–26, 71*. Gothenburg.

Humble, N. (2010a) "Parallelism and the humanists", in Humble (2010b), 237–265.

(2010b) *Plutarch's Lives: Parallelism and Purpose*. London.

(2013) "Imitation as commentary? Plutarch and Byzantine historiography in the tenth century", in Pace and Volpe Cacciatore (2013), 219–225.

Hunger, H. (1969–70) "On the imitation (MIMHΣIΣ) of antiquity in Byzantine literature", *Dumbarton Oaks Papers* 23: 15–38.

Hunter, R. (2018) *The Measure of Homer: The Ancient Reception of the* Iliad *and the* Odyssey. Cambridge.

Hunter, R. and D. Russell (eds.) (2011) *Plutarch: How to Study Poetry*. Cambridge.

Hutchinson, G. (2018) *Plutarch's Rhythmic Prose*. Oxford.

Ianziti, G. (2016) "Pier Candido Decembrio and the Suetonian path to princely biography", in Baker et al. (2016), 237–270.

Iglesias Montiel, R. (1991) "La recepción de Plutarco en el Comentario de De la Cerda a las *Geórgicas* de Virgilio", in García López and Calderón Dorda (1991), 173–182.

Immerwahr, H. (1960) "*Ergon*: history as a monument in Herodotus and Thucydides", *AJPh* 81: 261–290.

Indelli, G. (1992) "Plutarco, *Bruta animalia ratione uti*: qualche riflessione", in Gallo (1992), 317–352.

(ed.) (1995) *Plutarco. Le Bestie sono esseri razionali*. Naples.

Ingenkamp, H. G. (1971) *Plutarchs Schriften über die Heilung der Seele* (Hypomnemata 34). Göttingen.

(1999) "*Ou psegetai to pinein*. Wie Plutarch den übermässigen Weingenuss beurteilte", in Montes Cala et al. (1999), 277–290.

(2016) "De Plutarchi malignitate", in Opsomer, Roskam, and Titchener (2016), 249–242.

Inglese, L. (2003) "Aspetti della fortuna di Erodoto in Plutarco", *RCCM* 45: 221–244.

Innes, D., H. Hine, and C. Pelling (eds.) (1995) *Ethics and Rhetoric: Classical Essays for Donald Russell on His Seventy-Fifth Birthday*. Oxford.

Inwood, B. (ed.) (2003) *The Cambridge Companion to the Stoics*. Cambridge.

Irigoin, J. (1976) "Les manuscrits de Plutarque à 32 lignes et à 22 lignes", in *Actes du XIVe Congres International des Etudes Byzantins, Bucarest, 6–12 Septembre 1971*. Bucharest, 83–87.

(1982–3) "La formation d'un corpus: Un probleme d'histoire des textes dans la tradition des *Vies paralleles* de Plutarque", *RHT* 12–13: 1–13.

(1986) "Le catalogue de Lamprias: tradition manuscrite et éditions imprimées", *REG* 99: 318–331.

(1987) "II. Histoire du texte des *Oeuvres Morales* de Plutarque," in Flacelière et al. (1987), ccxxvii–cccx.

Irwin, E. (2006) "The biographies of poets: the case of Solon," in McGing and Mossman (2006), 13–30.

Isaac, B. (2004) *The Invention of Racism in Classical Antiquity*. Princeton, NJ.

Isaacson, W. (ed.) (2010) *Profiles in Leadership: Historians on the Elusive Quality of Greatness*. New York.

Jacob, C. (2013) *The Web of Athenaeus*. Trans. A. Papaconstantinou. Washington, DC.

Jacobs, S. (2018) *Plutarch's Pragmatic Biographies: Lessons for Statesmen and Generals in the Parallel Lives*. Leiden.

Jacquemin, A. (1991) "Delphes au IIᵉ siècle après J.-C.: un lieu de mémoire grecque", in S. Saïd (ed.), *Ellēnismos: quelques jalons pour une histoire de l'identité grecque*. Leiden, 217–231.

Jaeger, W. (1945) *Paideia: The Ideals of Greek Culture. Vol. I*. Oxford.

Jazdzewska, K. (2009–10) "'Not an innocent spectacle': hunting and *venationes* in Plutarch's *De sollertia animalium*", *Ploutarchos* 7: 35–46.

(2013) "A skeleton at a banquet: death in Plutarch's *Convivium Septem Sapientium*", *Phoenix* 67: 301–319.

(2015a) "Dialogic format of Philo of Alexandria's *De animalibus*", *Eos* 102: 45–56.

(2015b) "Tales of two lives in Xenophon's 'Hiero,' Plutarch's 'Gryllos,' and Lucian's 'Cock'", *Hermes* 143: 141–152.

(2016) "Laughter in Plutarch's *Convivium Septem Sapientium*", *CPh* 111: 74–88.

Jehne, M. (1999) "Cato und die Bewahrung der traditionellen *res publica*. Zum Spannungsverhältnis zwischen *mos maiorum* und griechischer Kultur im zweiten Jahrhundert v.Chr.", in G. Vogt-Spira and B. Rommel (eds.), *Rezeption und Identität. Die kulturelle Auseinandersetzung Roms mit Griechenland als europäisches Paradigma*. Stuttgart, 115–134.

Jenkins, R. (1948) "Constantine VII's portrait of Michael III", *BAB* 34.5: 71–77.

(1954) "The classical background of the Scriptores Post Theophanem", *Dumbarton Oaks Papers* 8: 11–30.

(1963) "The Hellenistic origins of Byzantine literature", *Dumbarton Oaks Papers* 17: 37–52.

Jennings, V. and A. Katsaros (eds.) (2007) *The World of Ion of Chios*. Leiden.

Jones, C. (1966) "Towards a chronology of Plutarch's works", *JRS* 56: 61–74. Reprinted in Scardigli (1995), 95–123.

(1967) "The teacher of Plutarch", *HSPh* 71: 205–213.

(1970) "Sura and Senecio", *JRS* 60: 98–104.

(1971) *Plutarch and Rome*. Oxford.

(1974) Review of Russell (1973a), *JRS* 64: 279–280.

(1978) *The Roman World of Dio Chrysostom*. Cambridge, MA.

(2004) "Multiple identities in the age of the Second Sophistic", in B. Borg (ed.), *Paideia: The World of the Second Sophistic*. Berlin, 13–21.

Jones, R. (1980) *The Platonism of Plutarch and Selected Papers (Ancient Philosophy. Editions, Commentaries, Critical Works)*, with an Introduction by L. Tarán. New York. [Reprint of the author's thesis, University of Chicago, 1913, originally published in 1916 by G. Banta Pub. Co.]

Jouan, F. (2001) "Quelques réflexions sur Plutarque et la tragédie", *SIFC* 95: 186–196.

Jouanna, J., L. Villard, and D. Béguin, D. (eds.) (2002) *Vin et santé en Grèce ancienne (Actes du colloque organisé à l'Université de Rouen et à Paris)*. Paris.

Jouët-Pastré, E. (2002) "Vin, remède et jeu dans les *Lois* de Platon", in Jouanna, Villard, and Béguin (2002), 222–232.

Jufresa, M. (1996) "La abstinencia de carne y el origen de la civilización en Plutarco", in Fernández Delgado and Pordomingo Pardo (1996), 219–226.

Jufresa, M., F. Mestre, P. Gómez, and P. Gilabert (eds.) (2005) *Plutarc a la seva època: paideia i societat (Actas del VIII Simposio Internacional de la Sociedad Española de Plutarquistas, Barcelona, 6–8 nov. 2003)*. Barcelona.

Jufresa Muñoz, M. (2007) "El amor de los animales en las *Vidas Paralelas* de Plutarco", in Nieto Ibáñez and López López (2007), 265–277.

Jung, M. (2006) *Marathon und Plataiai: Zwei Perserschlachten als leux de memoire im antiken Griechenland*. Göttingen.

Jüthner, J. (1923) *Hellenen und Barbaren*. Leipzig.

Kahle, M. (2017a) "Giannozzo Manetti: on famous men of great age, 'Life of Socrates'", in Baker (2017), 59–65.

(2017b) "Spoliating Diogenes Laertius: Gianozzo Manetti's use(s) of the lives of the philosophers", in Baker (2017), 38–89.

Kaldellis, A. (1999) *The Argument of Psellos' Chronographia*. Leiden.

(2007) *Hellenism in Byzantium: The Transformation of Greek Identity and the Reception of the Classical Tradition*. Cambridge.

Kalimtzis, K. (2012) *Taming Anger: The Hellenic Approach to the Limitations of Reason*. London.

Kammer, U. (1964) *Untersuchungen zu Ciceros Bild von Cato Censorius*. Frankfurt.

Karamanolis, G. (2006) *Plato and Aristotle in Agreement? Platonists on Aristotle from Antiochus to Porphyry*. Oxford.

Karpozilos, A. (ed.) (1990) *The Letters of Ioannes Mauropous Metropolitan of Euchaita*. Thessalonica.

Kassel, R. (1958) *Untersuchungen zur griechischen und römischen Konsolationsliteratur*. Munich.

Kasulke, C. (2000) "Hadrian und die Jagd im Spiegel der zeitgenössischen Literatur", in W. Martini (ed.), *Die Jagd der Eliten in den Erinnerungskulturen von der Antike bis in die Frühe Neuzeit*. Göttingen, 101–127.

Kazhdan, A. (ed.) (1991) *The Oxford Dictionary of Byzantium*. Oxford.

(2006) *A History of Byzantine Literature (850–1000)*, ed. C. Angelidi. Athens.

Kazhdan, A. and A. Wharton Epstein (1985) *Change in Byzantine Culture in the Eleventh and Twelfth Centuries*. Berkeley, CA.

Keaveney, A. (1992) *Lucullus: A Life*. London.

Kechagia, E. (2011a) "Philosophy in Plutarch's *Table Talk*: in jest or in earnest?" in Klotz and Oikonomopoulou (2011a), 77–104.

(2011b) *Plutarch Against Colotes: A Lesson in History of Philosophy*. Oxford.

Kechagia-Ovseiko, E. (2014) "Plutarch and Epicureanism", in Beck (2014a), 104–120.

Keller, A. (1939) "Plutarch and Rousseau's first *Discours*", *Publications of the Modern Language Association of America* 54.1: 212–222.

Kemezis, A. (2016) "'*Inglorius labor*? The rhetoric of glory and utility in Plutarch's *Precepts* and Tacitus' *Agricola*", *CW* 110: 87–117.

Kennedy, G. (1972) *The Art of Rhetoric in the Roman World*. Princeton, NJ.

Kennell, N. (1995) *The Gymnasium of Virtue: Education and Culture in Ancient Sparta*. Chapel Hill, NC.

Kessler, E. (1968) *Das Problem des frühen Humanismus; seine philosophische Bedeutung bei Coluccio Salutati*. Munich.

Kidd, I. (1992) "Introduction" and notes to R. Waterfield (trans.) and I. Kidd (ed.), *Plutarch: Essays*. London.

Kienast, D. (1964) "Die Homonoiaverträge in der römischen Kaiserzeit", *JNG* 14: 51–64.

Kim, L. (2009) "Historical fiction, brachylogy, and Plutarch's *Banquet of the Seven Sages*", in Ribeiro Ferreira et al. (2009), 481–495.

(2010) "The literary heritage as language: Atticism and the Second Sophistic", in Bakker (2010), 468–482.

(2017) "Atticism and Asianism", in Richter and Johnson (2017), 41–66.

King, C. (trans.) (1908) *Plutarch's Morals: Theosophical Essays*. London.

Kingston, R. (2022) *Plutarch's Prism. Classical Reception and Public Humanism in France and England, 1500–1800*. Cambridge.

Kirk, A. (2017) "Λόγος and φωνή in *Odyssey* 10 and Plutarch's *Gryllus*", in N. Slater (ed.), *Voice and Voices in Antiquity*. Leiden, 397–415.

Kirkland, N. B. (2019) "The character of tradition in Plutarch's *On the Malice of Herodotus*", *AJPh* 140: 477–511.

Kitchell, K. (2017) "Animal literacy and the Greeks: Philoctetes the Hedgehog and Dolon the Weasel", in Fögen and Thomas (2017), 183–203.

Kleczkowska, K. (2014) "Those who cannot speak: animals as others in ancient Greek thought", *Maska* 24: 97–108.

Kloft, H. and M. Kerner (1992) *Die Institutio Traiani: Ein pseudo-plutarchischer Text im Mittelalter*. Stuttgart.

Klotz, F. (2007) "Portraits of the philosopher: Plutarch's self-presentation in the *Quaestiones Convivales*", *CQ* 57: 650–667.

(2011) "Imagining the past: Plutarch's play with time", in Klotz and Oikonomopoulou (2011a), 161–178.

(2014) "The sympotic works", in Beck (2014a), 207–222.

Klotz, F. and K. Oikonomopoulou (eds.) (2011a) *The Philosopher's Banquet: Plutarch's Table Talk in the Intellectual Culture of the Roman Empire*. Oxford.

(2011b) "Introduction", in Klotz and Oikonomopoulou (2011a), 1–31.

(2011c) "Conclusion: reading (from) the *Table Talk* in Aulus Gellius' *Attic Nights*", in Klotz and Oikonomopoulou (2011a), 233–237.

Kneebone, E. (2008) "Τόσσ' ἐδάην: the poetics of knowledge in Oppian's *Halieutica*", *Ramus* 37: 32–59.

(2017) "The limits of enquiry in imperial Greek didactic poetry", in J. König and G. Woolf (eds.), *Authority and Expertise in Ancient Scientific Culture*. Cambridge, 203–230.

Knight, G. W. (1965) *The Imperial Theme: Further Interpretations of Shakespeare's Tragedies Including the Roman Plays*. London.

Knight, R. (1991) *Corneille's Tragedies: The Role of the Unexpected*. Cardiff.

Knox, B. (1964) *The Heroic Temper: Studies in Sophoclean Tragedy*. Sather Classical Lectures, vol. 35. Berkeley, CA.

König, J. (2005) *Athletics and Literature in the Roman Empire*. Cambridge.

(2007) "Fragmentation and coherence in Plutarch's *Sympotic Questions*", in J. König and T. Whitmarsh (eds.), *Ordering Knowledge in the Roman World*. Cambridge, 43–68.

(2010) "Conversational and citational brevity in Plutarch's *Sympotic Questions*," in Horster and Reitz (2010), 321–348.

(2012) *Saints and Symposiasts: The Literature of Food and the Symposium in Graeco-Roman and Early Christian Culture*. Cambridge.

Konrad, C. (1994) *Plutarch's* Sertorius*: A Historical Commentary*. Chapel Hill, NC.

Konstan, D. (1994) *Sexual Symmetry: Love in the Ancient Novel and Related Genres*. Princeton, NJ.

(2004) "The birth of the reader: Plutarch as a literary critic", *Scholia* 13: 3–27.

(2005) "The pleasures of the ancient text or the pleasure of poetry from Plato to Plutarch", in F. Cairns (ed.), *Greek and Roman Poetry: Greek and Roman Historiography*. Cambridge, 1–17.

(2006) "The active reader in classical antiquity", *Argos* 30: 7–18.

(2010–11) "A pig convicts itself of unreason: the implicit argument of Plutarch's *Gryllus*", *Hyperboreus* 16/17: 371–385.

Konstan, D. and S. Saïd (eds.) (2006) *Greeks on Greekness: Viewing the Greek past under the Roman Empire*. Cambridge.

Konstantinovic, I. (1989) *Montaigne et Plutarque*. Geneva.

Korhonen, T. (2012) "On human–animal sexual relationships in Aelian's *De natura animalium*", *Arctos* 46: 65–77.

Korhonen, T. and E. Ruonakoski (2017) *Human and Animal in Ancient Greece: Empathy and Encounter in Classical Literature*. London.

Kowalski, G. (1918) *De Plutarchi scriptorum iuuenilium colore rhetorico*. Krakow.

Krappe, A. (1933) "Solomon and Ashmodai", *AJPh*: 260–268.

Kraus, C. (ed.) (1999) *The Limits of Historiography: Genre and Narrative in Ancient Historical Texts*. Leiden.

Krauss, F. (1912) *Die rhetorischen Schriften Plutarchs*. Nuremberg.

Labarrière, J.-L. (1997) "*Logos endiathetos* et *logos prophorikos* dans la polémique entre le Portique et la Nouvelle Académie", in Cassin and Labarrière (1997), 259–280.

Lachenaud, G. (ed.) (1993) *Plutarque: Oeuvres Morales. Vol. XII*. Paris.

La Font de Saint-Yenne, É. (1754) *Sentimens sur quelques ouvrages de peinture, sculpture et gravure*. Paris.

La Matina, M. (1998) "Plutarco negli autori cristiani greci", in Gallo (1998a), 81–110.

Laird, A. (ed.) (2006) *Oxford Readings in Classical Studies: Ancient Literary Criticism*. Oxford.

Lakmann, M.-L. (1995) *Der Platoniker Tauros in der Darstellung des Aulus Gellius*. Leiden.

Laks, A. (2016) "The continuation of philosophy by other means?" in Weisser and Thaler (2016), 16–30.

Lamberton, R. (2001) *Plutarch*. New Haven, CT.

Larmour, D. (1992) "Making parallels: 'synkrisis' and Plutarch's *Themistocles and Camillus*", *ANRW* II.33.6: 4154–4200.

(2014) "The *synkrisis*", in Beck (2014a), 405–416.

Larmour, D. and D. Spencer (eds.) (2007) *The Sites of Rome: Time Space, Memory*. Oxford.

Lather, A. (2017) "Taking pleasure seriously: Plutarch on the benefits of poetry and philosophy", *CW* 110.3: 323–349.

Laurenti, R. and G. Indelli (eds.) (1988) *Plutarco: Sul controllo dell'ira (CPM 2)*. Naples.

Lauritzen, F. (2005) *The Depiction of Character in the Chronographia of Michael Psellos*. Diss., Columbia University.

Lavoine, S. (1986) "L'influence du Plutarque d'Amyot sur la tragédie française du XVIᵉ siècle", in Balard (1986), 273–283.

Law, R. A. (1943) "The Roman background of *Titus Andronicus*", *Studies in Philology* 40: 145–153.

Lee, H. (2009) *Biography: A Very Short Introduction*. Oxford.

Leeck, C. (2010) *Das Bild Roms in Plutarchs Römerbiographien. Schmeichelei oder ernsthafte Völkerverständigung?* Marburg.

Lefkowitz, J. (2014) "Aesop and animal fable", in Campbell (2014), 1–23.

Lefkowitz, M. (1981) *The Lives of the Greek Poets*. London.

(2012) *The Lives of the Greek Poets* (2nd ed.). London.

Legros, A. (2008) "Plutarque, Amyot, Montaigne et la 'superstition'", in Guerrier (2008), 275–291.

Lemerle, P. (1986) *Byzantine Humanism: The First Phase*. Trans. H. Lindsay and A. Moffatt. Canberra (French original 1971).

Lenfant, D. (2003) "De l'usage des comiques comme source historique: les *Vies* de Plutarque et la Comédie Ancienne", in G. Lachenaud and D. Longrée (eds.), *Grecs et Romains aux prises avec l'histoire: Représentations, récits et idéologies*, vol. 2. Rennes, 391–314.

(2007) "On Persian *tryphē* in Athenaeus", in C. Tuplin (ed.), *Persian Responses: Political and Cultural Interaction with(in) the Achaemenid Empire*. Swansea, 51–65.

Leo, F. (1901) *Die griechische-römische Biographie nach ihrer litterarischen Form*. Leipzig.

Leone, P. (ed.) (1991) *Maximi Monachi Planudis Epistulae*. Amsterdam.

Lerouge, C. (2007) *L'Image des Parthes dans le monde gréco-romain*. Stuttgart.

Lévy, E. (1984) "Naissance du concept de barbare", *Ktema* 9: 5–14.

Lewis, R. (1991) "Suetonius' 'Caesares' and their literary antecedents", *ANRW* II.33.5: 3623–3674.

Lhermitte, J.-F. (2015) *L'animal vertueux dans la philosophie antique à l'époque imperiale*. Paris.

Li Causi, P. (2009–10) "Strange animals: extremely interspecific hybridization (and *anthropopoiesis*) in Plutarch", *Ploutarchos* 7: 47–60.

(2010) "Granchi, uomini e altri animali. La genesi della violenza nel *De sollertia animalium* di Plutarco", in V. Andò and N. Cusumano (eds.), *Come bestie? Forme a paradossi della violenza tra mondo antico e disagio contemporaneo*. Caltanissetta, 189–208.

Licona, M. (2017) *Why Are There Differences in the Gospels? What We Can Learn from Ancient Biography*. Oxford.

Liebert, H. (2016) *Plutarch's Politics: Between City and Empire*. Cambridge.

Littlewood, A. (ed.) (1985) *Michael Psellus: Oratoria Minora*. Leipzig.

Ljubarskij, J. (1993) "New trends in the study of Byzantine historiography", *Dumbarton Oaks Papers* 47: 131–138.

(2000) "Why is the *Alexeid* a masterpiece of Byzantine literature?" in Gouma-Peterson (2000), 169–185.

Ljubarskij, J. et al. (1998) "Quellenforschung and/or literary criticism: narrative structures in Byzantine historical writings," *SO* 73: 5–73.

Lloyd George, R. (2016) *A Modern Plutarch: Comparisons of the Most Influential Modern Statesmen*. New York.

Lo Cascio, E. (2007) "Le città dell'impero e le loro élites nella testimonianza di Plutarco", in Volpe Cacciatore and Ferrari (2007), 171–186.

Lomas, K. and T. Cornell (eds.) (2003) *"Bread and Circuses": Euergetism and Municipal Patronage in Roman Italy*. London.

Long, A. (1988) "Socrates in Hellenistic philosophy", *CQ* 38: 150–117.

(1996) *Stoic Studies*. Cambridge.

López Férez, J. (2008) "Personajes históricos griegos o romanos en el *Quijote*", *Anales cervantinos* 40: 119–132.

López Rueda, J. (1973) *Helenistas españoles del siglo XVI*. Madrid.

Lorenz, G. (2013) *Tiere im Leben der alten Kulturen: Schriftlose Kulturen, Alter Orient, Ägypten, Griechenland und Rom*, 2nd ed. Innsbruck.

Luce, T. (1989) "Ancient views on the causes of bias in historical writing", *CPh* 84: 16–31.

Luppino Manes, E. (1989) "La traccia della biografia plutarchea di Agesilao: individuazione di una possibile indagine critica", in *Miscellanea greca e romana XIV*. Rome, 87–122. Reprinted as "Introduzione" in E. Luppino Manes and A. Marcone (eds.), *Plutarco: Vite Parallele. Agesilao – Pompeo*. Milan, 87–126.

Luttrell, A. (1960) "Greek histories translated and compiled for Juan Fernandez de Heredia, Master of Rhodes 1377–96", *Speculum* 35: 401–407.

(1970) "Coluccio Salutati's letter to Juan Fernández de Heredia", *IMU* 13: 235–243.

Mably, G. (1988) *De la manière d'écrire l'histoire*, ed. B. de Negroni. Paris.

MacCallum, M. (1910) *Shakespeare's Roman Plays and Their Background*. London. Reprinted 1967.

Mack, P. (2016) "Montaigne on reading", in P. Desan (ed.), *The Oxford Handbook of Montaigne*. Oxford, 415–433.

MacMullen, R. (1997) *Christianity and Paganism in the Fourth to Eighth Centuries*. New Haven, CT.

Macrides, R. (1996) "The historian in the history", in C. Constantinides, N. Panagiotakes, and A. Angelou (eds.), ΦΙΛΗΕΛΛΗΝ: *Studies in Honour of Robert Browning*. Venice, 205–224.

Maisano, R. and A. Rollo (eds.) (2002) *Manuele Crisolora e il ritorno del greco in occidente. Atti del Convegno Internazionale (Naples, 26–29 giugno 1997)*. Naples.

Malkin, I. (ed.) (2001) *Ancient Perceptions of Greek Ethnicity*. Cambridge, MA.

Manfredini, M. (1975) "Gli scolii a Plutarco de Areta di Cesarea", *Siculorum Gymnasium* 28: 337–350.

(1979) "Gli scoli alle *Vite* di Plutarco", *Jahrbuch der Österreichischen Byzantinistik* 28: 83–119.

(1983) "Gli scoli alle *Vite* di Plutarco e i lessici Bizantini coevi", in L. Leone and M. Pietro Luigi (eds.), *Studi Bizantini e Neogreci: Atti del IV Congresso nazionale di studi bizantini, Lecce, 21–23 aprile 1980-Calimera, 24 aprile 1980*. Galantina: 445–455.

(1987) "Codici plutarchei di umanisti italiani", *ASNP* 17: 1001–1043.

(1988a) "Codici plutarchei contenenti *Vitae* e *Moralia*", in Gallo (1988), 103–122.

(1988b) "Sulla tradizione manoscritta dei *Moralia* 70–77", in Gallo (1988), 123–138.

(1992) "Due codici de Escerpta Plutarchei e l'epitome di Zonara", *Prometheus* 18: 193–215.

(1993) "Due codici de Escerpta Plutarchei e l'epitome di Zonara II", *Prometheus* 19: 1–25.

Manfredini, M. and D. P. Orsi (eds.) (1987) *Plutarco. Le Vite di Arato et di Artaserse*. Milan.

Mango, C. (1975) "The availability of books in the Byzantine Empire, A.D. 750–850", in *Byzantine Books and Bookmen. A Dumbarton Oaks Colloquium*. Washington, DC, 29–45.

Mansfeld, J. (1992) *Heresiography in Context: Hippolytus' Elenchos as a Source for Greek Philosophy*. Leiden.

(1994) *Prolegomena: Questions to be Settled Before the Study of an Author, or a Text*. Leiden.

Manton, G. (1949) "The manuscript tradition of Plutarch *Moralia* 70–7", *CQ* 43: 97–104.

Manzini, F. (2019) "Plutarch from Voltaire to Stendhal", in Xenophontos and Oikonomopoulou (2019), 515–527.

Mariev, S. (ed.) (2008) *Ioannis Antiocheni Fragmenta quae supersunt omnia*. Berlin.

Marincola, J. (1994) "Plutarch's refutation of Herodotus", *AncW* 25: 191–203.

(1999) "Genre, convention, and innovation in Greco-Roman historiography", in Kraus (1999), 281–324.

(2010) "Plutarch, 'Parallelism' and the Persian-War *Lives*", in Humble (2010b), 217–235.

(2011) "Romans and/as Barbarians", in L. Bonfante (ed.), *The Barbarians of Ancient Europe*. Cambridge, 347–357.

(2012) "The fairest victor: Plutarch, Aristides and the Persian Wars", *Histos* 6: 91–113.

(2015a) "Plutarch, Herodotus and the historian's character", in Ash, Mossman, and Titchener (2015), 83–95.

(2015b) "Defending the divine: Plutarch on the gods in Herodotus", in A. Ellis (ed.), *God in History: Reading and Rewriting Herodotean Theology from Plutarch to the Renaissance. Histos* supplement 4: 41–83. https://histos.org /documents/SV04EllisGodinHistory.pdf.

(2018) "The strategies of Plutarch's *On the Malice of Herodotus*", in T. Thorsen and S. Harrison (eds.), *Dynamics of Ancient Prose: Biographic, Novelistic, Apologetic*. Berlin, 19–35.

Markantonatos, A. and C. Tsangalis (eds.) (2008) Ἀρχαία ἑλληνικὴ τραγῳδία: θεωρία καὶ πρᾶξη. Athens.

Markopoulos, A. (2003) "Byzantine history writing at the end of the first millennium", in P. Magdalino (ed.), *Byzantium in the Year 1000*. Leiden, 183–197.

(2009) "From narrative historiography to historical biography: new trends in Byzantine historical writing in the 10th–11th centuries", *Byzantinische Zeitschrift* 102: 697–715.

Marshall, L. (2017) "Gadfly or spur? The meaning of μύωψ in Plato's *Apology of Socrates*", *JHS* 137: 163–174.

Martin, H., Jr. (1960) "The concept of *prāotēs* in Plutarch's *Lives*", *GRBS* 3: 65–73.

(1961) "The concept of *philanthropia* in Plutarch's *Lives*", *AJPh* 82: 164–175.

(1979) "Plutarch's *De sollertia animalium* 959 B–C: the discussion of the encomium of hunting", *AJPh* 100: 99–106.

(1995) "Moral failure without vice in Plutarch's Athenian *Lives*", *Ploutarchos* 12.1: 13–18.

Martin, R. (1993) "The Seven Sages as performers of wisdom", in C. Dougherty and L. Kurke (eds.), *Cultural Poetics in Archaic Greece: Cult, Performance, Politics*. Cambridge, 108–128.

Martindale, C. (ed.) (2004) *Shakespeare and the Classics*. Cambridge.

Martindale, C. and M. Martindale (1990) *Shakespeare and the Uses of Antiquity*. London.

Martinelli Tempesta, S. (2013) "La tradizione manoscritta dei *Moralia* di Plutarco. Riflessioni per una messa a punto", in Pace and Volpe Cacciatore (2013), 273–288.

Martínez Benavides, M. (1999) "Plutarco en un comentario a Platón del siglo XVI", in Montes Cala et al. (1999), 301–308.

Martínez Fernández, A. (1994) "El vocabulario de los epigramas cretenses de época imperial", in *Actas del VIII congreso español de estudios clásicos: (Madrid, 23–28 de septiembre de 1991*. Madrid, 185–192.

Masaracchia, A. (1995) "Tracce aristoteliche nell' *An seni res publica gerenda sit* e nei *Praecepta gerendae rei publicae*", in Gallo and Scardigli (1995), 227–234.

Mason, H. (1970) "The Roman government in Greek sources", *Phoenix* 24: 150–159.

Massaro, D. (1995) "I *Praecepta gerendae rei publicae* e il realismo politico di Plutarco", in Gallo and Scardigli (1995), 235–244.

Matthiessen, F. (1931) "Sir Thomas North", in *Translation: An Elizabethan Art*. Cambridge, MA.

May, G. (1967) "Corneille and the classics", *Yale French Studies* 38: 138–150.

May, T. (1639) *The Tragedy of Cleopatra, Queen of Egypt*. London.

Mayer, K. (1997) "Themistocles, Plutarch, and the voice of the Other", in Schrader, Ramón, and Vela (1997), 297–304.

Mazza, M. (1995) "Plutarco e la politica romana. Alcune riconsiderazioni", in Gallo and Scardigli (1995), 245–268.

McCarthy, B. (1940–1) "Literary reminiscences in Psellus's *Chronographia*", *Byzantion* 15: 296–299.

McGing, B. and J. Mossman (eds.) (2006a) *The Limits of Ancient Biography*. Swansea.

(2006b) "Introduction", in McGing and Mossman (2006a), ix–xx.

McGrail, M. (ed.) (1997) *Shakespeare's Plutarch*. Tokyo.

McInerney, J. (2003) "Plutarch's manly women", in R. Rosen and I. Sluiter (eds.), *Andreia: Studies in Manliness and Courage in Classical Antiquity*. Leiden, 319–344.

McNamara, J. (1999) "Gendering virtue", in Pomeroy (1999a), 151–161.

Meeusen, M. (2016) *Plutarch's Science of Natural Problems: A Study with Commentary on Quaestiones Naturales*. Leuven.

(2017) "Egyptian knowledge at Plutarch's table: Out of the question?" in Georgiadou and Oikonomopoulou (2017), 215–226.

Mendels, D. (1986) "Greek and Roman history in the *Bibliotheca* of Photius – a note", *Byzantion* 56: 196–206.

Menéndez Pelayo, M. (1905) *Cervantes y El Quijote*. Whitefish, MT.

Méniel, B. (2008) "La réception en France, au XVIᵉ siècle, du traité *Comment il faut réfréner la colère*", in Guerrier (2008), 109–130.

Mérot, A. (1987) *Eustache Le Sueur 1616–1655*. Paris.

Mestre, F. (1999) "Plutarco contra el sofista", in Pérez Jiménez, García López, and Aguilar (1999), 383–395.

(2003) "Anacharsis, the wise man from abroad", *Lexis* 21: 303–317.

Michelini, A. (ed.) (2003) *Plato as Author: The Rhetoric of Philosophy*. Leiden.

Migne, J.-P. (ed.) (1928–45) *Patrologia Graeca*. Paris.

Miles, Gary (1989) "How Roman are Shakespeare's 'Romans'?" *Shakespeare Quarterly* 40: 257–283.

Miles, Geoffrey (1996) *Shakespeare and the Constant Romans*. Oxford.

Miletti, M. (2014) "Il *De laude ipsius* di Plutarco a la teoria "classica" dell'autoelogio", in P. Volpe Cacciatore (ed.), *Plutarco: linguaggi e retorica. Atti del XII Convegno della International Plutarch Society, Seziona Italiana*. Naples, 79–99.

Millar, F. (1964) *A Study of Cassius Dio*. Oxford.

Minon, S. (2015) "Plutarque (Thém. 24) transpose Thucydide (i.136): de l'harmonie austère au péan delphique. Pragmatique et rythmique de deux mode de composition stylistique", *REG* 28: 29–99.

Mittelhaus, K. (1911) *De Plutarchi Praeceptis gerendae reipublicae*. Diss., Leipzig University.

Moles, J. (ed.) (1988) *Plutarch: Life of Cicero*. Warminster, PA.

(1989) Review of Geiger (1985), *CR* 39: 229–233.

(1996) "Diatribe", in S. Hornblower and A. Spawforth (eds.), *Oxford Classical Dictionary*, 3rd ed. Oxford, 463–464.

Momigliano, A. (1949) "Notes on Petrarch, John of Salisbury and the *Institutio Trajani*", *Journal of the Warburg and Courtauld Institutes* 12: 189–190.

(1993) *The Development of Greek Biography*, 2nd ed. Cambridge, MA.

Monaco, M. (2011–12) "Folly and dark humor in the *Life of Demetrius*", *Ploutarchos* 9: 49–59.

Monaghan, L. and J. Goodman (eds.) (2007) *A Cultural Approach to Interpersonal Communication: Essential Readings*. Malden, MA.

Montaigne, M. (1987) *Michel de Montaigne: The Complete Essays*, ed. M. Screech. London.

Montchrestien, A. de (1943) *Les Lacènes: A Critical Edition*, ed. G. Calkins. Philadelphia, PA.

Montes Cala, J., M. Sánchez Ortiz de Landaluce, and R. Gallé Cejudo (eds.) (1999) *Plutarco, Dioniso y el vino*. Madrid.

Montiglio, S. (2011) *From Villain to Hero: Odysseus in Ancient Thought*. Ann Arbor, MI.

Mora, F. (2007a) "Greci e romani nelle *Vite parallele*", *Polifemo* 7: 135–92.

(2007b) "Nuclei d'interesse e strategie interpretative nelle *Quaestiones Romanae* di Plutarco", *Gerión* 25: 329–370.

Morales Ortiz, A. (2000) *Plutarco en España: Traducciones de Moralia en el siglo XVI*. Murcia.

Moravcsik, G. (ed.) and R. Jenkins (trans.) (1967) *Constantine Porphyogenitus: De administrando imperio*. Washington, DC.

Morgan, T. (2011) "The miscellany and Plutarch", in Klotz and Oikonomopoulou (2011a), 49–73.

Morrison, M. (1974) "Some aspects of the treatment of the theme of Antony and Cleopatra in tragedies of the sixteenth century", *Journal of European Studies* 4: 113–125.

Mossman, J. (1988) "Tragedy and epic in Plutarch's *Alexander*", *JHS* 108: 83–93. Reprinted in Scardigli (1995), 209–228.

(1992) "Plutarch, Pyrrhus, and Alexander", in Stadter (1992b), 90–108.

(ed.) (1997a) *Plutarch and His Intellectual World: Essays on Plutarch*. London.

(1997b) "Plutarch and Shakespeare's *HIV parts 1 and 2*", in McGrail (1997), 99–118.

(1997c) "Plutarch's *Dinner of the Seven Wise Men* and its place in *symposion* literature", in Mossman (1997a), 119–140.

(2005a) "Plutarch on animals: rhetorical strategies in *de sollertia animalium*", *Hermathena* 179: 141–163.

(2005b) "*Taxis ou barbaros*: Greek and Roman in Plutarch's *Pyrrhus*", *CQ* 55: 498–517.

(2010) "A life unparalleled: Plutarch's *Artaxerxes*", in Humble (2010b), 145–168.

(2014) "Tragedy and the hero", in Beck (2014a), 437–448.

(forthcoming) "Tragicomedy? Generic enrichment in Plutarch, *Demetrius* 38 and *Antony* 70", in Duff and Chrysanthou (forthcoming).

Mossman, J. and F. B. Titchener (2011) "Bitch is not a four-letter word: animal reason and human passion in Plutarch", in Roskam and Van der Stockt (2011), 273–296.

Moxon, I., J. Smart, and A. J. Woodman (eds.) (1986), *Past Perspectives: Studies in Greek and Roman Historical Writing*. Cambridge.

Muccioli, F. (2000) "La critica di Plutarco a Filisto e a Timeo", in Van der Stockt (2000b), 291–307.

(2012) *La storia attraverso gli esempi: Protagonisti e interpretazioni del mondo greco in Plutarco*. Milan.

Mueller-Goldingen, C. (1993) "Politische Theorie und Praxis bei Plutarch", *Würzburger Jahrbücher für die Altertumswissenschaft* 19: 201–213.

Müller, R. (1978) "Hellenen und Barbaren im Spiegel der hellenistischen Philosophie", *Klio* 60: 183–189.

Mullett, M. (2002) "New literary history and the history of Byzantine literature: a worthwhile endeavour?" in P. Odorico and P. Agapitos (eds.), *Pour une "nouvelle" histoire de la littérature Byzantine*. Paris, 37–60.

Murray, O. (1983) "The symposion as social organisation," in R. Hägg (ed.), *The Greek Renaissance of the Eighth Century B.C: Tradition and Innovation. Proceedings of the Second International Symposium at the Swedish Institute in Athens, 1–5 June, 1981*. Stockholm, 195–200.

(ed.)(1990) *Sympotica. A Symposium on the Symposion*. Oxford.

Murray, O. and M. Tecuşan (eds.) (1995) *In Vino Veritas*. Rome.

Naas, M. (2015) "American gadfly: Plato and the problem of metaphor", in J. Bell and M. Naas (eds.), *Plato's Animals: Gadflies, Horses, Swans, and Other Philosophical Beasts*. Bloomington, IN: 43–59.

Nagy, G. (1979) *The Best of the Achaeans*. Baltimore, MD.

Narro Sánchez, A. (2011) "Los valores de la buena mujer en Plutarco a través del De Institutione feminae christianae de Luis Vives", in Candau Morón et al. (2011), 569–584.

Neill, M. (ed.) (1994) *The Oxford Shakespeare: The Tragedy of Anthony and Cleopatra*. Oxford.

Németh, A. (2010) *Imperial Systematization of the Past: Emperor Constantine VII and His Historical Excerpts*. Ph.D. diss., Central European University, Budapest (www.etd.ceu.he/2010/mphnea01.pdf).

(2019) "The reception of Plutarch in Constantinople in the ninth and tenth centuries", in Xenophontos and Oikonomopoulou (2019), 187–204.

Nerdahl, M. (2007) *Homeric Models in Plutarch's Lives*. Diss., University of Wisconsin–Madison.

(2011–12) "Exiling Achilles: reflections on the banished statesman in Plutarch's *Lives*", *CJ* 107: 331–353.

Nesselrath, H.-G. (ed.) (2010) *Plutarch: On the Daimonion of Socrates – Human Liberation, Divine Guidance and Philosophy*. Tübingen.

Neville, L. (2012) *Heroes and Romans in Twelfth-Century Byzantium. The Material for History of Nikephoros Bryennios*. Cambridge.

(2016) *Anna Komnene: The Life and Work of a Medieval Historian*. Oxford.

Nevin, S. (2014) "Negative comparison: Agamemnon and Alexander in Plutarch's *Agesilaus–Pompey*", *GRBS* 54: 45–68.

Newmyer, S. T. (1992) "Plutarch on justice toward animals: ancient insights on a moral debate", *Scholia* 1: 38–54.

(1997) "Just beasts? Plutarch and modern science on the sense of fair play in animals", *CO* 74.3: 85–88.

(1999) "Speaking of beasts: the Stoics and Plutarch on animal behaviour and the modern case against animals", *QUCC* 63: 99–110.

(2003) "Paws to reflect: ancients and moderns on the religious sensibilities of animals", *QUCC* 75: 111–129.

(2006) *Animals, Rights and Reason in Plutarch and Modern Ethics*. New York.

(2008) "Animals in ancient philosophy: conceptions and misconceptions", in L. Kalof (ed.), *A Cultural History of Animals in Antiquity*. Oxford, 151–174.

(2014a) "Animals in Plutarch", in Beck (2014a), 223–234.

(2014b) "Being the one and becoming the other: animals in ancient philosophical schools", in Campbell (2014), 507–534.

(2017a) *The Animal and the Human in Ancient and Modern Thought: The "Man Alone of Animals" Concept*. London.

(2017b) "Human–animal interactions in Plutarch as commentary on human moral failings", in Fögen and Thomas (2017), 233–252.

Nieto Ibáñez, J. M. (2005) "Plutarco y la polémica antiestoica en las Academica de Pedro de Valencia", in Jufresa et al. (2005), 789–796.

(2007), "Plutarco en la *Monarquía Mística* de Lorenzo de Zamora: el amor a las humanas y divinas letras", in Nieto Ibáñez and López López (2007), 639–672.

Nieto Ibáñez, J. M. and R. López López (eds.) (2007) *El amor en Plutarco*. León.

Nikolaidis, A. (1986) "ΕΛΛΗΝΙΚΟΣ – ΒΑΡΒΑΡΙΚΟΣ: Plutarch on Greek and Barbarian characteristics", *WS* 99: 229–244.

(1988) "Is Plutarch fair to Nikias?" *ICS* 13: 319–333.

(1991) "Plutarch's contradictions", *C&M* 42: 153–186.

(1994) "Plutarch's contradictions", *AncW* 25.2: 213–222.

(1997) "Plutarch on women and marriage", *WS* 110: 27–88.

(1999) "Plutarch's attitude to wine", in Montes Cala et al. (1999), 337–348.

(ed.) (2008) *The Unity of Plutarch's Work: Moralia Themes in the Lives, Features of the Lives in the Moralia*. Berlin.

(2009) "*Philanthropia* as sociability and Plutarch's unsociable heroes", in Ribeiro Ferreira et al. (2009), 275–288.

(2011) "Plutarch's 'minor ethics:' some remarks on *De garrulitate, De curiositate* and *De vitioso pudore*", in Roskam and Van der Stockt (2011), 205–221.

(2012) "Aspects of Plutarch's notion of *philotimia*", in Roskam, De Pourq and Van der Stockt (2012), 31–53.

(2014) "Morality, characterization, and individuality", in Beck (2014a), 350–372.

(2017) "Past and present in Plutarch's *Table Talk*", in Georgiadou and Oikonomopoulou (2017), 257–270.

Nippel, W. (2002) "The construction of the 'Other'", in Harrison (2002), 278–310.

Nisbet, R. (1990) "Cola and clausulae in Cicero's speeches", in E. Craik (ed.), *Owls to Athens: Essays on Classical Subjects Presented to Sir Kenneth Dover*. Oxford, 349–359.

Noël, M.-P. (2002) "Vin, ivresse et démocratie chez Platon", in Jouanna, Villard, and Béguin (2002), 204–219.

Nora, P. (1984) *Les lieux de mémoire*. Paris (Trans. A. Goldhammer as *Realms of Memory: Rethinking the French Past*. New York, 1996).

North, J. and P. Mack (eds.) (2018) *The Afterlife of Plutarch*. London.

North, T. (1579) *The Lives of the Nobles Grecians and Romanes compared together by that grave learned Philosopher and Historiographer Plutarke of Chaeronea [. . .]*. London.

   (1595) *The Lives of the Nobles Grecians and Romanes compared together by that grave learned Philosopher and Historiographer Plutarke of Chaeronea [. . .]*, 2nd ed. London.

   (1603) *The Lives of the Nobles Grecians and Romanes compared together by that grave learned Philosopher and Historiographer Plutarke of Chaeronea [. . .]* 3rd ed. London.

Nussbaum, M. (1994) *The Therapy of Desire: Theory and Practice in Hellenistic Ethics*. Princeton, NJ.

   (2002) "The incomplete feminism of Musonius Rufus, Platonist, Stoic, and Roman", in M. Nussbaum and J. Sihvola (eds.), *The Sleep of Reason: Erotic Experience and Sexual Ethics in Ancient Greece and Rome*. Chicago, IL, 283–326.

Nyquist, M. (2022) "Tyrannicide, law, and sacrifice in *Julius Caesar*", *ELH* 89: 893–926.

Oakesmith, J. (1902) *The Religion of Plutarch: A Pagan Creed of Apostolic Times – An Essay*. London.

Odorico, P. 2009. "Byzantium, a literature that needs to be reconsidered", in I. Stănculescu (ed.), *Manuscrise bizantine în colecții bucureștene = Byzantine Manuscripts in Bucharest's Collections*. Bucharest, 64–77.

Oikonomopoulou, K. (2011) "Peripatetic knowledge in the *Table Talk*", in Klotz and Oikonomopoulou (2011a), 105–130.

   (2013a) "Plutarch's corpus of *Quaestiones* in the tradition of imperial Greek encyclopaedism", in J. König and G. Woolf (eds.), *Encyclopaedism from Antiquity to the Renaissance*. Cambridge, 129–153.

   (2013b) "Ethnography and authorial voice in Athenaeus' *Deipnosophistae*", in Almagor and Skinner (2013), 179–199.

   (2017a) "Space, Delphi and the construction of the Greek past in Plutarch's *Greek Questions*", in Georgiadou and Oikonomopoulou (2017), 107–116.

   (2017b) "Miscellanies," in Richter and Johnson (2017), 447–462.

O'Neill, E. (1997) "Plutarch on friendship", in J. Fitzgerald (ed.), *Greco-Roman Perspectives on Friendship*. Atlanta, GA, 105–122.

Opelt, I. and W. Speyer (1967) "Barbar", *JbAC* 10: 251–290.

Opsomer, J. (1994) "L'âme du monde et l'âme de l'homme chez Plutarque", in García Valdés (1994),33–49.

(1996) "Divination and academic 'skepticism' according to Plutarch", in Van der Stockt (1996), 165–194.

(1998) *In Search of the Truth: Academic Tendencies in Middle Platonism.* Brussels.

(2001) "Neoplatonist criticisms of Plutarch", in Pérez Jiménez and Casadesús Bordoy (2001), 187–199.

(2004) "Plutarch's *De animae procreatione in Timaeo*: manipulation or search for consistency?" in P. Adamson, H. Baltussen and M. Stone (eds.), *Philosophy, Science and Exegesis in Greek, Arabic and Latin Commentaries.* London, 137–162.

(2005) "Plutarch's Platonism revisited", in M. Bonazzi and V. Celluprica (eds.), *L'eredità Platonica: studi sul Platonismo da Arcesilao a Proclo.* Naples, 163–200.

(2006) "Eros in Plutarchs moralischer Psychologie", in Görgemanns (2006), 208–235.

(2007a) "Eros and knowledge in Plutarch's *Amatorius*", in Nieto Ibáñez and López López (2007), 149–168.

(2007b) "The place of Plutarch in the history of Platonism", in Volpe Cacciatore and Ferrari (2007), 281–309.

(2007c) "Plutarch on the One and the dyad", in R. Sorabji and R. Sharples (eds.), *Greek and Roman Philosophy 100 BC to 200 AD.* London, 379–395.

(2009) "M. Annius Ammonius: a philosophical profile", in Bonazzi and Opsomer (2009), 123–186.

(2012) "Plutarch on the division of the soul", in R. Barney, T. Brennan, and C. Brittain (eds.), *Plato and the Divided Self.* Cambridge, 311–330.

(2014) "Plutarch and the Stoics", in Beck (2014a), 88–103.

(2016) "Plutarch's unphilosophical *Lives*: philosophical, after all?" in M. Bonazzi and S. Schorn (eds.), *Bios philosophos: Philosophy in Ancient Greek Biography.* Turnhout, 101–126.

(2017) "Is Plutarch really hostile to the Stoics?" in T. Engberg-Pedersen (ed.), *From Stoicism to Platonism: The Development of Philosophy 100 BCE–100 CE.* Cambridge, 296–321.

(2020) "The Platonic soul, from the Early Academy to the first century CE", in B. Inwood and J. Warren (eds.), *Body and Soul in Hellenistic Philosophy.* Cambridge, 171–198.

Opsomer, J. and Steel, C. (eds.) (2012) *Proclus: Ten Problems Concerning Providence* (Ancient Commentators on Aristotle). London.

Opsomer, J., G. Roskam, and F. B. Titchener (eds.) (2016) *A Versatile Gentleman: Consistency in Plutarch's Writing.* Leuven.

Ortega Castejón, J. (1991) "Plutarco y el Comentario de Juan Luis de la Cerda a las *Georgicas* de Virgilio", in García López and Calderón Dorda (1991), 183–189.

Osborne, C. (2007) *Dumb Beasts and Dead Philosophers: Humanity and the Humane in Ancient Philosophy and Literature.* Oxford.

Oudot, E. (2010) "'Marathon, l'Eurymédon, Platées, laissons-les aux écoles des sophistes!' Les guerres médiques au second siècle de notre ère", in P.-L. Malosse, M.-P. Noël, and B. Schouler (eds.), *Clio sous le regard d'Hermès: L'utilisation de l'histoire dans la rhétorique ancienne de l'époque hellénistique à l'antiquité tardive.* Alessandria, 143–157.

Pacca, V. (ed.) (1996) *Petrarch: Trionfi, Rime, Codice degli abbozzi.* Milan.

Pace, B. and P. Volpe Cacciatore (eds.) (2013) *Gli scritti di Plutarco: Tradizione, traduzione, ricezione, commento.* Naples.

Padberg, F. (1933) *Cicero und Cato Censorius.* Bottrop.

Pade, M. (1995) "The Latin translations of Plutarch's *Lives* in fifteenth-century Italy and their manuscript diffusion", in C. Leonardi and B. Munk Olsen (eds.), *The Classical Tradition in the Middle Ages and the Renaissance: Proceedings of the first European Science Foundation Workshop on "The Reception of Classical Texts."* Spoleto, 169–183.

(1999) "Plutarch, Gellius and John of Salisbury in Humanist Anthologies", in M.-L. Rodén (ed.), *Ab Aquilone: Nordic Studies in Honour and Memory of Leonard E. Boyle, O.P., Skrifter utgivne af Riksarkivet 14.* Stockholm, 57–70.

(2007) *The Reception of Plutarch's Lives in Fifteenth-Century Italy.* 2 vols. Copenhagen.

(ed.) (2013) *Plutarchi Chaeronensis Vita Dionis Guarino Veronense interprete.* Florence.

(2014) "The reception of Plutarch from antiquity to the Italian Renaissance", in Beck (2014a), 531–543.

(2017) "Lives transformed: John Whethamstede's use of Plutarch's *Lives*", in Baker (2017), 93–118.

Palm, J. (1955) *Über Sprache und Stil des Diodoros von Sizilien.* Lund.

Panagopoulos, C. (1977) "Vocabulaire et mentalité dans les *Moralia* de Plutarque", *DHA* 3: 197–235.

Papadi, D. (2005) "Theatricality and dramatic vocabulary in Plutarch's *Moralia*: How to tell a flatterer from a friend", in Jufresa et al. (2005), 401–412.

(2008) "*Moralia* in the *Lives*: tragedy and theatrical imagery in Plutarch's *Pompey*", in Nikolaidis (2008), 112–123.

Papadodima, E. (2010) "The Greek/Barbarian interaction in Euripides' *Andromache, Orestes, Heracleidae*: a reassessment of Greek attitudes to foreigners", *Digressus* 10: 1–42.

Papakonstantinou, Z. (2014) "Sport, victory, commemoration and elite identities in archaic and early classical Athens", *C&M* 65: 87–126.

Paster, G. K. (1989) "'In the spirit of men there is no blood': blood as trope of gender in *Julius Caesar*", *Shakespeare Quarterly* 40.1: 284–298.

Patterson, C. (1992) "Plutarch's 'Advice on Marriage:' traditional wisdom through a philosophic lens", *ANRW* II.33.6: 4708–4723. Reprinted in Pomeroy (1999a), 128–137.

Paul, G. (1991) "*Symposia* and *deipna* in Plutarch's *Lives* and in other historical writings", in Slater (1991), 157–169.

Pavis d'Escurac, H. (1981) "Périls et chances du régime civique selon Plutarque", *Ktèma* 6: 287–300.

Payen, P. (2001) "Byzance", in F. Hartog et al. (eds.), *Plutarque: Vies parallès*. Paris, 1972–1973.

  (2014) "Plutarch the antiquarian", in Beck (2014a), 235–248.

Payne, M. (2010) *The Animal Part: Human and Other Animals in the Poetic Imagination*. Chicago, IL.

Pelegrín Campo, J. (1997) "La noción de barbarie en las *Vidas paralelas* de Plutarco de Queronea", in Schrader, Ramón, and Vela (1997), 367–378.

Pelling, C. (1973) "Plutarch, Alexander and Caesar: two new fragments?" *CQ* 23: 343–344.

  (1979) "Plutarch's method of work in the Roman *Lives*", *JHS* 99: 74–96. Reprinted in Scardigli (1995), 265-318; updated version in Pelling (2002a), 1–44.

  (1980) "Plutarch's adaptation of his source-material", *JHS* 100: 127–140. Reprinted in Scardigli (1995), 125-154; updated version in Pelling (2002a), 91–115.

  (1986a) "Plutarch and Roman politics", in Moxon, Smart, and Woodman (1986), 159–187. Reprinted in Scardigli (1995), 319–356 and in Pelling (2002a), 207–236.

  (1986b) "Synkrisis in Plutarch's *Lives*", in F. Brenk and I. Gallo (eds.), *Miscellanea Plutarchea*. Ferrari, 83–96; updated version in Pelling (2002a), 349–363.

  (ed.) (1988a) *Plutarch: Life of Antony*. Cambridge.

  (1988b) "Aspects of Plutarch's characterization", *ICS* 13: 257–274. Reprinted in Pelling (2002a), 283–300.

  (1989) "Plutarch: Roman heroes and Greek culture", in M. Griffin and J. Barnes (eds.), *Philosophia Togata: Essays on Philosophy and Roman Society*. Oxford, 199–232.

  (1990a) "Truth and fiction in Plutarch's *Lives*", in D. Russell (ed.), *Antonine Literature*. Oxford, 19–52. Reprinted in Pelling (2002a), 143–170.

  (1990b) "Childhood and personality in Greek biography", in Pelling (1990c), 213–244. Reprinted in Pelling (2002a), 301–338.

  (ed.) (1990c), *Characterization and Individuality in Greek Literature*. Oxford.

  (1992) "Plutarch and Thucydides", in Stadter (1992b) 10–40. Reprinted in Pelling (2002a), 117–141.

  (1995) "The moralism of Plutarch's *Lives*", in Innes, Hine, and Pelling (1995), 205–220. Reprinted in Pelling (2002a), 237–251.

  (1996) "Prefazione", in F. Albini (ed.), *Plutarco. Vita di Coriolano, Vita di Alcibiade*. Milan, xx–lviii.

  (1997a) "East is East and West is West – or are they? National stereotypes in Herodotus", *Histos* 1 (www.dur.ac.uk/classics/histos/1997/pelling.html).

  (1997b) "Introduzione", in C. Pelling and E. Melandri (eds.), *Plutarco: Vite parallele. Filopemene – Tito Flaminino*. Milan, 87–166, 249–331.

  (1997c) "Is death the end? Closure in Plutarch's *Lives*", in D. Roberts, F. Dunn, and D. Fowler (eds.), *Classical Closure: Reading the End in Greek and Latin*

*Literature*. Princeton, NJ, 228–250; updated version in Pelling (2002a), 365–386.

(1997d) "Plutarch on Caesar's fall", in Mossman (1997a), 215–232.

(1997e) "The shaping of *Coriolanus*: Dionysius, Plutarch and Shakespeare", in McGrail (1997), 3–32. Reprinted in Pelling (2002a), 387–411.

(1999a) "Dionysiac diagnostics: some hints of Dionysus in Plutarch's *Lives*", in Montes Cala et al. (1999), 359–368. Reprinted in Pelling (2002a), 197–206.

(1999b) "Epilogue", in Kraus (1999), 325–357.

(1999c) "'Making myth look like history:' Plutarch's *Theseus-Romulus*", in Pérez Jiménez, García López, and Aguilar (1999), 431–443. Reprinted in Pelling (2002a), 171–195.

(2000a) *Literary Texts and the Greek Historian*. London.

(2000b) "Rhetoric, paideia, and psychology in Plutarch's *Lives*", in Van der Stockt (2000b), 331–339. Reprinted in Pelling (2002a), 339–347.

(2001) Review of Ehlers (1998), *CR* 51: 273–276.

(2002a) *Plutarch and History: Eighteen Studies*. Swansea.

(2002b) "The *Apophthegmata Regum et Imperatorum* and Plutarch's Roman *Lives*", in Pelling (2002a), 65–90.

(2002c) "'You for me and me for you': narrator and narratee in Plutarch's *Lives*", in Pelling (2002a), 267–282.

(2004) "Do Plutarch's politicians never learn?" in de Blois et al. (2004), 87–103.

(2005a) "Synkrisis revisited", in Pérez Jiménez and Titchener (2005), 325–340.

(2005b) "Plutarch's Socrates", *Hermathena* 179: 105–139.

(2006) "Breaking the bounds: writing about Julius Caesar", in McGing and Mossman (2006a), 255–280.

(2007a) "*De malignitate Plutarchi*: Plutarch, Herodotus and the Persian wars", in E. Bridges, E. Hall, and P. Rhodes (eds.), *Cultural Responses to the Persian Wars*. Oxford, 145–164.

(2007b) "Ion's *Epidemiai* and Plutarch's Ion", in Jennings and Katsaros (2007), 75–109.

(2009) "Biography", in Boys-Stones, Graziosi, and Vasunia (2009), 608–616.

(2010) "Plutarch's 'Tale of Two Cities': do the *Parallel Lives* combine as global histories?" in Humble (2010b), 217–235.

(2011a) *Plutarch: Caesar. Translated with an Introduction and Commentary*. Oxford.

(2011b) "What is popular about Plutarch's 'popular philosophy'?" in Roskam and Van der Stockt (2011), 41–58.

(2012) "Plutarch on Roman *philotimia*", in Roskam, De Pourcq, and Van der Stockt (2012), 55–67.

(2014) "Political philosophy", in Beck (2014a), 149–162.

(2016a) "Herodotus, Polycrates – and maybe Stesimbrotus too?" *JHS* 136: 113–120.

(2016b) "Tragic colouring in Plutarch", in Opsomer, Roskam, and Titchener (eds.), 113–133.

(2020) "Fifth-century preliminaries", in De Temmerman (2020), 97–110.

(in press) "A doubles match: *Agis–Cleomenes and the Gracchi*", in Davies and Mossman (forthcoming in 2023).

Pérez Jiménez, A. (1990) "Plutarco y el humanismo español del Renacimiento", in Pérez Jiménez and del Cerro Calderón (1990), 229–247.

(1996) "ΔΕΙΣΙΔΑΙΜΟΝΙΑ: el miedo a los dioses en Plutarco", in Van der Stockt (1996), 195–226.

(1998) "Luisa Sigea y Plutarco", in Gallo (1998a), 377–388.

(2002) "Plutarco y la literatura española del XVII: Importancia actual de los estudios sobre Plutarco", in Ribeiro Ferreira (2002), 353–368.

(2003a) "Las *Vidas Paralelas* de Plutarco de la emblemática hispánica de los siglos XVI y XVII", *Humanitas* 55: 223–240.

(2003b) "El Plutarco de los *Moralia* en la literatura emblemática española", in G. Fernández Ariza (ed.), *Literatura Hispanoamericana del Siglo XX: Mímesis e Iconografía*. Málaga, 169–195.

(2003c) "Los héroes de Plutarco como modelo en la literatura emblemática europea de los siglos XVI–XVII", in Barzanò et al. (2003), 375–402.

(2005) "Usos didácticos de la imagen y la palabra: El Plutarco de Juan Francisco de Villava", in Jufresa et al. (2005), 797–808.

(2006) "Plutarco, Juan de Mal Lara y la Galera Real de D. Juan de Austria", in Aguilar and Alfageme (2006), 233–246.

(2007) "El Plutarco de Antonio Agustín", in Nieto Ibáñez and López López (2007), 673–686.

(2009) "Plutarco de Queronea", in F. Lafarga and L. Pegenaute (eds.), *Diccionario histórico de la traducción en España*. Madrid, 910–911.

(2014) "The reception of Plutarch in Spain", in Beck (2014a), 556–576.

(2019) "Plutarch's fortune in Spain", in Xenophontos and Oikonomopoulou (2019), 606–621.

Pérez Jiménez, A. and F. Casadesús Bordoy (eds.) (2001) *Estudios sobre Plutarco: misticismo y religiones místéricas en la obra de Plutarco. Actas del VII simposio Español sobre Plutarco, Palma de Mallorca, 2–4 de Noviembre de 2000*. Madrid.

Pérez Jiménez, A. and G. del Cerro Calderón (eds.) (1990) *Estudios sobre Plutarco: obra y tradición*. Málaga.

Pérez Jiménez, A., J. García López, and R. Aguilar (eds.) (1999) *Plutarco, Platón y Aristóteles. Actas del V Congreso Internacional de la I.P.S. (Madrid-Cuenca, 4–7 de mayo de 1999)*. Madrid.

Pérez Jiménez, A. and C. Macías Villalobos (2009) *Paradigmas de nuestra cultura: astrología y poder político en la Antigüedad : discurso pronunciado en el acto de ingreso en la Sociedad Erasmiana de Málaga por el Dr. D. Aurelio Pérez Jiménez, y contestación del Dr. D. Cristóbal Macías Villalobos: Málaga, 24 de abril de 2009*. Málaga.

Pérez Jiménez, A. and F. B. Titchener (eds.) (2005) *Historical and Biographical Values of Plutarch's Works: Studies Devoted to Professor Philip Stadter by the International Plutarch Society*. Málaga.

Pérez Martín, I. (2019) "Maximos Planoudes and the transmission of Plutarch's *Moralia*", in Xenophontos and Oikonomopoulou (2019), 295–309.

Pérez Molina, M. and C. Guzmán Arias (1991) "La presencia de Plutarco en la didascalia multiplex de F. Fernández de Córdova", in García López and Calderón Dorda (1991), 191–199.

Pertusi, A. (1964) *Leonzio Pilato fra Petrarca e Boccaccio: Le sue versioni omeriche negli autografi di Venezia e la cultura greca del primo Umanesimo.* Venice.

Petrarca, F. (1996) *Trionfi, Rime estravaganti, Codice degli abbozzi,* eds. V. Pacca and L. Paolino. Milan.

Petropoulou, M.-Z. (2008) "Humans treated as animals: human sacrifice real and metaphorical", in Alexandridis, Wild, and Winkler-Horaček (eds.), 99–118.

Petrucci, F. M. (2016) "Argumentative strategies in the 'Platonic section' of Plutarch's *De Iside et Osiride* (chapters 45–64)", *Mnemosyne* 69: 226–248.

Pfeiffer, S. (2008) "Der ägyptische 'Tierkult' im Spiegel der griechisch-römischen Literatur", in Alexandridis, Wild, and Winkler-Horaček (2008), 373–393.

Phillips, A. and M. Willcock (eds.) (1999) *Xenophon and Arrian, On Hunting.* Warminster.

Piccione, R. (1998) "Plutarco nell'*Anthologion* di Giovanni Stobeo", in Gallo (1998a), 161–201.

Piccirilli, L. (1989) "La tradizione 'nera' nelle biografie plutarchee degli Ateniesi del sesto e del quinto secolo", in A. Ceresa-Gastaldo (ed.), *Gerolamo e la biografia letteraria.* Genoa, 5–21.

(1990a) "Introduzione", in C. Carena, M. Manfredini, and L. Piccirilli (eds.) *Plutarco: Le Vite di Cimone e di Lucullo.* Milan, ix–xl.

(1990b) "Nicia in Plutarco", *AALig* 47: 351–368.

(1993) "Introduzione to *Nicia*", in M. Angeli Bertinelli, C. Carena, M. Manfredini, and L. Piccirilli (eds.), *Plutarco: Le Vite di Nicia e di Crasso.* Milan, ix–xxviii.

Pietsch, E. (2005) "The *Chronographia* of Michael Psellos: history of emperors, autobiography and apology", *Bysantinska sällskapets Bulletin* 23: 23–33.

Pimouguet-Pédarros, I. (2011) *La cité à l'épreuve des rois. Le siège de Rhodes par Démétrios Poliorcète (305–304 av. J.-C.).* Rennes.

Pineaux, J. (1986) "Un continuateur des *Vies parallèles*", in Balard (1986), 331–342.

Pinheiro, J. (2013) *Tempo e espaço da paideia nas Vidas de Plutarco.* Coimbra.

Plese, Z. (2005) "Platonist Orientalism", in Pérez Jiménez and Titchener (2005), 355–381.

Pomeroy, S. (ed.) (1999a) *Plutarch's Advice to the Bride and Groom and A Consolation to His Wife.* New York.

(1999b) "Reflections on Plutarch, *Advice to the Bride and Groom*: something old, something new, something borrowed", in Pomeroy (1999a), 33–57.

(1999c) "Reflections on Plutarch, *Advice to the Bride and Groom*", in Pomeroy (1999a), 75–81.

Pordomingo Pardo, F. (1996) "El Plutarco de la biblioteca Universitaria de Salamanca: Manuscritos e impresos de los siglos XV y XVI", in Fernández Delgado and Pordomingo Pardo (1996), 461–474.

(1999) "El banquete de Plutarco: ficción literaria o realidad histórica?" in Montes Cala et al. (1999), 379–392.

Porter, J. (ed.) (2006a) *Classical Pasts: The Classical Traditions of Greece and Rome.* Princeton, NJ.

(2006b) "Feeling classical: classicism and ancient literary criticism", in Porter (2006a), 301–352.

(2006c) "What is 'classical' about classical antiquity?" in Porter (2006a), 1–65.

Porter, W. (ed.) (1937) *Plutarch's Life of Aratus.* Dublin.

Powell, A. (1999) "Spartan women assertive in politics? Plutarch's *Lives* of Agis and Kleomenes", in S. Hodkinson and A. Powell (eds.), *Sparta: New Perspectives.* London, 393–419.

Powell, J. (ed.) (1988) *Cicero. Cato Maior De Senectute.* Cambridge.

Prandi, L. (2000) "Gli esempi del passato greco nei *Precetti Politici* di Plutarco", *RSA* 30: 91–107.

(2005) "Singolare e plurale nelle *Vite* greche di Plutarco", in de Blois et al. (2005), 141–156.

Preston, R. (2001) "Roman questions, Greek answers: Plutarch and the construction of identity", in Goldhill (2001b), 86–119.

Priestley, J. (2014) *Herodotus and Hellenistic Culture: Literary Studies in the Reception of the Histories.* Oxford.

Prior, W. J. (1991) *Virtue and Knowledge: An Introduction to Ancient Greek Ethics.* London.

Puech, B. (1983) "Grands-prêtres et helladarques d'Achaïe", *REA* 85: 15–43.

(1992) "Prosopographie des amis de Plutarque," *ANRW* II.33.6: 4831–4893.

Pütz, B. (2014) "Good to laugh with: animals in comedy", in Campbell (2014), 61–72.

Raaflaub, K. (2000) "Poets and lawgivers and the beginnings of political reflection in Ancient Greece", in C. Rowe and M. Schofield (eds.), *The Cambridge History of Greek and Roman Political Thought.* Cambridge.

Rabbow, P. (1914) *Antike Schriften über Seelenheilung und Seelenleitung auf ihre Quellen untersucht I, Die Therapie des Zorns.* Leipzig.

Rabelais, F. (1994) *Oeuvres complètes*, ed. M. Huchon. Paris.

Rabieh, L. (2006) *Plato and the Virtue of Courage.* Baltimore, MD.

Racine, J. (1966) *Oeuvres completes.* 2 vols., ed. R. Picard. Paris.

Radermacher, L. (1897) "Studien zur Geschichte der griechischen Rhetorik", *RhM* 52: 412–424.

Raeymaekers, J. (1996) "The origins of the rivalry between Philopoemen and Flamininus", *AncSoc* 27: 259–276.

Rajak, T. (2001) *Jewish Dialogue with Greece and Rome.* Leiden.

Ramírez-Araujo, A. (1954) "*Usque ad aras amicus*: Un adagio glosado por Cervantes", *HR* 22: 224–227.

Ramírez de Verger, A. (1990) "Plutarco en el *De orbe novo* de Juan Ginés de Sepulveda", in Pérez Jiménez and Del Cerro Calderón (1990), 271–276.

Ramón Palerm, V. (2000) "El *De Herodoti malignitate* de Plutarco come *epideixis* retórica", in Van der Stockt (2000b), 387–398.

(2011) "Plutarco y Juan de Pineda", in Candau Morón (2011), 621–632.

(forthcoming) "The irreligiosity of Herodotus: Plutarch's view", in Duff and Fletcher (forthcoming).

Ramos Maldonado, S. (1999) "Latin and vernacular in the works of Bernardino Gómez Miedes", in B. Taylor and A. Coroleu (eds.), *Latin and Vernacular in Renaissance Spain*. Manchester, 105–111.

Reeve, M. (1991) "The rediscovery of classical texts in the Renaissance", in O. Pecere (ed.), *Itinerari dei testi antichi*. Rome, 115–147.

Rehdantz, C. and F. Blass (1886) *Demosthenes' Neun Philippische Reden, 2.2, Indices*, 4th ed. Leipzig.

Reinsch, D. (2019) "Plutarch in Michael Psellos' *Chronographia*", in Xenophontos and Oikonomopoulou (2019), 234–247.

Reinsch, D. and A. Kambylis (eds.) (2001) *Annae Comnenae Alexias*. 2 vols. Berlin.

Relihan, J. C. (1992) "Re-thinking the history of the literary symposium", *ICS* 17: 213–244.

Renehan, R. (1981) "The Greek anthropocentric view of man", *HSCPh* 85: 239–259.

Renoirte, T. (1951) *Les "Conseils politiques" de Plutarque: une lettre ouverte aux Grecs à l'époque de Trajan*. Louvain.

Resta, G. (1962) *Le epitomi di Plutarco nel Quattrocento*. Padova.

(1986) "Francesco Filelfo tra Bisanzio e Roma", in R. Avesani, G. Billanovich, M. Ferrari, and G. Pozzi (eds.), *Francesco Filelfo nel quinto centenario della morte. Atti del XVII convegno di studi maceratesi, Tolentino, 27–30 settembre, 1981*. Padua, 1–60.

Reydams-Schils, G. (ed.) (2011) *Thinking through Excerpts: Studies on Stobaeus (Monothéismes et philosophie)*. Turnhout.

Reynolds, B. (1954) "Bruni and Perotti present a Greek historian", *BiblH&R* 16: 108–118.

Ribeiro Ferreira, J. (ed.) (2002) *Plutarco Educador da Europa*. Coimbra.

Ribeiro Ferreira, J. and D. Leão (eds.) (2003) *Os fragmentos de Plutarco e a recepção de sua obra*. Coimbra.

Ribeiro Ferreira, J., D. Leão, M. Tröster, and P. Barata Dias (eds.) (2009) *Symposion and Philanthropia in Plutarch*. Coimbra.

Ribeiro Ferreira, J., D. Leão, and C. Martins de Jesus (eds.). (2012) *"Nomos," "Kosmos," & "Dike" in Plutarch*. Coimbra.

Rich J. and G. Shipley (eds.) (1993), *War and Society in the Roman World*. London.

Richter, D. (2001) "Plutarch on Isis and Osiris: text, cult, and cultural appropriation", *TAPhA* 131: 191–216.

Richter, D. S. and W. A. Johnson (eds.) (2017) *The Oxford Handbook of the Second Sophistic*. New York.

Rist, J. (2001) "Plutarch's *Amatorius*: a commentary on Plato's theories of love?" *CQ* 51: 557–575.

Roberto, U. (ed.) (2005) *Ioannis Antiocheni Fragmenta ex Historia chronica*. Berlin.

Rodrigues, A. (in press). "Life of Lycurgus", in Davies and Mossman (forthcoming in 2023).

Roig Lanzillotta, L. and I. Muñoz Gallarte (eds.) (2012) *Plutarch in the Religious and Philosophical Discourse of Late Antiquity.* Leiden.

Roller, M. (2001) *Constructing Autocracy: Aristocrats and Emperors in Julio-Claudian Rome.* Princeton, NJ.
   (2003) "Horizontal women: posture and sex in the Roman *convivium*", *AJPh* 124: 377–422.
   (2006) *Dining Posture in Ancient Rome: Bodies, Values, and Status.* Princeton, NJ.

Rollo, A. (2002) "Problemi e prospettive della ricerca su Manuele Crisolora", in Maisano and Rollo (2002), 31–85.

Romano, R. (1994) "La *Lysis* inedita di Giovanni Grasso", *Koinonia* 18: 199–210.

Romeri, L. (2002) *Philosophes entre mots et mets: Plutarque, Lucien, Athénée autour de la table de Platon.* Grenoble.

Rosenmeyer, T. (1985) "Ancient literary genres: a mirage?" *Yearbook of Comparative and General Literature* 34: 74–84.

Rosivach, V. (1984) "The Romans' view of the Persians", *CW* 78: 1–8.

Roskam, G. (1999) "Dionysus sublimated", in Montes Cala et al. (1999), 433–445.
   (2004) "Plutarch on self and others", *AncSoc* 34: 245–273.
   (2004–5) "Τὸ καλὸν αὐτὸ [. .] ἔχοντας τέλος (*Praec. ger. reip.* 799a). Plutarch on the foundation of the politician's career", *Ploutarchos* 2: 89–103.
   (2005a) "Political education in the service of the public interest: Plutarch on the motivation of the statesman", in Jufresa et al. (2005), 133–138.
   (2005b) *On the Path to Virtue: The Stoic Doctrine of Moral Progress and Its Reception in (Middle) Platonism.* Leuven.
   (2007a) *A Commentary on Plutarch's "De latenter vivendo."* Leuven.
   (2007b) "Plutarch's attack on Epicurus' ideal of an 'unnoticed life': polemical strategies in *De latenter vivendo*", in Nieto Ibáñez and López López (2007), 867–876.
   (2009a) "Educating the young . . . over wine? Plutarch, Calvenus Taurus, and Favorinus as convivial teachers", in Ribeiro Ferreira et al. (2009), 369–383.
   (2009b) *Plutarch's* Maxime com principibus philosopho esse disserendum: *An Interpretation with Commentary.* Leuven.
   (2010) "Plutarch's 'Socratic symposia': the *Symposia* of Plato and Xenophon as literary models in the *Quaestiones Convivales*", *Athenaeum* 98: 45–70.
   (2010–11) "How to deal with the philosophical tradition? Some general rules in Plutarch's anti-Epicurean treatises", *Ploutarchos*: 8: 133–146.
   (2011a) "Ambition and love of fame in Plutarch's *Lives* of Agis, Cleomenes, and the Gracchi", *CPh* 106: 208–225.
   (2011b) "Aristotle in middle Platonism: the case of Plutarch of Chaeronea", in T. Bénatouïl, E. Maffi, and F. Trabattoni (eds.), *Plato, Aristotle, or Both? Dialogues between Platonism and Aristotelianism in Antiquity.* Hildesheim, 35–61.
   (2011c) "Plutarch against Epicurus on affection for offspring: a reading of *De amore prolis*", in Roskam and Van der Stockt (2011), 175–201.
   (2014) "Philanthropy, dignity, and euergetism", in Beck (2014a), 516–528.

(2017) "Discussing the past: moral vision, truth and benevolence in Plutarch's *On the Malice of Herodotus*", in Georgiadou and Oikonomopoulou (2017), 161–173.

(2021) *Plutarch: New Surveys in the Classics*, 47. Cambridge.

(forthcoming) "Dancing away the truth: Plutarch's polemical approach in *On the malice of Herodotus*", in Duff and Fletcher (forthcoming).

Roskam, G. and L. Van der Stockt (eds.) (2011) *Virtues for the People: Aspects of Plutarchan Ethics*. Leuven.

Roskam, G., M. De Pourcq, and L. Van der Stockt (eds.) (2012) *The Lash of Ambition: Plutarch, Imperial Greek Literature and the Dynamics of Philotimia*. Leuven.

Rossi, A. (2000) "The camp of Pompey: strategy of representation in Caesar's *Bellum Ciuile*", *CJ* 95: 239–256.

Rossi, V. and U. Bosco (eds.) (1933–42) *Le Familiari, I–IV. Edizione nazionale delle opere di Francesco Petrarca X–XIII*. Florence.

Rotroff, S. I. and M. C. Hoff (eds.) (1997) *The Romanization of Athens: proceedings of an international conference held at Lincoln, Nebraska (April 1996)*. Oxbow monograph; 94. Oxford.

Roueché, C. (2002) "The literary background of Kekaumenos", in C. Holmes and J. Waring (eds.), *Literacy, Education and Manuscript Transmission in Byzantium and Beyond*. Leiden, 111–138.

Rousseau, J. (1964) *Oeuvres completes: Vol. I*, eds. J. Spink, C. Wirz, P. Burgelin, H. Gouhier, R. de Vilmorin, and B. Gagnebin. Paris.

(1969) *Oeuvres completes: Vol. IV*, eds. J. Spink, C. Wirz, P. Burgelin, H. Gouhier, R. de Vilmorin, and B. Gagnebin. Paris.

Roux, P. de (ed.) (1986) *M.-J. Roland: Mémoires*. Paris.

Runciman, S. (1970) *The Last Byzantine Renaissance*. Cambridge.

Russell, D. (1963) "Plutarch's *Life of Coriolanus*", *JRS* 53: 21–28. Reprinted in Scardigli (1995), 357–372.

(1966a) "On reading Plutarch's *Lives*", *G&R* 13: 139–154. Reprinted in Scardigli (1995), 75–94.

(1966b) "Plutarch, 'Alcibiades' 1–16," *PCPhS* 12: 37–47. Reprinted in Scardigli (1995), 191–207.

(1968) "On reading Plutarch's *Moralia*", *G&R* 15: 130–146.

(1973a) *Plutarch*. London.

(1973b) "Remarks on Plutarch's *de vitando aere alieno*", *JHS* 93: 163–171.

(1983) *Greek Declamation*. Cambridge.

(1989) "Greek criticism of the Empire", in G. Kennedy (ed.), *The Cambridge History of Literary Criticism: Vol. I. Classical Criticism*. Cambridge, 297–329.

(1992) "ἦθος nei dialoghi di Plutarco", *ASNP* 32: 399–429.

(1993) *Plutarch: Selected Essays and Dialogues*. Oxford.

(1997) "Plutarch, *Amatorius* 13–18", in Mossman (1997a), 99–111.

(2010) "Introduction", in Nesselrath (2010), 3–15.

Said, E. (1978) *Orientalism: Western Conceptions of the Orient*. New York.

Saïd, S. (1994) "Lucien ethnographe", in A. Billault (ed.), *Lucien de Samosate.* Lyon, 149–170.

(2001) "The discourse of identity in Greek rhetoric from Isocrates to Aristides", in Malkin (2001), 275–299.

(2002) "Greeks and Barbarians in Euripides' tragedies: the end of differences?" in Harrison (2002), 62–100.

(2005a) "Poésie et éducation chez Plutarque ou comment convertir la poésie en introduction à la philosophie", in Jufresa et al. (2005), 147–176.

(2005b) "Plutarch and the people in the *Parallel Lives*", in de Blois et al. (2005), 7–25.

Saint-Évremond, C. de (1962) *Oeuvres en prose: Vol. I*, ed. R. Ternois. Paris.

(1969), *Oeuvres en prose: Vol. IV*, ed. R. Ternois (Paris).

Sainte-Beuve, C. A. (1839) *Critiques et portraits littéraires: Vol. 5* (Paris).

(1844) *Portraits littéraires: Vol. 2*, 2nd ed. Paris.

Salcedo Parrondo, M. (2005) "*Un león en la ciudad*: el perfil leonino del *Alcibíades* de Plutarco", in Boulogne (2005b), 135–141.

Salmeri, G. (2000) "Dio, Rome and the civic life of Asia Minor", in S. Swain (ed.), *Dio Chrysostom: Politics, Letters and Philosophy.* Oxford, 53–92.

(2011) "Reconstructing the political life and culture of the Greek cities of the Roman Empire", in van Nijf and Alston (2011), 197–214.

Salmon, P. (1984) "Racisme ou refus de la différence dans le monde greco-romain", *DHA* 10: 75–98.

Salutati, C. (1891–1911) *Epistolario*, I–IV, ed. F. Novati. Rome.

(1985) *De fato et fortuna*, ed. C. Bianca. Florence.

Sancho Montés, S. (2005) "Plutarc a la Primera Part de la *Història de València* d'en Pere-Antoni Beuter", in Jufresa et al. (2005), 835–842.

Sancisi-Weerdenburg, H. (2001) "Yauna by the sea and across the sea", in Malkin (2001), 323–346.

Sandbach, F. H. (1939) "Rhythm and authenticity in Plutarch's *Moralia*", *CQ* 33: 194–203.

(1941) "Some textual notes on Plutarch's *Moralia*", *CQ* 35: 110–118.

(ed. and trans.) (1969) *Plutarch's Moralia. Vol. XV* Cambridge, MA.

Sansone, D. (ed. and trans.) (1989) *Plutarch: The Lives of Aristeides and Cato.* Warminster.

Santese, G. (1994) "Animali e razionalità in Plutarco", in S. Castignone and G. Lanata (eds.), *Filosofi e animali nel mondo antico.* Pisa, 141–170.

(2005) "Plutarco, il linguaggio e la trasmissione delle conoscenze nel mondo animale", in Jufresa et al. (2005), 453–461.

Scannapieco, R. (2007) "'Voi che per li occhi mi passaste 'l core …': parola e imagine nell'*Amatorius* di Plutarco", in Volpe Cacciatore and Ferrari (2007), 125–170.

Scardigli, B. (ed.) (1995) *Essays on Plutarch's* Lives. Oxford.

Schadee, H. (2016) "Alfonso 'the Magnanimous' of Naples as portrayed by Facio and Panormita: four versions of emulation, representation, and virtue", in Baker et al. (2016), 95–120.

Schamp, J. (1995) "Le Plutarque de Photios", *AC* 64: 155–184.

(2000) *Les Vies des dix orateurs attiques*. Fribourg.

Schenkeveld, D. (1982) "The structure of Plutarch's *De audiendis poetis*", *Mnemosyne* 35: 60–71. Reprinted in Laird (2006), 313–324.

Schepens, G. (2000) "Plutarch's view of ancient Rome: some remarks on the *Life of Pyrrhus*", in L. Mooren (ed.), *Politics, Administration and Society in the Hellenistic and Roman World*. Leuven, 349–364.

Schmid, W. (1887–96) *Der Atticismus*, 4 vols. Stuttgart.

Schmidt, T. (1999) *Plutarque et les barbares: La rhétorique d'une image*. Leuven.

(2000) "La Rhétorique des doublets chez Plutarque: le cas de βάρβαρος καὶ [. . .]", in Van der Stockt (2000b), 455–464.

(2002) "Plutarch's timeless barbarians and the age of Trajan", in Stadter and Van der Stockt (2002), 57–72.

(2004) "Barbarians in Plutarch's political thought", in de Blois et al. (2004), 227–235.

(2008) "Les *Questions barbares* de Plutarque: un essai de reconstitution", *Recherches sur les rhétoriques religieuses* 8: 165–183.

(2011) "Sophistes, barbares et identité grecque: le cas de Dion Chrysostome", in T. Schmidt and P. Fleury (eds.), *Perceptions of the Second Sophistic and Its Times – Regards sur la Seconde Sophistique et son époque*. Toronto, 105–119.

Schmidt, T., M. Vamvouri, and R. Hirsch-Luipold (eds.) (2020) *The Dynamics of Intertextuality in Plutarch*. Leiden.

Schmitt Pantel, P. (1990) "Sacrificial meal and *symposion*: two models of civic institutions in the archaic city", in Murray (1990), 14–33.

(1992) *La cité au banquet: Histoire des repas publics dans les cités grecques*. Rome.

(1999) "Manger entre citoyens: les repas dans les cités grecques antiques", in Flandrin and Cobbi (1999), 39–57.

(2003) "Le Banquet et le 'genre' sur les images grecques, propos sur les compagnes et les compagnons", *Pallas* 61: 83–95.

(2009) *Hommes illustres: moeurs et politique à Athènes au Ve siècle*. Paris.

Schmitz, T. (1997) *Bildung und Macht: zur sozialen und politischen Funktion der zweiten Sophistik in der griechischen Welt der Kaiserzeit*. Munich.

(2014) "Plutarch and the Second Sophistic", in Beck (2014a), 32–42.

Schofield, M. (1999) *Saving the City: Philosopher-Kings and Other Classical Paradigms*. London.

(2003) "Stoic ethics", in Inwood (2003), 233–256.

Schoppe, C. (1994) *Plutarchs Interpretation der Ideenlehre Platons*. Münster.

Schorn, S. (2009) "Tears of the bereaved: Plutarch's *Consolatio ad uxorem* in context", in Fögen (2009), 335–365.

Schrader, C., V. Ramón, and J. Vela (eds.) (1997) *Plutarco y la Historia: Actas del V Simposio Español sobre Plutarco, Zaragoza 20–22 de junio de 1996*. Zaragoza.

Schriefl, A. (2013) *Platons Kritik an Geld und Reichtum*. Berlin.

Schröder, S. (ed.) (1990) *Plutarchs Schrift de Pythiae oraculis*. Stuttgart.

(2010) "Plutarch on oracles and divine inspiration", in Nesselrath (2010), 145–167.

Schroeter, J. (1911) *Plutarchs Stellung zur Skepsis.* Diss., University of Königsberg.

Schütrumpf, E. (1987) "The *rhetra* of Epitadeus: a Platonist's fiction", *GRBS* 28: 441–457.

Schwabl, H. (1962) "Das Bild der fremden Welt bei den frühen Griechen", in H. Schwabl, H. Diller, O. Reverdin, W. Peremans, H. C. Baldry, A. Dihle (eds.), *Grecs et barbares.* (Entretiens Hardt, VIII). Geneva, 1–36.

Schwartz, S. (2003) "Rome in the Greek novel? Images and ideas of empire in Chariton's Persia", *Arethusa* 36: 375–394.

Scott, R. (1981) "The classical tradition in Byzantine historiography", in M. Mullett and R. Scott (eds.), *Byzantium and the Classical Tradition.* Birmingham, 61–74.

Seager, R. (1980) "*Neu sinas Medos equitare inultos*: Horace, the Parthians and Augustan foreign policy", *Athenaeum* 58: 103–118.

Seavey, W. (1991) "Forensic epistolography and Plutarch's *de Herodoti malignitate*", *Hellas* 2: 33–45.

Sedley, D. (2012) *The Philosophy of Antiochus.* Cambridge.

Senzasono, L. (1997) "Health and politics in Plutarch's *De Tuenda Sanitate Praecepta*", in Mossman (1997a), 113–118.

Setton, K. (1956) "The Byzantine background to the Italian Renaissance", *PAPhS* 100: 1–76.

Ševčenko, I. (1962) *Études sur la polémique entre Théodore Métochite et Nicéphore Choumnos.* Brussels.

   (1975) "Theodore Metochites, the Chora, and the intellectual trends of his time", in P. Underwood (ed.), *The Kariye Djami, vol. IV: Studies in the Art of the Kariye Djami and Its Intellectual Background.* Princeton, NJ: 19–91.

   (1992) "Re-reading Constantine Porphyrogenitus", in J. Shepard and S. Franklin (eds.), *Byzantine Diplomacy: Papers from the Twenty-Fourth Spring Symposium of Byzantine Studies, Cambridge, March 1990.* Aldershot, 167–195.

   (ed.) (2011) *Chronographiae quae Theophanis Continuati nomine fertur liber quo Vita Basilii imperatoris amplectitur (Corpus Fontium Historiae Byzantinae 42).* Berlin.

Shepard, J. (ed.) (2008) *The Cambridge History of the Byzantine Empire c. 500–1492.* Cambridge.

Sheppard, A. (1984–6) "*Homonoia* in the Greek cities in the Roman empire", *AncSoc* 15–17: 229–252.

Shipley, D. (1997) *Plutarch's Life of Agesilaos: Response to Sources in the Presentation of Character.* Oxford.

Shumate, N. (1996) *Crisis and Conversion in Apuleius'* Metamorphoses. Ann Arbor, MI.

Simonetti, E. (2017) *A Perfect Medium? Oracular Divination in the Thought of Plutarch.* Leuven.

Simpson, A. (2019) "Precepts, paradigms and evaluations: Niketas Choniates' use of Plutarch", in Xenophontos and Oikonomopoulou (2019), 279–294.

Sinor, D. (1957) "Les Barbares", *Diogène* 18: 52–68.

Sion-Jenkis, K. (2000) *Von der Republik zum Prinzipat: Ursachen für den Verfassungswechsel in Rom im historischen Denken der Antike.* Stuttgart.

Sirinelli, J. (2000) *Plutarque de Chéronée: Un philosophe dans le siècle.* Paris.

Slater, W. (ed.) (1991) *Dining in a Classical Context.* Ann Arbor, MI.

Small, J. (1997) *Wax Tablets of the Mind: Cognitive Studies of Memory and Literacy in Classical Antiquity.* London.

Smith, R. (1992) "Photius on the ten orators", *GRBS* 33: 159–189.

Smith, S. (2014) *Man and Animal in Severan Rome: The Literary Imagination of Claudius Aelian.* Cambridge.

Snell, B. (1954) "Zur Geschichte vom Gastmahl der Sieben Weisen", in O. Hiltbrunner (ed.), *Thesaurismata: Festschrift für Ida Kapp zum 70. Geburtstag.* Munich, 105–111.

Sorabji, R. (1983) *Time, Creation, and the Continuum: Theories in Antiquity and the Early Middle Ages.* London.

(1993) *Animal Minds and Human Morals.* Ithaca, NY.

(1997) "Esprits d'animaux", in Cassin and Labarrière (1997), 355–373.

Späth, T. (2007) "Blick auf Helden statt Blick auf Rom: Plutarchs Rezepte für ein globales Bankett der Moral", in M.-L. Freyburger and D. Meyer (eds.), *Visions grecques de Rome: Griechische Blicke auf Rom.* Paris, 143–170.

Spawforth, A. (1994) "Symbol of unity? The Persian Wars tradition in the Roman Empire", in S. Hornblower (ed.), *Greek Historiography.* Oxford, 233–247.

Spencer, T. (ed.) (1964) *Shakespeare's Plutarch.* Harmondsworth.

Speyer, W. (1989) "Die Griechen und die Fremdvölker. Kulturbegegnungen und Wege zur gegenseitigen Verständigung", *Eos* 77: 17–29.

Stadter, P. (1965) *Plutarch's Historical Methods: An Analysis of the Mulierum Virtutes.* Cambridge, MA.

(1973a) "Planudes, Plutarch, and Pace of Ferrara", *IMU* 16: 137–162.

(1973b) "Thucydidean orators in Plutarch", in P. Stadter (ed.), *The Speeches in Thucydides.* Chapel Hill, NC, 109–123.

(1975) "Plutarch's comparison of Pericles and Fabius Maximus", *GRBS* 16: 77–85. Reprinted in Scardigli (1995), 155–164.

(1976) "Xenophon in Arrian's *Cynegeticus*", *GRBS* 17: 157–167.

(1987) "The rhetoric of Plutarch's *Pericles*", *AncSoc* 18: 251–269.

(1988) "The proems of Plutarch's *Lives*", *ICS* 13: 275–295.

(1989) *A Commentary on Plutarch's* Pericles. Chapel Hill, NC.

(1992a) "Paradoxical paradigms: Lysander and Sulla", in Stadter (1992b), 41–55. Reprinted in Stadter (2015a), 258–269.

(ed.) (1992b) *Plutarch and the Historical Tradition.* London.

(1995) "Subject to the erotic: male sexual behaviour in Plutarch", in Innes, Hine, and Pelling (1995), 221–236.

(1996) "Anecdotes and the thematic structure of Plutarchean biography", in Fernández Delgado and Pordomingo Pardo (1996), 291–303.

(1997) "Plutarch's *Lives*: the statesman as moral actor", in Schrader, Ramón, and Vela (1997), 65–81. Reprinted in Stadter (2015a), 215–230.

(1999a) "*Philosophos* and *philandros*: Plutarch's view of women in the *Moralia* and the *Lives*", in Pomeroy (1999a), 173–182.

(1999b) "Plato in Plutarch's *Lives* of Lycurgus and Agesilaus", in Pérez Jiménez, García López, and Aguilar (eds.) 1999), 475–486.

(1999c) "Drinking, table talk and Plutarch's contemporaries", in Montes Cala et al. (1999), 481–490. Reprinted in Stadter (2015a), 98–107.

(2000) "The rhetoric of virtue in Plutarch's *Lives*", in Van der Stockt (2000b), 493–510. Reprinted in Stadter (2015a), 231–245.

(2002) "Plutarch's *Lives* and their Roman readers", in E. N. Ostenfeld (ed.), *Greek Romans and Roman Greeks: Studies in Cultural Interaction.* Aarhus, 123–135. Reprinted in Stadter (2015a), 45–55.

(2003–4) "Mirroring virtue in Plutarch's *Lives*", *Ploutarchos* n.s. 1: 89–96.

(2004) "Plutarch: diplomat for Delphi?" in de Blois et al. (2004), 19–31. Reprinted in Stadter (2015a), 70–81.

(2005a) "Plutarco fra presente e passato", in Jufresa et al. (2005a), 653–658.

(2005b) "Revisiting Plutarch's *Lives* of the Caesars", in Pérez Jiménez and Titchener (2005), 405–422. Reprinted in Stadter (2015a), 56–69.

(2008) "Notes and anecdotes: observations on cross-genre *Apophthegmata*", in Nikolaidis (2008), 53–66.

(2010) "Parallels in three dimensions", in Humble (2010b), 197–216. Reprinted in Stadter (2015a), 286–302.

(2010–11) "How to deal with the philosophical tradition? Some general rules in Plutarch's anti-Epicurean treatises", *Ploutarchos* 8: 133–146.

(2011) "Competition and its costs: *philonikia* in Plutarch's society and heroes", in Roskam and Van der Stockt (2011), 237–255. Reprinted in Stadter (2015a), 270–285.

(2012) "The philosopher's ambition: Plutarch, Arrian and Marcus Aurelius", in Roskam, De Pourcq and Van der Stockt (2012), 85–98. Reprinted in Stadter (2015a), 199–211.

(2014) "Plutarch's compositional technique: the anecdote collections and the *Parallel Lives*", *GRBS* 54: 665–686.

(2015a) *Plutarch and His Roman Readers*. Oxford.

(2015b) "Friends or patrons?" in Stadter (2015a), 21–44.

(2015c) "Plutarch's Latin reading: Cicero's *Lucullus* and Horace's *Epistle* 1.6", in Stadter (2015a), 130–148.

(2017) "Discussing the past: moral vision, truth and benevolence in Plutarch's *On the Malice of Herodotus*", in Georgiadou and Oikonomopoulou (2017), 161–173.

Stadter, P. and L. Van der Stockt (eds.) (2002) *Sage and Emperor: Plutarch, Greek intellectuals and Roman Power in the time of Trajan (98–117 AD)*. Leuven.

Stamatopoulou, Z. (2014) "Hesiodic poetry and wisdom in Plutarch's *Symposium of the Seven Sages*", *AJPh* 135: 533–558.

Stanford, W. (1954) *The Ulysses Theme*. Oxford.

Stanton, G. (1973) "Sophists and philosophers: problems of classification", *AJPh* 94: 350–364.

Steidle, W. (1951) *Sueton und die antike Biographie*. Munich.

Steiner, G. (2005) *Anthropocentrism and Its Discontents: The Moral Status of Animals in the History of Western Philosophy*. Pittsburgh, PA.

(2008) "Das Tier bei Aristoteles und den Stoikern: Evolution eines kosmischen Prinzips", in Alexandridis, Wild, and Winkler-Horaček (eds.), 27–46.

(2009–10) "Plutarch on the question of justice for animals", *Ploutarchos* 7: 73–82.

Stem, S. R. (2012) *The Political Biographies of Cornelius Nepos*. Ann Arbor, MI.

Stevenson, R. (1997) *Persica*. Edinburgh.

Stok, F. (1998) "Le traduzioni latine dei *Moralia* di Plutarco", *Fontes* 1: 117–136.

Strachey, L. (1928) *Elizabeth and Essex*. London.

Striker, G. (1991) "Following nature: a study in Stoic ethics", *OSAPh* 9: 1–73.

(1994) "Plato's Socrates and the Stoics", in P. Vander Waerdt (ed.), *The Socratic Movement*. Ithaca, NY, 241–251.

Strobach, A. (1997) *Plutarch und die Sprachen: Ein Beitrag zur Fremdsprachenproblematik in der Antike*. Stuttgart.

Stronk, J. (2010) *Ctesias' Persian History: Introduction, Text, and Translation*. Düsseldorf.

Swain, S. (1988) "Plutarch's *Philopoemen and Flamininus*", *ICS* 13: 335–347.

(1989a) "Plutarch's *Aemilius* and *Timoleon*", *Historia* 38: 314–334.

(1989b) "Character change in Plutarch", *Phoenix* 43: 62–68.

(1990a) "Hellenic culture and the Roman heroes of Plutarch", *JHS* 110: 126–145. Reprinted in Scardigli (1995), 229–264.

(1990b) "Plutarch's *Lives* of Cicero, Cato, and Brutus", *Hermes* 118: 192–203.

(1992a) "Plutarchan *synkrisis*", *Eranos* 90: 101–111.

(1992b) "Plutarch's characterization of Lucullus", *RhM* 135: 307–316.

(1996) *Hellenism and Empire: Language, Classicism, and Power in the Greek World, AD 50–250*. Oxford.

(1997) "Plato, Plutarch, Athens and Rome", in J. Barnes and M. Griffin (eds.), *Philosophia Togata ii: Plato and Aristotle at Rome*. Oxford, 165–187.

Swift, L. (2010) *The Hidden Chorus: Echoes of Genre in Tragic Lyric*. Oxford.

Syme, R. (1958) *Tacitus*. 2 vols. Oxford.

Tagliasacchi, A. (1960) "Plutarco e la tragedia greca", *Dioniso* 34: 124–142.

Takho, T. and E. Lowe (2015) "Ontological dependence", in *The Stanford Encyclopedia of Philosophy* (https://plato.stanford.edu/entries/dependence-ontological).

Taplin, O. (1986) "Fifth-century tragedy and comedy: a synkrisis", *JHS* 106: 163–174. Reprinted in E. Segal (ed.) (1996) *Oxford Readings in Aristophanes*. Oxford, 9–28.

Tarrant, H. (1993) *Thrasyllan Platonism*. Ithaca, NY.

(2000) *Plato's First Interpreters*. Ithaca, NY.

Tartaglia, L. (1987) "Il *Saggio su Plutarco* di Teodoro Metochita", in *Talariskos: Studia graeca Antonio Garzya sexagenario a discipulis oblata*. Naples, 339–362.

Tatum, W. (2010) "Why *parallel* lives?" in Humble (2010b), 1–22.

Taufer, M. (1999) "Er e Tespesio: Plutarco interprete di Platone", *Lexis* 17: 303–318.

Taylor, A. (2003) *Animals and Ethics: An Overview of the Philosophical Debate.* Peterborough.

Teague, F. (1992) "Letters and portents in *Julius Caesar* and *King Lear*", *Shakespeare Yearbook* 3: 87–104.

Tecuşan, M. (1993) *Symposion and Philosophy.* D.Phil. thesis, Oxford University.

Teodorsson, S.-T. (1989) *A Commentary on Plutarch's Table Talks,* vol. I. Gothenburg.

  (1990) *A Commentary on Plutarch's Table Talks,* vol. II. Gothenburg.

  (1996) *A Commentary on Plutarch's Table Talks,* vol. III. Gothenburg.

  (1997) "Ethical historiography: Plutarch's attitude to historical criticism", in Schrader, Ramón, and Vela (1997), 439–447.

  (1999) "Dionysus moderated and calmed", in Montes Cala et al. (1999), 57–69.

  (2000) "Plutarch's use of synonyms: a typical feature of his style", in Van der Stockt (2000b), 511–518.

  (2005) "Plutarcho innovatore del vocabulario Greco", in Pérez Jiménez and Titchener (2005), 405–418.

  (2007–8) "Health is wealth: Plutarch on contemporary luxury", *Ploutarchos* 5: 81–90.

  (2009) "The place of Plutarch in the literary genre of *symposium*", in Ribeiro Ferreira et al. (2009), 3–16.

Terian, A. (ed.) (1981) *Philonis Alexandrini de Animalibus.* Chico, CA.

Theander, C. (1951) *Plutarch und die Geschichte.* Lund.

Thériault, G. (1996) *Le culte d'Homonoia dans les cités grecques.* Lyon.

Thompson, L. (1979) "Strabo on civilization", *Platon* 31: 213–219.

Thumiger, C. (2014a) "Animals in tragedy", in Campbell (2014), 84–98.

  (2014b) "Metamorphosis: human into animals", in Campbell (2014), 384–413.

Timotin, A. (2012) *La démonologie platonicienne. Histoire de la notion de daimōn de Platon aux derniers néoplatoniciens.* Leiden.

Titchener, F. B. (1991) "Why did Plutarch write about Nicias?" *AHB* 5: 153–158.

  (1999) "Everything to do with Dionysus", in Montes Cala et al. (1999), 491–499.

  (2008) "Is Plutarch's Nicias devout, superstitious, or both?" in Nikolaidis (2008), 277–283.

  (2009) "The role of reality in Plutarch's *Quaestiones Convivales*", in Ribeiro Ferreira et al. (2009), 395–401.

  (2011) "Plutarch's *Table Talk*: sampling a rich blend – a survey of scholarly appraisal", in Klotz and Oikonomopoulou (2011a), 34–48.

Tovar Paz, F.-J. (1996) "El motivo de la 'caza' en *De Sollertia Animalium* de Plutarco", in Fernández Delgado and Pordomingo Pardo (1996), 211–217.

Tozza, M. (2008–9) "Gli epiteti omerici nel *Grillo* di Plutarco: parallelismo simbolico tra animali e divinità", *Ploutarchos* 6: 45–52.

  (2012) "Animali parlanti e giustizia in Plutarco ed Omero", in Ribeiro Ferreira, Leão, and Martins de Jesus (2012), 191–199.

Trapp, M. (1999) "Socrates, the *Phaedo* and the *Lives* of Phocion and Cato the Younger", in Pérez Jiménez, García López, and Aguilar (1999), 487–499.

(2004) "Statesmanship in a minor key? The *An seni* and the *Praecepta gerendae rei publicae*", in de Blois et al. (2004), 189–200.

(2007) *Philosophy in the Roman Empire: Ethics, Politics and Society.* Aldershot.

Treadgold, W. (1980) *The Nature of the Bibliotheca of Photius.* Washington, DC.

Trego, K. (2012–13) "Competition in context: *philonikia* in *Agesilaus–Pompey*", *Ploutarchos* 10: 63–74.

Tritle, L. (1988) *Phocion the Good.* London.

Tröster, M. (2008) *Themes, Character, and Politics in Plutarch's Life of Lucullus: The Construction of a Roman Aristocrat.* Stuttgart.

(2009) "Banquet and philhellenism in the *Lives of Flamininus* and *Aemilius Paullus*", in Ribeiro Ferreira et al. (2009), 165–179.

(2012) "Plutarch and *Mos Maiorum* in the *Life of Aemilius Paullus*", *AncSoc* 42: 219–254.

(2014) "Cimone come benefattore panellenico e campione di concordia: Una proiezione di Plutarco?" *RSA* 44: 9–28.

Tsekourakis, D. (1983) Οἱ Λαϊκοφιλοσοφικὲς πραγματεῖες τοῦ Πλουτάρχου. Ἡ σχέση τους μὲ τὴ "διατριβὴ" καὶ μὲ ἄλλα παραπλήσια γραμματειακὰ εἴδη. (Ἀριστοτέλειο Πανεπιστήμιο Θεσσαλονίκης, Ἐπιστημονικὴ Ἐπετηρίδα Φιλοσοφικῆς Σχολῆς 34). Thessaloniki.

(1987) "Pythagoreanism or Platonism and ancient medicine? The reasons for vegetarianism in Plutarch's *Moralia*", *ANRW* II.36.1, 366–393.

Tsouvala, G. (2014) "Love and marriage", in Beck (2014a), 191–206.

Tuplin, C. (1996) *Achaemenid Studies.* Stuttgart.

Tutrone, F. (2012) *Filosofi e animali in Roma antica: Modelli di animalità e umanità in Lucrezio e Seneca.* Pisa.

Ullman, B. (1963) *The Humanism of Coluccio Salutati.* Padua.

Ungefehr-Kortus, C. (1996) *Anacharsis, der Typus des edlen, weisen Barbaren – Ein Beitrag zum Verständnis griechischer Fremdheitserfahrung.* Bern.

Ure, P. (1958) "Chapman's use of North's Plutarch in *Caesar and Pompey*", *Review of English Studies* 9.35: 281–284.

Usener, H. (1887) *Epicurea.* Leipzig.

Uthemann, K.-H. and H. Görgemanns (2006) "Diatribe", in H. Cancik and H. Schneider (eds.), *Brill's New Pauly: Encyclopedia of the Ancient World*, at https://referenceworks.brillonline.com/entries/brill-s-new-pauly/diatribe-e3 16870. Leiden.

Valgiglio, E. (1975) "Basilio Magno *Ad Adulescentes* e Plutarco *De Audiendis Poetis*", *Rivista di Studi Classici* 23: 67–85.

(ed.) (1976) *Plutarco: Praecepta gerendae reipublicae.* Milan.

(1982) "Alcuni aspetti di Cicerone come fonte di Plutarco", in *Studi in onore di Aristide Colonna.* Perugia, 283–299.

(1987) "Ἱστορία e βίος in Plutarco", *Orpheus* 8: 50–70.

(ed.) (1989) *Plutarco: Il progresso nella virtù (CPM 3).* Naples.

(1991) "La struttura del *De audiendis poetis* di Plutarco", in D'Ippolito and Gallo (1991), 375–380.

(1992) "Dagli 'Ethicà' ai 'Bioi' in Plutarco", *ANRW* II.33.6, 3963–4051.

Vallozza, M. (1990) "Alcuni motivi del discorso di lode tra Pindaro e Isocrate", *QUCC* 35: 43–58.

    (1991) "Osservazioni sulle techniche argomentative nel discorso di lode nel *De laude ipsius* di Plutarco", in D'Ippolito and Gallo (1991), 327–334.

Vamvouri Ruffy, M. (2011) "Symposium, physical and social health in Plutarch's *Table Talk*", in Klotz and Oikonomopoulou (2011a), 131–157.

    (2012) *Les vertus thérapeutiques du banquet: médecine et idéologie dans les* Propos de Table *de Plutarque*. Paris.

Van der Stockt, L. (1987) "Plutarch's use of literature: sources and citations in the *Quaestiones Romanae*", *AncSoc* 18: 281–292.

    (1990) "Plutarch on language", in P. Swiggers and A. Wouters (eds.), *Le langage dans l'Antiquité*. Leuven, 180–196.

    (1992) *Twinkling and Twilight: Plutarch's Reflections on Literature*. Brussels.

    (ed.) (1996) *Plutarchea Lovaniensia: A Miscellany of Essays on Plutarch*. Leuven.

    (1999a) "Plutarch on mania and its therapy", in Montes Cala et al. (1999), 517–526.

    (1999b) "A Plutarchan hypomnema on self-love", *AJPh* 120: 575–599.

    (1999c) "Three Aristotles equal but one Plato: on a cluster of quotations in Plutarch", in Pérez Jiménez, García López, and Aguilar (1999), 127–140.

    (2000a) "Aspects of the ethics and poetics of the dialogue in the Corpus Plutarcheum", in Gallo and Moreschini (2000), 93–116.

    (ed.) (2000b) *Rhetorical Theory and Praxis in Plutarch: Acta of the IVth International Congress of the International Plutarch Society, Leuven, July 3–6, 1996*. Louvain.

    (2002) "Καρπὸς ἐκ φιλίας ἡγεμονικῆς (Mor. 814 C): Plutarch's observations on the 'old-boy network'", in Stadter and Van der Stockt (2002), 115–140.

    (2003–4) "Odysseus in Rome: on Plutarch's introduction to *De cohibenda ira*", *Ploutarchos* 1: 107–116.

    (2004) "Plutarch in Plutarch: the problem of the hypomnemata", in I. Gallo (ed.), *La biblioteca di Plutarco*. Naples, 331–340.

    (2005) "'Excludens amator': Agesilaus fending off a kiss", in Pérez Jiménez and Titchener (2005), 441–450.

    (2007) "'God does not love birds' (*De gen. Socr.* 593A): theophilia in Plutarch", in Nieto Ibáñez and López López (2007), 199–207.

    (2008) "Self-esteem and image-building: on anger in *De cohibenda ira* and in some *Lives*", in Nikolaidis (2008), 285–295.

    (2011) "*Semper duo, numquam tres*? Plutarch's *Popularphilosophie* on friendship and virtue in *On having many friends*", in Roskam and Van der Stockt (2011), 19–39.

    (2013) "Loyalty divided or doubled? Plutarch's Hellenism saluting Rome", in P. Schubert (ed.), *Les grecs héritiers des romains*. (Entretiens Hardt, LIX). Geneva, 15–43.

    (2014) "Compositional methods in the *Lives*", in Beck (2014a), 321–332.

van Emde Boas, E., A. Rijksbaron, L. Huitink, and M. De Bakker (2019) *Cambridge Grammar of Classical Greek*. Cambridge.

Van Hoof, L. (2007) "Strategic differences: Seneca and Plutarch on controlling anger", *Mnemosyne* 60: 59–86.

(2008), "Genres and their implications: meddlesomeness in *On curiosity* versus the *Lives*", in Nikolaidis (2008), 297–310.

(2010) *Plutarch's Practical Ethics: The Social Dynamics of Philosophy*. Oxford.

(2014) "Practical ethics", in Beck (2014a), 135–148.

Van Meirvenne, B. (2002) "Plutarch on the healing power of (a tricky) παρρησία: observations on a political reading of *De adulatore et amico*", in Stadter and Van der Stockt (2002), 141–160.

van Nijf, O. (2011) "Public space and the political culture of Roman Termessos", in Van Nijf and Alston (2011), 215–242.

van Nijf, O. and R. Alston (eds.) (2011) *Political Culture in the Greek City after the Classical Age*. Leuven.

van Wees, H. (1992) *Status Warriors: War, Violence and Society in Homer and History*. Amsterdam.

Vasoli, C. (1972) "Bruni, Leonardo", in *Dizionario Biografico degli Italiani*. Vol. XIV. Rome, 618–633.

Vaughan, A. and V. Vaughan (1991) *Caliban: A Cultural History*. Cambridge.

Vela Tejada, J. (2019) "Atticism in Plutarch: a μίμησις τῶν ἀρχαίων or *diglossia*?", *Euphrosyne* 47: 295–308.

Verdegem, S. (2008) "Plutarch's *Quaestiones Romanae* and his *Lives* of Early Romans", in Nikolaidis (2008), 171–185.

(2010a) *Plutarch's Life of Alcibiades: Story, Text and Moralism*. Leuven.

(2010b) "Parallels and contrasts: Plutarch's *Comparison of Coriolanus and Alcibiades*", in Humble (2010b), 23–44.

Verger, J. (1997) "Guarino de Vérone", in C. Nativel (ed.), *Centuriae Latinae: Cent une figures humanistes de la Renaissance aux Lumières offertes à Jacques Chomarat*. Geneva, 409–415.

Vernière, Y. (1977) *Symboles et mythes dans la pensée de Plutarque*. Paris.

Vetta, M. (ed.) (1983) *Poesia e simposio nella Grecia antica: guida storica e critica*. Rome.

Veyne, P. (1976) *Le pain et le cirque: Sociologie historique d'un pluralisme politique*. Paris.

(1978) "La famille et l'amour sous le haut-empire romain", *Annales* 33: 35–63.

(1985) "L'empire romain, I", in G. Duby and P. Ariès (eds.), *Histoire de la vie privée, I: De l'empire romain à l'an mil*. Paris, 19–223.

(1988) *Did the Greeks Believe in Their Myths?* Trans. P. Wissing. Chicago, IL.

(1990) *Bread and Circuses: Historical Sociology and Political Pluralism*. Trans. B. Pearce. London.

(1999) "L'identité grecque devant Rome et l'empereur", *REG* 112: 511–567.

(2005) *L'Empire gréco-romain*. Paris.

Vickers, B. (ed.) (1996) *Francis Bacon: A Critical Edition of the Major Works*. Oxford.

Viti, P. (ed.) (1996) *Leonardo Bruni: Opere letterarie e politiche*. Turin.

Vlassopoulos, K. (2013) *Greeks and Barbarians*. Cambridge.

Volpe Cacciatore, P. (ed.) (2009) *Plutarco nelle traduzioni latine di età umanistica.* Naples.

Volpe Cacciatore, P. (2017) "Gli animale e gli uomini in Plutarco", in M. Sanz Morales, R. González Delgado, M. Librán Moreno, and J. Ureña Bracero (eds.), *La (inter)textualidad en Plutarco.* Cáceres, 383–389.

Volpe Cacciatore, P. and F. Ferrari (eds.) (2007) *Plutarco e la cultura della sua età. Atti del X Convegno plutarcheo, Fisciano-Paestum, 27–29 ottobre 2005.* Naples.

Voltaire (1957) *Oeuvres historiques*, ed. R. Pomeau. Paris.

von Arnim, H. (ed.) (1903) *Stoicorum veterum fragmenta. Vol. I.* Lepzig.

Waith, E. (1962) *The Herculean Hero in Marlowe, Chapman, Shakespeare and Dryden.* London.

Wälchli, P. (2003) *Studien zu den literarischen Beziehungen zwischen Plutarch und Lukian.* Munich.

Wallace-Hadrill, A. (1983) *Suetonius: The Scholar and His Caesars.* London.

(2008) *Rome's Cultural Revolution.* Cambridge.

Walsh, J. (1992) "Syzygy, theme and history: a study in Plutarch's *Philopoemen* and *Flamininus*", *Philologus* 136: 208–233.

Walter, G. (ed.) (1951) *Les Vies des hommes illustres. Traduction de Jacques Amyot.* 2 vols. Paris. 2nd ed. 1977.

Walton, F. (1965) "A neglected historical text", *Historia* 14: 236–251.

Wankel, H. (ed.) (1976) *Demosthenes: Rede für Ktesiphon über den Kranz.* Heidelberg.

Wardman, A. (1955) "Plutarch and Alexander", *CQ* 5: 96–107.

(1971) "Plutarch's methods in the *Lives*", *CQ* 21: 254–261.

(1974) *Plutarch's Lives.* London.

Warren, J. (2002) *Epicurus and Democritean Ethics: An Archaeology of Ataraxia.* Cambridge.

Waterfield, R. and P. Stadter (eds.) (1998) *Greek Lives: A Selection of Nine Greek Lives.* Oxford.

(1999) *Roman Lives: A Selection of Eight Roman Lives.* Oxford.

Webb, R. (2006) "Fiction, mimesis and the performance of the Greek past in the Second Sophistic", in Konstan and Saïd (2006), 27–46.

Wecowski, M. (2014) *The Rise of the Greek Aristocratic Banquet.* Oxford.

Wegehaupt, H. (1914) "Planudes und Plutarch", *Philologus* 27: 244–252.

Weidner, E. (1913) "Barbaros", *Glotta* 4: 303–304.

Weiss, R. (1953) "Lo studio di Plutarco nel trecento", *PP* 8: 321–342.

(1977) *Medieval and Humanist Greek: Collected Essays.* Padua.

Weissenberger, B. (1894). *Die Sprache Plutarchs von Chaironeia und die pseudoplutarchische Schriften.* Straubing.

Weisser, S. (2016) "The art of quotation: Plutarch and Galen against Chryisippus", in Weisser and Thaler (2016), 203–229.

Weisser, S. and N. Thaler (eds.) (2016) *Strategies of Philosophical Polemics in Greek and Roman Philosophy.* Leiden.

Wendel, C. (1950) "Planudes, Maximos", *RE* 20.2: 2202–2253.

Westerink, L. (ed.) (1948) *Michael Psellus: De omnifaria doctrina.* Utrecht.

(ed.) (1973) *Nicétas Magistros: Lettres d'un exilé (928–946)*. Paris.

Whitmarsh, T. (2000) "The politics and poetics of parasitism: Athenaeus on parasites and flatterers", in Braund and Wilkins (2000), 304–315.

(2001) *Greek Literature and the Roman Empire: The Politics of Imitation*. Oxford.

(2002) "Alexander's Hellenism and Plutarch's textualism", *CQ* 52: 174–192.

(2005) *The Second Sophistic*. Oxford.

(2006a) "Quickening the classics: the politics of prose in Roman Greece", in Porter (2006a), 353–374.

(2006b) "'This in-between book': language, politics and genre in the *Agricola*", in McGing and Mossman (2006a), 305–333.

(2006c) "The sincerest form of imitation: Plutarch on flattery", in Konstan and Saïd (2006), 93–111.

(2009) "Greece and Rome", in Boys-Stones, Graziosi, and Vasunia (2009), 114–128.

Whittaker, J. (1969) "Ammonius on the Delphic E", *CQ* 63: 185–192.

Wiedemann, T. (1986) "Between men and beasts: barbarians in Ammianus Marcellinus," in Moxon, Smart, and Woodman (1986), 189–201.

(1988) *Greek and Roman Slavery*. London.

Wildberger, J. (2008) "Beast or god? The intermediate status of humans and the physical basis of the Stoic *scala naturae*", in Alexandridis, Wild, and Winkler-Horaček (2008), 47–70.

Wilken, U. (1906) "Hellenen und Barbaren", *Neue Jahrbücher für das klassische Altertum* 17: 457–471.

Wilkins, J. (2008) "Animals in the Romano-Greek culture of the second century AD", in Alexandridis, Wild, and Winkler-Horaček (2008), 315–328.

Wilson, N. (1967) "The libraries of the Byzantine world", *GRBS* 8: 53–80.

(1970) "The church and classical studies in Byzantium", *A&A* 16: 68–77.

(1975) "Maximus Planudes and a famous codex of Plutarch", *GRBS* 16: 95–97.

(1992) *From Byzantium to Italy: Greek Studies in the Italian Renaissance*. Baltimore, MD.

(1996) *Scholars of Byzantium*. London. First published 1983.

Winkler, J. (1985) *Auctor and Actor: A Narratological Reading of Apuleius' Golden Ass*. Berkeley, CA.

Wirszubski, C. (1950) *Libertas as a Political Idea at Rome during the Late Republic and Early Principate*. Cambridge.

Witt, R. (1976) "Toward a biography of Coluccio Salutati", *Rinascimento* 16: 19–34.

(1978) "Salutati and Plutarch," in S. Bertelli and G. Ramakus (eds.), *Essays Presented to Myron P. Gilmore: Vol. I*. Florence, 335–346.

(1983) *Hercules at the Crossroads: The Life, Works and Thought of Coluccio Salutati*. Durham, NC.

(1996) "Introduction: Hans Baron's renaissance humanism" and "The crisis after forty years", *The American Historical Review* 101: 107–118.

(1999) "Hans Baron", in P. Grendler (ed.), *Encyclopedia of the Renaissance: Vol. V*. New York, 299–300.

(2000) *In the Footsteps of the Ancients: The Origins of Humanism from Lovato to Bruni*. Leiden.

Wofford, S. (1997) "Antony's Egyptian Bacchanals: heroic and divine impersonation in Shakespeare's Plutarch and *Antony and Cleopatra*", in McGrail (1997), 33–67.

Wohl, V. (1997) "Scenes from a marriage: love and logos in Plutarch's *Conjugalia Praecepta*", *Helios* 24: 170–192.

Woolf, G. (1993) "Roman peace", in Rich and Shipley (1993), 171–194.

Worth, V. (1986) "Les Fortunes de Jacques Amyot en Angleterre", in Balard (1986), 285–296.

Wyttenbach, D. (1843) *Lexicon Plutarcheum et Vitas et Moralia complectens*. Leipzig.

Xenophontos, S. (2012) "Comedy in Plutarch's *Parallel Lives*", *GRBS* 52: 603–631.

(2013) "Imagery and education in Plutarch", *CPh* 108: 126–138.

(2014a) "Resorting to rare sources of antiquity: Nikephoros Basilakes and the popularity of Plutarch's *Parallel Lives* in twelfth-century Byzantium", *Parekbolai* 4: 1–12.

(2014b) Review of Beck (2014a), *BMCR* 2014.09.38.

(2016) *Ethical Education in Plutarch: Moralising Agents and Contexts*. Berlin.

(2018) "The Byzantine Plutarch: self-identity and model in Theodore Metochites' Essay 71 of the *Semeioseis gnomikai*", in North and Mack (2018), 23–39.

(2019) "Plutarch and Theodore Metochites", in Xenophontos and Oikonomopoulou (2019), 310–323.

Xenophontos, S. and K. Oikonomopoulou (eds.) (2019) *Brill's Companion to the Reception of Plutarch*. Leiden.

Yaginuma, S. (1992) "Plutarch's language and style", *ANRW* II.33.6, 4726–4742.

Yunis, H. (2003) "Writing for reading: Thucydides, Plato and the emergence of the critical reader", in H. Yunis (ed.), *Written Texts and the Rise of Literate Culture in Ancient Greece*. Cambridge, 189–212.

Zadorojnyi, A. (1997a) "Tragedy and epic in Plutarch's *Crassus*", *Hermes* 125: 169–182.

(1997b) "The Roman poets in Plutarch's stories", in Schrader, Ramón, and Vela (1997), 497–506.

(2002) "Safe drugs for the good boys: Platonism and pedagogy in *Plutarch's De audiendis poetis*", in Stadter and Van der Stockt (2002), 297–314.

(2006a) "King of his castle: Plutarch, *Demosthenes* 1–2", *CCJ* 52: 102–127.

(2006b) "Plutarch's Themistocles and the poets", *AJPh* 127: 261–292.

(2007) "Cato's suicide in Plutarch", *CQ* 57: 216–230.

(2010) "ὥσπερ ἐν ἐσόπτρῳ: The rhetoric and philosophy of Plutarch's mirrors", in Humble (2010b), 169–195.

(2011) "The ethico-politics of writing in Plutarch's *Life of Dion*", *JHS* 131: 147–163.

(2012) "Mimesis and the (plu)past in Plutarch's *Lives*", in J. Grethlein and C. Krebs (eds.), *Time and Narrative in Ancient Historiography: The "Plupast" from Herodotus to Appian*. Cambridge, 175–198.

(2014) *"Kratein onomatôn*: language and value in Plutarch", in Beck (2014a), 304–320.

(2018a) "Plutarch à la Russe: ancient heroism and Russian ideology in Tolstoy's *War and Peace*", in North and Mack (2018), 149–178.

(2018b) "Plutarch's heroes and the 'biographical synecdoche'", in F. Cairns and T. Luke (eds.), *Ancient Biography: Identity through Lives*. Tallahassee, FL, 241–259.

(2019) "Heroism, apophthegms, and the Plutarchan hypotext in Tolstoy's *War and Peace*", in S. Tilg and A. Novokhatko (eds.), *Antikes Heldentum in der Moderne: Konzepte, Praktiken, Medien*. Freiburg, 17–34.

(2020) "Greek and Latin biography", updated version, in R. Scodel (ed.), *Oxford Bibliographies Online (Classics)* (https://www.oxfordbibliographies.com/page/classics).

Zanker, P. (1988) *The Power of Images in the Age of Augustus*. Ann Arbor, MI.

Zeller, E. (1868) *Die Philosophie der Griechen in ihrer geschichtlichen Entwicklung (Dritter Theil, Zweite Abtheilung, Die nacharistotelische Philosophie, zweite Hälfte)*. Leipzig.

Ziegler, K. (1949) *Plutarchos von Chaironeia*. (Separatdruck *RE* XXI.1). Stuttgart. Reprinted as Ziegler (1951).

(1951) "Plutarchos von Chaironeia", *RE* XXI.1: 636–962.

(1964) *Plutarchos von Chaironeia*. Stuttgart.

Zuiderhoek, A. (2008) "On the political sociology of the imperial Greek city", *GRBS* 48: 417–445.

# Appendix: Plutarch's *Moralia*

"short" English title

| | | | |
|---|---|---|---|
| *De liberis educandis** | 1A-14C | *On the education of children** | *On education** |
| *Quomodo adolescens poetas audire debeat* | 14D-37B | *How the young man should listen to poetry* | *Study of poetry* |
| *De recta ratione audiendi* | 37C-48D | *On listening* | |
| *Quomodo adulator ab amico internoscatur* | 48E-74E | *How to tell a flatterer from a friend* | *Flatterer and friend* |
| *Quomodo quis suos in virtute sentiat profectus* | 75A-86A | *How to understand that one is making progress in virtue* | *Progress in virtue* |
| *De capienda ex inimicis utilitate* | 86B-92F | *How to profit from one's enemies* | *Profiting from enemies* |
| *De amicorum multitudine* | 93A-97B | *On having many friends* | *Having many friends* |
| *De fortuna* | 97C-100A | *On chance* | |
| *De virtute et vitio* | 100B-101E | *On virtue and vice* | |
| *Consolatio ad Apollonium* | 101F-122A | *Consolation to Apollonius** | |
| *De tuenda sanitate praecepta* | 122B-137E | *Advice on health* | |
| *Coniugalia praecepta* | 138B-146A | *Advice to bride and groom* | *Marriage advice* |
| *Septem sapientium convivium* | 146B-164D | *Banquet of the Seven Sages* | |
| *De superstitione* | 164E-171F | *On superstition* | *Superstition* |
| *Regum et imperatorum apophthegmata* | 172A-194E | *Sayings of kings and commanders* | |
| *Apophthegmata Romana* | 194F-208A | *Sayings of Romans* | |
| *Apophthegmata Laconica* | 208A-236E | *Spartan sayings* | |
| *Instituta Laconica* | 236F-240B | *Customs of the Spartans* | |
| *Lacaenarum apophthegmata* | 240C-242D | *Sayings of Spartan women* | |
| *Mulierum virtutes* | 242E-263C | *Virtues of women* | |
| *Quaestiones Romanae* | 263D-291C | *Roman questions* | |
| *Quaestiones Graecae* | 291D-304F | *Greek questions* | |
| *Parallela Graeca et Romana** | 305A-316B | *Greek and Roman parallel stories** | *Parallel stories* |

*(cont.)*

| | | | |
|---|---|---|---|
| *De fortuna Romanorum* | 316C-326C | On the fortune of the Romans | Fortune of the Romans |
| *De Alexandri magni fortuna aut virtute* | 326D-345B | On the fortune or virtue of Alexander | Alexander's fortune or virtue |
| *De gloria Atheniensium* | 345C-351B | Were the Athenians more famous in war or in peace? | Glory of Athens |
| *De Iside et Osiride* | 351C-384C | On Isis and Osiris | Isis and Osiris |
| *De E apud Delphos* | 384D-394C | On the E at Delphi | E at Delphi |
| *De Pythiae oraculis* | 394D-409D | That the Pythia's oracles are no longer in verse | Oracles of the Pythia |
| *De defectu oraculorum* | 409E-438E | On the obsolescence of oracles | Decline of oracles |
| *An virtus doceri possit* | 439A-440C | Can virtue be taught? | |
| *De virtute morali* | 440D-452D | On moral virtue | Moral virtue |
| *De cohibenda ira* | 452F-464D | On controlling anger | Control of anger |
| *De tranquilitate animi* | 464E-477F | On tranquillity of mind | Tranquillity of mind |
| *De fraterno amore* | 478A-492D | On brotherly love | Brotherly love |
| *De amore prolis* | 493A-497E | On the love of offspring | Love of offspring |
| *An vitiositas ad infelicitatem sufficiat* | 498A-500A | Is vice sufficient to cause unhappiness? | |
| *Animine an corporis affectiones sint peiores* | 500B-502A | Are the passions of the soul worse than those of the body? | |
| *De garrulitate* | 502B-515A | On talkativeness | Talkativeness |
| *De curiositate* | 515B-523B | On being a busybody | Curiosity |
| *De cupiditate divitiarum* | 523C-528B | On love of wealth | |
| *De vitioso pudore* | 528C-536D | On compliancy | Bashfulness |
| *De invidia et odio* | 536E-538E | On envy and hate | |
| *De se ipsum citra invidiam laudando* | 539A-547F | On praising oneself inoffensively | Inoffensive self-praise |
| *De sera numinis vindicta* | 548A-568A | On the slowness of divine punishments | God's slowness to punish |
| *De fato\** | 568B-574F | On fate* | |
| *De genio Socratis* | 575A-598F | On the divine sign of Socrates | Socrates' sign |
| *De exilio* | 599A-607F | On exile | |
| *Consolatio ad uxorem* | 608B-612B | Consolation to my wife | |

*(cont.)*

| | | | |
|---|---|---|---|
| Quaestiones convivales | 612C-748D | Table talk | |
| Amatorius | 748E-771E | Dialogue on love | On love |
| Amatoriae narrationes* | 771E-775E | Love stories* | |
| Maxime cum principibus philosopho esse disserendum | 776A-779C | That a philosopher should converse especially with princes | Converse with princes |
| Ad principem ineruditum | 779D-782F | To an uneducated ruler | Uneducated ruler |
| An seni respublica gerenda sit | 783A-797F | Should an old man engage in politics? | Old man in politics |
| Praecepta gerendae reipublicae | 798A-825F | Rules of statesmanship | Political advice |
| De unius in republica dominatione, populari statu, et paucorum imperio | 826A-827C | On monarchy, democracy, and oligarchy* | |
| De vitando aere alieno | 827D-832A | That one ought not to borrow | Against borrowing |
| Vitae decem oratorum* | 832B-852E | Lives of the ten orators* | |
| Comparationis Aristophanis et Menandri compendium | 853A-854D | Comparison of Aristophanes and Menander (abridged) | |
| De Herodoti malignitate | 854E-874C | On the malice of Herodotus | Malice of Herodotus |
| De placitis philosophorum* | 874D-911C | Doctrines of the philosophers* | |
| Quaestiones naturales | 911C-919E | Natural questions | |
| De facie quae in orbe lunae apparet | 920A-945D | On the face which appears in the orb of the Moon | Face in the Moon |
| De primo frigido | 945F-955C | On the principle of cold | |
| Aqua an ignis utilior sit* | 955D-958E | Is water or fire more useful?* | |
| De sollertia animalium | 959A-985C | Are land or sea animals more intelligent? | Cleverness of animals |
| Bruta animalia ratione uti, sive Gryllus | 985D-992E | That irrational animals use reason, or Gryllus | Gryllus |
| De esu carnium | 993A-999B | On the eating of meat | Eating of meat |
| Platonicae quaestiones | 999C-1011E | Platonic questions | |

*(cont.)*

| | | | |
|---|---|---|---|
| *De animae procreatione in Timaeo* | 1012A-1030C | *On the creation of the soul in the 'Timaeus'* | |
| *Epitome libri de animae procreatione in Timaeo* | 1030D-1032F | *Abridgement of the book On the creation of the soul in the 'Timaeus'* | |
| *De Stoicorum repugnantiis* | 1033A-1057C | *On the contradictions of the Stoics* | *On Stoic contradictions* |
| *Stoicos absurdiora poetis dicere* | 1057C-1058D | *That the Stoics talk more paradoxically than the poets* | |
| *De communibus notitiis adversus Stoicos* | 1058E-1086B | *Against the Stoics on common conceptions* | *Common conceptions* |
| *Non posse suaviter vivi secundum Epicurum* | 1086C-1107C | *It is not possible to live pleasantly according to Epicurus* | *Epicurean pleasant life impossible* |
| *Adversus Colotem* | 1107D-1127E | *Against Colotes, in defence of the other philosophers* | *Against Colotes* |
| *An recte dictum sit latenter esse vivendum* | 1128A-1130E | *Whether "Live unknown" is good advice* | *Live unknown* |
| *De musica\** *fragmenta* | 1131A-1147A | *On music\** Fragments | |

\*The text is ascribed to Plutarch, but the Plutarchan authorship is unlikely or suspect.

# Index Locorum

# Index

# Index

493

*Index*

Pyrrhus, 180, 185, 272, 286, 317, 329, 341, 401
Pythagoreanism, 79, 85, 89, 100, 106, 284, 290
Pythia, 173
Pythiad, 3, 122
Python, 300

Quintilian, 179, 325

Rabelais, 384, 385
Racine, J., 383, 384, 390, 398, 399, 400
reason, 50, 53, 55–57, 61, 62, 71, 93, 96, 97, 99, 113, 164, 181, 195, 199, 200, 205, 218, 229, 232, 238, 276, 283, 285, 289, 294, 297, 300, 371. *See* intellect, *logos*
animal, 282, 290, 292–294, 298, 301
reception, 1, 7, 83, 308, 314, 339
Platonic, 96
Plutarchan, 3, 152, 304, 308, 310, 316, 321, 322, 335, 338, 339, 340, 383
Shakespeare, 382
Suetonius, 335
revolution, 63
French, 7, 383, 401, 402
oligarchic, Athens, 188
Rhodes, 308, 326
Richelieu, 384, 397, 399, 400
riddles, 86, 148, 150
rivalry, philosophical, 101, 106, 116
rivalry, political, 35, 45, 53, 190, 192, 195, 256, 378, 398. *See* ambition, *philonikia*
Rinuccini, A., 334
Robespierre, 401
Roland, J.-M., 402
Rome, 15, 16, 30, 32, 36, 39, 41–45, 48, 55, 59, 60, 63, 65, 140, 143–145, 149, 150, 160, 180, 183–185, 206, 207, 222, 244–247, 250–252, 254–258, 261–263, 266–270, 272–276, 280, 281, 284, 287, 288, 331, 333, 334, 361, 363–365, 369, 370, 378–380, 399
Roman Greece, 1, 6, 179, 274
Romulus, 9, 31, 65, 183, 207, 333, 399, 400
Rousseau, J.-J., 383, 391, 393
Roville, G., 395
Rufo, J., 349
Ruiz de Virués, A., 341

Saavedra, 346
Sabines, 235, 399, 401
Saint-Evremond, 392, 393
Salamis, Cyprus, 272
Sallust, 40, 251, 255
Salutati, C., 325, 328, 337
Sappho, 238
satire, Roman, 244
satraps, 146, 249, 269

Satyrus, 13, 15
scholia, 313, 314
Scipio Aemilianus, 16, 64, 213, 252
Scipio Africanus, 36, 224, 362, 363, 394
Scylla, 302
Second Sophistic, 6, 22, 30, 32, 177, 261, 266, 290
Seleucids, 269
Seleucus, 249
self-control, 42, 53, 74, 145, 186, 193, 201, 203, 216, 219, 224, 232, 256, 278
self-presentation, 19, 54, 139, 274, 284, 332
Senate, Roman, 40, 71, 140, 183, 366
Seneca, 223, 284, 325, 344, 346, 349, 387, 392, 394, 396, 398
Septuagint, 83
Serapion, 5
Serranus, 16
Sertorius, 185, 232, 265, 266, 287, 329, 342, 398, 399
Servius, 43
Seven Sages, 129, 149, 150, 151, 182
sex, sexuality, 3, 16, 53, 57, 74, 146, 191, 194, 226, 237, 239, 240, 242, 256, 265, 291, 314
Sextus Pompey, 364, 375
Sforza, F., 336
Shakespeare, 4, 25, 357–382
Shelley, M., 338
Sibylline books, 275
Sicilian expedition, 22, 76, 188, 190, 192
Sicily, Sicilian, 42, 104, 183, 186, 188, 190, 272, 273, 306, 307, 332, 335
Sigeros, N., 324
similes, 107, 163, 165, 175, 240, 268, 285, 299, 341
Simmias, 164, 165
Simón Abril, P., 341, 342
simplicity, 5, 90, 146, 157, 183, 189, 209, 211, 244, 258, 264, 293, 391
skills, 197
communication, 207
interpersonal, 201
language, 375
military, 41
oratorical, 62
slaves, slavery, 56–58, 73, 139, 161, 186, 191, 202, 210, 211, 262, 265, 266, 278, 285, 286, 322, 372, 388
Soclarus, Plutarch's friend, 143, 241, 292
Soclarus, Plutarch's son, 5
Socrates, 12, 17, 19, 24, 67, 80, 114, 115, 128, 129, 136, 181, 183, 191, 203, 204, 214, 216, 224, 239, 240, 265, 289, 294, 300, 302, 336, 337, 385, 394
Socrates of Argos, 178
Soli, 108

CAMBRIDGE COMPANIONS TO . . .

## AUTHORS

*Edward Albee* edited by Stephen J. Bottoms
*Margaret Atwood* edited by Coral Ann Howells (second edition)
*W. H. Auden* edited by Stan Smith
*Jane Austen* edited by Edward Copeland and Juliet McMaster (second edition)
*James Baldwin* edited by Michele Elam
*Balzac* edited by Owen Heathcote and Andrew Watts
*Beckett* edited by John Pilling
*Bede* edited by Scott DeGregorio
*Aphra Behn* edited by Derek Hughes and Janet Todd
*Saul Bellow* edited by Victoria Aarons
*Walter Benjamin* edited by David S. Ferris
*William Blake* edited by Morris Eaves
*Boccaccio* edited by Guyda Armstrong, Rhiannon Daniels, and Stephen J. Milner
*Jorge Luis Borges* edited by Edwin Williamson
*Brecht* edited by Peter Thomson and Glendyr Sacks (second edition)
*The Brontës* edited by Heather Glen
*Bunyan* edited by Anne Dunan-Page
*Frances Burney* edited by Peter Sabor
*Byron* edited by Drummond Bone
*Albert Camus* edited by Edward J. Hughes
*Willa Cather* edited by Marilee Lindemann
*Catullus* edited by Ian Du Quesnay and Tony Woodman
*Cervantes* edited by Anthony J. Cascardi
*Chaucer* edited by Piero Boitani and Jill Mann (second edition)
*Chekhov* edited by Vera Gottlieb and Paul Allain
*Kate Chopin* edited by Janet Beer
*Caryl Churchill* edited by Elaine Aston and Elin Diamond
*Cicero* edited by Catherine Steel
*J. M. Coetzee* edited by Jarad Zimbler
*Coleridge* edited by Lucy Newlyn
*Wilkie Collins* edited by Jenny Bourne Taylor
*Joseph Conrad* edited by J. H. Stape
*H. D.* edited by Nephie J. Christodoulides and Polina Mackay
*Dante* edited by Rachel Jacoff (second edition)
*Daniel Defoe* edited by John Richetti
*Don DeLillo* edited by John N. Duvall
*Charles Dickens* edited by John O. Jordan
*Emily Dickinson* edited by Wendy Martin
*John Donne* edited by Achsah Guibbory

*Christopher Marlowe* edited by Patrick Cheney
*Andrew Marvell* edited by Derek Hirst and Steven N. Zwicker
*Ian McEwan* edited by Dominic Head
*Herman Melville* edited by Robert S. Levine
*Arthur Miller* edited by Christopher Bigsby (second edition)
*Milton* edited by Dennis Danielson (second edition)
*Molière* edited by David Bradby and Andrew Calder
*Toni Morrison* edited by Justine Tally
*Alice Munro* edited by David Staines
*Nabokov* edited by Julian W. Connolly
*Eugene O'Neill* edited by Michael Manheim
*George Orwell* edited by John Rodden
*Ovid* edited by Philip Hardie
*Petrarch* edited by Albert Russell Ascoli and Unn Falkeid
*Harold Pinter* edited by Peter Raby (second edition)
*Sylvia Plath* edited by Jo Gill
*Plutarch* edited by Frances B. Titchener and Alexei Zadorojnyi
*Edgar Allan Poe* edited by Kevin J. Hayes
*Alexander Pope* edited by Pat Rogers
*Ezra Pound* edited by Ira B. Nadel
*Proust* edited by Richard Bales
*Pushkin* edited by Andrew Kahn
*Thomas Pynchon* edited by Inger H. Dalsgaard, Luc Herman and Brian McHale
*Rabelais* edited by John O'Brien
*Rilke* edited by Karen Leeder and Robert Vilain
*Philip Roth* edited by Timothy Parrish
*Salman Rushdie* edited by Abdulrazak Gurnah
*John Ruskin* edited by Francis O'Gorman
*Sappho* edited by P. J. Finglass and Adrian Kelly
*Seneca* edited by Shadi Bartsch and Alessandro Schiesaro
*Shakespeare* edited by Margareta de Grazia and Stanley Wells (second edition)
*George Bernard Shaw* edited by Christopher Innes
*Shelley* edited by Timothy Morton
*Mary Shelley* edited by Esther Schor
*Sam Shepard* edited by Matthew C. Roudané
*Spenser* edited by Andrew Hadfield
*Laurence Sterne* edited by Thomas Keymer
*Wallace Stevens* edited by John N. Serio
*Tom Stoppard* edited by Katherine E. Kelly
*Harriet Beecher Stowe* edited by Cindy Weinstein
*August Strindberg* edited by Michael Robinson
*Jonathan Swift* edited by Christopher Fox
*J. M. Synge* edited by P. J. Mathews
*Tacitus* edited by A. J. Woodman
*Henry David Thoreau* edited by Joel Myerson

*Tolstoy* edited by Donna Tussing Orwin
*Anthony Trollope* edited by Carolyn Dever and Lisa Niles
*Mark Twain* edited by Forrest G. Robinson
*John Updike* edited by Stacey Olster
*Mario Vargas Llosa* edited by Efrain Kristal and John King
*Virgil* edited by Fiachra Mac Góráin and Charles Martindale (second edition)
*Voltaire* edited by Nicholas Cronk
*David Foster Wallace* edited by Ralph Clare
*Edith Wharton* edited by Millicent Bell
*Walt Whitman* edited by Ezra Greenspan
*Oscar Wilde* edited by Peter Raby
*Tennessee Williams* edited by Matthew C. Roudané
*William Carlos Williams* edited by Christopher MacGowan
*August Wilson* edited by Christopher Bigsby
*Mary Wollstonecraft* edited by Claudia L. Johnson
*Virginia Woolf* edited by Susan Sellers (second edition)
*Wordsworth* edited by Stephen Gill
*Richard Wright* edited by Glenda R. Carpio
*W. B. Yeats* edited by Marjorie Howes and John Kelly
*Xenophon* edited by Michael A. Flower
*Zola* edited by Brian Nelson

## TOPICS

*The Actress* edited by Maggie B. Gale and John Stokes
*The African American Novel* edited by Maryemma Graham
*The African American Slave Narrative* edited by Audrey A. Fisch
*African American Theatre* by Harvey Young
*Allegory* edited by Rita Copeland and Peter Struck
*American Crime Fiction* edited by Catherine Ross Nickerson
*American Gothic* edited by Jeffrey Andrew Weinstock
*American Horror* edited by Stephen Shapiro and Mark Storey
*American Literature and the Body* by Travis M. Foster
*American Literature and the Environment* edited by Sarah Ensor and Susan Scott Parrish
*American Literature of the 1930s* edited by William Solomon
*American Modernism* edited by Walter Kalaidjian
*American Poetry since 1945* edited by Jennifer Ashton
*American Realism and Naturalism* edited by Donald Pizer
*American Travel Writing* edited by Alfred Bendixen and Judith Hamera
*American Women Playwrights* edited by Brenda Murphy
*Ancient Rhetoric* edited by Erik Gunderson
*Arthurian Legend* edited by Elizabeth Archibald and Ad Putter
*Australian Literature* edited by Elizabeth Webby
*The Beats* edited by Stephen Belletto
*Boxing* edited by Gerald Early

Printed in Great Britain
by Amazon

56662546R00294